MYTHOLOGY
A VISUAL ENCYCLOPEDIA

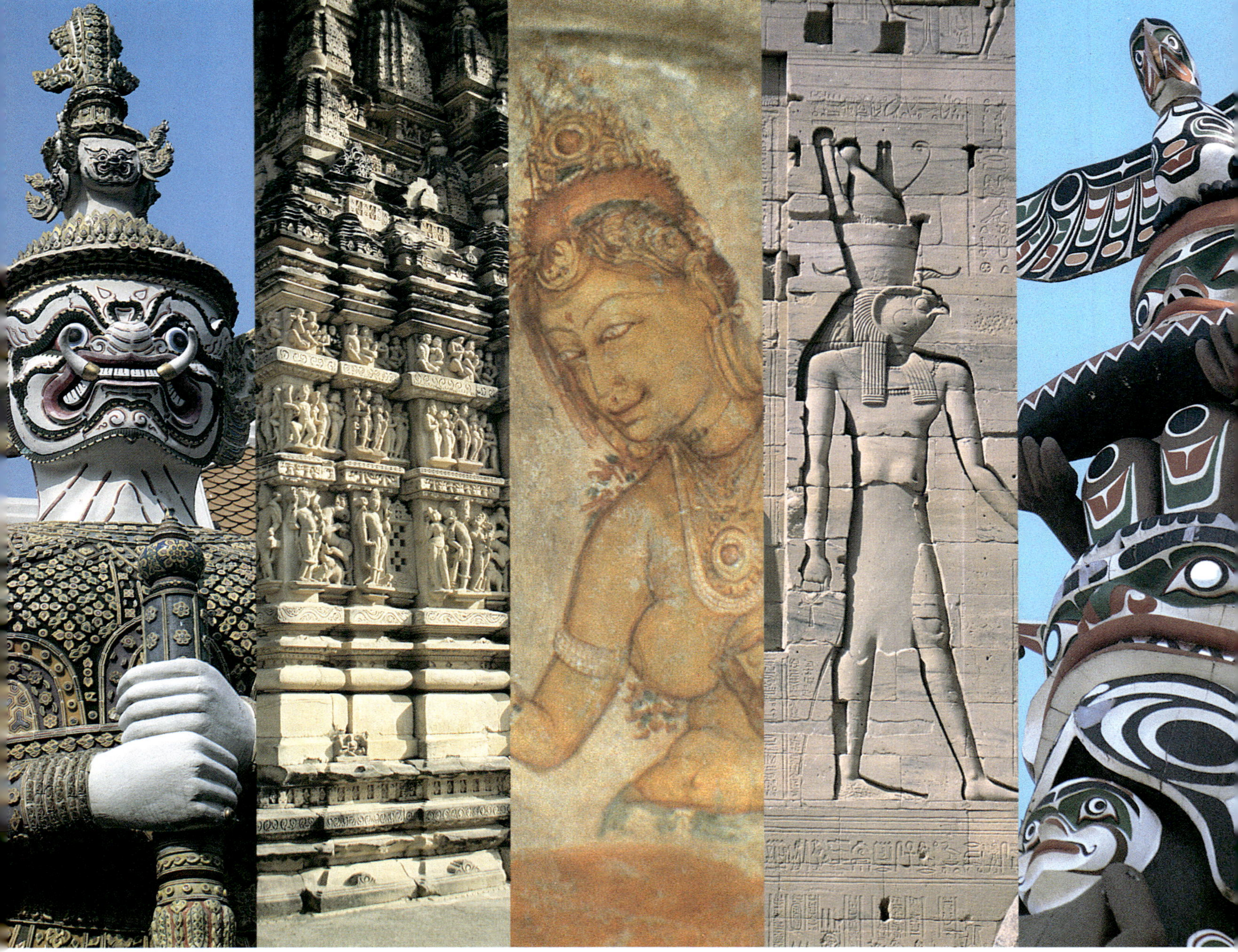

MYTHOLOGY
A VISUAL ENCYCLOPEDIA

JO FORTY

PARKGATE
BOOKS

The publishers acknowledge the kind assistance of
C.M Dixon who supplied a wealth of photographs and
captions for this book

First published in 1999 by
PRC Publishing Ltd,
Kiln House, 210 New Kings Road, London SW6 4NZ

This edition published in 1999 by
Parkgate Books
London House
Great Eastern Wharf
Parkgate Road
London
SW11 4NQ

© 1999 PRC Publishing Ltd

All rights reserved. No part of this publication may
be reproduced, stored in a retrieval system, or transmitted
in any form or by any means, electronic, mechanical,
photocopying, recording, or otherwise, without the prior
written permission of the Publisher and copyright holders.

British Library Cataloguing in Publication Data:
A catalogue record for this book is available from the British Library.

ISBN 1 902616 53 7

Printed and bound in China

CONTENTS

INTRODUCTION 6

EGYPT AND THE MIDDLE EAST 34
Egypt Mesopotamia Iran Canaan Arabia Israel Asia Minor A-Z

INDIA, SRI LANKA 120
Hinduism Buddhism Jainism Tibet Sri Lanka

CHINA, JAPAN AND SOUTH-EAST ASIA 170
China Japan South-East Asia Siberia Mongolia A-Z

EUROPE 228
Pre-Classical Crete and Mycenae Rome Celts The Northern Lands Christianity A-Z

THE AMERICAS 338
North America Inuit Northwest Plains Southwest Southwest Woodlands Central America
Maya Toltec/Chichimec Aztec The Caribbean South America Mochica Tihuanaco
Chimor and Chuicuito Inca A-Z

AFRICA 412
World Origin Pygmies Bushmen (San) Hottentots (Khoi) Khoisan Bantu
West Africa Ashanti Fon Yoruba Hamio-semitic Nilo-Saharan A-Z

OCEANIA 462
Polynesia Melanesia Micronesia Australia A-Z

GLOSSARY 510

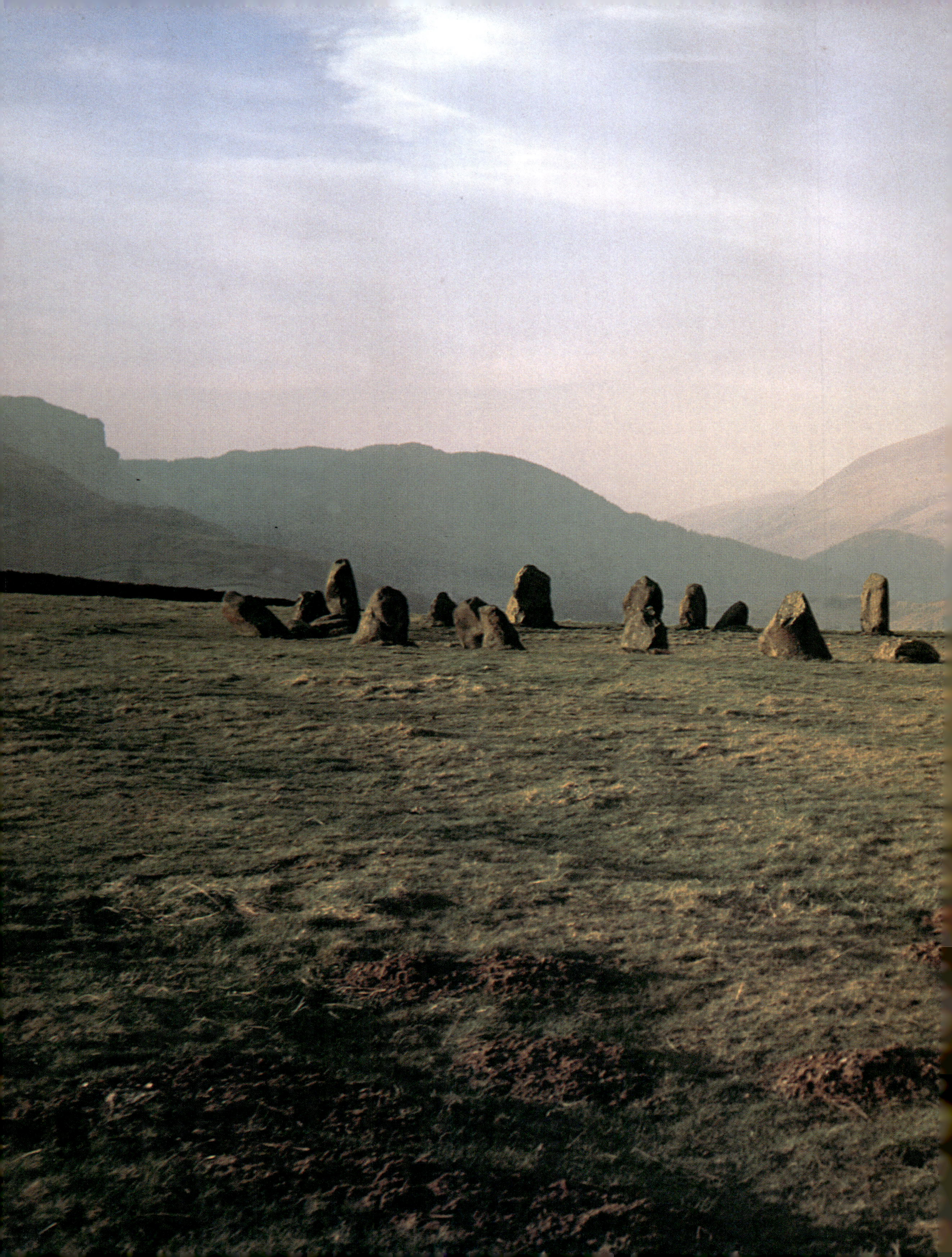

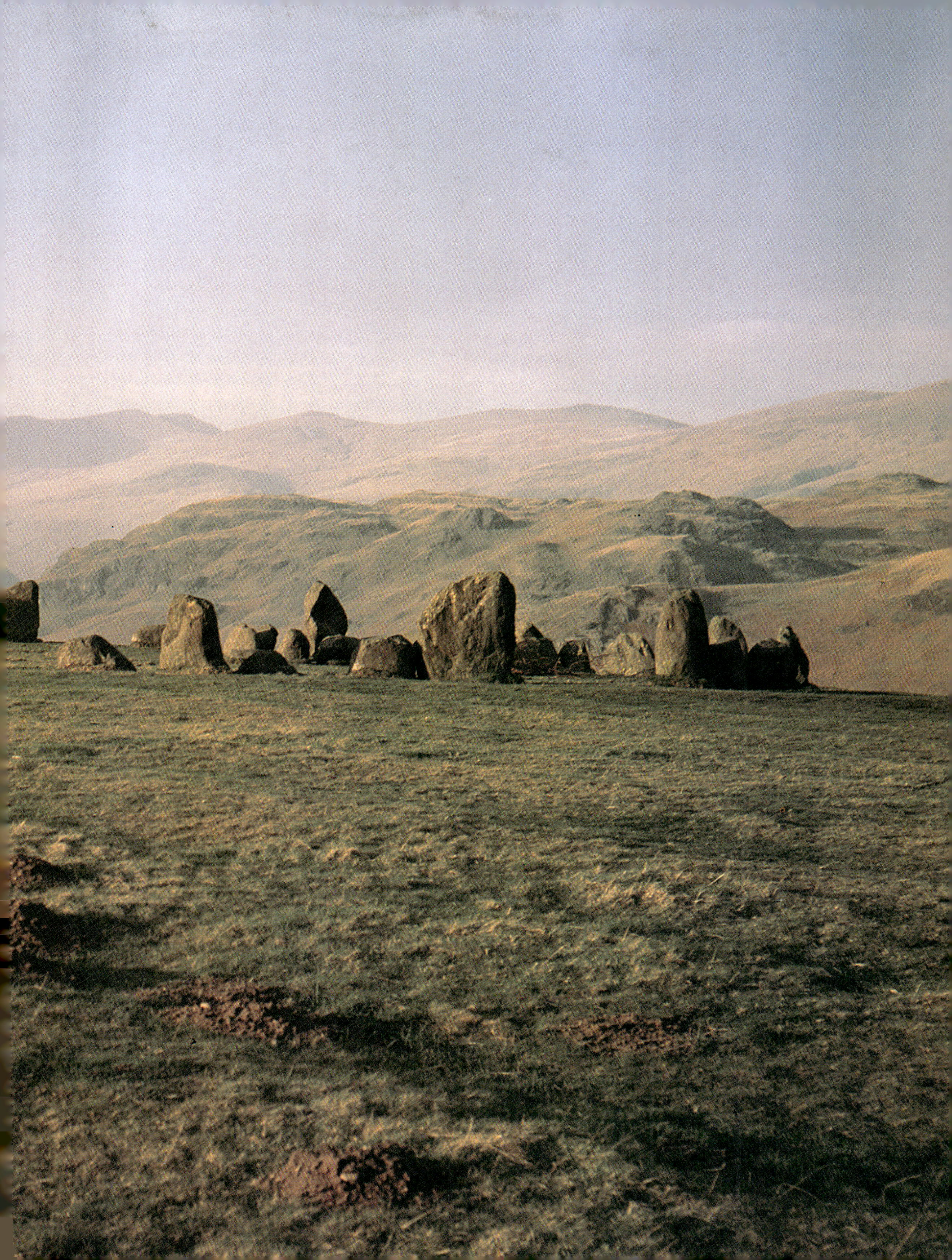

INTRODUCTION

BELIEF in anything is guaranteed to be alien to someone else, and it is as easy to dismiss other people's beliefs as irrational or misguided as it is rare to have no thoughts at all about our existence or consciousness, or even what comes after it. In fact, the myths and gods posited by humankind through the ages are virtually endless, and on the surface quite different, yet all reflect the basic human need to make outside forces responsive — forces which can be invoked, placated or challenged and which as a result of human action and belief can manifest a shape and personality.

For some today faith and belief are considered primitive and weak, putting religion on a par with idiocy, neurosis and insecurity. Others seek to prove that the divine is merely a projection of the human need to believe in some kind of design or purpose in an otherwise hostile life and universe. Equally persuasive arguments are put forward by those with faith in the validity of their own particular system. Whatever one's personal views there can be no denying the power and potential of belief itself.

Mythology is intrinsic to mankind, and all races without exception possess one. To study these at a worldwide level is to trace the pattern of man's spiritual and intellectual development, for there has been no age nor civilization that has not attempted to understand and interpret the mysteries of this strange life, using the "software" of myth, religion and philosophy. The fundamental questions have never changed: how was the world brought into being? What forces govern human life? And how can these be adapted and made favorable? The answers have varied as much as the societies that have produced them. From the time when nomadic hunters sought to improve their chances of success with ritual target-bonding and spirit identification, to the more modern

Previous pages: A winter view of Mt Helvellyn from the Castlerigg Druids' circle in Northern England (Neolithic & Bronze Age). Right: This stone image of a seated Buddha is carved from the solid rockface at Polonnaruwa, Sri Lanka.

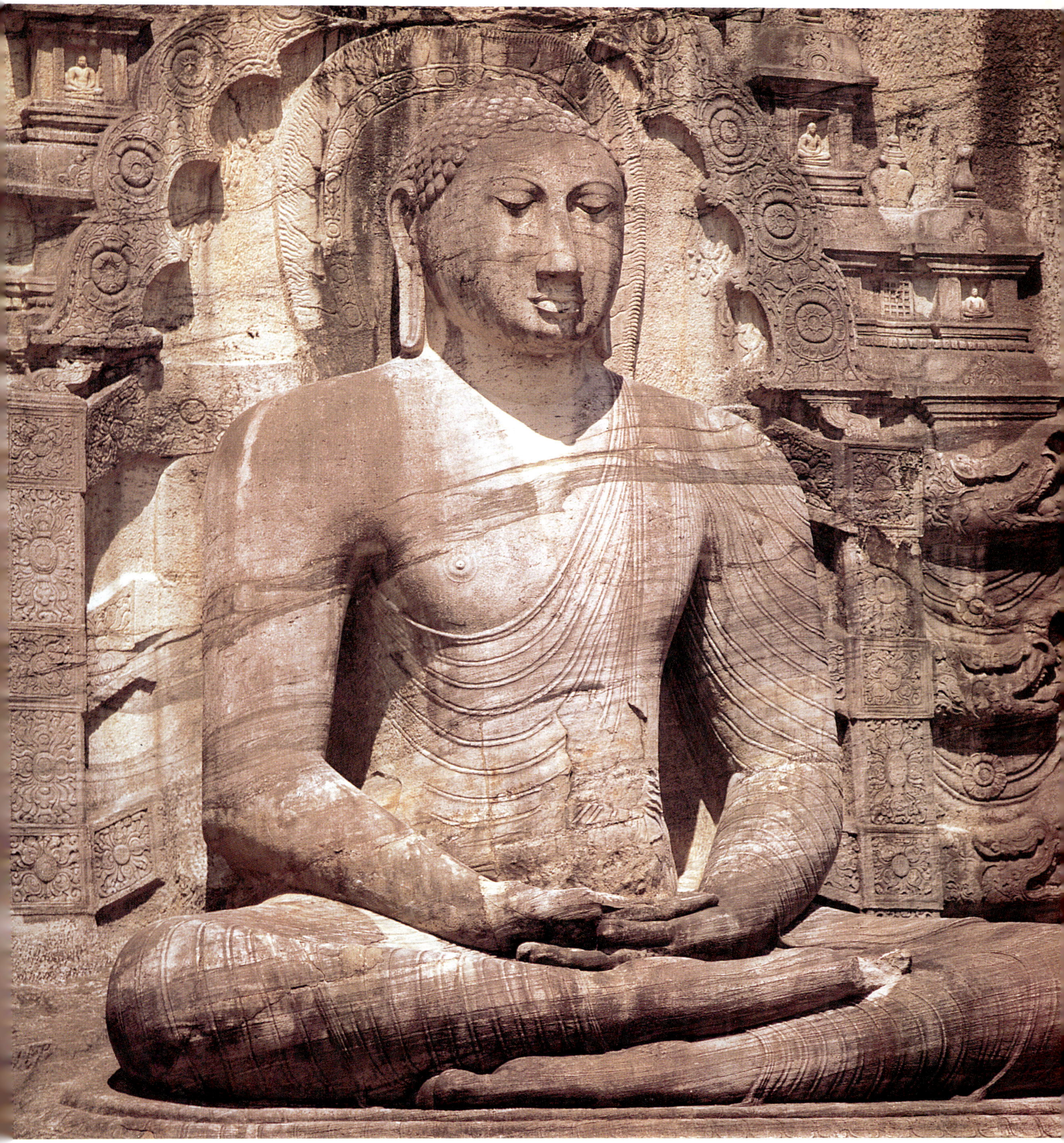

preparation of training for a specific purpose, all reflects the focus system of desire and need, which can lead to success and fruition in reality. Myth makes a direct connection to our unconscious, working through an intuitive process that, like the universe, is always one step beyond logic. However "the agony of the quest is superseded by the joy of vision...the power of the flash of insight which illuminates the narrowness of the matter-of-fact explanation, and compels the intellect to acknowledge the need for a more adequate understanding. Mythology possesses an intensity of meaning that is akin to poetry." (Arthur Cotterell)

Modern comparative studies of religion and mythology confirm the necessity and vitality of myths, which are universally accepted as expressing axiomatic and intrinsic truth — not just of existential detail but of a basic and eternal reality. Myth is both profane and sacred — setting definitions, examples, patterns and sequences for human behavior. Modern myths sometimes contain the disguised revival of older mythologies, but are so often constantly metamorphosing and updating that they lack the ancient symbolism and inadequately represent true eternal reality. However, psychology has proven that the dreams and fantasies of modern man often reflect the Classic mythical themes. Myth is fictional narrative, yet it does not project false images of the world, but rather cyphers of the unchanging, hidden core of existence. It has the serious and worthwhile function of allowing people expression of their deepest feelings and intuitions about the significance of their lives. Nowadays people are beginning to recognize the power of these ancient lyrical tales, for the function of myth in primitive societies is not just entertainment but "edutainment." Interpretive and didactic in purpose, it reveals a deeper reality

Above left: An Inuit face mask found in East Greenland.
Right: This illustration of the Raga Panchaduya (India, 18th century AD) sees Radha and Krishna seated in a grove, attended to by cowherds and female musicians.

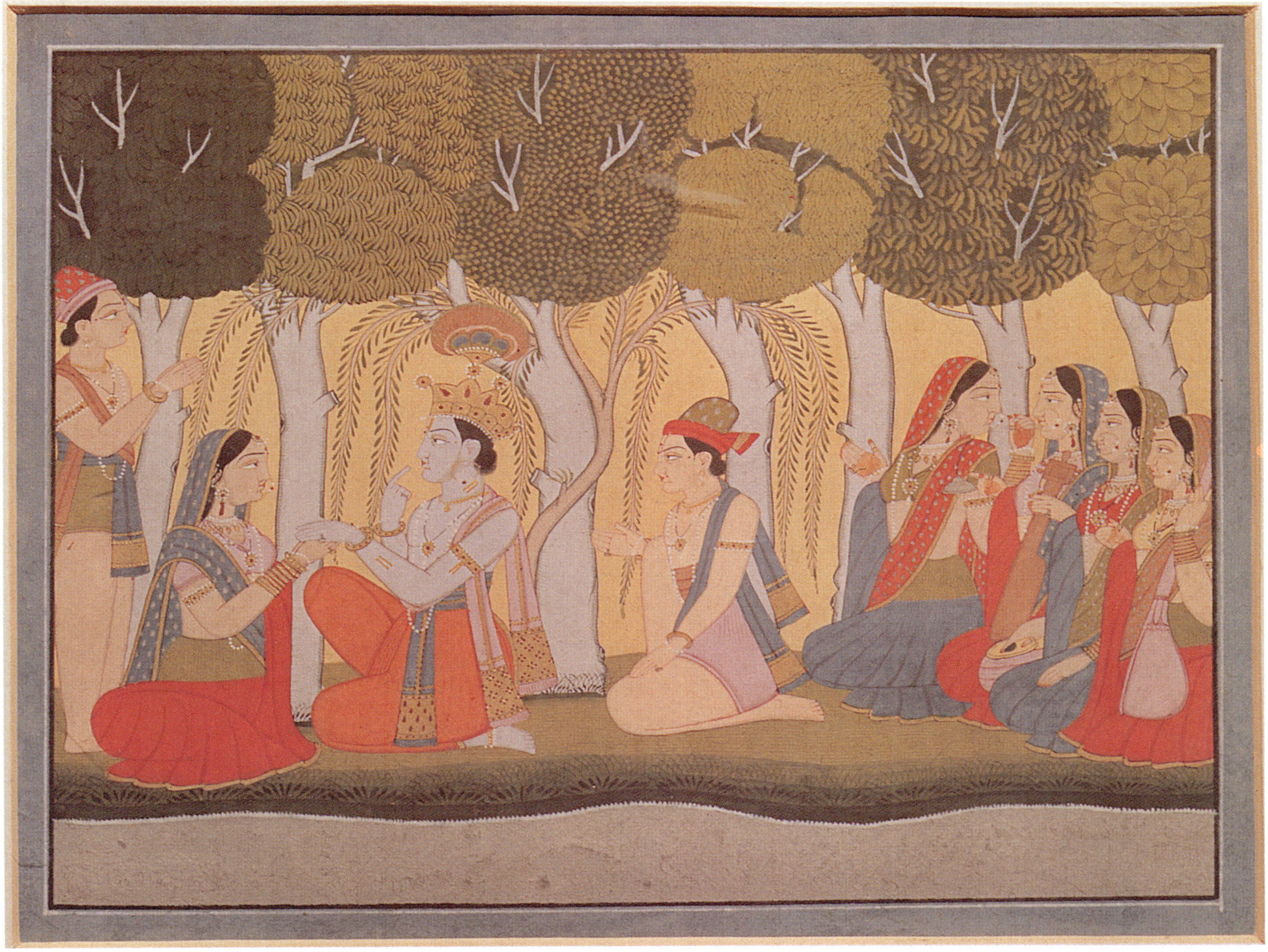

through which the present life, fate and work of humankind is controlled, and it is the acknowledgement of the link between the past and the present that is enacted in daily life.

There has also always been an automatic association of myth with ritual and religion, and although many did originate this way, it definitely does not account for them all. Certain myths that are worldwide — the cosmic egg, the flood, the quest for fire, the battle against monsters and the ladder up to heaven, all appear to have a special, potent significance for humankind. These worldwide themes were noticed by Jung and led to his theory of the collective unconscious, which has done much to aid our understanding of world mythology. Each society gives its own particular form to such archetypes. In this way mythology shapes the culture and reflects the insight and intuition of the society that sources it, and the ancient myths that trace a line forward to the present remain potent and active in our own societies as well as our personal psyches.

The disciplines of archeology, linguistics, psychology, anthropology, ethnography, sociology, comparative mythology, comparative religion and religious history have all played a part in our understanding of world mythology. Gradually it is unraveled and itemized by an increasing number of refined disciplines. At the beginning of the 20th century the view of Western rationalism concerning mythology was that myths were exclusive to primitive societies and had no place in modern civilization — which had supposedly evolved through reason and the burgeoning sciences away from such imaginative explanations. It was said that in more primitive times the world had been interpreted emotionally, as a conflict between the contrary personalities, which all uncontrollable phenomena were given by an imaginative and interactive

Above left: This relief shows the god Thoth on the Egyptian Temple of Ramesses II. Right: The Venus de Milo at the Louvre, Paris.

· INTRODUCTION ·

13

humankind. Ironically even at that time within Western society, religion and its related mythology were a much stronger part of everyday life. However, the closer one looks into the origins of any modern nation the more mythical it becomes. If this is the case then mythologies are merely cultural explanations that are alien to our own.

Freud and Jung both began to develop the modern understanding of myths, linking them to our subconscious. Freud interpreted dreams and myths as being a reflection of our often thwarted or sublimated sexual desires and needs. Jung saw them as being a part of a collective unconscious that was shared by all mankind, containing the archetypes of our various evolutionary states that combine to work our conscious minds through to new thresholds of transformation. Jung disagreed with Freud's simplistic sexual analysis, positing this collective unconscious as well as each human's uniquely personal one. The latter is filled with material particular to the individual; the former houses the common mental inheritance of man — the archetypes and primordial images which bring into our ephemeral consciousness an unknown psychic life belonging to a remote past. When we look at active mythological interfaces that continue with ancient paradigms we see an eloquence of incident rather than word — they are not the product of individual minds, but are produced, controlled and treasured by the collective unconscious, effected on a subconscious level, touching intuition, feeling and imagination, constantly refashioned and reshaped and layered with new relevant meaning. Their details impress themselves on the memory and soak deep into the psyche.

A more recent development is structural comparative mythology, as propounded by Levi-Strauss. This is a

Above left: A replica of Athena à la Ciste, (originally 5th century BC). Right: Norse chess pieces carved from walrus ivory.

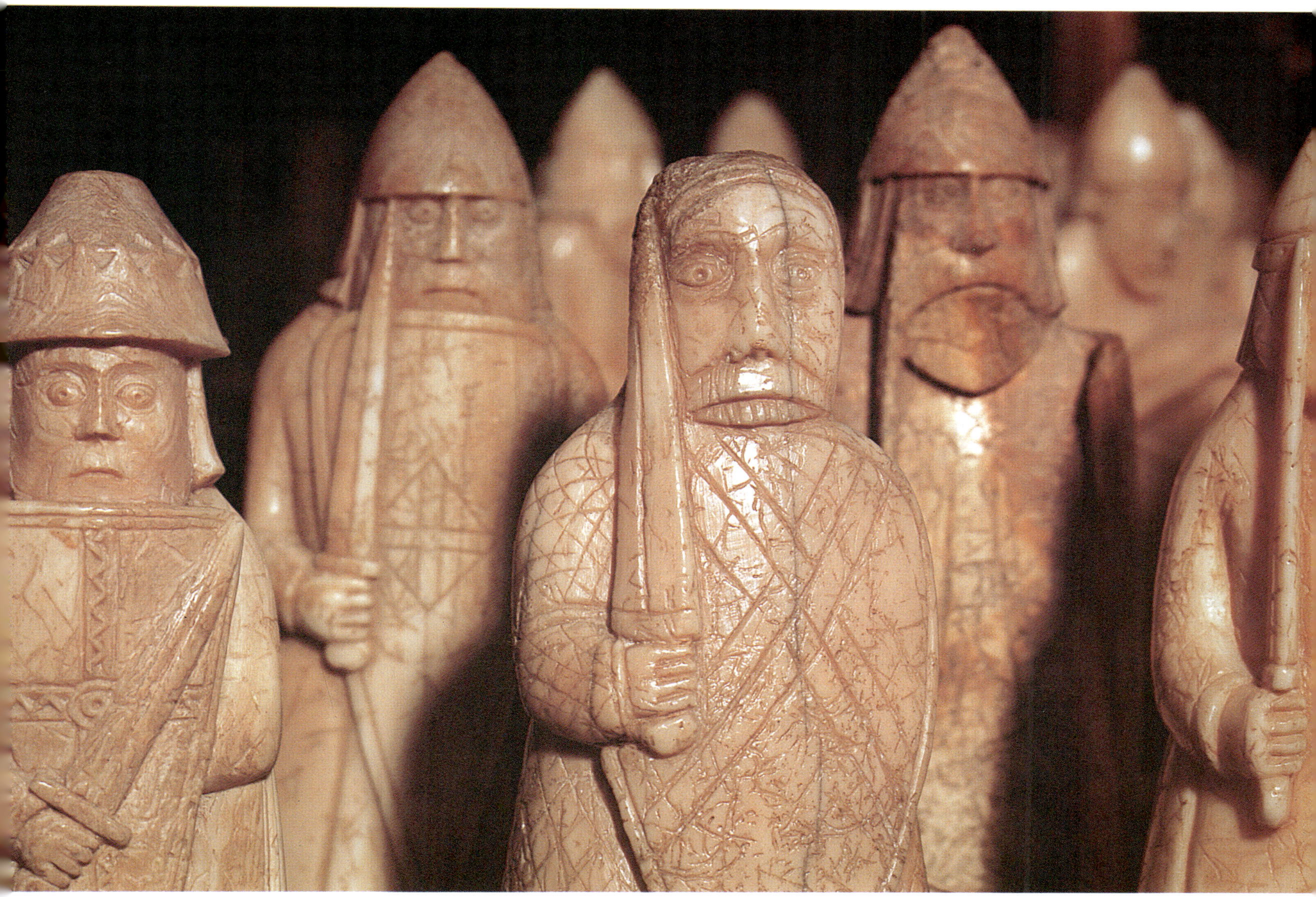

progression or continuation of Freud and Jung, which analyses myths by breaking each one down into its constituent parts to reveal the structure of archetypes beneath. The structural mythologists believe that the basic idea behind most myths is the reconciliation of opposites in order to overcome the contradictions that naturally manifest in daily life. A process of "If you can conceive it you can achieve it."

Thus mythologists realize that all societies, no matter how ancient or contemporary have their own mythologies, as integral as their own mores and fashions — all of which combine to form a contemporary matrix of factors that make each phase of time unique. Just as time moves forward so these paradigm shifts are in a constant process of becoming. As older constructs fade, the warp and weft of our world changes and mutates. Have we now a burgeoning world mythology or is it that almost all humankind's belief systems are currently operational at present, giving a truly spectacular breadth to our vision and imagination, with wider parameters than ever before? All seek to explain and decode the world around us, and our own often contradictory drives and needs within it. The object of myth is to explain the world, (as is the object of science), to make it more friendly and accessible to us. Yet one's belief is tempered by one's own self knowledge and awareness — at a personal or social level. None of us individually know how to operate or function scientifically — it is merely the pooled use of cumulative data, a particular way of interpreting the world, which falls far short of explaining its mystery. In reality science is a kind of modern myth, with every fact merely a working hypothesis until augmented, corrected or disproved by further advances or changes of thought. Also within our own much larger and more complicated societies, in the absence of an effective general

Above left: Rahu, swallower of the sun and moon and author of Eclipses. (13th century AD). Right: The Cross of the Scriptures (c. 900 AD) in Eire.

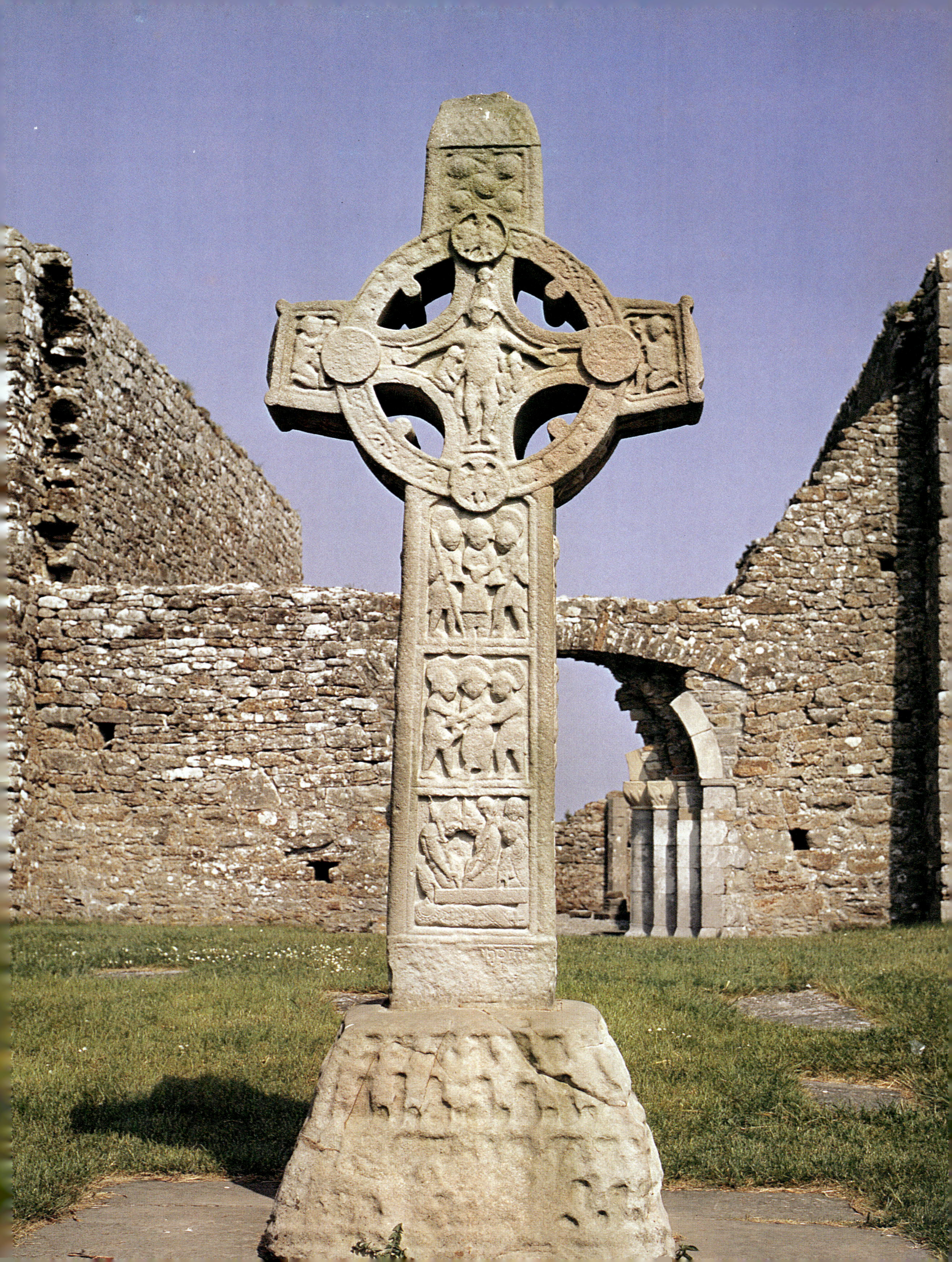

mythology, each of us has his "private, unrecognized, rudimentary, yet secretly potent pantheon of dream," one's own secret mythology. Being aware and at the center of our own existence, we are everything we believe ourselves to be, and perhaps a little more besides.

Over the millennia of man's historical culture the stories have wended, mutated and metamorphosed, carried on irresistibly as time tracks forward. Beguiling in their diversity, despite having outward differences they resonate with an intrinsic similarity — a thread of continuity that runs through them all. Myths are made to explain the world, to make sense of it, and to take possession of the world in conceptual symbolic forms in order to achieve a physical possession too — a target-bonding system of the desires and needs of our own individual selves and their external manifestation — societies. By explaining the world through stories we overcome our fears and uncertainties, and attach meaning and logic to illogical things, slowly getting a grip on them. Also myth appeals to the subconscious, intuitive world of feelings — impressions gained from all our senses and our cell awareness at a subvocal, intuitive level.

When myths are finally superseded they are remodified again, or collected as stories with which to entertain ourselves, increase knowledge and gain new awareness. When old myths finally lose the meaning of their form, new ones are needed and made — the hybrids of a world culture in constant fusion. Based in reality they explain, illustrate and justify. Where they are still implicitly believed they live and are used to integrate and illustrate our thoughts and arguments, exorcise our demons and inspire confidence, example and reflection.

The clothing of mythology — gods, beasts, physical places — all are ciphers and symbols, avatars of intangibles which

Above left: This Roman relief The Apotheosis of Augustus shows the deification of the emperor. Right: A mask made by the North American Iroquois people.

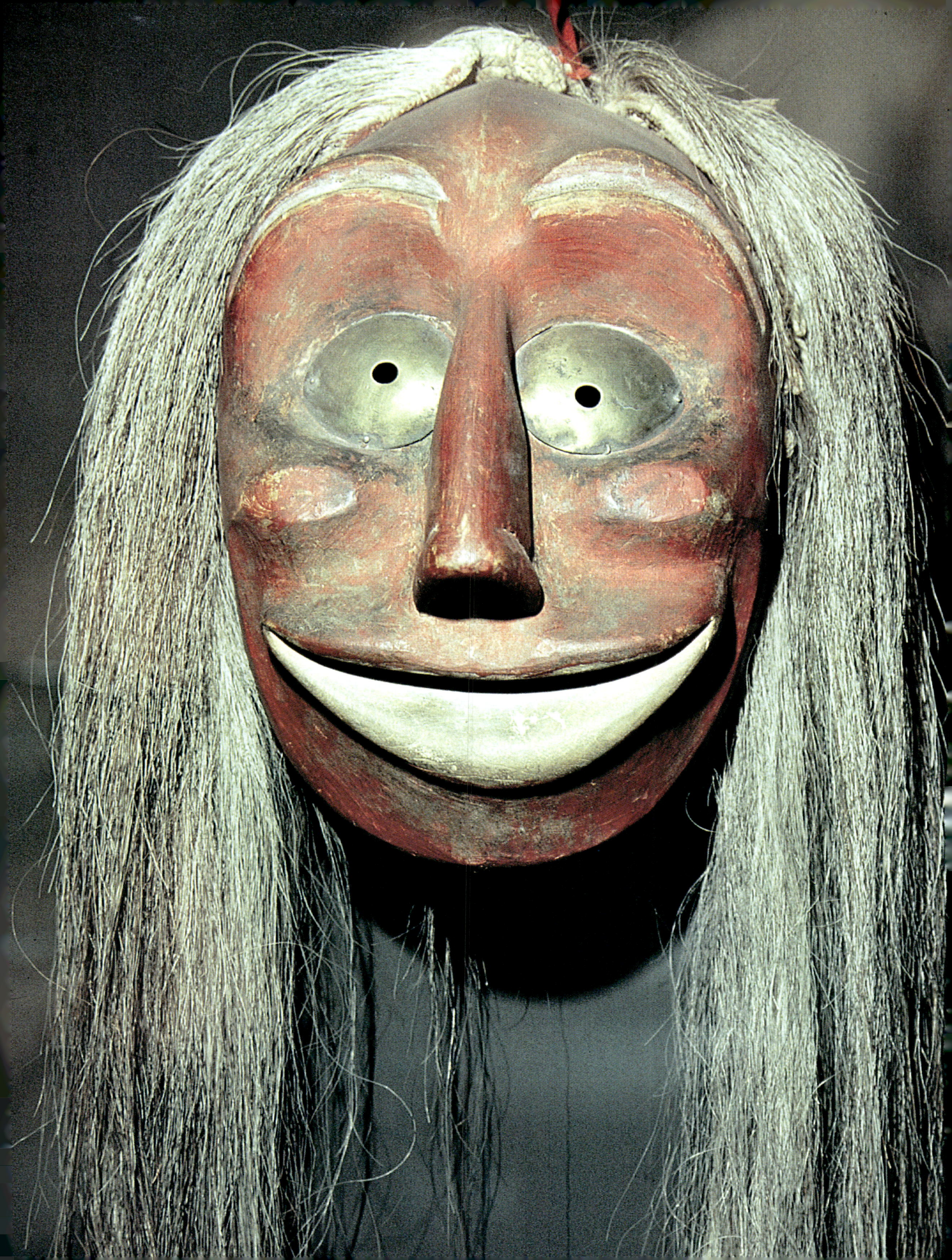

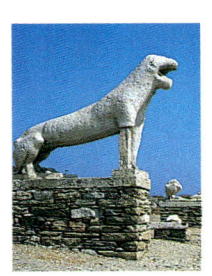

can manifest in new ways or remain almost eternally the same — a case of "the symbol restores the theme," and so convey the sacred axiomatic truths of existence. The word "myth" (*mythos*) originally meant story and was used to differentiate such from the factual (*logos*) accounts of real events. Herodotus wrote his history and called it fact, differing from the fiction of mythology. Myths that refer to the remote past and seem to be irrelevant in fact have a radical purpose — to reflect the natural order of things; the conventional hierarchy underpinned through mythological prototypes. Levi-Strauss showed that myths sought to resolve those contradictions natural to a person's life by reconciling the natural extremes. His analysis showed how the questions raised and dealt with in myth continue to resonate by being picked up by neighboring cultures and passed on. It has also been shown that narrative structure is fundamentally important with regular and repeated elements that are not always included all together but that do always occur in a perceivable order.

Myth and folklore come from the same explanatory source and are communal products that often exist in multiple versions. They seek to explain the origins of the world, including the origin of society and culture. They occur in both primitive unstratified hunter-gatherer societies and in the more complex hierarchical ones. Folktales on the other hand come from intermediate societies, usually from an agricultural source, dealing with social conflict and human problems rather than the cosmic origins addressed by myth.

Modern research has proved that myths are not dead and gone but alive and well. They emanate from the dynamic and ever-changing nature of oral narrative. Perhaps literary data cultures with the fixity of print actually curtail this process. The myths remain in an oral part of the culture, or in

Above left: The Naxian marble Terrace of Lions (7th century BC).
Right: A female dancer of Hoysala (Central India 12th century AD).

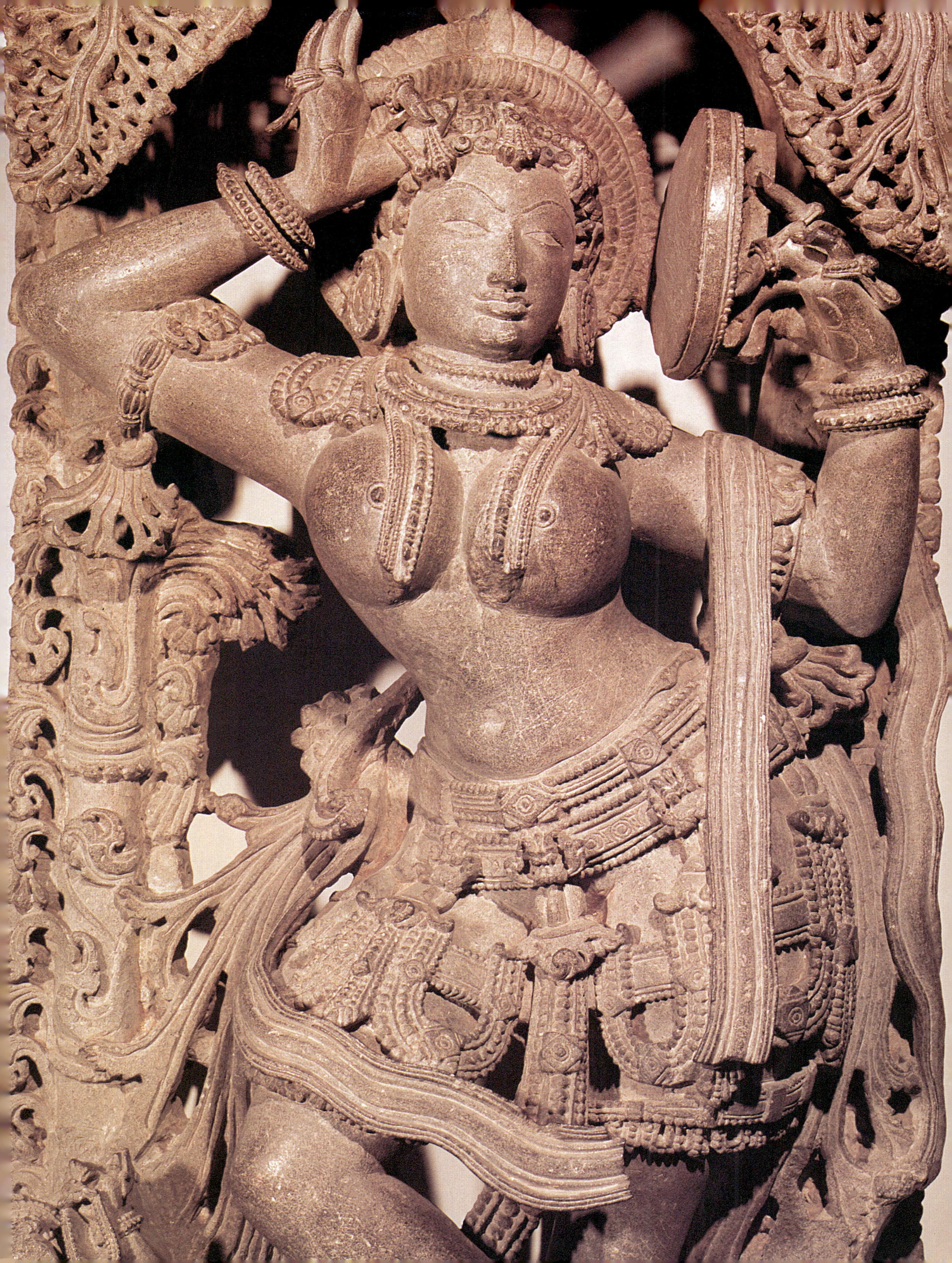

other areas where the emphasis is on the ephemeral. The moment of composition is the point, therefore everything must be regularly retold and made anew. In oral cultures there are communal frames of reference and word patterns recognized by all, where even those who listen are participating in a proactive way — asking and answering questions in call and response mode or joining in at the chorus, they therefore become an intrinsic part of the process rather than passive listeners to a fixed version of events. Legends are literary and based on old historical events distorted by time, where the layered accretion of each successive dominant group has purloined the myth for their own purposes. All overlap and shade into each other.

Shamans accumulate first hand experience through experiment and observation, like priests they are concerned with the domain of the spirit. Unlike scientists they enjoy a certain creative and artistic freedom and their sequencing is redolent of the creative process. Children do this when at play, rehearsing future roles by what they know and what they surmise or see as possible — including reasons for things that they do not yet fully comprehend, but nevertheless observe and attempt to understand. This playfulness never leaves the mythological process, even though its subjects can also be dangerous, because it is about interconnecting all aspects of life and it seeks to unify all into a coherent totality. Thus it registers and conveys meaning in its deepest sense, surviving because of its varied aspects that entertain as well as instruct.

The main themes of mythology seek to decode the origins of the world, positing water, void or a giant personality which contains the potentiality that is put in motion — land rising from the waters, mud making people, cosmic eggs cracking open, heaven and earth formed through primal sacrifice.

Above left: A Celtic wooden idol from France.
Right: The Sphinx, the Valley Temple and the Pyramid of Khafre (26th century BC).

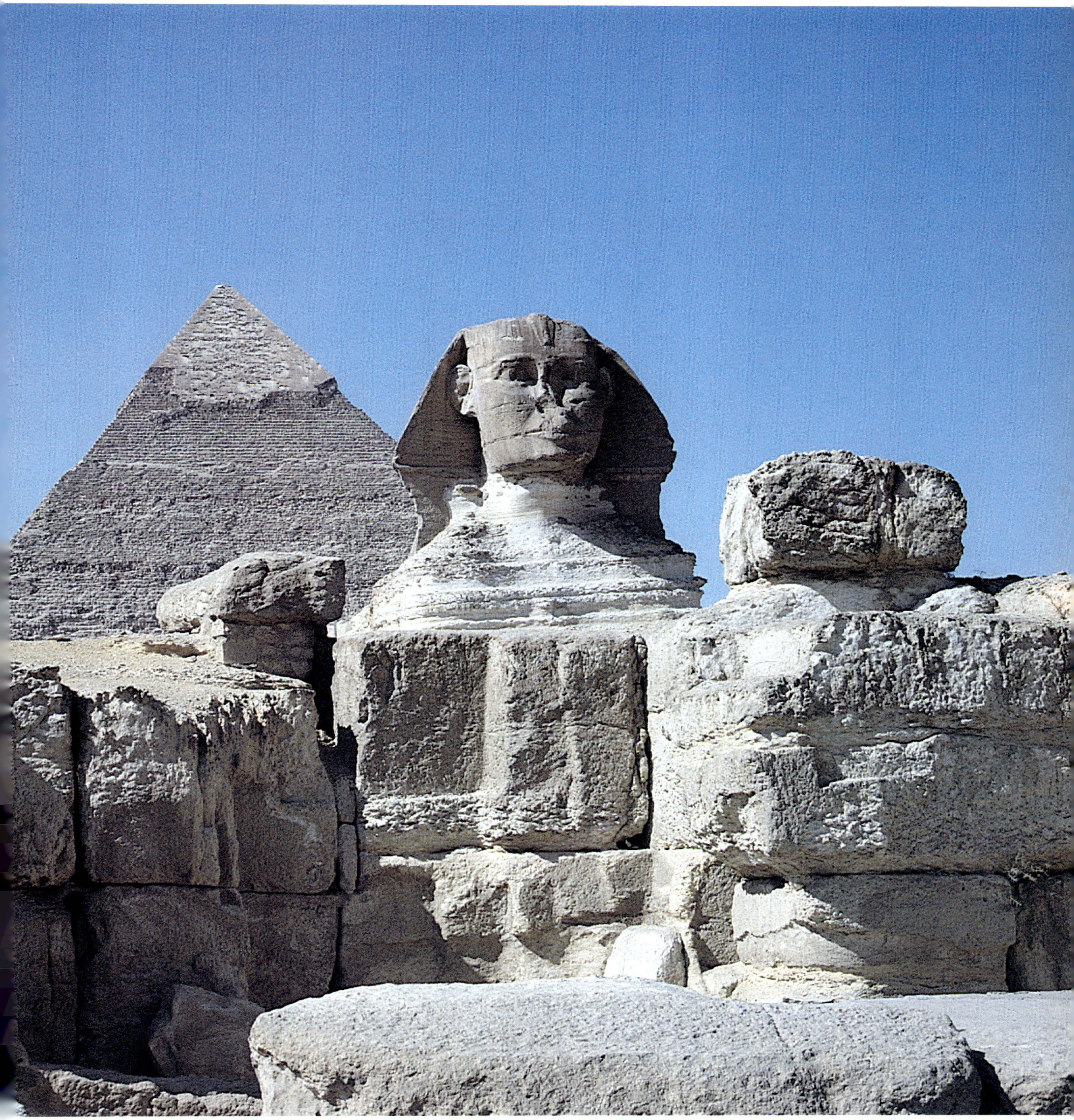

From this singularity, duality then follows — separation and plurality rather than oneness and undifferentiaition. Often either a couple or single god are broken apart or separated in order that the many may take up life. (Ouranos and Kronos ate their children until overthrown, an omen of their inevitable passing through life's constant rotating processes.) Often sexuality first rears its head as a sign of immanent plurality — gods locked in a timeless embrace until forcibly separated. Also sacrifice and sacrificial death bring about change and new life. Giants who voluntarily explode their body parts to form geographical features and terraform the planet. Or else the cosmic serpent or the World Tree — all these myths formalize the constructive and destructive aspects of life and are therefore part of a process that reconciles opposites in a perpetual cycle of mutual need — one state anticipating another. Almost all cultures have this formative period prior to progression toward some kind of climax and then the process starts again with a renewal. The Aztec five suns and Hindu Kalpas illustrate this process of renewal and destruction. In myth, numerology represents the codification of dimension — lateral and universal structure that requires definition and therefore dimension with its accompanying numerical sequences. Hence the endless fascination with numbers which seek to convey and define space, physical processes within it and the mystical cosmic reality that underpins it. Color coding becomes another way of differentiation and therefore is similar to numerology.

In myth the visible world is merely the visual part of an inestimably more complicated system which involves other elements not immediately visible to human observation. The spirit world intermediary connects to heaven and hell, the psychic manifestations of everything that is there in

Above left: An Egyptian papyrus (12th century BC) showing Khons the moon god of Thebes and his mother Mut. Right: A bronze Poseidon found in the sea off Cape Artemision, Greece.

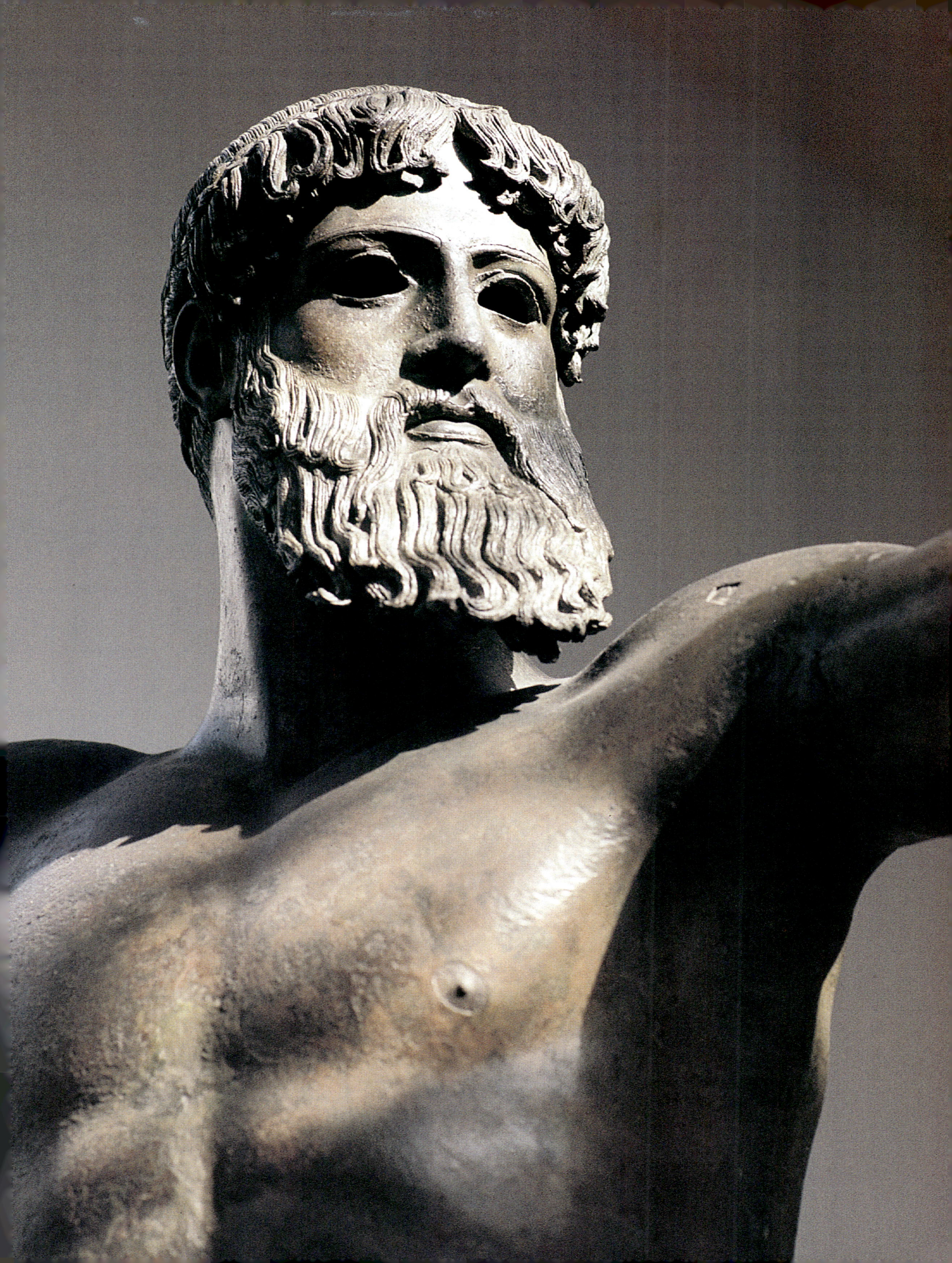

actuality. This can also be seen in reverse as a dream world, where the motivating ideas and icons are acted out. It's life that's the dream, constantly renewed by a sleeping god or celestial creator who can appear in divine, human or animal formats — male sun/sky divinities and female earth/moon deities, influenced by climate, inclination, geography and personality. Also relevant and visible stars are personalized and linked to some cultural purpose, such as crop sewing, irrigation and harvesting. Buildings too often reflect the groundplan of the universe as perceived by a particular culture, along the same lines as features — to be isolated and explained or recognized. Man himself can manifest in his limbs and organs the universe and its processes at large in a micro-macro reflection. All things actually are based on similar precepts and formulas — it is merely a matter of scale and permutation that define the exact dimensions and characteristics. Water going down a plug is a whirlpool, a hurricane is a slow-moving atomic explosion, an earthquake is an orgasm and the fight against infection is a flesh landbattle.

Creator gods compel, but in fact the overall lack of real specifics indicate an acceptance — we are here after all. Sometimes our existence is defined as a requirement by these gods for servants, to perform sacrifices, feed and worship in an almost ironic way — for which came first the chicken or the egg? Did god create man or vice versa? Certainly the gods of man seem modeled in his image, just as a crocodile would have a crocodilic-god — if it had the imagination in the first place. So the gods experience all the rage, desire, jealousy and sorrow we do — almost endlessly — until killed with unbelief. Are they merely a projection upon which our anxieties and fears are portrayed — another kind of target-bonding system?

Above left: A reconstruction of an Anglo Saxon helmet (7th century AD).
Right: This Mayan relief shows a priest cutting his tongue on a rope of thorns.

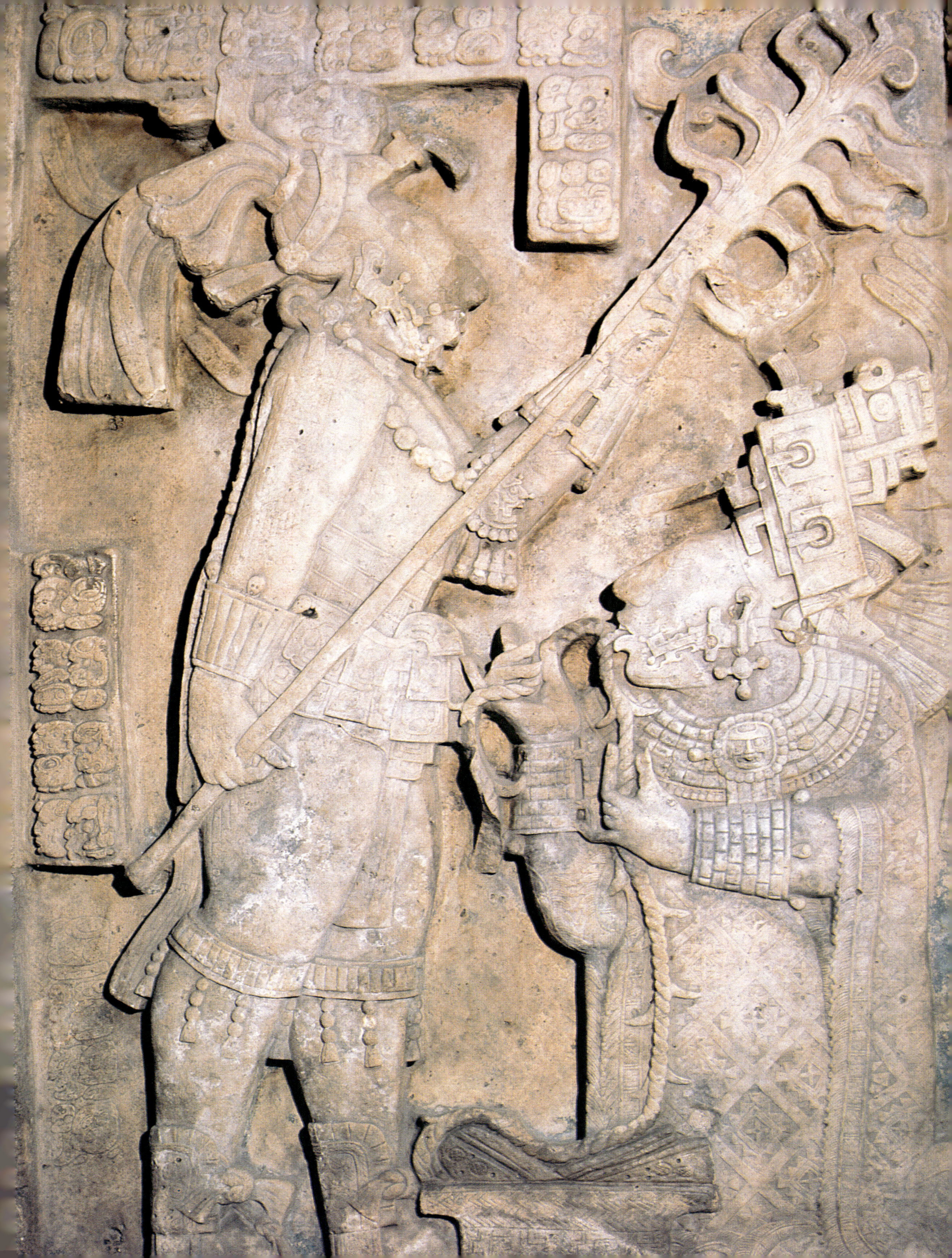

Misfortune often originates through some breaking of some cultural taboo, wars occur because someone's wife is unfaithful or snubs someone else and steals their things — all these common and trivial reasons denoting the inevitable competition between individual units and cultures, often put down to man's own stupidity and spite or lack of vision. Sometimes lazy or mischievous animals do the same too. In the end death is necessary or life would choke itself in its ever-changing diversity and expansion, or else reduce to singularity once more. Plurality must have its own system controls to prevent irretrievable chaos and break down — or those very things are manifested in a controlled way which in turn limits and controls life and its processes. Disease is put down to imbalance or a deliberate evil attack from intruders and requires medico-religious help from one skilled in such matters — perhaps initially people with more creative imagination who could see a way out.

Disaster and global catastrophe are often seen as deserved through evil behavior, non-conformity to the natural order, the challenging of a god's will, disobedience, selfishness or transgression from natural or tribal laws. The flood myth variants are a classic example of this. Punishment for sexual transgression occurs when a person disobeys tribal law with incest, for sex within the clan carries visible evil consequences and therefore requires prohibition and punishment.

Agents of change, heroes and tricksters occur in all cultures — another blurring of the border between the gods and men and an illustration of the source of myth which arises from within ourselves in an attempt at explanation. These forms follow an age old tendency still very much alive to invest important people with mythological significance — the cult of the individual who becomes a culture hero. Some heroes work

Above left: The theater of ancient Sparta.
Right: A Celtic deity holds two stags (Denmark, 100 BC).

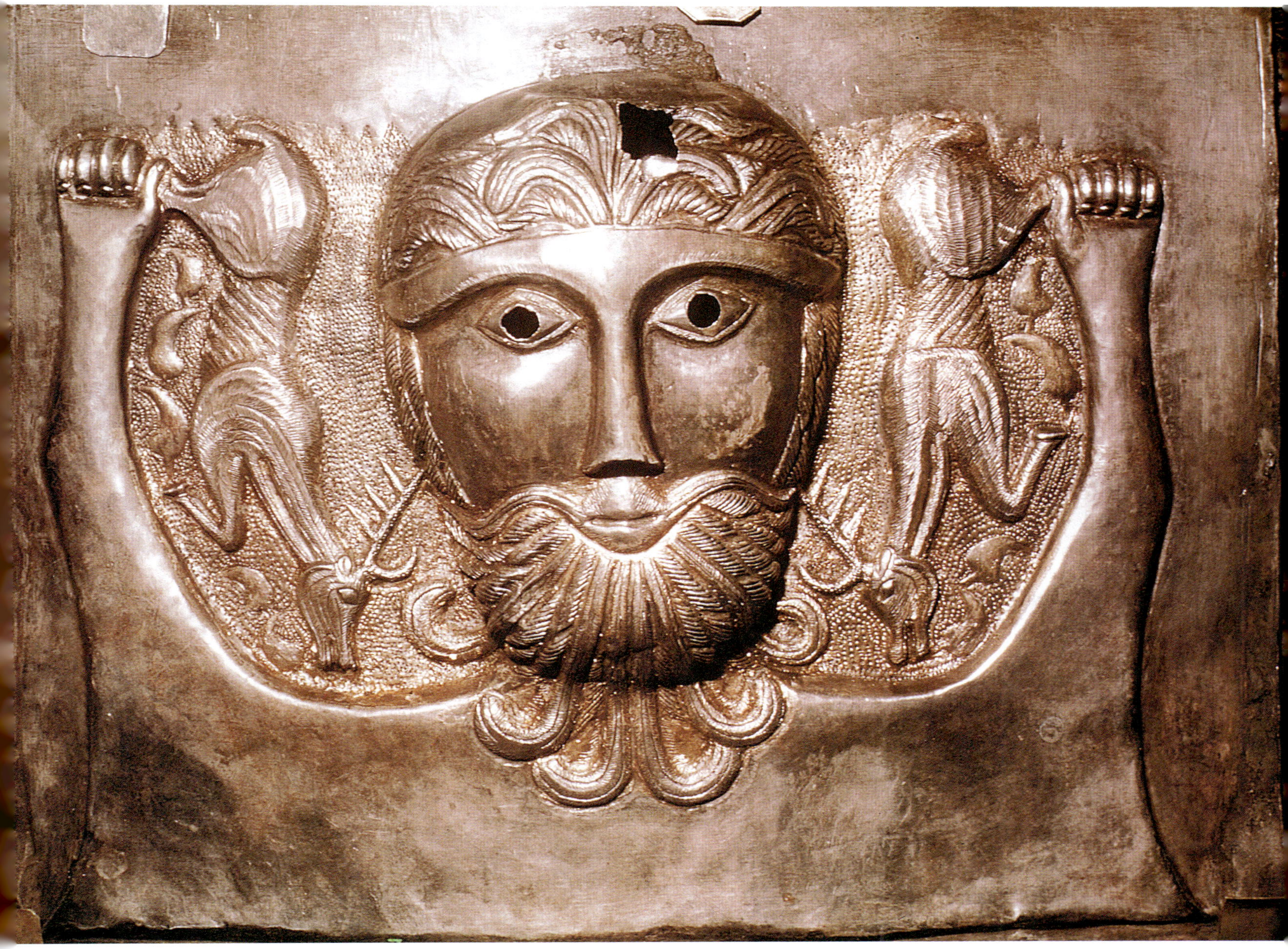

tirelessly for the benefit of mankind, others are more ambivalent and mischievous — manifesting the random principle within the world. These cultural icons bring language, fire, food, farming and any other requirements and skills that are needed to be learnt. Others just travel using their brains and personality to eventually triumph over all kinds of adversity, and represent man's ability and capacity to learn. Though these humorous ones manifest man's restless, questioning spirit they are also often selfish or impractical. Sometimes they attempt to subvert the cosmic order and are divinely punished, still other times they undermine the social order and represent a criticism of the social structure. Cultural heroes can also occur in animal format, for animals are often given equal status with man, along with speech capability. They represent a bridge between the worlds, or else define clan and family loyalties with their allegiances. At other times humans metamorphose into them or mate with animal consorts, who share their lives for a while and acknowledge a common spiritual bond, for visible life contains an overmap of the mythological and spirit worlds. The soul is often conceived as another copy of the body but insubstantial or different in certain basic ways. After death, provisioned by the living for a similar world thereafter, the soul journeys to another domain – the Underworld or spirit world. Shamans and shape shifters journey into this spirit world too, as experts for the mass of the populace, leaving their bodies whilst in a trance to visit as a spirit, free from the physical limitations. These dream journeys also provide another prime example of the propensity to imagine and mythologize. — the purpose dependent on the environment and culture. Sometimes, due to the manner of their death, spirits may linger in Limbo, trapped to continue interaction on the human plane, with judgement of their past

Above left: Agamemnon and Clytemnestra of Sparta.
Right: Ossian's Grave a Neolithic Court Cairn, above Glen Aan, County Antrin, Northern Ireland.

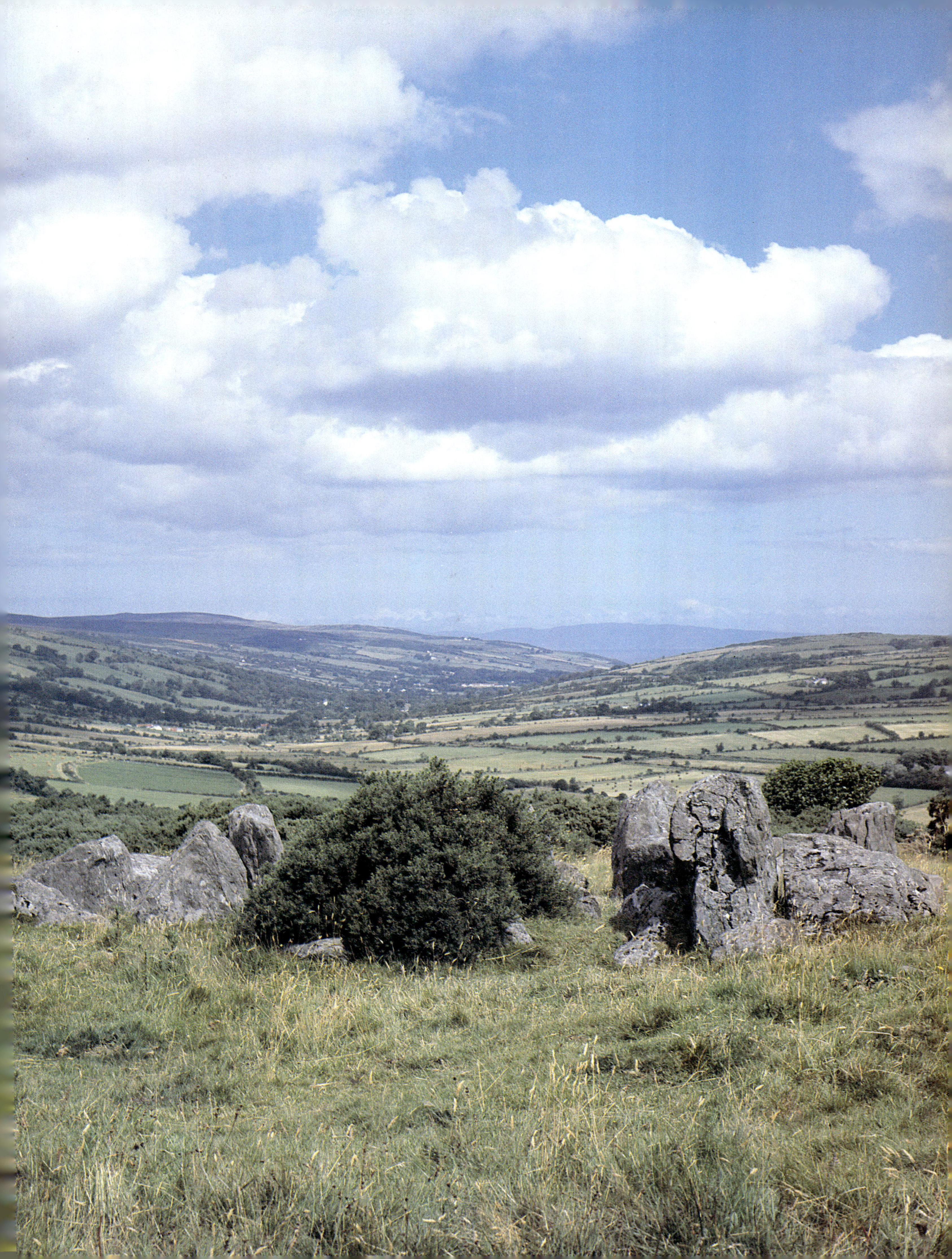

life a usual occurrence. Reincarnation however is a different belief format, where one's new form is dependent on previous old behavior. Heaven or the Afterlife is where the good and moral go. And these rewards of good behavior are manifested if one follows "company policy," and are as a result reunited with your particular god in his particular heaven. If not, one rots in hell or starts all over again. Ancestry, rank and kingship myths are used to justify rule and the seizure or imposition of power, with kingship validated by comparison to the most prestigious features around it — usually divinity. Incarnations of gods and previous famous kings, are shown to be linked to contemporary monarchies or rulers and their administration. In some ancient societies the king was seen as a manifestation of the god, in others he just "minded the shop," or was chosen for his (usually martial) ability.

The decision to include in this book figures from the major world religions — particularly Christianity and Islam — was made in order to illustrate their mythological aspects and not to undermine any prevailing belief systems. All religions rely to lesser or greater extent on the use of symbolic narratives to demonstrate abstract concepts and in this way can be termed "mythological." The line between myth and religion is often fine — for example one would expect to see the inclusion of Classical gods in any work on the subject of mythology, yet these clearly formed the basis of Ancient Greek religion and were venerated and worshipped as assiduously as any later deity. It is not my intention to disparage any religion, merely to trace its relationship to myth.

Jo Forty
Bryantspuddle, Dorset

Above left: This Anglo-Saxon relief shows Christ rescuing Adam and Eve from Hell.
Right: A Gorxio mask of polished stone from Mexico.

33

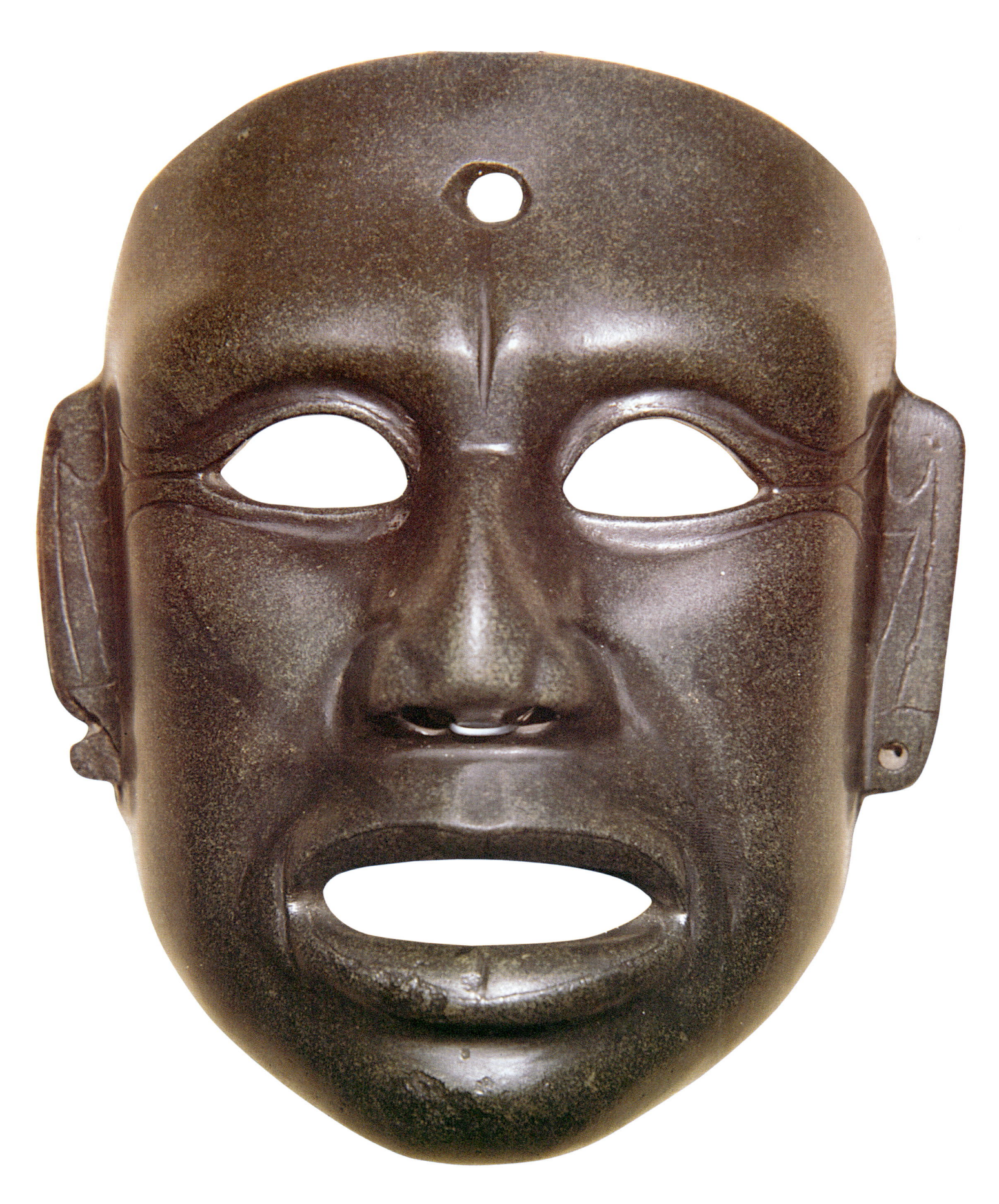

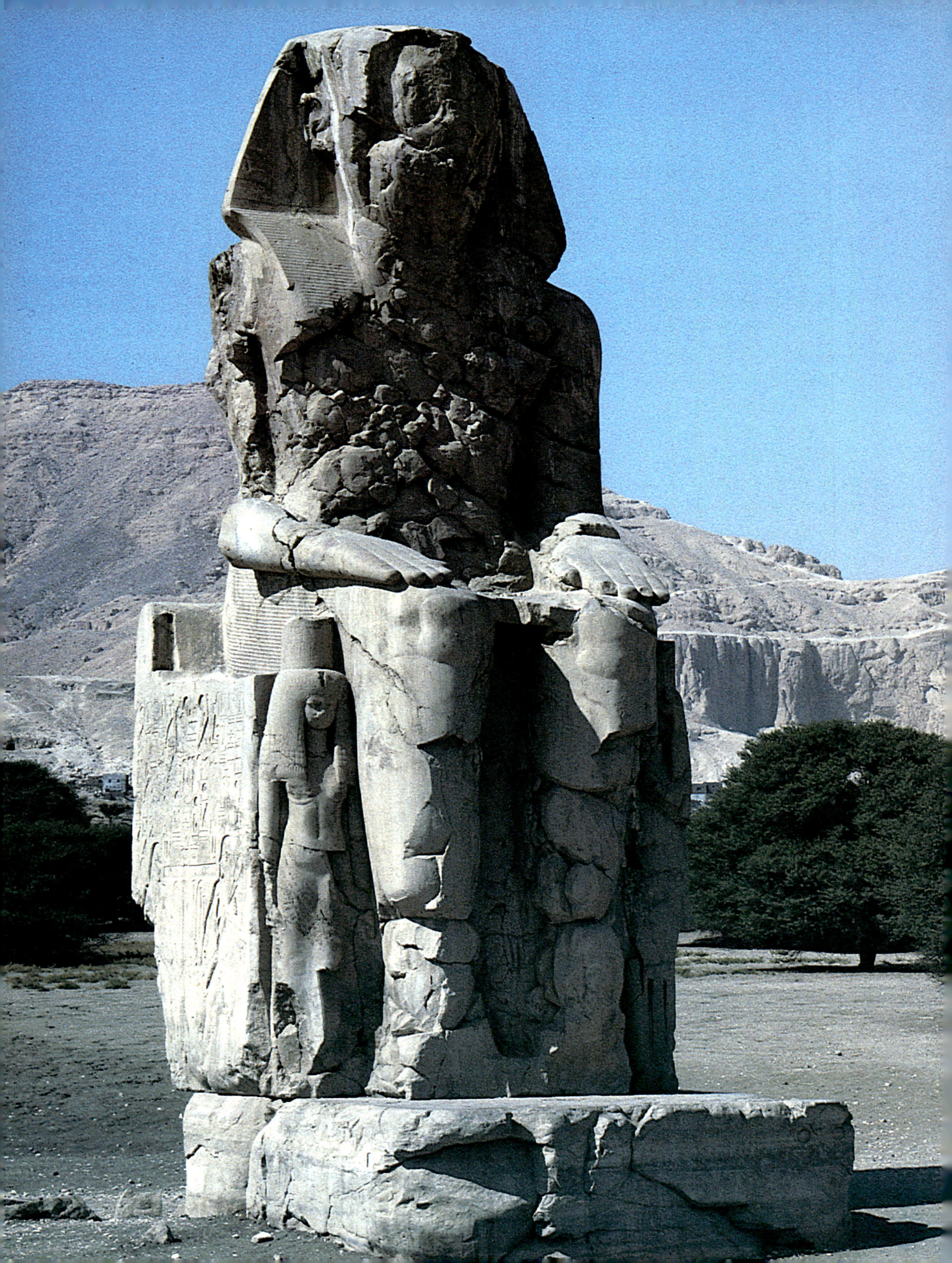

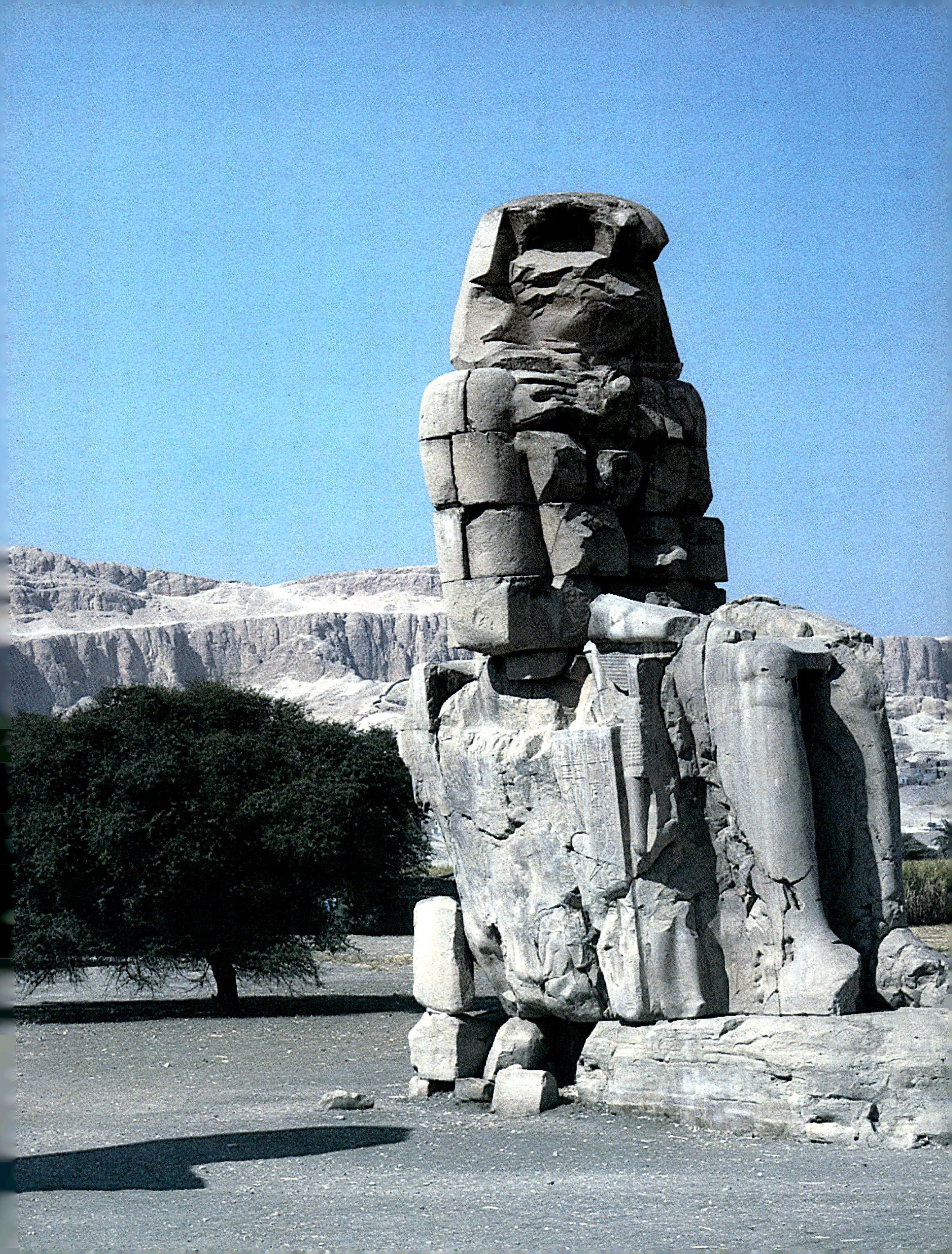

EGYPT & THE MIDDLE EAST

SUMER and Egypt were two of the four great centers of early civilization (China and India being the other two). Their achievements included working in stone and metals, design of a written language, and the development of cities. The latter were set in the alluvial plains of great rivers, and their religions and protocols were concerned with the organization of the vital resource of water and its use in irrigation.

Writing and other specialized occupations were radical new steps for these new communities. City dwellers were often not directly involved with subsistence agriculture and so had the time to develop skills that would not have been possible for the farmer. Also the potential abundance of crops allowed a surplus with which to trade, and trade brought communication with other cultures.

So began the development of hierarchical societies. In Egypt the Two Lands were held by one pharaoh when strong — a divine being who was worshiped as a manifestation of the god — whereas in Mesopotamia kingship was viewed as granted by the gods; the kings were only their stewards on Earth. Cities were based around a temple or holy area, and replacing and renewing this central structure gradually led to a mound with walls built around it for protection. In Mesopotamia mudbricks were used due to the scarcity of stone, which stimulated inventiveness and trade as well as new building techniques. Increased population levels and the growth of trade also gave craftsman the opportunity to begin making luxury items, requiring raw materials. The workshops of Mesopotamia and Egypt consequently traded commodities and ideas, leading to a new phase in the

Previous pages: The statues of Pharaoh Amenhotep III with the Valley of the Kings in the background. Right: The step-pyramid of King Zozer (c. 2600 BC), Saqqara, Egypt, and remains of the Valley Temple.

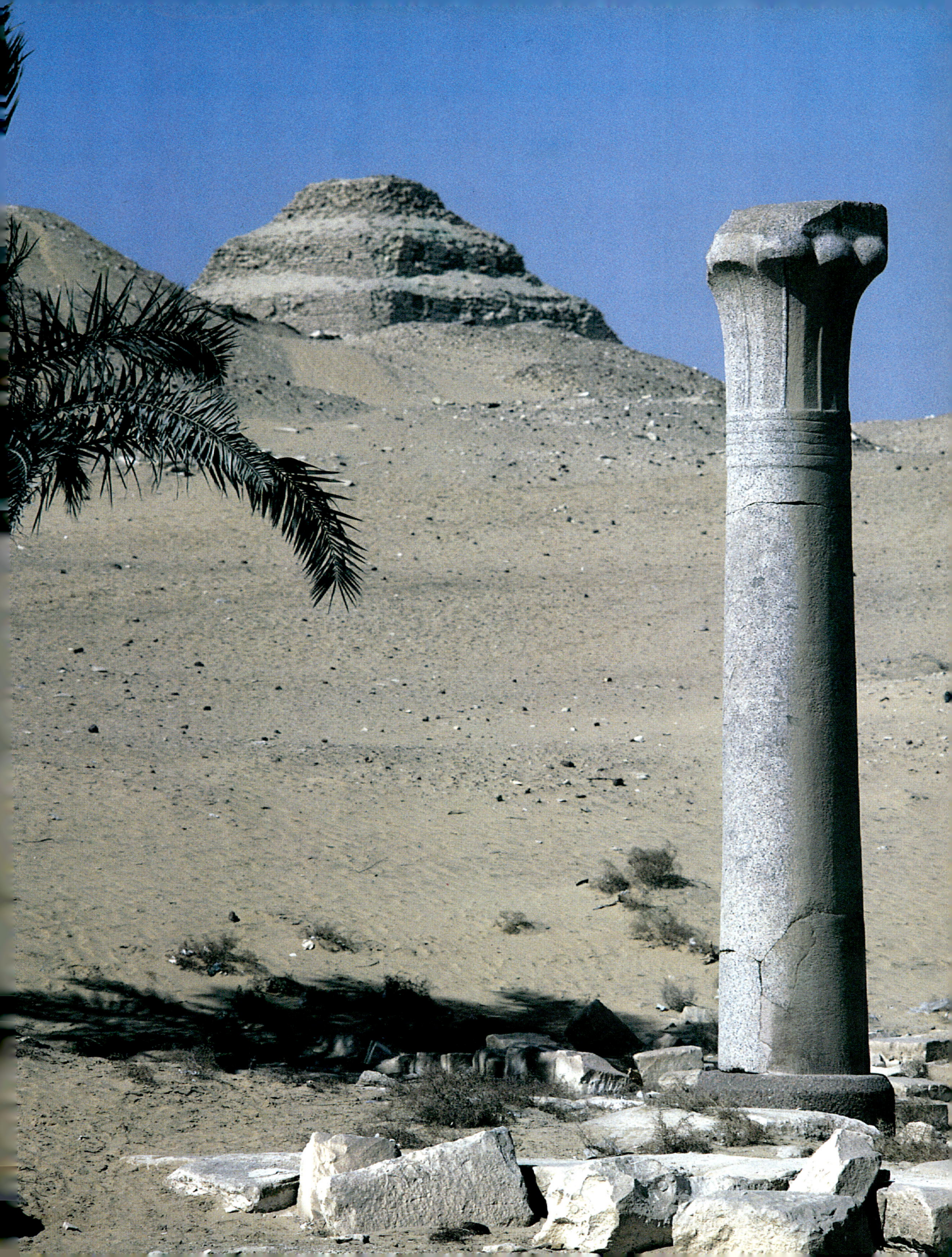

development of human society. Their inheritors in turn continued this development, bequeathing to us, their descendants, a thread of continuity that links us back to those first civilizations.

EGYPT

The gargantuan temple complex at Karnak and Luxor, the ancient Egyptian capital of empire ruled over by the composite deity Amun-Re and the result of accretion over two millennia, stunned the Classical tourist Herodotus. Egypt, after some initial early Mesopotamian input, had taken time to develop distinctively in isolation, with the deserts that surrounded it an effective insulation. It was one of the world's first river valley civilizations, with its wonderfully synchronized annual inundation that made crop-growing easy and left time for the lasting cultural preoccupations of stone construction and afterlife protocols.

The geographical differences between the upper Nile and its lower delta were reflected in the population and the name of the country itself — the "Two Lands," which had been united in about 3500 BC. Upriver being more isolated and conservative, the delta was always the interface between Egypt and the Mediterranean world — source of trade, immigration and technology. The man who united these two disparate geographical elements was the pharaoh — a deity made manifest and the bridge between the human and divine worlds. The first pharaohs cemented the union with the creation of a new capital city, Hutkaptah (called Memphis by the Greeks) and gods of the larger and more influential cities acquired national status as the Two Lands fused.

Egypt's history swings on the pivot of this geographical division — when the pharaoh was strong the country

Above left and Right: Carved papyrus leaves emerge from a pillar at the Temple of Amun, Karnak, Egypt.

• EGYPT & THE MIDDLE EAST •

prospered and expanded, when weak it broke back down into its constituent parts or was occupied by outsiders. These times were later called Intermediate periods. In time the priesthood also became so powerful that it was able to intermarry with royalty and create a line of priest-kings.

The timeframe of Egyptian history is divided into three main periods — the Old, Middle and New Kingdoms, each separated by an Intermediate period. The Old Kingdom saw the dynamic development of art and architecture that would become the blueprint for the future — for it was never really excelled. The Middle and New kingdoms saw the rise of Waset (also known as Thebes), the god Amun-Re and an Egyptian empire. By this time the country was no longer isolated but rather part of a vortex of human activity as the early civilizations and other migratory peoples intermingled on a scale hitherto unseen.

Intermediate periods occurred when there was either a weak or disputed royal line, which led to simultaneous pharaohs competing from, upriver and the delta, or else through foreign occupation. Finally, the newly forming Classical world rudely erupted into this ancient land. Assyrians, Persians, Greeks and Romans all in turn occupied and manipulated Egypt with their own agendas and the creative dynamic that had sustained it over three millennia wound down and moved west. Egypt had been sidelined.

There are no complete primary sources for the Egyptian myths — in fact most of our knowledge of them comes secondhand, from the later Greeks and Romans. There does not seem to have been the same emphasis on narrative within the religious culture, and no texts have been found that recount entire myths, but there are different native versions of episodes of particular ones. Presumably interpretation of the

Above left and Right: Amun-Ra (right) gives life to Ramses II who wears the headdress of a deity in the Temple of Ramses II, Luxor, Egypt.

· EGYPT & THE MIDDLE EAST ·

mythology over Egypt's long history was subject to the demands of the time, the location and the political motives of those who left their stories to posterity.

The most widespread creation myth is that of Re-Atum — the sun god with a bewildering array of names and aspects, who emerged from the dark primeval waters of Nun, creating light and the first land, a mound called the Benben. Re-Atum then conceived the first generation of gods himself, spitting out or ejaculating Shu and Tefnut, the deities of air and moisture. Setting the divine precedent that the pharaohs would mimic, brother and sister married and produced Geb and Nut, the Earth and the Sky, who in their turn gave birth to Osiris, Isis, Set and Nepthys.

These nine gods and goddesses are grouped together as the Great Ennead, and originated in Iunu (or Heliopolis as it is also known), one of three great early cities (the others were Hutkaptah and Khmun, also called Memphis and Hermopolis respectively) each of which had its own creation myth. Also in that pantheon was the son of Osiris and Isis, Horus, of whom the pharaoh was believed to be an earthly manifestation. In Memphis it was Ptah who emerged from the primeval mound. He was given a wife, Sakhmet, and a son, Nefertu, to make up the Memphite Triad, though Sokar, the god of the Memphite necropolis, is also linked with them. Apis was seen as a manifestation of Ptah, reflecting the legend that in the form of celestial fire Ptah impregnated a heifer that gave birth to the god in the shape of a bull.

In Khmun (Hermopolis), there was a set of eight deities — an ogdoad — representing the primeval chaos before the coming of the sun god. There were four frog-headed gods paired with four snake-headed goddesses: Nun and Naunet represented the primordial abyss; Heh and Hauet were a

Above left and Right: The Temple of Horus in Edfu, Egypt.

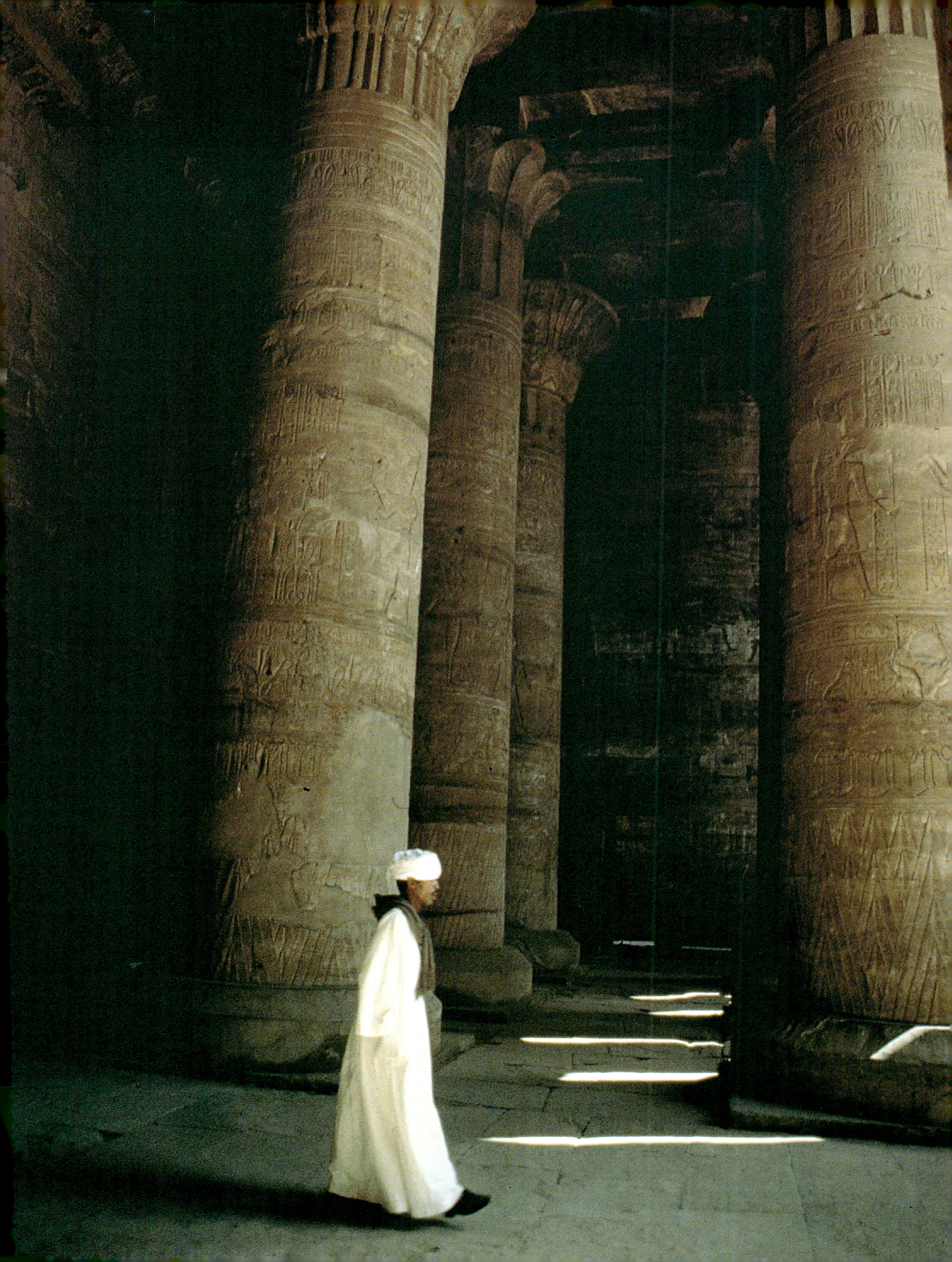

manifestation of infinity; Kek and Kauket personified darkness and Amun and Amaunet were the essence of hidden power — omnipresent yet invisible. Reflecting the inherent duality of the Two Lands, these male and female forms produced from themselves the mound out of chaos, upon which lay the egg containing the young sun god Re.

In Waset (Thebes), another great city — destined to be the religious and political capital from the Middle Kingdom period onward, the creation myth centered on Amun. Once he had ousted Montu, the older god of the Theban Nome, Amun went on to combine with Re, the chief god of the Old Kingdom, and become the supreme god of the Egyptian pantheon. He was given a consort, Mut, and a son, Khons, to make up the Theban Triad. The largest and most impressive Egyptian temples were raised in their names at Karnak and Luxor.

At Elephantine, Khnum was said to have created life on his potter's wheel. He too had a consort, Satis, and Anukis made up the triad as their divine child.

Over a long period of time all these gods combined and coalesced into new incarnations. Thus Re, Amun and Atum were put together in a seemingly endless variety of formats. All the gods had this ability to regenerate and renew, demonstrating the Ancient Egyptians' veneration of the past.

Just as there were many creator god myths, so too were there a great number of solar cycle myths — with the same essential imagery and motifs, yet endless variation. Their meaning was the cycle itself. The sun god was born anew each dawn, and crossed the sky in his solar boat, gradually ageing and finally dying (although this is never specifically mentioned). He then traveled during the night through the Underworld, in a cycle of regeneration.

Above left and Right: The sacred temple of the Triad of Thebes — Amun, Mut and Khons — in Luxor, Egypt.

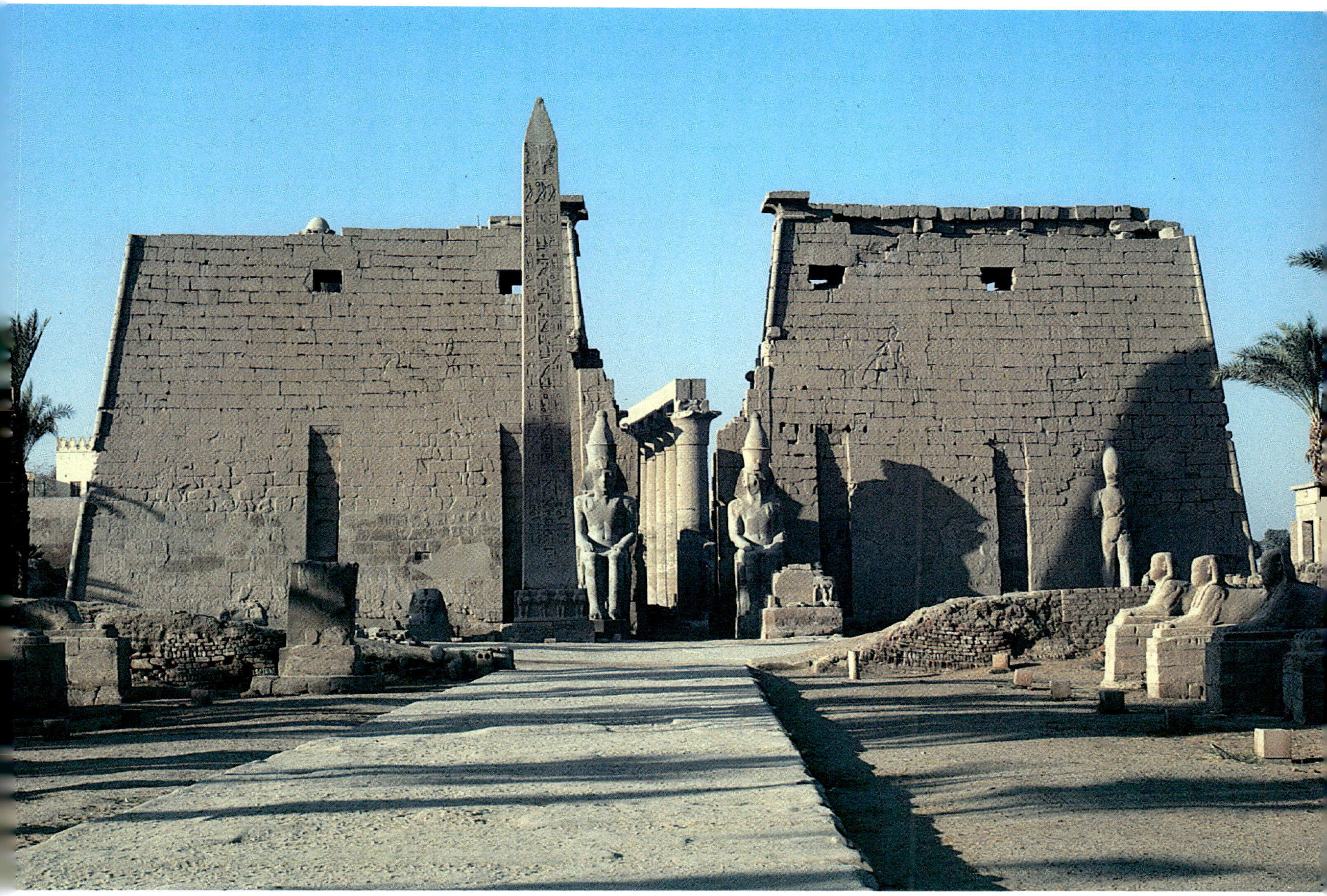

One of the main mythological cycles was that of Osiris, which was closely interwoven with the evolution of the Two Lands and the institution of divine kingship, and also probably reflects and interprets actual past events. Osiris was the acknowledged heir of Atum, married to his sister Isis. However his brother Set was jealous of him and, inviting him to a banquet under the guise of friendship, imprisoned Osiris in a chest, which was then thrown into the Nile. The chest drifted down river to Byblos, where it lodged in the branches of a tree. Isis, who had been searching everywhere, found the chest and hid it in the marshes of the delta; but Set discovered it once again whilst out hunting and, angrily breaking it open, he cut the body of Osiris into pieces, scattering them far and wide. Isis then called her sister Nepthys to help collect all the pieces together and make the first mummy. Despite her great magic powers, Isis could not bring Osiris back to life, yet she managed to impregnate herself on him, taking the form of a hawk to do so, and gave birth to Horus. Set discovered what had taken place and hoped to murder Horus as well, but Isis invoked the protection of Re, who then sent Thoth to arbitrate. Osiris remained a king, but king of the Underworld.

When Horus became a man, he claimed his father's rank and inheritance, and aspired to leadership of the gods, but Set contested his claim and challenged him. Re favored Set, but most of the other Gods preferred Horus, and so Re retired from the debate in a bad temper. Eventually battle ensued between Horus and Set, and being older and more experienced, Set began to dominate. But he lacked an ally equal to the one Horus could call on — the great Isis — who was determined her son would triumph. She guided him through all the stages of the struggle, yet still Horus could

Above left and Right: From left to right, statues of Osiris, Horus and Isis.

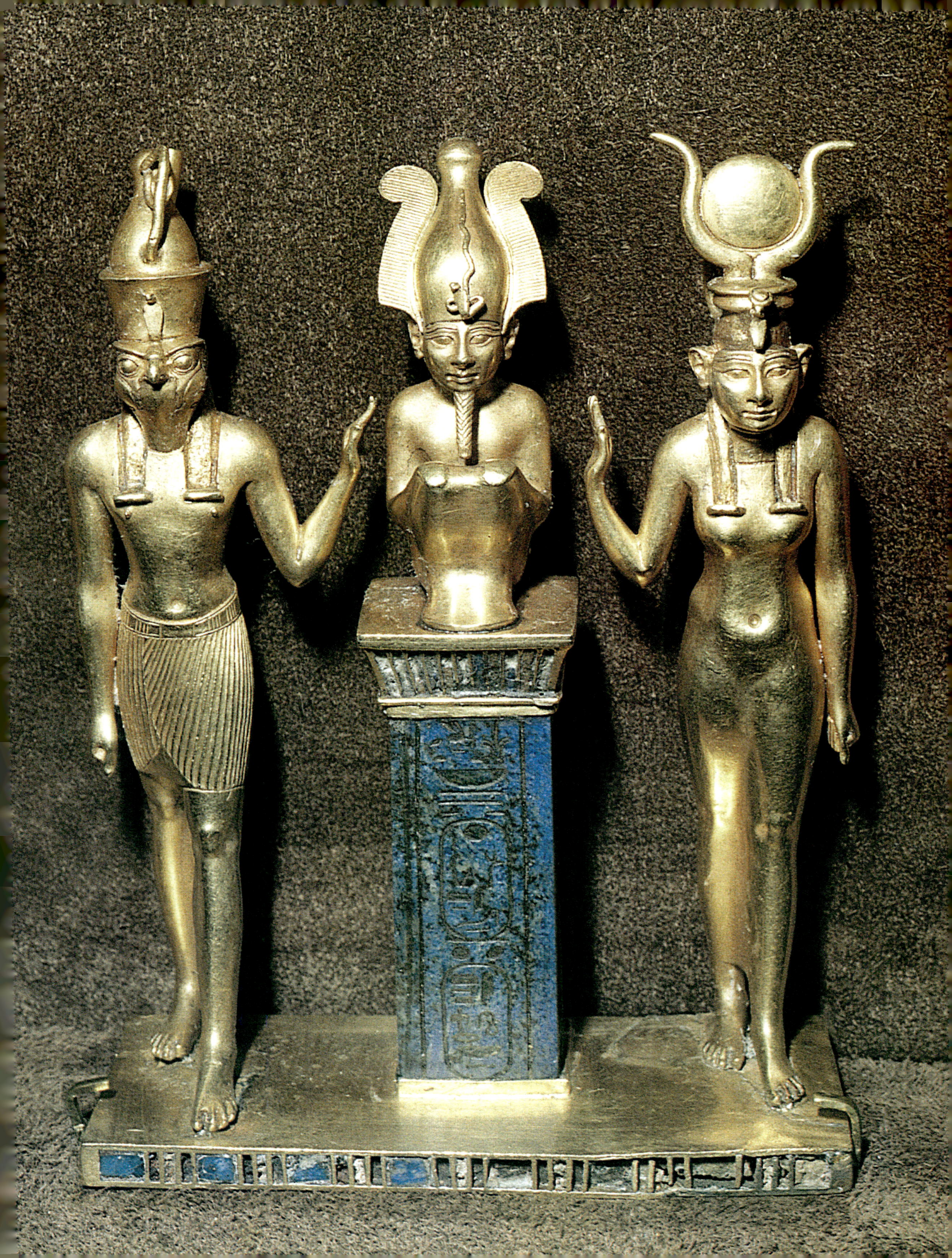

not completely vanquish Set, so in the end all the gods decided to appeal to Osiris himself. Osiris rebuked them and championed his son as his rightful heir, and so Horus finally came to his inheritance. The pharaoh came to be seen as the incarnation of Horus in life, and of Osiris in death, although as time went by Osiris-hood was open to any pure heart. Other versions of this myth had Osiris and Set ruling over separate parts of the country, but Set mismanaged his region, which turned to desert, and he decided to do away with Osiris and have it all, thus leading to their conflict. Both Set and Horus did many vile things to each other in their struggle for dominance including rape, castration, amputation and blinding, as well as various less harmful tricks to try and outwit each other. Horus even savagely attacked his mother Isis, when she prevented him from finishing Set off when he had the chance. Although there are many versions of their struggle, all these Horus-Set myths end with arbitration from Thoth, and a collective decision on the part of all the gods in favor of Horus.

MESOPOTAMIA

Mesopotamia had a different kind of geography from Egypt, with its two main rivers turbulent and lacking the consistency of the Nile, and with closer mountains making the climate stormy and full of change. The Sumerians were the earliest city people in the region and they were pivotal to the whole of Mesopotamian mythology thereafter. Their period of supremacy from c. 3000–2500 BC saw the growth of diverse city-states linked by trade, with their independent and individual gods. Gradually these cities evolved into a loose federation with regular changes in overall leadership and, though local cults remained, the best known gods of the

Above left and Right: A close-up of the Temple of Inanna, the Sumerian goddess of love and war, at Uruk (c. 1475 BC).

• EGYPT & THE MIDDLE EAST •

larger cities became universally recognized. Although not an absolute theocracy (for they farmed and manufactured individually), the Sumerians regarded themselves as stewards of the gods, holding the city and land in fief only. City-states, thus owned by deities, grew up around the main temple or ziggurat, which gradually accreted in layers upward. Originally, Mesopotamia consisted of independent city-states that each had their time of prominence: Ur (c. 4500 BC), Uruk, Eridu, Umma, Ebla, Mari, Adab, Nippur, Akshak, Sippar, Der, Nuzi, Nineveh, Akkad, Susa and Babylon. Usually independent, they gradually linked together through alliance and conquest. Eventually they were all linked after being conquered by the upland Iranians.

Writing initially developed through the keeping of temple accounts and data concerning agricultural sowing and harvesting times. The earliest writings in the form of clay tablets were made at Uruk in 3100 BC. Marking wet clay with the end of a reed stalk made the first letters. A pictographic script then developed, slowly metamorphosing into cuneiform. Literary compositions and poetry followed. These cities were temple and palace bureaucracies, a feature they had in common with all the early civilizations. Trade was vital, as Mesopotamia lacked all kinds of commodities. Semites eventually swamped the non-Semitic Sumerians, but their influence on future cultures was lasting. Their agriculture was based on irrigation, not rainfall, and cultivation that stimulated organization and cooperation. Sumerian religion was chthonic — worshipping earth rather than sky powers, with Enlil at the apex. The creation of mankind was credited as a deliberate act on the part of gods, who needed retainers to observe the rites and practices that kept them sustained. The Sumerians believed that after death

Above left and Right: A glazed brick lion relief follows the Sacred Way to the Ishtar gates at Babylon.

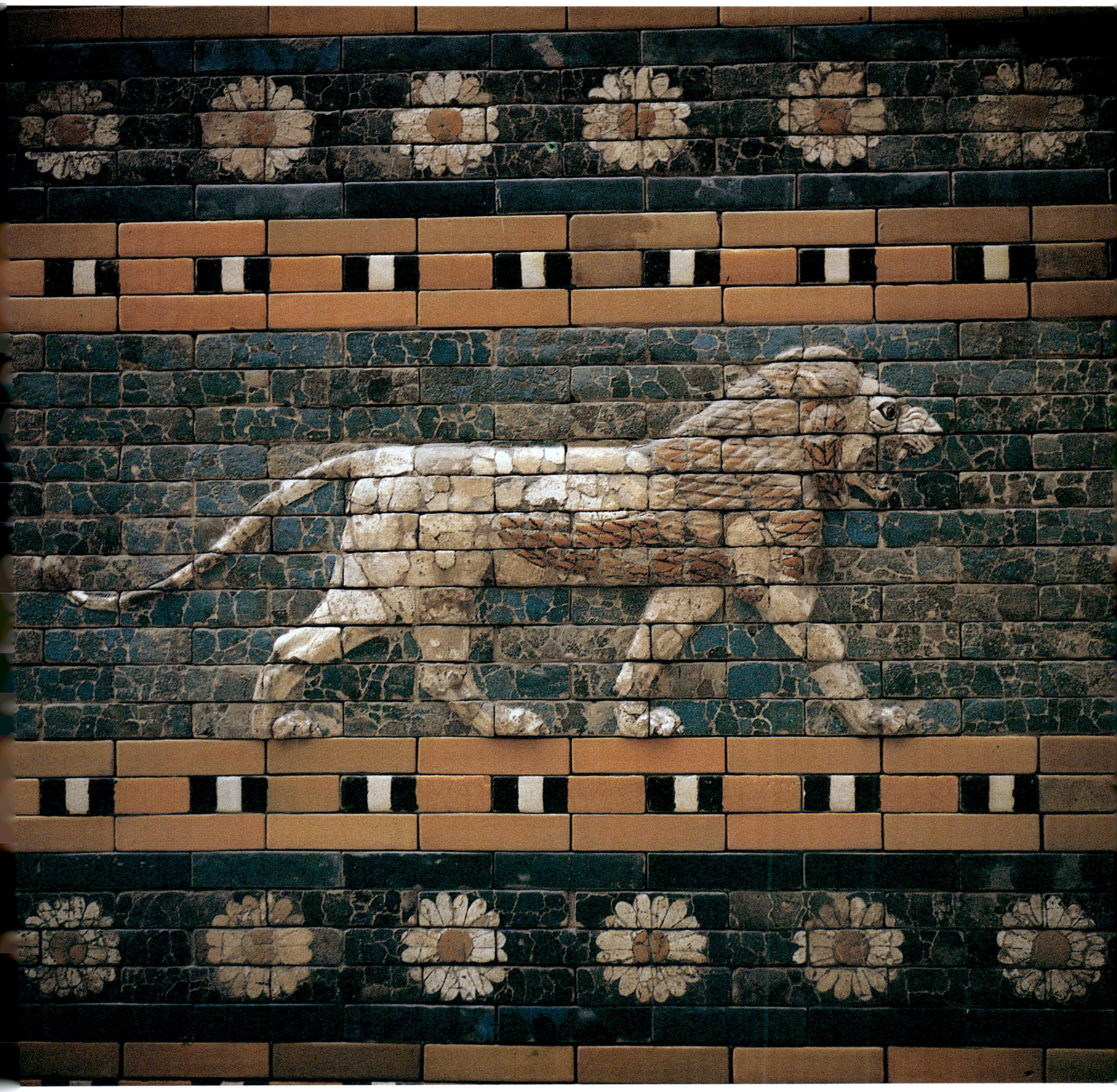

man went to a shadowy netherworld that was certainly not paradisiacal. In their mythology there were battles against dark powers, huge storms and hurricanes, foreign invasion, internal competition, external conflict and uneven river flow — all of which went to mold an outlook that accepted struggle as a part of life and as necessary as divine order.

Babylon and Assyria were influenced by the Sumerians in turn, as the interactions of the Old World speeded up. Many Hurrite and Hittite records have been found at Babylon, detailing the extent of trade and intimating the large size of the administration. The Babylonian king Hammurabi united the whole area into a single country through conquest and went on to underpin it with his Law Code. The Babylonians were interested in Sumerian religion and mythology, which they modified and incorporated into their own religious system. Still later the Assyrians carried out a similar process when they in turn revitalized Babylonian culture and formed the idea of a single universal empire.

IRAN

The Mesopotamian mythologies pale somewhat when compared to the heavy black and white dualism of opposites belonging to Iranian Zorastrianism, which changed the whole feel of contemporary religion. No longer did good and evil originate from the same source of being, transcending and reconciling opposites; instead there was divine open warfare. This extreme dualism had a profound effect on West Asian religious processes.

The Iranians were Aryans, the same people who went east into India and west into Mesopotamia and Europe. Zorastrianism developed slowly from the early Aryan sky gods, as they were modified on the journey west. Rejecting

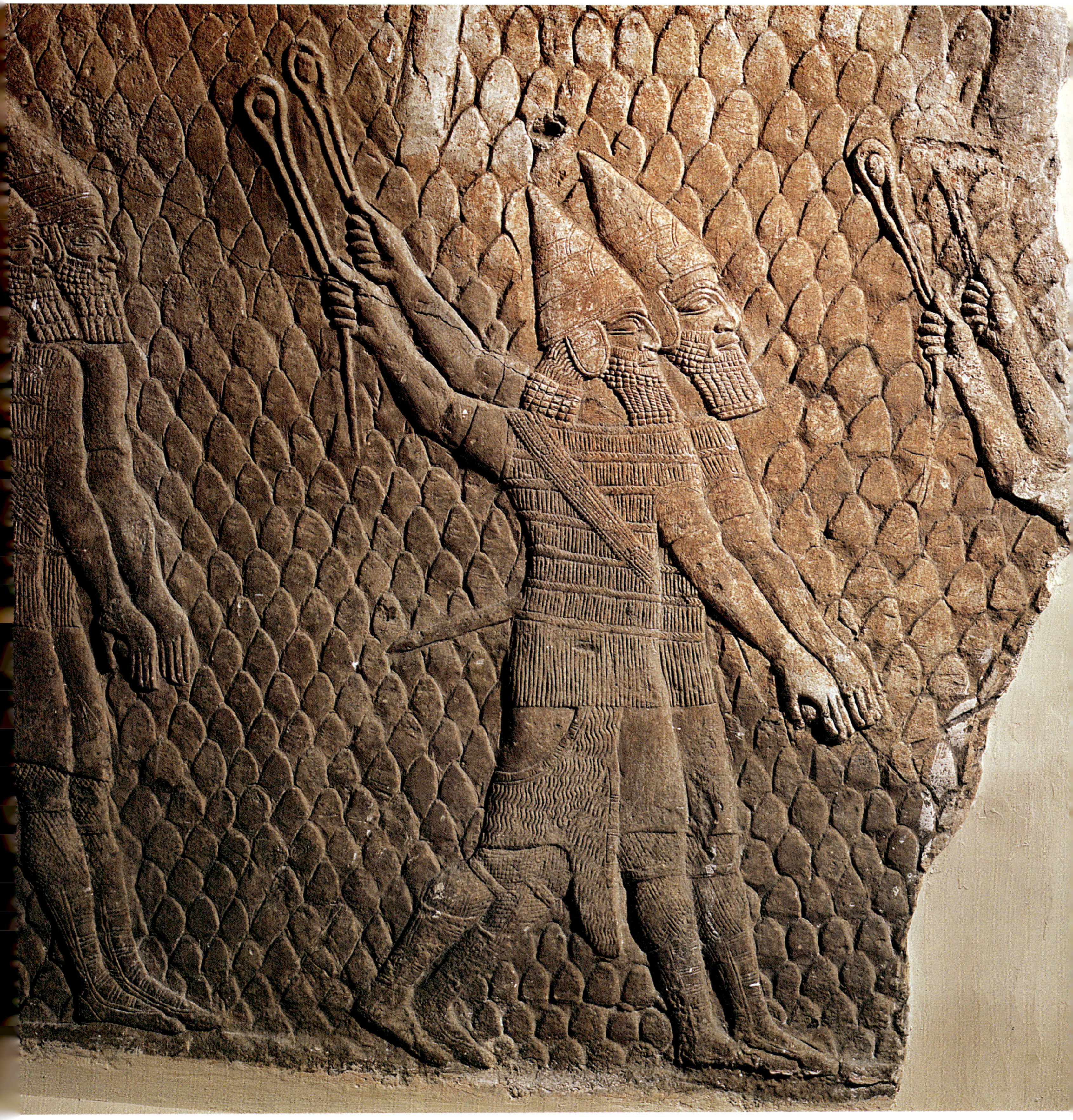

the amoral war gods (who became the Zorastrian evil *daevas*) in favor of a more balanced worship of moral truth and right (manifested in the *ahuras*) the new religion was guided by a highly trained priest elite. The cosmological view of this religion interpreted the world as a battleground between good and evil forces, fighting toward a conclusion. At the end of time, evil would be defeated and the universe complete its development of perfection. Man was seen as the only creature capable of choice — all other living things having predetermined good or evil natures. The elements of creation were seen as inherently good, particularly fire.

First evolving in eastern Iran, Zorastrianism came to dominate with the rise of the Achaemenian royal dynasty (559–323 BC). As it became the religion of an empire, it also came into contact and was influenced by other West Asian cultures. Briefly eclipsed by the Hellenistic age but deeply rooted in Iranian culture and with a coherent body of teaching which survived, it experienced a resurgence with the rise of the indigenous Sassanian dynasty (226 BC–800 AD). When Moslem arms finally defeated the Sassanians, Zorastrianism became virtually extinct in its homeland. In the 10th century AD however, a hardcore group left for India, where they still exist as the Parsees. It is reported that since the recent Islamic revolution in Iran and the throwing off of outside influences, Zorastrianism is making something of a return.

CANAAN, ARABIA, ISRAEL

Canaan (also called Phoenicia) was a land of ancient Semitic peoples which included most of the area that makes up modern Israel and Syria. Like its West Asian neighbors it was made up of city-states (Tyre, Sidon, Ugarit and Byblos) which traded with all the larger empires around them. In fact

Above left and Right: This Phoenician ivory panel is a reminder of the burned palace at Nimrud (8th century BC).

• EGYPT & THE MIDDLE EAST •

55

the Canaanites or Phoenicians were talented sailors who spread far and wide, connecting disparate cultures through trade as well as transmitting their own ideas. They were eventually taken over by other powers in that ever-changing area of migration and conflict, and being of the same Semitic racial stock they were absorbed by Hebrew culture.

The Canaanite polytheistic religion contained a large pantheon, headed by the gods El and Baal and goddesses Asherah and Astarte. The emphasis was on fertility, reflecting the importance of water for agriculture in that dry region. Deities were sacrificed to in high places and at temples and shrines in ways similar to Israel and other Semitic cultures.

The Hebrews, shifted and shunted through war and conquest, melding the ideas of the moment and those of the great civilizations around them. They emerged from the nexus of a dynamic and changing world to form through ordeal and trial the masterplan of their religion — which would penetrate geographical distance and time to become, along with its similarly-sourced cousin, Islam, one of the two most dominant religions of the modern world. For the Hebrews perfected the West Asian tendency toward monotheism. El and Yaweh had similarities that were eventually curtailed, both gods were detached and omnipotent, hiding a jealous and competitive sensitivity. Yaweh evolved perhaps from various city gods including Sin, the chief deity of Abraham's home city of Ur, and Akhenaten's Aten about whom Moses would have heard. At this time people were seriously mixing and exchanging data and theory. The Hebrew creator god even told Jonah that the Hebrews held no exclusive rights to him — he was a worldwide god whose message was for all humankind. There were to be no others, no images and therefore little mythology,

Above left and Right: A Canaanite supreme deity in bronze.

• EGYPT & THE MIDDLE EAST •

although mythological elements were modified to fit this desert-honed religion. The Hebrews withstood the outside influences of settlers in Canaan's urban civilizations.

Islam, the other great West Asian monotheistic religion, again originated in the desert. In 610 AD Mohammed began the last great wave that assimilated and obliterated West Asian history. Monotheist and straightforward, with no mythology as such, it ended a cultural heritage that stretched back to the Sumerians. From West Asia, Islam burst out across the world into Spain, Central Asia and beyond. Its adherents regard it as the final revelation by God to mankind, superior to both Judaism and Christianity. It requires total submission to the "Will of God." The prophet Mohammed was the exclusive channel for this communication. Until middle age a merchant from Mecca, he then experienced a series of divine revelations that form the basis of the Koran. Originally this message was intended for the Arabs alone, but it came to include a universal message for all humankind. Mohammed experienced various initial difficulties from his pagan compatriots, but after a few setbacks he successfully organized his followers so that by the time of his death his authority extended over the whole Arabian Peninsula, leaving Islam poised for further military and religious conquest.

ASIA MINOR

The civilizations of Asia Minor — Hurrian, Hittite and Phrygian — turned on the West Asian concept of the sacrificed and resurrected male fertility god, which continued to appeal as it drifted west toward Greece and Rome.

The Hurrians were an ancient people of unknown origin who had migrated into northwest Mesopotamia by c. 2500 BC. A later Hurrian kingdom based in northern Syria and

Above left and Right: An ancient Assyrian stone carving.

• EGYPT & THE MIDDLE EAST •

known as Mitanni existed by 2000 BC, at which time it came into conflict with Egypt. With the expansion of the Hittites, the Hurrians were absorbed in much the same fashion as the Sumerians, who lost precedence to Babylon, though they left a similarly profound influence on their descendants.

The Hittite Empire in Asia Minor lasted from c. 2000–1200 BC, before being absorbed in turn by the Assyrians. Their pantheon was immense and chaotic, with gods behaving much as humans. The Hittites expanded their territory, attracted by the wealth of the city civilizations over the Taurus Mountains and this exposed them to West Asian religion and culture. Ultimately their empire achieved a similar size and status as its contemporaries: Egypt, Babylon and Assyria. Hittite state organization centered on military and political power at their capital Hattustas, but allowed local religious variation. There were the state supreme sun god and goddess, who ruled the pantheon with an important weather god who was betrothed to the female sun deity. The Hittites shared a Mesopotamian fascination with elemental deities whose behavior had such direct impact on their everyday lives.

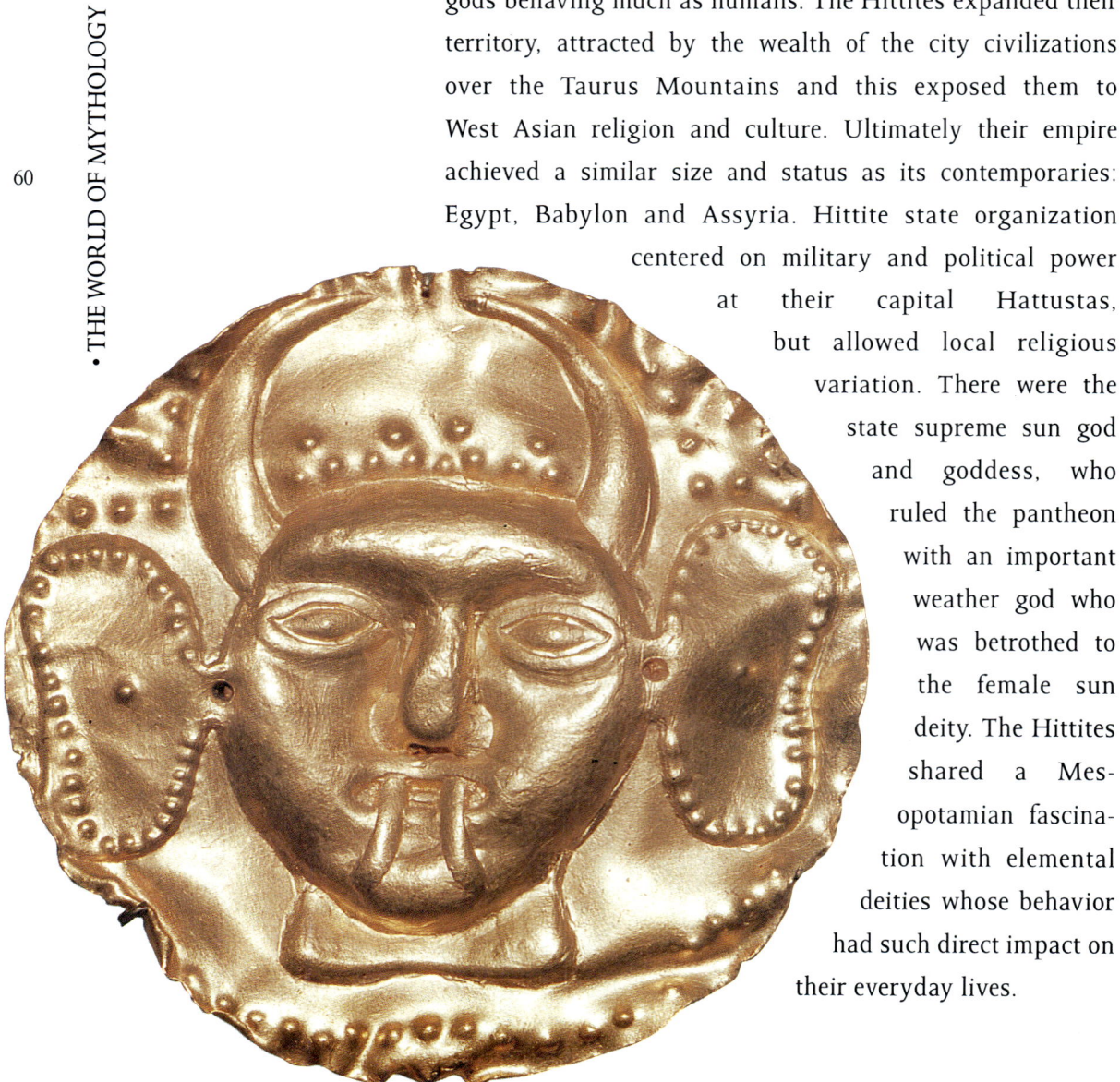

Above left and Right: This gold plaque was discovered in a Persian temple (c. 5th–3rd century BC).
Above left and Left: This Persian gold medallion represents Ahriman (c. 5th–3rd century BC).

EGYPT & THE MIDDLE EAST

A-Z
CODEX GODS

ADAD
"Canal inspector of Heaven and Earth"
A Mesopotamian weather and fertility god. In Adad was the manifestation of the huge storms that swept over the lands of the Near East. A son of An, in myths and religious texts he was portrayed as a bull or a lion, while in human form he was a warrior, racing a chariot harnessed to the storms. Adad had temples in Enegi near Ur, Babylon and Assur. His symbol was a forked lightning bolt, and there is some evidence that he was involved with his brother Shamash in the administration of oracles.

ADAPA
Sumerian Adapa was a son of the god Ea, the first man (equivalent to the Biblical Adam), one of the Seven Sages of Mesopotamian mythology and King of Eridu. While fishing in his boat, Adapa was wrecked by the South Wind and in magical retaliation he broke its wings. Anu, supreme god of the pantheon, summoned Adapa to heaven to explain himself. Ea, wishing to save his son's life life, advised that he dress down and be polite, and told him to reject any offered hospitality. Through this advice and being honest and upfront, Adapa managed to reassure Anu and was returned to earth. However, by having refused food and drink in heaven he had lost his chance for eternal life. Adapa subsequently found it difficult to forgive his father for this.

ADONIS
"Lord"
A Syrian fertility god, adopted successfully by the Greeks, whose mythical roots are firmly based in West Asia — around Syria and the Lebanon — where there was a river named after him. His main temples were at Byblos and Paphos, where his annual death and resurrection were celebrated, his reappearance manifesting in the bloom of the anemone flower. He was the object of Aphrodite's affections and the goddess repeatedly tried to dissuade him from his favorite leisure pursuit of hunting. He was, however, deaf to her pleas and died in a hunting accident soon after being warned.

AHRIMAN
The personification of evil in ancient Iranian mythology, in counterpoint to Ahuramazda. Ahriman ruled over death and manifested Angra Mainya — the destructive spirit who was contrasted with the manifestation of Ahuramazda's Spenta Mainya, or Holy Spirit. The two were locked in a cycle of mutual exchange and cancellation until the eventual foretold triumph of good over evil. Ahriman knew of the phrophecy and thus strove hard to fulfil his role by introducing an opposing evil for each of Ahuramazda's efforts, making all the calamities and suffering that beset mankind — illness, disease, extremes of weather, destructive dragons and even the influential planets, in

Right: A stone relief of King Ashurnasirpal II, his attendants and the winged Ahuramazda above.

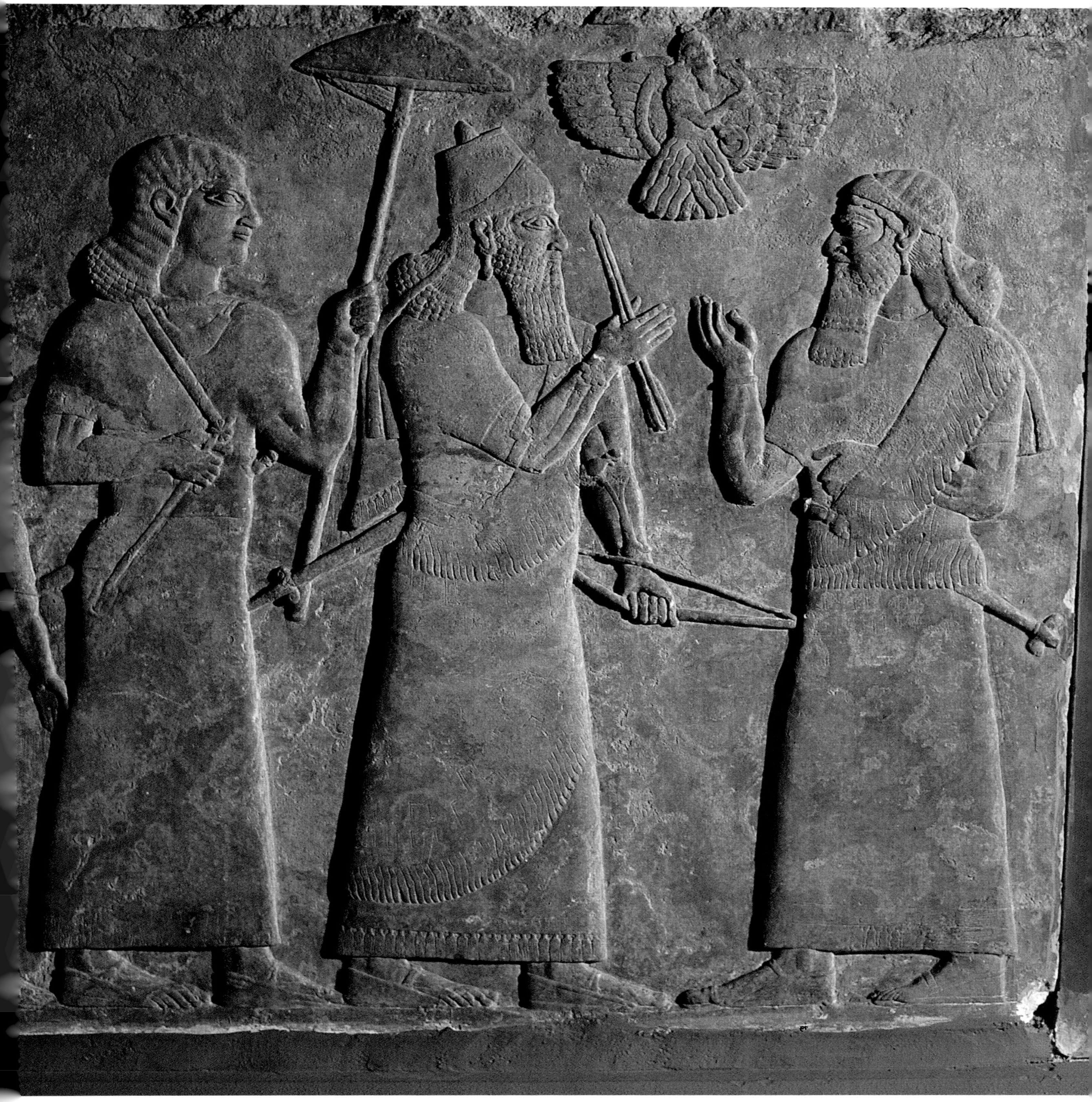

A-Z
CODEX GODS

contrast to Ahuramazda's stars. His source of power was the destructive female principle called Az, which through undermining the intellect, brought about baseness and bestiality.

AHURAMAZDA
"Wise Lord"
Also known as: Ahura, Ormuzd

Originally known only as Ahura (Lord) before the addition of Mazda (Wise) and later called Ormuzd, Ahuramazda was the principal deity in Zorastrianism, the religion of ancient Iran. This doctrine, propounded by Zarathustra (Zoroaster) and traditionally dated to 628–551 BC, entails a dualistic system of good, created by Ahuramazda, opposed by evil, embodied in Ahriman. These two were the offspring of Zurvan Akarna (Infinite Time). Fire was the symbol of Ahuramazda and was therefore central to Zoroastrianism, as is evident from the excavations of Sassanian fire temples and the recurrence of fire altars on Sassanian coins.

Ahuramazda represented the metamorphosis from polytheistic to monotheistic beliefs, anticipating the Semitic montheisms that were eventually to dominate the region and later the world. He was a god of prophecy and revelation whose development incorporated the older polytheistic gods as manifestations of himself and his opposite Ahriman in what then evolved into dualism, prefiguring the eventual single all-encompassing deity.

ALILAT

An Arabian mother goddess, worshiped in Nabataean kingdom based at Petra in present day Jordan. These warrior-merchants, with the new technology of saddles considerably upgrading their military capabilities, spread her influence in their vicinity. She was manifested at their capital by a squarish stone, reflecting the Middle Eastern affinity with distinctive stone landmarks (usually aerolites) and their tendency to imbue them with religious significance. Her son, Dusura, eventually eclipsed her in importance.

AMMUT
"Devouress of the Dead"

Ancient Egyptian Underworld monster goddess. Egyptians believed that everyone was judged after death, descending into the Underworld, to the Hall of Two Truths. There a tribunal of forty-two assessor gods examined the dead to decide if they were worthy of eternity in the realm of Osiris. This test consisted of the heart, considered to be the "blackbox" data recorder of all past deeds, being weighed in a pair of scales against Ma'at, the goddess of Truth, manifested as a feather. Provided the dead man's statements were truthful the scales balanced and the god Thoth declared him "True of voice" and fit for the kingdom of Osiris. Ammut sat by the scales during the proceedings. She had the head of a crocodile, the body of a lion or leopard and the

Right: An Egyptian papyrus of Anhai (c. 1150 BC).

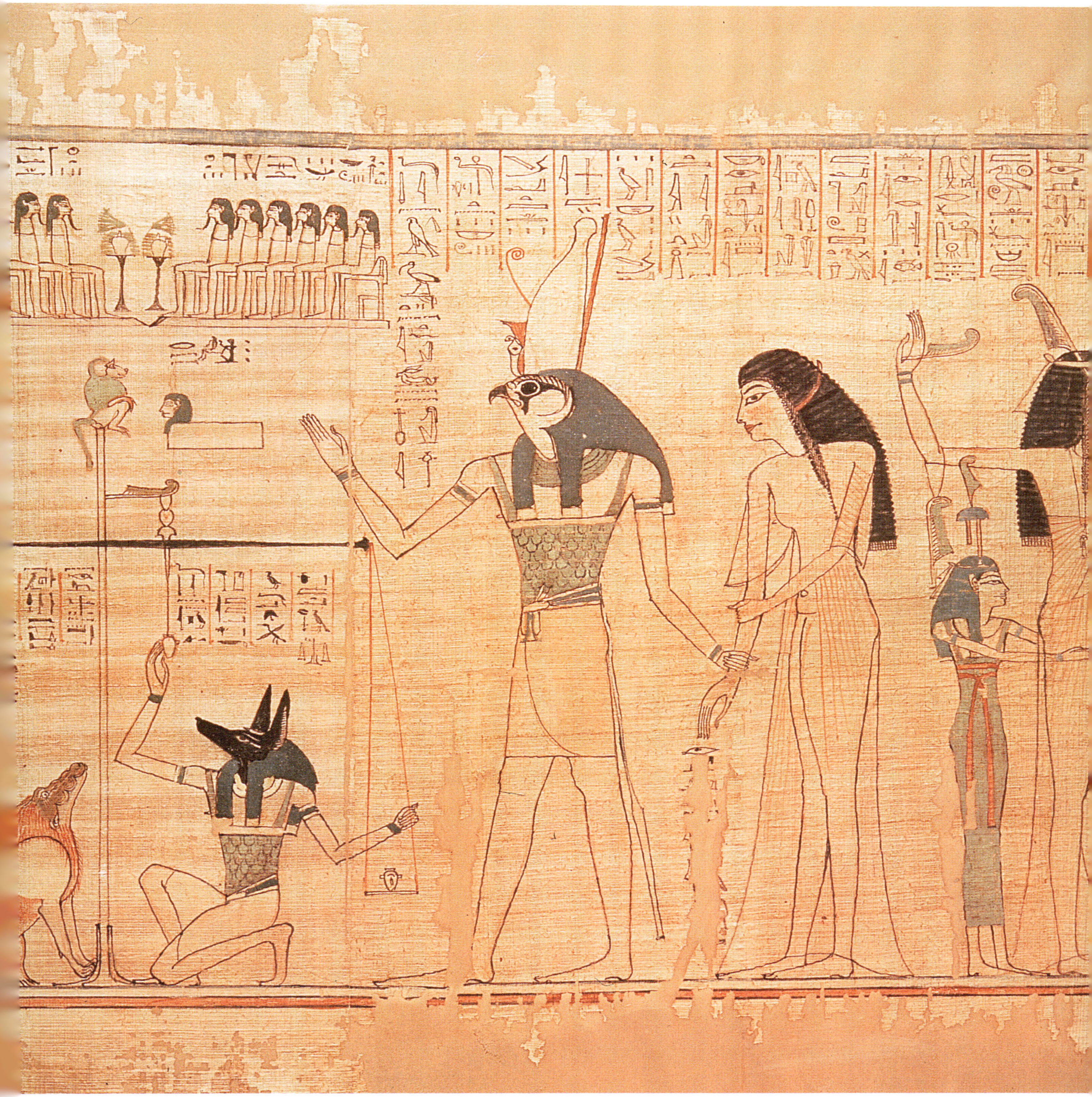

A-Z
CODEX GODS

rear-end of a hippopotamus, and she devoured those hearts that did not balance, causing all other parts of the soul to instantly disintegrate.

AMUN
"The Hidden One"

An Egyptian sky and war deity who combined with the sun god Re to become Amun-Re, the prime creator god. He developed into the empire's main war god during the height of the pharaonic empire, and was portrayed anthropomorphically, sporting a crown of two tall plumes, often carrying a spear, although sometimes also as a man with a ram's head. He was associated with the military operations of the pharaohs, particularly Tutmose III, when Egyptian dominion stretched from the Sudan to Syria. Scenes on the walls of temples stress this close relationship. His main cult center was at Thebes, where the tribute pouring in from the empire went to build a magnificent complex of temples and treasuries at Luxor and Karnak — which until their sack by the Persians were the oldest, largest and most famous of the Classical world.

AN
Also known as: Anu

An was the Mesopotamian personification of heaven, portrayed anthopomorphically — as were all Mesopotamian gods. Known as An to the Sumerians, he was the overlord of all the other gods whose importance gradually declined as younger more aggressive or proactive deities such as Enlil arose, until he took a back seat as a creative principle and a holy place within which the newer gods functioned. An then became a remote, celestial "grandfather" deity. The stars were his soldiers and the Milky Way his royal road. He intercedeed on behalf of the lesser gods when Enlil became overbearing in his demands, and was referred to for his wisdom and experience. By the time of the Assyrio-Babylonian pantheon he had receded to concept status as the manifestation of heaven, giving way to the more violently active and military Marduk and Ishtar.

ANHUR

Egyptian sky and war god, who was popular in 18th–24th Dynasties. He manifested the creative power of the sun, and was also a warlike aspect of Ra. Anhur enjoyed a unusual popularity with the ordinary peasants.

ANDJETY

Andjety was a precursor of Osiris and closely related to the monarch. He was portrayed as a ram-headed man — a symbol of fertility.

ANTI

The sky hawk god associated with Horus, Anti was a guardian deity who protected the regions of the east, where the sun god rose.

Right: A corridor in the Temple of Amun at Karnak, Egypt.

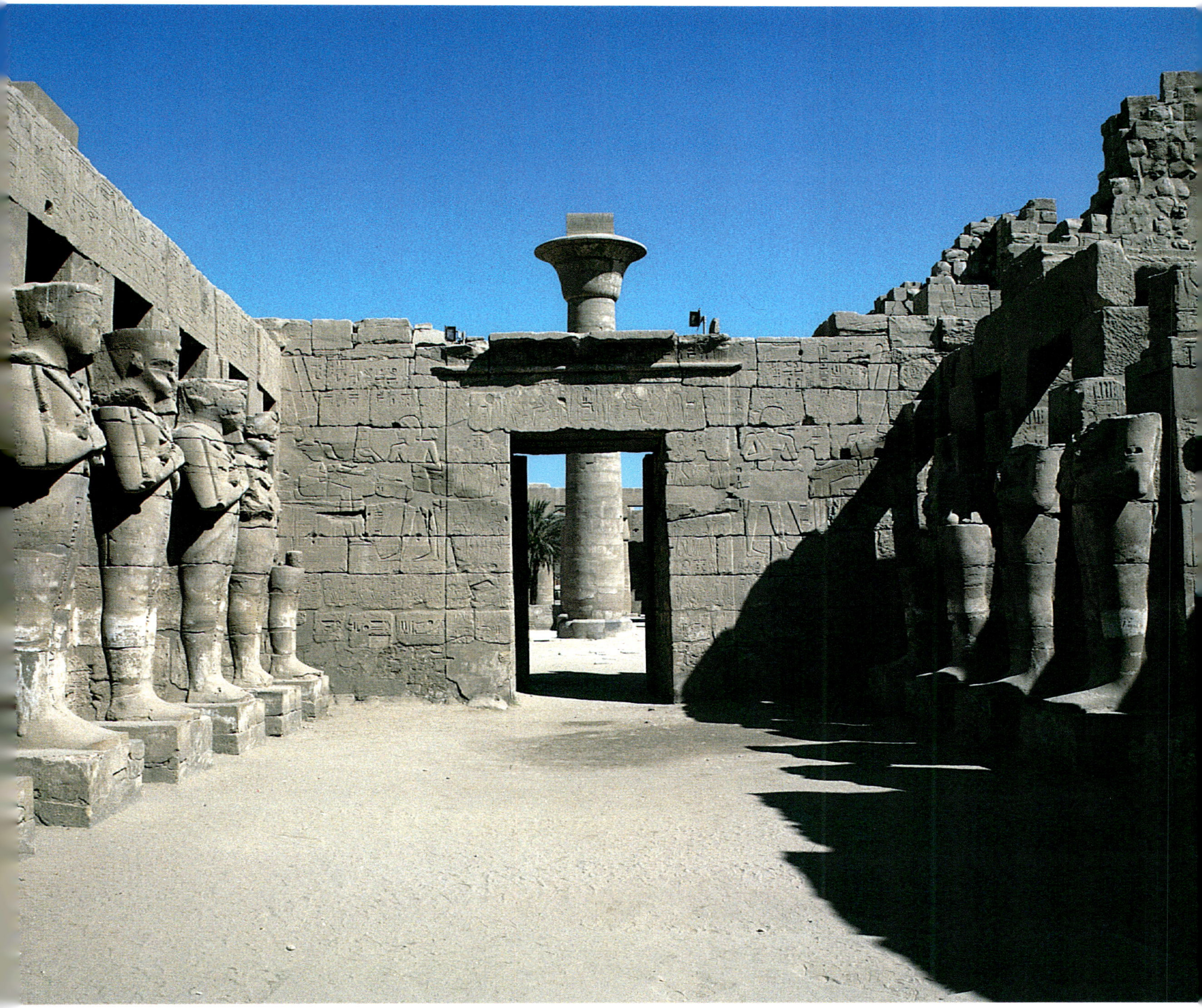

A-Z
CODEX GODS

ANUBIS
"Lord of the Sacred Land"

Anubis, the ancient Egyptian god of embalming and the desert necropoli, was portrayed as a sleek black jackal or anthropomorphically with a jackal's head. Before the rise of Osiris, Anubis was the dominant funerary god. As "The one in front of the gods pavilion," he presided over the embalming tents and workshops, while as "Lord of the Sacred Land" his jurisdiction over the tombs was acknowledged. It was from him that the necessary fragrant oils for the embalmers to rub into the corpses came and he was also responsible for the wrapping of the body in linen bandages, woven by the goddess Tayet. Beyond the tomb, once the Weighing of the Heart ceremony had been successfully negotiated, Anubis guided the deceased towards the throne of Osiris.

ANUKET
Also known as: Anukis, Anket

Goddess of the cataracts of the lower Nile. Dual-tempered, she was embracer or strangler. Her sacred animal was the gazelle. In the New Kingdom she was designated the role of divine child of Khnum and Satis.

ANZU/ZU
Also known as: Imdugud

Anzu was the Thunderbird of Sumerian mythology, later conceived as a manifestation of the gods Ningirsu and Ninurta. He took the form of a giant bird with a lion's head. It was Anzu who stole "The Tablets of Destiny" from Enlil, recovered later by Ninurta. A Sumerian temple relief at Ubaid in southern Iraq, which dates to the early third millennium BC, gives a good idea of his appearance.

ARK
Noah's ship in the Jewish Flood variant. Also the wooden chest or container for keeping the commands set in stone by Yaweh — the Ark of the Covenant. Following the Golden Calf episode and the destruction of the first tablets Moses was instructed to build this ark to contain the new versions. The Ark was kept in the main temple at Jerusalem. Myth tells of it being once stolen by the Philistines who returned it swiftly when they suffered plague wherever they subsequently kept it. Similar to the Holy Grail, the ark is manifested for Jews in their chunky Torah containers and is a mythic treasure of other Christians.

APIS
The bull god Apis in Egyptian mythology was the herald and communicator manifestation of the Memphite creator god Ptah, involved on his behalf in the delivery of oracles. Memphis was the administrative and political capital of The Two Lands, so the cult of the Apis bull became the most prestigious animal cult in

Above left: Tomb painting of Anubis, the jackal-headed god. Right: This detail of an Egyptian box shows Anubis with the scribe Thoth as they weigh the heart.

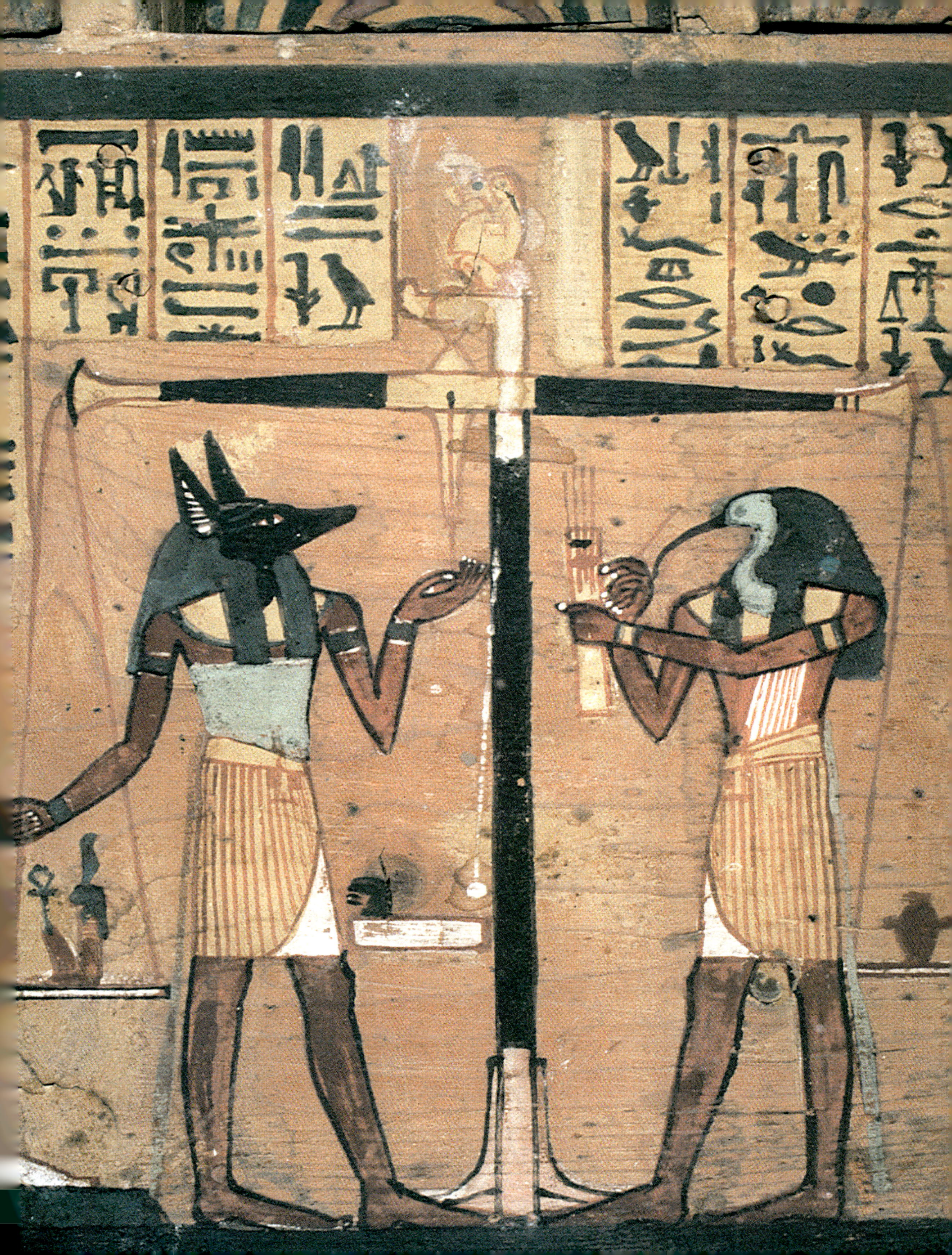

A-Z
CODEX GODS

the land. Traditionally the Apis bull bore particular markings, consisting of a completely black hide except for a white triangle on its forehead, and the tip of its tail divided into two thick strands. Huge catacombs under Memphis (modern Cairo) contain carefully mummified bulls.

APOPHIS
Also known as: Apep

An awesomely destructive Underworld serpent whose nature symbolized the idea of chaos and non-existence — the ultimate fear of the ancient Egyptians. When Re the sun god descended, to travel the twelve hours of night through the Underworld, Apophis was one of the major hazards encountered en route. As the sun god was towed along in his nightboat, his crew became hypnotized by the serpent's baleful stare. The rescuer of Re was the tamed renegade god Set.

ASHUR
With the coming of Assyrian domination in Mesopotamia, Ashur merged the roles of Anshar, Marduk and Enlil to become the paramount war god of this military civilization, ruling from the capital city named after him. He was portrayed as a winged disc within which was a tautly-stretched bow with an arrow cocked and ready for firing — military insignia of his martial status.

ASSESSOR GODS
The forty-two Underworld deities who assessed the earthly life of the dead. Each one was associated with a particular sin or crime, and to each one in turn the deceased had to deny involvement, known as the Negative Confession.

ASTARTE
Also known as: Athart, Anat, Athirat, Tanit

Mother, fertility and war goddess, Astarte was the Phoenician manifestation of the planet Venus and consort and sister of the sky war god Baal.

She was worshiped at Sidon, Jerusalem, Mizpah and at Carthage in Carthaginian form as Tanit. She was also introduced into Egypt by the Hyksos and is linked to Hathor through her wide horns. She was known to the Hebrews as a moon goddess of Sidon and given worship until Yaweh became jealous.

Astarte was rather more than a bimbo fertility goddess — she could be fierce, merciless and bloodthirsty, often being portrayed armed and dangerous. Also through her eloquence and flattery of El, Baal was allowed to build a house on Mt Saphon, the home of the gods. In a nutshell, she was the apocalypse in a skirt.

ATEN
"Sun Disk"

A manifestation of the creator sun god Re, invisible to man. In an official revolution Akhenaten (Amenhotep IV) forced him into a

Above left and Right: This Egyptian papyrus shows the cat Ra killing Apophis, the snake of evil (c. 1300 BC). Right: A stone carving of Astarte, the goddess of fertility and war.

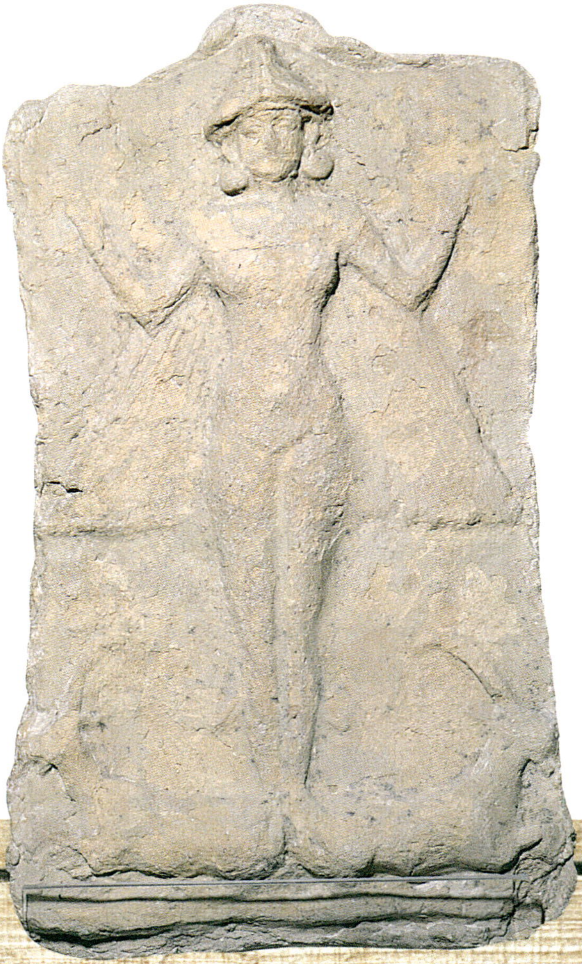

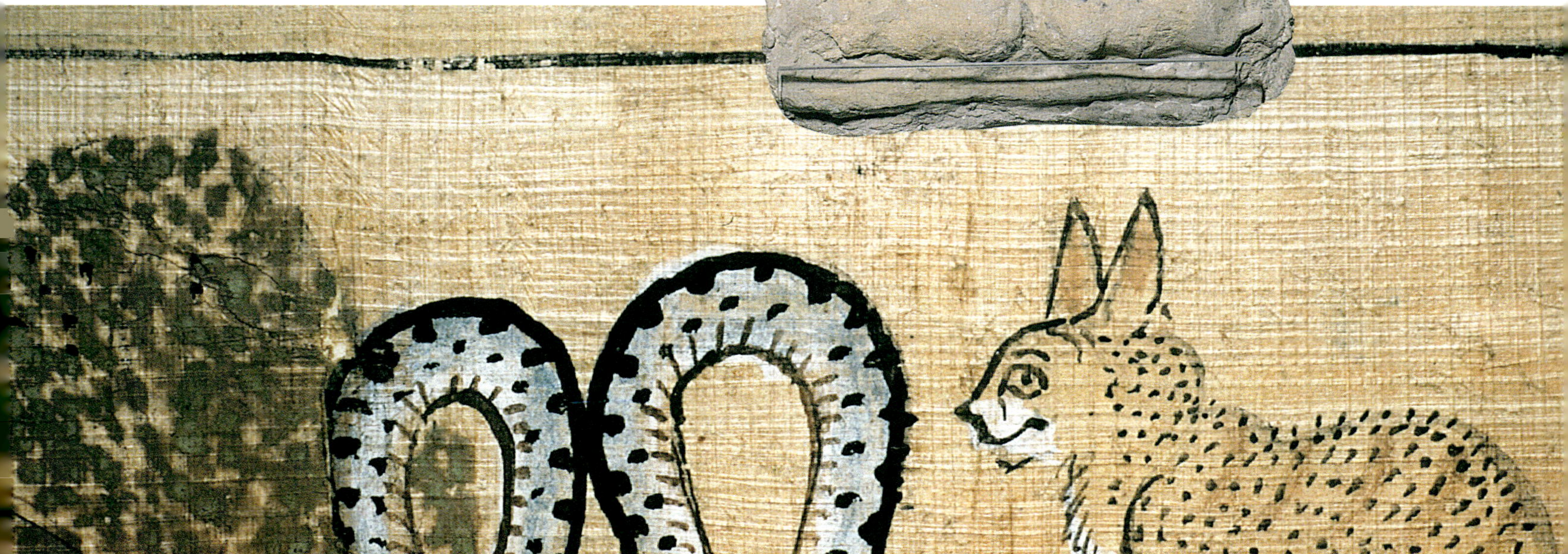

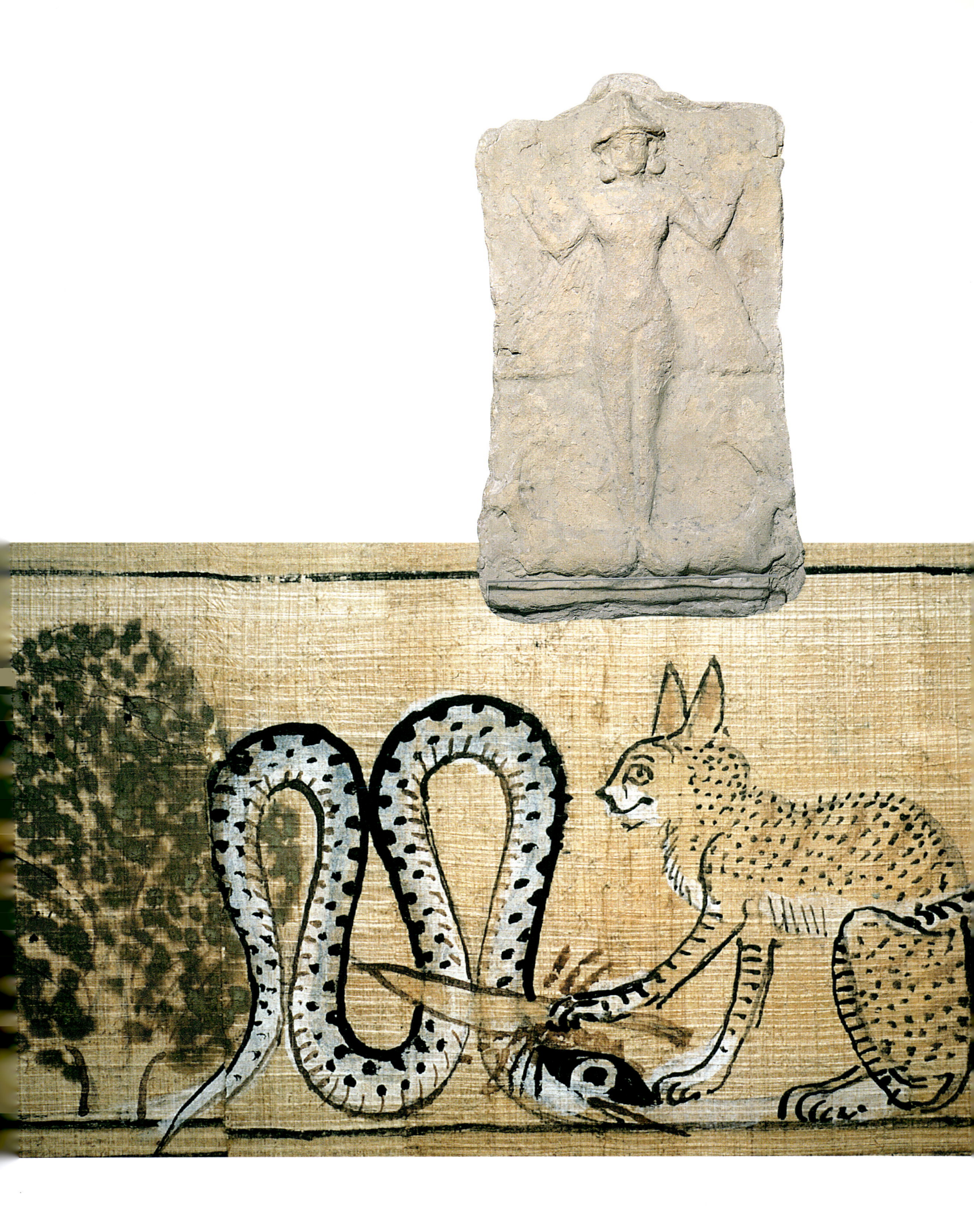

A-Z
CODEX GODS

paramount monotheistic position. Yet in a way the exclusive worship of Aten was the climax of a religious quest by the pharaohs of the 18th Dynasty for an ultimate god, all-powerful and omnipresent. It was also a way to curb the power of the Theban priesthood at Karnak. However, it went entirely against the grain of a polytheistic culture, and lasted no longer than its prime instigator. Aten was an aspect of the sun-creator, his name literally meaning "disk," and was portrayed as such, with a Uraeus — the cobra goddess of royal insignia — and rays emanating from the disc's lower arc ending in hands, some holding Ankh, the hieroglyph for "life." Aten as a manifestation of the sun god occurred far back in history, prior to his brief ascension in the New Kingdom, but it was in this period that he began to be associated with royalty and have an active cult under their patronage. Given the power and autonomy of the priesthood of Amun-Re at the time, one can sense a motive behind the pharaoh's promotion of Aten, to offset that power. When Akhenaten moved the capital from Waset (Thebes), he built a new one which he called Akhetaten and, in keeping with his religious revolution, he encouraged a similar revolutionary approach in the arts. He himself was depicted in this new distinctive and realistic style, the only known break from the tradition, illustrating how closely linked state art was with religious belief. When Akhenaten died, he and the cult of Aten were expunged from Egyptian history.

ATRA-HASIS
"Exceedingly Wise"

Hero of the Akkadian Flood myth, first attested in cuneiform tablets of the 17th century BC, concerning the creation of mankind. Enki made humans in order to help the gods but soon their numbers and noise became too intrusive. Plague, drought and famine were unsuccessfully tried by Enlil to wipe the humans out, but each time he was foiled by Enki, who was determined to protect the human race through Atra-Hasis, the king. Finally Enlil resolved to destroy mankind with a flood. Atra-Hasis, guided by Enki, built a boat and took on board his family, belongings, and healthy examples of animals and birds, before the flood arrived destroying all life on Earth. Eventually the continuing chaos of the rain and the lack of order and offerings upset the gods. Straight after he landed Atra-Hasis craftily sacrificed at once to the hungry deities, who were attracted "like flies" to the smell of the food.

ATTIS

Phrygian fertility god and son of Cybele. His myths tell of self-mutilation and resurrection. In one, harassed by an affectionate monster he castrates himself — a rather drastic way of solving the problem. Attis equates with Tammuz:

Left: An Akhenaten statue from Karnak, Egypt, (c. 1375 BC).
Right: This limestone relief shows Akhenaten holding one of his daughters under the rays of Aten, the sun god.

73

A-Z
CODEX GODS

the annual ceremony celebrating his castration, death and rebirth was a time of major bloodletting and sacrifice with his eunuch priests piercing themselves into frenzy. Rome took eagerly to this bizarre religion, in which initiates achieved union with the god through self mutilation and sacred marriage.

ATUM

Anthropomorphic creator sun god of Heliopolis, the paramount center of sun worship in Ancient Egypt, who combined with Re to make the supreme solar deity and father of the Heliopolitan Ennead. Atum willed himself into being, and went on to make the universe in the form of Shu — air — and Tefnut — moisture, through masturbation or expectoration. They in turn made Geb — earth — and Nut — sky. The story goes that Geb and Nut were making love when they were separated at Atum's command. Nut, on top, arched her back upward to form the sky; Geb formed the earth. Atum was seen as the father of the pharaoh, to whom the pharaoh returned and depended on for protection after death. The lion, the bull, the snake and the lizard were all sacred to Atum, serving as his avatars.

BAAL
"Lord"
Also known as: Baal-Hadad

Phoenician fertility and water god, sometimes known as Baal-Hadad, the paramount weather and war god, well known from the mythological texts of the 2nd millennium BC from Ugarit (Ras Shamra). He was the son of Dagon, brother and wife to Anat/Astarte and the hero of a complicated mythological epic, written on seven cuneiform tablets. In this, as the manifestation of fresh water, it is told that he defeated Yam, the god of the salty sea, and hubristically built his house on Mt Saphon. His pride then lead him to defy death and so Baal was slain by Mot the god of Death and taken to the Underworld, with the result that all life on earth went into stasis. His sister/consort Anat hunted Mot down and slaughtered him after a fierce battle. Mot's body was then cut up, winnowed, burned, ground up and sowed in the ground, and by this method Baal was revived.

Baal was a popular god who eventually lost out to Yaweh, whose priests and phrophets purged Israel of his presence, and concocted myths to prove Yaweh's dominance.

BABI

An extremely fierce, bloodthirsty Underworld baboon god, associated with male virility. A testosterone

Left: A bronze Canaanite sculpture of Baal (c. 15th century BC).
Right: An Egyptian papyrus depicting the allegory of the cosmos: sky goddess Nut above the earth god Geb, with the boat of sun god Re sailing between them.

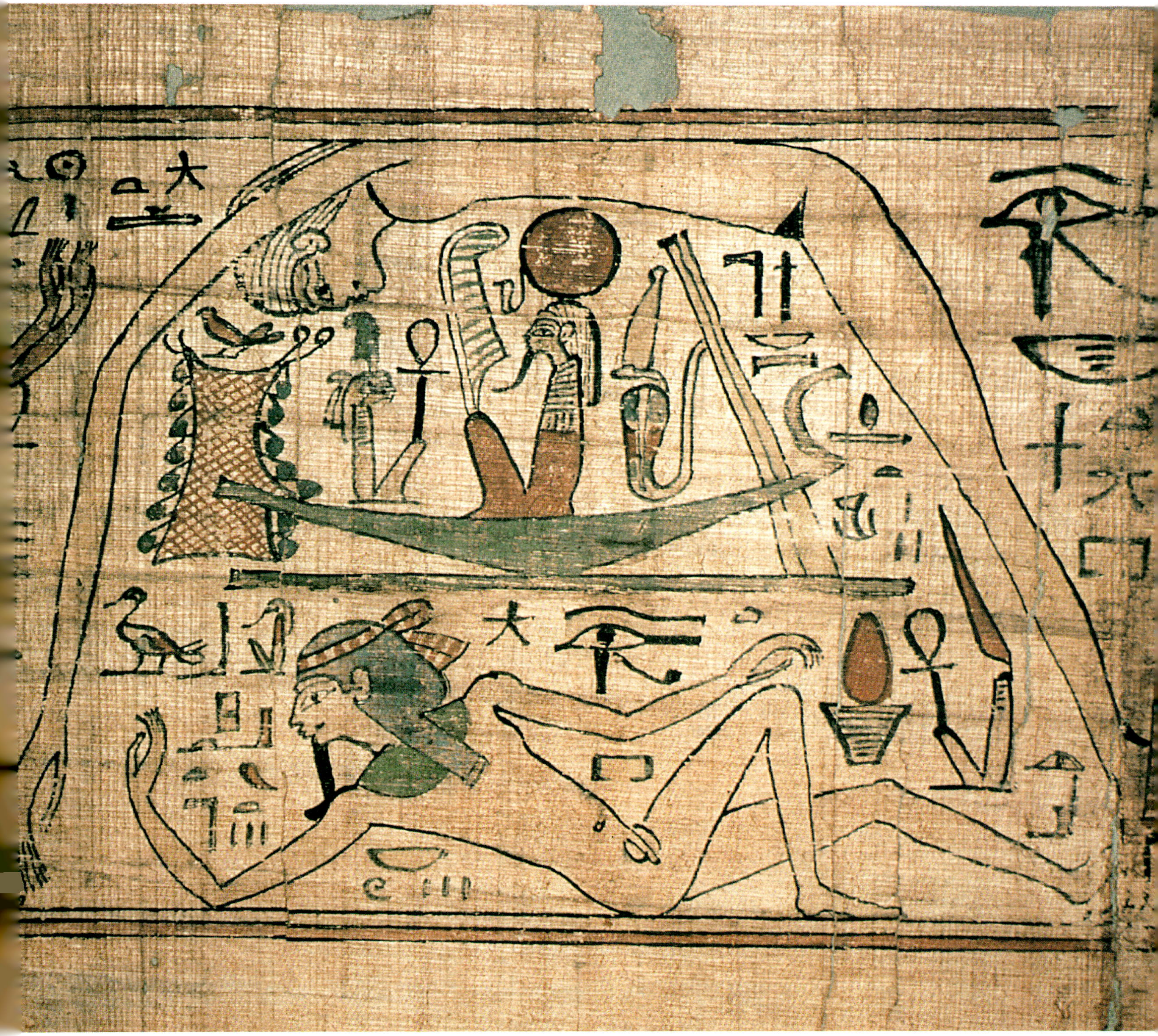

A-Z
CODEX GODS

nightmare, Babi lived on those judged unfit for the realm of Osiris, and was capable of murder on sight, though he did also have a protective aspect — against snakes and other dangers.

BANEBDJEDET

Also known as: Ba Neb Tetet, Banebdedet, Banaded

Banebdjedet was the ram god of Mendes in the northeast of the Nile delta associated with Khnum. He was the level-headed arbiter among the gods. When Horus and Set were at an impasse, it was Banebdjedet who paved the way towards arbitration, by recommending the goddess Neith be consulted. Though Banebdjedet preferred the claim of Set, Neith found in favor of Horus.

BASTET

Also known as: Bas, Bast

Bastet was the feline sun goddess of Bubastis, and daughter of the sun god Re. She became very popular, especially in Ptolemaic times. Bubastis was the ancient capital of Lower Egypt, and Bastet was an ancient deity, elevated to national status when the 22nd Dynasty made her city the capital. She was first represented as a woman with a lioness's head, holding a sistrum or rattle, but later a cat's head replaced that of the lioness. She was originally a manifestation of the anger of Re but in time her nature softened, and during the Ptolemaic period she was a goddess of pleasure, and consequently much more popular. In her temples cats were kept and at death were mummified and buried in catacombs (although there is no reason to suppose that this is the etymological starting point for that word! — in fact catacombs has a latin root). The Ancient Egyptian sense of humor comes across in the faces painted on these cat mummies, expressing bewilderment, indignation or charm with an enchanting smile. She was closely linked to the king as nurse and protectress, and was identified and confused with both Mut and Sakhmet. Bastet had a son, the lion-headed Mihos.

BES

Bes was an immensely popular household deity of the common people in ancient Egypt, responsible for the prosperity of the family and in particular the welfare of children. A grotesque but benign dwarf god, he was a protector of childbirth and guardian of the night. In contrast to the other gods, Bes was considerably less than immaculate. Hairy, bandy-legged, plump, his good nature and love of fun and music made him popular with the poor and he became universal as a protective deity of the family and conjugal union, as well as a defender against dangerous animals and the night. He was also the god of cosmetics and female adornment, and utensils in general.

Above left: A stone carving of the Egyptian god Bes. Right: An Egyptian pottery head of Bes.

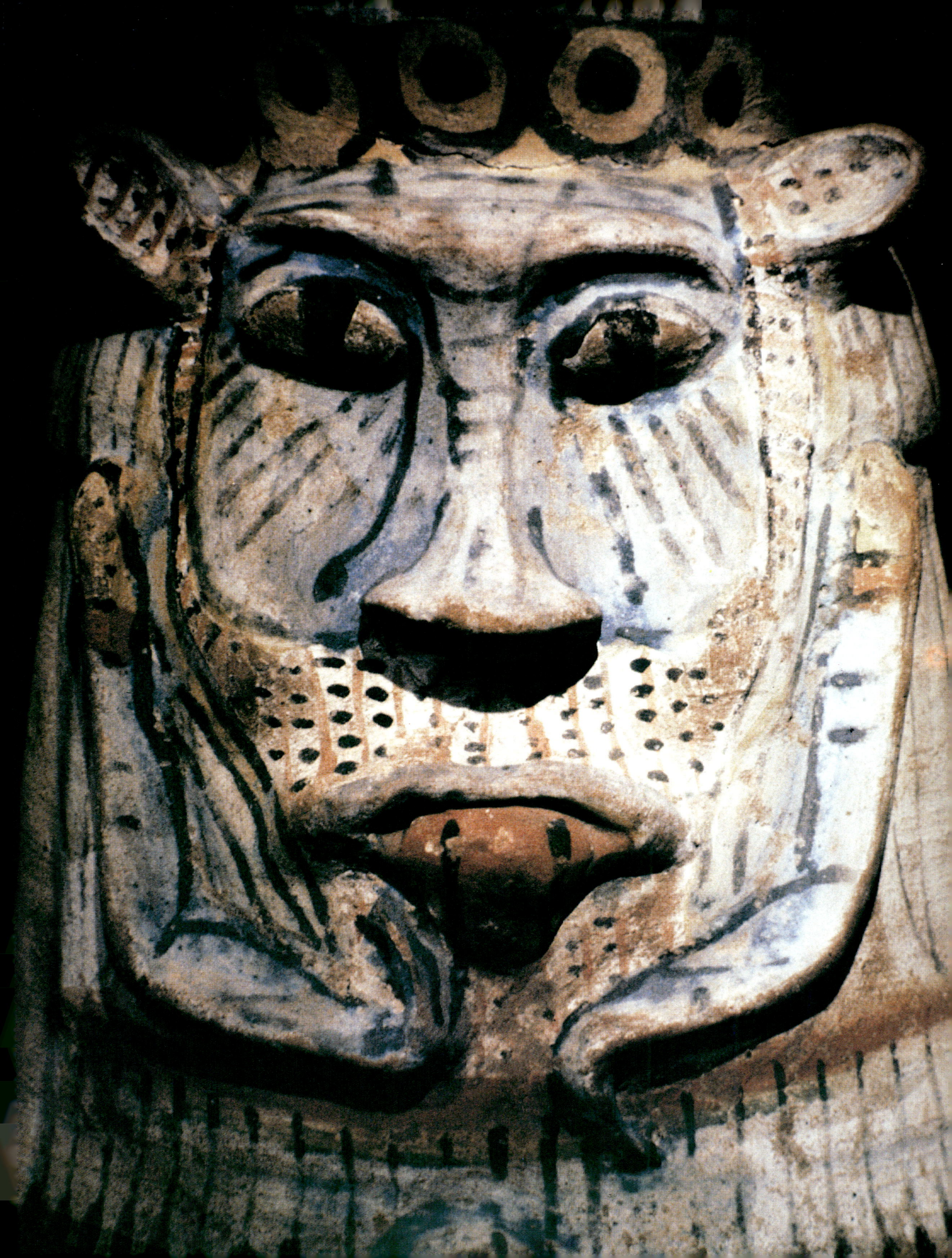

A-Z
CODEX GODS

CYBELE
Phrygian mother and earth goddess, described as the mother and sometimes the lover of the resurrected god Attis. She was portrayed attended by lions, and the castration, death and rebirth of her son/lover was celebrated annually as part of the seasonal cycle of decay, fertility and regeneration. The ceremonies were bloody with sacrifices and blood used for baptism, in which initiates used a symbolical sickle-shaped knife for ritual castration. The cult of Cybele was introduced into Rome in 205 BC, and like those of Isis and Mithras, attracted many devotees.

DANIEL
The myths concerning Daniel center on his stay at Babylon. Here he experienced apocalyptic visions as the future was revealed to him — that Israel would have to be purged of all impurity before being brought to their their true god. Daniel's adventures concern the vindication of his faith and humbling of the corrupt Babylonian king, Nebuchadnezzar.

Jeremiah and Ezekiel warned of this too, but the conquest of Israel by Babylon in 597 BC, culminating in the capture and destruction of Jerusalem a decade later, almost lost the Hebrews their confidence in Yaweh. Mass deportation to Babylon followed. Their prohpesised redemption began when the Persian king Cyrus captured Babylon in 539. His policy of restoring exiled peoples to their own lands and culture helped the Hebrews to return, although the following centuries were full of complications and tests of their resolve as various armies and peoples annexed them into several empires.

The Book of Daniel represents apocalyptic literature at its earliest, written during a critical time, to keep Hebrew culture from being overwhelmed and absorbed by the Hellenistic culture of the Seleucids, following the death of Alexander and the division of his empire by his generals.

DUAMUTEF
One of the four sons of Horus. A jackal-headed funerary god responsible for the stomach. (See Sons of Horus.)

DUMUZI
Also known as: Attis, Tammuz

Sumerian shepherd and fertility god, better known by the Hebrew form Tammuz. Dumuzi was probably originally a historical individual (he is referred to in the Sumerian King List), who also merges with traditions about other Mesopotamian gods. Sumerian poetry speaks of Dumuzi as the lover and husband of Inanna (Ishtar). In Innana's "Descent to the Netherworld" he is sacrificed by her so that she may escape and return to Uruk. Dumuzi's death through Inanna also features in the story "Dumuzi's Dream."

Right: The breathataking Ishtar gates of Babylon. (c. 604–562 BC).

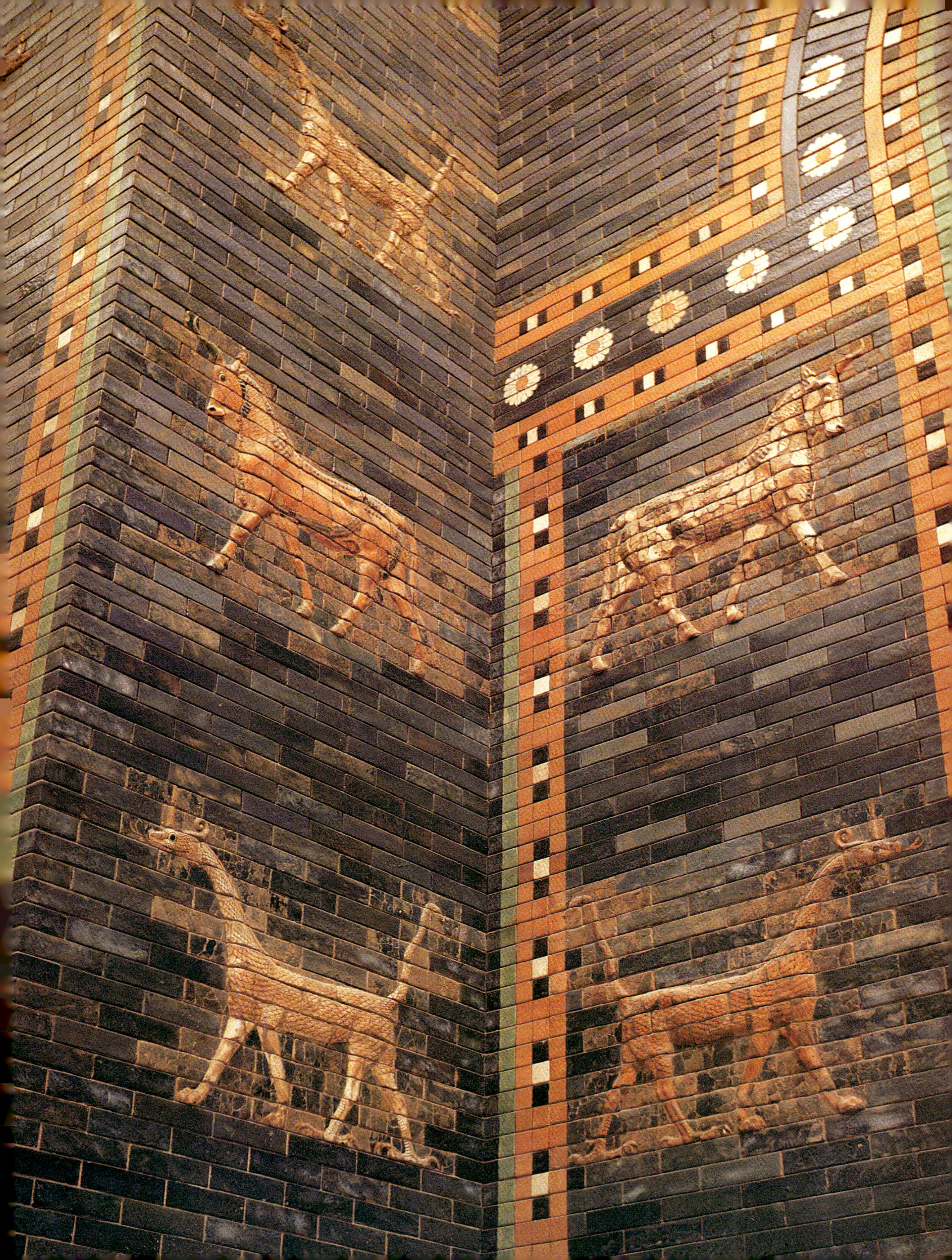

A-Z
CODEX GODS

His annual death, resurrection and marriage indicate a fertility ritual connected with the agricultural cycle. The fertility of Sumer was encouraged in this sacred ritual, in which the king enacted the role of Dumuzi and the high priestess that of Inanna.

EL

El, the supreme Semitic Canaanite god, who ruled Canaan for many years until finally ceding precedence to Yaweh. El lived on Mt Saphon and was the benevolent and merciful father of time, the gods and men. Like many older creator gods he eventually became a personification of power — a manifestation of the concept. In the Old Testament there is a reference to El and Yaweh as one and the same ultimate god. As master of wind and wave he kept the rivers flowing. He was represented as a bull — a title and description of power.

ENKI

Also known as: Ea

A Sumerian water and fertility god of Eridu, Enki was a high ranking creator deity on a par with An (heaven), Enlil (air/sky) and Ninhursaga (earth mother). His priests often wore garments that simulated fish, signifying his mastery over that medium. His main story has him analoguous to Adam in the Garden of Eden, in Dilmun — the Sumerian equivalent, where Enki dwelt with Ninhursaga, providing the water that turned it into a fruitful paradise. When Enki ate eight of Ninhursaga's plants a quarrel erupted, she cursed him with death and stormed off. Her curse worked all too well and Enki was expiring rapidly until Ninhursaga was persuaded to return and cure him. Although there are Biblical similarities (Eve and Ninti) it seems certain that the first Eden myths were obviously Sumerian in origin, where the tree also played a role in symbolizing life/existence. Enki is credited with the creation of man after the gods complained about the lack of food offerings. It was also he who warned of the impending flood to Adapa, King of Sippar, when the gods tried to destroy their mortal helpers.

ENLIL

"Lord Wind"

Sumerian sky and earth deity and one of the principal gods of the Mesopotamian pantheon, worshiped especially in his home city of Nippur. Many of the more important gods are described as his offspring, including Ishtar/Inanna, Sin/Nanna-Su'en, Nergal, Ninurta, Ningirsu (his prime son) and Shemash/Utu. His wife was usually Ninlil, although the grain-goddess Sud had this status in some contexts. Enlil was praised above all as cosmic administrator and he possessed both the Tablets of Destiny and the power of the storm. In some myths he is portrayed as benevolent, but in the myth of Enlil and Ninlil, he rapes the young Ninlil, thus

Right: The Canaanite supreme deity El in bronze.

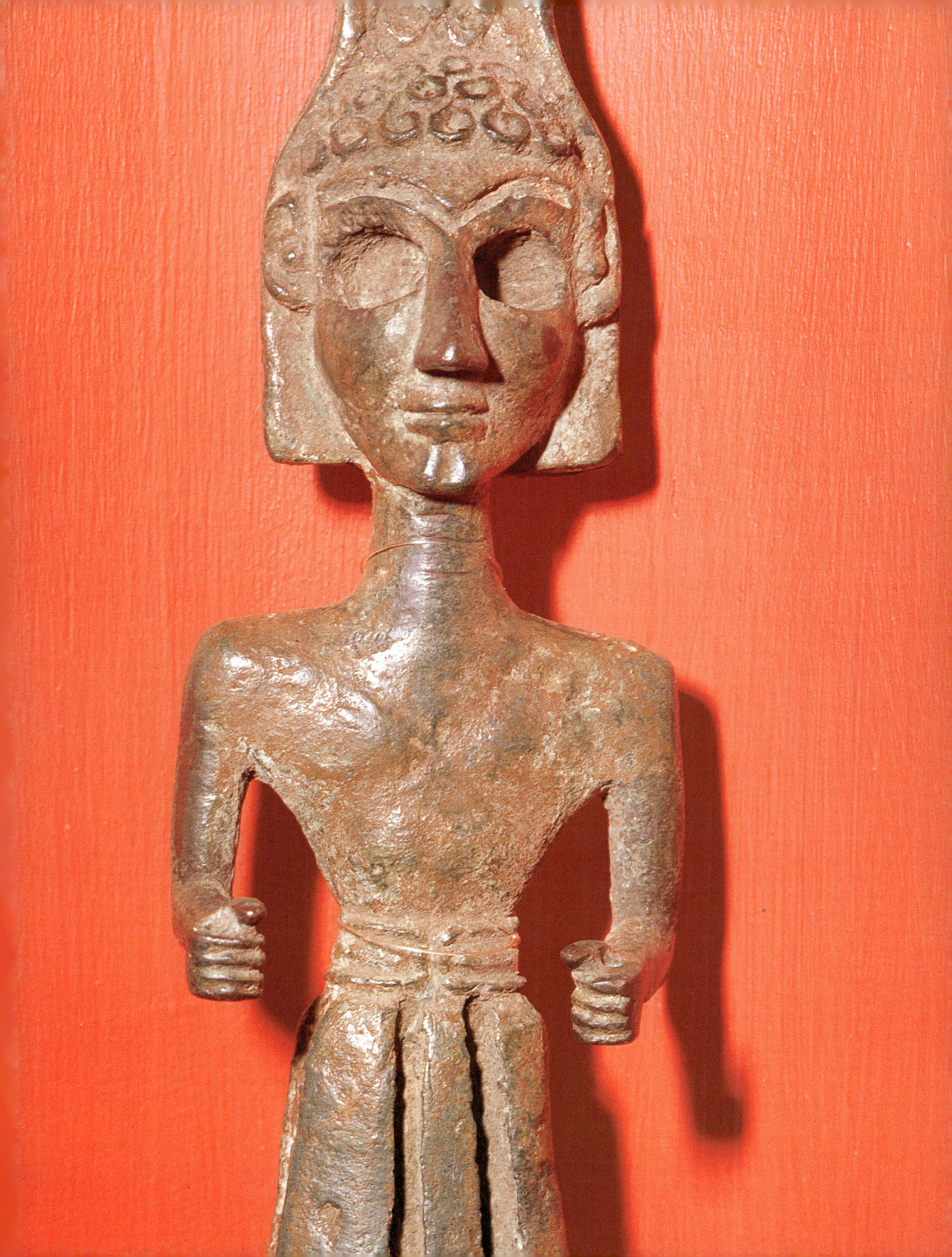

A-Z
CODEX GODS

begetting Nanna-Su'en, and is banished from Nippur to the Underworld for his crime. His first son Nanna, the result of Ninlil's rape, became the moon god of Ur. In the Sumerian Flood stories it is Enlil who takes the decision to destroy mankind.

THE GREAT ENNEAD

A pantheon of nine gods originating in Iunu (Heliopolis), the ancient religious capital of Egypt. Consisting of Atum-Re, the sun creator god and his descendants: Shu, Tefnut, Geb, Nut, Osiris, Isis, Set, Nephthys and Horus.

ETANA

According to the Sumerian King List, Etana was a king of Kish ruling in the early 3rd millennium BC. The myth tells of Etana's childless wife dreaming of the "plant of birth," which her husband then resolves to find for her. To do this he uses an eagle trapped in a pit, as suggested to him by Shamash. Etana rescues the eagle, which transports him up to Heaven on its back, where he collects the "plant of birth." The result is that Etana and his wife do finally have a son.

GAYOMART
"Dying Life"

In Persian mythology, Gayomart was the prototype man, created by Ahuramazda. It took over 3,000 years for him to achieve corporeal form. He then lived for three decades before being poisoned by Ahriman, at the instigation of Jeh — the whore. From his seed grew the plantlike father and mother of the human race, Mashye and Mashyane, who forsook Ahuramazda for Ahriman, and were damned to hell as a result.

GEB

Ancient Egyptian fertility god, the son of Atum and president of the divine tribunal on kingship in the dispute between Horus and Set. Just as he vindicated the claim of Horus, so does he support the ruling pharaoh. In his role as an earth god of fertility Geb appeared green-colored and sometimes ithyphallic. Perhaps Geb's most interesting point is that he is a male earth figure, it being much more common in ancient cultures to view the earth as female.

GILGAMESH

Legendary King of Uruk, half human and half divine, and the hero of the "Epic of Gilgamesh" — the original and oldest written myth to survive from ancient Mesopotamia — or anywhere else for that matter. Fragments of various texts exist, the ancient Sumerian one being preoccupied with the fear of death and attempts to overcome it, the more complete and later Akkadian version involving Gilgamesh in a series of adventures including the life and death Enkidu, the rejection of Ishtar, the

Right: This Akkadian seal (c. 2400–2200 BC) shows Gilgamesh and Enkidu fighting boars.

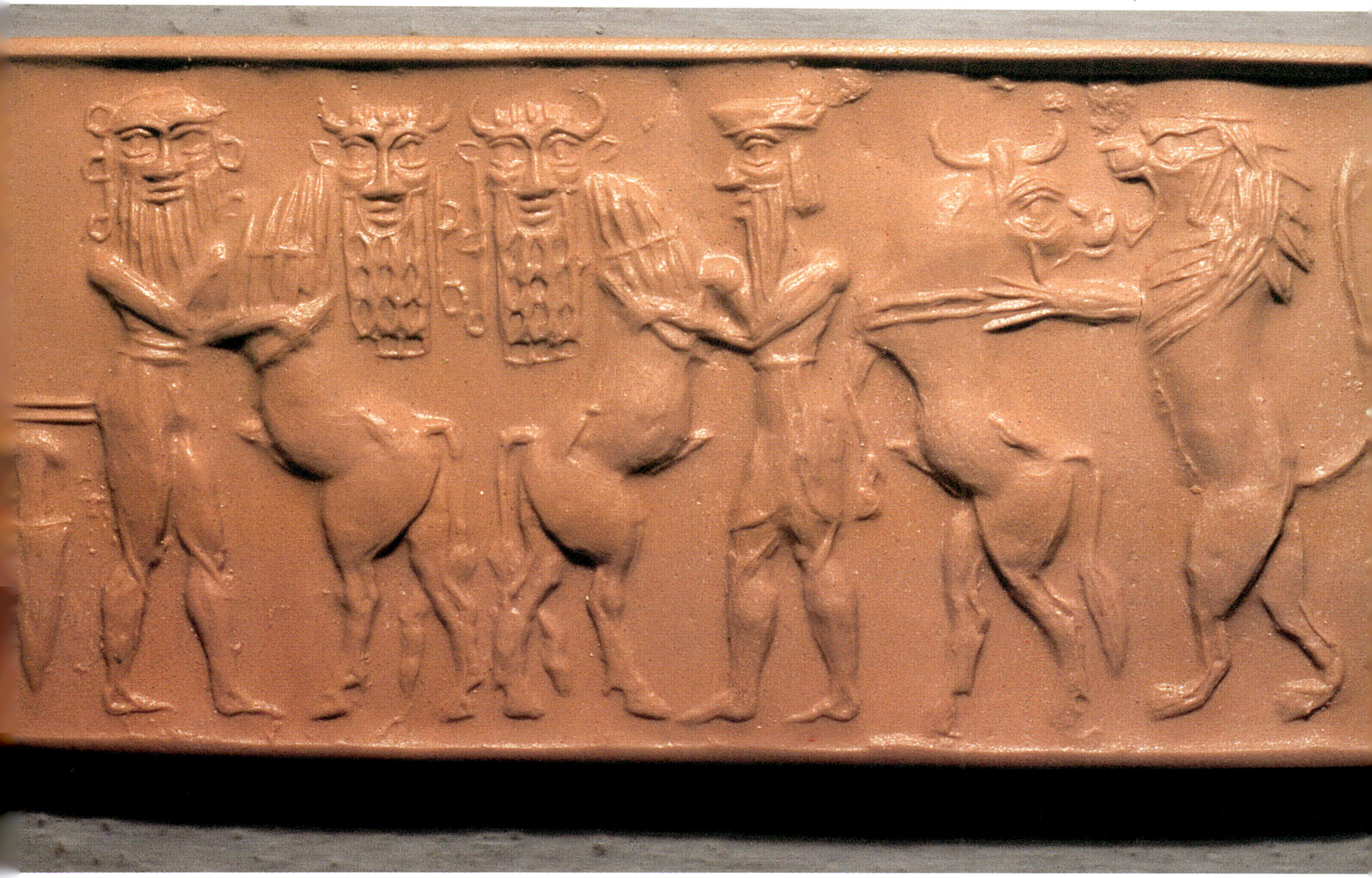

A-Z
CODEX GODS

quest for Utnapishtim and the gain and loss of the Plant of Eternal Life. Because of his half humanity Gilgamesh cannot resist sleep, let alone death; so this oldest epic in the world concerns the ever-contemporary questions and Gilgamesh is in fact the world's first existential hero.

HAPI

Personification of the waters of the Nile, especially the inundation. Dwelling near the first cataract, Hapi is portrayed in well-fleshed anthropomorphic form, with a large paunch and pendulous breasts, suggesting plenty, and a crown of aquatic plants, often carrying a tray of food or pouring water from urns. Although he was featured in the reliefs of other deities' temples, Hapi had none of his own, and no priesthood.

HAPY

Also known as: Hapi

Ancient Egyptian personification of the waters of the Nile, especially the inundation. Dwelling near the first cataract, Hapi is portrayed in well-fleshed anthropomorphic form, with a large paunch and pendulous breasts suggesting plenty, and a crown of aquatic plants, often carrying a tray of food or pouring water from urns. Although he was featured in the reliefs of other deities' temples, Hapy had none of his own, and no priesthood.

HATHOR

Multi-aspected sky goddess, symbolic mother of the pharaoh. In funerary aspect as Lady-guardian of the Western Lands of the Dead, she was protectress of the necropolis and the dead. She was also goddess of destiny, healing, childbirth, love, music and dance, and protectress of women. When Re became disgusted and disillusioned with mankind, he ordered Hathor to destroy all men. She set about her task with such fury and zeal that he had second thoughts, and had to resort to trickery in order to stop her. Despite this frightening negative capability, Hathor was predominantly a benign mother-goddess. Portrayed anthropomorphically as a cow, her temples were at Dendera, Edfu and Ombos.

HEKET

Ancient goddess of childbirth, creation and grain germination, she took the form of a frog or a frog-headed woman.

HERYSHAF

"He who is upon his lake"

Ram god of mid-Egypt, personification of Re and associated with Osiris. His city of Hnes was the capital of Northern Egypt during the first Intermediate period, at which time he was associated with Re and Osiris.

Heryshaf was portrayed as a man with a ram's head.

Right: The Egyptian goddess Hathor wears a headdress with the ears of a cow.

• EGYPT & THE MIDDLE EAST •

85

A-Z
CODEX GODS

HORUS
"The one far-off" or "He on high"
Many-aspected, falcon-headed, sky sun god. Son of Osiris and Isis, who fought Set to reclaim his father's inheritance. (See The Great Ennead.) His hawk's head insignia was used far back in predynastic times, as a symbol of identity and leadership. Horus could be portrayed as either a hawk, or a hawk-headed man. The unification of the Two Lands saw him ascendant — merging with other deities to become a state god at Memphis. He was a symbol of unification, strength, divine kingship (the pharaoh is Horus alive), perfection, protection (the Eye of Horus), and purification; some of his manifestations are listed below:

Harpokrates
Horus the child, the child of Osiris and Isis
Haroeris
Harwer
Horus the Elder; mature, claiming his
 father's throne, fighting Set
Harakhty
Horus of the horizon: the sun god.
Harsiesis
Horus son of Isis: Avenger of Osiris.
Harsomtus
Horus of the Two Lands; uniter of Upper and
 Lower Egypt.
Harendotes
Horus father-protector; battling against Set.

IMHOTEP
Scribe, architect, courtier and designer and builder of the first pyramid at Saqqara, which led to his deification and adoption as a son of Ptah. He was revered as a god of learning, knowledge and healing. He was portrayed seated, with an open manuscript scroll on his knees, and with the shaven head of a priest.

INANNA
Also known as: Ninanna
In ancient Sumeria temples were constructed in pairs, where a consort couple of god and goddess were worshiped to reflect the obvious duality of life. Innana, the most important goddess of the Sumerian pantheon was linked with her consort Dumuzi. Daughter of An or Enlil and identified with the planet Venus, she was a war deity, but mainly a goddess of fertility and love.

She challenged her opposing goddess — Ereshkigal (Light and Darkness), making a bid for the hegemony of the Land of no Return beneath the sweet waters of the earth. Once there she was turned into a corpse and left on a stake. Her vizier having unsuccessfully tried the other gods, finally appealed to Enki, who then created two sexless avatars to go to her aid, with the water and food of life. When she revived and was led back she could not get rid of a pursuing host of demons, who demanded a substitute. She chose Dumuzzi, her partner with whom she was angry for not doing more to help.

Right: This Egyptian mummy in the shape of a hawk represents Horus.

· EGYPT & THE MIDDLE EAST ·

87

A-Z
CODEX GODS

ISHTAR
"Lady of Heaven"
Also known as: Mylitta, Inanna.
The multi-faceted Ishtar is the most important of all the Mesopotamian goddesses, occurring in the cuneiform texts of all periods. The Akkadian name Ishtar is related to the Syrian Astarte and the biblical Ashtaroth. Ishtar is usually considered to be a daughter of Anzu, with her cult located at Uruk, but there are other traditions as to her ancestry, and it is probably that these reflect originally different goddesses that were identified with her. Ishtar is the subject of a cycle of texts describing her tragic love affair and ultimately fatal relationship with Tammuz. She is generally viewed as the goddess of love and sex, and textual evidence exists to indicate her general connection with prostitution. She also had a role to the Assyrians as a war goddess, who accompanied kings into battle, filled with bloodlust. Ishtar is also a manifestation of the planet Venus, though her earliest symbol was a reed bundle.

ISIS
Great mother goddess of Egypt. The wife of Osiris, mother of Horus and symbolic mother of the pharaoh. Isis was an idealized woman and mother: loving, faithful, resourceful; she was the possessor of mind-boggling magical powers and was the only person ever to discover the true name of the great sun god Re. Her cult originated in Perehbet, and spread over the whole of Egypt. Her image is that of an attractive, mature woman, with a miniature throne on her head, or with cows horns and a sundisk between them. The sistrum was sacred to her, and a magic knot called Tat. She was shown in many attitudes: suckling Horus the child, enthroned next to Osiris, and protecting both her husband and the souls of the dead with her winged arms. Her persistence and cunning were illustrated in the struggle between her son Horus and Set, when she caused Set to betray his sexual assault on Horus. Her continuity stretches down through mother goddesses to the Virgin Mary.

JESUS
Son of God and Mary by immaculate conception and militant activist. Though he undoubtedly existed as a real person and his followers have successfully spread his ethos of love and forgiveness throughout the Western world, the intense mythic web built around him justifies his inclusion here. His miracles, his testing, his

Left: Isis stands guard at the tomb of Tutankhamun, (c. 1350 BC).
Right: A stone relief of Isis with cow's horns and a sun disc.

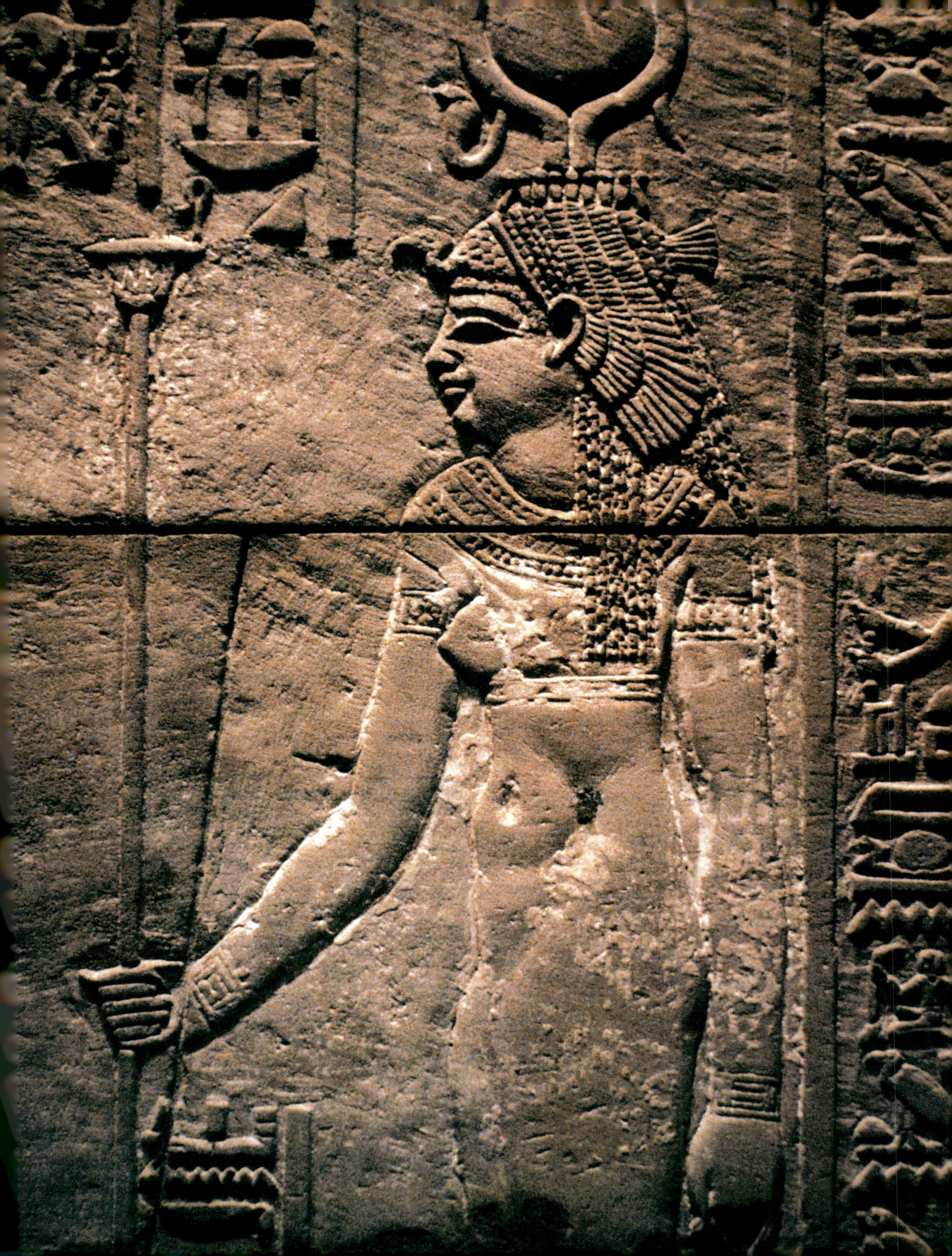

A-Z
CODEX GODS

parables, teaching and lastly his trial, death and resurrection touch on many themes which he shared with older gods of the Semitic regions coupled with input from the great river civilizations of Mesopotamia and Egypt.

KHEPRI

"He who is coming into Being"
Also known as: Khepra, Khepren.
Khepri was a manifestation of the sun god creator Re in the form of a scarab beetle, or a man with a complete beetle instead of his human head. Khepri rolled the sun before him like a scarab beetle with its dungball, from which emerge its young. The Ancient Egyptians saw in this the act of self-creation, and thus this creature was believed to be a manifestation of Re. Khepri was often used in amulets, seals and pectorals as a motif of the sun god, and as a protective charm against evil.

KHNUM

Ram-headed creator god of Elephantine and war-champion of the sun god Shu, Khnum guarded the source of the Nile, and controlled the annual inundation. In his capacity as guardian of the cataract region he was grouped with Satis and Anukis to make the Elephantine Triad, and, regarded as the soul of the sun god, his name became Khnum-Re. His other aspect was that of creator god; linked to the procreative power of the ram and the life-giving waters of the Nile, Khnum was said to have made mankind, and indeed all life, on his potter's wheel.

KHONSU

Also known as: Khons
Egyptian sky and moon deity. Son of Amun and Mut. One of the Theban Triad. Khons had various manifestations over the centuries; his nature underwent a change from bloodthirsty war god of the Old Kingdom, to divine child and healer in the New Kingdom. He was represented as a royal child, wearing the side plait (a sign of youth), and carrying the crook and flail. He was also shown as a falcon-headed youth surmounted by the lunar disk and crescent combined. Khons had a temple dedicated to him in the precinct of Amun at Karnak.

LEVIATHAN/BEHEMOTH

"Coiled"
Also known as: Lotan
Gigantic sea serpent of Hebrew mythology, and a recreation of the chaos dragon Tiamat. Leviathan was the female aspect and Behemoth the male counterpart. Both occur in the Talmud and are concerned with the defence, and end, of the world. The Book of Job mentions the awesome power of this evil monster, who became associated with hell in Christian imagery.

Right: A tomb painting of the Egyptian God Khnum in the Valley of the Queens (12th century BC).

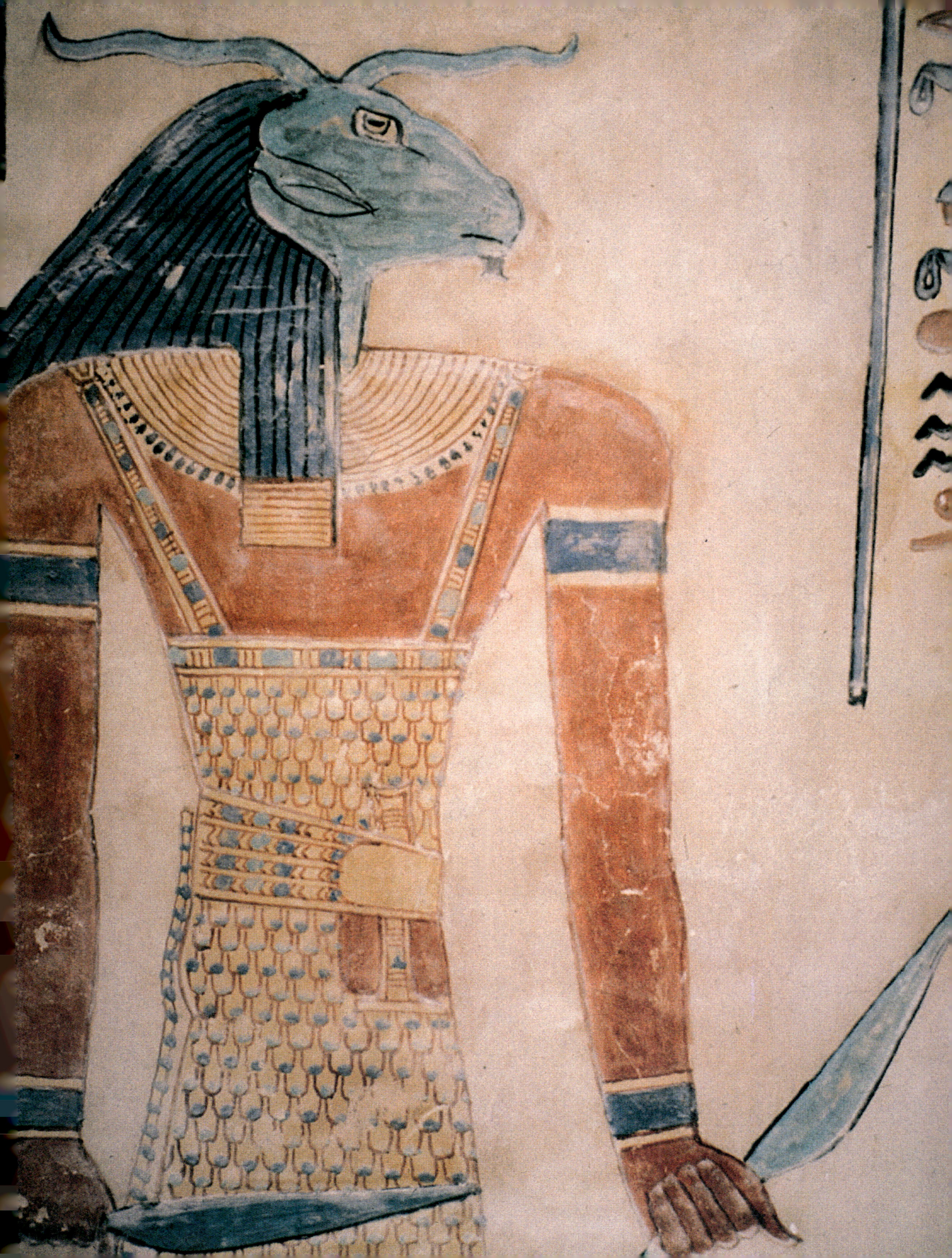

A-Z
CODEX GODS

MA'AT

Personification and goddess of truth, justice, and cosmic harmony, she was the wife of Thoth. Ma'at, manifested as a feather sat in the other scale, opposite the heart of the deceased, in judgement. Failure to balance the scales resulted in the most feared second death, and the loss of the possibility of the afterlife with Osiris in his kingdom. Ma'at was portrayed as a woman wearing an ostrich feather on her head, which could also by itself represent the goddess. The pharaohs saw Ma'at as their authority to rule, and were often represented holding a miniature version of her in their hands, displaying their truthfulness and integrity to the major deities.

MARDUK

"Bull calf of the Sun"

In the Babylonian creation epic, it was Marduk who conquered the chaos dragon Tiamat and saved the gods from destruction. The other gods had failed to subdue her, so the young Marduk undertook the battle in exchange for recognition as the highest of the gods. His successful conquest of Tiamat then led to his creation of the cosmos and the life within it, including humankind, from her body.

In the 1st millennium BC Marduk was often referred to as Bel, translating as "Lord" and the increasing synchronization of Marduk with other important gods of the pantheon is exemplified in a small cuneiform tablet which lists each god as a particular aspect of Marduk himself. His particular symbols were the pointed triangular spade, found commonly on cylinder seals and boundary stones, and the mythical beast called Mushhushshu. This was a composite leonine monster with a horned snake's head, a scaly body and eagle's talons, well-known from the glazed brick representations on the Ishtar Gate at Babylon, built by Nebuchadnezzar II.

MELQART

The Semitic Canaanite version of the hero Heracles and the city god of Tyre, he was linked to the sea and navigation. Melqart died by fire and his festival of awakening was once held annually in January. Originally a solar god, in time he became more associated with matters nautical (with Tyre being so close to the sea). The Greeks adopted Melqart under the name Melicertes, creating the evocative image of a boy riding a dolphin.

MERETSEGER

Cobra goddess of Thebes, guardian of the royal tombs. She was portrayed as a coiled cobra, or as a cobra with the head of a woman, and had the reputation of being a dangerous but merciful goddess. Her abode was the peak of the mountain that overlooks the Valley of Kings in western Thebes.

Right: An Egyptian relief of Ma'at the goddess of truth.

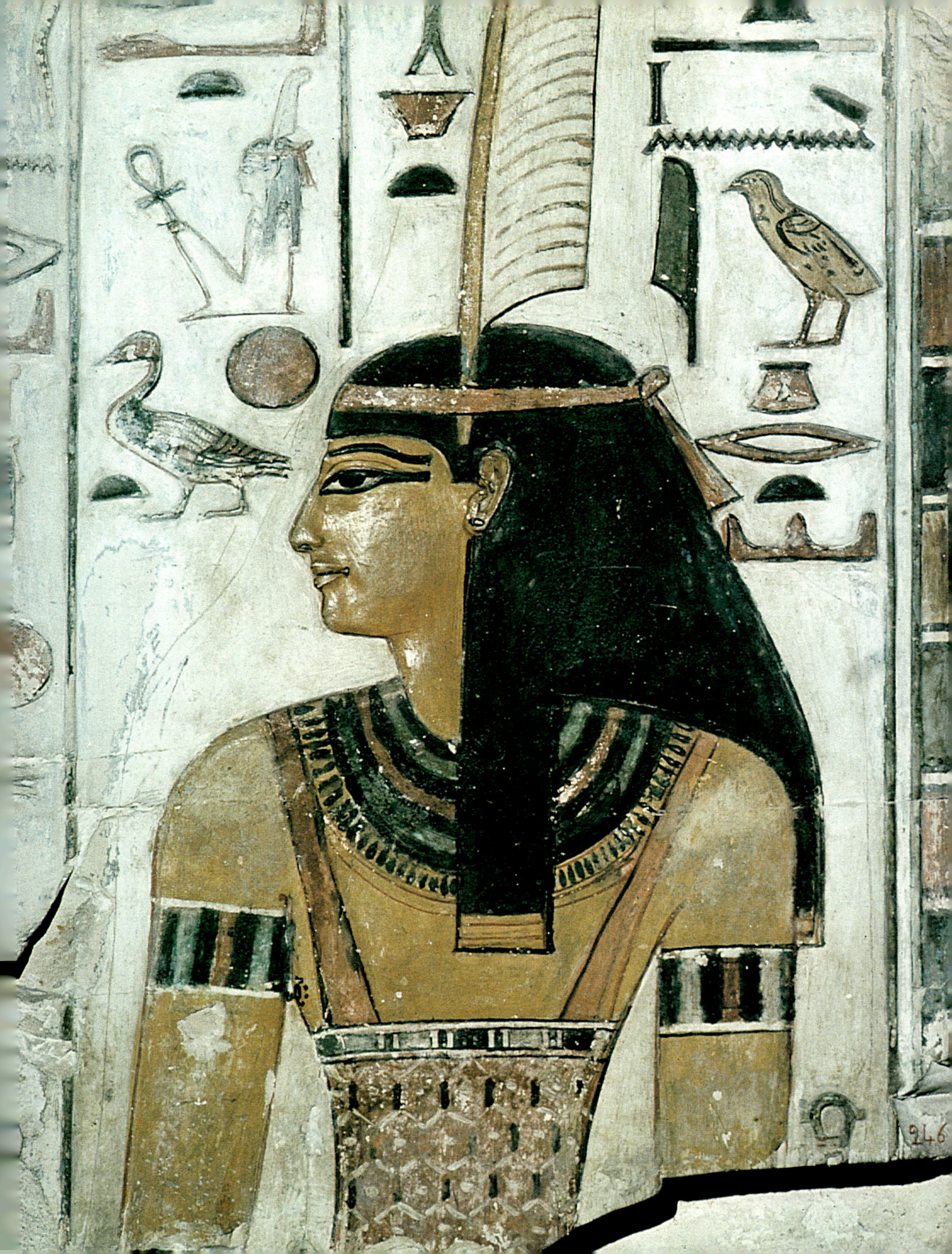
246

A-Z
CODEX GODS

MIN
Min was the god linked to the phallus — the symbol of sexual procreativity and fecundity. He also combined with Horus as a protective deity of the eastern desert, roads and travelers. Min was seen as another manifestation of Amun, and wore his plumed headdress while holding a whip-like sceptre. He was also sometimes shown holding his erect phallus in his left hand. His sacred animal was the white bull, and his main centers were at Coptos and Panoplis.

MITHRA
"Friend"
Also known as: Mitra, Mithras.
An ancient Indo-Iranian solar god whose cult spread via Greece to the Roman world in the second half of the first century BC. In pre-Zorasterian times he was a paramount deity, who represented light and from whose gaze nothing could hide. Originally twinned with Ahura he was finally supplanted by him in the religion propounded by Zoraster, though Ahuramazda referred to him in an equal context as himself. Mithra also possessed war god capability, as an implacable, merciless and furious opponent regarded with awe. However his mien was just and friendly and he encouraged honor among gods and men. When he partook of the sacred Haoma drink he underwent ritual intoxication, paving the way for his later status as his cult spread into the Roman world. By the time it reached Rome, this was a secretive cult, the sacrifice of bulls and washing in their blood was a vital part of their ceremonies.

MOLOCH
Originally mistakenly linked to Melqart, Moloch was in fact the manifestation of early Semitic religious child sacrifice. Yaweh commanded Abraham to perform this rite, but only to test his obedience, since he then substituted a ram in place of his firstborn child.

MONTU
Also known as: Mont
Falcon-headed war god of Thebes and the Theban Nome, Montu was the embodiment of the martial vigor of the pharaoh, and as a war god was portrayed holding the *khepesh* — a curved saber. Also manifested as a Buchis, a bull, kept in a shrine at Hermonthis, Montu was eventually superseded by Amun at Thebes.

MUT
Sky war goddess of Thebes, wife of Amun and symbolic mother of the pharaoh, Mut was often linked with Bastet. She was portrayed as a woman wearing a vulture headdress surmounted by the *pshkent* — the double crown of Egypt. She could also be lioness-headed, hence her association with Bastet.

Above right: This Egyptian papyrus shows Rameses III receiving Amun, Mut and Khons (12th century BC).
Right: A Roman relief of marble found in Hungary (1st–2nd century AD).

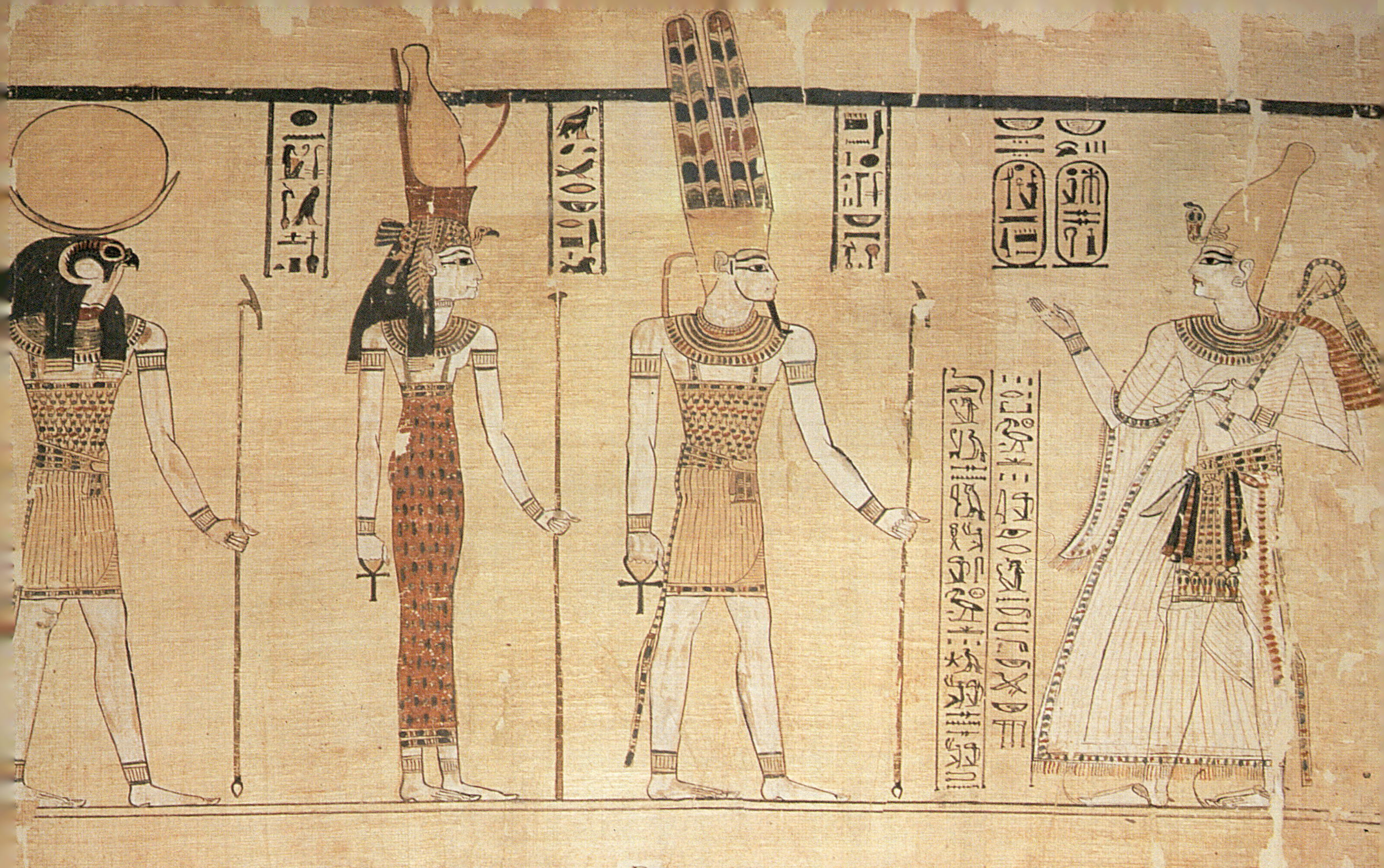

B

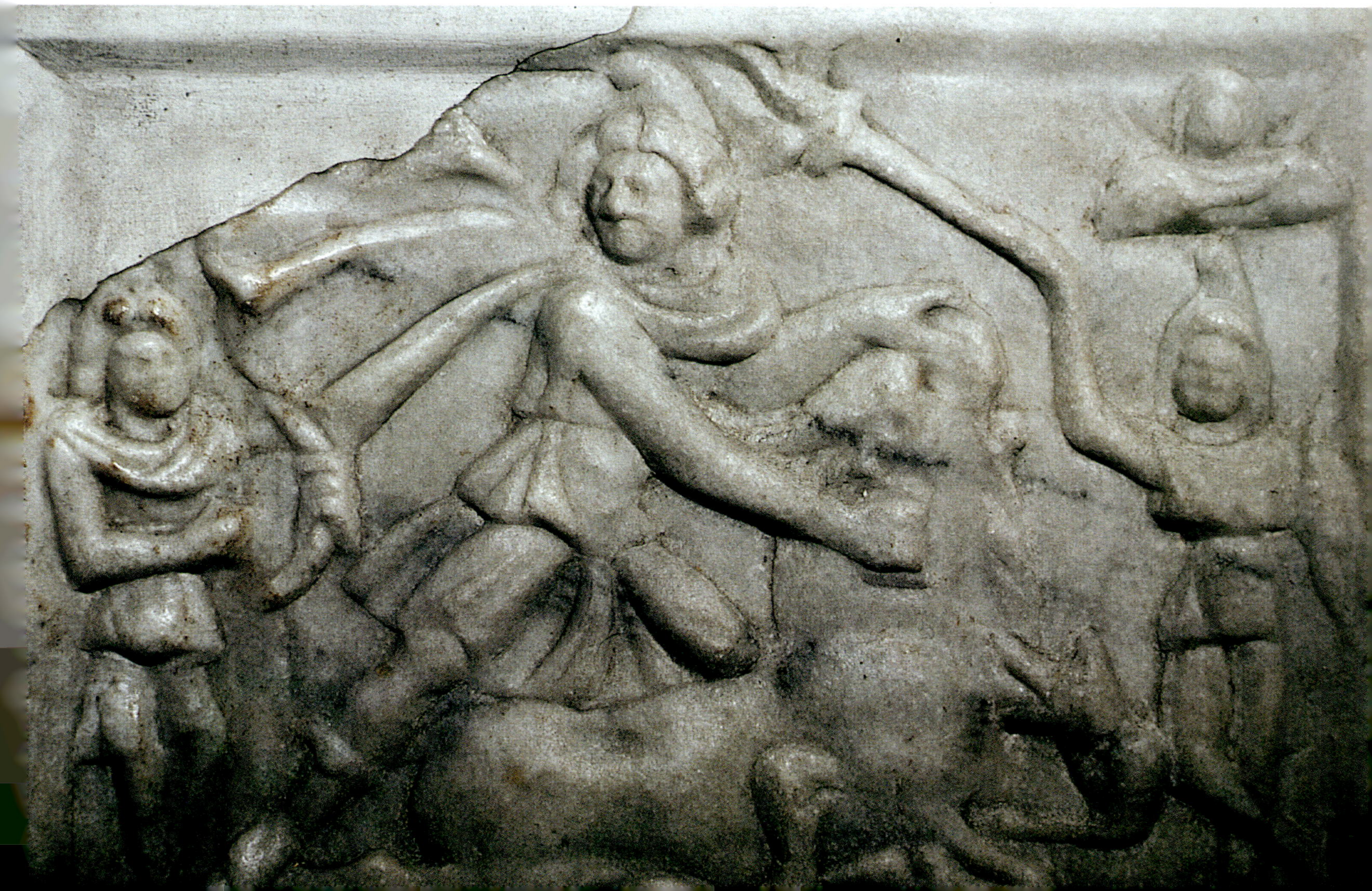

A-Z
CODEX GODS

NEBETHETEPET
Heliopolitan goddess, the feminine counterpart to the male creative principle of the sun god Amun. She was the hand with which Atum brought the world into being.

NEFERTUM
Son of Ptah and Sekhmet, Nefertum was the god of rebirth, symbolized by the lotus blossom. Nefertum was portrayed wearing a stylized lotus flower on top of his head.

NEHEBKAU
The Invincible Underworld snake god of protection. Represented as a snake but with human arms and legs, Nehebukau protected the pharaoh in the Underworld after death.

NEITH
"Lady of the bow and ruler of arrows"
Sky creator goddess of Sais, in the delta and consort of Set, Neith was also the goddess of war and weaving. Her red crown was absorbed into the crown of the pharaoh — the *pshkent* but her oldest symbol was the shield with crossed arrows. It was claimed that Neith wove the world with her shuttle, and that Re was her son.

NEKHBET
Vulture goddess of Upper Egypt, protector of mothers and children. She occurs as a heraldic device above the pharaoh, balancing the Lower Egyptian cobra goddess, Wadjet. She was also represented as a vulture at rest. At royal births she was the protective nurse to the monarch.

NEPHTHYS
"Mistress of the Mansion/Temple"
Also known as: Nebthet
Funerary goddess of the Dead, sister of Osiris and Isis and consort of Set, Nephthys seduced Osiris and gave birth to Anubis. She wore on her head the ideogram of her name: Neb, — a basket, and Het — a palace. Together with Isis she was a protectress of the pharaoh in the Underworld. She could also take the form of a kite guarding the funerary bed of Osiris.

NERGAL
Also known as: Erra
Mesopotamian god of death and the Underworld, the son of Enlil and Ninlil and a warrior rather similar to Ninurta. His cult city was Kutha in southern Iraq, where he was worshiped with his consort Laz. As ruler of the realm of the dead his wife was Ereshkigal, and the Myth of Nergal and Ereshkigal, explains the circumstances under which Nergal came to rule there.

NIMROD
Mythical king of Shinar in Hebrew mythology. Nimrod became a byword for godlessness and blasphemy. Through possession of Adam and Eve's clothing he became vastly powerful,

Right: A wooden figure of the goddess Nephthys.

EGYPT & THE MIDDLE EAST

A-Z
CODEX GODS

controlling animals and the destiny of all conflicts. His success led to his deification, but he was still dissatisfied and ordered the construction of a huge tower in preparation for an assault on heaven itself. Yaweh frustrated this attempt by mixing up all speech (Babel), causing the original unity of mankind to be broken as different languages arose. In later versions the tower of confusion remained but Nimrod slipped into obscurity.

NINHURSAG
"Lady of the Mountain"
A Mesopotamian mother goddess, ranking as one of the top four Mesopotamian deities. Ninhursag's symbol was the uterus and she represented productivity of the earth and animals, as well as birth and the institution of kingship. She dwelt in Dilmun with her consort Enki although their relationship was stormy.

NINURTA
"Lord of the Earth"
A major Mesopotamian deity, the son of Enlil, worshiped especially in the city of Nippur in the temple Eshumesha. His adventures featured prominently in two mythic poems. The first concerned with rainfall and irrigation tells of his defeat of the mountain monster Asag by using stones to control the water flow of the Tigris and the Euphrates rivers. The second describes Ninurta's triumphant return to his home city of Nippur. His character is multi-faceted; initially agricultural it became more and more militaristic as time went on — his warrior prowess being celebrated particularly by later Assyrian kings.

NOAH
The origin of the Flood myth is Mesopotamian, where it was sent because the gods had tired of all the trouble and strife emanating from man. In Hebrew mythology the Flood was caused by Yaweh in response to the sin of Adam. Noah the son of Methusalah's grandson was above reproach at a time when his contempoararies had been seduced by the corruption of fallen angels. He was chosen by Yaweh to build an ark that would save him and the animals: all others were to be destroyed. He was also credited with the introduction of agriculture and its techniques and with having introduced the vine.

NUN
"Father of the gods"
Nun was the personification of the primeval watery chaos in Egyptian mythology, and was one of eight deities manifesting this state before the coming of the sun god. Once Atum had emerged spontaneously out of Nun in order to create the cosmos, Nun had no further role to play. This concept of Nun as the primeval water is preserved in Egyptian temples where a sacred lake symbolized Nun and provided a practical service for ritual ablutions.

Right: An Iranian goddess in terracotta (c. 1500–1100 BC).

EGYPT & THE MIDDLE EAST

A-Z
CODEX GODS

NUT
Sky goddess of the Heliopolitan Ennead. Daughter of Shu and Tefnut, Nut was represented as a slim-limbed girl, stretching her body, balanced on her fingers and toes, over her consort Geb. Like all Egyptian sky goddesses, she could assume the form of a sacred cow. She was also thought to swallow the sun each evening, and give birth to it again each dawn. As a funerary deity she was believed to enfold the pharaoh in her soul at his death, so that he would dwell in the sky with her, and she also provided sustenance for the dead in the Underworld.

ONURIS
Egyptian spear-carrying god of war and hunting, Onuris was portrayed as a bearded man wearing a crown of four high plumes. He was most frequently identified with Shu, but also Horus, whose cause he supported wholeheartedly. His consort was Mekhit, a lioness-headed woman whom he brought back from the south.

OSIRIS
Supreme god of the Underworld and the dead and firstborn of Geb and Nut, Osiris was murdered by his jealous brother Set. Counterpart to the sun god below ground, and manifestation of the pharaoh after death, he civilized Egypt, and taught the people how to cultivate crops — hence his manifestation as a grain god, as well his more usual funerary and mortuary incarnations. Osiris was portrayed in human form, mummified, holding the sceptres of kingship. He wore a crown which consisted of ram's horns and a tall centerpiece, with a plume on each side. His skin had a greenish tint. Osiris became increasingly important from the first Intermediate period onward, offering as he did the chance of resurrection to any pure soul regardless of wealth or position. His main center was at Abydos.

PTAH
Anthropomorphic creator god of Memphis, part of the Memphis triad, consort of Sekhmet and Father of Nefertem (though he also adopted Imhotep). Apis, the sacred bull, was another manifestation. God of architects, artisans, artists and masons, he created the skills of design and sculpture. Ptah was represented as a shaven-headed mummiform man holding a sceptre. He was most popular with the pharaohs of the 19th Dynasty. His funerary aspect was in combination with Sokar, the guardian of the Memphite necropolis, where he created the life-restoring ceremony of "The Opening of The Mouth." He was said to have created himself, and then spoken the universe into existence.

RASHNU
The wise and impartial judge of Iranian mythology, who along with Mithra and Sraosha judged the souls of the dead. During the time

Above left: A 6th century Egyptian deity in bronze and gilt. Above right: The eye of Osiris from an ancient Egyptian papyrus. Right: A bronze image of Osiris, supreme god of the Underworld.

101

A-Z
CODEX GODS

after death before the soul had left the environs of the corpse, Rashnu would reach his decision and decide the fate of the soul in question. Those who were to be saved were then accompanied by an angel to heaven, those who had failed walked a bridge as fine as a knife edge from which they inevitably plummeted into the abyss of hell.

RE/RA

The Heliopolitan creator sun god, (see the Great Ennead), Re was the apex of all sun god manifestations and was symbolized by a falcon with the sun on its head surrounded by a cobra, and by a scarab rolling the sun before him like a ball of dung. Also, in the Underworld, he became a ram-headed god. Re often combined with other gods: Atum, Benu, Harakhti and Osiris. His cult escalated during the 5th Dynasty and, after merging with Atum, he became the supreme solar deity. Re was said to have created mankind from his tears, a symbolic birth, for humankind, with its deceit, wickedness and violence, was nothing but a problem to the gods. Finally Re had enough and, becoming angry, he ordered Hathor to kill mankind. She took on the shape of Sakhmet and was so diligent in her task that Re was shocked by the indiscriminate slaughter, and commanded her to stop. But Hathor-Sakhmet was so intent she ignored him, and he had to resort to trickery to stop her. By mixing beer with pomegranate juice he simulated blood, and left it on the battlefield. Hathor thought it was blood, and drank so much of it that she became drunk and unable to continue.

RENENUTET

Cobra goddess of agriculture, protection, fertility and linen, especially bandages, she was also guardian of the Pharaoh. Renenutet was represented as a cobra rearing up to strike, or as an enthroned goddess. Embodying the role of divine motherhood, she was also portrayed as a woman suckling a child. Along with Shait she gave each child a destiny, an allotted span of years and she attended the weighing of men's hearts in the Hall of Two Truths. Her cult flourished in the fertile Faiyum, where she was connected to the Sobek.

SAOSHYANT

"Savior"

Saoshyant was the redemptive savior figure of Iranian mythology. His task was to remove from the world all the evils of Ahriman, introducing the second stage of existence and uniting souls with their bodies once again. This would include both the good and bad, the good would go to Ahuramazda's paradise and the bad would dwell in the darkness of Ahriman's hell. A torrent of molten metal would then envelop everything and everyone, though to the just it would seem like warm milk. The sins of the

Right: An Egyptian bronze with golden eyes.

• EGYPT & THE MIDDLE EAST •

A-Z
CODEX GODS

damned would be purged by this conflagration and all would return to Ormzdud in great joy. In another myth there are four Zorastrian stages — the fourth and present age enjoys the teaching of Zoraster and will terminate with the advent of Saoshant.

SATIS

Goddess of the southern frontier and the consort of Khnum. Associated with the annual inundation, Satis was represented as a woman wearing the long white crown of Upper Egypt, with antelope horns or plumes.

SATAN

Man has always peopled his fear of darkness with a crew of demons and other malevolent beings. The Hebrews were no exception. At first Satan meant only adversary, and is recorded as being sent by Yaweh to test Job. Later, with Enoch, he became the manifestation of evil incarnate. Satan was jealous of Adam and refused to acknowledge him — or his creator. For this he and his supporters were ejected from Heaven and Satan's bitter emnity with humankind began. Christianity then developed this idea into a spiritual demonology to counterbalance the paganism it struggled against and thus the dualism of good and evil inherent in all the middle eastern religions was validated in one of the world's contemporary creeds.

SAKHMET
"Powerful One"
Fierce lion-headed goddess of Memphis, daughter of Re, consort of Ptah and one of the Memphis Triad, she was Hathor's instrument for the destruction of mankind, until Re made Hathor too drunk to continue. Sakhmet, as Re's daughter, represented the destructive power of the sun but she also had a protective and healing side, and seemed happily married to Ptah — the most creative of the gods.

SARAPIS

A composite national god of the Ptolemaic period, created to symbolize the synthesis of the Greek and Egyptian cultures. A god of the sun, fertility, healing and the afterlife, Sarapis was portrayed as a bearded man.

SARGON OF AKKAD

Historical ruler and founder of the Semitic Old Akkadian Dynasty, which united the cities of Mesopotamia into an effective empire for the first time. Sargon is the subject of a whole cycle of stories and traditions, but also occurs in a myth called the "Sargon Legend." This tells how he was born in secret to a high priestess who placed him in a reed basket sealed with pitch and deposited it in the river. A irrigation worker called Aqqi rescued the boy and brought him up, teaching him to be a gardener. The boy went on to became king. This theme, the so-called "infant

Right: This goddess, with the head of a lioness, was found at Thebes.

EGYPT & THE MIDDLE EAST

A-Z
CODEX GODS

exposure" motif, has echoes in other literatures, notably that of the Hebrew Moses in the Bible.

SELKET

Also known as: Serket, Selkis

Protective scorpion goddess, a daughter of Re, she watched over the sky with Neith to prevent anyone interrupting Amun and his wife, and so became a guardian goddess of conjugal union. Selket was represented as a woman with a scorpion on her head, or as a scorpion with a woman's head. In her funerary aspect she was the helper and guard of Qebehsenuef, custodian of the viscera. She also helped the deceased orient themselves in the Underworld, and was believed to bind Apophis, the evil snake who was a manifestation of darkness and death. In the world of the living she was a kind of patron-saint for healers and witchdoctors, and a protective deity against venomous bites and poison.

SESHAT

Horned-goddess of writing and archives, she was married to Thoth. It was Seshat who measured time, kept the royal accounts and helped the pharaoh with the the layout and foundations of temples. She also audited the booty and tribute from foreign lands and military expeditions. Seshat was shown as a woman wearing a panther skin robe, holding a pen, a palette and sometimes a tally-stick. On her head she wore a headband with a seven-pointed star on a stick.

SET

Also known as: Seth, Setekh, Setesh, Suty, Sutekh

God of chaos and disorder, thunder and storm, violence and the desert, Set was the second son of Geb and Nut, who tore himself out of his mother early. He was jealous of his brother Osiris and, killing him, usurped the throne, until he was finally ousted in favor of Horus. The personification of evil, Set most often appeared anthropomorphically, with the head of an animal that the Greeks identified with their Typhon. He was portrayed as a composite creature with four legs, an erect tail and a gently curving snout. On his head rose two squared-off ears or horns; his skin was white and his hair red.

Each month Set attacked and consumed the moon, the hiding place of Osiris, and preyed on the souls of the deceased, yet still Set was championed occasionally by various pharaohs, until he was adopted by the Hyksos invaders who settled in the delta. After their expulsion, Set's already battered reputation took a further drop, his statues were destroyed and his name became anathema. When he lost out to Horus, Set went to live with the sun god, becoming his weather controller. He traveled with Re in his solar boat and, standing in the prow, speared Apophis when he attacked. His two main centers of worship were Ombos and Kus.

Above left: Selket, a protective goddess, discovered in King Tutankhamen's tomb.
Right: Four more protective goddesses — Isis, Nephthys, Selket and Neith — also found in Tutankhamen's tomb.

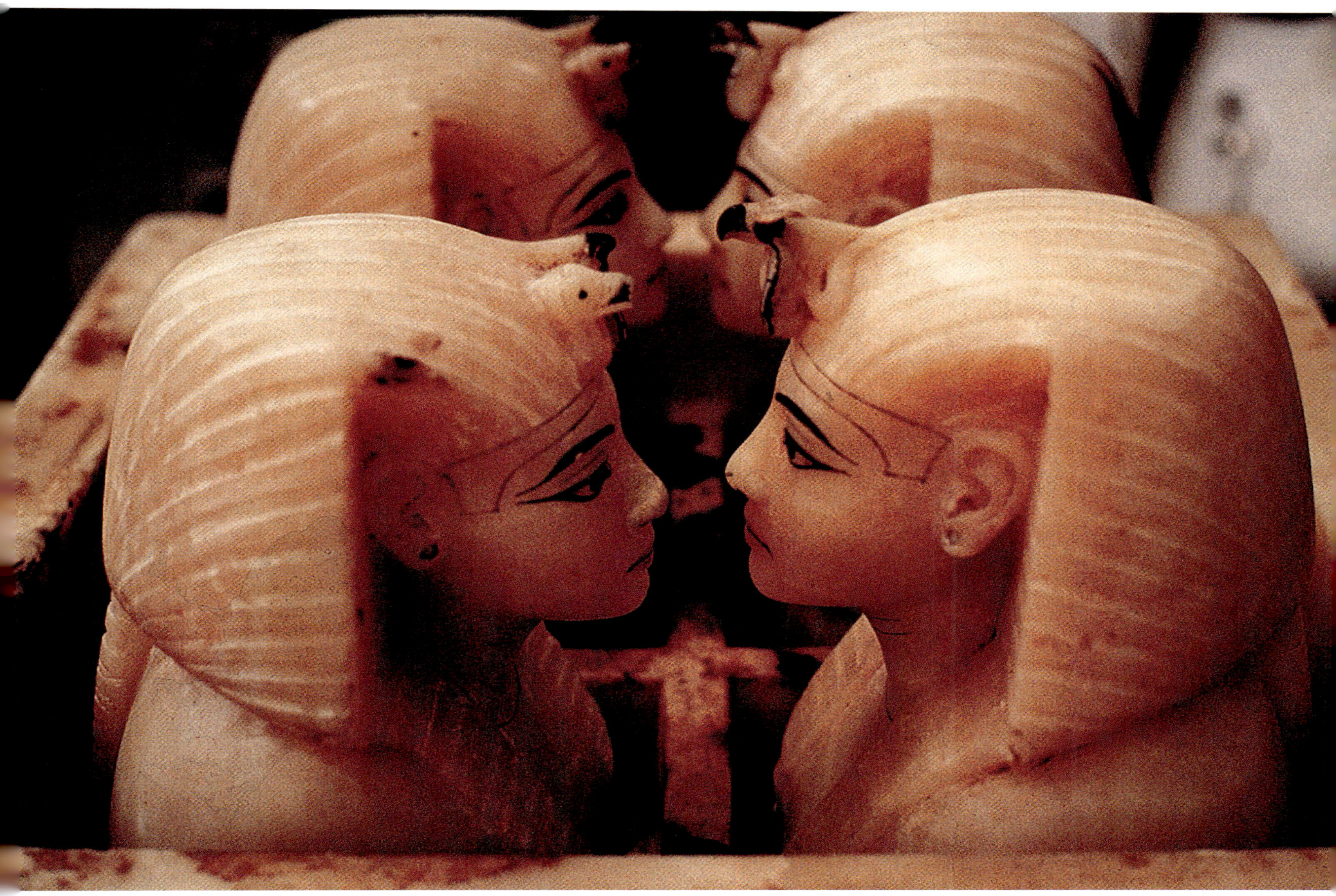

A-Z
CODEX GODS

SHAMASH
Also known as: Utu

The benevolent Mesopotamian sun god of justice, Shamash was in charge of the spiritual link between thr gods and man. He was the son of the moon god, Sin, and the brother of Ishtar. He was believed to cross over the heavens in the day and traverse the underworld by night. While in the Underworld Shamash was considered responsible for the spirits of the dead, and he played an important role in protective magic against ghosts and witches.

SHAY
Also known as: Shait

The Ancient Egyptian personification of destiny. When the deceased reached the hall of judgement, Shay was present to give a true account of all sins and good works. Against her testimony there was no appeal.

SHU

Air god of sunlight and the atmosphere. Husband of Tefnut, they made up the first couple of the Heliopolitan Ennead. At the command of Re, Shu forcibly separated Geb and Nut from their endless loving embrace, and held Nut up to make the sky. Shu was represented anthropomorphically, wearing a plume on his head and with his arms raised (supporting Nut). After Re, Shu was king of the world. But he was ambushed by the children of Apophis, and though he beat them he was left weakened and exhausted by the encounter. So he abdicated in favor of Geb, and retired to heaven. Shu had the usual dual aspect of punisher or protector: in the Underworld he was a very dangerous god who led a band of killers, and was a great peril for the deceased. In protective mode he could defend against Apophis and other demons.

SIA
Also known as: Saa

The personification of mind and intelligence, created by the blood dripping from the phallus of Re. Sia aided the sun god on board his boat during the night journey through the Underworld.

SIMON THE MAGUS

Gnostic Canaanite sorcerer. The gnostics were a heretical sect of Christians abominated by the mainstream. St Peter rebuked Simon the Magus for his attempt to purchase magical powers which he presumed to have been supplied by the Holy Spirit. When Simon flew, St Peter brought him down. Simon the Magus was an alter ego for St Paul during the bitter schism between him and St Peter. The real opponents of Paul were the Jewish converts in Jerusalem, including the original disciples of Jesus. They rejected the faith propounded by Paul, who was a Hellenistic Jew and the first saint not to have actually known the Messiah. He viewed Christianity as a

Above left: This papyrus shows the gods pulling the sun god in a boat through the Underworld during the 11th hour of night. Right: A papyrus showing the god of air supporting the boat of Khepri while the sky-goddess accepts the sun.

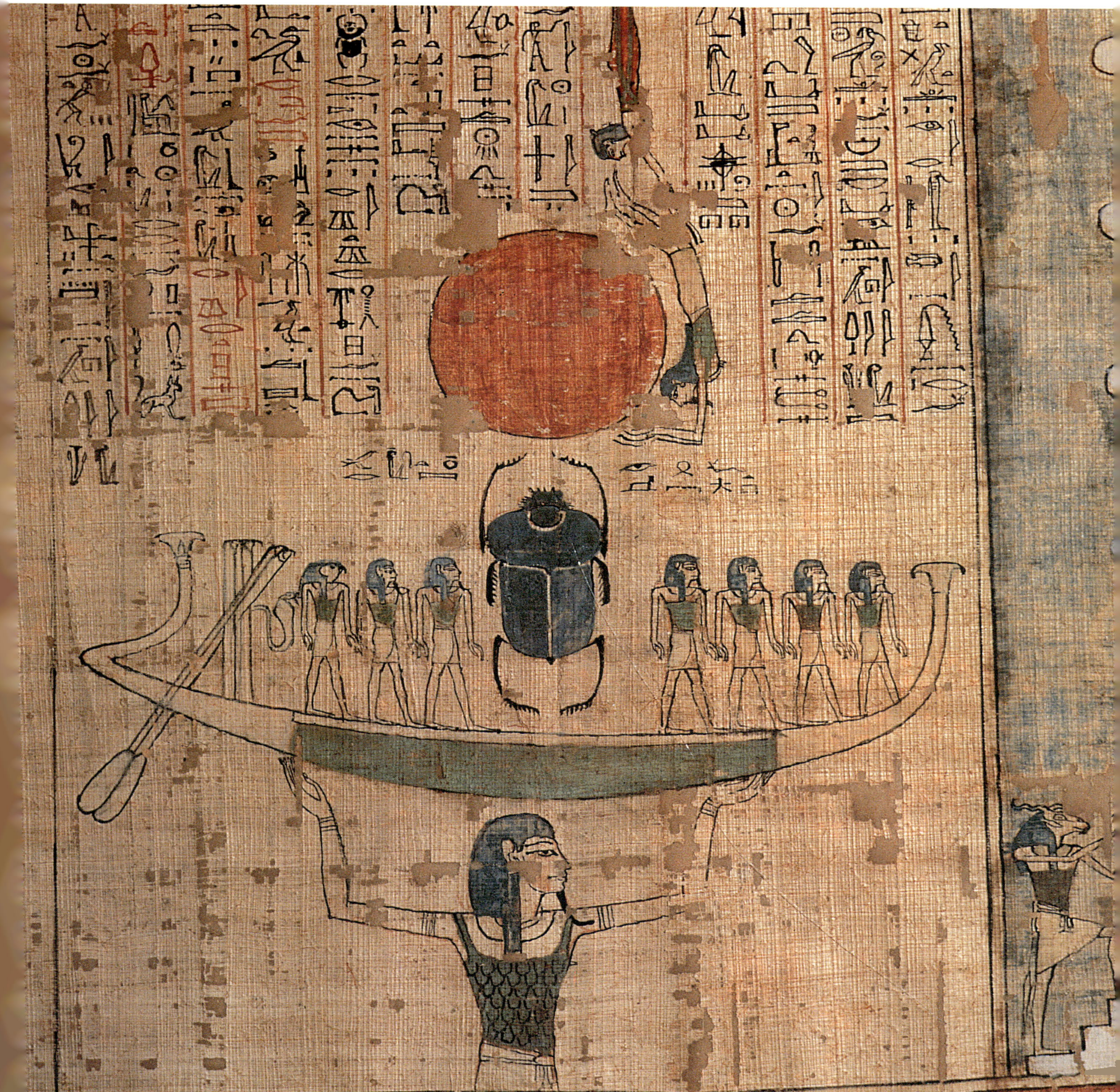

A-Z
CODEX GODS

new religion which had jettisoned Jewishness. Following the Roman destruction of Jerusalem in 70 AD, these challenges ceased and non-Jewish converts were freely accepted. Simon the Magus became the origin of all heresies in Christian iconography.

SIN
Also known as: Suen, Nanna, Nanna-Su'en
The Mesopotamian moon god of Ur, son of Enlil and Ninlil, husband of Ningal and father to Shamash and Ishtar. His principal cult was located in the ancient city of Ur. A fertility god of earth and air, Sin's cult tended toward monotheism. One of the myths that tell of Sin's adventures relates the wooing of Ningal, which is consistently rejected until he has irrigated the land and seen the crops grow. When all around is in abundance only then does Ningal consent to live with Sin, worshiped as Nanna-Suen from the great Ziggurat at Ur.

SOBEK
Also known as: Sebek, Suchos
Egyptian crocodile god with links to royalty and the symbol of instant destruction for any enemy. His mother was the creator goddess Neith of Sais. In Upper Egypt at the temple complex of Kombo on the banks of the Nile, he was worshiped along with his wife Hathor and their child Khonsu.

SOKAR
The Egyptian hawk god worshiped in the Memphite necropoli. He amalgamated with the great creator god to become "Ptah-Sokar." In Underworld scenes Sokar became the "lord of the mysterious region" and his head emerged from the sand mound over which the sun god passed in a gesture of resurrection. His festival emphasized the resurrection of the god-king.

SONS OF HORUS
Horus's sons — Imsety, Hapy, Duamutef and Qebehsenuef — were the four funerary gods responsible for protecting the internal organs that were removed, embalmed and kept in canopic jars, the stoppers of which were fashioned in their images.

Imsety was anthropomorphically portrayed, he looked after the liver and was watched over in turn by Isis.

Hapy was represented as a baboon, his province was the lungs, and his guardian goddess was Nephthys.

Duamutef was interpreted as a jackal, he guarded the stomach and was protected by Neith.

Qebehsenuef, who took the form of a hawk, had the intestines under his jurisdiction. Serket was his guardian goddess.

Right: The Egyptian god Sobek sits with Pharoah Amenhotep III.

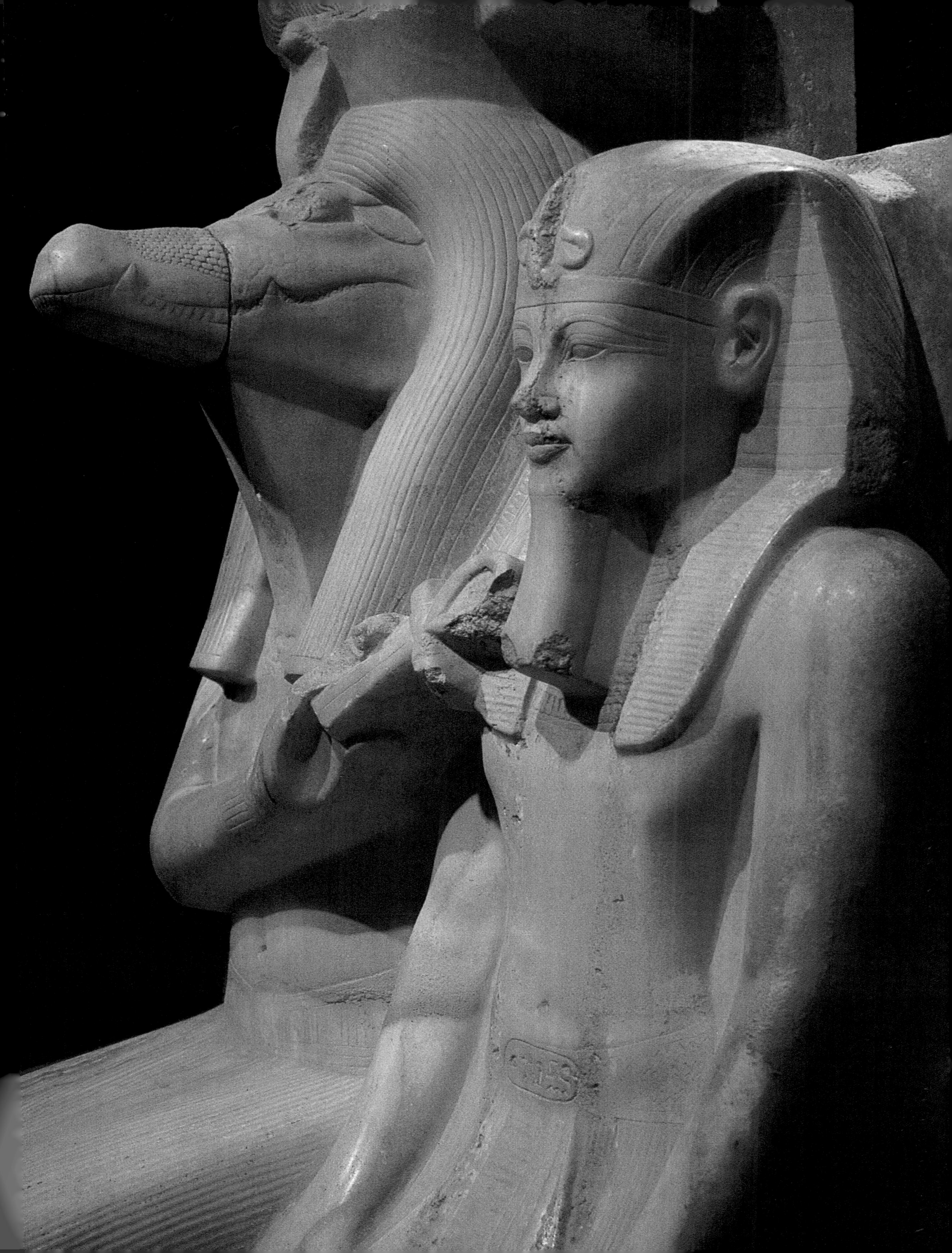

A-Z
CODEX GODS

SOPEDU
Also known as: Septu, Sopd

Falcon border-patrol god, protector of the Eastern Desert. Linked with Horus. Sopedu the "Smiter of Asiatics" was portrayed as a man with foreign features, wearing two feathers on his head, or as a falcon wearing the same feathers. In his cosmic aspect Sopedu combined with another hawk deity, Horus. His area of influence included the turquoise mines of the Sinai Peninsula, though his main center was in the northeastern delta.

SOULS OF PE AND NEHKEN
These were gods who symbolized the pre-dynastic rulers of the Two Lands prior to unification: Pe or Buto in the delta, and Nehken or Hierakonpolis in Upper Egypt. They were considered the protective ancestors of the living pharaoh. Those of Pe were visualized with the heads of falcons, and those of Nehken with the heads of jackals.

SPHINX
An image of the sun god, the earliest known Sphinx is the huge statue near the pyramid of King Chephren on the Giza plateau necropolis. It takes the form of a recumbent lion with a human head wearing the Nemes headdress. Other avenues of sphinxes linked temples and their precincts. Sphinxes could have almost any kind of head — human or animal.

SRAOSHA
"Hearken"

The herald of ancient Iranian mythology, he survived the Moslem conquest as Surush, the messenger of Allah sometimes equated with Gabriel. In Zorastrian times he was Ahuramazda's all-hearing ear, (like Re's eyes) listening out for the evil of Ahriman. Because evil is most active at night, he would descend to earth during darkness to pursue the demons and wrongdoers. His main enemy was Aeshma, the destructive spirit, whom he pursued relentlessly. Sraosha was also a mediator who manifested obedience to the divine will of Ahuramazda.

TATENEN
Also known as: Tanen, Tathenen

The personification of the very fertile Nile silt, left after the waters of the annual inundation. In this aspect of fertility deity Tatenen was combined with Geb. He also combined with Ptah in a creator god mode, and was guardian of the royal dead. Tatenen was portrayed as a man with a crown consisting of two feathers and two ram's horns.

TAWERET
Aka: Tauret, Thoueris

Protective hippopotamus goddess. Along with her consort Bes the dwarf god, Taweret was the protector of women in pregnancy and childbirth. Very popular with the ordinary people, like her

Above left: The Sphinx and the pyramid of Cephren.
Right: One of the Sphinxes found on the way to the Luxor Temple.

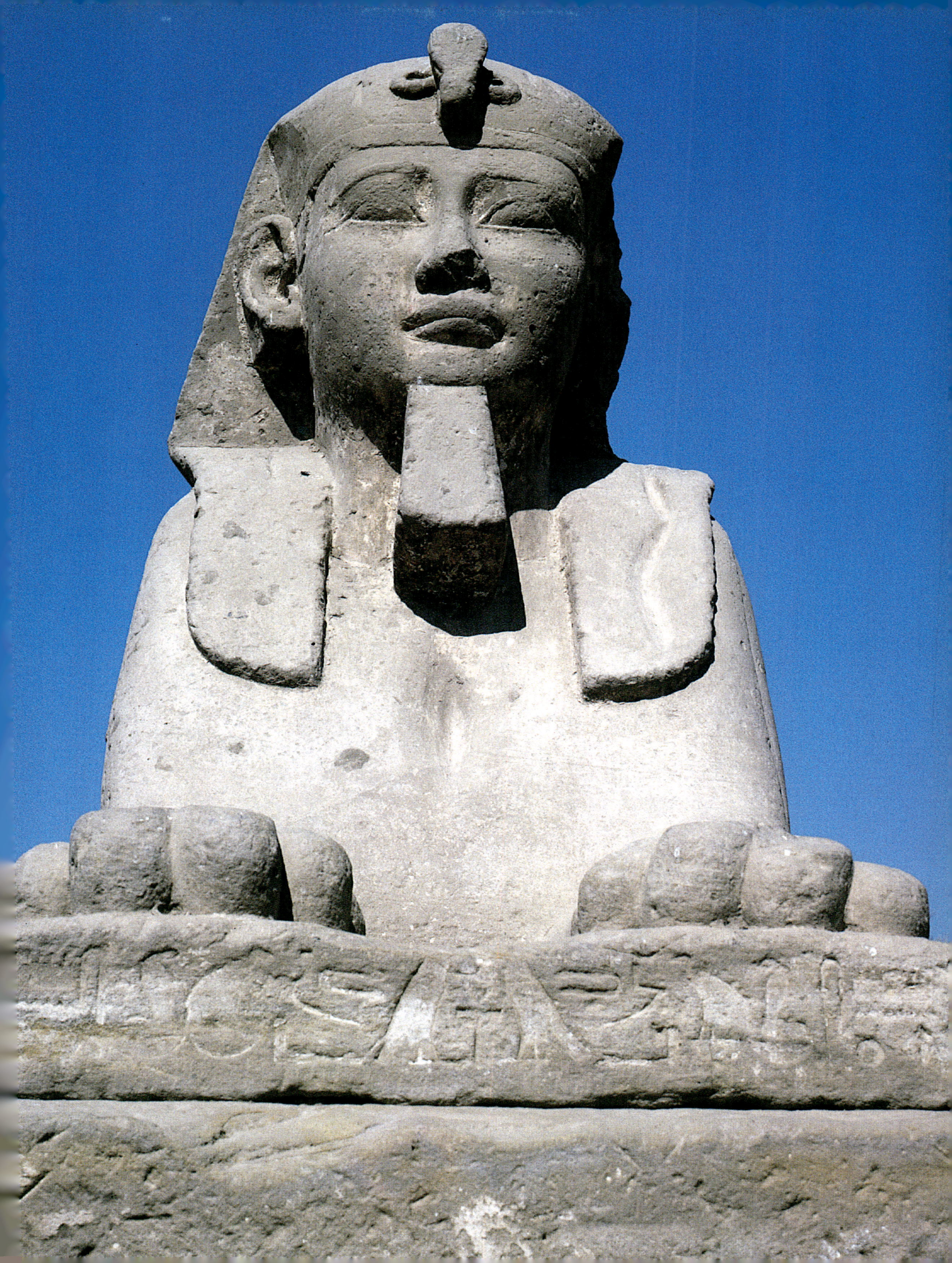

A-Z
CODEX GODS

husband she had a bizarre appearance — a female hippopotamus with human breasts, lion's feet, and a crocodile's back and tail. She wore a wig of straight hair that fell to her shoulders. Her alarming appearance belied her benign nature and frightened off malevolent spirits.

TIAMAT
Also known as: Labbu, Lobat

The Mesopotamian dragon and manifestation of chaos. In the account of the universe prior to Marduk's remodeling there were only the sweet waters (Abzu), the salt ocean (Tiamat) and the mist hovering above both (Mummu). Abzu and Tiamat were the parents of the first gods — Lahmu and Kahamu, who begat Anshar and Kishar who begat Anu and Ea. The noise of these new gods oppressed and enraged Tiamat and Abzu to the point where they decided to destroy their progeny. Hearing of this Ea pre-empted them and killed Abzu. Final deliverance from this danger came from Ea's son Marduk. As Tiamat prepared for war with a new husband (Kingu) and a new army of demons, Marduk was chosen as divine champion and his precedence over all other gods was acknowledged. Armed with weapons and winds he launched his attack, slaying Tiamat and capturing her forces. He then split the monster in two, placing one half into the air to form the heavens and the other down to make a floor over the deep. The world between was created from the blood of Kingu.

TEFNUT
Primeval sky goddess of moisture and consort of Shu, Tefnut was one of the Heliopolitan Ennead and the Eye of Re. The goddess of dew, rain and mist, Tefnut assumed leonine form or remained anthropomorphic, except for her lioness's head.

TELIPINU
The Hittite weather and fertility god, whose enraged withdrawal from the world sparked a panic in both gods and men. As everything began to wither and die an eagle was sent out by the sun god to find Telipinu. The eagle failed, so the goddess Hannahanna sent out a bee with orders to sting Telipinu, envelope him in wax and bring him back. The bee found the missing god, but its stings enraged him so much that he sent massive floods to destroy his teasers. It took a special ceremony of magic conducted by Kamrusepas, the goddess of spells, to allay his anger and persuade him to return to his temple and care for the earth again.

TESHUB
The Anatolian weather god, Teshub was depicted driving in a chariot pulled by bulls. In the Hurrian pantheon, his wife was Hebat. Teshub had usurped his father, Kumarbi, and the "Song of Ullikumni" tells of a conspiracy launched by Kumarbi against Teshub to regain his position. Kumarbi recruits the sea into this contest, from which a child, Ullikumni, is born

Right: An Egyptian wall painting from the Tomb of Nebamun in Thebes.

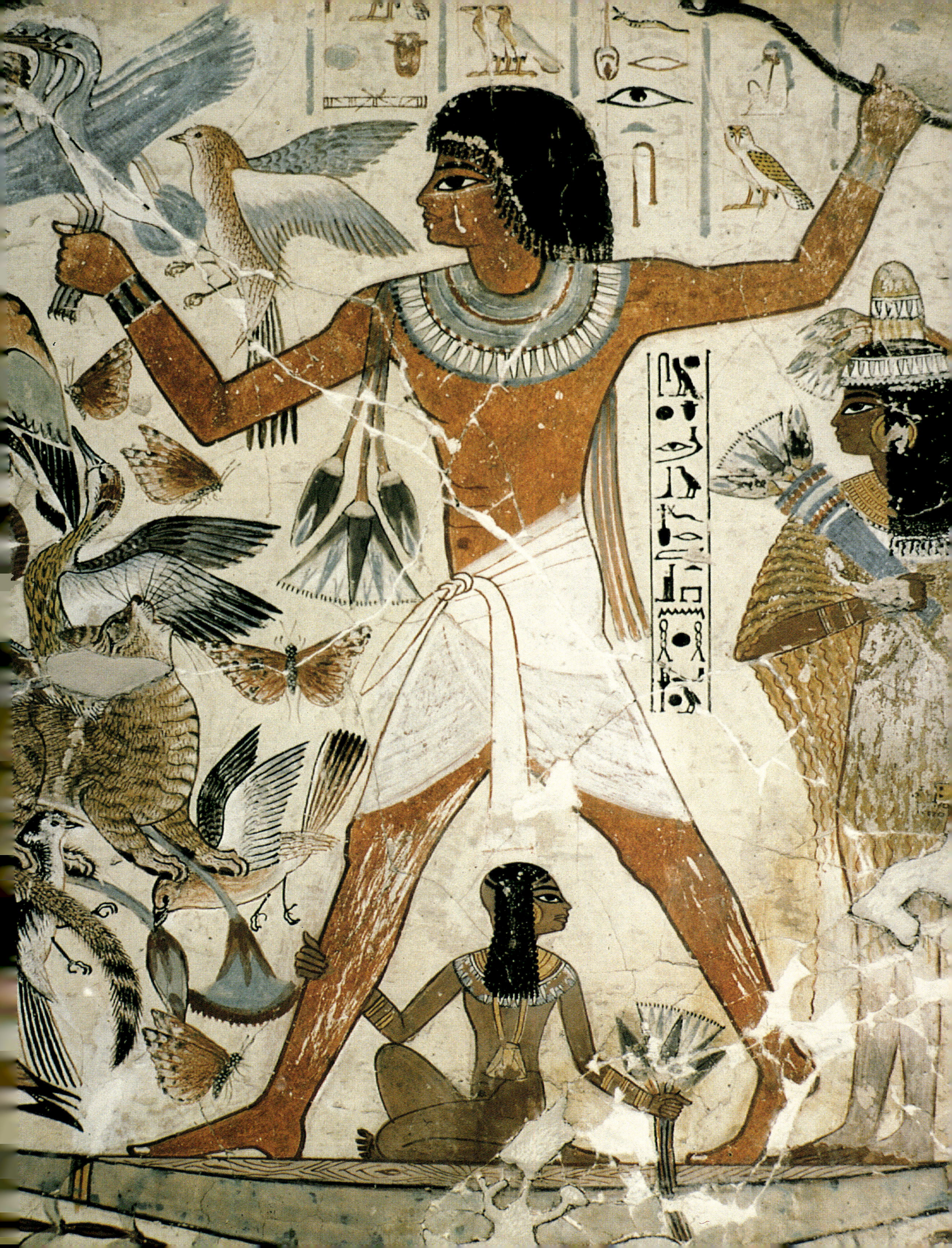

A-Z
CODEX GODS

and set on the shoulders of Upelluri in the sea, who then attains enormous size. Teshub however uses an ancient knife to combat Ullikumni's magic diorite stone, and renders him powerless.

THOTH

Moon god of data, Thoth was credited with inventing writing, the calendar, science, music, magic and art, medicine, maths and astronomy. He was also the Divine Recorder; conciliator and arbiter among the gods. Thoth was the divine regulative force, present throughout the funeral rites and involved in the judgement of the soul. He was a staunch supporter of Horus, but healed the wounds of both gods after their combat. Thoth displaced the eight creator deities of Hermopolis to become paramount — hailed as a creator god in his own right. He was depicted anthropomorphically with the head of an ibis, or just as an ibis or a baboon. In each case on his head he wore the combined lunar disc and crescent. He was esteemed particularly by scribes, and gave the knowledge of hieroglyphs to man.

ULLIKUMMI

A Hurrian monster who threatened earth and heaven until finally cut down to size by Ea. He was part of a psychotic group of Mesopotamian gods struggling for predominance, and was the progeny of Kumarbi and the sea god's daughter. When Ullikummi was born he was placed on the shoulder of Upelluri who held up all the world. He grew alarmingly in size, heading heavenward, until he forced Teshub to abdicate again. Teshub then appealed to Ea, who eventually severed the stone giant's feet with an ancient and magical knife. In this story the myth of sacred combat between the cthonic and sky gods is played out.

VAHAGN

The paramount solar god of war and state belonging to the ancient Armenians, who entered Asia Minor from Thrace in the 7th century BC. Following the conquest of the Armenians by Cyrus all other gods except Vahagn were replaced with the Iranian pantheon. Vahagn was associated with the sun, lightning and fire and he was a great slayer of dragons and demons, sometimes compared to Hercules.

UTANAPISHTIM

Also known as: Ziusudra

A Sumerian king and Noah-type flood hero who appeared in the Mesopotamian Flood story variants and was credited with saving mankind from destruction. For his piety and goodness he was rewarded with eternal life in the land of Dilmun. In a different Sumerian composition, "The Instructions of Shuruppak," Ziusudra received advice from his father Shuruppak in the form of short proverbial sayings. Utanapishtim also occurs in the "Epic of Gilgamesh."

Above left: An ibis-headed god leads the deceased to the Underworld. Right: Thoth, the moon-god of data, as seen on a papyrus.

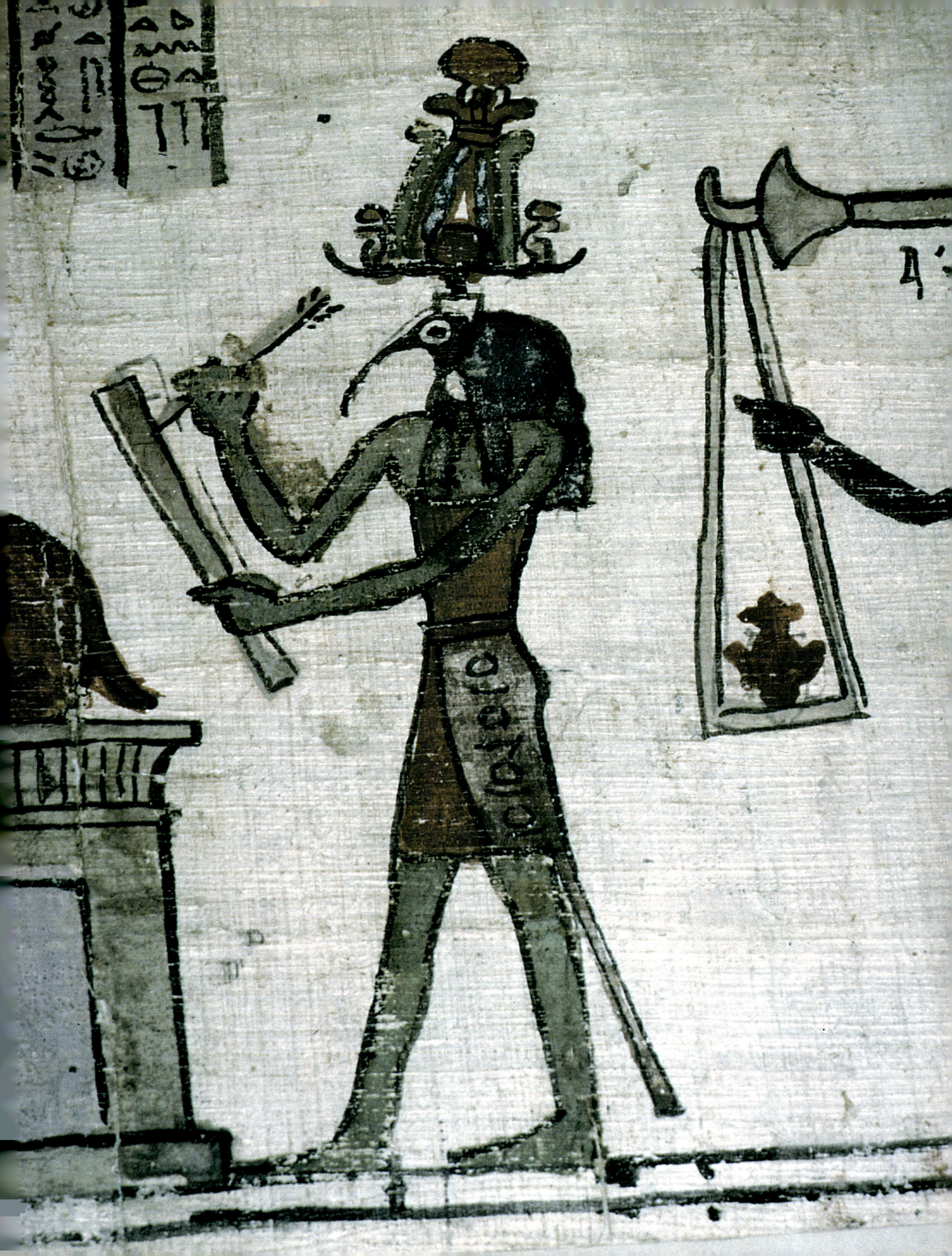

A-Z
CODEX GODS

WADJET
Also known as: Uajyt

Cobra goddess of the delta, preserver of the royal authority. Along with her southern counterpart, Nehkbet, she was part of the royal insignia, protecting the pharaoh — the Uraeus cobra of the Double Crown. Her cult center was at Buto, also known as Pe. Wadjet was depicted as a cobra rearing up as if ready to strike. In her role as eye of Re, she could also be portrayed as a lioness.

WENEG
A son of Re, Weneg personified cosmic order, and was thus the judge of other gods and a male counterpart to Ma'at.

WEPWAWET
Jackal headed god of Upper Egypt. Wepawawet lived in the west and was the guide of the dead, leader of expeditions, and war-champion of the pharaoh. He was identified with Horus. Wepawawet also guarded the sun boat of Re on its nightly journey through the Underworld. He was represented anthropomorphically, with a jackal's head, and dressed as a soldier, carrying various insignia.

ZU
In Sumerian mythology Zu was a lion-headed storm bird who stole the sacred tablets of destiny on which the universal laws were inscribed. He thus threatened the very fabric of existence and considerably unnerved the gods. Whoever wore these tablets (originally belonging to the chaos-dragon Tiamat) around their neck was in command of the world. Finally Ninurta, the son of Enlil and god of war and hunting, tracked Zu down to her nest on the mountain of Sabu and rescued the tablets. Later Zu came to be seen as a manifestation of Ninurta.

Left: Wepawawet, the jackal-headed god of Upper Egypt.
Right: Wadjet, the preserver of royal authority was part of the royal insignia.

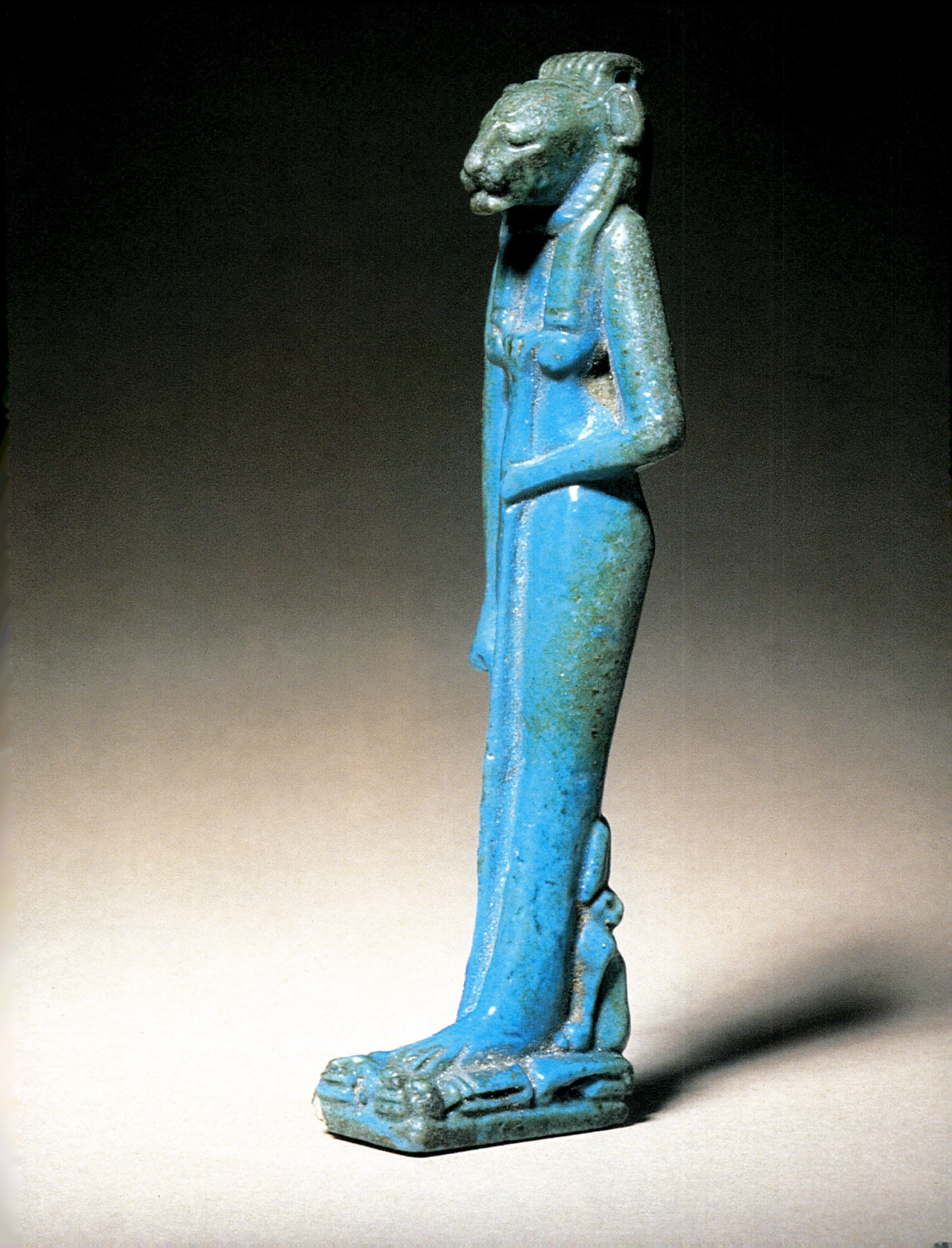

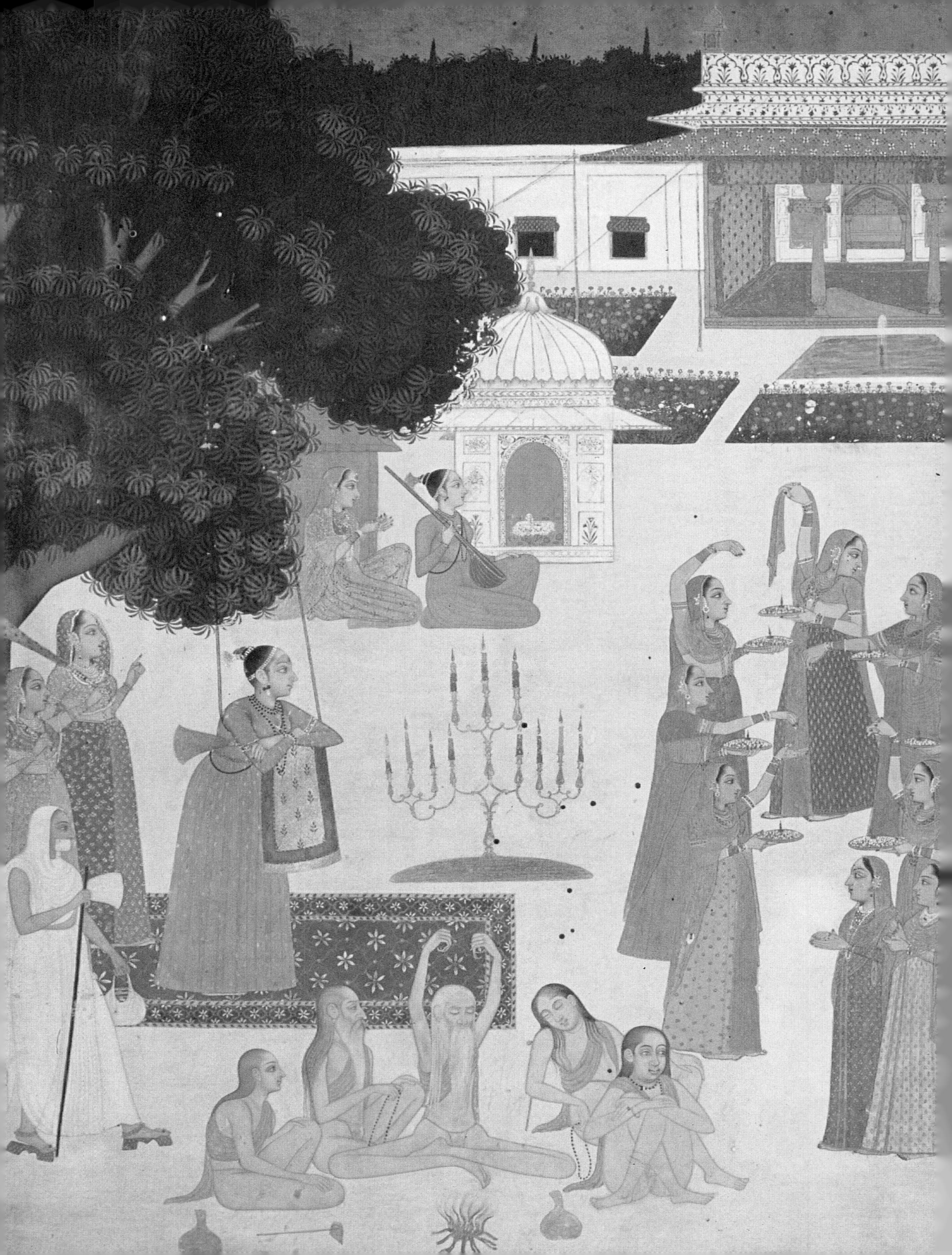

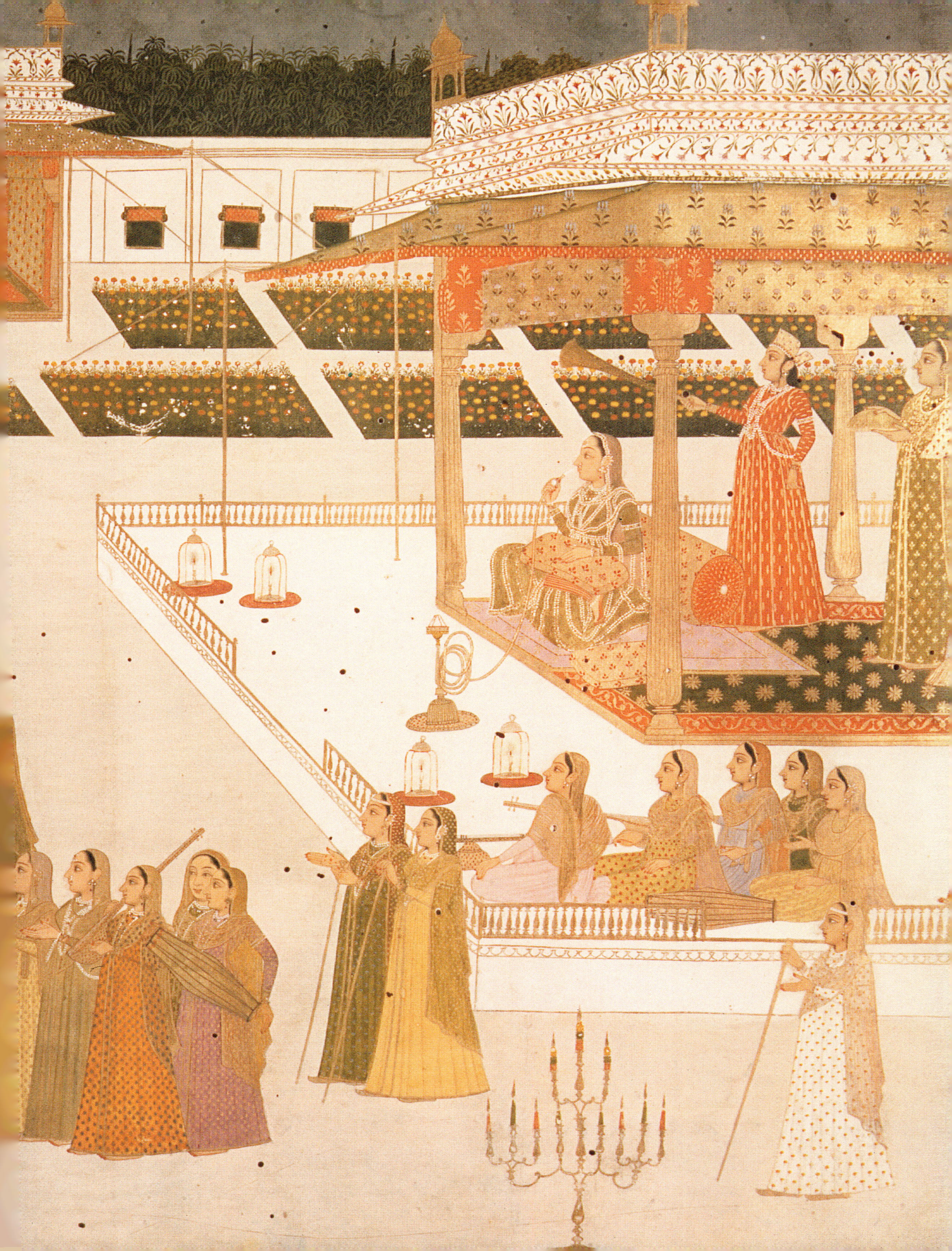

INDIA

INDIA blurs the borders between gods and men. In Hindu mythology men often seem to become semi-divine — especially sages, kings or priests — while the gods are anthropomorphic and motivated by human desires. They are often no better than men, just more powerful, able to indulge themselves in their predilections and choosing to enact them on earth. Myth in India has remained archaic; a collective heritage which even today continues to refashion and reshape what is one of the most complex living cultures in the world.

The overriding factor differentiating the mythologies of India from other advanced countries is that her mythology is still vibrantly alive and continuous, and accepted as scriptural history on a par with the Bible or the Koran.

India — the Holy Land of the East and second of its great river valley civilizations — extended over a much wider area than its counterparts. Many of the elements visible today were already in existence over four thousand years ago. It seems that like many ferocious wandering tribes, the Aryans who moved into the area in about 1500 BC, were civilized by the culture they conquered, for Vishnu, Shiva and Devi ultimately prevailed over Indra, Brahma and their kin.

In India there has been an almost continuous cultural flow, reaching back into the unrecorded past and continuing through the whole of recorded history. It is alive with images, visually stunning and richly polychromatic in their textures — "an inextricable jungle of luxuriant growths. A continuous thread of potent symbolism runs through this ancient yet vibrant culture, never diluted by philosophy or science, it has remained as a consequence more true to its ancient parameters, and though in a constant state of flux it stays bound within its ancient heart." Its hierarchical but tolerant society has absorbed foreign invasions of people and ideas, and it has grown into the world's

Previous pages: An Indian princess and her ladies celebrate Diwali—the Hindu festival of light—in a palace garden. Right: The Elephant Wall, a Buddhist shrine found in Ruvanvalisaya, Sri Lanka.

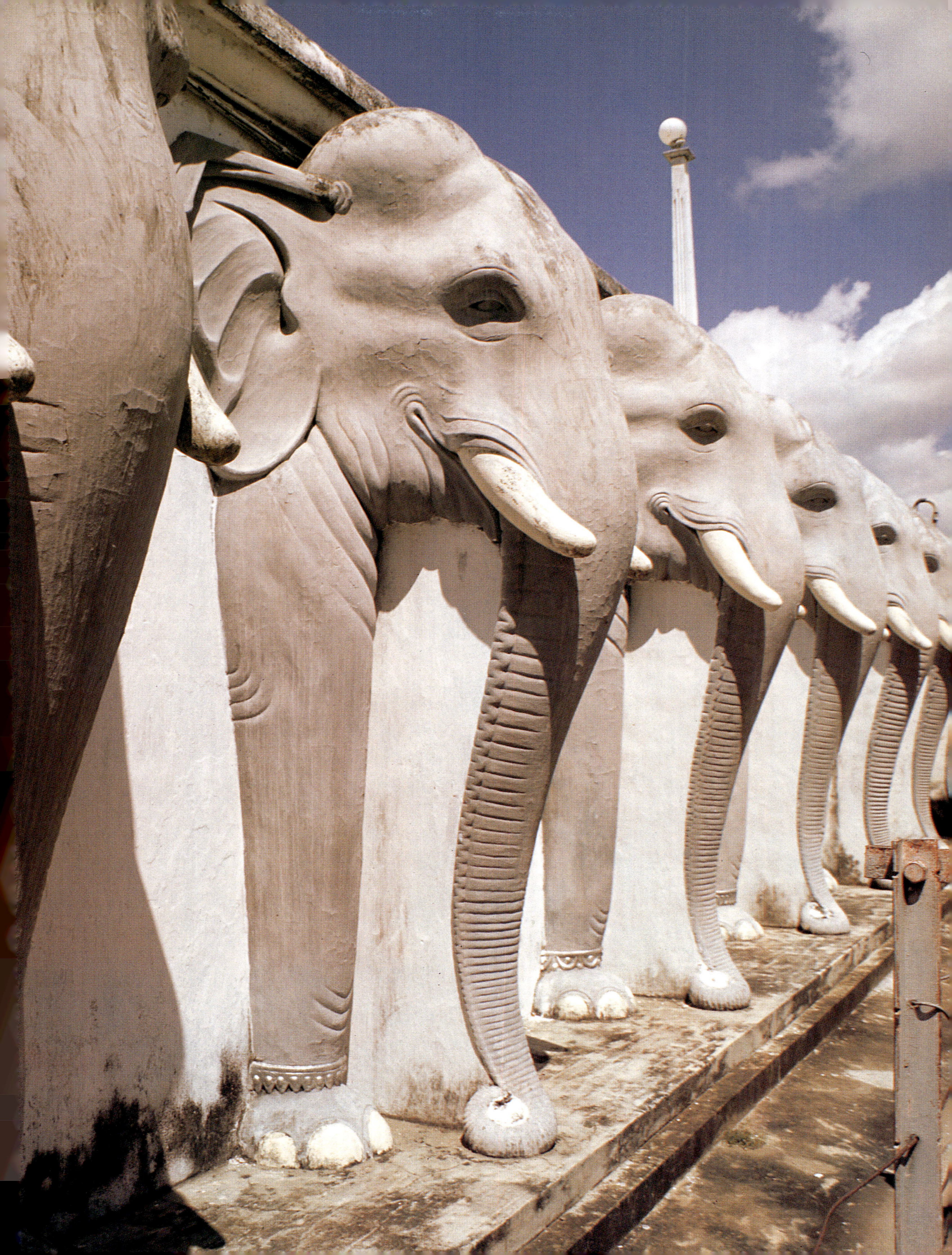

oldest continuous flow of monist myth. Nothing is discarded, all is accreted.

Such manifestation and plurality of detail is at the core of Hinduism, which seeks to comprehend the inherent unity of existence — for this multiplicity can be boiled down to aspects of the Hindu Trinity, the *Trimurti*, creation, duration and dissolution. It is further reduced by the sage and the ascetic, who seek to leave the wheel of endless transformation and escape the infinite cycle of rebirth contained within it. All head to the same god. "Beyond aversion and desire lies the union and coincidence of all opposites in one transcendent source. Birth, love, friendship, beauty, anger, pain, betrayal, terror and death all have their rightful place in the constant evolution of reality."

All this mythology is in the moment, not of it. It is easy to be intimidated by its sheer size and overlapping multiplicity, for the monist Indian religious culture is fundamentally opposed to West Asian dualism. It seeks to emphasize the "oneness" and unity of all reality as opposed to a landscape of black and white opposites. Instead there is eternal tension between creation and destruction, an immense pattern of the one endlessly fusing into the other.

Another theme is that things are not what they seem and that reality is in some way illusory. Through the constant metamorphosis or stylization of the same things, the symbol highlights and restores the theme. In India we can see the ancient tradition long since gone in our Western civilization of an oral tradition kept alive and fresh through constant updating and renewal.

Thus to approach Indian mythology from the direction of history would fundamentally miss the point; it must be viewed from a different "live" angle, and from within the context of Indian religious philosophy, with its wide speculation into the nature of the world and of human existence.

Above left and Right: A colossal Buddha cut from a solid rockface at Awkana, Sri Lanka.

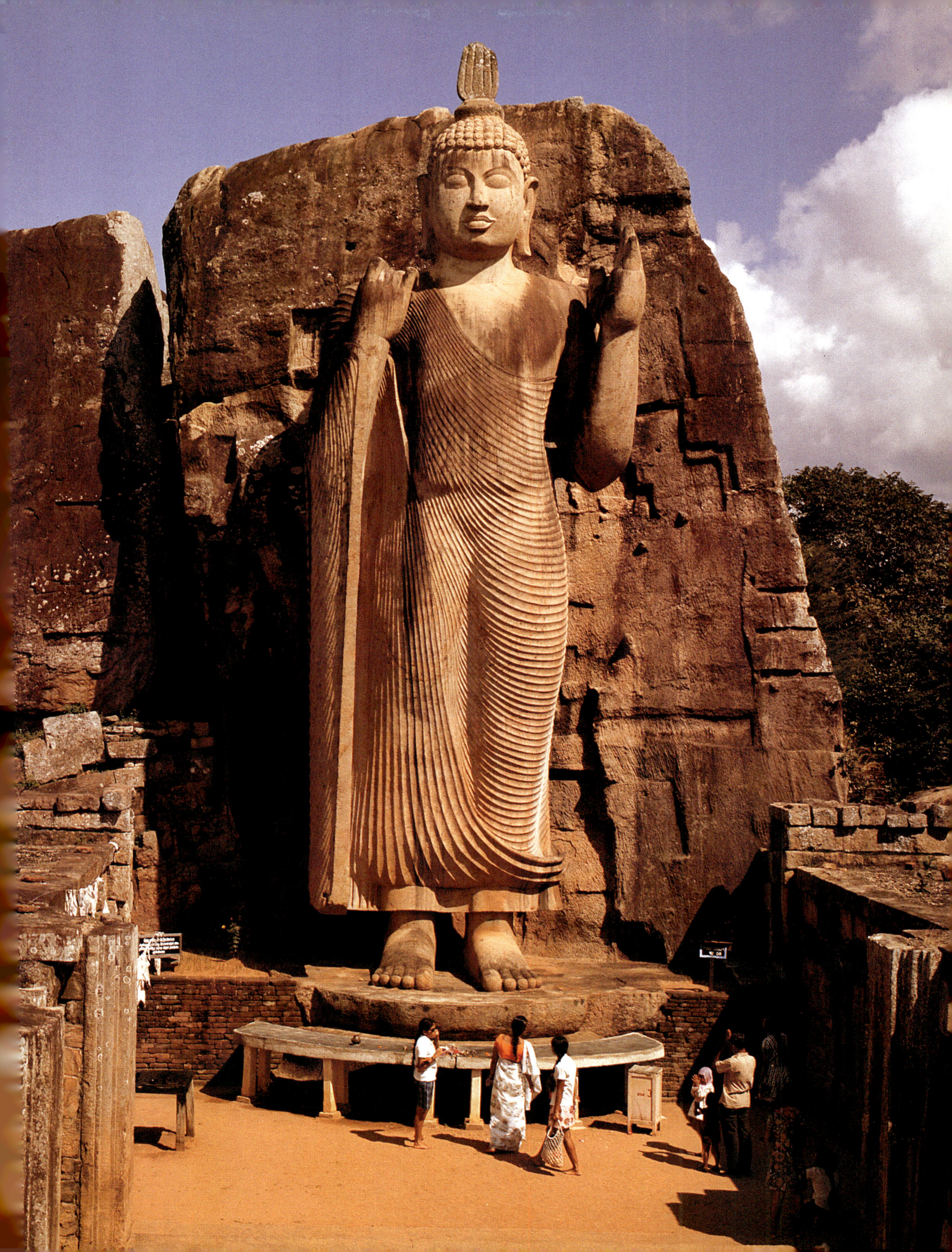

Beginning with the *Vedas*, the sacred knowledge of the Hindus was set down, detailing hymns of praise, correct ritual procedure, spells and charms. With the *Upanishads*, the beginnings of systematic thought occur, laying the foundations for later philosophical systems and providing some of their primary data. The Upanishads acknowledge the intrinsic energy and essence common to all existence. They also develop the ideas behind the original *Vedas*, with the many gods reduced to single concepts. This represents a shift towards the internalization and spiritualization of many ideas and the de-mythologizing of the Vedic tradition, transforming it into more of a philosophical discipline. Liberation must be gained through a combination of knowledge and developed awareness, in a proactive approach that required intelligence, effort and commitment and not merely the repetition of various words and actions.

The highest value is placed on liberation — to escape the cycle of rebirth and reincarnation. Indian philosophies have been traditionally divided into six orthodox systems called *astika* and three unorthodox or radical systems known as *nastika*. The six astika list as: *Samkhya* — a dualist system which maintains a distinction between matter and nature; *Yoga* — physical and mental techniques to promote meditation and free the mind; *Purva Mimamsa* — the interpretation the *Vedas* as a series of injunctions for action; *Vedanta* — emphasizing renunciation and the search for salvation; *Nyaya* — a logic system concerned with methodology and reasoning; and *Vaisheshika* — another logic system, sometimes linked with Nyaya, but with the emphasis on physics. The three nastika are skepticism, Buddhism and Jainism. All three nastika emphasize a detachment from worldly existence and salvation through conquering physical existence with strict ascetic discipline.

Above left and Right: A Sri Lankan Buddhist shrine at Anuradhapura Ruvanvaliseya (c. 161–137 BC).

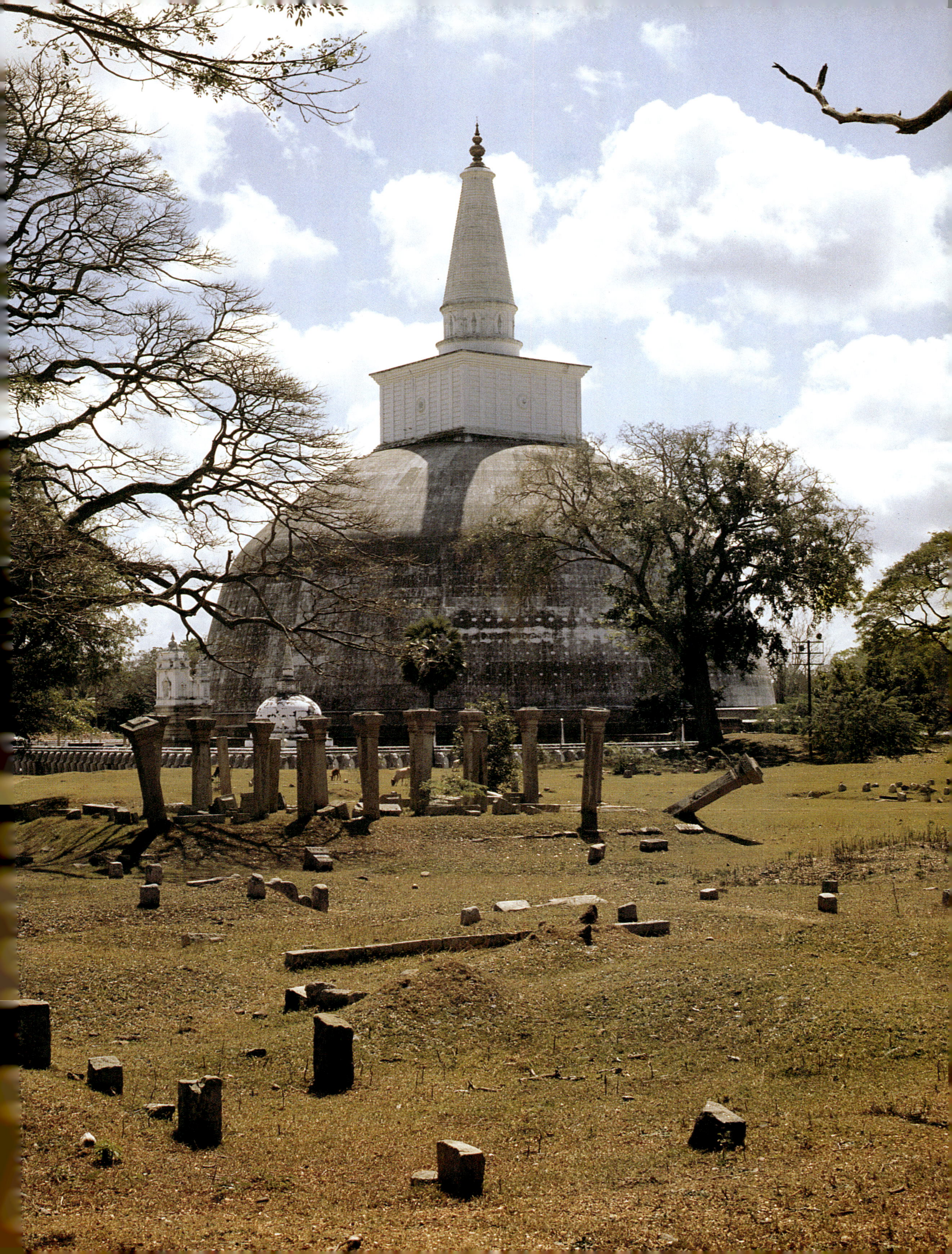

The Indus, Ganges and Deccan plains were the wombs of Indian civilization, containing the original population tidemarks of its early history: Munda, Dravidian and Aryan. It was the interaction of these different social and linguistic groups that formed the religious character of these areas. The supra-regional language that linked everything and enabled this development was Sanskrit.

The oldest god grouping was the Vedic pantheon (mother earth goddess and phallic sky god), which gave way to the Hindu Trimurti concept of the three elements of the cycle of existence, contained within a trio of gods: originator, maintainer and destroyer. This places the creation of the world as an arrangement not a creation.

The aboriginal religions have remained within India but Buddhism and Hinduism swept well beyond their boundaries. Hinduism penetrated to Cambodia and Java. Buddhism (extinct in its mother country) penetrated the whole of the Far East, and interwove with the indigenous religions of Tibet and Sri Lanka, especially in its Tantric mode.

Non-Aryan religious aspects were manifested in the Munda and other aboriginal peoples, practicing the totemistic animism of early human groupings. Features of this culture were sacrifices absorbed by spirits as commodities, combined, perhaps, with cannibalism.

The matriarchal Dravidians were more evolved — no blood and raw meat, but the veneration of idols instead. These were hung with scented flowers, perfumed and watered. This peaceful worship belied the overriding preoccupations: Durga and Kali demonized destructive female principles and symbolized the ambiguous fecundity of nature, with the male principle symbolized in the lingam — a phallic representation something similar to the modern concrete road bollard.

Above left and Right: This meditating Buddha is seated on a lotus with two disciples (1st century AD).

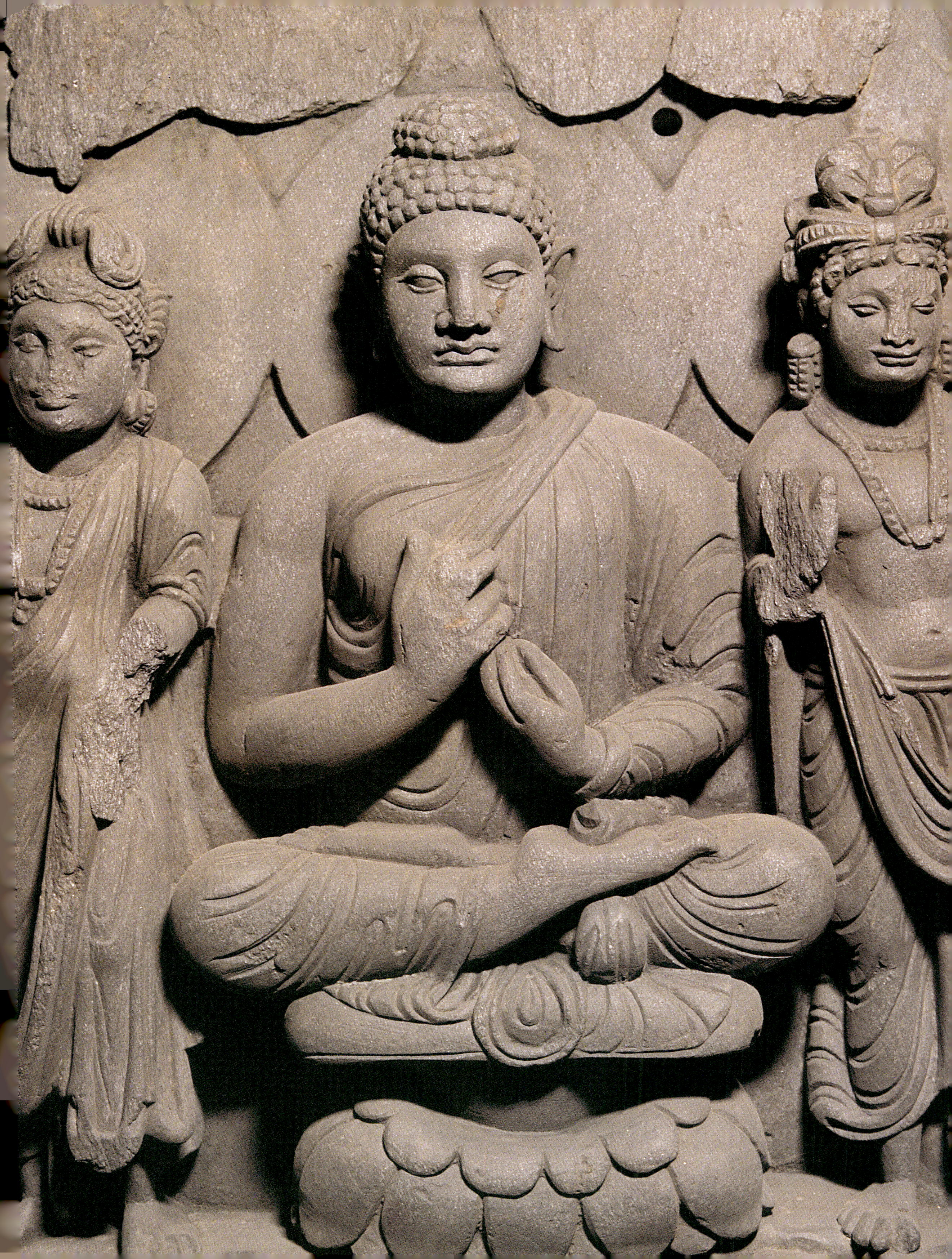

Aryan aspects were marked by tight family groups, showing an invader's wish and will to remain different and dominant. This primarily military society, organized in small clans and tight structures — the product of a defense mentality — helped the Aryan social structure evolve into a recognizable caste system of warriors, priests and commoners and reflected the metamorphic change from Vedism to Brahmanism: Ahas changed to Dharma — religious protocol to social organization.

Even with modern commentaries and reflections, all Hindus today still acknowledge the *Rig Veda* as the oldest documentation of the highest truth in its totality and emblematic of a myriad yet coherent whole. To remove one single factor would perhaps upset the balance.

"Instead of looking for some historical evolution, one would do better to reflect on the fact that, in the earliest recorded times, the sages had a direct vision of things unimpaired by mental reasoning, and were content to make elliptical allusions to the planes of consciousness which they wished to share with their disciples."

It is also fruitless to seek a social distribution "key" to unlock this sacred spectrum, for the worship of deities is pan-caste and not prone to such arbitrary dissection and analysis.

HINDUISM

In around 1500 BC Indo-Aryan pastoral nomads invaded northwest India; conquering the early Indus valley civilization and drifting slowly further east, they eventually settled in the Ganges plain. Here they introduced their tripartite Brahman social structure, which went on to become the basis of the Hindu caste system. Also at this time the *Rig Veda* was composed in Sanskrit. By about 500 BC this Sanskrit culture was firmly established in its heartland of the central Ganges plain. This

Above left and Right: This Hindu temple in Banglore is distinctly South Indian.

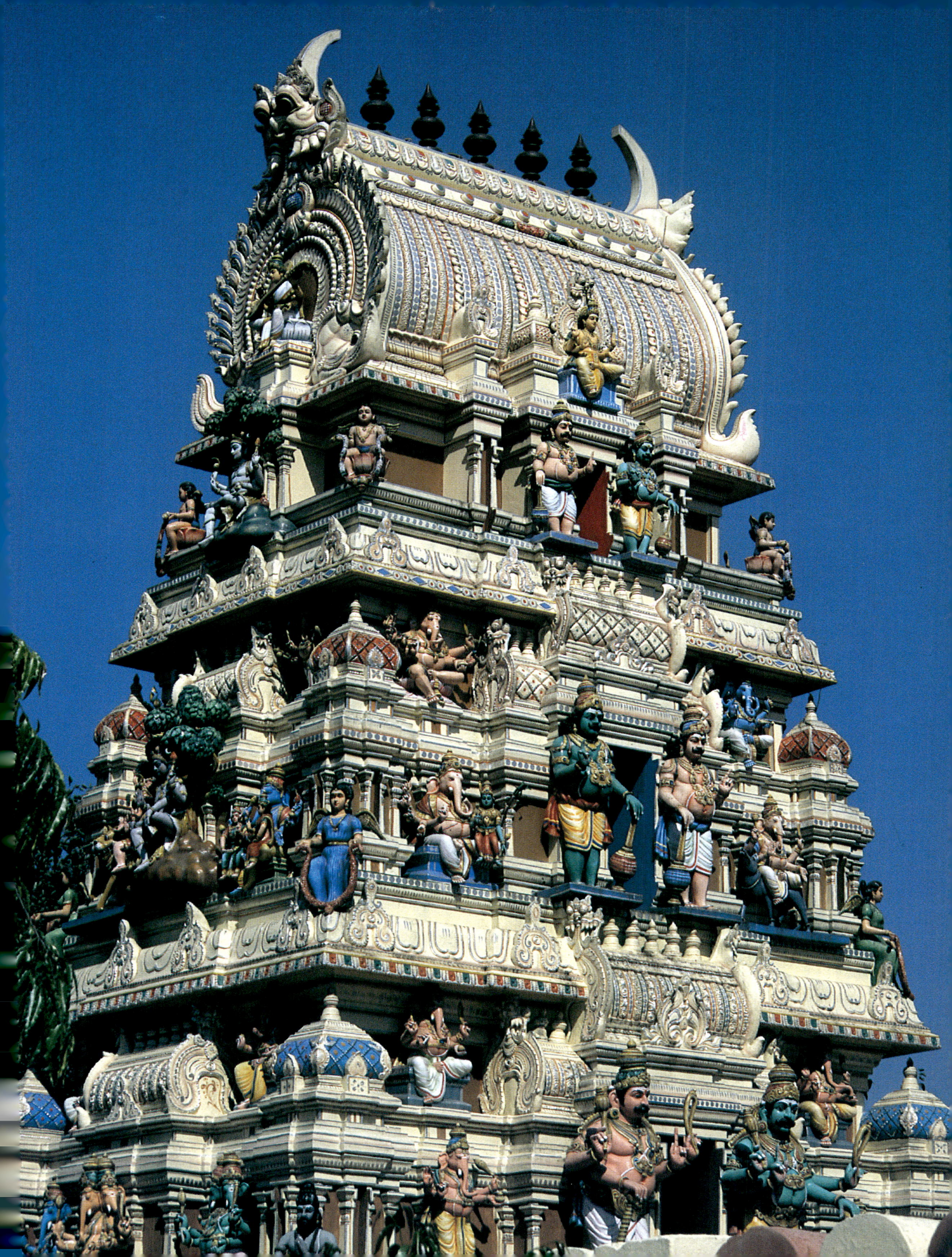

time also saw the beginnings of Buddhism. Siddhartha Gautama was born, into a wealthy royal family of the Sakya tribe in Kapilavastu, north of Benares. At the age of 30 he left it all behind to find the Middle Way.

From around 500–501 AD There was further Aryan expansion southward as far as Sri Lanka, and eastward to Bengal and Assam, and by 1500 AD Sanskrit culture had left by boat to Burma, Thailand, Cambodia, Sumatra and Java. At this time the *Puranas* were composed. These sacred compositions dealt with the mythology of Hinduism and covered other subjects such as festivals, pilgrim sites, caste obligations etc.

The Hindu religious tradition has thus developed over thousands of years, with integral links to the social system and history of India. It does not trace its origins back to a specific founder or prophet; it has no set creed and no specific institutional structure. What it does emphasize is *dharma* — the correct way of living rather than a doctrine, and so it can encompass a wide range of custom and belief. Within India itself there is a wide variation of people who call themselves Hindus and through new developments there is a constant updating of Hindu thought.

The Hindu caste system began with three levels but continued to extend to four castes: *Brahmins* (priests), *Kshatriyas* (warriors), *Vaisyas* (peasant farmers) and *Sudras* (slaves and servants). The "Untouchables" were added still later. It seems that the older pre-Aryan culture had a sizeable influence on the newcomers because the focus and content of its religious ideas did not vanish with the Aryan conquest, but combined and resurfaced later. Then it is found that the Aryan god Indra is demoted to the second rank, beneath the older Trimurti. Brahma was always more a concept than a god like Vishnu and Shiva, who initiate a lot more, but he does supply

Above left and Right: Krishna, atop the bird god Garuda fights the god Indra on an elephant (c. 1590 AD).

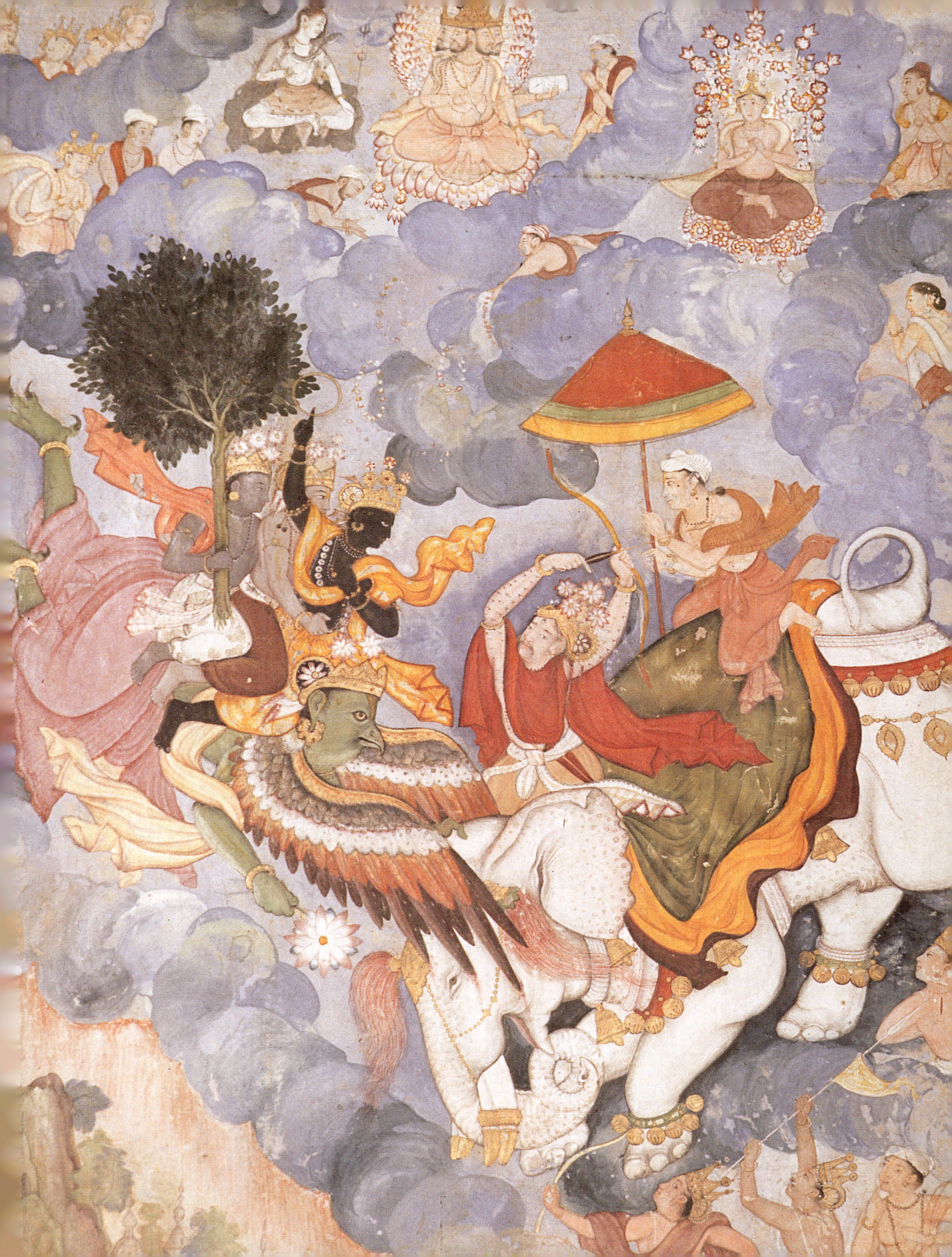

time to the equation, and thus number. Indian time phases are as labyrinthine as their pantheon A day and night of Brahma (called a *kalpa*) is calculated at 8,640,000,000 years, which would last for a 100 years of these time periods, before the dissolution of the universe and subsequent recommencement. The message driven home is one of endlessness and continuity: even the gods would dissolve at the end of a kalpa before it all came round again; the wheel of oneness — *Maya* — is also seen as illusion imposed upon the everlasting soul, *Jiva*.

BUDDHISM

This thought and practice system originated with the teachings of Siddhartha Gautama (563–479 BC), who awoke from life's dream-state and got off the merrygoround of illusory experience — *samsara*. His life and ministry were an example of the direction to be followed. Buddha — like Lao Tzu — knew that his mission could not be explained in words and so restricted the recording of his words and deeds. Despite this, an intricate mythology developed, integrated with Hinduism and spread along with Buddhism across Asia. The teachings of the Buddha are summarized in the four Noble Truths and set out in the eightfold path or way to enlightenment, known also as the "Middle Way" for its route lay between sensuality and asceticism. The eight requirements were: perfect understanding, perfect aspiration, perfect speech, perfect conduct, perfect means of livelihood, perfect endeavor, perfect mindfulness and perfect contemplation. Through observation and effort a person can break out of the laws of *karma*, which states that a person's actions have consequences that are carried forward into their next life. The aim of Buddhists is to step outside this wheel of karmic rebirth and attain *nirvana*, or release from it and reunification with the One.

Above left and Right: Prince Siddhartha, later Buddha, travels with his attendants in a carriage.

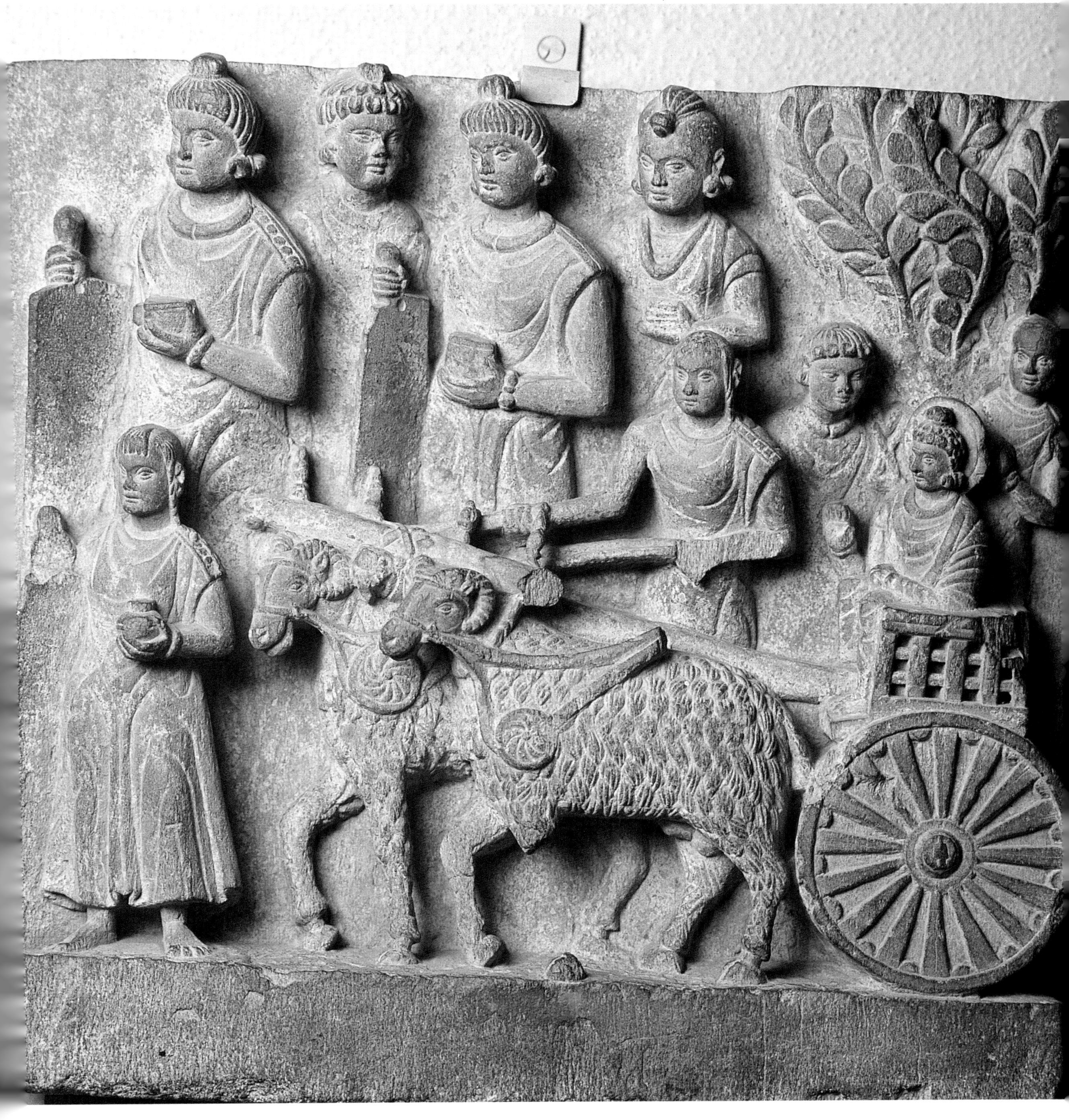

JAINISM

Jainism is another indigenous Indian thought system, which perhaps originated in the older pre-Aryan Dravidian culture and its reaction against the evolving Hindu elitist caste system and animal sacrifice. Buddhism and Jainism have sympathetic precepts and parallels, including a belief in karma and rebirth, withdrawal from the world, liberation and Nirvana. Another refined Jain principle is the concept of *Ahimsa*, or not harming any other living being, for it was believed that the wheel of rebirth could bring one back as an animal or even an insect — the inadvertent death of which could effect one's own karma. So Jains covered their mouths to prevent breathing in a fly and gently swept the road in front of them so they might not kill anything.

Like Buddha and Lao, was Mahavira (599–526 BC), last of the 24 Jain Tirthankaras or "river crossing makers." These austere ascetics, acknowledging no creator nor source, reached the Jain Nirvana where the soul floats in infinite knowledge and bliss. Jainism makes even Hindu and Buddhist numerology minute with their endless eternity. Its pre-Aryan roots indicate a dualsitic nature. For the Jains matter held karma, so there's no escape other than in withdrawal, and even fasting to death was an accepted and evolved process.

TIBET, SRI LANKA

In almost complete contrast is Tibetan and Tantric Buddhism and Hinduism. In Tibet and Sri Lanka erotic religious sculpture and mysticism were practiced, and sexual intercourse was seen as an accepted and a legitimate form of worship and a route to higher awareness. This precept was known as Mithuna — "the state of being a couple" and Yab-Yum — sexual union to surpass non-duality and erase all distinctions of self. Through

Above left and Right: Ambika a mother goddess as seen on a Jain Temple in Orissa. (11th century AD).

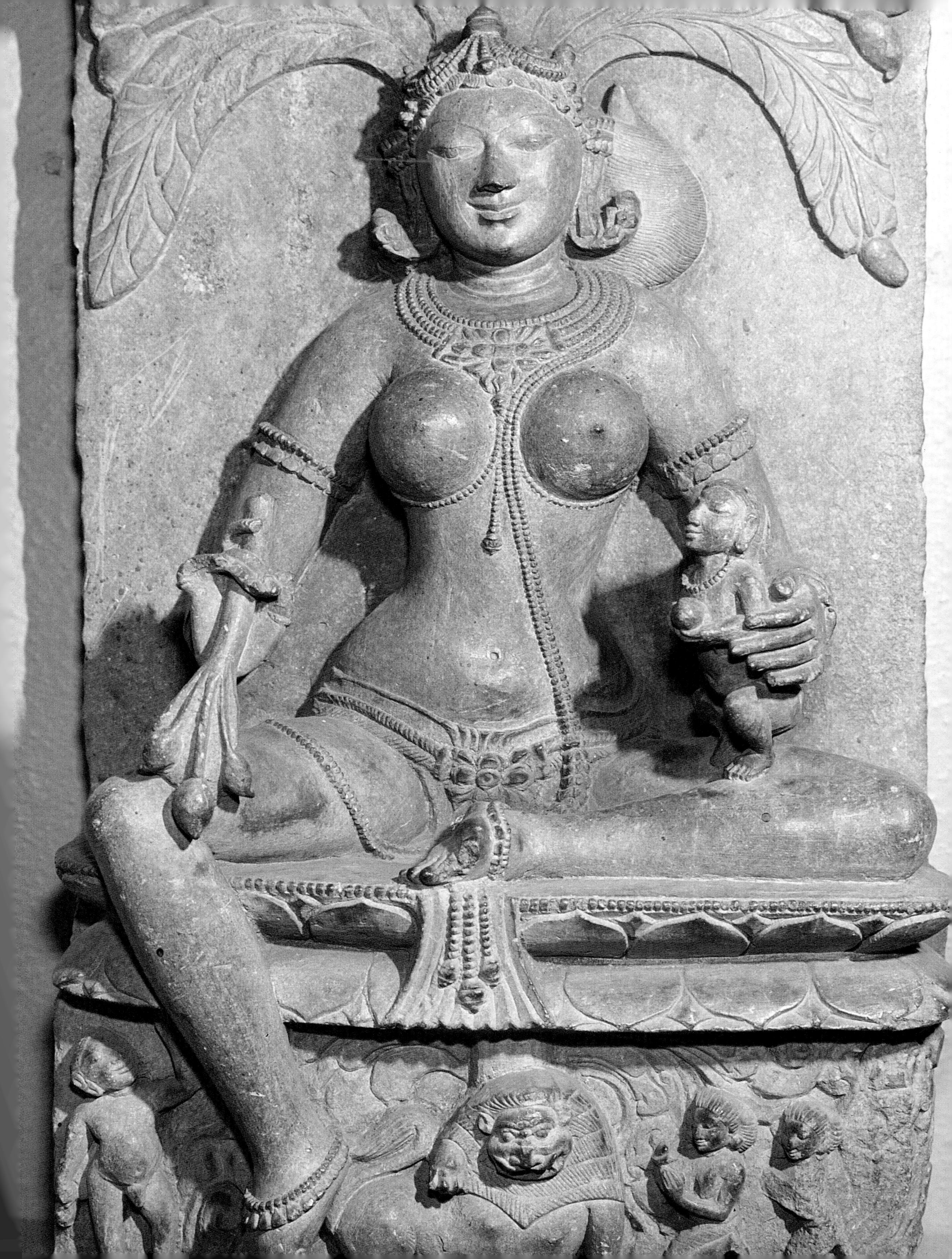

refined sexual awareness, these opposing creative principles could be aligned and cancelled out, giving rise to a religious perception. This was reflected mythologically with Shiva and his shakti Devi.

Hinduism and its mythology also influenced Cambodia, but its greatest influence was felt in Sri Lanka and Tibet, where following the revival of Hinduism, Buddhism in its mother country faded, leaving Sri Lanka and Tibet to combine with their own indigenous elements to create a new fusion with the inevitable doctrinal differences, leading to the eventual emergence of Mahayana Buddhism, with the emphasis on compassion and the Christ-like savior figures of the bodhisattvas — the Buddhas to be. The older tradition was Hinayana (Lesser Vehicle), more austere, withdrawn and meditative. This was the Sri Lankan choice. Tibet chose Mahayana (Greater Vehicle), Their vigorous art influenced by their own nature and land, wild and harsh, with a fair bit of violence intimated, befitting their dangerous landscape. The old animist-shamanist Bon religion of the Tibetans, Siberians and Mongolians combined with the smoother fluid Hinduism to form this distinctive branch. The relative merits of Indian and Chinese Buddhism were discussed at Lahsa in 792, with the Indian variant chosen as the dominant one. Teachers did not come till after 1040. The Tibetans converted the Mongols to their form of Buddhism, which ultimately mellowed their menace and aided their absorption into Chinese civilization. The bodhisattva Avalokitesvara was reborn as each successive Dalai-Llama, with the idea gradually spreading to other abbots.

Above left and Right: This statue made of clay, flour and bone ash depicts Maha Kala, a defender of Tibetan Buddhism.

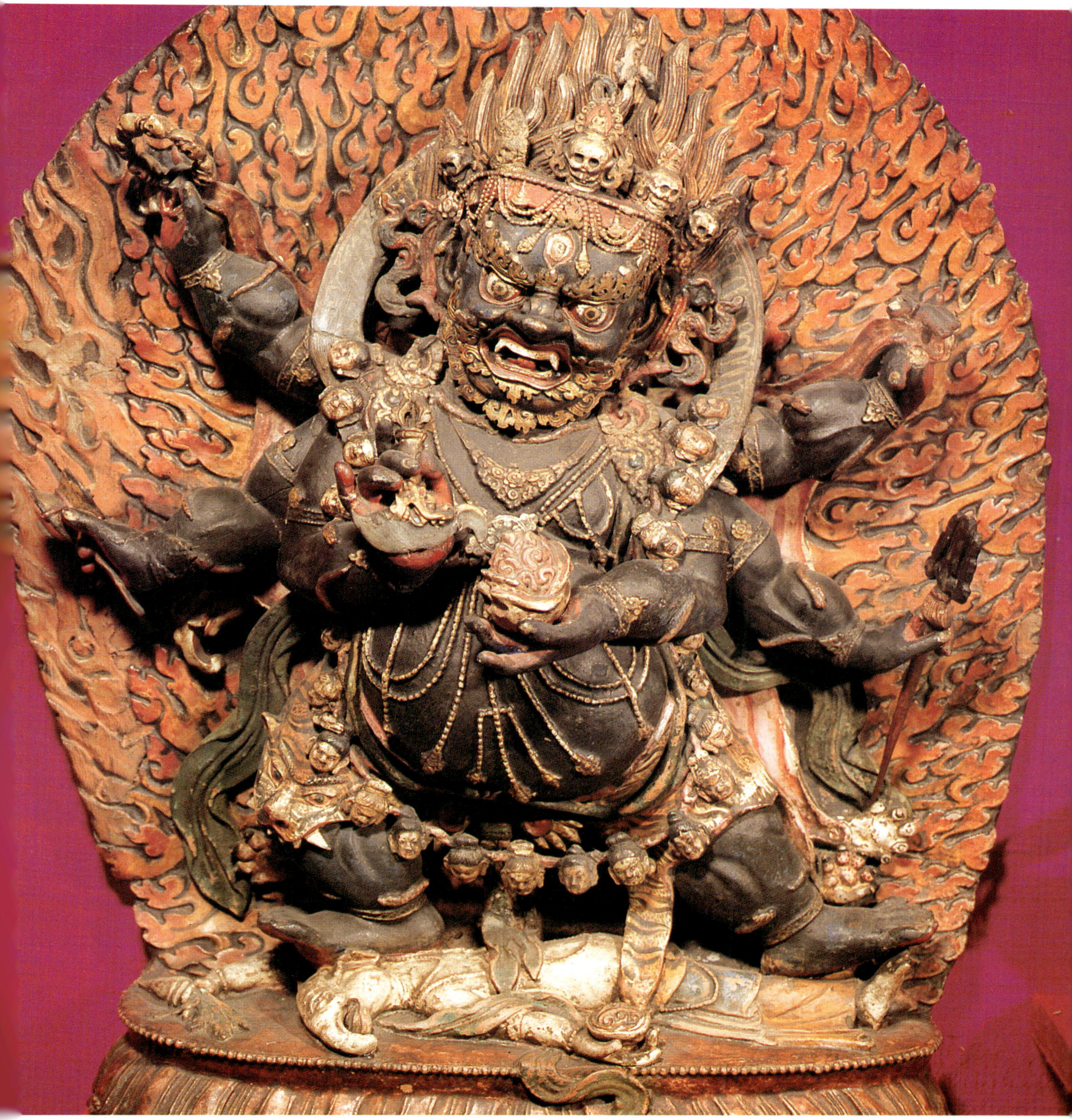

A-Z
CODEX GODS

ADITI

A Hindu sky-goddess and creatrix, Aditi is Nature supreme and mother of all the worlds and gods, representing the infinite consciousness infused in all forms and things. She is another female counterpart to Vishnu, with similarities to Ushas, and also to her son Surya. Whereas she binds or unites all things together, her opposite, Diti, manifests the divisive awareness of self, which separates people and things from each other, raising the potential for discord. The Adityas, the children of Aditi and Kasyapa, vary in number from two to fifteen, but include many of the major Hindu gods, sometimes even Vishnu and Shiva. Their job was to protect the world against chaos and evil by maintaining the absolute truth of the universe.

AGNI
"Fire"

Hindu fire-god, who appeared in various guises: as a red man with many arms and legs, riding a ram, with his face covered in butter, hair awry and many-tongued and toothed, belching and emitting light. His birth has various legends too: that he emerged spontaneously from water as a calf, from the sky as an eagle as well as from kindling wood. He had other roles as well, primarily as messenger of the gods, but also as a sky-god, creating storms to fertilize the earth. He represented fire in its different constructive and destructive forms, but also represents the manifestation of divine will and the energy of the cosmos present in all things. Agni had a beneficent side, which welcomes all who come to him, offering guidance and support. He was nevertheless feared for his powers by the other gods.

AMITABHA
"Infinite Light"

The boddhisattva of infinite light, who represents the pre-existent Buddha who already spontaneously exists. Amitahba is the manifestation of the essence of all six of the Meditation Buddhas, who sprung from the lotus. Foregoing his own Nirvana he remains behind to aid the weak and suffering. His only prayer is the formula of his name and this convenience appealed to the worldly Chinese. The archetype of compassion, Amitabha became the popular, gentle and almost effortless way of salvation for Mahayana Buddhists, all of whom expected to be reborn to a lotus throne each in the Pure Land.

AMRITA
"Not dead"

Amrita represents the ecstasy-inducing water of life in Hindu mythology, formed as the primeval ocean churned. When the demon Ra to decapitate him lest he obtain complete impregnability and so his severed manic swollen head adorns Hindu temples as a talisman to ward off evil spirits. Amrita is similar to Soma, the drink of

Right: A bronze of Agni, the Hindu god of fire.

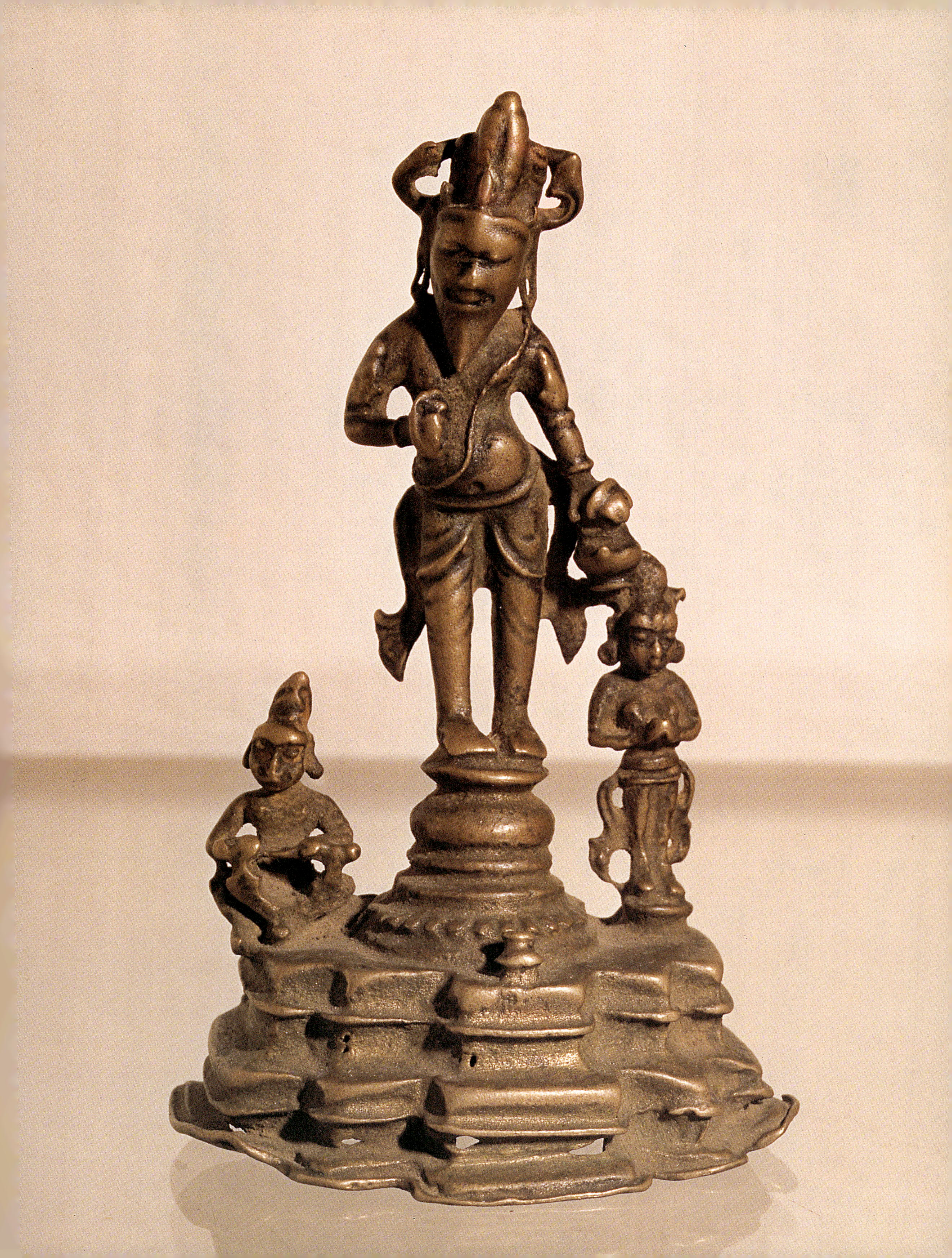

A-Z
CODEX GODS

the gods favored by Indra. The heat in India is often the enemy and the cool moon god Soma, with his radiance and moisture and water-controller became a creator deity. The *Vedas* extol him/it in an exhilaration of ecstasy that underlines the importance of transcendent drugs in the ancient religions.

ANANTA
"Endless"

Ananta is the World Serpent motif of Hindu mythology. While the cosmos is in stasis Vishnu sleeps upon the gargantuan snake Ananta, the manifestation of primordial essence. Sometimes portrayed anthropomorphically, Ananta can take the form of Balarama — its android avatar and half-brother to Krishna. Ananta's poison destroys physical reality, reducing matter back to its essence at the end of each cycle of existence. A kind of awesome conditioner that makes the dirt not come out of the wash, but instead melts the whole wash back into the water.

ARJUNA

Son and incarnation of the Hindu god Indra. His mother was Indrani. A hero and warrior, he plays a key role in the Bhagavad-gita, a philosophical poem that tells of his dialogue with Krishna during the war of the Mahabharata, between the Pandavas and the Kurus. Hesitating to become involved in such a senseless slaughter among relatives, Arjuna is finally convinced by Krishna of its particular inevitability and the redeeming eternity of the soul.

ASURAS

Although originally possessing a divine connotation, the Asuras in time inverted to become its opposite morphing into Hindu devils, the enemies of the Devas. The dividing line between gods and demons is not always clearly marked, and far from being mutually exclusive, they complement one another. The term Asura, usually applied to a demon, can in some instances be applied to a god in devilish mode. Their main weapon was their piety. After all, they are carrying out an important function, set by the creator to maintain the balance of the cosmic order, — without evil and chaos how could good and order exist? Thus they can even rival gods at certain moments, and in these contests the higher concept always triumphs, yet needs the lower as a catalyst for progress, in order to ascend, transcend and succeed.

AVALOKITESVARA

The Buddhist epitome of compassion. Like Amitabha, Avalokitesvara too forwent Nirvana to help the weak and suffering lesser mortals. He empathized powerfully with all living and suffering, always leading by example and effort, he represents the Mahayanan ideal of commitment and involvement. Fitting nicely with his advanced form-changing facility

Right: An 8th century carving of Anuradhapura, found at the Ratna Prasada in Sri Lanka.

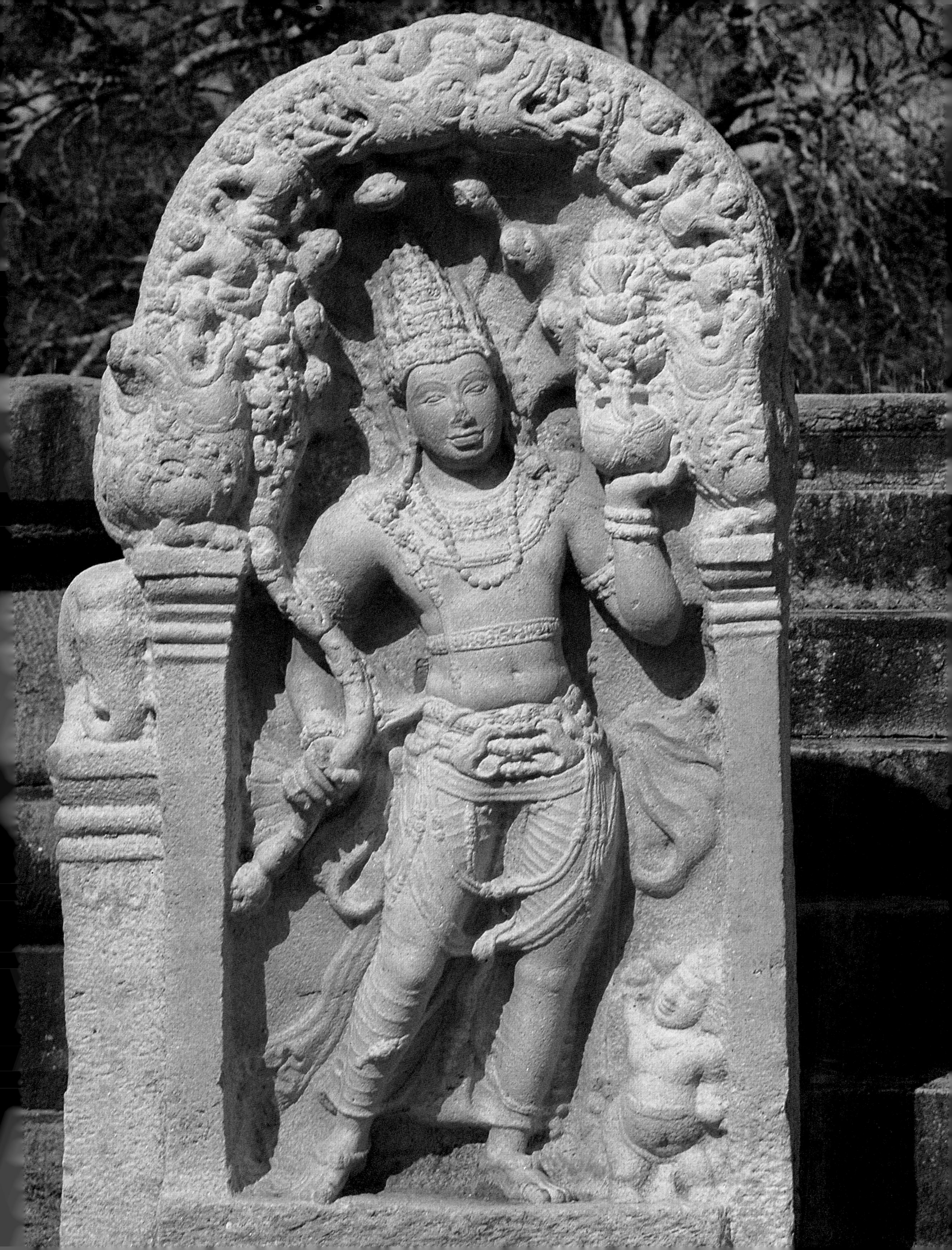

A-Z
CODEX GODS

(animals, people, objects, surreal hallucinations) he was portrayed as a rather handsome young man holding a lotus flower in Indian iconography, yet appeared as a merciful goddess to the Chinese. His female consort was the white-clad Tara. In Tibet he became the national deity, of whom the Dalai-Lama is a living incarnation.

BALARAMA

Another human avatar of Vishnu. Wise and faithful friend and brother of Krishna, to whom he was the main childhood companion, Balarama is almost always included in Vishnu's avatar directory yet rarely occurs in anything other than secondary roles. He was also the avatar of Ananta, the world serpent.

BODHISATTVAS

Buddhist gods, whose advanced awareness, spirituality and virtue has earned them divinity, yet who refrain from Nirvana to remain in the wheel of reincarnation so that they may help others. Gautama Buddha is the prime example, choosing to remain and preach for another fifty years after his enlightenment. There were many others though, including the five Dhyani-Bodhisattvas; also Manjusri, Maitreya, Kaspaya and Kshitigarbha, to name but a few in a strong Buddhist tradition of teachers and the knowledge and example they passed on.

BRAHMA

The supreme creator-god of the Hindu mythology, who came from the Absolute — all manifested reality, called Brahman ("One that is multiple"), manifested in the three major forms of Brahma, Vishnu and Shiva, who correspond to the creative, conservative and destructive actions carried out by the divine. Brahma is the first god, who thinks up the world whilst in meditation and then sets it in motion He is also the father of both the gods and men, personifying the creative aspect of Life he was worshiped as such in many forms. He is usually portrayed with four faces, which formed as his gaze followed his beautiful consort when she first emerged from his side, and four arms. From his union with her the first man was born. Partly because he was an older more generalized manifestation, Brahma developed into a beneficent old deity and lost his prime role to Vishnu, the protective and nurturing aspect of the Trimurti, or triad of Brahma, Vishnu and Shiva. Though he ceded importance to Vishnu and Shiva he still ultimately has the most vital role, for he has

Left: A 16th century Nepalese bodhisattva in gilded bronze.
Right: An 11th century Brahma carving.

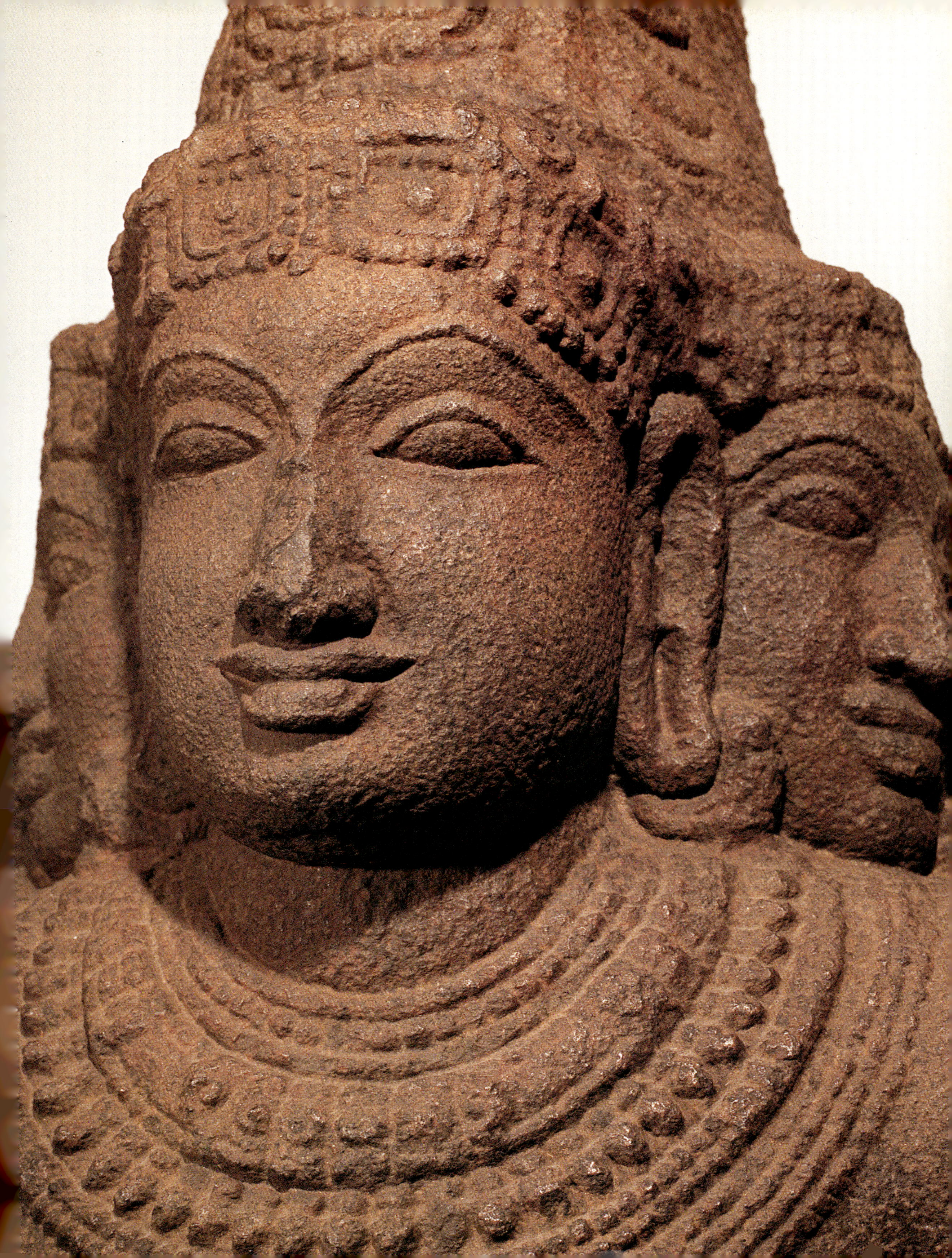

A-Z
CODEX GODS

spoken the world and all in it into existence, and it is his life and being that is the clock mechanism of it all. The kalpa time frame is defined by Brahma's life. Nevertheless he his worship has declined.

BUDDHA

The future Buddha/Bodhisattva, avatar of Vishnu, was born by "Immaculate Conception" into the royal family of the Sakyas and named Siddhartha. (In Japan he is known as Sakyamuni) The legend tells of a prophecy that should the young prince ever see old age, sickness or death he would devote his life to asceticism, so great trouble was taken by his family that this should not occur. However the inevitable did eventually happen and despite desperate delaying tactics (culminating in marriage and a son), Siddhartha left to begin his renunciation and evolution into Buddhahood. In his search for the Middle Way between the two extremes of asceticism and sensuality he learnt that to be free of the wheel of reincarnation one must renounce desire, and yet live in the world with compassion for all other things, actively involved in helping life flow and not set apart in judgement. Following his enlightenment he eventually was persuaded from entering Nirvana by the pleas of all — man and god — to remain and aid others. He then converted his family to the Middle Way, and began to preach throughout the land, a doctrine of compassion and moderation, with legends and miracles attributed to him throughout his life.

DEVAS

Some categories of gods exist only collectively and the Devas was the collective grouping of the gods with celestial powers. There are various other categories: Rudras, Visvas, Vasus, and Maruts. The Devas were the counterparts of the Asuras.

DEVI

The great mother goddess of Hindu mythology, female counterpart and consort of Shiva, avatar-equipped (Durga, Kali, Chandi, Parvati, Bhairavi), dynamic and complex quintessence of the female entity and manifestation of the dualism inherent in all existence. Perhaps she represents the coalescence of a myriad goddesses, but she may also be the mother goddess of the original Indus Valley civilization. As Durga "the inaccessible," she possesses vampire-like teeth and rides a lion, her many hands holding weapons As Kali the "black mother" she is the ogress wife of Shiva, complete with skulls and severed hands and battle frenzy. The highpoint of her worship was at the time of the Tantras, when because of the sexual aspect of religious awareness and technique female shaktis or manifestations attracted worshippers intrigued by the idea of mithuna — "the state of being a couple', a way to religious insight through sexual union.

Right: This Buddha sits, protected by a three-headed cobra, in a Buddhist temple in Sri Lanka.

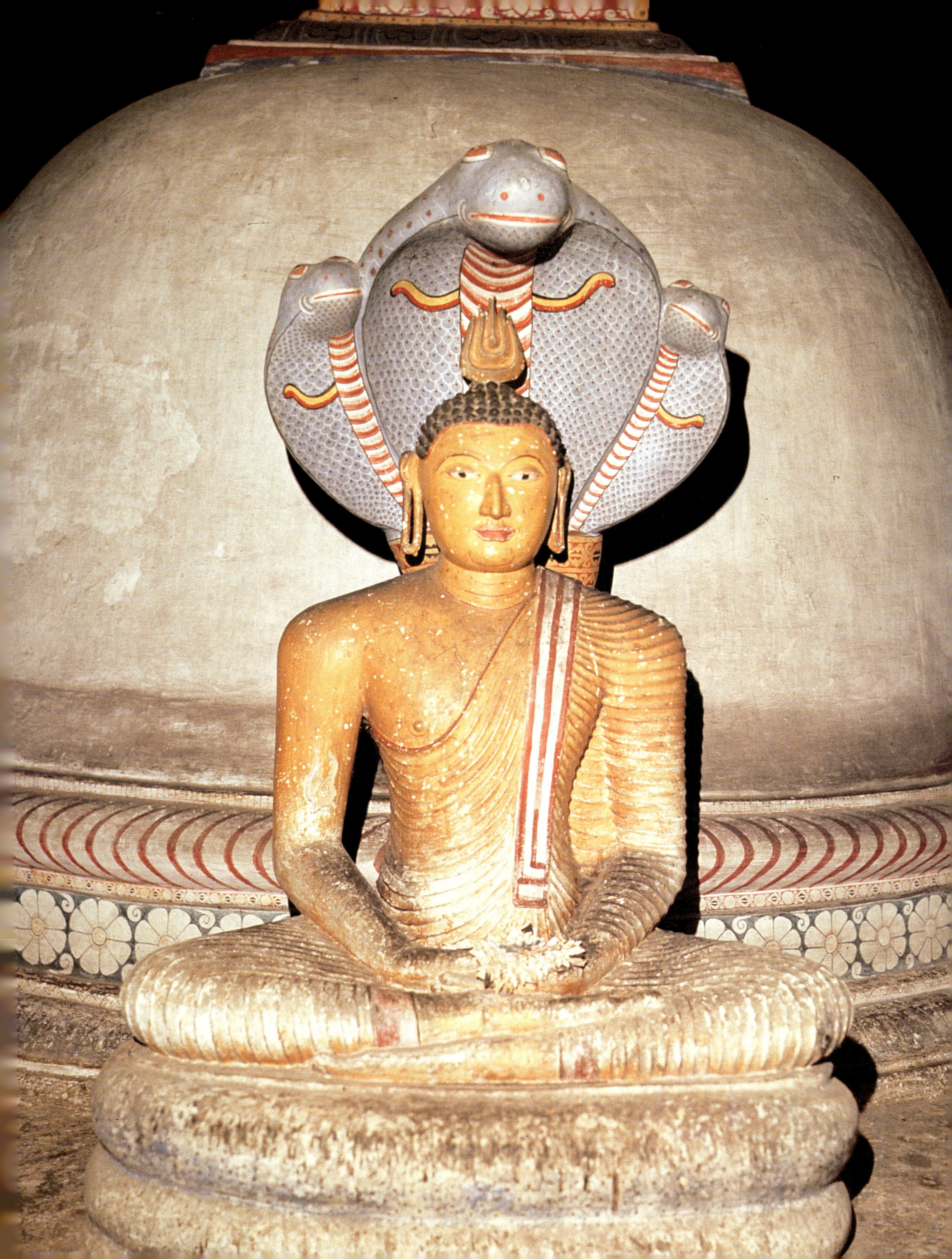

A-Z
CODEX GODS

DURGA

Durga was another manifestation of the mother goddess in destructive female mode. She was portrayed as a beautiful but fierce yellow woman riding a buffalo or a tiger and usually armed. Again she represents certain aspects. The female forms of male principles first became shaktis of the male prototypes but as time progressed they were worshiped as individual goddesses in their own right. This enabled Indian culture to absorb variants and assign foreign elements a position within their own culture, as well as balance positive and negative manifestations. Durga's precise origins are unclear but a local source in Southern India seems likely.

GANGA

The Hindu water-goddess of purification and the divine manifestation of the sacred river Ganges, Ganga was an aspect of Parvati, which implies ritual purification through bathing, and the cleansing of the body. In myth Ganga was married to the Ocean from which union Jalamdhara resulted, who went on to make war against the gods, and who was only finally beaten when they all combined to make a weapon strong enough to defeat him. Even then he possessed the capacity to reconstitute himself, which was only stopped when Shiva's female counterparts drank all his blood, preventing him from regenerating.

GANESH

The elephant-headed Hindu god of wisdom and literature. Along with Karttikeya he was a child of Shiva and Parvati. Ganesh represents the call to spiritual power in Hindu mythology. He was portrayed anthropomorphically, with the head of an elephant on a corpulent human body, denoting prosperity and plenty. The myth concerning the loss of his human head has various versions, including that of his father Shiva, who decapitated him when he would not let him have access to his wife, Parvati, whom Ganesh guarded. Shiva then relented and promised a new head from the first thing to come their way — an elephant. Ganesh is one of the most popular of Hindu deities, who aids the devout by removing obstacles in their path.

GARUDA

Hindu bird-god, and eater of serpents, the guardians of spiritual truth in the terrestrial plane in opposition to Garuda's manifestation of spiritual truth and strength on higher planes. He was Vishnu's mount and took the form of a giant bird. In order to free his mother from a curse, Garuda had to supply his serpent cousins with the Elixir of Immortality. He fetches it but orders them to ritually purify themselves before consuming the potion. Whilst the devout serpents are thus engaged Indra steals the Elixir (as arranged beforehand with Garuda), in order

Above left: Hindu pilgrims bathing in the Ganges River at Varanasi, India. Right: A 13th century carving of the Hindu goddess Durga killing the buffalo demon.

· INDIA ·

A-Z
CODEX GODS

to prevent the truth he represented remaining on the physical plane of existence. So Garuda represents man's higher spiritual aspirations, which in order to flower must leave the terrestrial plane.

GOMMATESVARA

The son of the first Jain saint or savior Bahubali, was known as Gommatesvara. In the myths there is as struggle for their father's kingdom between the brothers Bahubali and Bharaba. At the point of victory Bahubali has an insight into the pointlessness of his purpose and gives up the kingdom to his brother to retire into nature and meditate for a year. To commemorate this feat his brother commissioned the colossal statue. This myth explains the 60-foot high statue of Bahubali still in existence today at Sravana Belgola in India.

HANUMAN

Hanuman was a Hindu monkey-god possessed of immense physical strength and cunning, who was the companion to Rama in his quest for the return of his wife and consequent war with her captors, including Ravana the king of the demons. In this war Hanuman performs various feats of strength and agility, including leaping over to Sri Lanka from the Indian continent and preventing the female demon Surasa from swallowing him by enormously elongating himself. He was the son of Vayu, the source of his great strength, but was also possessed of great humility and chastity, a true devoted follower of Rama. He is often portrayed holding open his chest to reveal the flaming letters of Rama's name written in his heart. For his unswerving loyalty and bravery Rama rewarded him with eternal life and youth.

INDRA

King of the Rig Veda Hindu gods and chief god of the air and storms, the effective' head of the Hindu pantheon until supplanted by the triumvirate of Brahma, Vishnu and Shiva. Indra was represented as golden in color, with four arms, driving a golden chariot or upon an elephant. Indra loved the intoxicating drink soma — the nectar of the gods, which he drank in copious quantities. He was regarded as a sensuous deity in celestial paradise, and like Zeus was constantly having amours, which included even Gautama's wife, Ahlya. For this sin he was punished twice. Gautama marked him with a thousand yoni signs, and Brahma allowed the demon king Ravana to defeat and capture him. Indra the rain-giver was also a fertility aspect. He also manifested a type of beneficent, heroic power struggling against evil demons, such as Vritra, a great dragon who challenged him for supremacy. Like Zeus and Thor he strikes his enemies with thunderbolts.

Right: This rock image shows Buddha before his enlightenment. He sits emaciated after years as an ascetic while the four daughters of Sena try to bring him food.

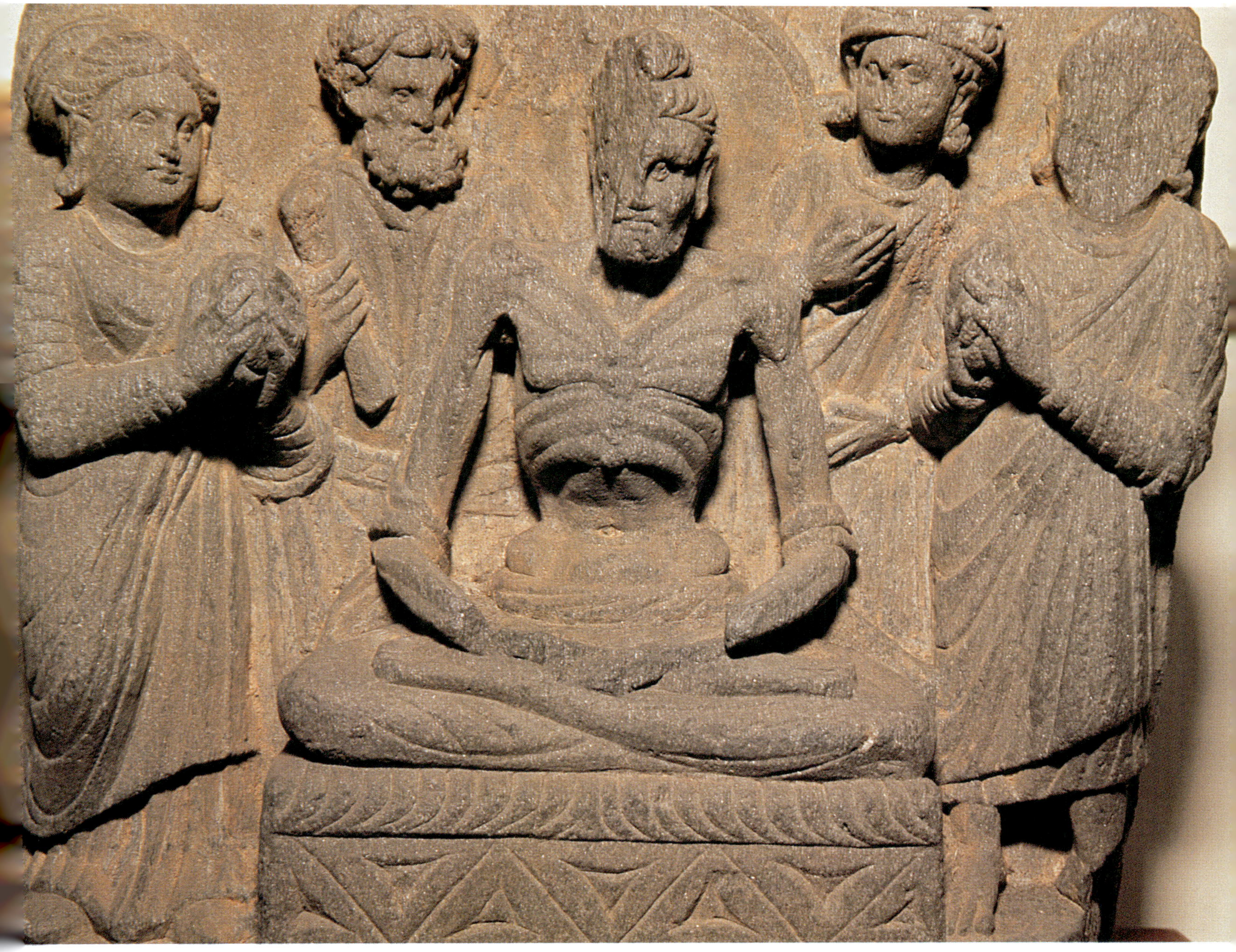

A-Z
CODEX GODS

JATAKA
Birth stories of the Buddha, telling of his past lives/previous births in various incarnations — bird, animal or man, the Jataka were assembled soon after the Buddha had passed into Nirvana. They serve a didactic purpose, to reveal the continuous moral dialogue that threads through them.

KALI
Female manifestation of the principle of destruction, although in the typical conciliatory fashion of Indian mythology Kali can also be seen as the mother of life, in that the destructive process is a vital principle of existence. Kali is the shakti and consort of Shiva and she is sometimes portrayed dancing on top of him. Her appearance was terrifying for she wore a belt of severed hands and a necklace of skulls, her four arms carried weapons and she was smothered in blood. She also had a huge mouth with sharp teeth and a drooling tongue, which seemed to relish her work as well as convey divine madness and intensity of purpose. Kali was a more recent arrival to the pantheon, with Durga preceding her, both manifestations of a female destructive principle that trace ultimately to Devi, but grew from more localized origins in the syncretistic mythological process.

KAMA
Kama the Hindu god of love was first born of all creation, for desire for existence is the prime feeling of the universal mind. He is portrayed as a lithe and handsome youth with a bow and flower-tipped arrows. In fact Kama lost his corporeal form after he was commanded by Indra to give Shiva a passion for Parvati, in the exchange he caught a full blast from Shiva's third eye chakra (a power-node in the body) and was reduced to ashes. Later Kama succeeded in hitting Shiva with a love-arrow, this time at the behest of Brahma.

KARTTIKEYA
Hindu god of war and twin brother of Ganesh, who represents the call to physical power, as his brother is spiritual power incarnate. Whereas Ganesh represents Will, Kartikkeya manifests the Means. He was created by Shiva, originally as six separate beings, but was hugged so fiercely by his mother Parvati that the bodies were squeezed into one, leaving the six heads with which he is portrayed. He rides a peacock, with a rooster as his standard, and is sometimes also known as Skanda, a contraction of Alexander, in acknowledgement of that great Greek general's martial prowess.

KRISHNA
Krishna was called "the Adorable" by his worshippers, and he is certainly the most well known avatar of Vishnu. In a Greek-like twist Krishna when born was brought up away from

Right: A painting of Radha and Krishna wandering through a grove

· INDIA ·

153

A-Z
CODEX GODS

his true home after his uncle the king had been warned that one of his sister's children would assassinate him. He was thus raised by cowherds, whom he later turned from the worship of Indra and protected. Krishna was always portrayed dark-skinned or blue. He was renown from his beginnings as a beguiler with a great sense of humor and a practical joker. He developed from mischief making into the great lover and god of eroticism. Like Achilles he met his end with an ankle-arrow, mistaken by a hunter for a deer as he rested in the forest. He represented the perfect deification of life. The most charming and human of Vishnu's incarnations, women were all magnetically attracted to him. When he danced he grew many hands so that each one thought she danced only with him. Krishna became Arjuna's partner in the Mahabharata, the philosophic exchange fundamental to Hinduism.

LAKSHMI

Also known as: Sri

An avatar and female counterpart of Vishnu, Lakshmi was the Hindu goddess of love and beauty, prosperity and good luck — the Indian equivalent of Aphrodite, for she was born on a lotus from the churning of the milky sea when Vishnu was manifested in the tortoise avatar. She was not generally worshiped separately, but paired with Krishna. Like Aphrodite her beauty made her desirable and she was somewhat unstable in her attachments, eventually ending up with Indra, who at her own request divided her into four parts in order to make her more manageable. She has strong associations with the fall festival of Divali.

MAITREYA

"The Kind One"

The Buddha who is yet to come. The Maitreya is the Buddhist analogy of the savior figure that occurs in religions and mythologies worldwide — from the resurrected pagan fertility gods to the monotheistic Messiahs. He dwells in the Tusita sky or heaven from whence the Sakyamuni descended earlier, and is portrayed in gold, wearing the robe of his predecessor. He is the final savior of mankind, waiting in the wings for his moment on the stage.

MANU

The Hindu Noah, who received warning of the impending flood from a small fish (a manifestation of Vishnu) which begged his help, promising pointedly to return it. Manu helped the creature, and then as a result had a magical expanding fish to cope with. Instructing him to build an ark, the fish then towed Manu on a long journey, also answering his prayers for a wife with whom he had children who in turn became the ancestors of humankind.

Right: Vishnu and Lakshmi ride on the bird god Garuda.

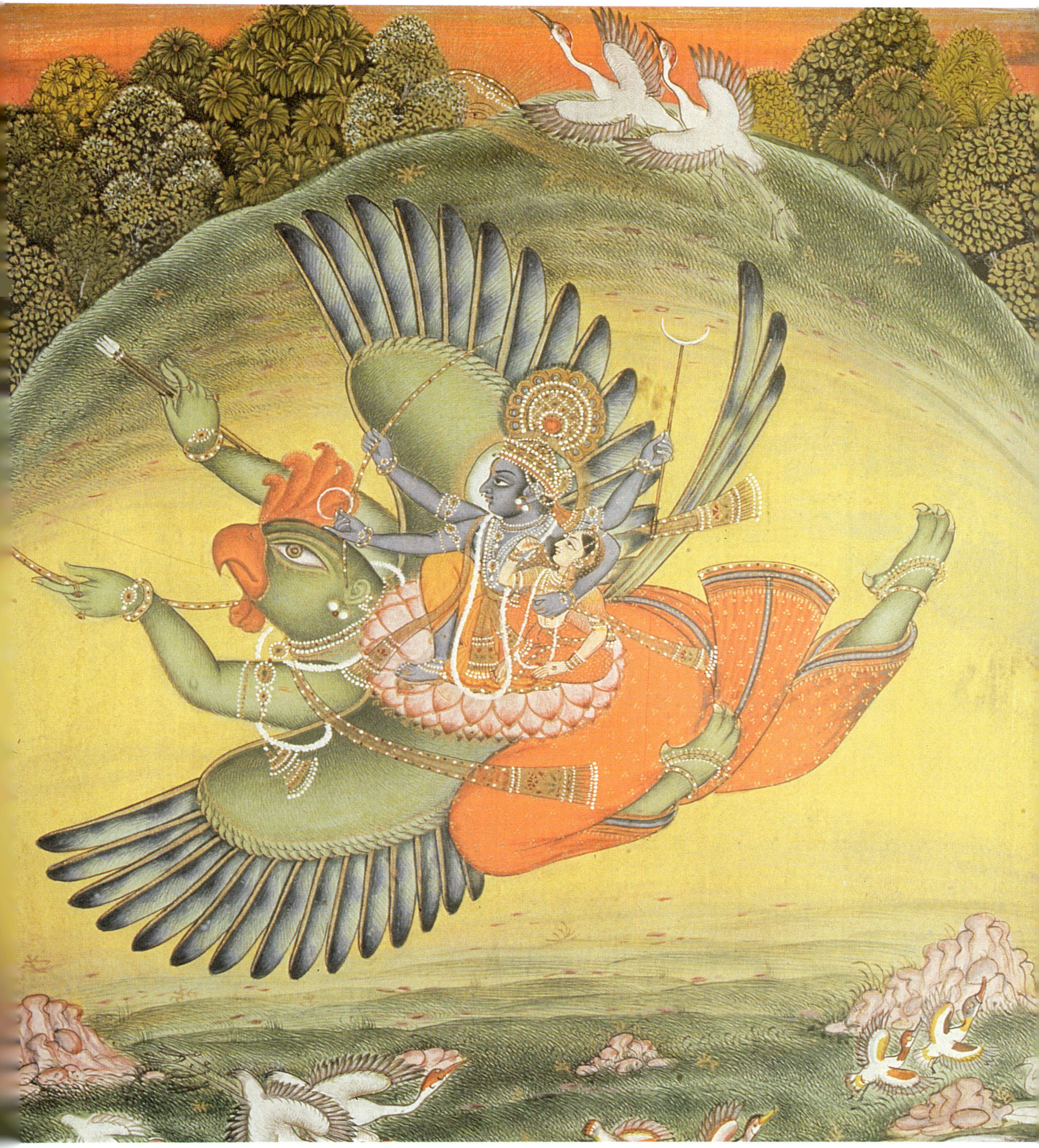

A-Z
CODEX GODS

MARA
The demon Mara was a magician, a master of illusion, who through his magic could lead further astray the souls of those lost in the cycle of the senses.

The Buddhist devil-equivalent, Kama and Mara are linked — the two sides of life (desire for) and (fear of) death. These two powers rule the world for most of us — the unawakened or unconscious. For us the Buddha offered his doctrine known as a vehicle — for transporting/saving our eternal souls through the development of spiritual wisdom. Mara was Buddha's tempter too, though in this he failed, for he could not reach him as he sat composed beneath the Bodhi tree.

MITRA
Hindu sun god and twin brother of Varuna, Mitra was the manifestation of intellect and beauty and the perfection of the divine being — the joy of life so to speak. The two sons of Aditi complemented each other in their aspects of the concept of higher states and universal being, with Mitra shaping and leading on from Varuna, structuring life and illuminating it with divine joy and truth.

NAGAS
A benevolent snake race who live in the underworld kingdom of Patala, the Nagas are well disposed towards man and life and serve as a protective talisman to ward off evil — a striking contrast to the serpents of most other mythologies. They occur in the Hindu, Buddhist and Jain mythology and are often featured architecturally as temple guardians.

NARADA
An avatar of Vishnu, who represents the communication of divine intention and the realization of each thing according to its unique nature. He was both the messenger between the gods and of them to man. Narada was a divine sage, a manifestation of Vishnu, yet also a fervent worshiper who through a life of devotion led by example. He originally upset his father Brahma by refusing to marry and after an exchange of curses was condemned to a life of sensuality, during which time he became a master of music and invented various instruments. After this he took up yogic meditation and evolved into his role of divine sage, messenger and counselor.

NATARAJA
Nataraja is another avatar of Shiva. Master of the dance and the determiner of the rhythm of the worlds, he danced the creation of the universe. Nataraja is usually portrayed dancing his mystic dance of transcendence, to which all living things must succumb. In one myth the god converted the ten thousand hermits (*rishis*) who at first rejected him and his joyfulness, but who

Right: Parvati, Shiva's consort, stands with her right hand raised as if holding a flower.

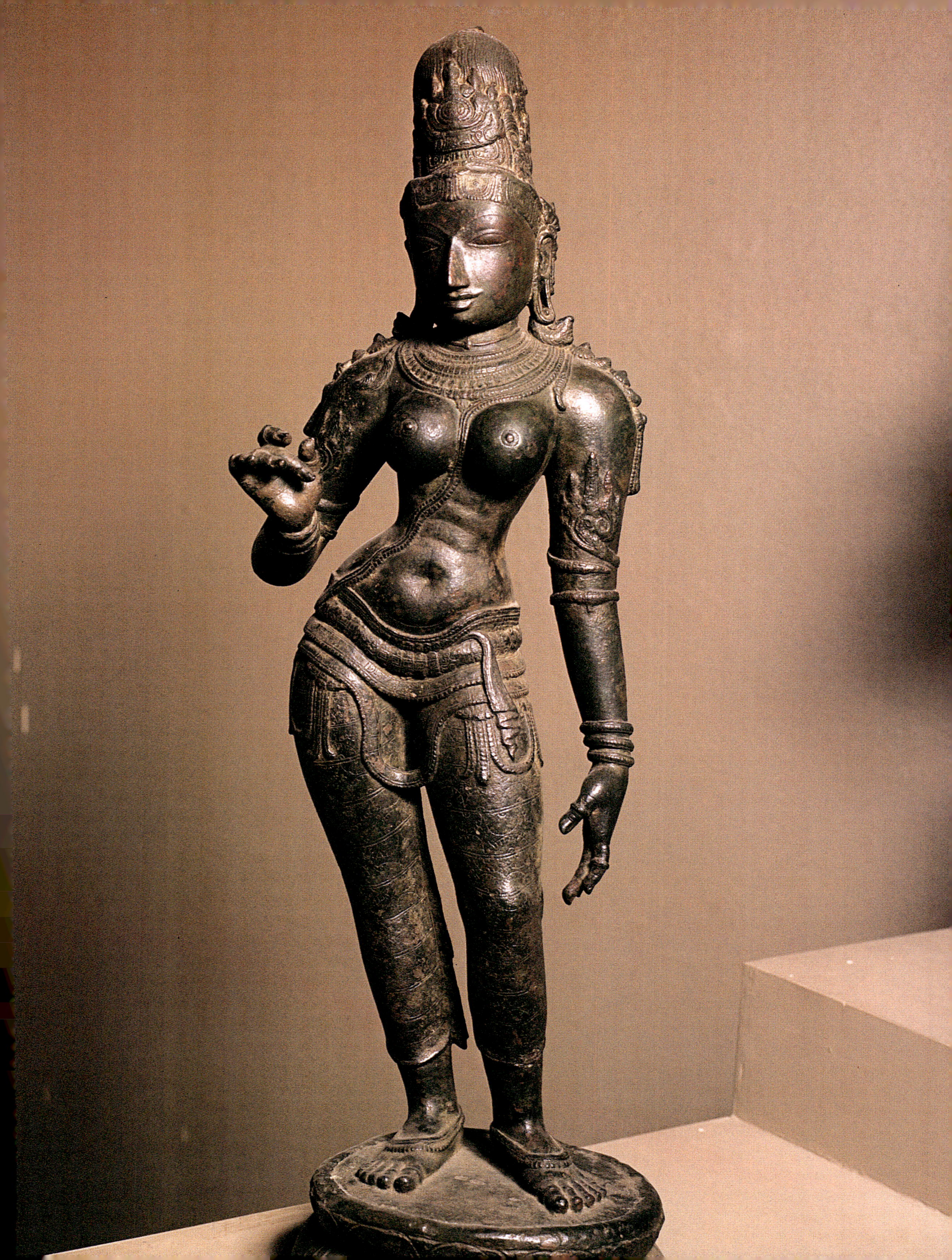

A-Z
CODEX GODS

were won over with a new awareness by his mystic dancing, representing the interaction of the individual with the divine.

PARVATI
"Mountain"

The mountain mother goddess, daughter of the Himalayas and another female manifestation and consort of Shiva, with whom she is often portrayed in an idealized divine family, along with their children Ganesh and Skanda. Parvati is mainly a benevolent goddess who absorbs Shiva's spiritual and sexual energy to release into the world for the benefit of all. One myth tells of her initial rejection by Shiva on account of her dark skin, which she overcomes by making her body glow. This hints at a pre-Aryan origin as an aboriginal mother goddess.

PRAJAPATI

A Hindu creator sky god and Lord of all Creation — both divine and terrestrial — Prajapati was a father figure, and many others gods and sages were also addressed with this name, which represented the concept of generation and the manifestation of forms. In the *Vedas* he incestuously mates with his daughter, pursuing her with spilling semen from which all life springs as she flees his embrace. Two of Prajapati's daughters, Kadru and Vinata, were both wives of the great sage Kasyapa. Kadru gave birth to the serpents and Vinata to Garuda and Aruna — the dawn glow, the latter only half complete due to her mother's impatience.

RAMA

An avatar of Vishnu, and as such an aspect of a magnificent whole too great to comprehend and thus requiring subdivision. The epic "Ramayana" recounts his exploits in countless tongues, making him perhaps the most popular of the gods. He is the ultimate moral archetype of Hindu thought, and in his heroic stories unfold the quandaries of life and the upright man's approach to them. Perhaps the main story of Rama concerns his wife's abduction by Ravana the demon king. Aided by the faithful Hanuman the monkey king, he finally crosses to Sri Lanka where the two armies meet, and after slaying Ravana with a magic arrow, he then requires proof of his wife's fidelity. Sita climbs on a funeral pyre but the flames will not touch her, thus proving her worth and Rama takes his wife back again.

RISHABHA

One of the semi-legendary founders of Jainism, Rishabha possessed semi-divine status, as his father was one of the fourteen Manus. He was the first Tirthankara ("makers of the crossing"). Rishabha was the king of Bharata — a kingdom he relinquished in order to become a hermit/sage, living a life of austerity and asceticism. This was in keeping with the central tenets of

Right: A 16th century bronze of Rama with his bow.

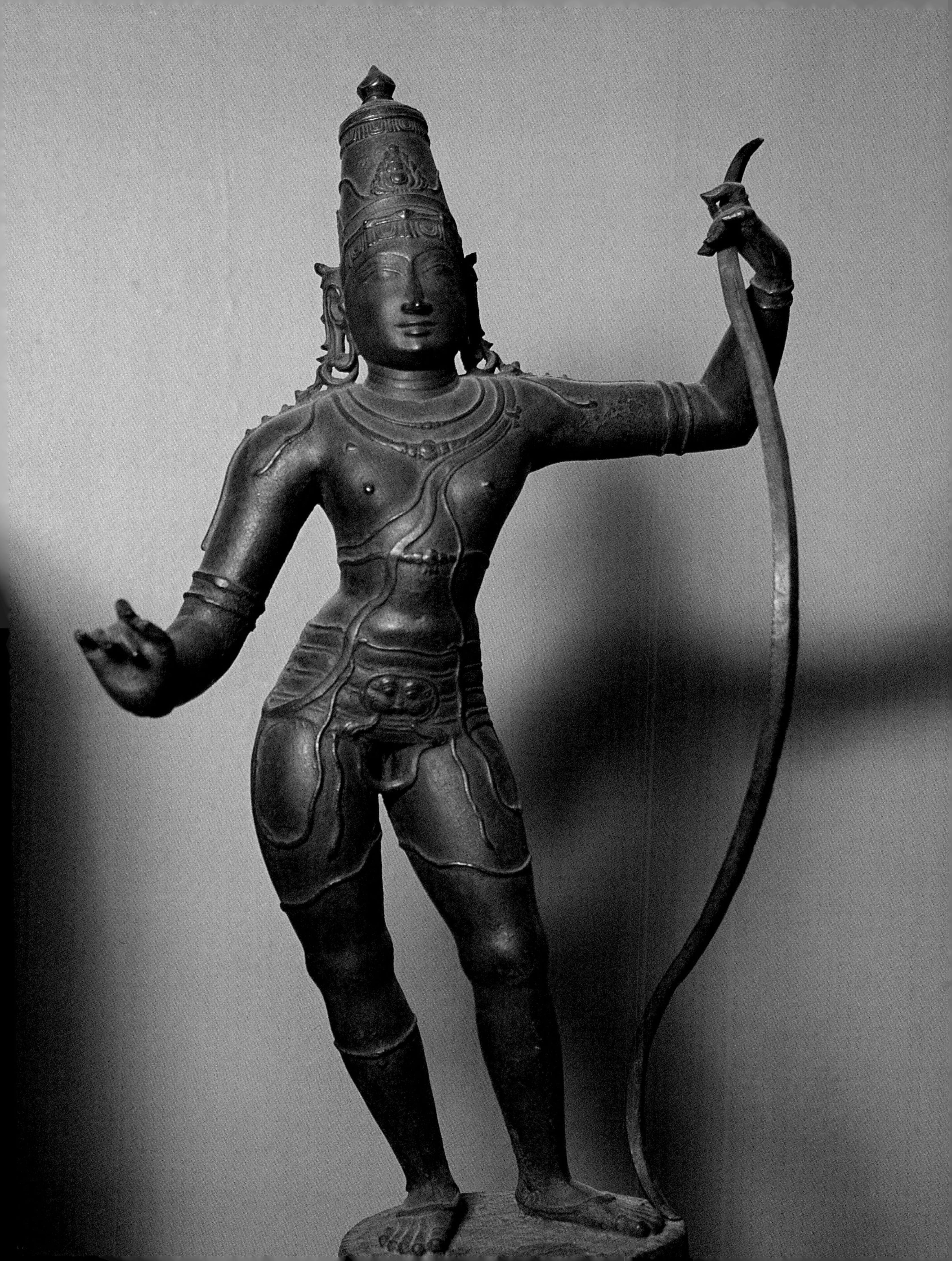

A-Z
CODEX GODS

Jainism, which sees the world as so polluting one has to retire from it in order to limit contamination. The origin of Jainism was rooted in the older pre-Aryan Indus valley civilization, which was to experience a resurgence once the Aryan invaders had became more aware of the level of the culture they had conquered.

RISHIS

The seven divinely inspired sages and authors of the sacred hymns known collectively as the *Vedas*. They were the forerunners of the Brahmins and their poetry extended the religious horizons of the invading pastoralists.

The seven Rishis were: Gotama, Bharadwaja, Viswamitra, Jamad-agni, Vasistha, Kasyapa and Atri. Through visions they saw the cosmic unity of the universe. Their inward revelation was then transferred into poetry.

They eventually became semi-divine, marrying various deities and producing divine progeny. They are sometimes seen as human or of human origin and at other times they are treated as avatars of a greater god.

SACRED RIVERS

The Ganges, Jumna and Saraswati are the three most sacred rivers of Hindu mythology, and all of them possess anthropomorphic manifestations as goddesses. The Saraswati was the original border of the early Aryan homeland. Myth tells of the divine marriage of Vishnu, who kept Jumna and gave Sarawati to Brahma and Ganga to Shiva.

SARASVATI

Ancient agricultural fertility mother goddess of learning and music, Sarvasvati was credited with the invention of Sanskrit. Terracotta figures dating to 2500–2000 BC have been found in the Indus valley denoting her prevalence and importance. In the Vedic period less emphasis was placed on the worship of female deities, although the mother goddess figure certainly did not die out, but remained on a popular level with the worship of female tree spirits. At a higher level in society she metamorphosed into conceptualism, being personified as a creative idea. Later she associated with Vak — the goddess who symbolized speech and sound as a streamlike process. Ultimately these powerful mother goddesses would have a profound effect on Hinduism, muscling their way back into the pantheon to assume their rightful positions.

SAVITRI

Savitri was one of the kings of the Hindu heaven, worshiped as the creator of the true and the just. He was the celestial, golden "brilliant god" who represented the soul of all beings with a body, and he ruled over time and governed the movement of all things. His aspect is one of calm order, punctuality and organization, with truth and justice paramount on his agenda.

Above left: A Nepali image of Shiva, one of Hinduism's supreme gods. Right: Shiva seen as lord of the dance.

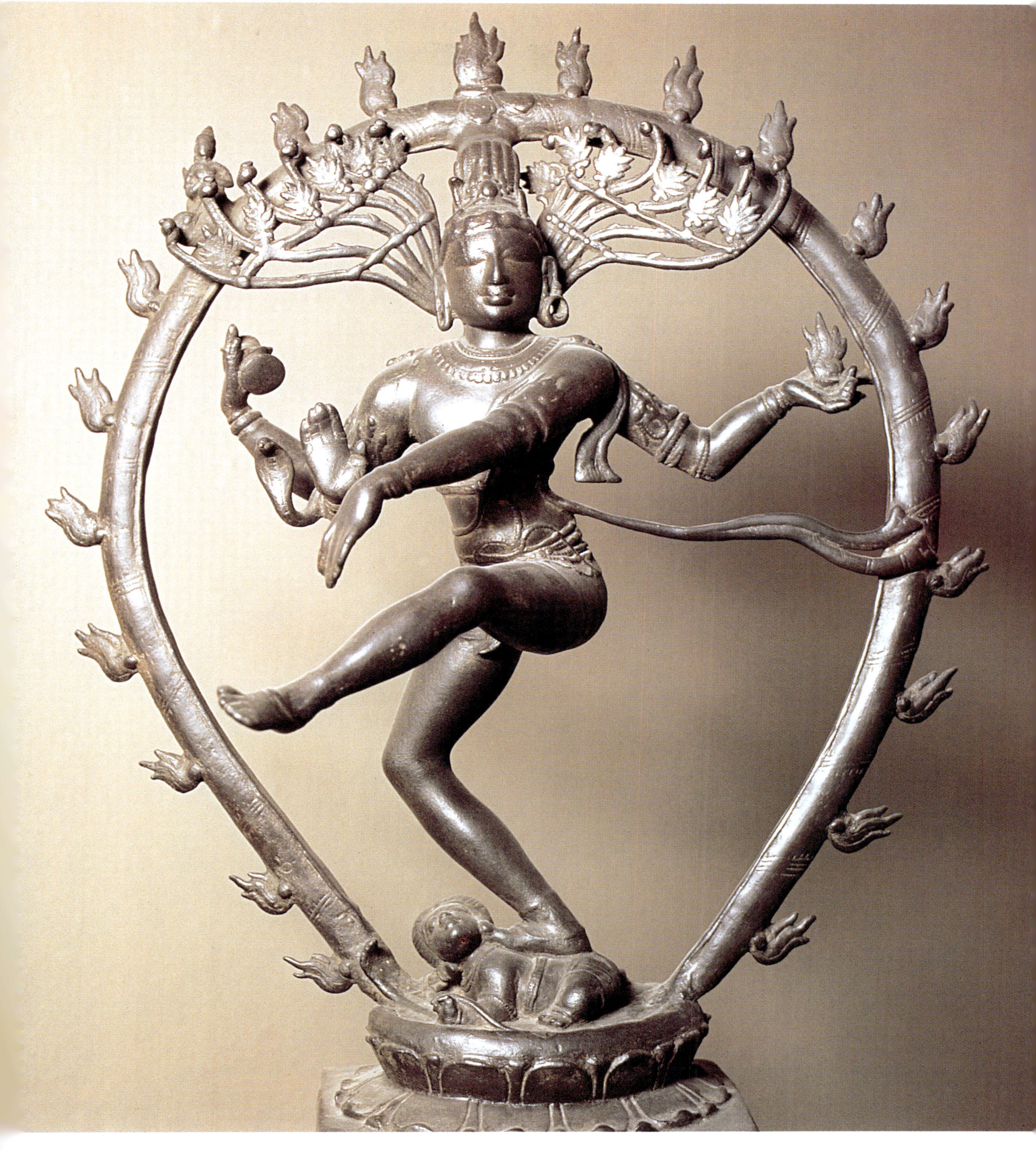

A-Z
CODEX GODS

SHIVA

One of the supreme gods of the Hindu pantheon, third deity of the triad of which Brahma and Vishnu are the other members. He represents the principle of destruction and the regeneration that follows it and has countless forms and names. Shiva was ambivalent in nature, a creator and destroyer, as well as a fertility-god. Hindu art portrays him in many ways; as a man he has four arms, a third central eye (sometimes with three horizontal lines), wrapped in a tiger's skin with serpent necklaces and with his hair tied up and ornamented with a crescent moon. He is also pictured as lord of the cosmic dance and in one terrifying aspect as the violent Rudra, lord of beasts, fighting against evil in any form. In this form he lives, wearing a necklace of skulls, in a hell of burning tortured bodies inhabited by vampires, demons and monsters. Shiva's overall aspect was inimical to man and his prayers, his role precluded sympathy in the necessity of his fundamental destructive principle. His female counterpart occurs in up to four avatars: Parvati, Kali, Durga and Uma. His main symbolic representation is the *lingam* — a phallic column in the shape of a modern traffic bollard.

SOMA

Soma is the multi-faceted Hindu moon-god, whose aspects vary enormously. He is the creator and father of the gods, the Supreme Being created before the *Vedas*, yet he also represents the moon and alcoholic intoxication. He corresponds to beatitude, the possibility of enjoyment and the very diversity of life in its myriad forms. One myth confirms this role, in which divine will (*Agni*) and beatitude (*Soma*) meld together to become a single entity that pervades the everything and forms the rest of the universe. *Soma* also manifests anthropomorphically the ecstasy of intoxication in the form of the Hindu gods' "ambrosia," called *soma*. This is an indispensable potion with which they perform all their heroic feats and trials of strength, and which gives them immortality. (Indra especially loves his *soma*, and is portrayed with a swollen belly full of it.)

SUMERU

Also known as: Meru

Sumeru is the World Mountain of Hindu mythology, through which runs the vertical axis of the universe. With its head in the clouds, on its slopes sport the gods, while around it sun and moon revolve. The Vindhya Mountains at the northern extremity of the Deccan, and the Himalayas were both seen as the home of the gods. Shiva's holy mountain is Kailasa, in the Himalayas, from which also flows the waters of life and the Holy Rivers.

SURYA

The Hindu sun god, Surya was originally one of the three deities (the other two were the rain god

Above left: The holy family — Shiva, Ganesh, Parvati, Kartikeya — at the burning ground. Right: Shiva with Nandi and his consort Parvati.

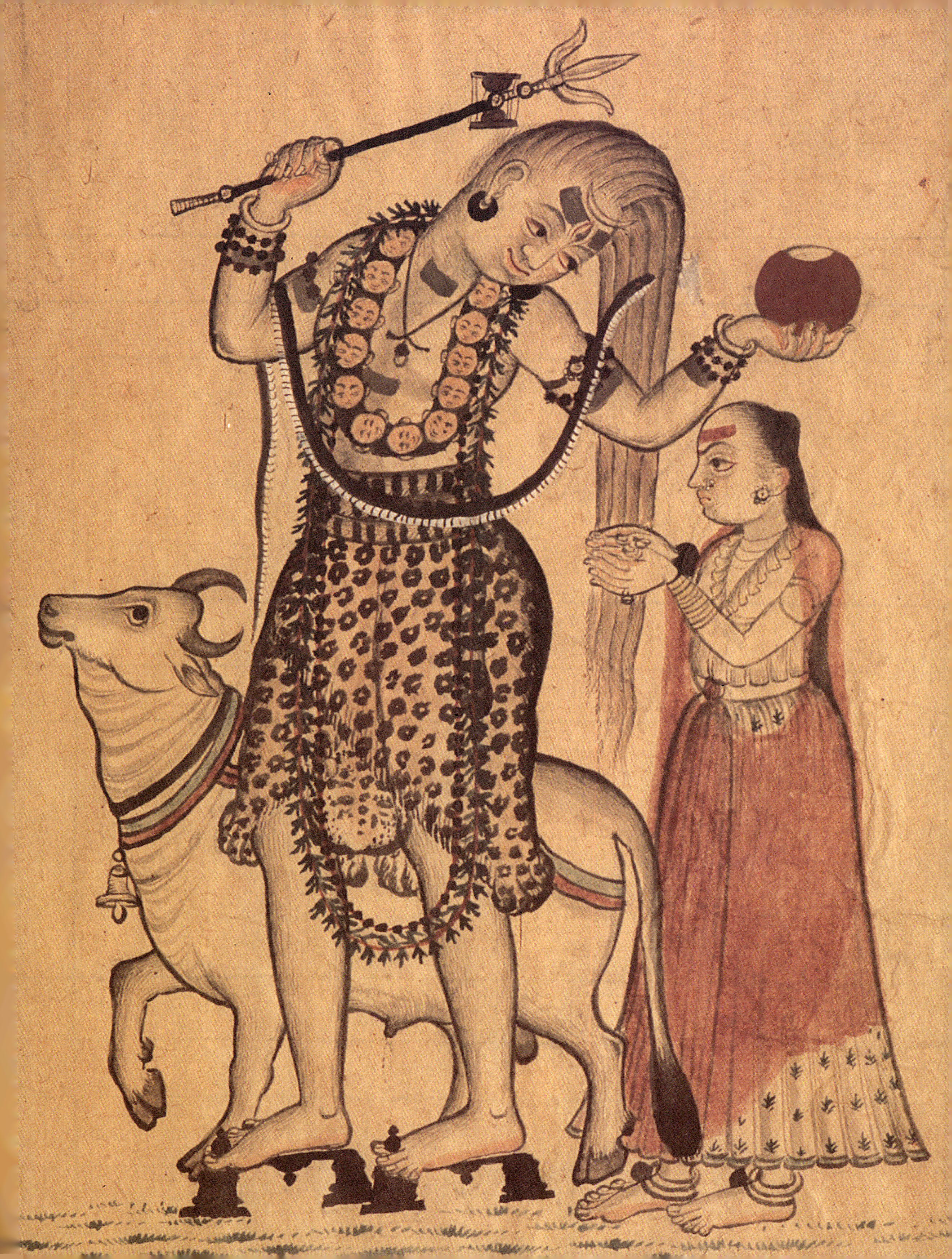

A-Z
CODEX GODS

Indra and the fire god Agni) that held sway before the Trimurti of Brahma, Vishnu and Shiva. He was of a small stature with a copper body, and rode through the sky in a chariot drawn by seven horses driven by his consort Aruna, the dawn. He was also the father of Yama and Yamuna. This Hindu sun god possesses the most complex mythology resulting from the variety of personages associated with the sun. He was the Enlightened, who made up the triad with Indra and Agni, throwing the light of truth on thought, freeing man from his ego in his capability of abstraction and perception. He was portrayed as a dark red man with three eyes and four arms, sometimes seated on a red lotus with rays emanating from his body. Surya was married to Sanja, daughter of the smith-god Visvakarma. In one myth she found the glare of his presence altogether too bright and dazzling and replaced herself with Shaya the goddess of Shade, and there followed a gap of some years before Surya noticed the subterfuge. In order to regain his wife he allowed her father to clip away part of his radioactive substance, from which Visvakarma fashioned various extraordinary artifacts, and reduced his son-in-law's brightness sufficiently for his daughter to be able to cope.

TVASHTRI
Also known as: Visvakarma

Visvakarma or Tvashtri is the Hindu smith-god, representing the divine power of construction in the world, the carpenter and modeler who adapts and assembles all its individual pieces, sometimes using his team of helpers known as the Ribhus. It is he who makes the thunderbolts of Vishnu. He overlaps with other gods and goddesses too, such as Prajapati. He was a prime character in the myth of Surya, the sun, whose brilliance he clipped at the behest of his dazzled wife, making various divine objects for the gods from the clippings.

USHAS

Ushas is the Hindu goddess of the dawn and a female counterpart of Surya the sun god, occurring with equal importance to him in the *Vedas*. She is the daughter of the sky and mother of both the gods and of light itself, manifested as the sun's rays. She wakens the other gods from sleep, thereby allowing them to act and develop. Through her illumination man is enlightened with truth and awareness. Also, like Surya, she rides a shining chariot — drawn by cows across the sky. She smiles always, bringing the light with her, waking gods and men to their roles and duties. Although ancient and immortal, being reborn each day she is young and youthful in appearance.

VAIROCANA

There are two Vairocanas in Hindu mythology. One is the king of the demons, the balance of

Right: A stone carving of Surya the sun goddess, holding lotuses.

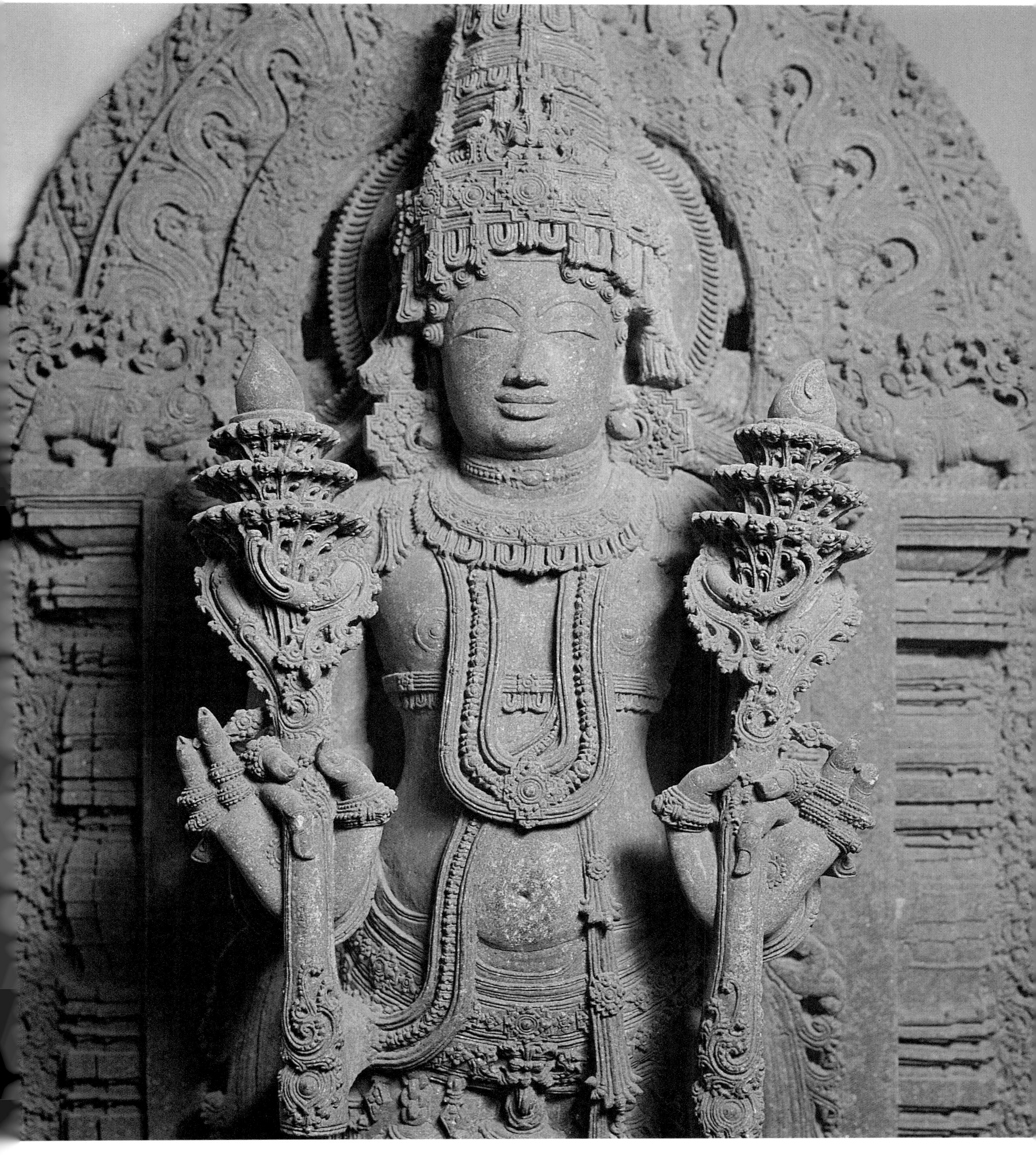

A-Z
CODEX GODS

Indra, the other the sun-Buddha important in Japanese and Tibetan Buddhism. As the sun-Buddha, Vairocana manifests the higher truth and the source of the cosmos, and is important as an object of meditation. (In Japan he became associated with the Shinto sun-goddess Amaterasu but is also of great importance to the Shingon sect.)

Vairocana the king of the demons, is the counterpart of Indra, king of the gods. Both are instructed by Brahma to carry out their functions of order and chaos respectively. Vairocana is thus only doing his duty, and like many Indian demons respects the scriptures and holy law, carrying out his job — of being a demon and so evil — to the best of his ability.

VARUNA

An ancient Hindu creator sky god of cosmic law and order, and the spiritual image of an infinity that embraces and illuminates. Varuna is witness to all actions and events everywhere. He is also Lord of the Waters, portrayed sometimes riding on the back of a giant sea-monster. Although his iconography was anthropomorphic, he represents more a concept of the energy intrinsic to all existence, or a state of awareness of this process.

VEDAS

The four Sanskrit books forming the oldest sacred literature of the Hindus along with the *Brahmanas*, the *Aranyakas* and the *Upanishads*. These were the *Rig Veda* (sacred hymns of praise), the *Sama Veda* (clerical sacrificial chants), the *Yajur Veda* (sacrificial formulae) and the *Athara Veda* (charms and protective spells). The *Brahmanas*, *Aranyakas* and *Upanishads* became known as the "Vedanta" — a summation or conclusion to the *Vedas*, progressing from correct ritual procedure to the development of philosophy and wisdom.

VISHNU
"The Wide-Strider"

Vishnu is the Hindu solar god of love, and savior of the world, representing the preservative, protective aspect of the principal Trimurti triad (Brahma, Vishnu, Shiva) of Hindu gods, who are the three manifestations of the single entity of the Absolute (Om or Brahman). Whenever order and justice are threatened Vishnu intervenes. He also has innumerable names, aspects and avatars, and occurs in a great many myths and legends in various animal forms or as a man, a dwarf or a lesser god. He was a companion and ally of Indra in his struggle against Vritra. He is generally portrayed as dark-skinned, but also as a blue-skinned adolescent. His female counterpart was Lakshmi, also known as Sri, who was the goddess of prosperity and good fortune. It is recounted in the *Rigveda* that he measured the universe or cosmos, crossing it in three strides, thereby affirming it as habitable

Right: Vishnu in his 10th incarnation as the white horse.

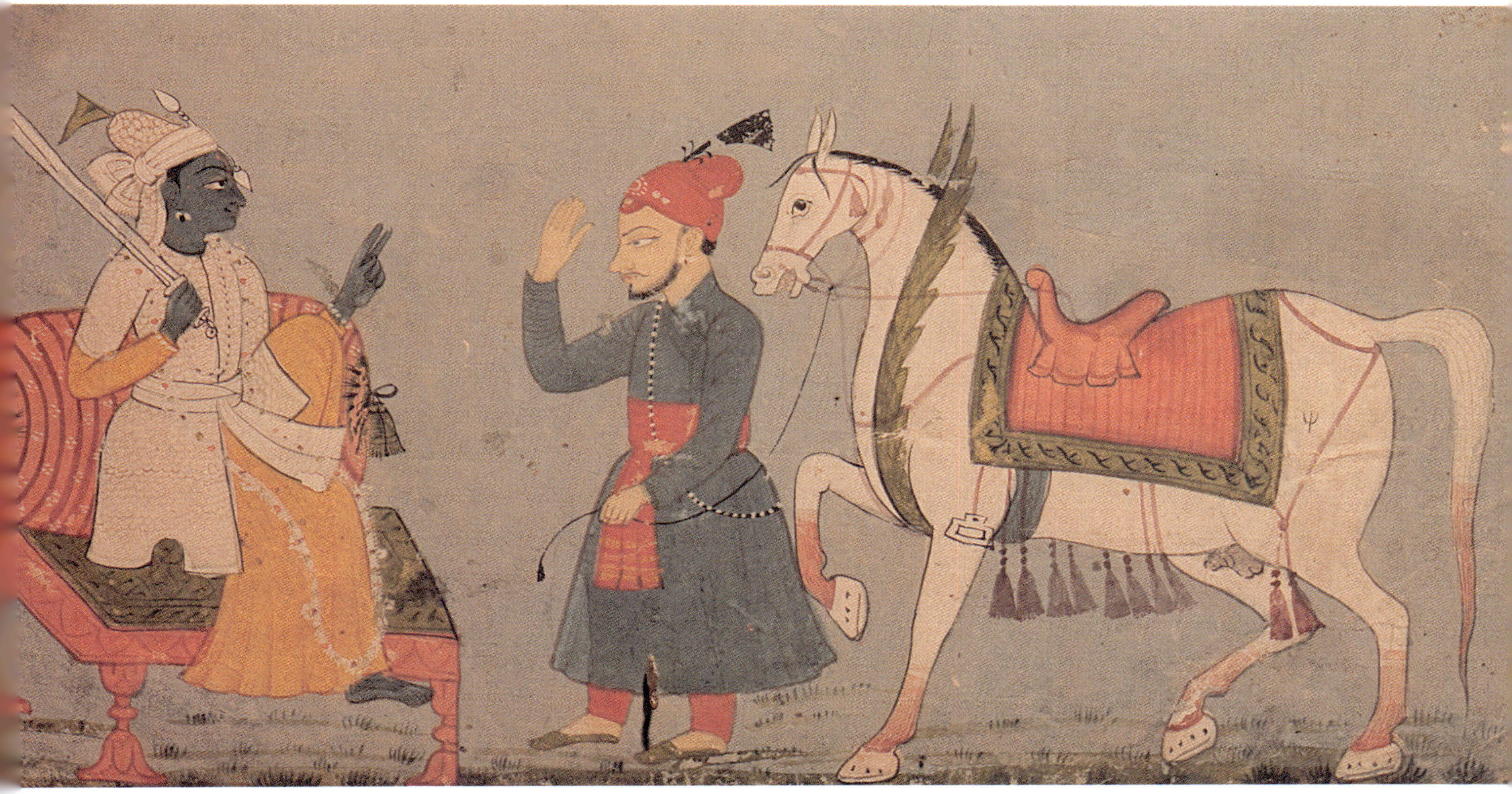

A-Z
CODEX GODS

territory. Being the creative and sustaining aspect of the Trimurti, Vishnu is seen by his devotees as the ultimate god, since Brahma is too passive and Shiva too destructive.

VISHNU'S AVATARS

Varaha was an avatar of Vishnu, manifesting as a boar to help form the earth. Along with the fish (Matsya), the turtle (Kurma), the lion-man (Narasimba), the dwarf (Vamana), these non-human avatars were causal in the formation of the world and aided in various wars between the gods and the demons, with Vishnu assuming each one of their forms for some specific purpose. The divine/human avatars — Krishna, Rama and Gautama Buddha — merit their own entries.

The final non-human avatar of Vishnu, Kalki, is the one that has not yet manifested — the one that is to come — in the shape of a giant with a horse's head, a horse itself or a man upon a white horse. He will close the present age of iron and put an end to the wicked.

YAMA

Yama is the Hindu god of the dead, whose jurisdiction covers all those who have died, to whom he represents judgement. He brings happiness to the righteous and virtuous, and bestows suffering on sinners and there is no escape from him when he comes at his appointed time. He is portrayed anthropomorphically, wearing red clothes and with green skin. He also sports a crown and rides on a buffalo, with a flower in his hair and a lasso in his hand. He is also known as Dharma-raja, the applier of the law, and Dandadhara, the applier of punishment. When he was the first man, he had a twin sister, called Yami, who had an incestuous desire for him, to which he did not succumb. This virtue earned him his immortality and the right to judge all those who seek to enter the Underworld.

Left: A late-10th century version of Vishnu.
Right: A 7th century version of Vishnu.

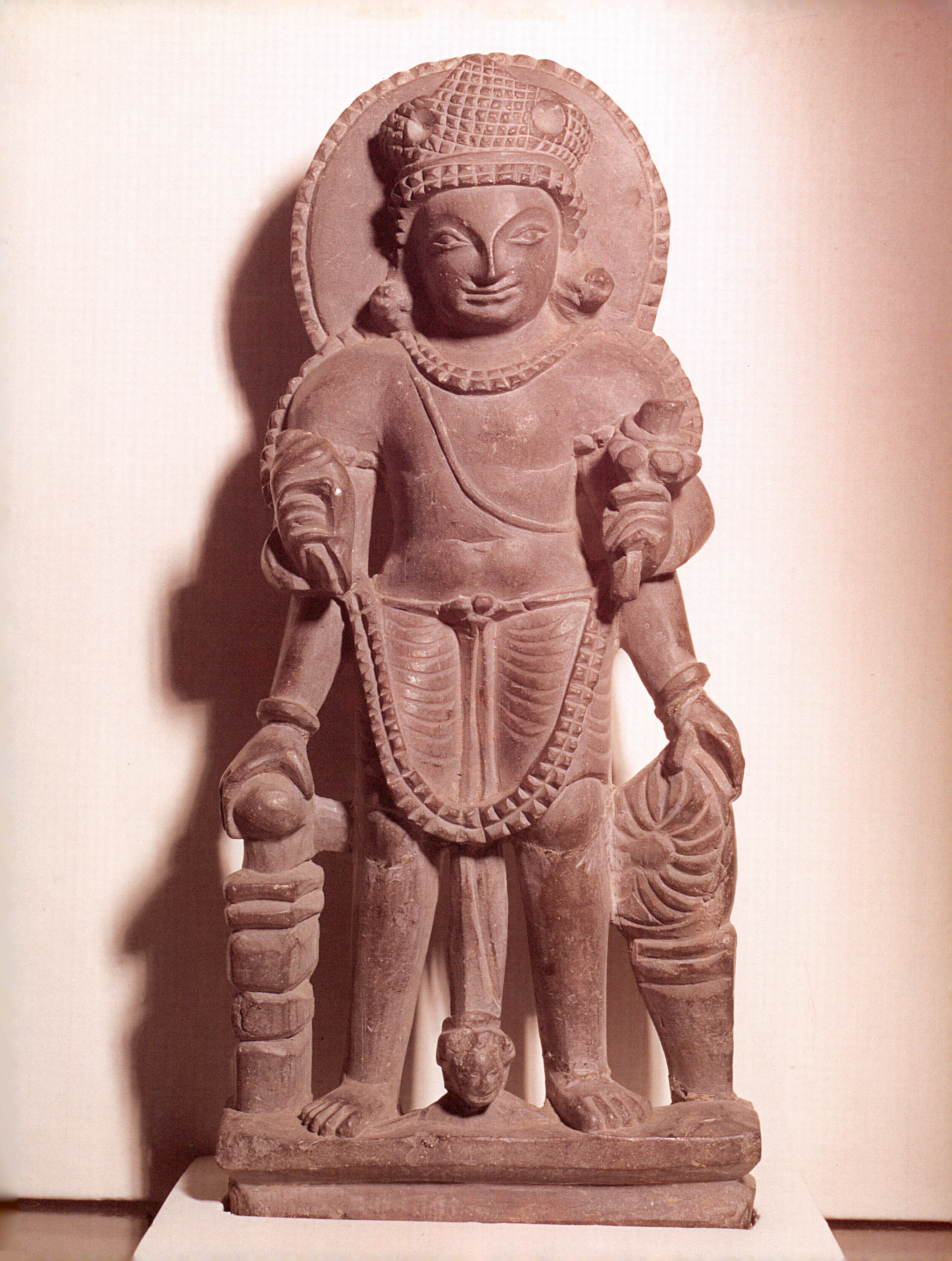

江南第一
千古無雙

民之父母

嘉定縣姜煋士民同立

CHINA, JAPAN & SOUTH-EAST ASIA

THE one religion that has the scope and range of this whole area is Mahayana Buddhism, known as the Greater Vehicle. In every country it combined with indigenous belief to yield each one their own distinct variation. Certain concepts however were shared by all, such a one being the Dhyani Buddhas and Bodhisattvas. As an idea gradually developed of a supreme (Adi) Buddha into that of a creator god, he was attributed with the creation of five celestial Dhyani Buddhas or Buddhas of meditation, who although Indian in name originally, occur in all countries with their own native nomenclatures. These celestial Buddhas in turn evolved into five human Buddhas, who each derived from the communal thoughts of all the five celestials, though each remained associated with one in particular, along with an accompanying Bodhisattva. These figures occur time and time again across all borders.

CHINA

China and India are the two ancient Eastern river civilizations, which along with their now vanished but still recognizable western counterparts in Mesopotamia and Egypt, are the oldest recorded. Interestingly, in China religion and mythical function took a turn toward rationalism, though accommodating the ancient animism and foreign imports such as Buddhism too. Taoism and Confucianism were the two indigenous products of great significance. Coupled with veneration of ancestors, Chinese religion focused on individual salvation through effort and observance. The first philosophers of the Warring States prior to any unification often withdrew to remote forests and mountains in order to divorce themselves

Previous pages: This Chinese painting is from a series on the governor Chao Hsia, considered a wise mandarin and perfect Confucian official. Right: This Chinese Buddhist stele was produced during the Ch'i period (550–571 AD).

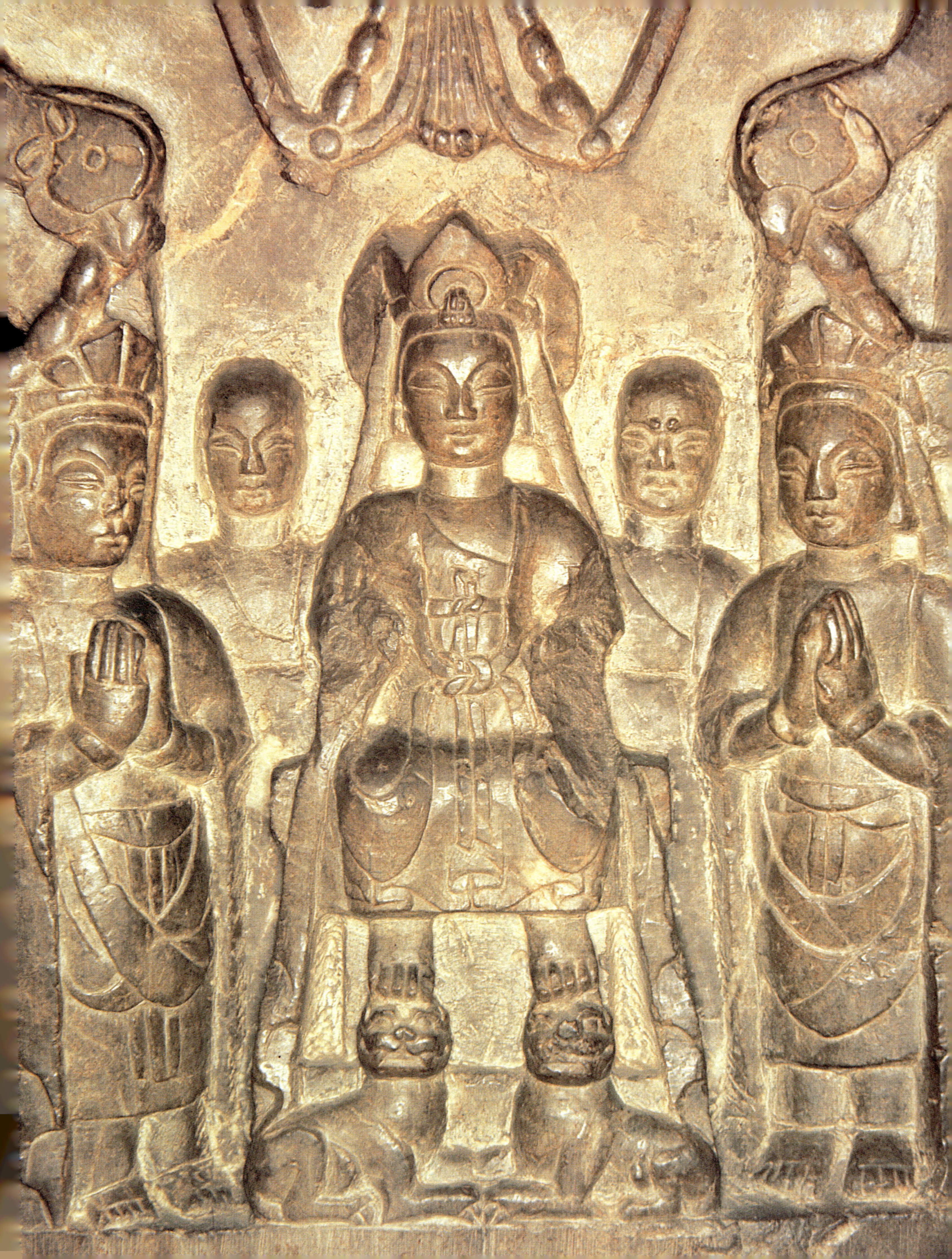

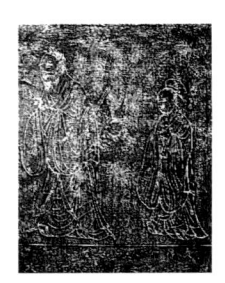

from material concerns and incessant warfare; they went back to meditate and find an answer in the equilibrium of nature. Lao Tzu withdrew, whereas Confucius, suspicious of mysticism, remained within society. Taoists were more instinctive and rejected the ornate customs and duty of society in favor of simplicity and directness in the contemplation of nature through observation in a dispassionate and prototype scientific mode.

The other root of Taoism was Wu magic, performed by sorcerers who connected to an animist spirit world to decode replies from ancestors, obtain advice, interpret oracles, perform divination and read omens. These Wu traditions and animist peasant belief were beyond the pale of the administration and nobility, who had their stake in the centralized core of society. They absolutely rejected such irrational belief in favor of the civically dutiful Confucians, although the form of some ceremonies and rituals were gone through more as a matter of public performance. Taoism was to draw great strength from the Mongolian invasions from the Steppes, whose shamanist tendencies naturally bolstered the indigenous version, following conquest.

Buddhism, coming from the holy-land of India, has been the only influence on China until more modern times. It made a great impact on Chinese religious thought, becoming the national religion and transforming Taoism into a much more organized church. Its effect at every level of Chinese society was prodigious. But the refined Chinese skill of absorption was exercised again, and rather than China modify to Buddhism, Buddhism was modified to fit the Confucian state.

The birth of Confucius is recorded as 551 BC. No single character has had as much influence on Chinese thought, although in life he was content to be an obscure teacher. As a

Above left and Right: A Chinese drawing of Confucius and a disciple.

夫子於聖人之屈伸得仰而有若德安木
政名

moral philosopher, he required "noblesse oblige" from a nobility, who could only justify their rule if it was exercised with wisdom, consideration and humility. The Emperor was the Son of Heaven, who ensured correct links were maintained with the divine. Bad kingship could wreck the natural order and therefore cause disaster. Thus primitive rites of ancestor worship were made into a moral formula underpinning authority and encoded in the national matrix that linked the divine and human worlds. This was almost the only religion necessary, as the concerns of Confucius were exclusively temporal. While paying respectful lip service to conventional religious protocols, he nevertheless maintained a distance from matters spiritual. This natural caution gave balance. When religion grew too powerful it was curtailed by the state, which afterward ensured it never became so large as to threaten again. There have thus been no religious wars to speak of in Chinese history, which has conversely suffered from a lack of imaginative speculation. Confucius was content for mythology to remain the preserve of Taoism and Buddhism.

The structure of the Chinese divine pantheon reflected its earthly equivalent, appearing a vast administrative bureaucracy, complete with a strict hierarchy of major and minor deities and engulfed in paperwork, and even including an annual internal report by which all were assessed for promotion or demotion. The functions persisted but the functionaries could change — even gods could be demoted. This practical and realistic aspect of Chinese mythology and religion reflects the concerns with real life rather than the origins of it — the requirements of a stable and to some degree secular society. It also explains why the majority of Chinese deities were in fact originally men, who were deified for conscientious service.

Above left and Right: This Chinese wood carving (c. 14th century) is of a Buddhist disciple.

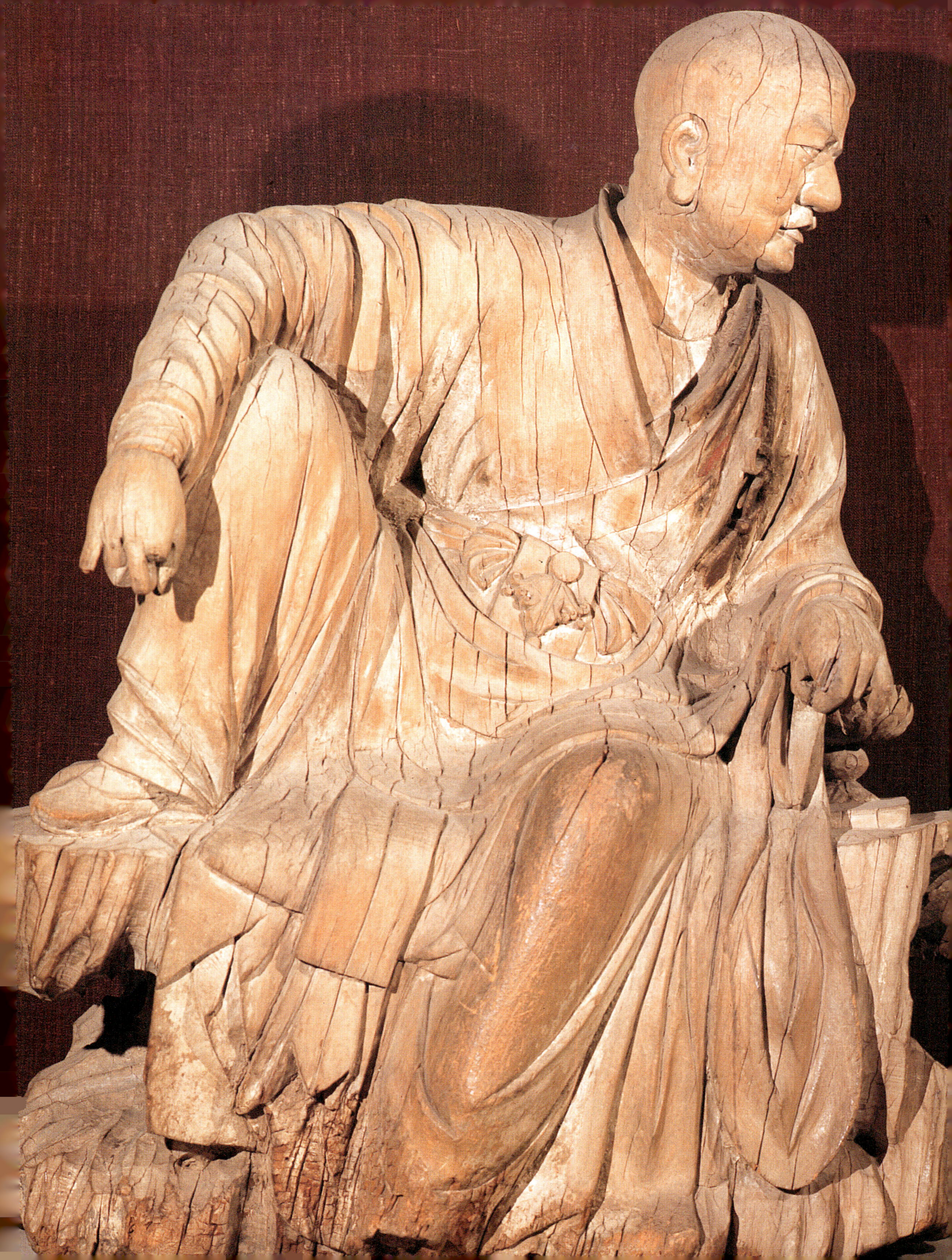

Accompanying the demise of the Manchu royal dynasty at the beginning of this century was that of the the civil service exam based on Confucianism that had been in existence for 2,000 years. Taoist, Buddhist and Chinese religious tradition and folklore survived and continued, along with the newer imports of Islam and Christianity. With the advent of the Communist government in 1949, the major religions were tolerated, but Chinese folk religion was dismissed as superstition and persecuted. All the religions were, however, much effected by the government's secularization of their lands and later exile of their leading members in the Cultural Revolution — which lasted a decade and resulted in driving religion underground. Since 1978, there has been a political shift and more religious tolerance, with the churches permitted to run their own affairs, re-consecrate buildings and hold open services. New Confucian colleges have opened, and the imported religions have been absorbed and modified to suit the Chinese character.

JAPAN

The ancestors of the Japanese originated from the continental mainland — probably Korea. They met and fought the original inhabitants of the islands — the Ainu, whom they subdued and assimilated. At first they lived in tribal clans, usually headed by a matriarch, gradually developing into the male-dominated feudal system which became the archetype of Japanese society for almost two millennia. The continent continued to exert great influence; although not slavishly copied, it was the source of new ideas which then underwent intense modification — a facility still possessed by the Japanese today. Japan experienced its own unique development in relative isolation except for these occasional mainland transfusions.

Above left and Right: A Japanese warrior.

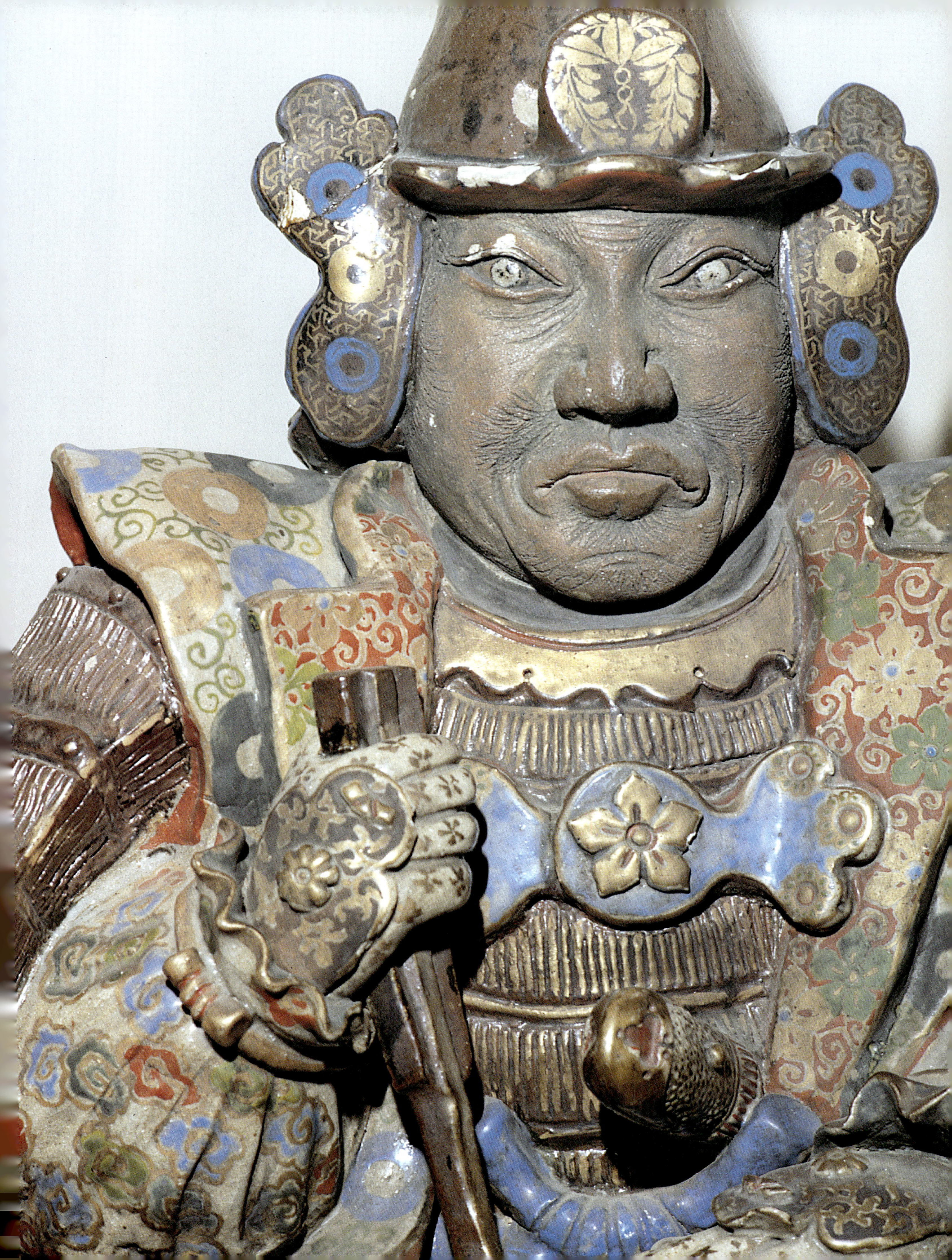

Its indigenous belief system was known as Shinto. This evolved from the nature worship of the native folk religions, with their belief in a spirit world of the *kami* — who could inhabit a feature of landscape or take a specific bodily form, and could be either benevolent or malicious. State Shinto developed with the acknowledged divinity of the Japanese royal family from the 8th century onward. From this time Shinto myths were written down, outlining the creation of the cosmic egg and the mythological creation of the gods and subsequent creation of the world order, including the Japanese Islands and royal family.

The natural island isolationist tendency coupled with native imagination led to the refinement of Buddhism and its resultant sects. Particular credit for the establishment of Buddhism in Japan must go to Prince Shokotu (573–621 AD), who was of critical importance. Instrumental in the importation of Buddhism and Confucianism, he is also credited with the creation of the first Japanese constitution in 604. As a Buddhist himself, though with no preference for any particular sect, he commissioned new temples and helped set up six Buddhist philosophic centers in Nara, the Japanese capital at that time. These schools eventually became so powerful that the emperor moved his capital to Kyoto in 741 AD in an attempt to counteract their influence, going on to encourage the development of the alternative Tendai and Shingon sects which were more syncretistic in their approach. They therefore combined easily with the indigenous Shinto, consequently making Buddhism more popular and prevalent. Jodo Shinshu, Ryobu Shinto, Shingon, Tendai, Rinzai and Soto Zen and Nichiren were all Buddhist derived sects that the Japanese absorbed in quick successsion as they modified this critical foreign import. Jodo Shinshu (Pure Land) emphasized the

Above left and Right: This Japanese mandala was produced during the Kamakura period (13th century AD).

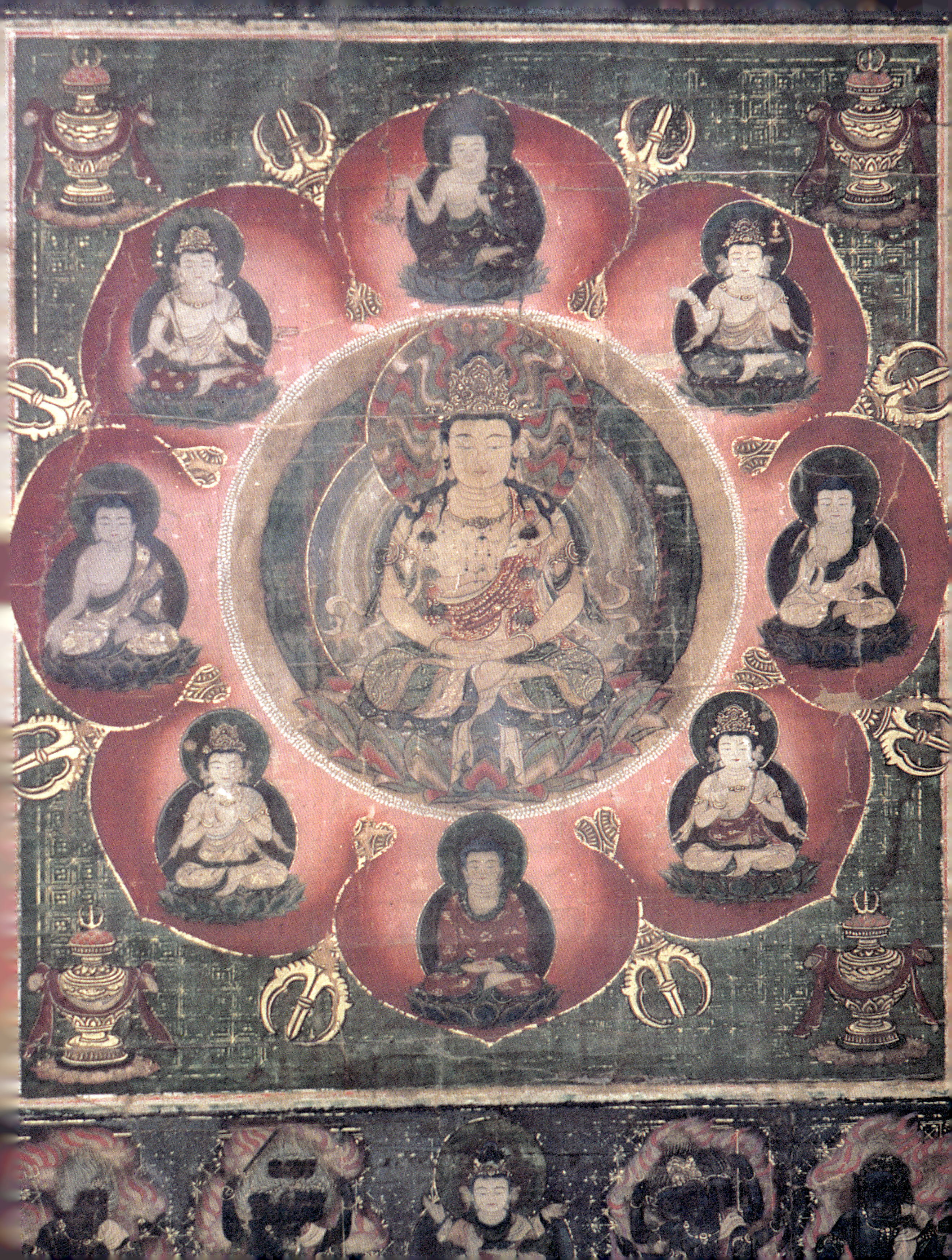

possibility of rebirth through Amida Buddha and the exclusive chanting of his name, Zen gave the potential of either instant or gradual enlightenment through meditation and awareness, Nichiren more narrowly advocated the chanting of a specific (Diamond) sutra, Shingon was more esoteric and mystical, Tendai emphasized the Lotus Sutra but was more broadly based, Rinzai was a Zen sect that appealed especially to the Samurai nobility with its focus on *koans* (riddles) and practical life, whereas Soto emphasized study of the sutras and Zazen meditation.

SOUTH-EAST ASIA

Cambodia, Laos, Vietnam, Thailand, Burma, Malaysia, Java, Indonesia, Sumatra and Bali — all have the Indian/Chinese mix which is proportionately varied in each country. In Cambodia, Confucianism took hold, but beyond this direct Chinese influence faded in contrast to the religious dynamism of India, capable of firing the imagination in a way that Confucianism could not hope to match. All these countries and peoples were influenced by Hinduism, probably initially through trade, then conversion through pilgrim saint adventurers spreading their missions. Others came and settled to sustain the influence. This was all still further strengthened by the arrival of Buddhism, fleeing the resurgence of Hinduism in India itself. The Lesser Vehicle (Hinyana) brought by monk missionaries emphasized self-discipline, and although it got off to a good start it was eventually eclipsed by its later, bigger brother — the Larger Vehicle of Mahayana, advocating salvation for all and with easier steps to accomplish this. Hinyana still retains a foothold only in Burma and Thailand.

The decline of the Hindu-Buddhist states in the Indonesian Islands resulted from a breakdown of the conventional order

Above left and Right: This Malayan (modern-day Indonesia) shadow puppet of Rama was inspired by the Hindu epic the Ramayana

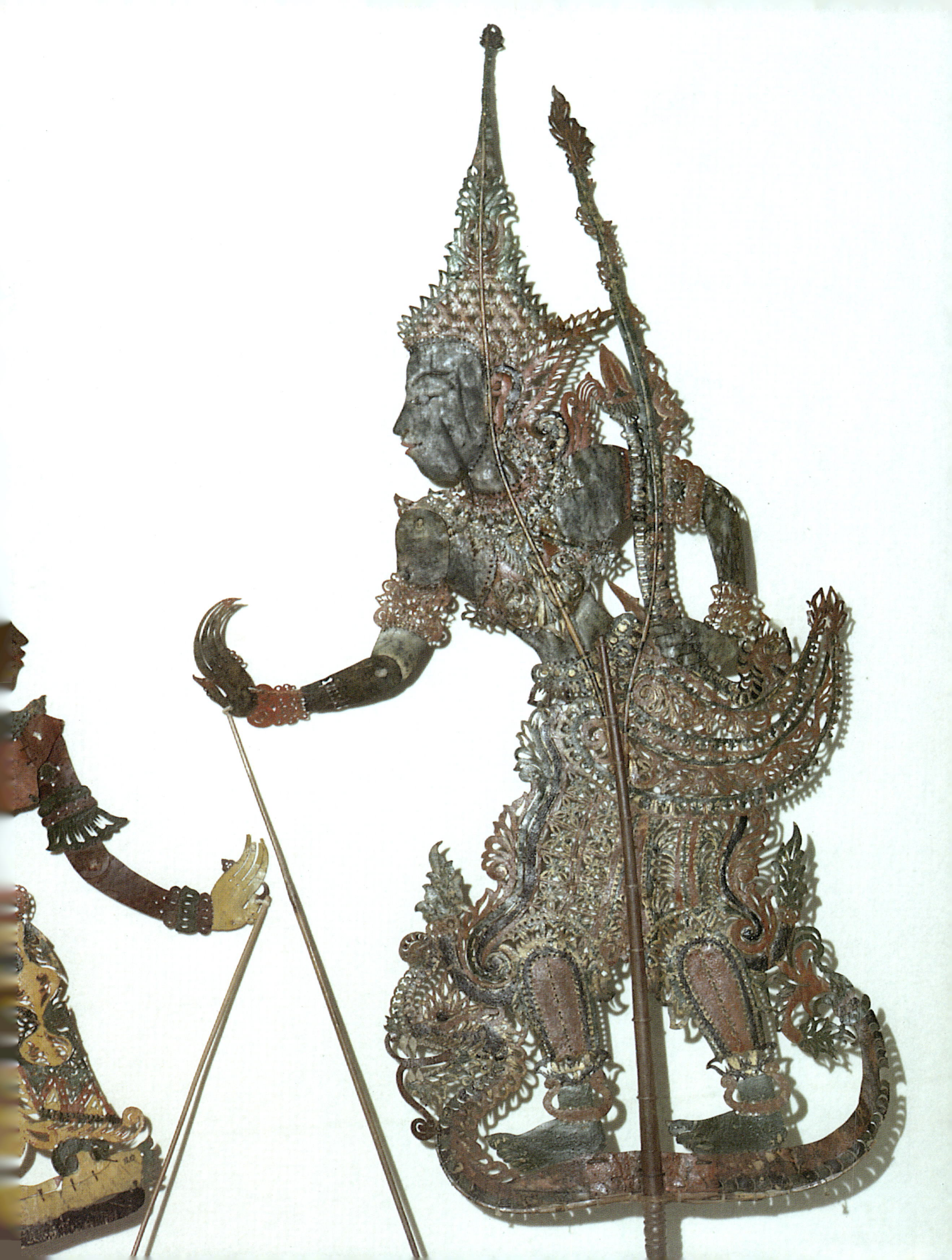

caused by the physical disruption of earthquakes, volcanoes and war, coupled with the steady rise of Muslim infiltration. From the 13th century onward this presence grew to eventually absorb the whole area under Islam in a largely peaceful evolutionary conversion process. Only on the East Asian continent did Hinduism or Buddhism survive.

The only other parts of South East Asia which neither Chinese or Indian influence reached were the Philippines, Borneo, Indonesia and other smaller less significant islands unknown even at the time. These had to wait for the later European waves of settlement, bringing the West Asian and Semitic monotheisms that were blazing their paths worldwide.

SIBERIA, MONGOLIA

A massive territory divided into four main population groups: Finno-Ugrians, Turko-Mongols, Tungus and Paleo-Siberians — all of which break down in an ever-increasing complexity of sub-groups and tribes too numerous to mention. A fifth major grouping on the fringes of this area is that of the Paleo-Arctic Inuit.

The universe, according to these Siberian peoples, takes the form of a vast symmetrical egg, which is divided vertically into two equal sections. On the far side heaven and earth meet and clash to produce violent winds. The three main worlds or Upper, Lower and Middle Earths are all interconnected by a pivotal World Tree, whose canopy stretches to Heaven, and whose roots go down into the Underworld. An ancient earth goddess dwells in the roots and the souls of unborn children live in the branches. Sometimes as an alternative or an addition to this view there is another horizontal axis, which denotes a river people's acknowledgement of their most important resource, and makes a variant analogy of life as upstream and

Above left and Right: This Chinese Buddhist woodcarving was produced during the Juan dynasty (12th–13th century AD).

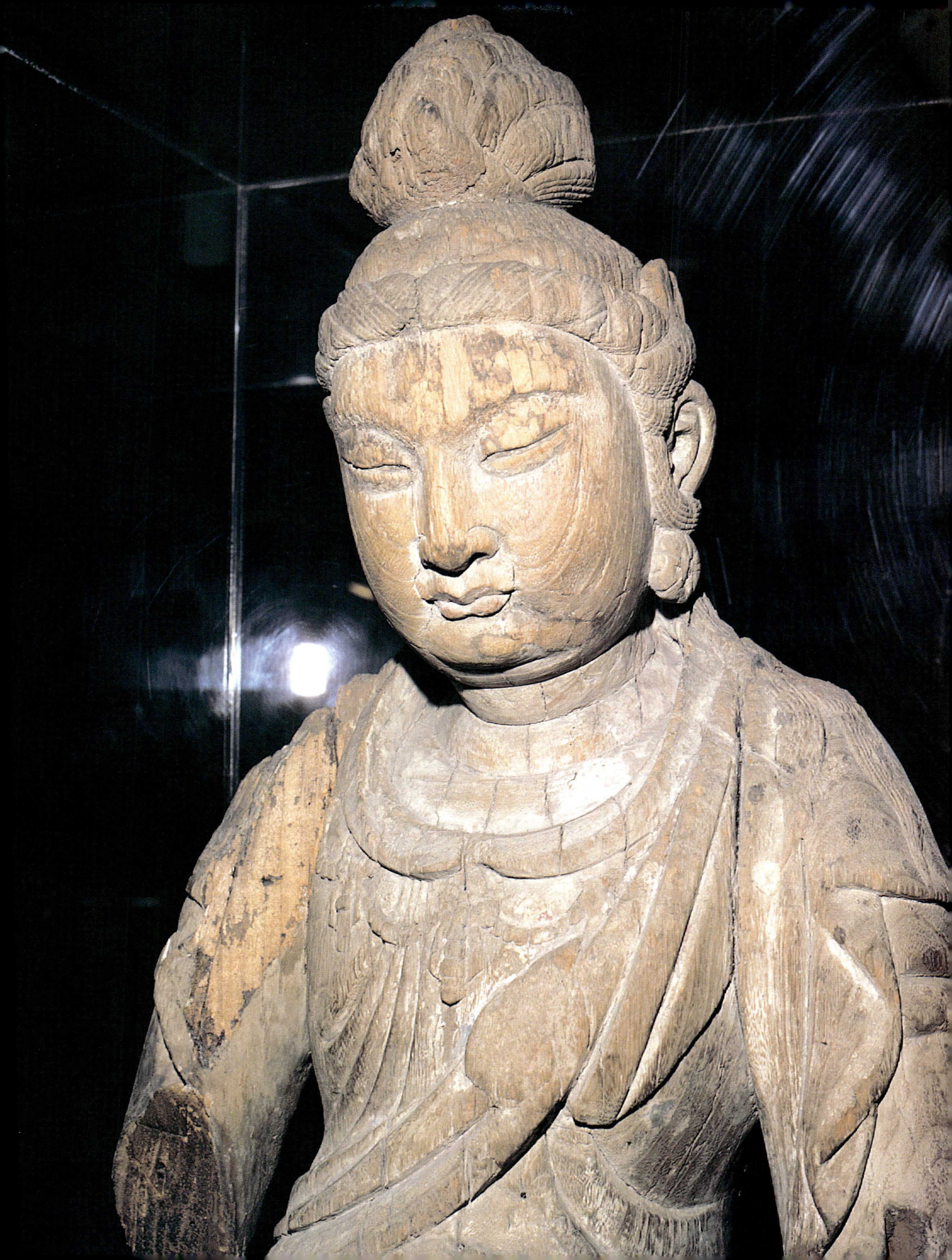

death downstream. Though primarily shamanist and animist in belief, there was room for sky creator divinities who sometimes created the original man or who alternatively developed alongside him, regulating the universe so that all things may continue in their cycles of life and death. Even Shamanism was sometimes explained as the gift of a great god in the form of an eagle, so that man might be protected against illness. Other explanations insist that Shamanism was a product of the inverse devil personality, or the development of man himself, impatient with his wait for divine aid. The ever-growing powers of the live and present Shamans eventually eclipsed the remote Great God although his adherents fought back tooth and claw. Some common myths recount the battle between the Great God and his ally Death and humankind with its Shamans. Earth creator gods were worshiped too, who made and maintained the features of the landscape and were the source of water and food. But it was primarily the ancient animist spirit world that held the true attention of the Siberians. That is until later migrations and incursions led them further toward conventional sky god supremacy.

Once outside his unique tribal environment a man was confronted by the spirits of other tribes and territories who were inevitably hostile, and therefore had to be either defeated or appeased. Sometimes though, spirits were seen as being neither specifically, but randomly vulnerable to either approach. It was always a gamble to attempt to overcome these spirits voluntarily or for one's own advantage, as things could easily go the wrong way. Spirits were rather similar to people in that they liked to be entertained and given presents, but they also liked to fight, coveted others possessions and could become angry, drunk and devious.

Above left and Right: Phoenixes glide among the peonies and rocks of this beautiful silk tapestry (16th–17th century AD).

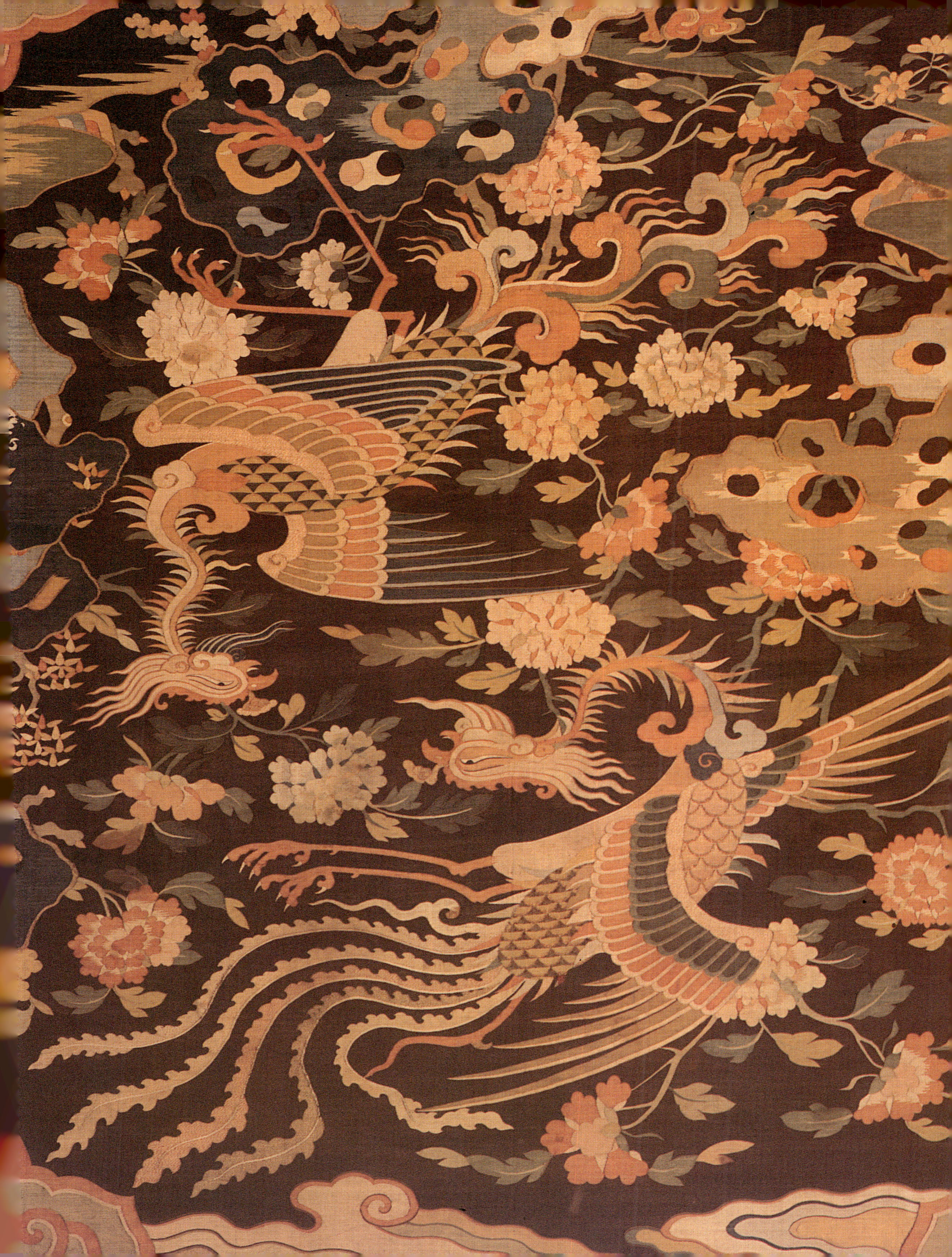

A-Z
CODEX GODS

AMATERASU

Amaterasu was the sun goddess from whom the Yamato tribes and the Japanese imperial family claim descent. The main myth involving her is the standard "seasonal" story that occurs worldwide. In this Japanese variant it concerns Amaterasu's manic storm god brother Susanoo, who through his outrageous behavior drove her to hide away in a cave. He first of all visited his sister in the sky telling her of his plan to visit their mother in hell. In a competition to decide who was the more powerful, they agreed to create a few gods and goddesses. Amaterasu chewed up Susanoo's sword and blew out a trio of goddesses, so in reply Susanoo ate some of his sister's jewels and promptly exhaled five gods. Pleased with himself he then got so excited and enraged he ran off, destroying anything he could reach and causing considerable damage. In conciliatory fashion Amaterasu made excuses for her brother, but his misbehavior continued to escalate. He next polluted temples and shrines, and then, in order to intimidate his rival sibling still further, he threw a flayed horse through the roof of the weaving shed where she was making divine clothes for the other gods. This was the final straw for Amaterasu, who broke down and fled, eventually hiding herself away in a cave. Of course without the sun's radiance things went from bad to worse — nothing would grow and devils and demons were everywhere afoot. Finally the rest of the gods decided something must be done to remedy this appalling situation. They consequently organized a flamboyant party just outside Amaterasu's cave, where they hung jewels and mirrors in the trees in order to tempt her and Ama-No-Uzume, a fertility goddess, danced such a sexy dance that the gods were soon highly stimulated and in an uproar. Amaterasu's curiosity inevitably got the better of her and she took a peek outside the cave. As she did so her own light was reflected back from the mirrors, and intrigued, she came out still further. She was then quickly grabbed by the waiting gods and prevented from returning into her bolt-hole. Thus the sun was brought back out into the world once more and life could continue.

AMIDA-NYORAI

Also known as: Amida

The Japanese version of Amitahba Buddha, the "Lord of Light," of especial significance to the Jodo or "Pure Land" school of Buddhism. Following the harder, esoteric approach of Hinyana Buddhism, with its life of asceticism and withdrawal so difficult to achieve, a more simple Mahayana method was put forward for the masses: plain faith. Through simple prayers and chants the faithful could achieve the salvation offered by one who had attained Nirvana. Other Japanese Buddhist sects advocated variations on this approach — Tendai: the Lotus Sutra, Nichiren: the persistent

Right: An apsara (celestial being) possibly from the cave temples of Lung Men, China (6th century AD).

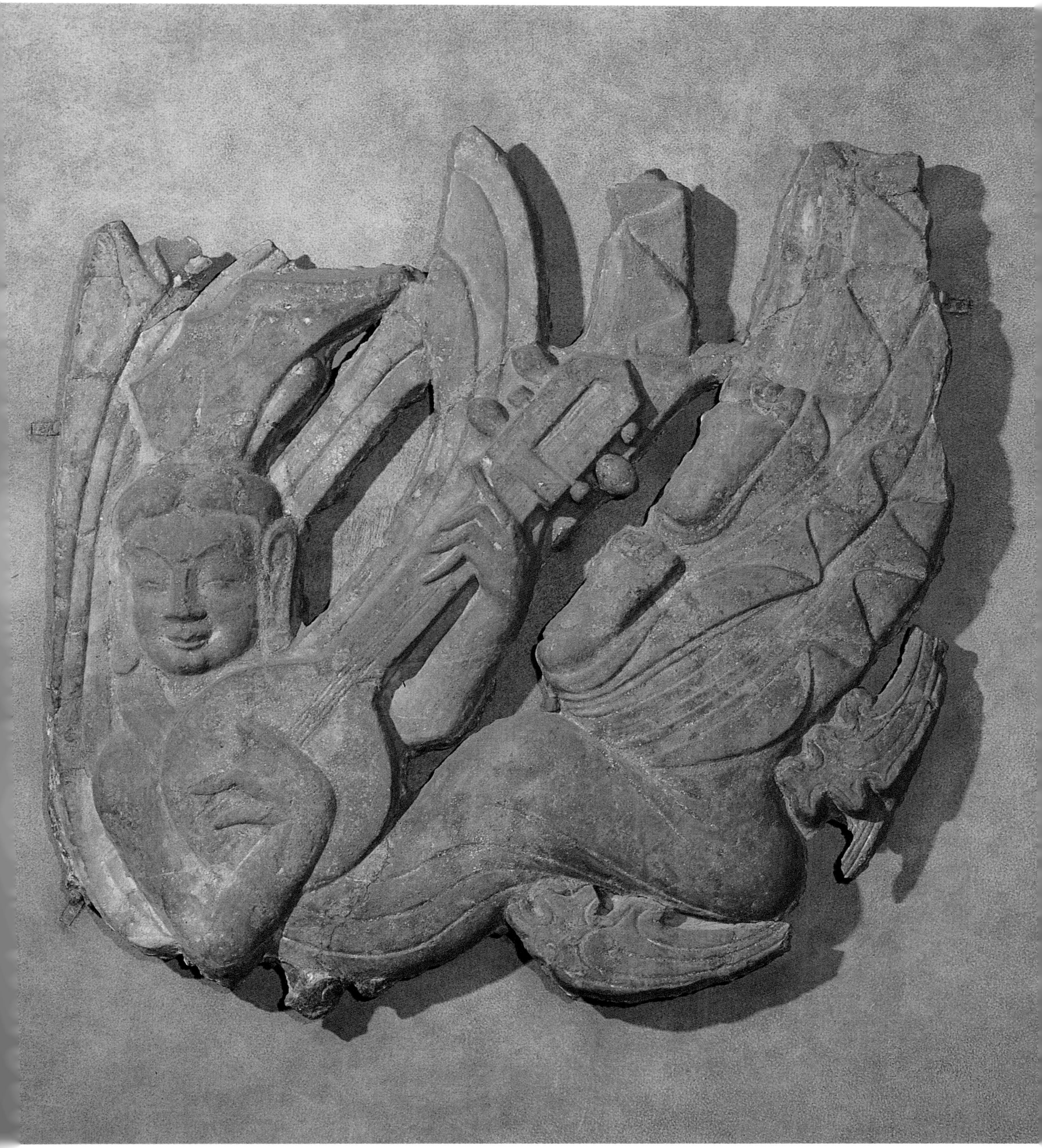

A-Z
CODEX GODS

chanting of the Diamond Sutra. The Shingon and Zen sects were more esoteric and mystical, advocating enlightenment through the more usual meditation and asceticism. Amida was portrayed enthroned on a lotus seat with a huge halo. His pure land was a paradise in which people remained until they attain Nirvana.

ANCESTOR WORSHIP

An ancient element of Chinese religious life which has survived the Communist period to remain very much current. Ancestral importance is a worldwide phenomenon, used to achieve continuity and justify dominance as well as underline identity. In China it began with the Shang dynasty c. 1500 BC. A manuscript, *The Classic of Rites*, details the rituals performed. Confucian philosophy absorbed these aspects easily, as they tied in with its conservative approach to maintaining the order and structure of society. It was therefore acknowledged by the administration and enacted in public rituals for state occasions. This co-existed with the more personal and familial worship of one's own ancestors, reflecting the Chinese emphasis on the family.

THE FOUR AO

The Four Ao were Chinese guardian water gods of the rain and sea, who took the form of dragons. Their names were Ao Ch'in, Ao Jun, Ao Shun and Ao Kuang. They were under the command of Huang Shang-Ti, the Jade Emperor, and each was assigned a corresponding area of land and sea as his fief.

BENTEN

Benten was the Japanese deity of luck and wealth, who was also associated with eloquence and music. She was a popular goddess with all who sought good fortune and consequently had many local shrines. Although she eventually married a prince of the disconcerting snake people who dwelt in the seas around Japan, Benten had a painfully shy and innocent nature. Due to her natural delicacy she found it hard at first to fulfil her marriage vows, succeeding ultimately because of her sense of *giri* — duty.

BODHIDARMA

Also known as: Ta-Mo, Daruma.

The founder of the Ch'an Tsung "Inner Light" school of Buddhism — one of the most distinctive and original products of the Chinese mind, which culminated as Zen in Japan and has now penetrated worldwide. In 520 BC Bodhidarma arrived in Nanking from India and had an unsettling effect on the state sponsored Buddhist mainstream. This fierce, uncompromising character was famous for his cryptic awareness, as displayed in the short sharp shock of an interview with the Jade Emperor. He then retired to a monastery and passed his years in meditation.

Above left and Right: The Taoist immortal, Chung Li Ch'uan in Chinese ivory (17th century).

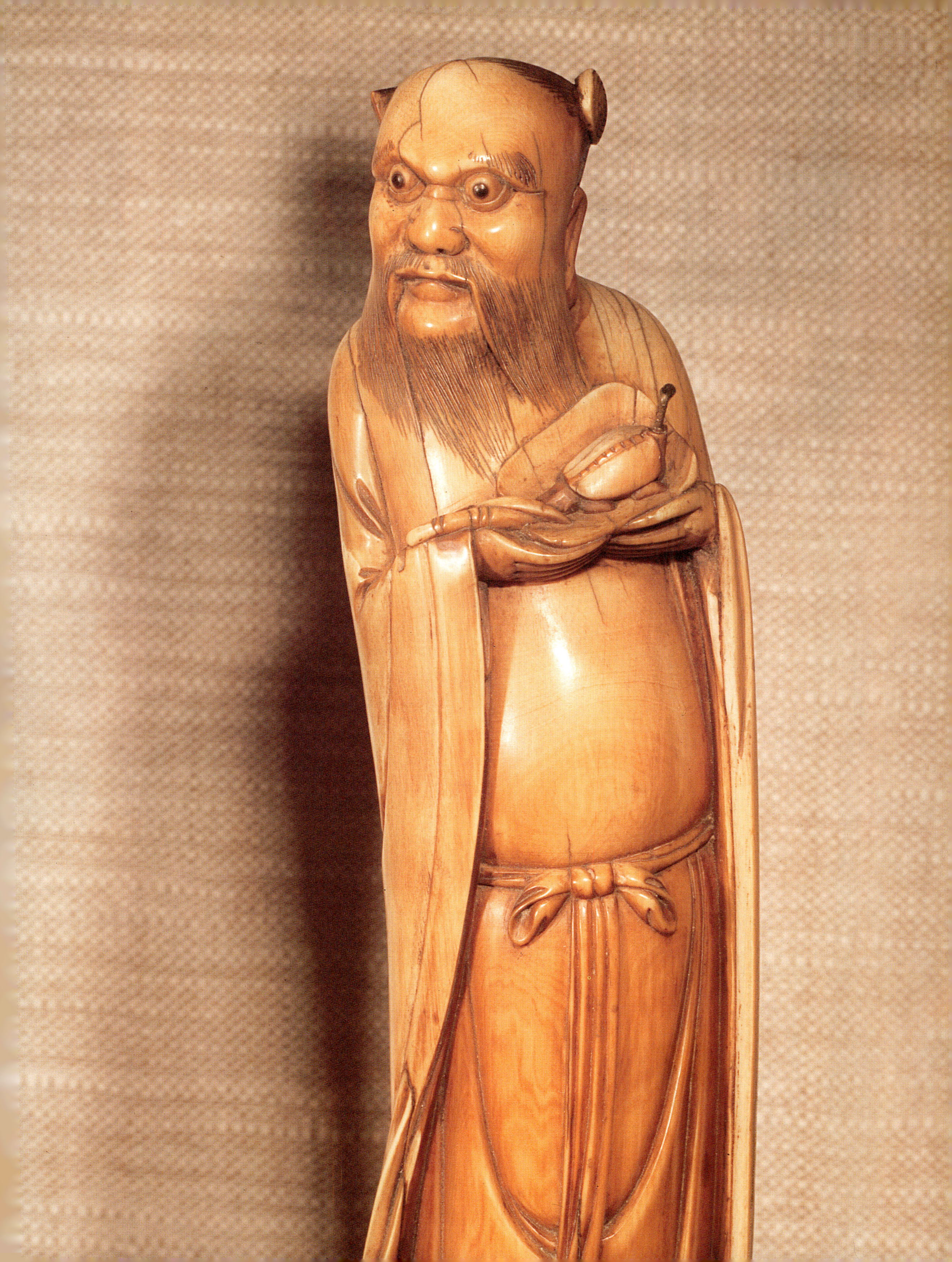

A-Z
CODEX GODS

The second patriarch of Ch'an Tsung was Hui-k'o, who sought out Ta-Mo to become his disciple. Initially his requests for instruction were always turned down, but he remained outside Bodhidarma's door in meditation. Finally unable to bear the suspense of waiting any longer, he cut off his left hand, and sent it in to the master. He later experienced *satori* — sudden illumination through a flash of insight.

The Zen tradition eschews all the inherent dogma of scriptures and words, advocating instead the development of a supra-rational awareness that points directly to the soul in order to perceive the Buddha within all.

BUGA
"God"
Buga was the paramount deity of the Tungus people of Siberia. He created the first human beings out of fire, water, earth and iron. This was achieved by converting elements into human compositional features. From the earth were made flesh and bones, from iron the heart was forged, water was then converted to blood by the divine process and finally from fire the warmth was supplied to animate the results.

CH'ANG-O
Ch'ang-O was the Chinese moon goddess and the wife of I — both of them were condemned to live on earth following the killing of the nine suns by I. She enraged her husband so much when she stole his immortal elixir given to him by the gods, that she had to flee to the moon and beg the aid of the Celestial Hare in mollifying her husband. After a few slaps from the Celestial Hare and a reappraisal of his wife's beauty, I was soon converted. Ch'ang-O however, was not convinced and elected to remain in her custom-built luxury palace on the moon, where I visited her regularly. In another version of the myth Ch'ang-O turns into a toad when she consumes the elixir, and remains on the moon with only an old man and a hare for company, whilst the aggrieved I returns to heaven.

CONFUCIUS
Also known as: K'ung Fu-Tzu, Master Kung
Top Chinese philosopher (551–479 BC), who founded the oldest school of Chinese thought. Confucius was born into an impoverished but aristocratic family in the state of Lu (modern Shantung). There he became an official of the government administration with a retinue of disciples. Initially his fortunes prospered, to the extent that through jealousy there was a breach with those above him. He thus renounced his position and became a wandering sage and teacher. His philosophy advocated social and political responsibility sustained through high moral values, benevolence and reciprocity, all without recourse to religion, which he instinctively mistrusted. His teachings and aphorisms were written down after his death by

Right: Another painting from the Chao Hsia series: here the kind governor encourages farmers to plant mulberry trees.

還望次歲豐稔神祐厥米黃
酒勸農再
黃霸發金
穋重見景

飲竭力鋤茅稂

A-Z
CODEX GODS

his followers and augmented over time to serve the Confucian ideal of state service.

DAINICHI-NYORAI
"The Great Illuminator"

For the Shingon ("True Word") sect, the Buddha Mahavairocana was the ultimate Enlightened One. This mysterious sect was founded by Kukai, who is better known by his posthumous name of Kobo-Daishi. He came to prominence when appointed abbot of the great monastery at Miyako, where after about ten years he considered his mission at an end. He was then buried alive seated in meditation, awaiting the final solution with the advent of the Maitreya Buddha, known in Japan as Mirokubosatsu, the Buddha to come.

Dainichi-nyorai was the cosmos made manifest, his energy lurking in the merest mote, intrinsic to the universal paradigm. He was portrayed seated on a lotus in deep and serene contemplation. Around him his avatars and emanations — "indestructible potentialities destined to manifest themselves in the dynamic aspects of the universe." Shingon adherents believed it possible to evoke magic powers that enable Dainichi-nyorai to manifest his form on earth.

DRAGONS
Fabulous mythical beasts, dragons were of great significance in Chinese mythology. As with other countries, they were used as a symbol of royalty and in China the emperor's royal emblem was the dragon. Many gods also took this form, or could assume it at certain relevant times. Originally the serpent was a royal symbol and worshiped as divine, because it renewed itself and seemed immortal. The dragon — an embellished cousin of the serpent — gradually superseded it in Chinese iconography.

ERH-LANG
Also known as: Chao Ching

A widely worshiped Chinese guardian god and protective spirit, Erh-lang was born Chao Ching and became the governor of Kuan-chou province when it was being destroyed and flooded by a camouflaged dragon acting incognito. Eventually after a grueling battle he defeated and beheaded the monster, gaining the new title Erh-Lang.

Another legend made him the nephew of the Jade Emperor, who could assume any one of up to seventy different forms, including animal, human and mythical hybrid shapes. This was probably due to his association with Yi and Chien, the latter a protective spirit famous for many brave feats.

ERLIK
The evil master and underworld god of Siberian mythology, yet also the original prototype man. Tartar myth tells of the god Ulgan's discovery of some mud with human features floating on the

Right: This 19th century silk robe with embroidered dragon — the symbol of royalty — was once worn by an emperor.

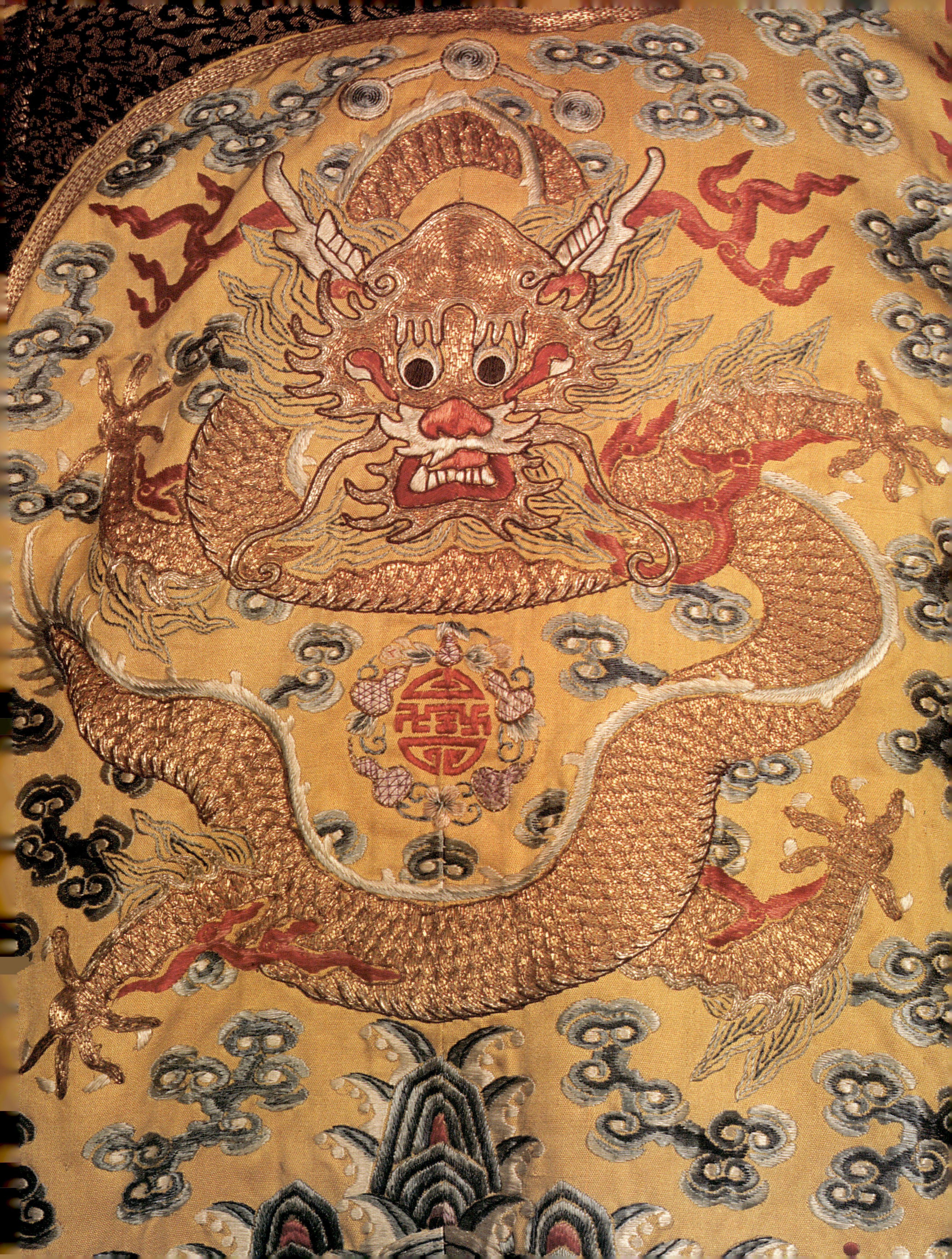

A-Z
CODEX GODS

ocean, to which Ulgan input spirit energy. Having animated this prototype man, Ulgan named him Erlik. However, after this, their relationship was all downhill, for Erlik's pride ensured his own downfall — a familiar worldwide theme. Erlik consequently ended up as king of the Underworld, yet despite this he was still viewed and worshiped as the father of humankind.

FIVE

Five was a number of particular significance in Chinese mythology. There were the Five Elements, the Five Emperors, the Five Buddhas, the Five Holy Mountains and the Five Cardinal Points, all of which could have a divine form. These consisted of the usual four directional elements and the central point or origin. Numerology is a particular aspect of Chinese myth, which contains a bewildering variety of sequences — perhaps indicating the vastness of this nation's geographical area and thus its syncretism and absorption of disparate elements which in turn give rise to multiple variants and sequences of similar or related aspects.

FU-HSING/SHU-HSING/LU-HSING

Also known as: Pei Tou

The Pei Tou were the celestial spirits of the Ursa Major constellation, the three most important were called Fu-hsing, Shu-hsing and Lu-hsing — a trio of Chinese gods who represented happiness, long life and money respectively. Like many Chinese deities they were originally human, but were granted divine status. Fu-Hsing's symbol was a bat, Shu-Hsing was portrayed as an old man with one of the Peaches of Immortality as his sign and Lu-Hsing's symbol was a deer. They were all popular domestic gods of fate and fortune worshiped and propitiated by the common folk.

FU XI

Fu Xi was an ancient Chinese creator god, who was linked to Nu Gua. They were often portrayed as a married couple. It is also said that Fu Xi was one of the first emperors, who later became a mythological hero figure to whom various discoveries and skills were attributed, including teaching mankind the arts of fishing and farming, and the invention of writing and music.

GIMOKODAN

A giant female personification of the Underworld and manifestation of Limbo for the Babo tribes from Mindano in the Philippines. Gimokodan was covered in nipples and her two sides varied in color — red proclaimed her possession of those killed in combat while the white side was a negative image of the world above. In Gimokodan everything was inverted: spirits came out at night, and in daylight turned to dew, resting on vegetation. Along with the

Right: A Japanese netsuke shows a man and child following the tradition of scattering beans at New Year in an effort to ward off evil spirits.

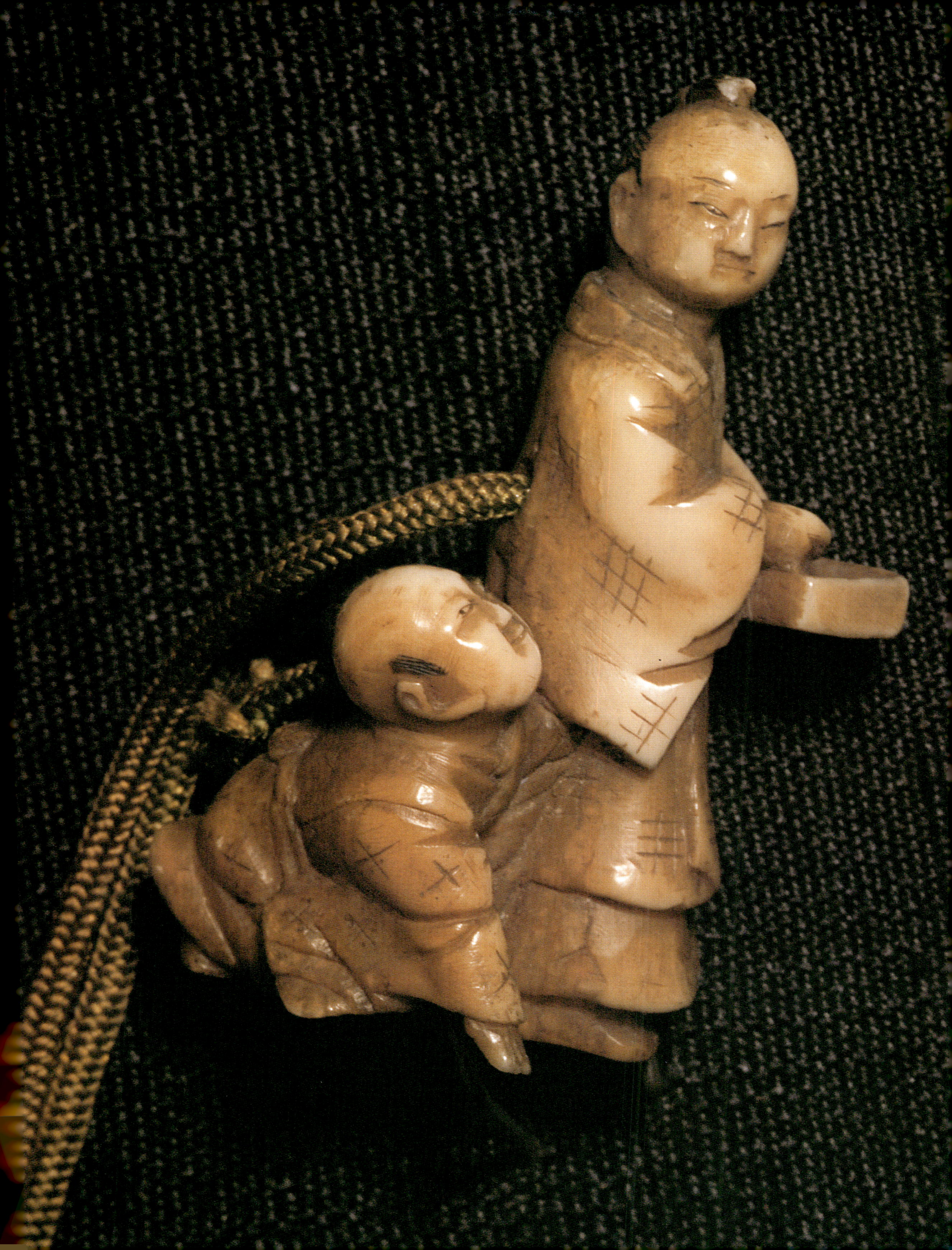

A-Z
CODEX GODS

larger animals, human beings were believed by these tribes to have several souls or *gimokod*, which at death would separate, with some going to heaven and others to Gimokodan.

HACHIMAN
Also known as: Ojin

Hachiman was the popular Japanese Shinto god of war, especially dear to the military. Like Mars, his Roman counterpart, he was also a god of agriculture and a protective deity, especially of children. Almost a third of Shinto shrines were dedicated to this war *kami*, as befitted a martial system of competing *daimyo* or feudal lords. One myth explains his origin as that of the deified emperor Ojin who was associated with Hachiman on account of his pugnacity. Rather surprising is another divine connection between Hachiman and the gentle Bodhisattva Kannon, which evolved as the dual strands of Shinto and Buddhism interwove.

HARI-HARA
"Grower/Remover"

Hari was another name for Vishnu and Hara for Shiva in their capacities as creator and destroyer respectively. Hari-Hara manifested these two aspects in a single figure in which it is possible to see a supreme god, symbolizing the two opposing life-principles manifested and reconciled in each other.

At Angkor Thom, the ancient Khmer capital in present day Cambodia, is the colossal temple of Angkor Wat, which features representations of Hari-Hara that indicate he was an important hybrid or avatar of the Indian Trimurti concept as it penetrated eastward. Hari-Hara was connected to and portrayed as royalty, underlining the Khmer kings right to rule. One myth accounts for the existence of Hari-Hara as a result of Vishnu and Shiva combining to take on a particularly fierce and powerful demon named Guha.

HENG-HA/ERH-CHIANG
Two Chinese guardian gods of Buddhist temples, known as the Sniffing General and the Puffing General. One emitted through his nose and the other through the mouth, deadly steam and rays with which to combat evil and protect the temples from sacrilege or attack. They were eventually superseded by the Heavenly Kings, who were four in number, each one guarding one of the four cardinal points and directions.

HOU T'OU
"Prince of the Earth"
Also known as: She, Ti

An agricultural and fertility deity of Chinese mythology, Hou T'ou was the god of the earth, although as a manifestation of the whole planet he was better known as Ti. A yearly ritual called the "Rites of the Eight Gods" was enacted by the

Above left and Right: This T'ang Dynasty (7th–10th century) statue stood guard outside a Chinese tomb.

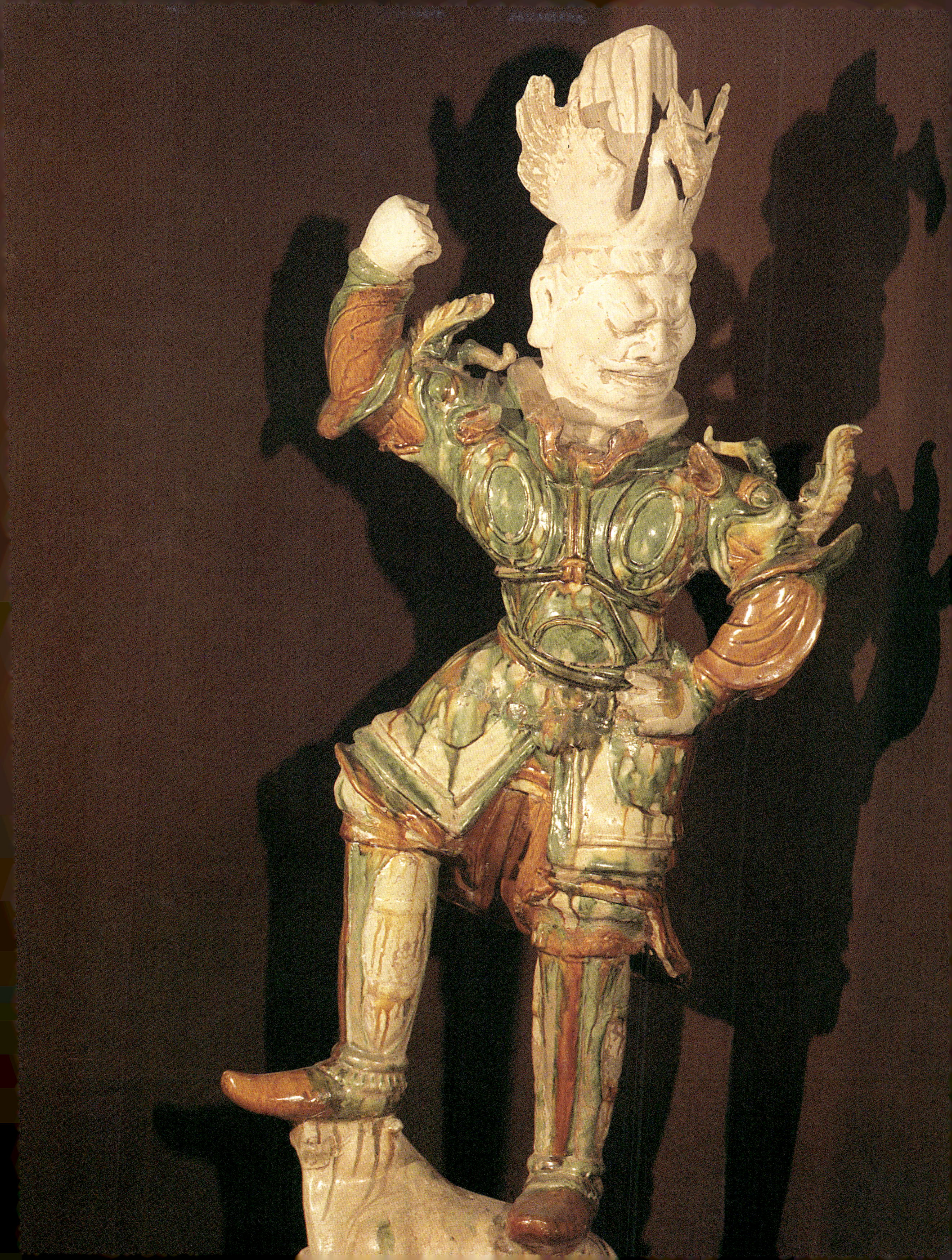

A-Z
CODEX GODS

emperor each spring and mirrored in every Chinese village. This consisted of the ceremonial digging of the first spadeful of earth, performed with accompanying prayers, in order to encourage fertility. That this particular rite should be cleverly appropriated by Confucius from China's ancient past reflects agricultural China's preoccupation with feeding itself.

HSIEN
"Immortal"
Also known as: Jen

In Chinese Taoism the Hsien were immortals who dwelt just off-planet and dressed in feathers, their technical means to this immortality was a dual-dose elixir. Taoists believed that each soul consisted of two parts: the Hun came from the sky and returned there after death, the Pho came from the earth and was reabsorbed. The balance of these two elements inside the body corresponds with the Yin-Yang universal theory. In Taoist alchemy two elixirs could restrain these souls from departing, hence conferring immortality. This was part of a process of transformation/metamorphosis only open to masters of the highest category, who became celestial immortals or T'ien Hsien. Those who remained earthbound dwelling in forests and mountain peaks were called Ti Hsien. A third category existed, called the Shih Chieh Hsien, who would slough off their bodies after death and became corpse-free. Aged but undying, the Hsien roamed the universe at will, performing various actions and miracles. Yuan shi, the son of Pa'an Ku, was a Hsien.

HUANG-TI
"Yellow Emperor"

Huang-Ti was the patron saint of Taoism, an ancient legendary emperor often associated with Lao-Tzu. Stories tell of his gradual development into a Taoist saint-equivalent — from a typically self-indulgent monarch with a kingdom full of problems and his senses dulled and blunted, he finally made an effort and began to fast and meditate. In a dream he saw the kingdom of a mythical ruler Wu Hsing, which functioned without desire or fear, but was above the realm of the senses, its people composed. Huang-Ti then followed this path and his kingdom became orderly and composed. After a long reign he ascended into the firmament as a Hsien.

Huang-Ti was also seen as a Wu Hsing — one of the Five groupings, manifested in color-coded emperors of elements and directions.

INARI
"Moon god"
Also known as: Uke-Mochi ("good genius")

The Japanese rice god of Shinto mythology, he was also god of wealth and friendship. When Uke-Mochi entertained Tsuki-yomi she filled the land with food, the sea with fish and the hills with game. Disgusted that all these things had

Above left: A 17th century Ming ivory of the Taoist immortal Chang Kuo Lao. Right: Another Ming ivory, this time of Taoist immortal Han Hsi Ang Tzu.

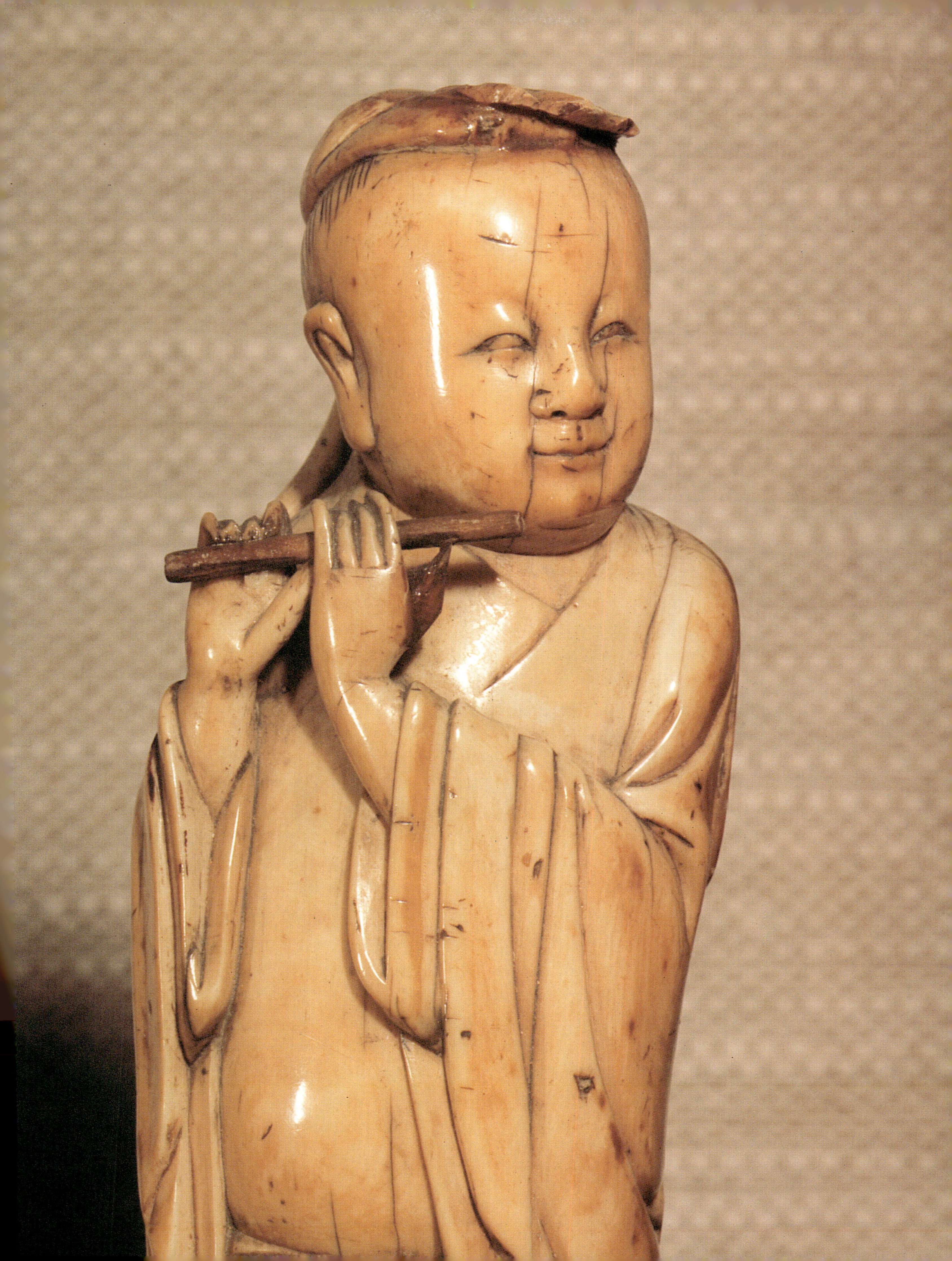

A-Z
CODEX GODS

emerged from her mouth he killed her, but from her corpse grew plants and cattle, even silkworms. This myth (an attempt to explain the introduction of sericulture) lacks any historical validity — the art of making silk was stolen from the Chinese by Koreans and others and passed on to other societies.

IZANAGI/IZANAMI

Izanagi was the male half of the Japanese creator god partnership with his sister, Izanami, being his female counterpart. They were the seventh generation of creator gods, who produced many others themselves. It was their job to solidify the earth and form the landmass, and then people it. When they first began to make other things they were not very successful, breeding monsters and more islands, but this was due to a wrong protocol: Izanami had spoken first, whereas Izanagi should have initiated the mating sequence. When they corrected this mistake all went well in a series of god births, until the final one, the fire-god Ho-Masubi, who gave his mother so much pain in the delivery that as a consequence she died. Izanagi was inconsolable at his wife's death, and followed her down to hell. However, she had already partaken of food there and was decomposing. Izanagi had disobeyed her when he had followed her and had caught sight of her ugliness, for which she was furious, sending a horde of she-demons after him, then following herself. Izanagi only just managed to escape, and rolled a huge stone to block the entrance to hell. Exchanging insults and threats Izanami promised to kill 1,000 people a day, and Izanagi to cause 1,500 women to give birth. As he bathed himself after this close call, the dirt of hell washed off him and formed harmful spirits and gods, so Izanagi made some beneficent gods to compensate, including all the sea gods. From his left eye came Amaterasu the sun, and from his right Tsuki-Yomi the moon god. From his nose came the infamous Susanoo, who straightway started trouble and had to be chased away.

JIZO-BOSATU

Also known as: Ti-tsang, Jizo

Ti-tsang in China and Jizo in Japan, the bod-hisattva Ksitigarbha roams through the realms of hell giving comfort to the tortured souls and rescuing them merely by his presence. Although not popular in India his association with the dead attracted Chinese Buddhists with their ancestor worship tendencies. He was portrayed as a gentle monk, bald and robed, equipped with a staff possessing rings on one end that announced his presence. Apart from this he was silent, neither asking nor thanking for alms and food given. He was also sometimes portrayed as a Chinese soldier.

Right: A Ch'in dynasty (12th century) statue in gilt bronze of the bodhisattva, Kuan-Yin.

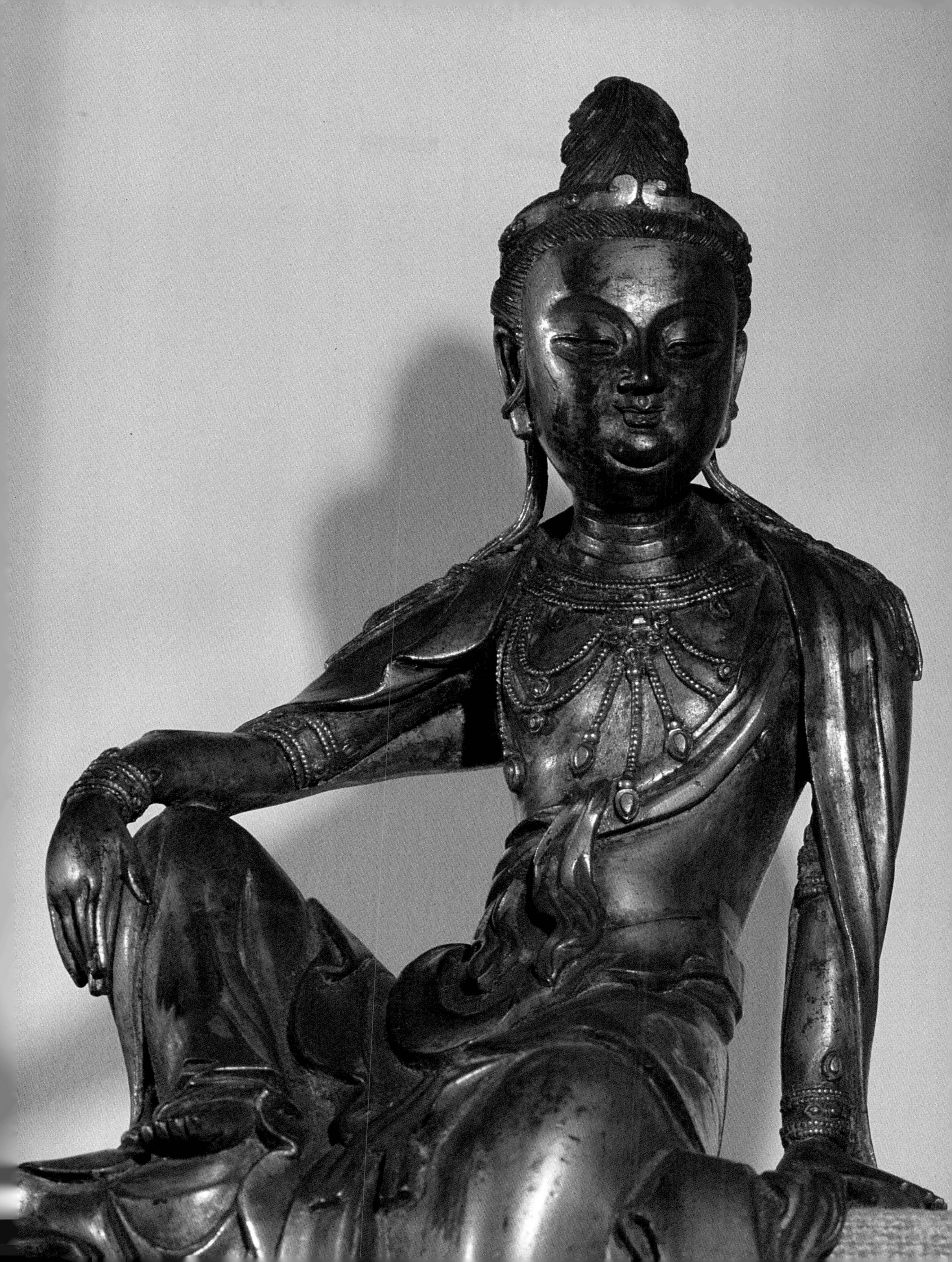

A-Z
CODEX GODS

KADAKLAN

The supreme deity of the Tinguian people lived in the mountainous interior of the Phillippine Island of Luzon. Kadaklan was a thunder and storm god, who dwelt in the sky with his faithful hound Kimat — his lightning weapons manufacturer and acolyte in various rituals. Kadaklan's origins are somewhat obscure and he was not held in as a high regard as the tribal ancestors. Complex funeral ceremonies were the prime events of Tinguian ritual — the most vital point being the safe arrival of the dead into the Underworld.

KAMI

Kami were the Japanese Shinto spirits of all things or the manifestation into personality of the life-force that was seen to be inherent in everything — the divine essence. Kami could therefore occur in an infinite variety: as rivers, rocks, mountains, lakes and trees, or as animals, deified men, devils, goblins and spirits. Gods too were Kami but not all Kami were gods. These spirits represent an early attempt to anthropomorphize nature — to assign personality and therefore protocol to all aspects of day to day life and to attribute character to inorganic objects and features of landscape. As Shinto and Buddhism integrated Kami were increasingly seen as protectors of the Buddhas and bohdisattvas.

KISHIMO-JIN

The Japanese Kishimo-Jin was a protectress of children, who like her Indian counterpart began life as the reverse — a demon with a special taste for children with whom she would abscond. Ultimately, through the good example of the Buddhist concept of *Ahimsa*, or non-injury she forswore her old ways and became the benefactor of children instead. Popular in India and China, she was an archetypal mother goddess who bestowed life, nourished it and destroyed it. The balance of creation, preservation and destruction is slightly shifted in Buddhist myth, emphasizing family life and benevolence. Her cult became popular in Japan toward the end of the 13th century AD. Legend says she was even occasionally seen and she was portrayed as a mother suckling an infant, with her symbol being a pomegranate.

KUAN-TI

Also known as: Kuan Yu, Kuan Kung.

As the Confucian Chinese god of war and fate, Kuan-Ti had a very auspicious red face, for red is considered by the Chinese to be a lucky color. He was seen as beneficent god to whom humans could call for advice through divination, although this could occasionally transform into judgement. Originally a famous human Han general called Kuan-Yu at a time of the Warring States, through military success and the

Above left: A K'ang-Hsi (1662–1722) statue of Kuan Ti, the Chinese god of war.
Right: Another image of Kuan Ti, the Chinese god of war, made between the 17th and 18th centuries.

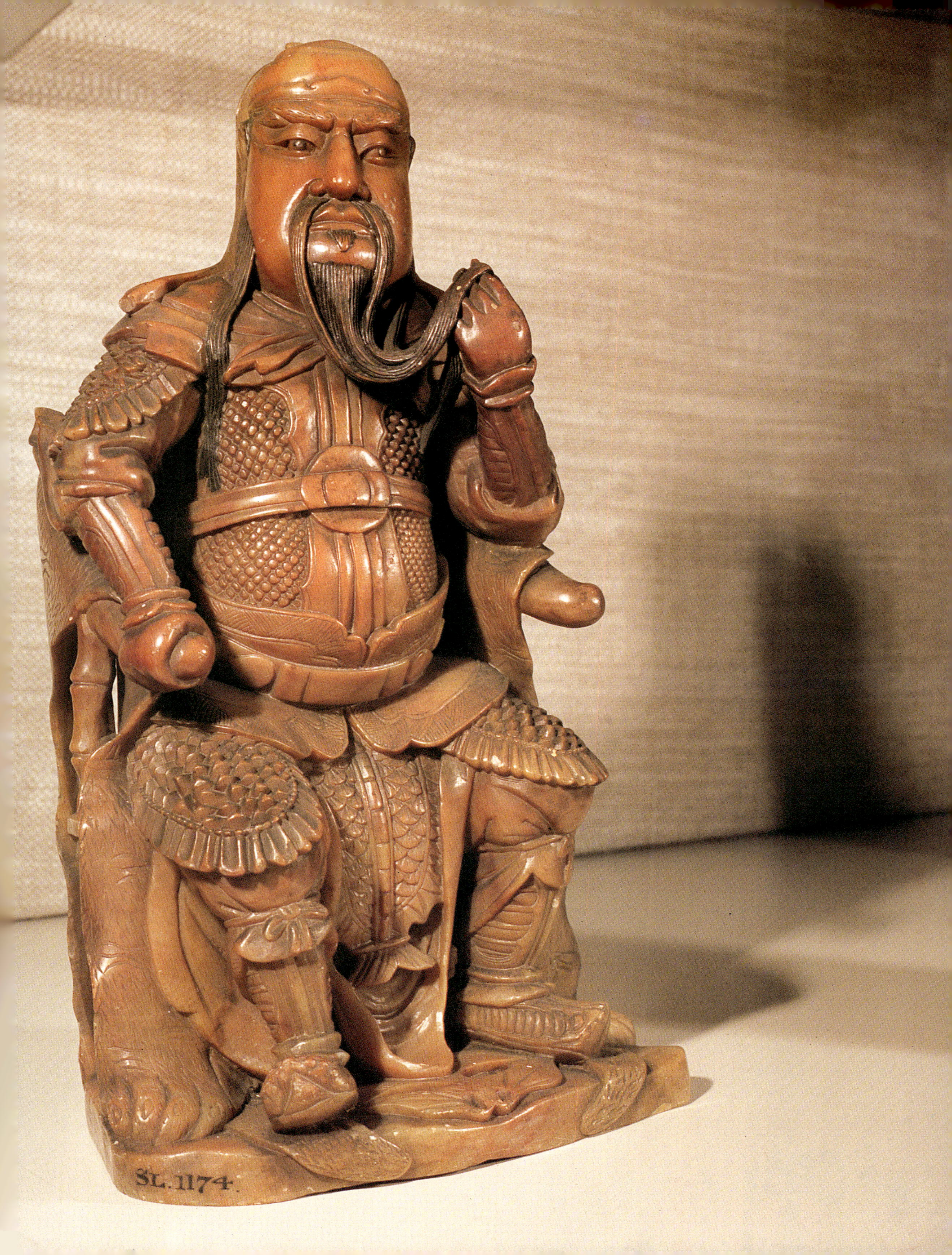
SL.1174

A-Z
CODEX GODS

resulting royal patronage Kuan-Ti was slowly promoted and simultaneously elevated in importance. His warlike aspect became in time secondary to his civilian role of counselor and judge, his skill and experience actually preventing war. He was eventually killed by the evil machinations of the powerful Sun clan, but enjoyed increasing cult worship until ultimately deified as a divine champion and protector.

KUMANG

The mother goddess of the Ibans — the sea Dayaks of Borneo. Kumang was in charge of the Iban heavenly paradise that was the home of Bujang, the legendary first Iban. Their mythology tells of an original homeland situated in the Arabian Peninsula from where the Ibans supposedly migrated, but this could merely reflect the important flow of cultural ideas from West Asia rather than a full-scale migration. The Iban live in village-sized long houses with a single roof. In Iban culture headhunting was seen as proof of a warrior's courage and prowess, and the grisly prize acted as a talisman for their Tua or guardian spirit. These spirits were usually in snake format, but could sometimes be a deer or a cat.

KUAN-YIN

Kuan-Yin was the compassionate Chinese Buddhist goddess of mercy and fertility — the Madonna figure of East Asia. She seems to once have been an indigenous deity who became linked with the Indian male bodhisattva, Avlokitesvara. She is portrayed dressed in white, sometimes with a child on her lap and her myths range from putting the goodness and nutrition into rice using milk from her breasts to the relief of suffering. Pilgrims — especially people with otherwise incurable diseases — came to pray and seek a cure at her temple on one of the Five Holy Mountains, called Miao Feng Shan. In Japanese Buddhist mythology she switched gender to take a male form, and became known as Kannon. Images of him possess many eyes and arms that convey infinite power and awareness. Other myths tell of Kuan-Yin's original human life and the suffering she underwent on account of her father, who was enraged when she refused to marry. She was allowed to become a nun but had to do the most menial tasks and when this did not dissuade her he then had her murdered. Her soul then went to hell, but on arrival spontaneously turned the underworld into a paradise revealing her purity. She later healed her father when he was sick and was reconciled with her peculiar parent.

LAO-TZU
"Old Master"
Also known as: Lao Chun, Lao Tan, Li Erh, "The madman of Ch'u"

According to Confucian legend the first of the "irresponsible hermits" was Li Er, but it has

Above left: Kuan-Yin, the Taoist goddess of mercy from the Kang Hsi (1662–1722) period. Right: A wooden carving of Kuan-Yin from the Song dynasty (12th and 13th century).

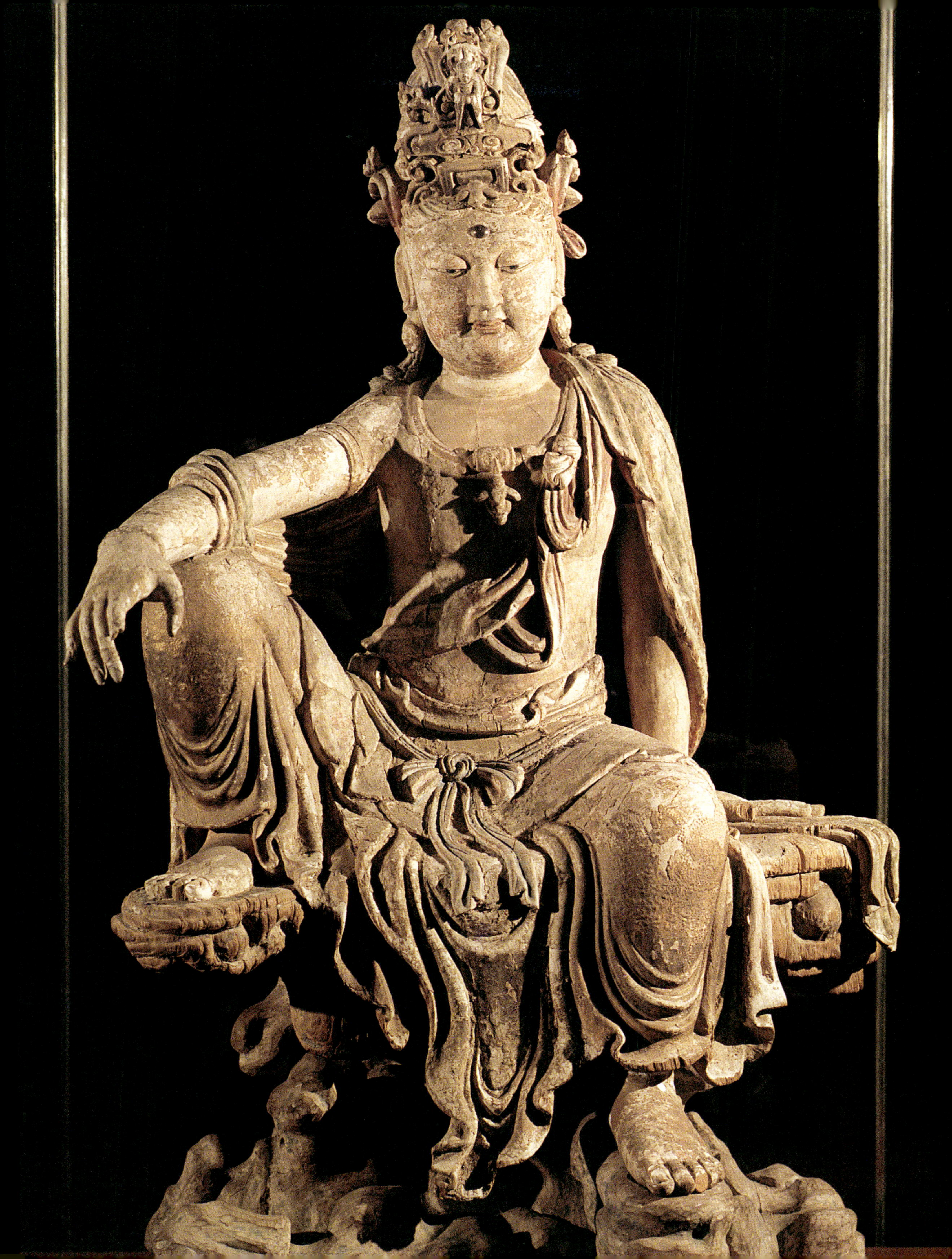

A-Z
CODEX GODS

become conventional call Lao Tzu the father of Taoism. Legend tells of his birth from his mother's left side after a gestation period of eighty years! In fact very little is actually known of Lao Tzu's life. Spurning wordly acclaim and reputation it is said that he searched for truth in a far place. He found it and remained a hidden master, though he is credited with the authorship of the *Tao Te Ching* — the classic Taoist philosophical text poem. Lao Tzu was canonized and worshiped as one of a trinity of Taoist deities which included Pa'an Ku and Yu-Huang Shang-Ti.

LI CHING

Also known as: Li, T'o-T'a-Li

Li Ching was the Chinese divine Prime Minister/President and chief guardian of Heaven, whose name originally derived from that of a famous Chou general deified for exemplary service. His other name, T'o-T'a-Li commemorated the gift of a pagoda given him by his son in reconciliation for a family feud. (His son had brought disgrace on the family by killing the Dragon King's messenger.) Li Ching was originally a Taoist deity who was absorbed by Chinese Buddhism, being represented in many temples.

LIEH-TZU

A semi-legendary sage and another archetypal low-key Taoist master, Lieh-Tzu minded his vegetable garden for most of his life, a hidden master who after death became a Hsien. The lesson he taught was that it is not in the great palaces nor the crowd that true awareness lies but rather in nature and the observation of the minutiae of life in all its great depth and its process of constant change. A later book attributed to Lieh-Tzu contains the reworking of earlier Taoist myths combined with a slice of Chinese history.

LUNG

The dragon of Chinese folklore. Unlike other cultures who viewed these legendary creatures as malevolent and ferocious monsters, the dragons of Chinese legend were essentially benevolent and therefore honored. These composite mythical beasts, made up of parts of almost every other creature, were seen as water gods — the manifestation of irrigation and water. They were associated with clouds, mist, rain, rivers and seas and were also propitiated for successful farming. They possessed varied powers, including a scaling facility, through which they could control their size from mini to mega, and also flew and had submarine capabilities in line with their water deity status. In time the dragon became the royal emblem, identified with the emperor in his benevolent paternal sustaining role.

MI-HUNG-T'ANG

The Broth of Oblivion, brewed by the Lady

Right: Dragons and phoenixes in enamel paint embelish this porcelain dish from the Kang Mai period (1661–1722).

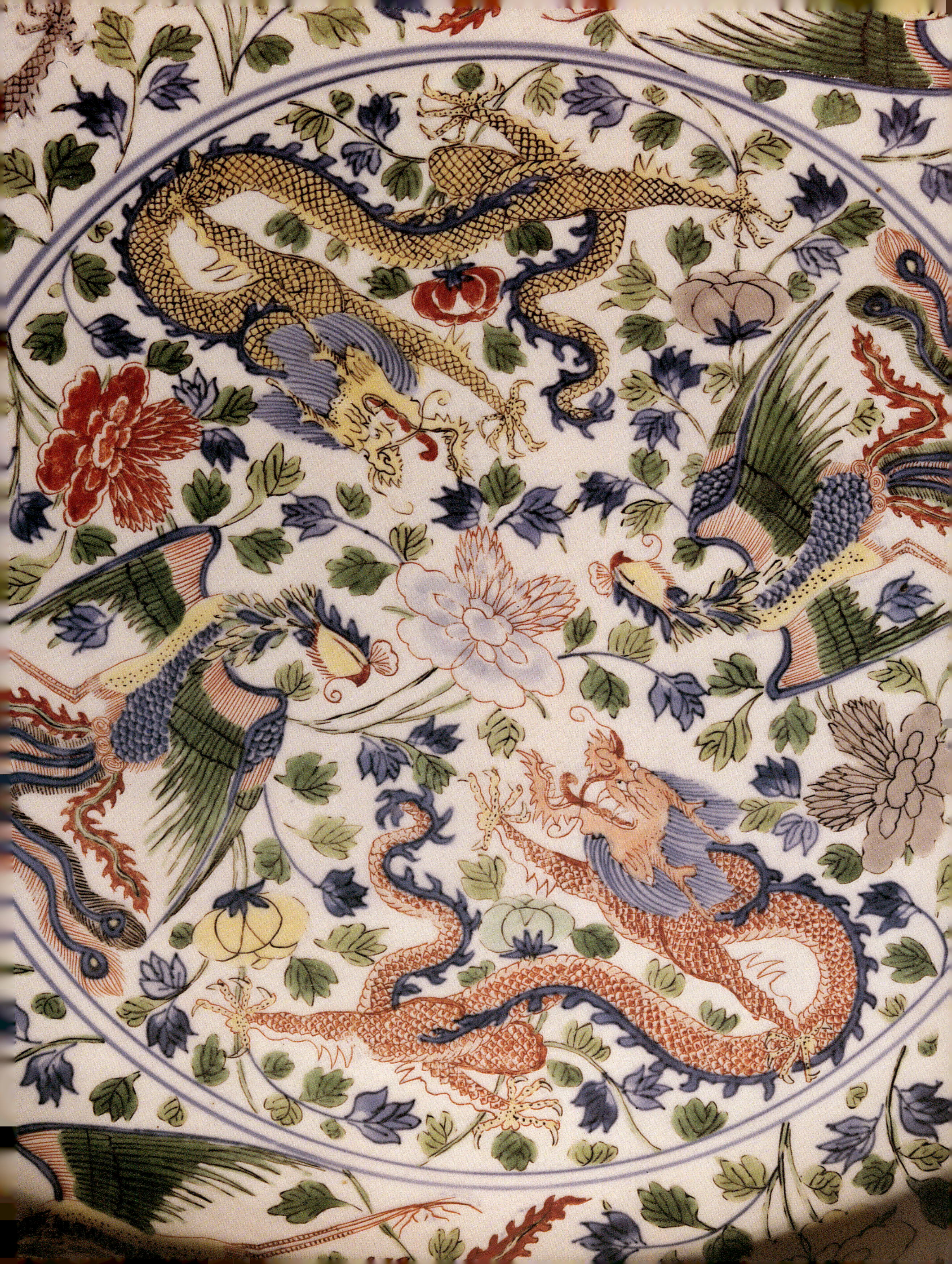

A-Z
CODEX GODS

Meng, who dwelt on the border of Hell. Once drunk it made anyone forget all about their former life, erasing the mind so that even the power of speech and knowledge of language was lost. This was in preparation for the soul to be born once again into the world, virgin and unsullied by past experience or memory. Only the ability to feel pain was retained after a draught of the Oblivion Broth.

MI-LO-FO
Also known as: Mi-Lo-Shen-Chi, Maitreya, Miroku-Bosatsu

Mi-Lo-Fo was the Chinese version of the Maitreya Buddha — the future Buddha living in the Tusita heaven who has yet to come. As with almost all mythological Buddhist figures, Mi-Lo-Fo is a native adaptation of the original Indian archetype — for the Chinese variant the archetype is overlapped with that of a large humorous monk surrounded by children and known as the Laughing Buddha. His status in China is far higher than that of his Indian counterpart.

Miroku-Bosatsu is the Japanese variant of the same original Maitreya. In Japan he is usually portrayed seated in thoughtful or meditative mode.

MONKEY

A Chinese Buddhist animal hero, Monkey was Sun Wukong the Monkey King, a trickster-hero who took on the rest of Heaven. He stole the Peaches of Immortality and fought all who came his way in his bid for power until finally overcome by the Buddha, and sent to accompany the monk Tripitaka (T'ang Seng) on his voyage to India. Their adventures form the story of the 14th century "Journey to the West," and illustrate the easy mix of indigenous and imported mythologies.

NIRVANA
Also known as: Nibbana

Nirvana is an Indian word meaning the condition of complete inner release and freedom. Western interpretations have incorrectly interpreted this state as that of personal annihilation, for Nirvana is seen by its adherents as a positive process that is both creative and liberating. Originally not specifically defined other than as an ultimate state, in later Mahayanan times it came to simultaneously represent the cosmic energy distributed universally and an emptying of personal definition. A re-absorption into the One from which plurality emerges.

NU GUA

Nu Gua was the wife of the ancient Chinese creator god Fu Xi, although she was also a creator goddess in her own right. She was portrayed as a serpent with a female human head. Her myth of humankind's creation has her feeling lonely one day soon after the earth had been formed, and deciding she needed company she took some mud and made a copy of herself,

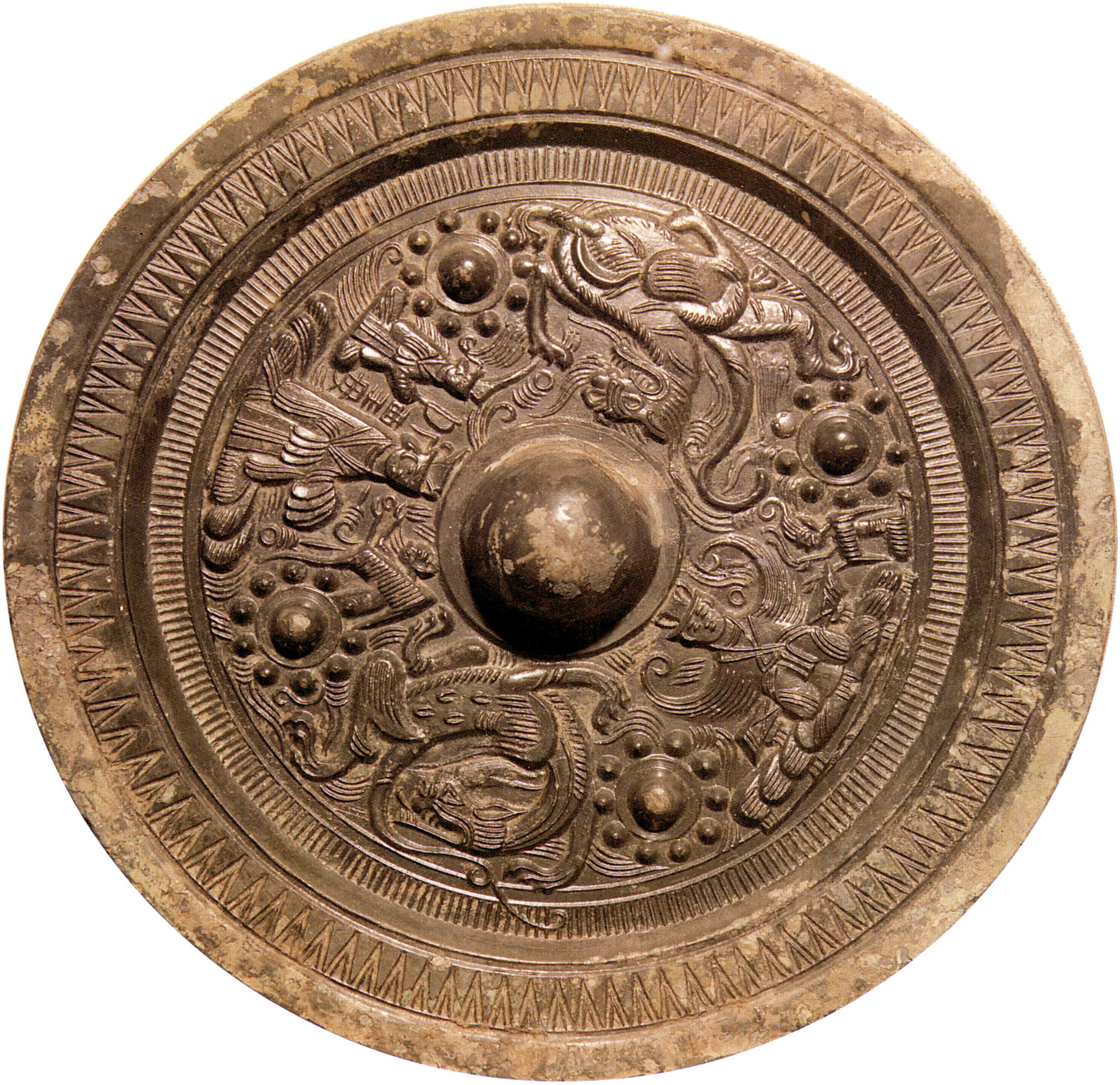

A-Z
CODEX GODS

which became the first human. She then made more copies, and speeded up the process by flicking mud everywhere — each piece coalescing into a person as it landed. She then taught them how to survive and reproduce, and as a result she was also worshiped as a protector goddess

OKUNINUSHI

Okuninushi was the Japanese god of medicine and sorcery, who struggled against Amaterasu's attempts to rule the Yamato lands of central Honshu. Okuninushi had eighty brothers, all competing for the hand of the princess Suseri-Hime, the daughter of Susanoo and his wife Kusanada-Hime. On their way to woo the princess, all eighty of them passed and ignored or taunted an agonized hairless rabbit, which was in fact a deity in disguise. The only exception was Okuninushi, who successfully cured the unfortunate creature. Through this compassionate display he gained the princess Yagami-hime as his bride, though it cost him the benevolence of his brothers, who according to legend fought and killed him in various ways. Okuninushi however, would always regenerate. A much sterner test came from his father-in-law Susanoo, who also tried to kill him with subterfuge, snakes and fire. Okuninushi survived these attempts, sometimes with help, and finally escaped along with the storm god's sword and bow, with which he quelled his brothers. He ultimately had to cede first place to Amaterasu, but joined the pantheon as an immortal. The sword, along with the mirror used to lure Amaterasu from her cave and her magatama beads became the three divine objects that conferred legitimacy on the Japanese royal line.

ONI

The Oni were the evil demons of Japanese mythology — interfering spirits who brought about catastrophe, disease and ill luck. They were anthropomorphic, but had three eyes apiece and horns, with wide leering mouths and talons on both their hands and their feet. They also had a hawk-like ground-attack flight capability, swooping down to steal the souls of the cursed and evil. Buddhist monks therefore developed a psychic air-defense to cope with this malevolent anti-human weapons system. It involved exorcism and safeguard procedures designed to prevent the Oni gaining footholds from which to operate opportunistically. Though not as state of the art as the Oni in military terms, the Tengu — perhaps originating through the Indian Garuda — were a similar breed. Seen as the reincarnations of particularly unpleasant and arrogant nobility, they were naturally ill disposed towards humanity in general, and were endowed with a large vicious streak that made violence and depravity enjoyable.

Right: This bronze Chinese mirror depicting, Heng-O on the moon was produced during the T'ang Dynasty (618–906 AD) and shows Heng-O under the Cassia tree while a hare pounds the elixir of life.

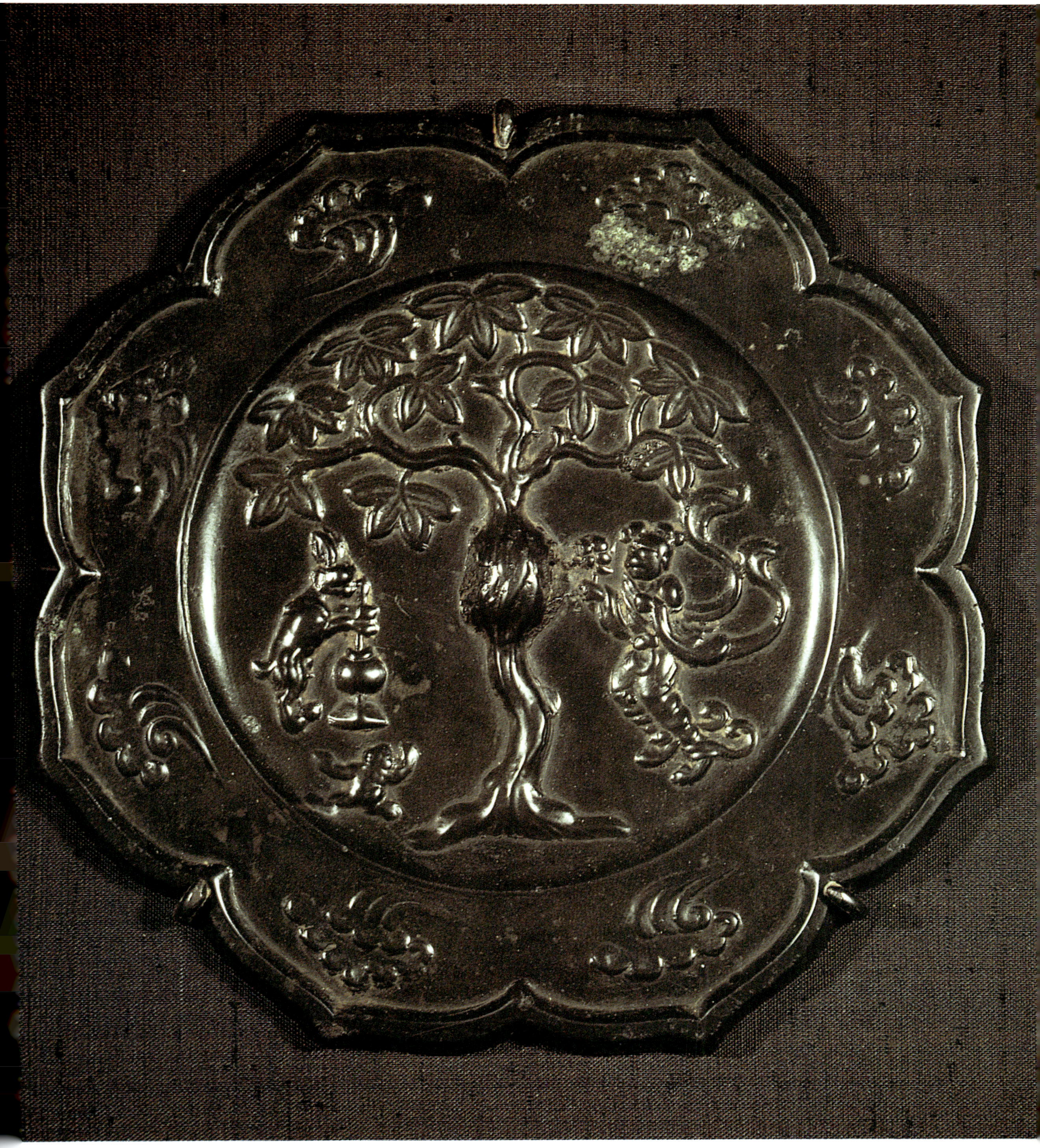

A-Z
CODEX GODS

O-WATA-TSUMI

O-Wata-Tsumi was the chief Japanese sea and water god, one of the deities created by Izanagi as he purified himself after his visit to hell. He aided Amaterasu's great grandson Yamasachi in his dispute with his brother Umisachi. The two brothers had swapped their traditional occupations of hunting and fishing, but Yamasachi had failed to catch any fish and lost his brother's special fish-hook into the bargain, so he descended under the sea in an attempt to recover it. There he met and fell in love with Toyotama-Hime, the sea-god's daughter. O-Wati-Tsumi approved of the match and helped Yamasachi find the missing fish-hook, also providing him with a magic jewel which he later used to subdue his arrogant elder brother. The child of the union was the ancestor of the first Emperor, Jimmu.

P'AN-KU
Also known as: Pan-Gu

Pan-Ku was a primal Chinese creator god, the child of the fusion between the elemental forces of Ying and Yang. For thousands of years he germinated inside an egg, which, when it finally hatched, broke into two pieces and became the heavens and the earth. Then, in order to increase the distance between these two, he stood up, remaining upright for a few more thousand years until the two sections had hardened into place. Then he lay down and died, and, as his corpse disintegrated, the individual parts changed, becoming various features of the landscape. His head formed the sun and moon, his blood became the rivers and seas, his hair grew into forests and his sweat became moisture and rain, his breath the wind, his voice thunder and his fleas the ancestors of mankind! This is, in fact, in keeping with the Chinese attitude concerning man and nature. For them man is merely a single element in the complex pattern of life — just one creature of many and his position is not center-stage. Instead he should strive for balance and harmony with the outside that he finds and the inside he discovers. This theme is reflected in the relative proportions of the Chinese figurative arts such as their landscape painting and sculpture.

RADIN

Radin was a legendary leader of the Sea Dayaks of Borneo, to whom later myth attributes the introduction of smallpox to his home island. For a deliberate, arrogant and hubristic error in correct ritual procedure for the god Sengalang Burong following a great victory over a rival tribe Radin was punished, with a plague of smallpox killing his people. He sought to atone for his sin as much as he could by attempting to slay the hungry ghost which hunted his people at night, singing of flesh's sweetness. Radin lay in wait for this spirit one night and slashed at it in the dark with his *golok* (machete), feeling the resistance of what he took to be the ghostly body. However the next

Right: This Chinese "chueh" or pitcher is made of bronze and dates back to the Shang dynasty (12 BC).

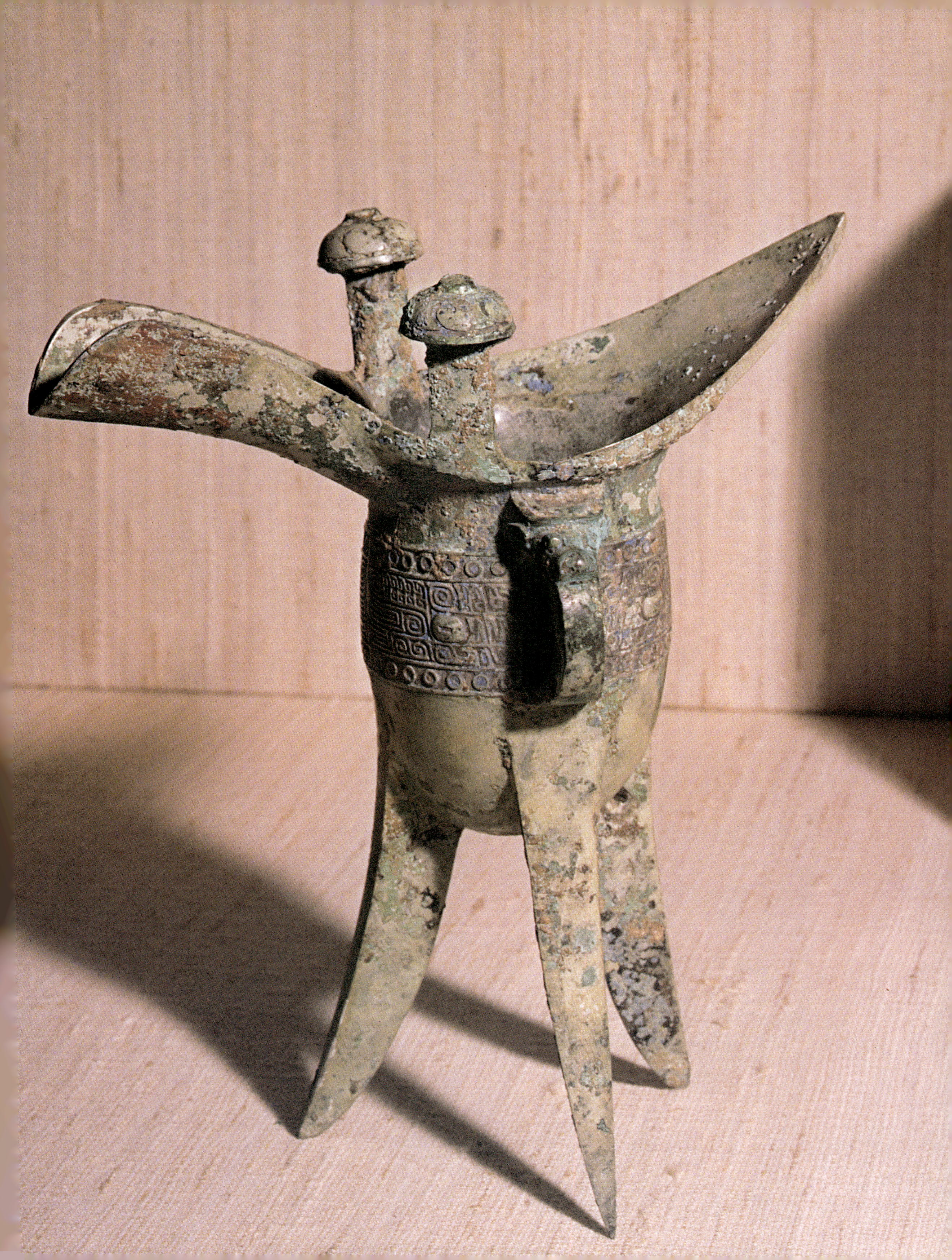

A-Z
CODEX GODS

day he discovered that the image of Sengalang Burong had received a huge wrent from a *golok* strike. On seeking the advice of the tribal elders Radin was told that the image of Sengalang Burong was too dangerous and unpredictable to remain inside the village and should therefore be swiftly exported. This task was achieved and the plague passed, Radin had learnt his lesson and resumed correct ritual procedure.

RATI
"Erotic desire"
Rati is the Balinese version of a Hindu fertility goddess, portrayed as heavily pregnant yet still lascivious. She is a surreal mix of the maternal and the sexual, depicted as she is as a large mammaried, maternal woman with a juxtaposing vampish voluptuousness. Bali's old animist links survive with a mythology packed with demons, of which Rati is an example. This goddess taunts and mocks those ascetic religious males who abstain from feminine company, and is guaranteed to get hardcore puritans riled. Rati is a manifestation of female energy in all its forms and reflects the more realistic and imaginative Indian approach to mythology and religion, which allows and acknowledges considerably more variation than the sole role permitted a female deity within Christianity and the other Semitic monotheisms.

SAN KUAN
"The Three Rulers"
This trio of elemental gods consisted of T'ien (Heaven), Ti (Earth) and Shui (Water). Taoist belief considered them transcendent powers who were the source of happiness, sins repented and protection from evil respectively, whereas Buddhist myth connected them with the Three Immortals T'ang Huang, Ko Yung and Chou Wu, who were the deified ministers of a Sung emperor and whose role was as protective spirits.

SHEN NUNG
Legendary ruler of China, who introduced the benefits of agriculture and taught the skills of medicinal herbs, which illustrates the Chinese connection between cooking and medecine. Shen Nung possessed a see-through stomach which enabled him to observe the effects of his experiments and refine his treatments, though ultimately he became too experimental and came to grief when testing a kind of grass which caused his intestines to burst.

SHITENNO
Indomitable astral guardians of the planet, portrayed as a kingly figures wearing body armor and carrying various hand weapons. The Shitenno were the sentinels of the four cardinal points and directions. To the East was Jikoku, to the South Zocho; in the West dwelt Komoku and in the North Bishamon, also known as Tamon.

Right: Wooden models such as this one of the main Shinto shrine at Ise, are common in Japanese homes.

217

A-Z
CODEX GODS

SHOTEN
Shoten was the Japanese Ganesha variant — the elephant-headed Hindu god of wisdom and literature and remover of obstacles In Japan he was associated with Tantric ritual, including one in which he was manifested in the sexual union of both male and female versions of himself. Shoten and Kwannon were thus joined in "non-duality" as a divine couple, representing the manifestation of enlightenment.

SUKUNA-BIKO
"The Small Lord of Renown"
The Japanese dwarf god, Sukuna-Biko was the ally and confederate of Okuninushi, the son-in-law of Susanoo and king of Izumo. He was highly skilled in both agriculture and medicine. His size belied his knowledge and energy as he traveled continuosly and knew almost everything that was going on in the world.

SUSANOO
"Valiant, Swift, Impetuous Deity"
Susanoo was the Japanese thunder, rain and storm god, who, from the moment of his spontaneous birth as his father Izanagi rinsed himself off after returning from hell, retained some essence of his hellish origins; beginning his career with trouble and interference. Susanoo's trickster pranks were initially more down to his ebullient over-the-top character than any great malice, but as time progressed he became increasingly malign. He competed endlessly with his sister, the sun goddess Amaterasu, and when she would not acknowledge his supremacy he terrified her so much that she hid herself away. He was thus the author of the resulting chaos, and later also slew the earth goddess Ogetsu-no Hime. For these crimes he was expelled from Heaven and banished to the earth, where he wandered for some time before he fought and overcame a monster, winning the magical sword from within its tail and gaining the hand of Princess Kusanada-Hime as well inheriting the kingdom he had saved in the process. He later obstructed his son-in-law Okuninushi in any way he could, until the latter's perseverance and ingenuity won him over.

TAOISM
One of the two main branches of Chinese belief systems, the other being Confucianism. Both were philosophic approaches to the problems of existence, emphasizing balance and moderation, tempered with wisdom leading to enlightenment in everyday dealings with the world. This "Way" or "Tao" anticipated the Buddhist "Middle Way," and, in fact, when Buddhism came to China it was incorporated into this indigenous philosophic religion quite seamlessly — just as with Buddhism and the local Shinto religion in Japan. Lao Tzu was the mythical author of the *Tao te Ching*; a book of maxims that offers observations and advice tinged with philosophic

Right: A 17th century soapstone carving of Shou-Lao, the Chinese god of longevity. Visible are the crane and the deer which are both symbols of immortality.

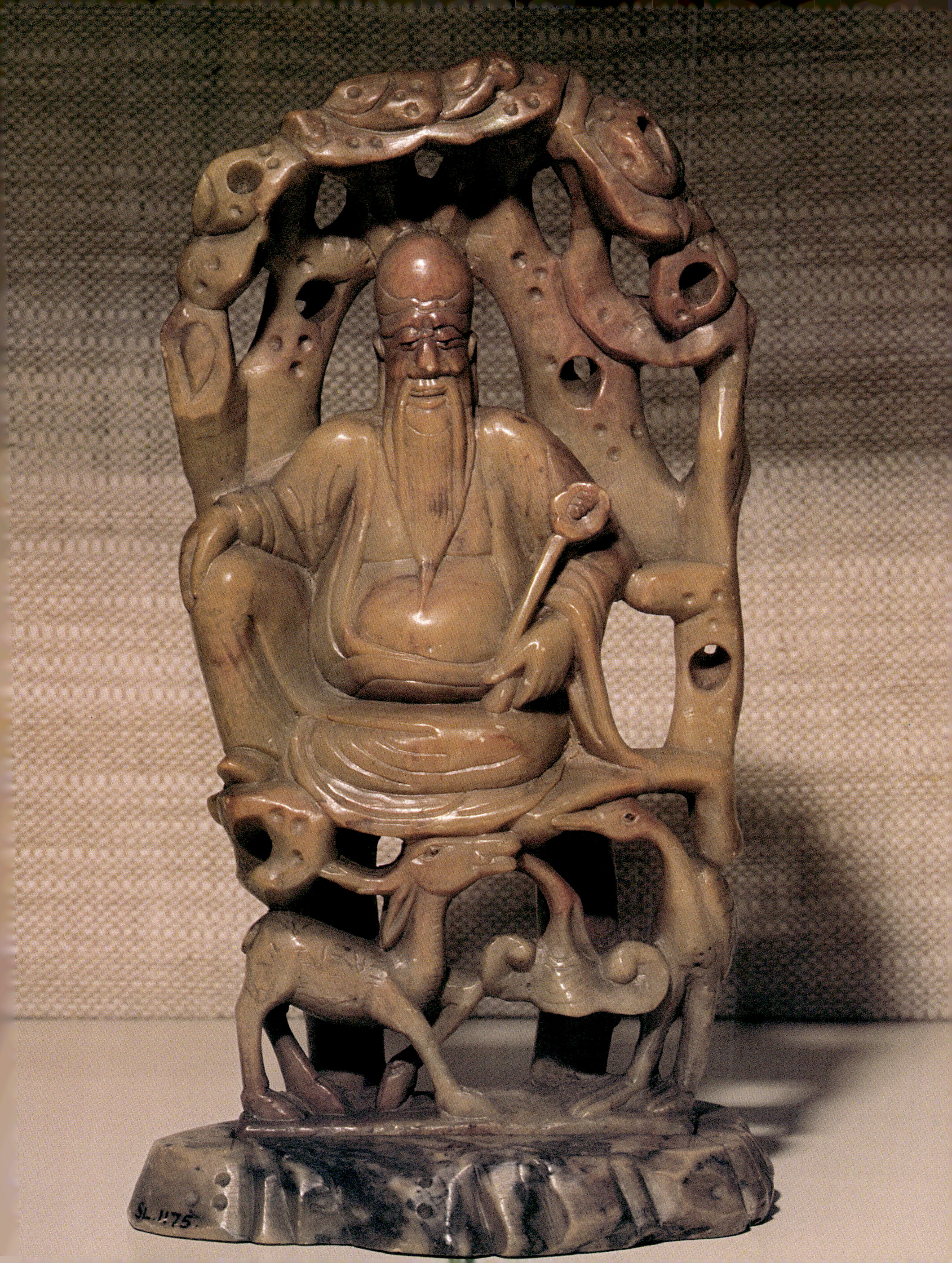
SL.1175.

A-Z
CODEX GODS

objectivity, which along with the *Chuang Tzu* and *Lieh Tzu Tao* were central to both Taoism and Confucianism. In Taoism the I-Ching is used for divination, through the reading of the pattern of yarrow-stalks (or coins nowadays) when shuffled and thrown down. The resulting hexagrams can then be built up and referred to in the commentary that accompanies the I-Ching, which is attributed to Confucius. As Buddhism spread, Taoism became more of a national religion and an organized church than a philosophic system, adopting and incorporating local gods and myths into a native pantheon. It already had a syncretistic base of animism and ancestor worship combined with an underpinning of philosophic theory and action which gave it the confidence and the capability to mix and merge with philosophical and religious imports.

T'AI SHAN
"Holy Emperor"

The sacred mountain T'ai Shan was honored by Taoists, Confucians and Buddhists alike. The annual spring sacrifices to Shang-Ti on the summit was performed by the emperor, and for centuries it was the premier attraction for pilgrims. The mountain manifests the supreme terrestrial deity to Taoists, who named it Shang-ti — "Holy Emperor." He controls destiny, apportions birth and death and is Lord of the Yellow Springs — the Chinese underworld.

TENGRI
"God," "Sky" or "Heaven"

The supreme sky god of the Mongols, Tengri was held to have created the whole of visible and invisible reality, over which he then ruled. He was also in control of destiny and fate, factoring them into each individual's life equation. Meteorites and other natural sky phenomena were seen as Tengri's portents and communications, and the Mongols had an expression which indicated his supreme status: "The Sky Decrees."

TRIPITAKA
Also known as: Hsuan-tsang, Yuan-tsang and T'ang-seng

Best known affectionately as Tripitaka, Hsuan-tsang was the pilgrim incarnate. In 629 AD he began his awesome overland trek accompanied by Monkey to the holy land of India to fetch manuscripts of Buddhist doctrine and where for sixteen years he studied and underwent instruction, eventually returning home to take the Buddha's teaching with him. No one knows the exact date of Buddhism's introduction into China but there is record (from around 65 AD) of a Shantung prince who incorporated the union of Taoism and Buddhism into his religious observance and protocols, which is the first instance of such a paradigm. In the beginning though little literature was available, which left the teachings somewhat shrouded in mystery

Right: A Chinese ivory of T'ien Kung, master of the heaven made during the famous Ming dynasty (16th–17th century).

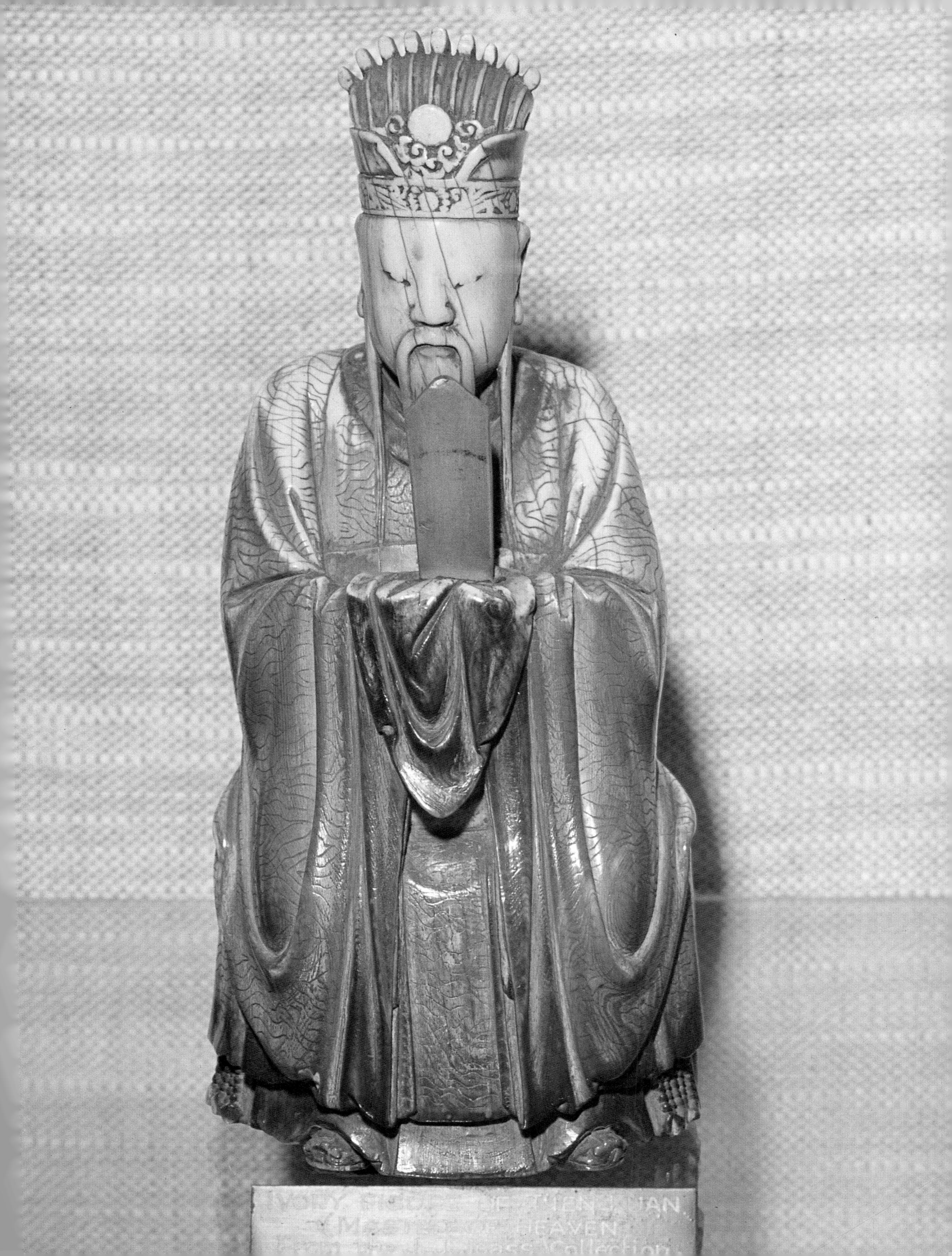
HEAVEN
Collection

A-Z
CODEX GODS

and open to incorporation, interpretation and improvisation, which made the mix of Taoism and Buddhism that much easier. Clearing these mists was the prime role of Tripitaka's Indian mission, and his journey itself threw up a cycle of adventures and legends. In fact Tripitaka's pilgrimage mythology became an extraordinarily popular part of Chinese folklore. Incorporating many other characters and deities, the stories are filled with fantastic events including magical encounters, matter transformation, psychic warfare, and telekinesis. Accompanied by Hanuman the monkey god, and sometimes other animals or deities, his adventures were entertaining yet educational. In time they became almost children's stories of knockabout, slapstick humor.

TSAO CHUN

Tsao Chun was the domestic kitchen god of Chinese mythology. Very ancient, his normal place was a small niche close to the vital cooker in Chinese houses, from there he supplied a kind of spiritual electricity that aided successful physical and therefore mental nourishment and ensured the prevention of negative energy and psychic pollution of food sources. He was in other words a kind of psychoactive Food Commission or Health and Safety standards inspector, who monitored and modified the kitchen and food preparation. He was portrayed as a kindly old man surrounded by children.

UKULAN-TOJON

Ukulan-Tojon was the water god or spirit of the Yakuts. Like all Mongolians and Siberians, the Yakuts held beliefs similar to the shamanist and animist views of the North American Indians, to whom they were related. They believed that the world was controlled by manifestations of animistic energy, and that all living things — from a tree to an animal — possessed a spirit. The Altai Tartars referred to this spirit as *Kut*, which was possessed by natural phenomena and animals, as well as by humankind. A strong master-spirit had command over lesser ones, with the more powerful and pertinent natural features dominating. Ukulan-Tojon was the mighty water lord of great importance, for water was particularly venerated by the Mongols, who conducted complex rituals and sacrifices in order to cross rivers safely, with some tribes even having taboos on washing. Others believed that certain rivers disgorged into a hell ruled by soul-eating animal spirits with transforming capabilities.

URASHIMA

Urashima was a fisherman of Japanese legend, who married a mermaid and dwelt with her in an undersea luxury palace. For a while their lives were blissful, but eventually he began to pine and miss his life on land, whereupon he begged his wife to enable him to see his famil, and visit

Right: This head of the Japanese god Haniwa was unearthed from a 6th century tomb.

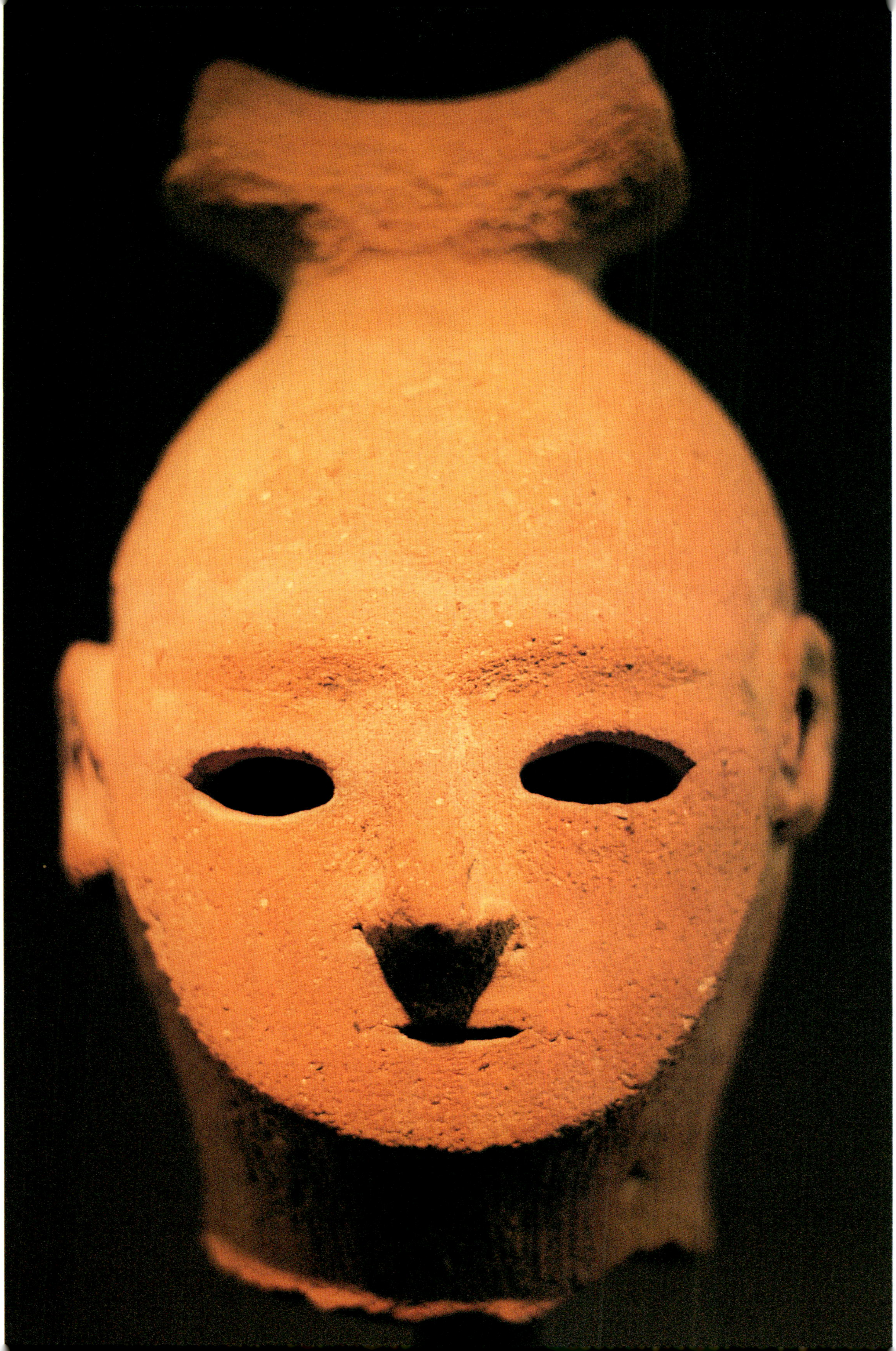

A-Z
CODEX GODS

the world of air again. To allow him to do this without mishap his undersea wife gave him a black box which would ensure a safe outward journey and return provided its integrity remained intact. Urashima set off, but when he arrived onshore he discovered to his chagrin that centuries had passed by and his family and everyone else he knew were dead, and in bitterness broke open the black box. As he did so a small explosion occurred, and instantly his body caught up with time — ageing, withering, dying and turning to dust in the equivalentnumber of seconds.

YENG-WANG-YEH

Also known as: Emma-O, Yama

Known in India as Yama the Hindu god of death, and exported to China as part of Buddhist mythology he became Yeng-wang-yeh, the foremost Lord of Death in the Yellow Springs — the Chinese underworld. His mission was the implication of the law of retribution, but as this was an automatic system it left him as a mere tormentor of souls in transit, and thus somewhat limited in scope.

There were ten of these deathlords altogether, and at Yeng-wang-yeh's court it was decided to what part of the underworld each of the dead would be assigned, for there were also ten courts, each presided over by a deathlord, and each specializing in a particular area of sin or crime. Having metamorphosed in China, in Japan he changed again — into Emma-O, the merciless, black-faced judge of souls, and the ruler of a kingdom that was the antithesis of Heaven. Ever unswayed, Emma-O cynically but correctly assumed that those who ended up being processed by his administration were persona non grata anywhere else, giving him free rein to indulge his own cruel foibles.

YI

Also known as: I, Hou I, Hou Yi.

I was the Chinese god of bowmen, who killed the Nine Suns and was exiled from Heaven as a result along with his wife, Ch'ang-O. There were originally Ten Suns, but when their schedule got mixed up they all shone at once and their heat became so fierce that the world began to burn up. So I, the "Excellent Archer" shot down nine of them, leaving only the remaining one. As a result of this he was exiled to earth. I then went in search of the Elixir of Immortality. He was eventually given it by the Queen Mother of the West, who lived on the slopes of the holy mountain named Kunlun. The elixir was to be of little use to him though, for his wife stole it in an attempt to become immortal and return to Heaven. As it was she was destined to remain on the moon and become its goddess, but I himself was eventually readmitted to Heaven. At that time in China science and sorcery co-existed and combined amicably — somewhat like alchemy. Wizards and astronomers all

Right: This Japanese wooden figure served as a guardian at the temple gates.

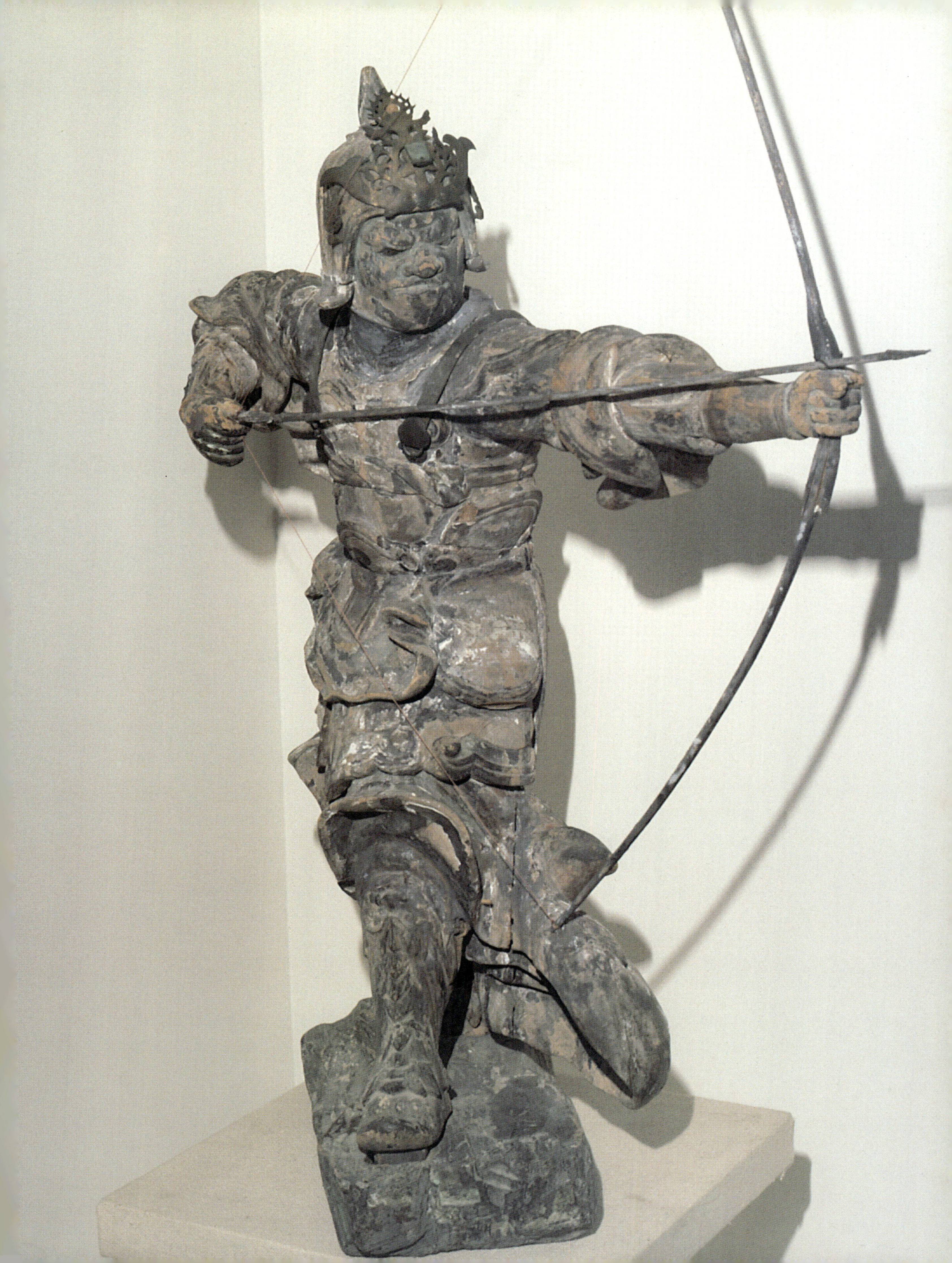

A-Z
CODEX GODS

acknowledged the underlying union of man with his enviroment and were drawn into the administration.

YIN AND YANG

Yin represents the female, cold, dark, earth and sustenance; and Yang the male, heat, light, Heaven, creation and dominance. Together they represent the concept of the two balancing, interactive, cyclically operating cosmic forces of Chinese philosophy and religion. From these two conciliatory opposites everything else is produced — all of which contains the Yin-Yang essence in various formulas and ratios. Within each one is an aspect or element of the other, revealing them to be complementary as well as contradictory. Thus they manifest the duality of the universe and represent the opposing but mutually dependent tones and textures of life.

YU

Also known as: Yu-huang-shang-ti

Yu is Father of Heaven and the supreme Jade Emperor in Chinese mythology. He was the divine equivalent of the earthly human emperors, and as such was especially and significantly worshiped by them. His court in Heaven was also a replica of that on earth, complete with an administrative bureaucracy. Yu-huang-shang-ti is said to have created humankind out of clay, but when he left the clay figures outside to dry it began to rain, and by the time he rescued them some had melted a little (the ancient Chinese saw this as the reason that some people were born deformed). He then introduced the science of irrigation to humankind, becoming famous for his aquatic technology. When asked by the divine monarch to help limit the damage during a deluge, he set about complex hydraulic engineering operations that culminated in the successful containment of the floodwaters.

Yu-huang-shang-ti was also the legendary ancestor of the first Hsia dynasty. Esteemed as a paragon of virtue and public service by the Confucians, he was regarded somewhat dubiously by Taoists who feared the repercussions of his industrial incursions into the natural world, with its artificial control systems that overrode the natural laws.

ZODIAC

Along with a dating system now used concurrently with the dominant Western (Gregorian) timeframe, the Chinese from ancient times have also assigned animals to each year as well as the hours of the day. These are Rat, Ox, Tiger, Hare, Dragon, Snake, Horse, Sheep, Monkey, Fowl, Dog and Pig. Thus the year of one's birth was the operative astrological factor. In fact their indigenous calendar is based upon lunar rather than solar cycles.

Above left: A netsuke of the rat, one of twelve animals in the Japanese zodiac.
Right: A close-up of a Chinese plate produced during the K'ang Hai (1661–1722) period showing Chinese sages using the yin-yang symbol to read the future.

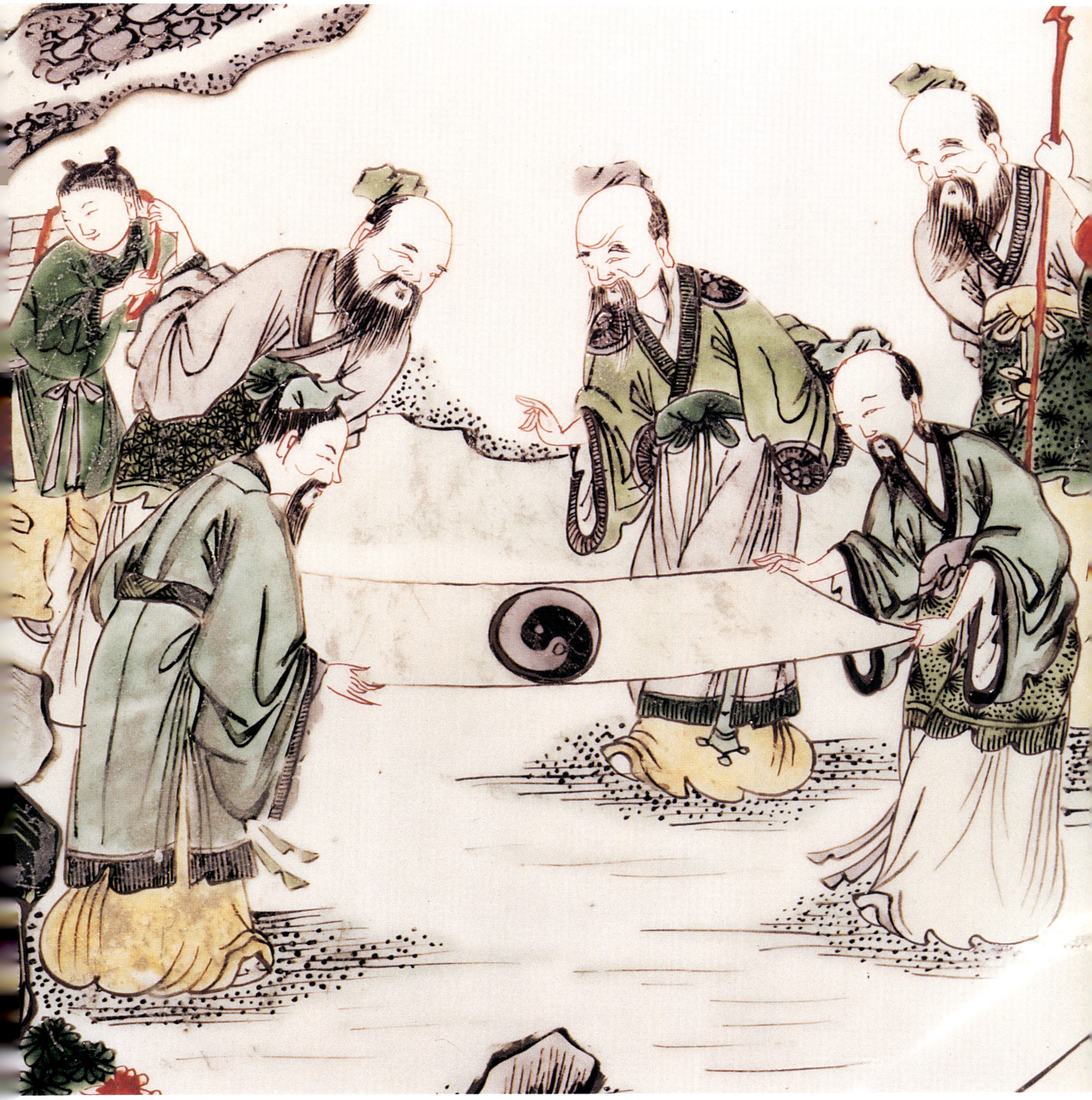

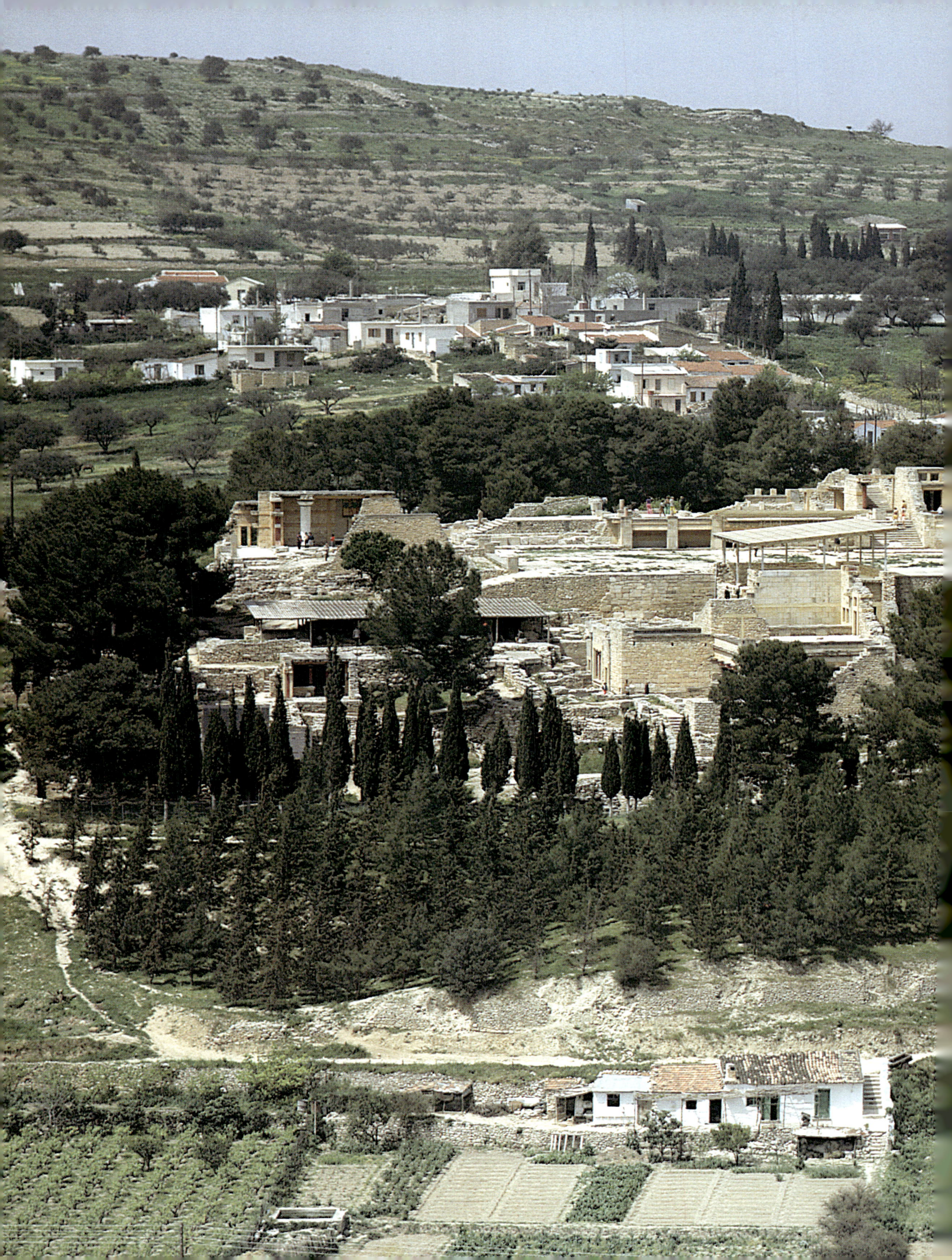

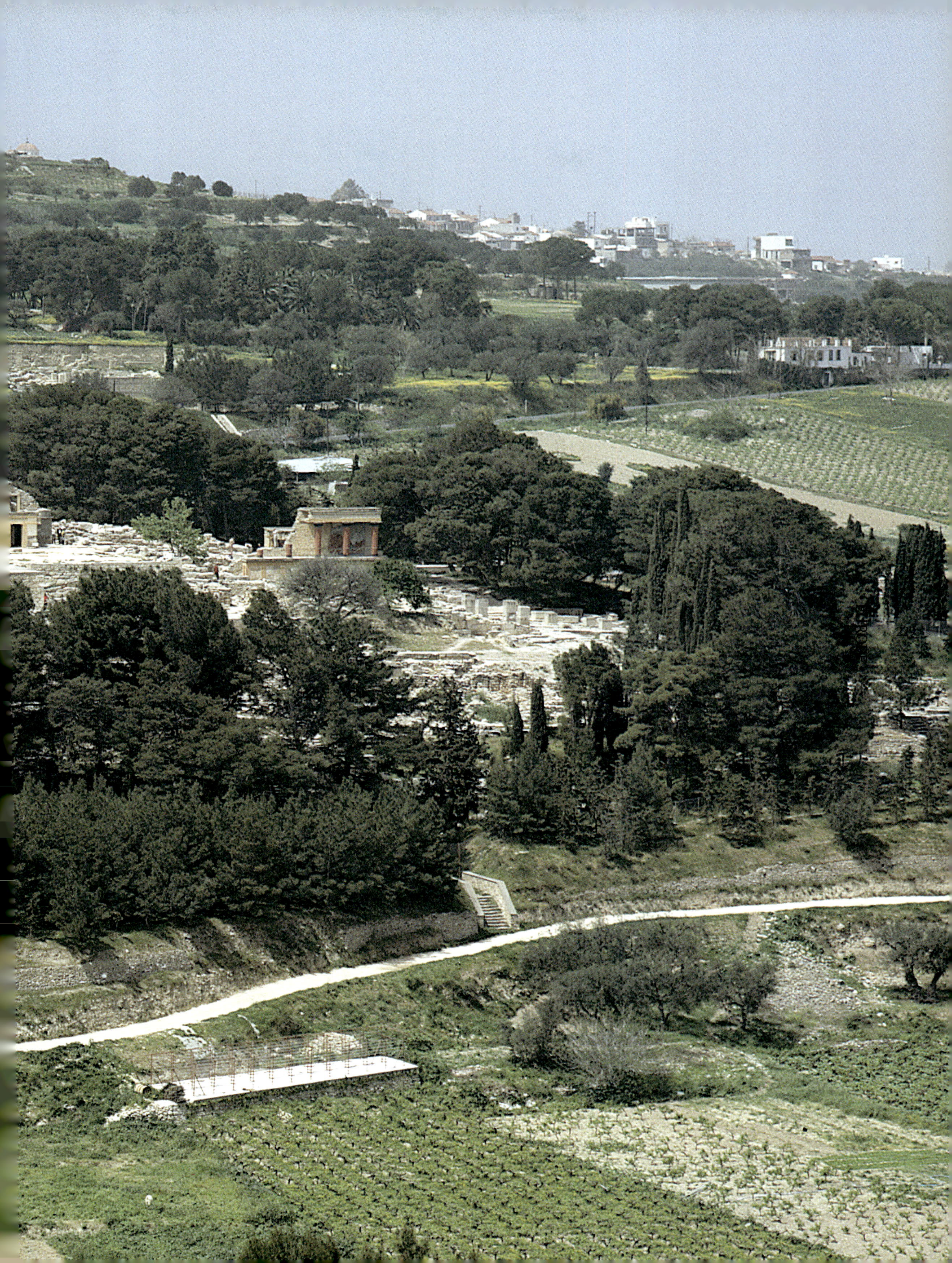

EUROPE

PRE-CLASSICAL

The pre-classical pantheon of ancient Europe had more in common with other ancient areas of the globe, and can only really be pieced together by the meticulous analysis of relatively few primary sources and clues. There are archeological sites which reveal much information concerning the practical aspects of day to day life — structures, food, farming, weapons and burial contents and techniques — but of the people's oral culture nothing remains other than visual representations — the artwork — with which to attempt interpretation of those mental processes that constitute a human's life — the prevalent hopes, fears and beliefs.

The chief deities were obviously the chthonic mother and fertility goddesses, centering on the vital requirement of continuity and fertility to counter the reality of short life-spans. The emphasis upon the mother indicates a human grouping not dissimilar to our closest primate relatives — monkeys and chimpanzees. They too live in matriarchal societies dominated by a few guardian, sperm bank males who defend tribal areas and provide breeding material for a female dominated core. The latter then evolve complex communication, organizational procedures and hierarchies.

CRETE AND MYCENAE

Gradually, fertility deities and rituals became more complicated, combined perhaps with growing settlement, farming and observation of natural phenomena, including increased awareness of time and season, sun, moon, stars and tides. Even the earliest recorded "data" civilization, known as Minoan and hailing from Crete (poised centrally in the Mediterranean it had West Asian and African influences), was mother-dominated, chthonic, and fertility based.

Previous pages: The Minoan Royal Palace in Crete, Greece. Right: The Lion Gate at Mycenae, Greece

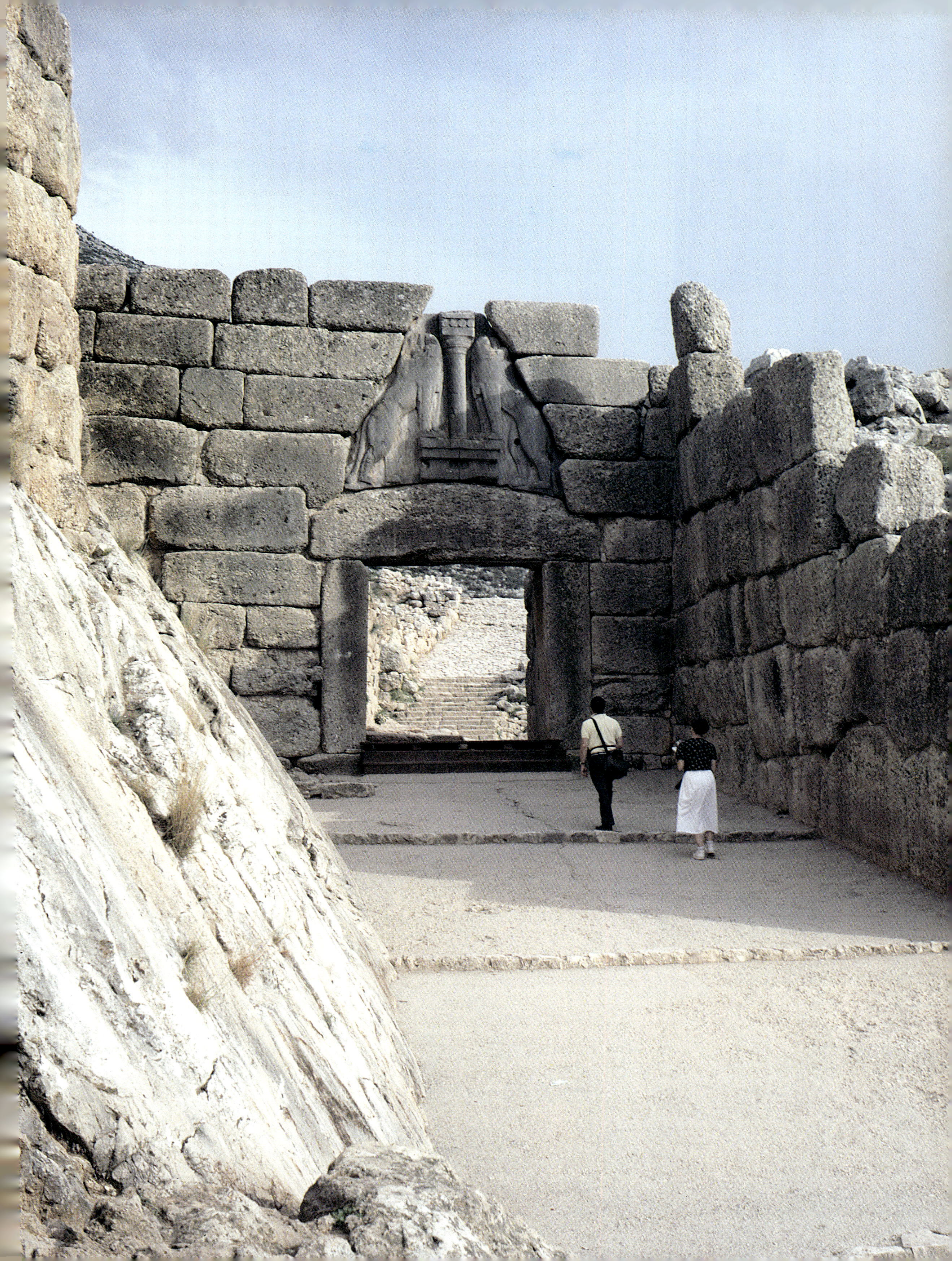

The next developments included the influx of new Aryan pastoralist warriors who worshiped male sky gods. Beginning around 2000 BC the Greeks of the Mycenaean Age, with their metallurgy and social organization, conquered and absorbed the smaller, darker native peoples. There followed the first golden age of Greece — the founding of the first city-states that Homer later mythologized and which became the legendary prototypes of the later Classical Age. After this a mysterious Dark Age ensued. Very little is known about this period, but it brought about the demise of Mycenaean civilization. Perhaps volcanic eruption and earthquake contributed to the breaking down of communications, but also new Greek peoples — the Dorians — came surging in to push the Mycenaeans eastward into Asia Minor, the Cyclades and the Dodecanese. For two hundred years there was an unrecorded chaos until eventually (c. 800 BC) there was a resurgence of the Greek city-states. With their own original and distinctive cultures coupled with West Asian influence, these began to sow the seeds of a civilization that is at the root of our present Western culture.

The Greeks were myth makers par excellence, and much more besides — they developed sciences and arts that continue to resonate in the modern world. However, myth was appropriated by artists, politicians, philosophers, poets and playwrights to illustrate and prove moral, political and intellectual points. These tales were accepted as true, and were widely utilized as a resource to justify expediency and whatever other political purposes — almost like statistics or a point of law today.

In Greek myth the tension between male and female deities is often palpable, and this reflects the wider population changes taking place at the beginning of Europe's recorded

Above left and Right: This soapstone libation vessel is in the shape of a bull's head (1700–1450 BC).

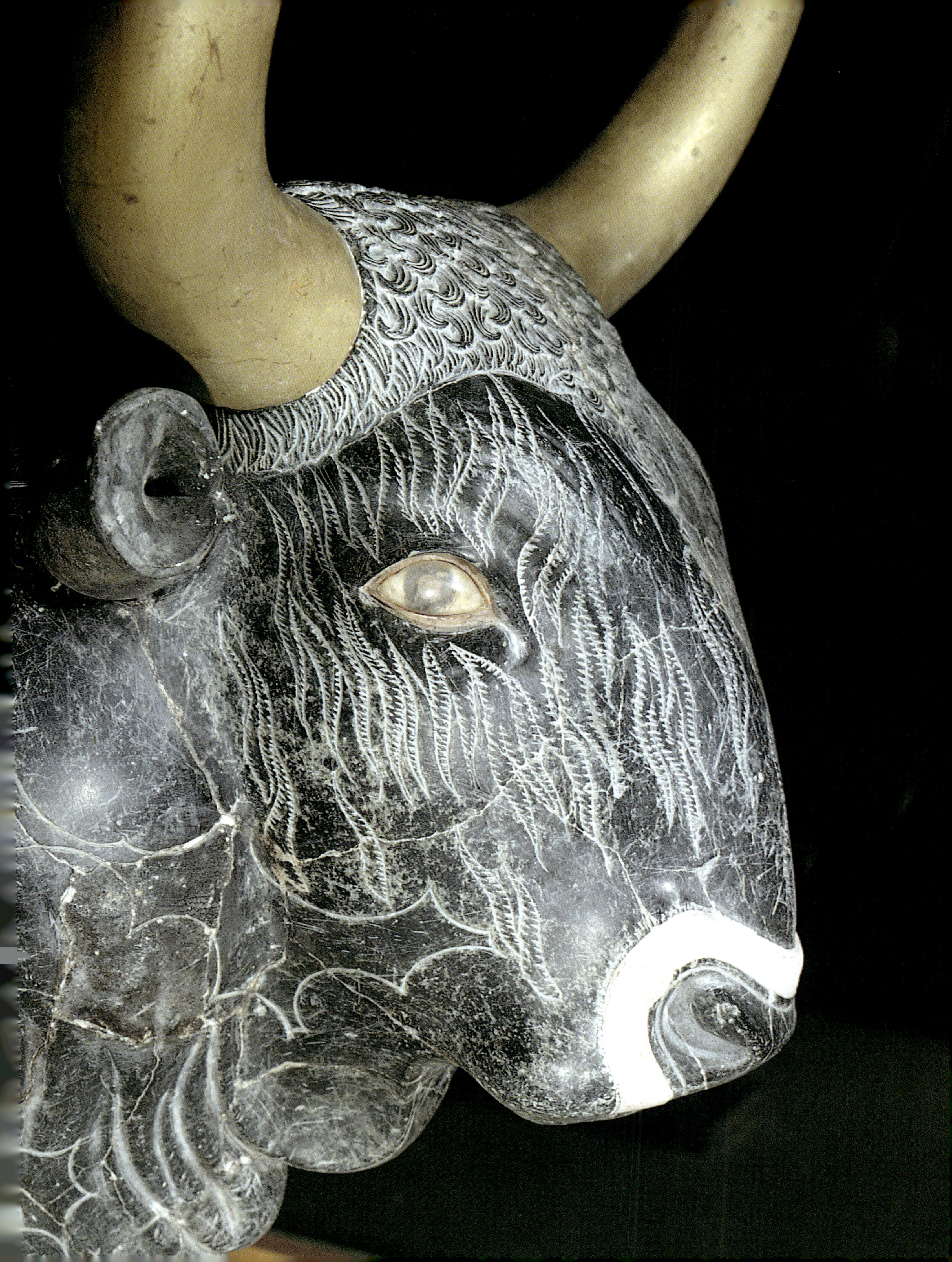

history. There were huge influxes of aggressive warrior based societies to whom movement was both necessary and attractive. Often pushed on by other, fiercer, tribes behind them, they were looking for new pastures. As they spread, the old fertility based matriarchies were conquered and absorbed (although not entirely and not without exceptions); their mother goddesses entering a combined pantheon that had a strong and capable female contingent. The stories that have been passed down, though amusing, belie the deep tension and violence of an unwilling female demotion and male conquest. Even after millennia the remains of the old religions can be seen in tales of the little folk, witches and spirits of the countryside. Earth belief runs deep.

With the development of Greek civilization, an increasingly sophisticated society sought to define and develop its history. Thus Hesiod, one of antiquity's greatest writers and thinkers, attempted to unravel the thick knotted ball of the Indo-European, West Asian and ancient chthonic belief systems that had merged and mutated through migration and war into the extensive mythology of Greece. His task was complicated by a large amount of local variation in the myths due to the Greek geography — scattered islands and short coastal plains cut off by high hinterland — as well as the independent Greek nature that encouraged an individual, cosmopolitan approach to life.

In Mycenaean times each ruling house of a city had its mythic lineage, tracing back to the gods and underlining the inherent justification of specific rule. Later heroes began to set a new precedent, for they relied upon human attributes rather than those of the gods — becoming human rather than divine. This was part of a process whereby humans started to realize ambitions within their own sphere — an intellectual

Above left and Right: A bust of Hesiod, the (8th century BC) Greek poet.

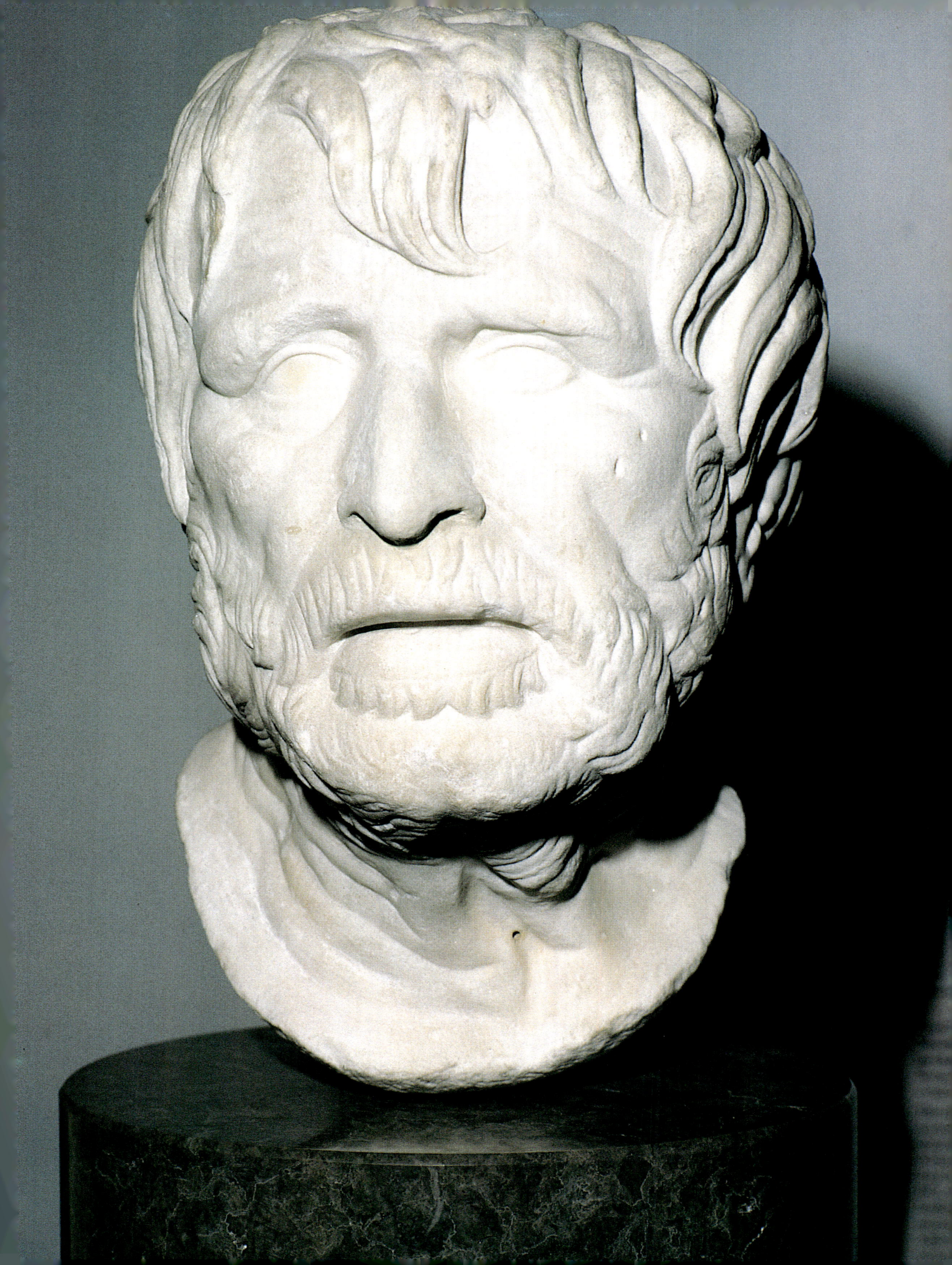

distancing from the previously ubiquitous supernatural forces that had been seen as the fount of all knowledge and in control of human endeavors. Subsequent philosophies broke reality into different fields and became more reliant on dispassionate observation and intellectual effort than divine causality, which increasingly became secondary to human expediency. This was arguably the most important movement of thought in Western history, paving the way for the scientific thought that has so obviously influenced European history. Eventually a combination of Greek arts and sciences, Roman law and organization and West Asian Semitic monarchism and monotheism became the major foundation stones of Western society and European civilization.

Though unique in this intellectual revolution, mythically Greece borrowed heavily from West Asia. Mesopotamia, Egypt, Canaan and Asia Minor all imbued their gods and goddesses with the human impulses and realities that required divine aid for success. Thus the characteristics of the Ancient Sumerian goddess of love Inanna were present in Phoenician Astarte, and as time progressed so Aphrodite took on many of Astarte's responsibilities in refined form. Such a system of human desire and requirement has unceasingly evolved throughout humankind's history.

By the 6th century BC, prototype scientist philosophers were undermining the old ways and arguing new theories and approaches to explain their universe. Though not often accepted at the time by the mass of the population, their ideas were mental dynamite, ticking away like time-bombs to eventually detonate with shattering implications. Meanwhile Greece played out her strength in almost permanent warfare. Refining the arts of war in the process, she nevertheless fell to the subtle machinations of the first grandmaster — Phillip of

Above left: A bronze monument to Leonidas, King of Sparta, who perished in 480 BC while defending the area against invading Persian armies. Right: A bronze hoplite or Spartan soldier, the most feared warrior of the 5th century BC.

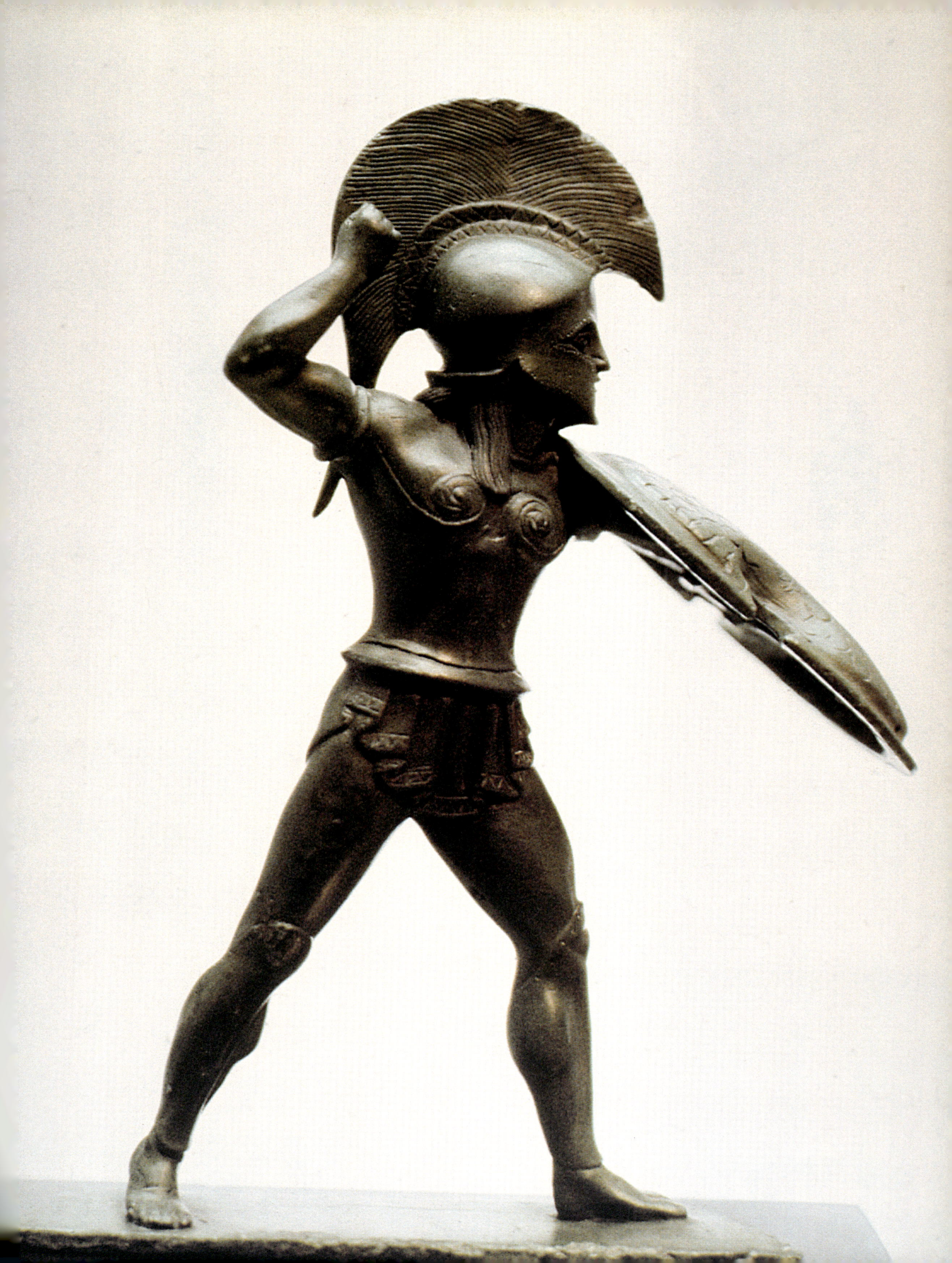

Macedon — who was succeeded after his arrogant demise by his equally extraordinary son, Alexander, the seed of the Hellenistic age. (The power of mythology has still to be acknowledged for the ideals it sets — ideals that inspire dreams of heroism from which empires are made. Alexander was never separated from his copy of Homer's *Iliad*.) Due to Alexander's success in building an empire, the Greek reconvened and restructured West Asian pantheon was launched back across the source countries, to refine and redefine many of the ideas and prototypes that had initially come the other way. The Hellene and Hellenistic culture, equipped with radical new schools of thought would continue to penetrate many societies. These vivid tales and philosophies were the final exuberant releases of an energy that had used its people up, though not their ideas.

ROME

It was left to the early Roman Empire to continue the evolution. Admirably suited to the task in an already discernibly stoical European sense, they seemed to combine utter practicality with a naïvety toward areas into which they were either afraid or incapable of looking. Perhaps they were so realistic as to be completely nonchalant when it came to other gods — for they had no defense against theological invasion from their many conquests. Running such a huge and varied society inevitably involved compromise, and it was in the religious area that the Romans did indeed make concessions, whereas militarily, strategically and economically they did not. The paucity of the Roman spiritual imagination can be gleaned from their behavior and history. They took many of gods and mythologies as direct imports from Greece, in addition to other bizarre deities from

Above left and Right: This theater was built at the ancient site of Ephesus in Turkey (3rd–1st century BC).

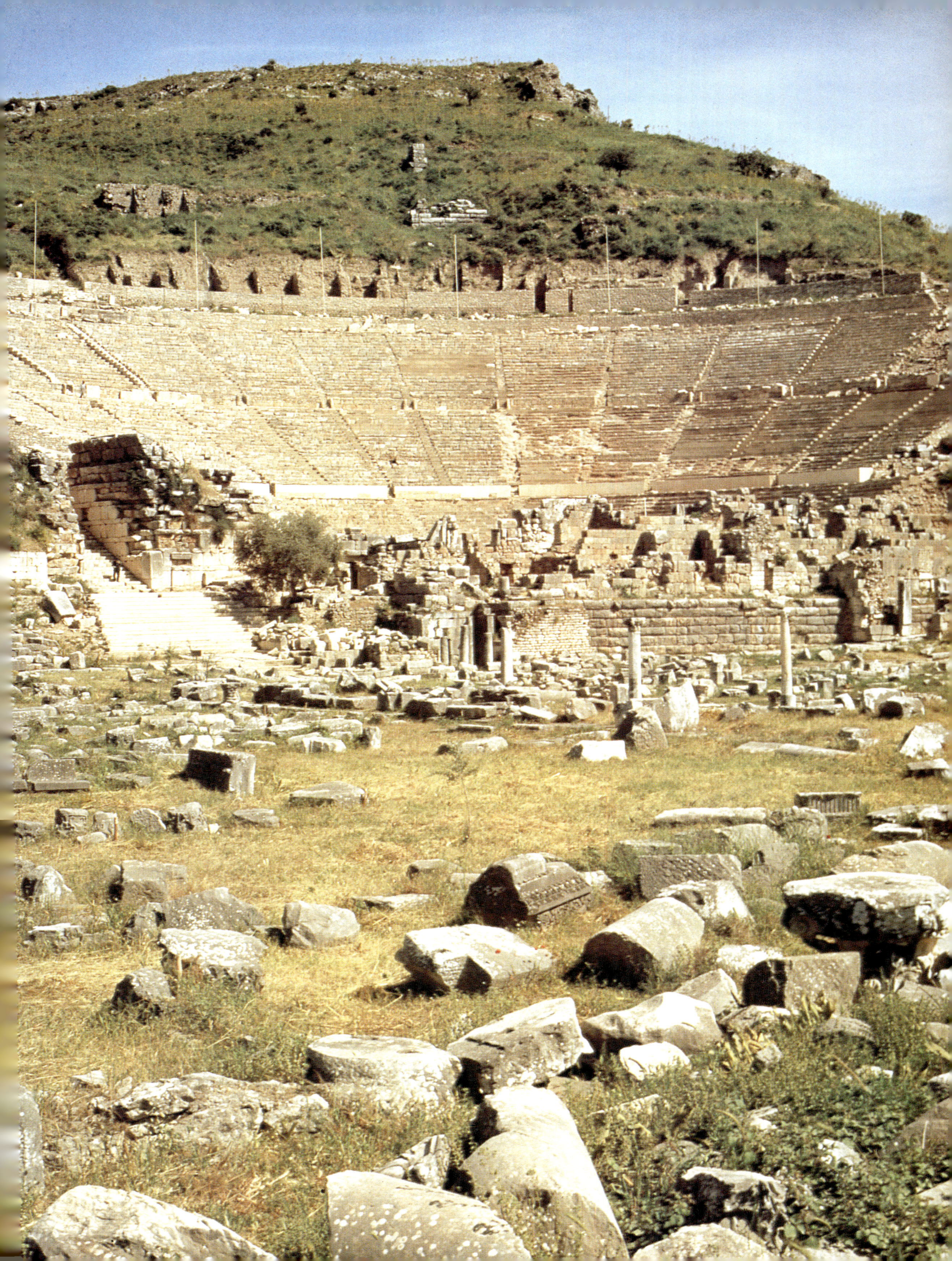

further afield. In their defense it must be said that they were in origin only a single city state whose personal myths were held dear, though such myths could not cover the vast range of empire over which they ended up masters. On another level too, the Romans were so practical that they did not concern themselves overmuch with mythological and philosophical questions, their realities resided in the material benefits of the world, while paying lip service to the gods. That this seems all too similar to modern society is not so surprising when it is accepted that Western civilization is the child of Greece and Rome. Greece supplied the imagination and Rome the more practical aspects of organization. For in organizational, political and legal forms they achieved more than ever before and their hegemony drew the blueprint of the Europe to come.

Roman paranoia following Hannibal's devastating twelve year raid, ensured that Rome became the policeman of the Mediterranean, thereafter attacking anyone who grew large enough to be at threat. They balanced Parthia's western pretensions with eastern ones of their own. They also struck north into Gaul and Germany, stabilizing the borders and holding back the relentless barbarian flood — for a time. Ultimately however, Rome too fell prey to dissension and disunity. The Empire finally split in two and began its slow descent into religious and political anarchy. The Western Empire would fall to the Germanic barbarians in 476 AD while the East would hold out another thousand years as the Byzantine Empire, before finally being eclipsed by the Turks.

CELTS

Celtic culture being oral not much has survived and such that has comes from secondary sources. The Celts first appeared from Germany. Gradually raiding further and further into

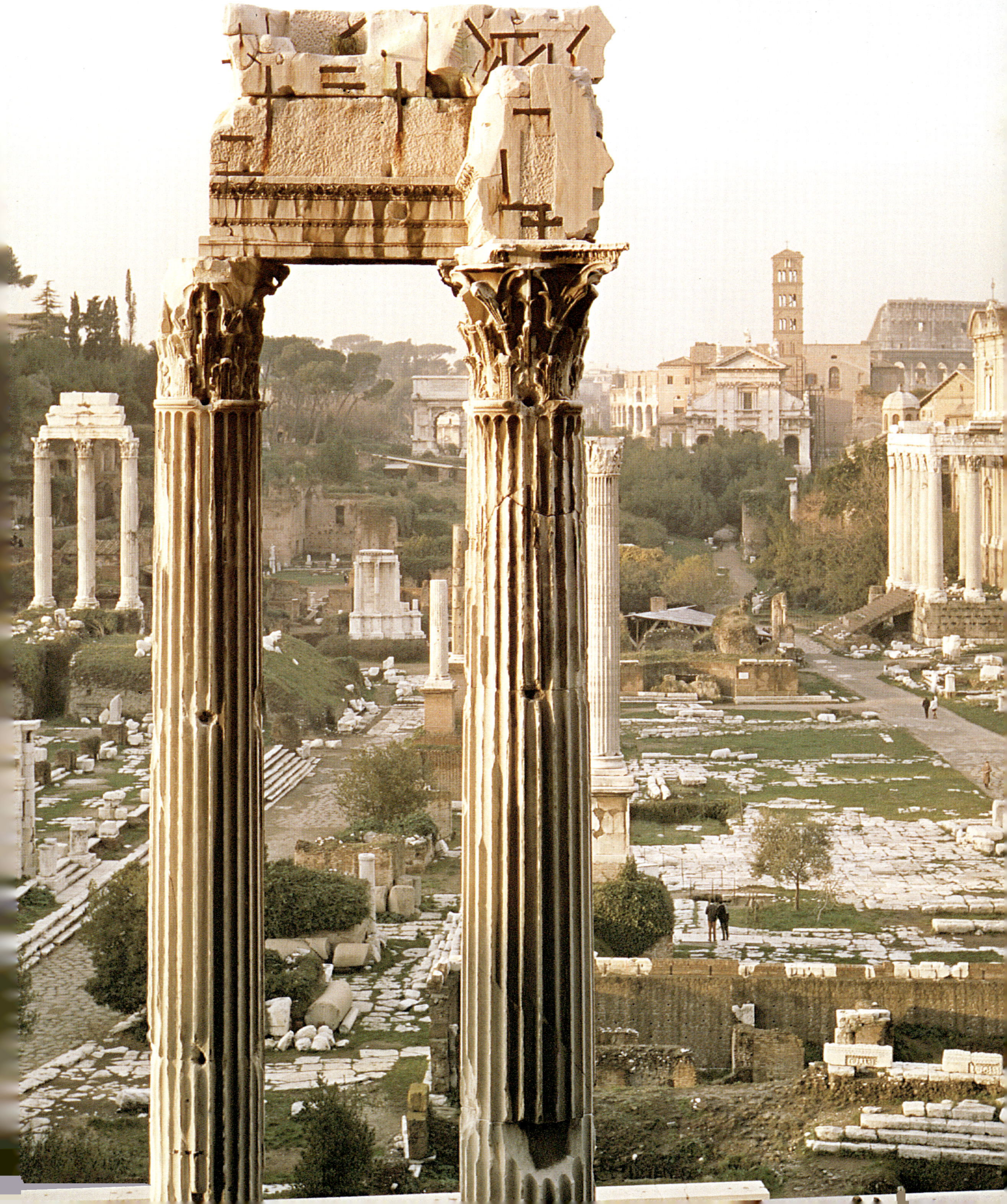

Europe, they eventually had settlements in Gaul, Spain, Britain, Italy and the Balkans. Due to such widespread colonization, their beliefs and customs varied widely and given their independent nature it is perhaps not very surprising there was no Celtic Empire. Gaul, their biggest settlement area, was not in fact even a single state until conquered by Rome. After the mainland Celts had been absorbed there remained only Britain and Ireland — even after Roman conquest Britain remained primarily Celtic speaking. Ireland remained the only Celtic country free from any major outside influence until Christianity and the Vikings arrived. In some ways Ireland is indicative of the Celtic lack of the organization necessary to achieve nation status. Here, though forming a civilization of great artistic and military merit, they remained in loose tribal groups, endlessly at war for a High kingship that remained mythical.

THE NORTHERN LANDS

The Germanic peoples of the Northern Lands originated in a heartland enclosed by the Rhine, Danube and Vistula rivers, from where they spread out in all directions, though their progress south was held up by the Roman Empire for a few centuries. They were fierce and feared fighters who remained pagan long after the rest of Europe had converted to Christianity. In the south they became the inveterate enemy of the Romans, to whom were unknowingly related — to Rome they were literally the barbarians at the gates. In the north they settled into Scandinavia, to burst forth again as waves of awesome sea-raiders who would voyage far and wide in their quest for gold and land. These invaders settled extensively in Britain, Ireland, Coastal Europe, Greenland, Iceland and Russia — where it is said that they began the Slav kingdom

Above left: A Celtic stonehead, uncovered in the former Czechoslovakia (3rd–2nd BC). Right: This headpost shows the detail early Vikings would apply to their ships.

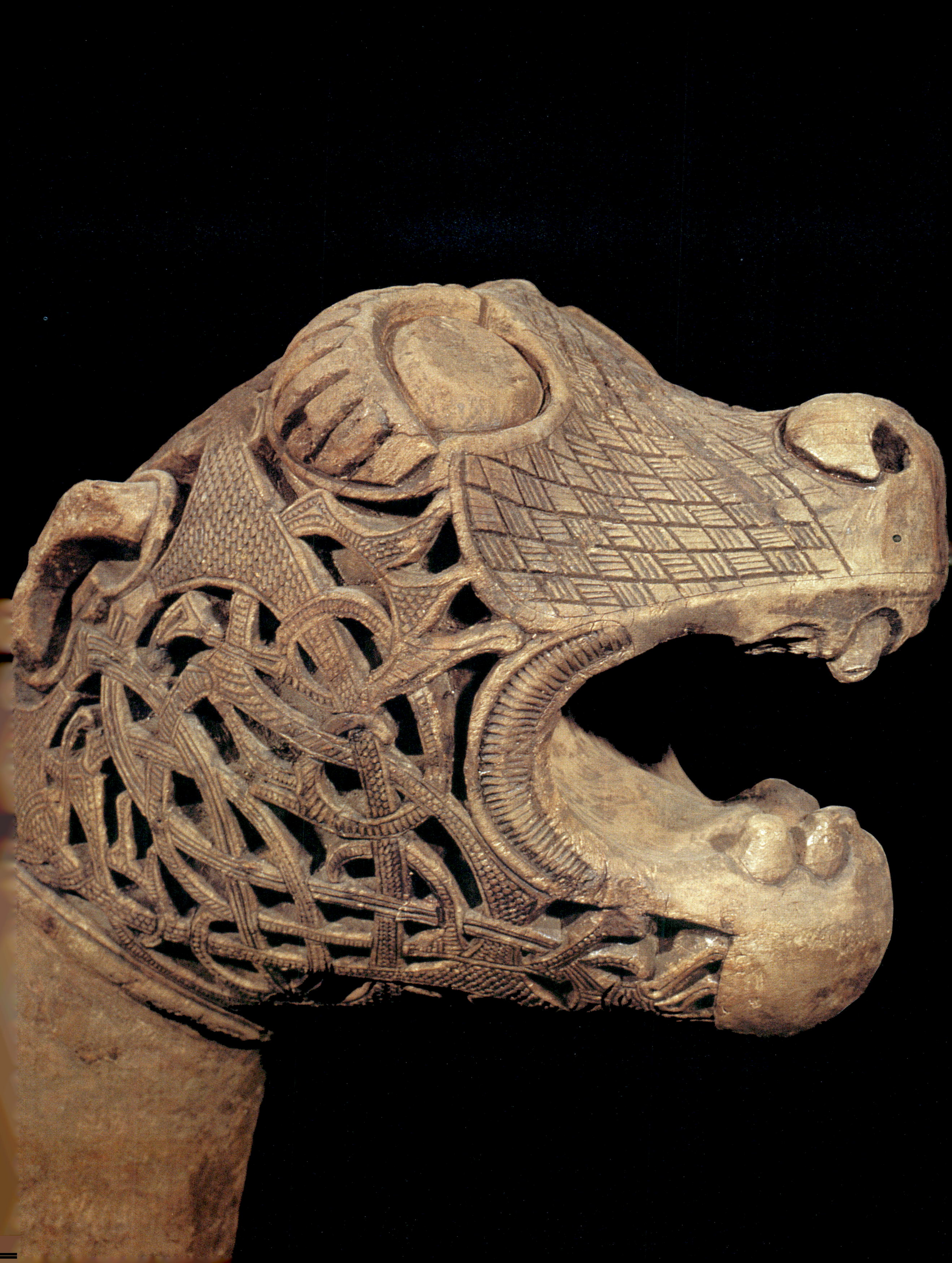

and royal house. These Norsemen worshiped Odin the one-eyed and the other gods of the Aesir and Vanir. Their myths told of Ragnarok, the final battle between the Gods and Ice Giants that would herald the end of the world. They prized bravery and battle above all else, although they also had a passion for the sea and gold. The ancient and decadent civilizations of the east and west thus lured them irresistibly.

CHRISTIANITY

When Flavius Valerius Aurelius Constantinus, better known as the Roman Emperor Constantine, issued the Edict of Tolerance at Milan in 313 AD a momentous step was taken, the consequences of which could not have been forseen by many at that time. Christianity, which up until then had been persecuted by the state was granted religious freedom, and although the emperor did not himself convert till just four years before his death in 337 AD, this Semitic monotheist religion began an ascendancy, which would culminate in its penetration throughout the Roman Empire. Although the Norsemen and Russians took longer to accept this new religion, and continued raiding into Christianized Europe, they too eventually fell for its promise of forgiveness and of a heaven beyond death. However, the conversion of Europe did not take place overnight. Paganism lingered in the superstition and folklore of Medieval Europe, with witches and demons entering a Christian iconography. The Church did its best to eradicate these semi-heresies, but the population seemed to require a folklore it could get its teeth into. Even today, especially in the Catholic and Greek Orthodox Churches, there is an emphasis on idols and fetishes; saints are still made, miracles acknowledged and exorcisms carried out to dispel demons.

Above left and Right: An 8th century church in Ireland, shows the stone carving tradition that would begin with the Celts and continue into the Christian era.

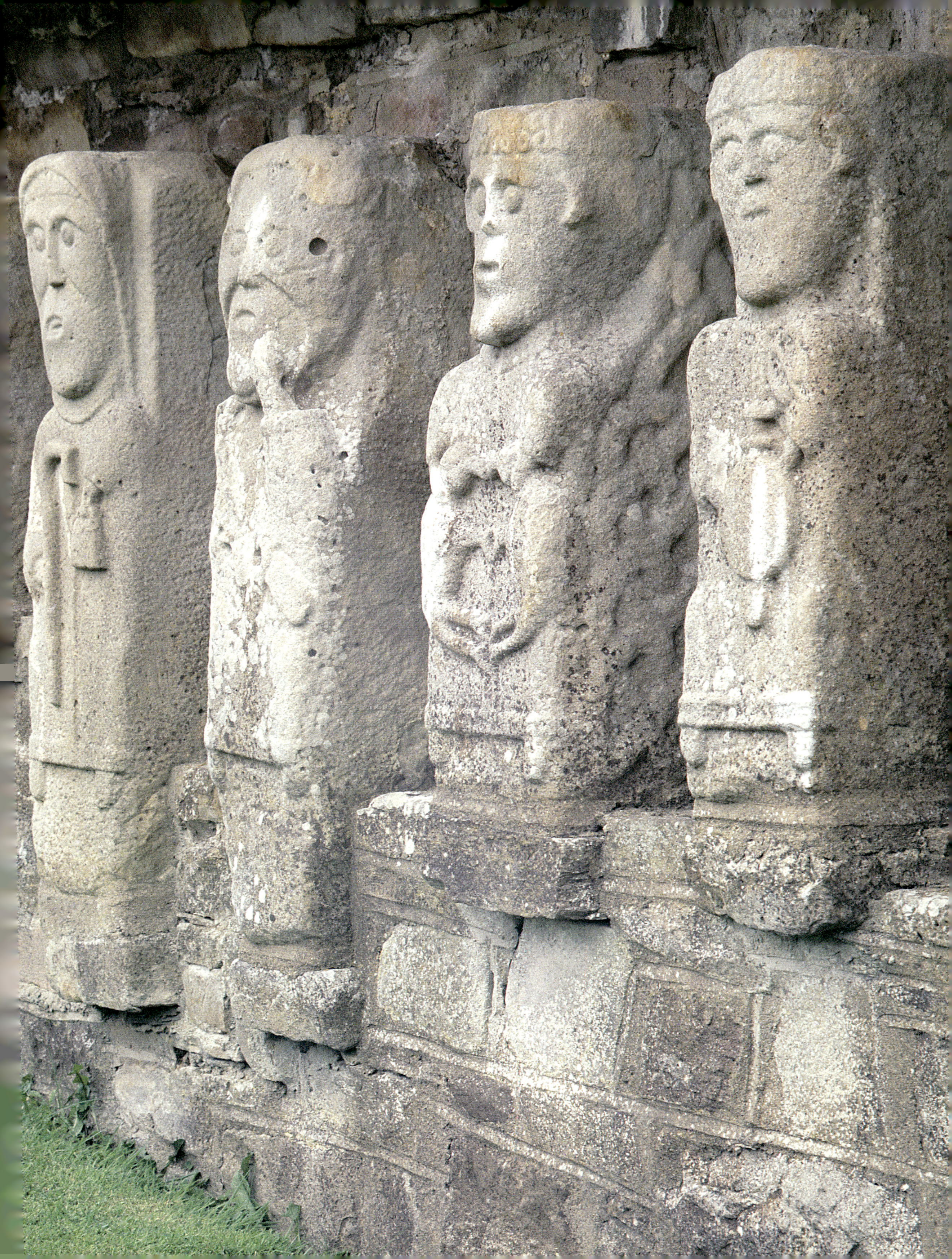

A-Z
CODEX GODS

ACHILLES
"Lipless"

The hero of Homer's *Iliad* and owner of an extraordinary temper. Achilles was the son of Peleus, king of Phthia in Thessaly, and Thetis, daughter of Oceanos. While still a child, his mother plunged him into the river Styx to ensure his invulnerability. In doing so however, she retained hold of him by his heel, which would later be the cause of his downfall and the origin of the phrase for someone's weak spot — the "Achilles heel."

Achilles knew that he would die at Troy — he had the option of a short but glorious life if he went, or of a long inglorious existence if he did not. During the siege of Troy his foul temper and pride were crucial to the plot of the myth — his arguments with Agamemmnon, neglect of Patrocles, killing of Hector and final fatal wounding by Paris are the major actions of Homer's *Iliad*, which was in fact subtitled "The Wrath of Achilles."

AEGIR
Norse god of the sea, the counterpart of the Greek Poseidon, but darker and far more frightening. Aegir was a giant who had nine wave daughters, and, like Poseidon, was linked with earthquakes and storms. His Northern raider devotees were known to sacrifice captives to ensure safe journeys. He was also called "the ale-brewer" since he became the owner of a vast bronze cauldron (stolen from the giant Hymir) in which he made the divine brew of the gods.

AENEAS
A Trojan prince, the son of Anchises by the goddess Aphrodite and mythical ancestor of Rome. Aneas was one of the elite Trojan warriors always in the thickest of the fighting. When Troy eventually fell he rescued his father and son and embarked on farflung travels — to Sicily, where Anchises died and was buried; Carthage, where he was loved by Queen Dido and finally Rome, where he fused the Trojans and Latins into a single race. He also visited the underworld at the Sybl's behest. These adventures form the *Aeneid*, Virgil's epic poem concerning the mythical origins of Rome. According to Roman tradition, Aeneas drowned in the river Numicus during a battle against the Etruscans. Roman tradition also gave him four sons, Ascanius, Euryleon, Romulus and Remus, two of whom feature prominently in Rome's foundation myth. Thus Virgil, and the Latin poets who followed him, could produce a lineage for the Roman emperors that stretched back into prehistoric time and also included a relationship with the gods.

AESIR/VANIR
The Aesir and the Vanir were the two races of gods in Norse mythology. Odin commanded the Aesir, while Freya was his Vanir counterpart. It

Right: This pot (c. 540–530 BC) shows Achilles and Ajax playing a game.

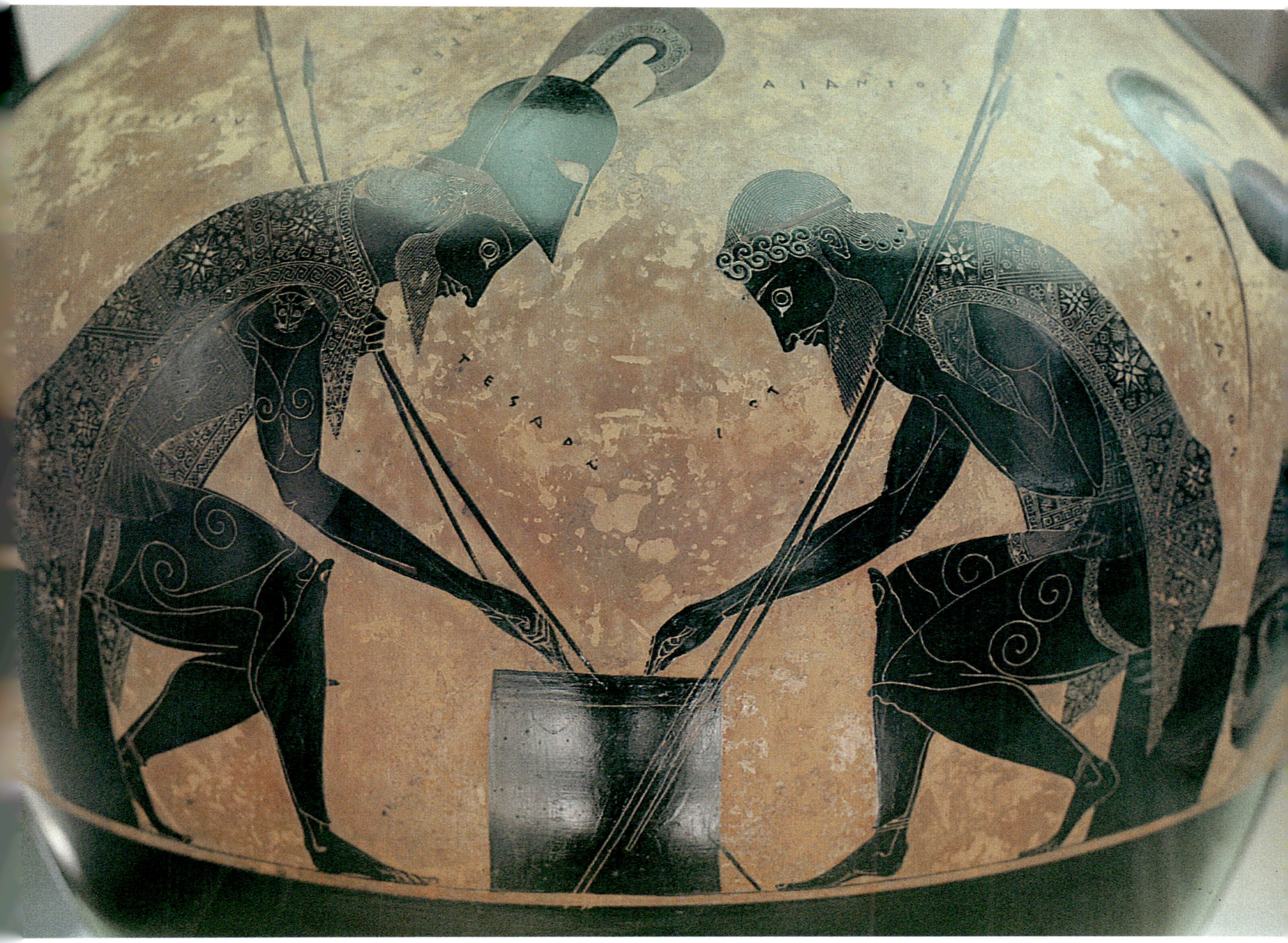

A-Z
CODEX GODS

seems the Vanir actually predated the Aesir with a war being fought between the two before peace was made. There were greater battles to fight, for in the war against the Frost Giants the gods themselves were bound by Fate, moving inexorably toward their doom at Ragnarok, when the forces of evil would destroy them. Only two human beings would remain after this apocalypse — Lif and Lifthrasir — to repopulate the world and worship Odin's son, Balder, in a new Heaven.

AGAMEMNON

Legendary king of Argos based at the citadel of Mycenae and brother of Menelaus, king of Sparta. The brothers married two sisters, Clytemnestra and Helen, the daughters of Leda by Zeus. Clytemnestra had previously been married to Tantulus, but Agamemnon killed her husband and son in order to have her. Her brothers, the Dioscuri, vowed revenge but were eventually mollified. With a start like this it seems obvious that the marriage was cursed.

Agamemnon was elected as the leader of the Greeks in the Trojan trade war, and, apart from his quarrels with Achilles which often jeapordized the whole campaign, he served and led well. After Troy had fallen he returned home to his fate, for his wife had taken a lover and hatched a murder plot which was soon put into action. Following Agamemnon's murder his son Orestes then took over the curse of the Atridae when he "did his duty" and killed his mother and her lover.

AMAZONS

The Amazons were a race of mythical female warriors. Their name derives from the practice of amputating their right breasts to make it easier to fire a bow in battle. According to the *Iliad*, King Priam went to war against them but in post Homeric legend they come to aid the defense of Troy after the death of Hector and their queen, Penthesilea, was killed by Achilles. Heracles also fought against them after he had killed Hippolyte and taken her girdle. Hippolyte in later legend was the wife of Theseus.

ANNA PERENNA

The role of Carthage in early Roman mythology was great. It was from Carthage that Aeneas fled, leaving a distraught Dido. Dido's sister, according to Ovid, was called Anna and after Dido's death she followed Aeneas to Italy. However, she was threatened by Aeneas's wife Lavinia and being warned in a dream by her dead sister, she again fled. Ultimately she became a river goddess and was also associated with vegetation. Her festival — celebrated on March 15 (the first month of the old Roman calendar) — was marked in a grove near Rome. Because of her links to vegetation, she was often associated with Ceres.

Right: This 8th century Viking runestone includes Odin's eight-legged horse Sleipnir and a ship in its etchings.

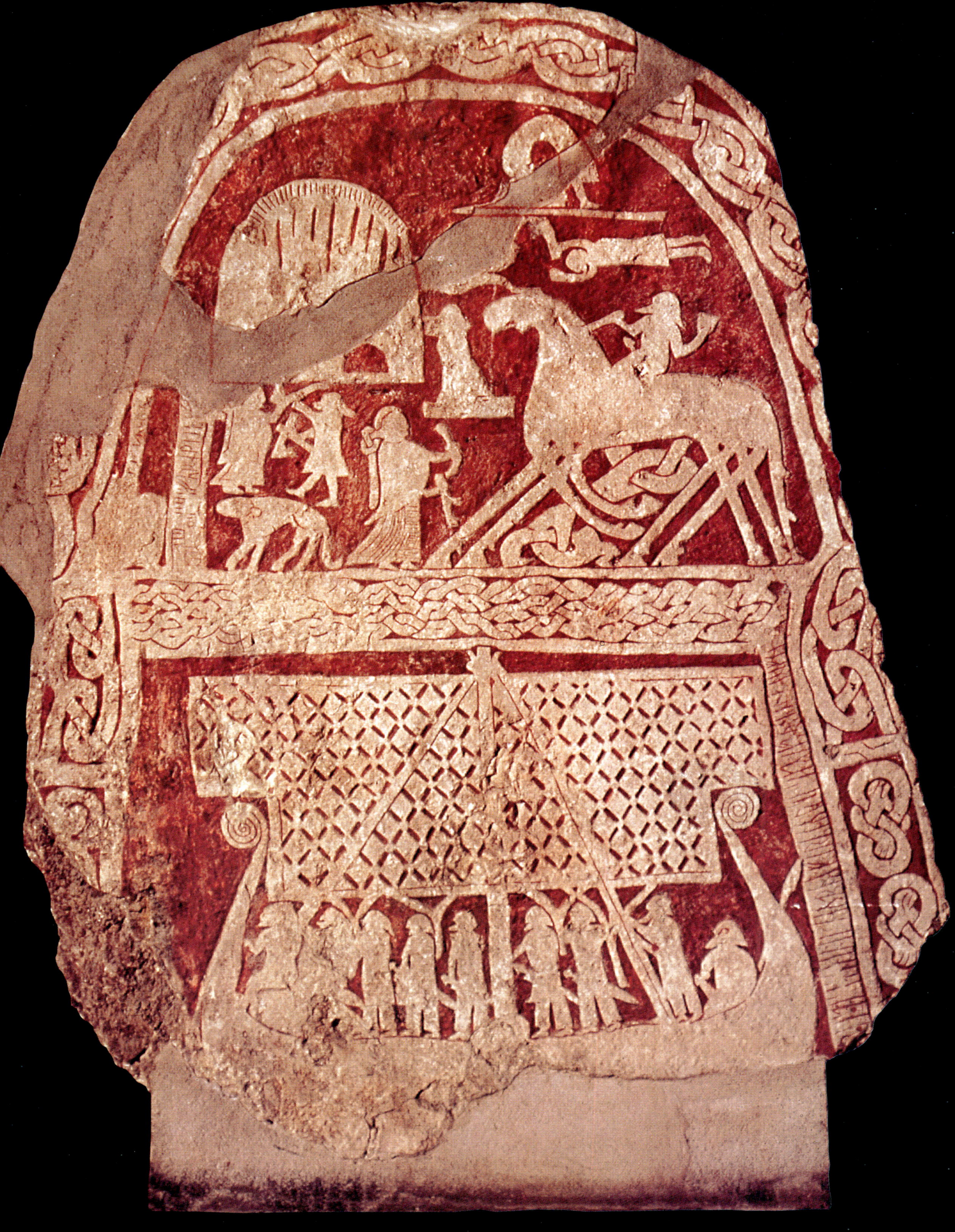

A-Z
CODEX GODS

ANTICHRIST

The counterpart of Christ in medieval Christianity and ruler of the last days of debauch before the Day of Judgement. The Antichrist is a reflection of the syncretism of West Asian religion, a combination of Persian dualism and Judeo-Christian apocalypse. An Antichrist first appears in the Hebrew Book of Revelations as a pseudo-messiah manipulating men and opposing God. Evil incarnate, through disinformation and media manipulation he would gain and hold power until righteously toppled. He was portrayed as a human tyrant but also had a bestial avatar armed with a huge head, searchlight eyes and large steel teeth, as well as having flight capability. His coming was fatalistically expected but equally feared, and this helped to launch the first crusade, which was tasked with the recapture of the holy city of Jerusalem from the Arab invaders.

In Europe named Satan he was seen as the father of the maligned Jews, who had helped in the death of Jesus, thus justifying a policy of prejudice and the pogroms launched against them. But although people believed the Antichrist was a Jew, they readily transferred their hostility toward a clergy that conferred with those in authority and comprimised its integrity with corruption and materialism. For many Puritans and Protestants the Pope became the manifestation of the Antichrist, a policy still followed by extreme sects to this day. The Catholics followed the same route with the demonization of Luther and other religious and political Protestant leaders.

The Antichrist is the manifestation of dualistic opposites that complement and cancel each other, then transform into new variants according to the cultural context. His next inevitable arrival is still awaited with varying degrees of expectation, just prior to the next big extinction.

ANTIGONE

The daughter of Oedipus, king of Thebes, and his mother Jocasta, Antigone looked after her blinded father in his self-imposed exile but returned to Thebes after the deaths of her brothers Eteocles and Polynices. After Oedipus had cursed his sons and departed into exile the brothers agreed to reign alternate years, but Eteocles refused to give up the throne at the end of his year. Polynices gathered together six chieftains to aid him and this was known in Theban legends as the "Seven against Thebes." Polynices led his army against the city and in the ensuing battle all of the Seven against Thebes, except Adrastus, were killed. Adrastus managed to escape thanks to his magic horse, Arion. Ten years later he led the sons of the seven back to Thebes to avenge their fathers' deaths and sack the city, but died of grief when his own son was killed in the battle. On her return to Thebes after the deaths of her brothers, Antigone committed suicide.

Right: A gold mask of an Achaen king found at Mycanae.

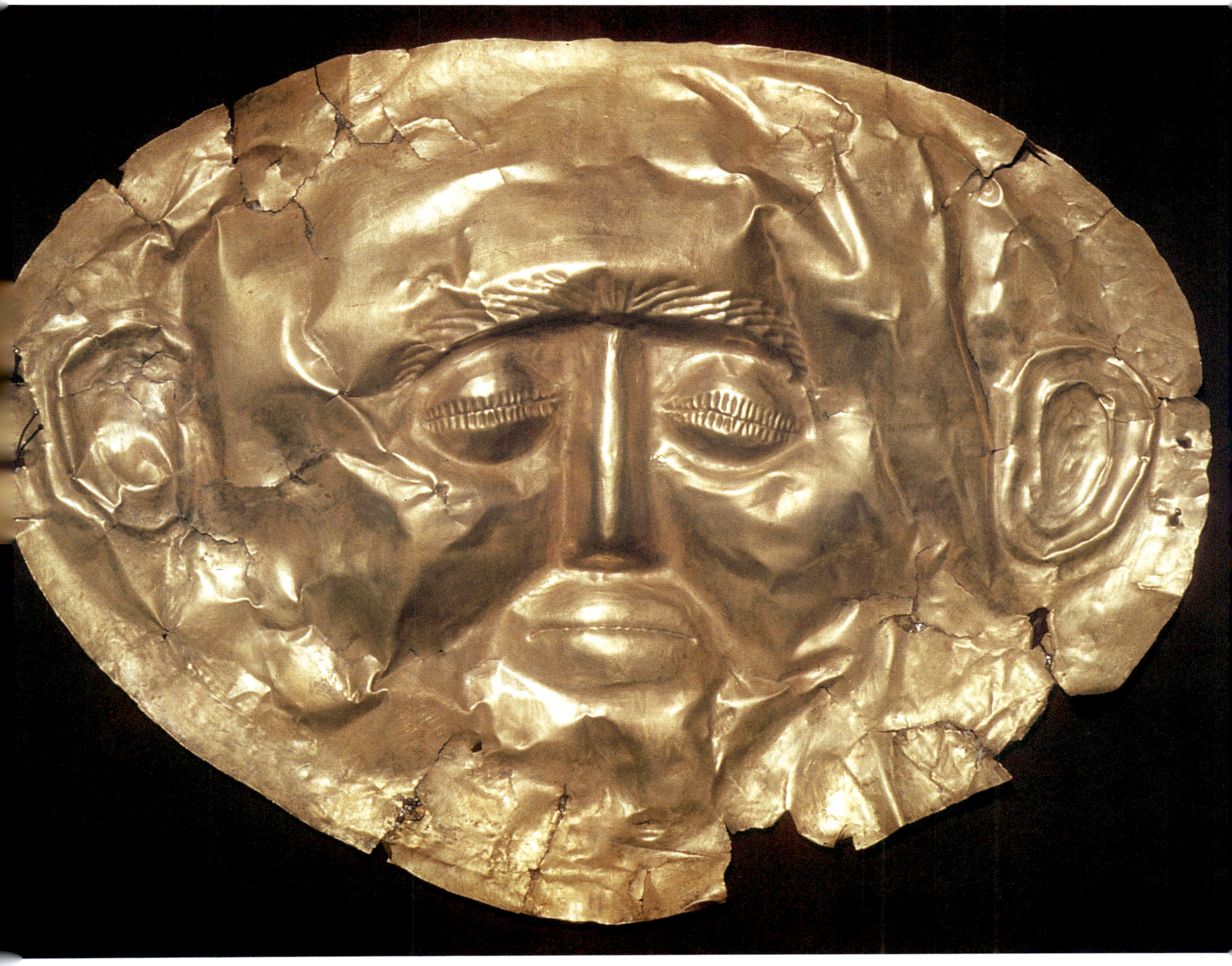

A-Z
CODEX GODS

APHRODITE

Also known as: Venus

Greek goddess of love and beauty, the daughter of Zeus and Dione, born from the sea foam at Paphos on the coast of Cyprus, she was initially married to Hephaestus the smith god, but left him for the Ares, god of war. by the latter she had five children, including the famous Eros. Among her other lovers were Adonis and Anchises, by whom she had Aneas. It was her winning of the Apple of Discord in the "Judgement of Paris" (between the goddesses Hera, Aphrodite, and Athena) which led to the Trojan War, and she was instrumental in saving Aneas and his Trojan group, who went on to become the mythic ancestors of Rome. In fact, Aphrodite predates Greek civilization — she drifted slowly westward from West Asia. There are strong traces of her Mesopotamian roots in her varied names. In turn her Roman counterpart — Venus — was originally a minor nature deity who transformed into a recognizable Aphrodite variant. Her history reflects the sycretism inherent in all religion and myth.

APOLLO

Also known as: Phoebus ("Shining")

Apollo was the Greek god of wisdom, medicine, prophecy and music, the son of Leto by Zeus, and twin of Artemis. The two were born on the island of Delos out of jealous Hera's reach, but Apollo's major shrine was constructed at Delphi after he had destroyed the chthonic serpent/dragon Python. Delphi became renowned throughout the ancient world for its oracular advice, delivered by a priestess called the Pythia. Apollo, as with many Greek gods seems to have originated in West Asia and drifted westward, changing into a handsome Greek when he reached this destination. He had many amours, including Coronis (mother of Ascelpius), Dryone, Daphne and Kyparissos.

ARES

Also known as: Mars

Greek god of war, the son of Zeus, and brother of the smith god Hephaestus whose wife he stole, Ares was not a particularly popular god. His nature was too fickle to warrant deep feeling and he had a nasty temper, tending to throw himself into things without much thought of the consequences. He could just as easily be treacherous as brave, and was not above cowardice and selfishness. He was always portrayed armed and due to his rivalry with his half sister Athena he supported the Trojans in the war. His main areas of worship were central and northern Greece.

The Roman counterpart was Mars, whose status as paramount war god was far above that of Ares — he ranked second in the Roman pantheon after his father Jupiter. His fathering of Romulus and Remus by the vestal virgin Rhea Silvia, founded the Roman race. Originally

Right: A statue of Apollo stands at a temple resurrected in his honor in Pompei. Mount Vesuvias is in the background.

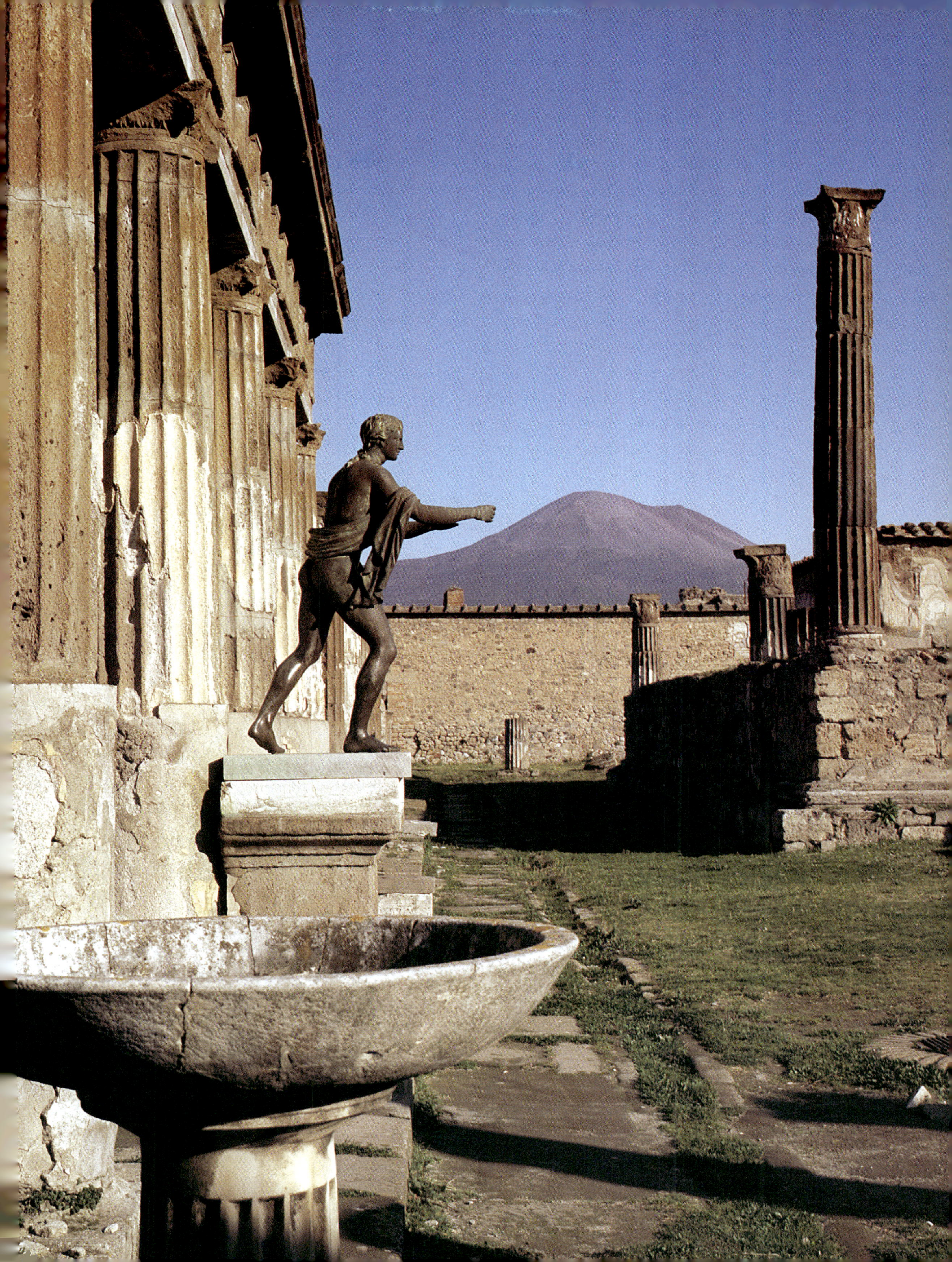

A-Z
CODEX GODS

an agricultural/fertility god, he gradually evolved into war deity, mirroring Rome's own development from a tribe of farmers to a nation of soldiers. These mutually exclusive roles are in fact synchronized in the seasons, for both professions depended upon similar conditions and March, originally the first month of the Roman year, saw both the beginning of the agricultural year and the start of the campaigning season.

ARGONAUTS

The name given to the famous crew of the ship *Argo* who accompanied Jason on his mythic quest for the Golden Fleece. Heracles and the Dioscuri were among their number, as well as Argos the shipbuilder, Tiphys the pilot, eagle-eyed Lynceus, Orpheus with the magical musical powers, Polydeuces the boxer and even the Attican prince Theseus. The construction of the *Argo* was supervised by Athena, who included a piece of Zeus' sacred Dodonian Oak in the prow, which subsequently possessed the power of speech and acted as a lookout and early warning system for Jason and his crew.

On their eventful quest they voyaged up the Black Sea to Colchis, returning home via southern Italy, North Africa and Crete before finally reaching Iolchos again with the Golden Fleece. The story is a great navigational epic which has parallels in other mythologies, particularly Celtic.

ARTEMIS
Also known as: Diana

Artemis was the Greek moon goddess, daughter of Zeus and Leto, and twin sister of Apollo. Diana was the eternal virgin huntress, possessed of a rather vindictive temperament. The deaths of a number of people were attributed to her: Actaeon, Callisto, Meleager, as well as the children of Niobe and Orion.

At Ephesus, Artemis betrayed her West Asian roots, being worshiped more as the Asiatic mother-goddess she originally was. Her temple there was one of the Seven Wonders of the ancient world.

ARTHUR

The semi-legendary Romano-British king who opposed the first Viking invasions. In Corwall, Britanny and Wales, legends tell not of his death but of his suspended animation until summoned to save his people again. The Arthurian myths have been constantly overlaid and layered into a sedimentary ocean of related myths. He began as a Romano-British *Dux Bellorum* or war leader, whose brain and brawn saved the Romano-Celts from being overwhelmed by the invasions of Norsemen that occurred following the departure of the Romans from Britain. Son of Uther Pendragon and his illegal liaison with Ygraine the wife of Duke Gorlois of Cornwall, which was managed through the magic of Merlin, Arthur was then brought up by the wizard. When he

Right: Apollo and Artemis sit in a chariot in this stone relief, which was removed from a Greek temple at Selinunte.

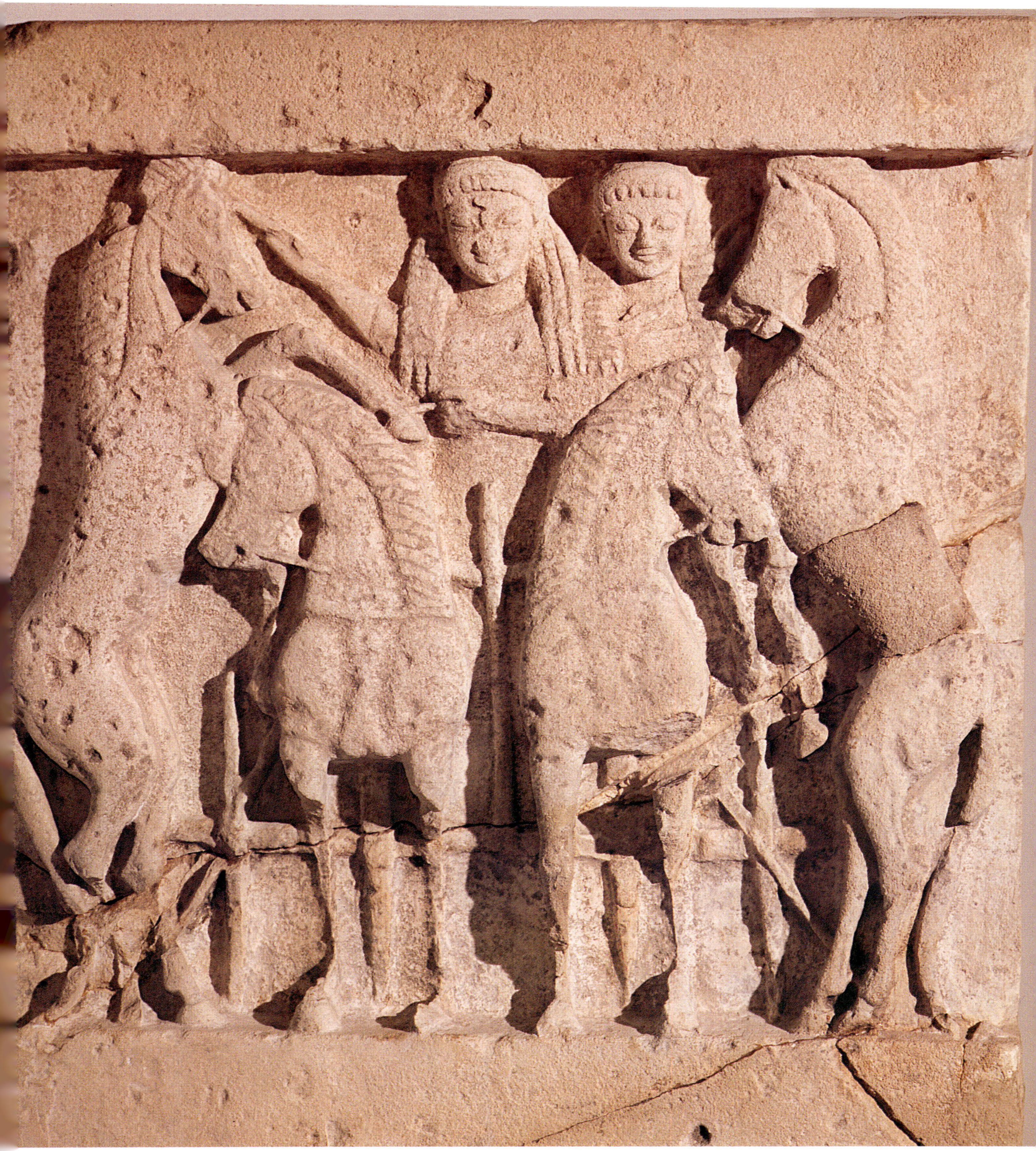

A-Z
CODEX GODS

pulled the enchanted sword Excalibur from the stone in which it had been set, he was revealed as the predestined king. Though still only a teenager he drove his enemies back, established his kingdom and then married Guinevere against Merlin's advice, for she was in love with Lancelot and ultimately betrayed Arthur. A greater disaster was finally enacted as his nephew Mordred rebelled against him. In a huge battle almost all the Knights of the Round Table were slain, and Arthur fatally wounded. Excalibur was then returned to the Lady of the Lake, and Arthur was conducted to his final resting place on the island of Avalon. Later writers constantly embellished and modified elements of the Arthur legend, introducing their own agendas and cultural preoccupations into what remains one of the more potent European myths.

ASCLEPIUS

Also known as: Aesculapius

Asclepius was the son the Greek god Apollo and the mythical founder of medicine. He was educated in the healing arts by the centaur Chiron and was an exceptional pupil, even able to re-animate the dead. Ultimately this facility annoyed Pluto, god of the dead. He complained to his brother Zeus, who threw a thunderbolt at Asclepius and killed him. Apollo was enraged at the death of his son but could do nothing against his father Zeus, so instead he killed the Cyclops, the manufacturer of Zeus's thunderbolt weapons.

After his death, by way of a peace offering, Asclepius received divine honors and was transformed into a constellation.

ATARGATIS

Known in Rome as Dea Syria (the Syrian goddess), Atargatis was an example of a deity from the conquered provinces that continued to have an importance after Roman conquest. Her cult was widespread in the Middle East (in places like Baalbeck and Damascus), but it also spread through Greece, Egypt and later Italy.

ATHENA

Also known as: Pallas Athene, Minerva

Athena was the warlike virgin goddess of wisdom, the daughter of Zeus and Metis, who sprang fully grown and armed to the teeth from her father's head in a bizarre birth. Following a negative prophecy Zeus had emulated his father and grandfather in swallowing his latest progeny. He then developed a headache, which was only relieved when Hephaestus hit him on the head and Athena emerged.

Her cult city Athens was won from Poseidon through her practical gift of the olive tree, and she held faith with the city ever after. Her animal avatar was the owl, which, along with her profile, became the city badge. She wore a breastplate and on the front of her shield she carried the head of the Gorgon, Medusa, which Perseus had given her.

Right: This beautiful statue of Athena, the Greek goddess of wisdom, was taken from the Athenian Acropolis. (c. 525–520 BC).

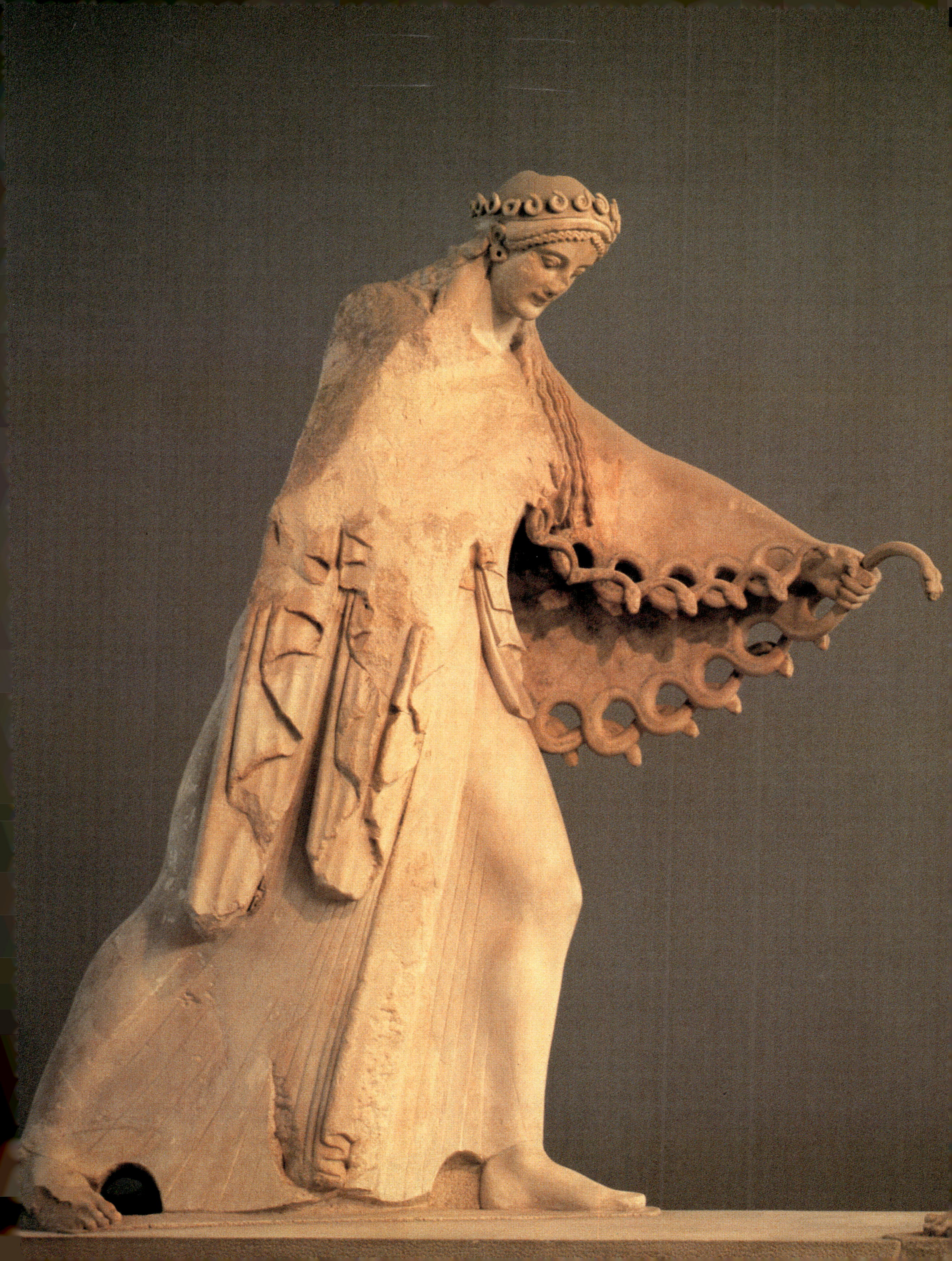

A-Z
CODEX GODS

The Roman counterpart, Minerva, inherited Athena's martial characteristics, but was also the goddess of crafts, trade and intellectual activity. With Jupiter and Juno she made up the great Capitoline triad and was introduced to Rome by an Etruscan contingent which came to the aid of Romulus.

ATLAS

The Titans were a race of giants that ruled the world before the gods of Olympia. It was Atlas who led the Titans in the war against Jupiter and was punished by having to bear the weight of the heavens upon his shoulders. He appears in a number of myths. In the Labours of Heracles (Hercules), Atlas is temporarily relieved of the pressure of bearing the heavens by being approached by Heracles in his search for the apples of Hesperides.

ATTIS

Originally an early vegetation god with a spring festival of death and resurrection which originated in Phrygia, central Asia Minor. He was the consort of Cybele.

BACCHUS

See Dionysius.

BALDER

"The Beautiful"

Heroic son of the Norse god Odin and his wife Freya, Balder was known for his looks and wisdom — he seemed to have it all. He was in fact a northern Adonis variant with similarities to Atis, Osiris and Tammuz — a dying/resurrecting fertility god who would rule the Heaven to come.

Balder was killed by a mistletoe dart hurled by the blind god Hoder, though it had been carefully set up by the evil Loki who was jealous of the high esteem in which Balder was held by the other gods. When an emissary sent to the underworld returned saying Balder could only be rejuvenated if every living thing would cry for him, Loki undermined that too, by disguising himself as an implacable old woman.

BELLEREPHON

Many of the tales of Bellerophon are similar to those of Heracles and Theseus and probably originated from primitive folklore before they became part of Greek legend. He is best known for his association with the fabulous winged horse Pegasus which helped him when he killed the Chimera and afterward when he defeated the Amazons. Later Bellerophon made the mistake of flying to Olympus on Pegasus. Zeus was so outraged at this presumption of a mortal that he sent a gadfly which stung Pegasus under the tail whereupon he reared up and sent Bellerophon crashing to earth. He spent the rest of his days wretched, lame and blind always shunning the company of other men.

Right: The owl would become synonymous with Athena. The bird, along with Athena's profile, was on the city's badge.

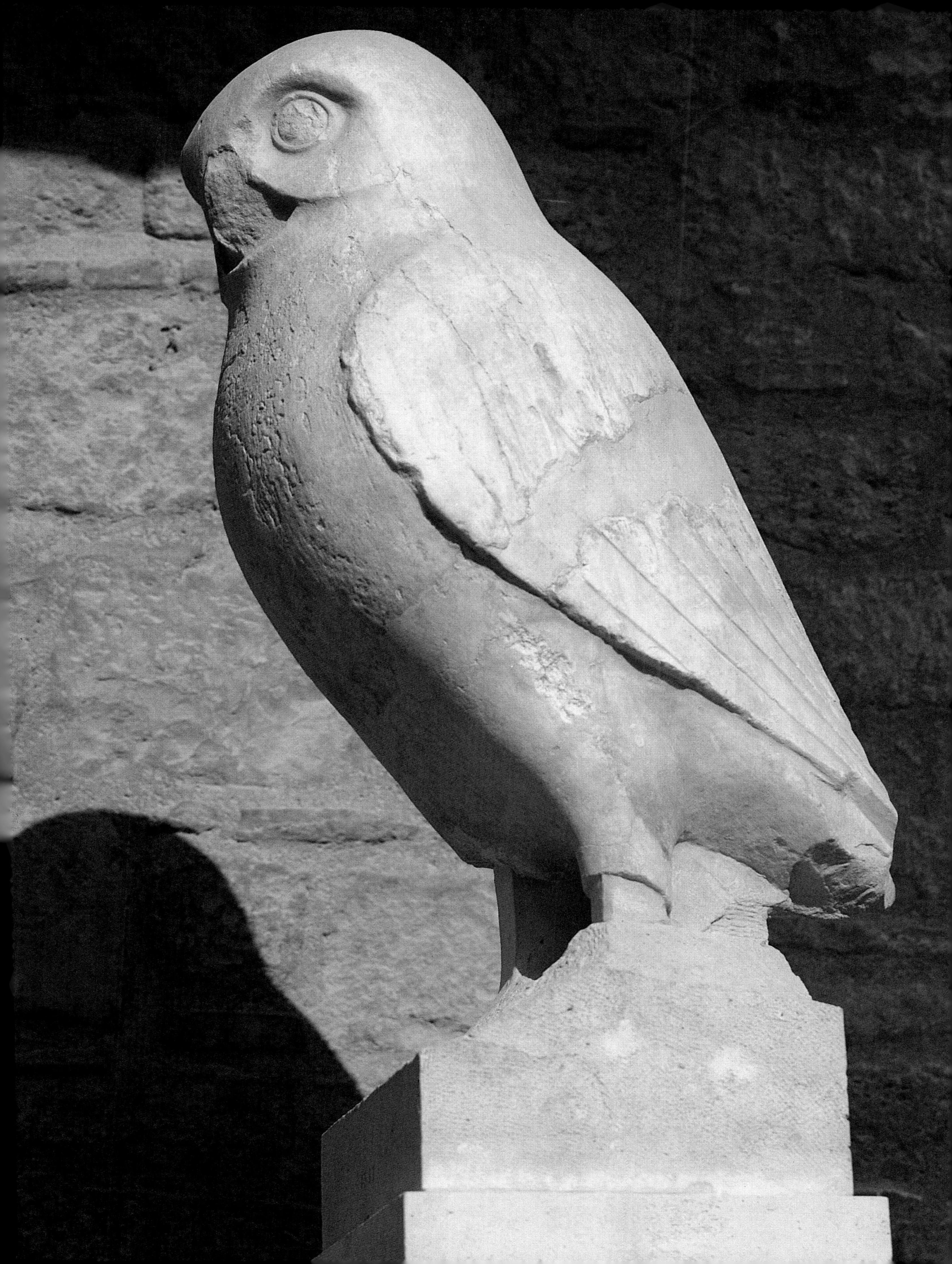

A-Z
CODEX GODS

BELLONA

The old Roman goddess of war, who is traditionally associated with the Greek goddess Enyo. She was an important deity, although her cult was relatively small. Her temple, built in the Campus Martius, was used by the senate for its meetings outside the sacred lines of the city (the "Pomerium"). The temple was also used to welcome ambassadors and victorious generals. In legend she was supposed to prepare the chariot of Mars.

BEOWULF

Hero of one of the longest epic poems, and certainly the most important to have survived complete in Old English, in which Beowulf the Geat goes to the aid of the Danes and destroys the monster Grendel and her son. He later went on to become king of the Geats, and after a reign of fifty years he died gloriously, fighting and killing a dragon that had been attacking his kingdom.

BESTIARIES

Illustrated collections and manuscripts concerning legendary animals. A bestiary was a coffee table book for the Middle Ages, full of mythological beasts such as the Unicorn, the Basilisk and the Bonnacon: composite animals of varying degrees of danger — some of them were harmless and beautiful, while others were bizarre, toxic and deadly. These illustrated books relied more upon the imaginative power of their creators than any actual animals, but provided educational entertainment, as well as possessing a certain style and literary merit. At a time when books were rare, the handmade and precious bestiaries gave kudos to any who owned them, representing wisdom and knowledge though filled only with what amounted to cartoon characters — potentialities of the fertile Medieval imagination. Christianity was at this time also full of such imagery, for the Renaissance had yet to make its huge impression on European culture, providing as it did a new paradigm for the imagination, with especial reference to the older classical model with its artistic and investigative arts.

BONA DEA

Also known as: Fauna,

Bona Dea (which translates as "Good Goddess") was the wife (or daughter) of Faunus. Men were excluded from her cult and an annual nocturnal ceremony was held in her honor every December. This ceremony was conducted in part by the Vestal Virgins and included the sacrifice of a sow along with much dancing and wine. In 62 BC there was a major scandal when Clodius (an important political contemporary of Julius Caesar, with whose wife Clodius was having an affair) was caught at the ceremony dressed in women's clothing.

Right: These chess pieces of walrus ivory are fashioned after Norsemen.

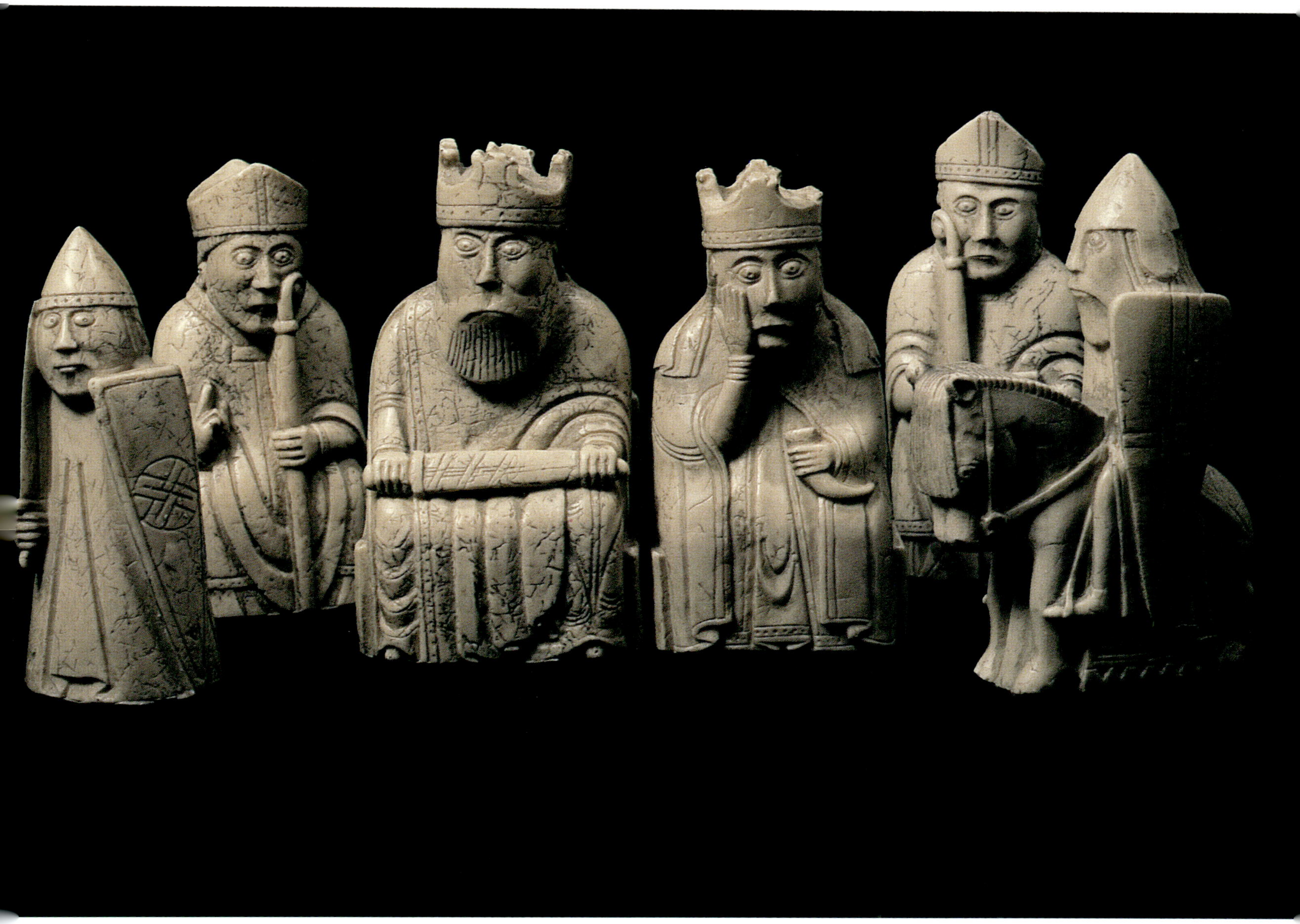

A-Z
CODEX GODS

BOR
"Born"

The father of Odin as well as Vili and Ve. Norse legend tells of the primeval cow Audumla "the Nourisher" who licked at an ice wall until gradually more and more parts of a strong, attractive man appeared. He was named Buri and soon after he begat Bor, who took a frost giant's daughter named Bestla as his wife. Their three children changed the nature of existance when they killed the old giant Ymir, creating the world from his corpse. Almost everyone else was drowned in the giant's blood at the time of the murder.

BRAN

Bran was the son of Febal and a royal hero of an 8th century Irish epic that celebrated his numerous adventures. Sea voyages in particular held a fascination for the ancient Irish, who even distinguished between a voyage to somewhere real and others to places mythical. The tale of Bran mixes both of these as he plied his way through an ocean of delight peopled with islands of beautiful women from whom he found it difficult to separate. When finally he returned to his homeland he found to his consternation that he was unknown except as an almost mythical voyager. Rather disgruntled by this reception he promptly set sail back off on his adventures.

BRES

Also known as: Eochaid ("The Beautiful"), and Gormac ("Dutiful Son").

Bres was a legendary Irish king, the son of a Tuatha woman, Eriu, and Elatha, who was of a race of mono-limbed people. As he grew twice as fast as other boys he was soon a proud and beautiful man who was given the High Kingship in the hope that his rule would bring prosperity and peace. Bres however proved unworthy, oppressing and humiliating his Tuatha kin until he was ousted from power. He fled and raised an army from a rival tribe, the Fomoire. A huge mythical battle was then fought for the High Kingship, which the Tuatha won.

BRIGIT
"Exalted One"

Fertility and war goddess of the Celts, Brigit is exceptional in that she seems to have undergone a smooth transition from pagan goddess into Christian saint. She was in fact a triple goddess, linked to two other horse goddess sisters. A deity of healing, crafts and poetry, she was also invoked by those in childbirth. Her home area of worship seems to have been Leinster in Ireland, but she was worshiped all over that country.

When she became a Christian saint, Brigit absorbed aspects of Celtic pagan goddesses, becoming a patron of agriculture and fertility. Her saint's day festival was on the same day as that of her previous incarnation — February 1st.

Right: This ogham stone, found in Ireland, is proof of the early movement away from paganism towards Christianity, as a crucifix is visible on the rock.

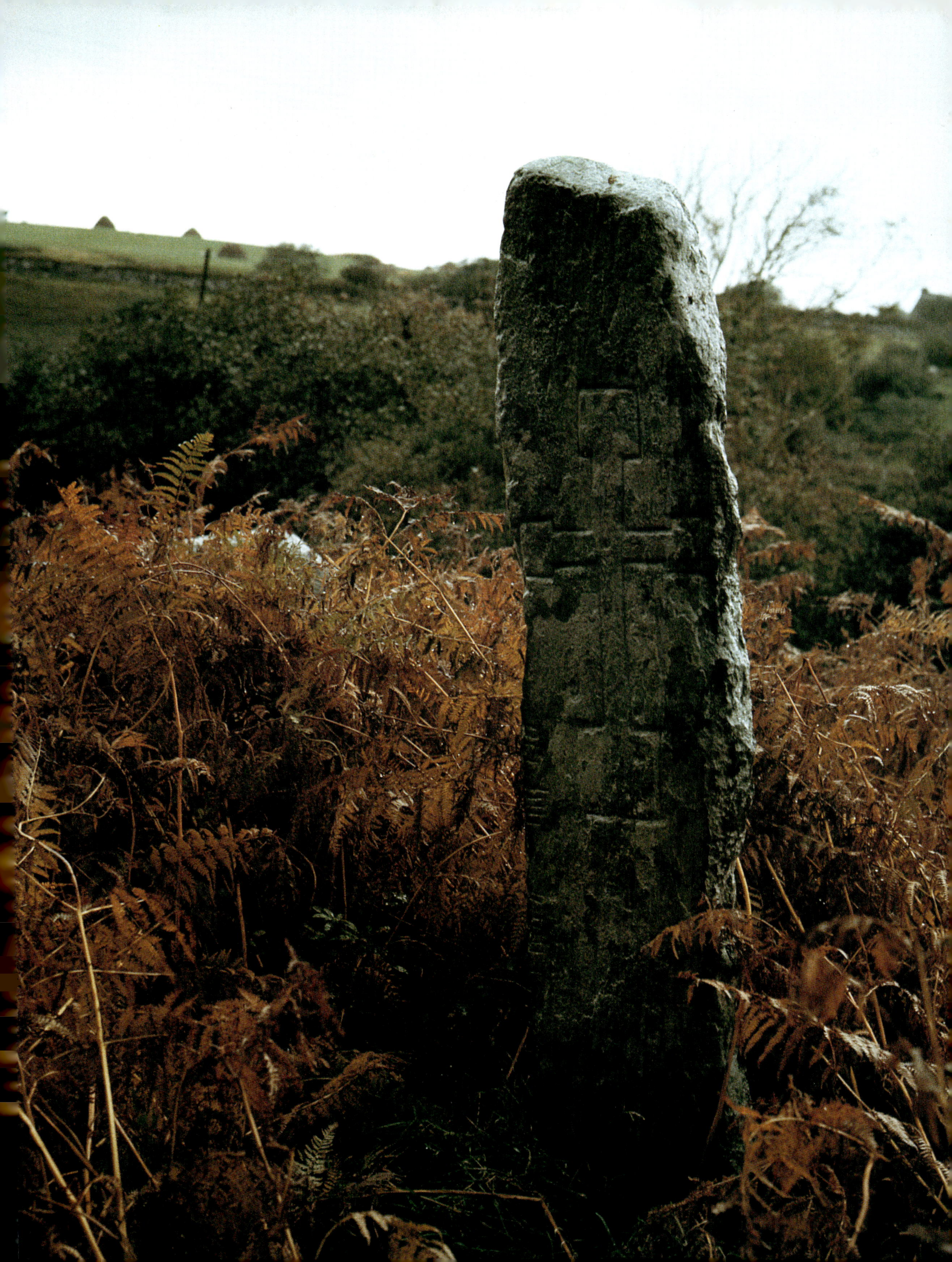

A-Z
CODEX GODS

BRUNHILDA
A Norse Valkyrie — a warrior priestesses of Freya. Brunhilda was the prototype mythical princess condemned to sleep in a castle surrounded by flames until a warrior prince braved the fire to wake her. All this came about when she defied Odin. She was eventually woken by Sigurd and fell in love with him. Sigurd subsequently lost his memory and agreed to impersonate Gunnar so that he could win Brunhilda for his friend. When she discovered the deception Brunhilda had Sigurd killed and then killed herself.

CADMUS
Legendary hero and founder of Thebes, Cadmus was perhaps a Phoenician, for he is credited with the introduction of their alphabet to Greece. When his sister Europa was abducted by Zeus disguised as a bull, Cadmus' father sent him and his brothers in search of her, with orders not to return unless successful. Such a quest was doomed from the start and Cadmus obeyed the Delphic oracle's advice to follow a cow, and found a city — Thebes — in Boeotia. Access to water supplies was gained through the conquest of a dragon who guarded the local lake, its blood sprouting warriors as it fell. Cadmus outwitted these grisly soldiers by hurling a stone in their midst, and they promptly began to fight each other. The survivors joined him in his new city. When ancient, Cadmus and his wife Harmonia left Thebes, to live in Illyrium or on Thera (legends vary), but this perhaps indicates his foreign nationality and return to his homeland.

CASSANDRA
Cassandra was one of the daughters of King Priam of Troy and regarded as the most beautiful. She was given the power of prophecy by Apollo, but was then doomed to be disbelieved because she refused him her love. Cassandra tried in vain to warn the Trojans about the wooden horse. After the sack of Troy she was brought home by Agamemnon and murdered along with him.

CENTAURS
The Centaurs were a tribe of wild creatures, half horse half human, living particularly in the wooded mountains of Thessaly. They are probably pre-Homeric, and for the Greeks they represented primitive desires and anti-social habits. They were noted for continual drunkenness, chasing women and fighting.

CERBERUS
Cerberus was the monstrous dog which guarded the entrance to the underworld. In some stories he has fifty heads but is usually depicted as having three. He had to be retrieved from Hell as one of Heracles' tasks.

Above left: After slaughtering his family, Hercules could only find redemption by undertaking the "Twelve Labors," such as the one shown here where he fetches the three-headed Cerberus from the underworld.
Right: Centaurs, described as half human and half horse, were known to be unruly.

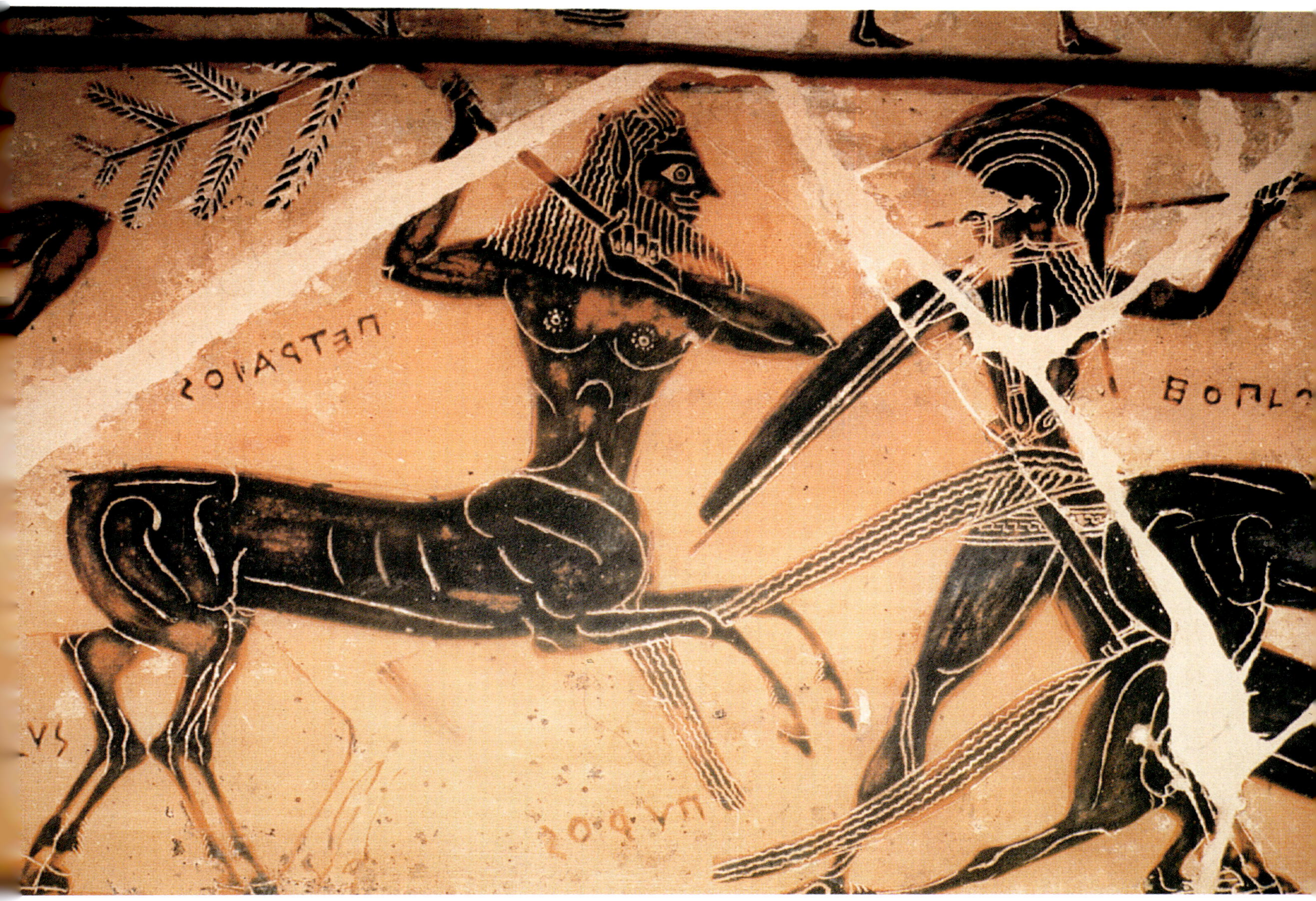

A-Z
CODEX GODS

CERES
See Demeter.

CERNUNNOS
A horned fertility god, Cernunnos is probably the oldest of the Celtic deities, and his origins may lie in the horned god of Paleolithic cave paintings. He was usually portrayed seated cross-legged, complete with his distinctive horns and surrounded by animals. On the famous silver cauldron from Gundestrup in Denmark, he is shown wearing and also holding in his right hand a torc (a Celtic neck-ring) and in his left a snake with a ram's head. His aspect as an agricultural and pastoral god holding sway over animals is always emphasized.

CHARON
Charon, son of Erebus and Nox, the children of Chaos, was the disgruntled old ferryman in Greek myth who took the souls of the dead on their journey across the river Styx to the underworld. He charged a fee for this service, and often intimidated his passengers by charging them to row themselves. One of the more popular myths concerning Charon tells of how he was soundly thrashed by Heracles when he refused the hero passage. Charon was forced to give way — with the result that he was chained up a year for allowing one of the living to enter the realm of the dead.

CIRCE
This legendary Greek princess is found in the *Odyssey*, the daughter of the Sun and Perseis, and a famous witch related to Medea. Circe lived on the island of Aeaea and when Odysseus and his crew landed there she turned his scouting party into different animals. With the help of Hermes, Odysseus was able to thwart her magic and threaten her safety, causing her to rescind her spells and become rather attached to him — he ended up staying there a while and Circe had two children by him, Telegonus and Casiphone.

COMUS
The son of Bacchus and Circe, Comus was a Roman god of feasts. As the son of Bacchus, he was portrayed as a young drunkard.

CORMAC MAC AIRT
During the legendary Cormac mac Airt's years as king, Ireland experienced a highpoint of peace and prosperity. His famed Solomon-style wisdom derived from the possession of a great golden cup; three lies would shatter it and three truths reassemble it once more. He also possessed a magic musical branch with three apples growing upon it which could heal the sick and aid the suffering. These gifts came to him from Manaanan mac Lir, a famous merchant and trader from the Isle of Man. With the death of Cormac his magical equipment vanished.

Above left: Cernunnos sits with a Celtic neck ring in one hand and a snake in the other (c. 100 BC). Right: Cernunnos again, this time on a stone relief from France.

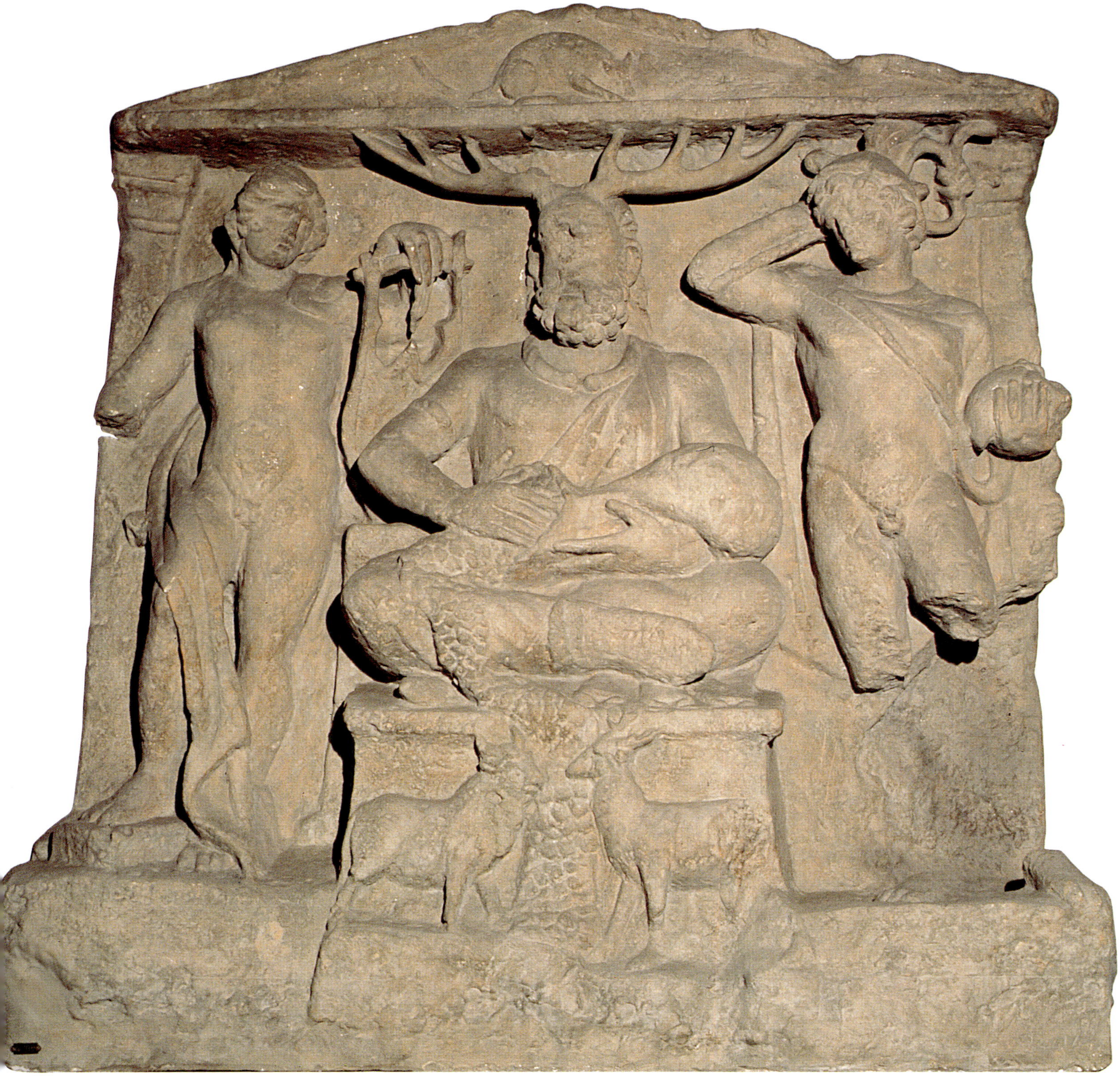

A-Z
CODEX GODS

CUPID
See Eros.

CYBELE
Cybele is a classic illustration of the way that provincial cults could be subsumed into the worship of one of the major Roman deities. Originating in Phrygia (part of the Roman empire in Asia), Cybele was a mother goddess who became linked with Rhea. Initially her cult in Rome was conducted by non-Roman priests who were ritually self-castrated before being able to act in the ceremonies associated with the cult. Until the reign of Claudius it was prohibited for Roman citizens to take part in these rituals. An annual festival was held in her honor between March 15 and 28; part of the ceremony included bathing in the blood of a freshly sacrificed bull. In legend, she was believed to have been born with both female and male genitalia, but the threat that this represented prompted the gods to castrate her. From the fallen male organs a tree grew, which ultimately caused the pregnancy of a nymph. The resulting child, Attis, was drawn to Cybele but he was unfaithful and ultimately took his own life. Following Cybele's prayers, Attis's body is not allowed to decay and he became a symbol of rebirth and purification.

DAEDALUS
This mythical Greek master craftsman was famed for his original thoughts and designs. In Crete Daedalus constructed the artificial cow by which the queen Pasiphae gratified her unnatural passion for her husband's prize bull. When the fruit of this union, the Minotaur was born, Daedalus then designed the Labyrinth in which to contain it. Later, for his helping Theseus escape the Labyrinth and win Ariadne, Minos imprisoned Daedalus and his son, Icarus.

They effected their escape by means of large artificial wings held together with wax, which Daedalus had designed and built. However tragedy ensued when Icarus flew too near the sun, the wax in his wings melted and he crashed into the sea and drowned. Daedalus made it to Sicily, where he then worked for King Cocalus.

DAGDA
"The Good God"
Also known as: Aed ("Fire"), Ollathair ("All-father"), Ruad Rofessa ("Lord of great Knowledge")

Dagda was an ancient Irish god, the ruler over life and death. He possessed some extraordinary equipment, including a magic staff with opposing functions — one end had awesome destructive capability, the reverse great life enhancing and restorative powers. His other magical artifacts included an inexhaustibly full cauldron and ever-laden fruit trees, as well as constantly ready and limitless food supplies. King of the Tuatha, Dagda was of vital import at the second battle of Mag Tuired. He was described as the Good God

Above left: According to legend, the Roman deity Cybele was born both man and woman.
Right: This rock carving shows Cybele in a chariot being pulled by lions and her consort Attys.

M·D·M·I· ET ·ATTINIS

·L·CORNELIVS·SCIPIO·ORFITVS
·V·C·AVGVR·TAVROBOLIVM·
SIVE·CRIOBOLIVM·FECIT·

A-Z
CODEX GODS

on account of his prowess at almost everything although he is sometimes made to look foolish by Lug. His daughter was the triple goddess Brigit and his wife Morrigan.

DANANN

Mother goddess of the ancient Irish and patroness of the mythical Tuatha, her name also infers aquatic connections. Originally one of the dominant people the tribes of Danann's Tuatha were eventually supplanted by the next influx — the Sons of Mil, who usurped their position and lands. Thus were the old gods and myths supplanted by new blood, being relegated to the more isolated and distant position as the "Little People" of Irish folklore.

DEMETER

Also known as: Ceres

Demeter was the essential Greek mother/fertility goddess and had many legends and consorts associated with her, the latter including Zeus and Poseidon. She was also related to other major mother goddess figures of the earlier religions of West Asia, principally Isis. Demeter's greatest sanctuary was at Eleusis just outside Athens.

DEUCALION

Deucalion was the equivalent of Biblical Noah and Mesopotamian Utanapishtim in the Greek version of the prevalent Flood myth. In this, Zeus displays his customary ambivalent behavior by first of all flooding the world to remove a vice-ridden humankind and then granting Deucalion's wish for companions by giving him the capacity to create people from stones dropped over his shoulder. Deucalion ultimately became king of Thessaly.

DIANA

Also known as: Artemis

Diana was a Roman goddess, closely associated with women, fertility and woodland. This last attribution also led her to be regarded as the goddess of hunting. The picture of the bathing Diana (Artemis) being spied on by Actaeon is one of the most familiar in art. In the story, which the Romans inherited from Greek myth, the hunter came upon the naked goddess whilst she was at her ablutions. As a punishment, she changed him into a stag, whereupon he was torn apart alive by his own hounds. One of her most important shrines was reputed to have a runaway slave as priest. The priest was supposed to have killed the previous occupant of the post and would himself face death if challenged by a subsequent runaway.

DIONYSIUS

Also known as: Bacchus

Fertility god of vegetation, wine, ecstasy and transcendence, Dionysius has his roots further east in West Asia. In Greek mythology he came late to the pantheon. As another son of Zeus, he

Right: This Roman period sculpture of Diana, the goddess of fertility and hunt, can be seen in the Vatican.

• EUROPE •

A-Z
CODEX GODS

was kept alive in his father's thigh after his mother vanished through the manipulations of an inevitably jealous Hera. One considerable myth concerns his journey to and return from India as a kind of *jihad* — a religious and military conquest. His triumphal return, complete with frenzied scenes, is often featured in both Greek and Roman art. A major feature of his cult involved exclusively female worshipers in an orgiastic and bloodthirsty rite of religious ecstasy and sacrificial murder. The Bacchanalia, an alcoholic celebration of the god, reached such heights (or depths) that it was eventually banned by an outraged Roman Senate in 186 BC.

DRUIDS

The mysterious religious caste of the ancient Celts, who performed a multi-functional role within Celtic society, as priests, teachers and diviners. They have associations with oak groves in which they conducted their ceremonies and with mistletoe, a mysterious and poisonous parasitical plant which grows on oak. The only present day evidence of their organization and rites are from Roman sources, and these merely comment on a few facts with no analysis. Thus today they remain a shadowy unknown organization, whose knowledge was very deliberately not recorded but transmitted orally and consequently died with them. However, their pagan rites are belived to have involved sinister rituals including blood sacrifice.

EPONA

A Celtic horse, war and mother goddess, worshiped mainly in Gaul but also in Britain during Roman times. In her horse goddess avatar she was always portrayed mounted or close to her equine familiars. An indication of her high status is inferred by over 300 monuments to her discovered in Gaul alone. The horse was a vital totem in the Celtic culture and therefore much represented in their art and mythology. Her cult was also adopted by Roman cavalry units along the Rhine, Danube and Scottish frontiers, emphasizing her military connections. As a mother goddess manifesting earth's fertility, Epona was shown with *paterae* (dishes of fruit) and *cornucopiae* (horns of plenty).

EROS

Also known as: Cupid, Amor

The god of love, son of Aphrodite by either Zeus, Ares or Hermes, Cupid is recognized today by his late poetical portrayal as a mischievous chubby winged child. Earlier legends are more ambiguous, suggesting complicated roots and snycretism. His tool was the bow, used to shoot love-arrows, against which nothing and no-one had any kind of defense. This power over both gods and men was indicated by showing him riding on a lion or dolphin, or breaking the thunderbolts of Zeus. Due to his appearance and the personal nature of his power he was benevolently tolerated by the other gods, despite

Right: This mural found in Tunisia (3rd century AD) shows Dionysius with a leopard.

ΔIONYCOC

A-Z
CODEX GODS

his constant tricks and minor misdemeanors, although they also feared his power — for anyone, gods included, could be made a fool for love.

EUROPA

Europa was the daughter of Agenor, King of Phoenicia and her most famous brother was Cadmus. She was yet another conquest of Zeus, who disguised himself as a bull to kidnap her and by whom she bore three sons: Minos, Sarpedon and Rhadamanthys, all of whom became kings. Also from Zeus, prior to her being married off, Europa received three presents: the bronze man Talos who guarded the shores of Crete, a hunting spear that could never miss and a dog that always ran its quarry down. She eventually gave her name to the European continent.

FATES

Also known as: Moirai (Greek), Parcae (Roman), Nornir (Norse)

Atropos, Lachesis and Clotho were three sisters and together they made up the three aspects of Fate. They were the daughters of Zeus and Themis, goddess of Law. Maidenly Clotho ("the spinner") spun the thread of each human's life, while middle-aged Lachesis ("the apportioner") selected the length of each thread, and the hag Atropos ("the inflexible") cut through it, thus ending each life. The Fate sisters stood above the interplay between gods and men, taking little active part; indeed they were almost outside time itself. They did occasionally help Zeus in his battles against giants and monsters and were also once tricked by Apollo who got them drunk, so allowing his friend Admetus to live beyond his allotted lifespan.

In Norse mythology the golden age ended when three giantesses arrived from the land of giants, manifesting time: Urdr (past), Vedandi (present) and Skuld (future). Collectively known as the Nornir they lived in the roots of the World Tree Yggdrasil and controlled the *wyrd* — the fate or destiny — of each human.

Belief in Time and Fate represented by an indifferent or spiteful female trio enjoyed a long life, even after the introduction and spread of Christianity.

FAUNUS

Faunus was the grandson of Saturn and the son of Picus and was worshiped as a god of fields and shepherds. Also seen as a god of prophecy he was the Roman equivalent of the Greek god Pan. An annual festival — the Lupercalia — with which Faunus was associated was held on February 15. The ceremony took place at the Lupercal, a cave situated at the foot of the Palatine Hill in which, according to legend, the she-wolf fed Romulus and Remus. The ceremony was undertaken by the Luperci — young boys who wore nothing save a belt — who wielded whips made of goat skin. After the sacrifice of a goat and a dog, the Luperci

Right: This spectacular 16th century tapestry illustrates the three fates—Atropos, Lachesis and Clotho—as they triumph over Chastity.

atropos lachesis cloto

A-Z
CODEX GODS

beat bystanders around the Palatine Hill. Anyone who was whipped was believed to gain improved fertility. Faunus was normally portrayed as half man with the legs of a goat. Linked with Faunus were the Fauns, who were the Roman equivalent of the Satyrs.

FELICITAS
A goddess of success who first came to prominence in the mid-2nd century BC when a temple was dedicated to her in recognition of Roman success in the conquest of Spain. Her importance grew with the empire as a means of bringing success to a new emperor and, as such, she often appeared on imperial coinage.

FIDES
The Latin word *fides* translates as faith, and Fides was a goddess of good faith. Her cult was popular and stretched back to the earliest days of Rome. Her figure was often used on coins and, like Felicitas, she became much more important with the rise of the empire as a mark of the loyalty of the army. In ceremonies commemorating her, it was normal practice for the sacrificer to don white gloves, and gloved hands were one of her symbols.

FLORA
The Roman goddess of flowers who was supposed to have received her first altar from the Sabine king Titus Tatius. Initially she had no festival, but later she was honored on April 28, when games — the Floriala — were held. The festivities featured various elements of debauchery, including coarse mime. In legend she was originally a nymph (called Chloris) who was pursued by the wind god Zephyr. When the pair married she was transformed into Flora, from whom sprang breath that became petals and following whose footsteps grew flowers. In the Roman myths of Juno (Hera), Flora reacted to Juno's anger over the birth of Minerva by rubbing herbs onto Juno's stomach. This resulted in pregnancy and the subsequent birth of Mars.

FORTUNA
Fors Fortuna was an old Roman goddess, seen as the equivalent of the Greek god Tyche, who was a deity of luck and success. Given her attributes, Fortuna was a popular deity and there were temples to her in many places. At the temple at Praeneste she was called the daughter of Jupiter. She was normally portrayed holding a *cornucopia* — a horn of plenty —and a rudder — indicating her power to direct lives. On occasions she was shown blindfolded symbolizing blind chance.

FENRIR
The monstrous wolf of Norse legend said to be the son of Loki. Fenrir lived in Asgard, the home of the gods, but his increasing size and ferocity terrified everyone. Eventually Odin arrived at a

Right: This Roman wall painting tells the story of Zeus who disguised himself as a bull to seduce Europa, the daughter of Agenor.

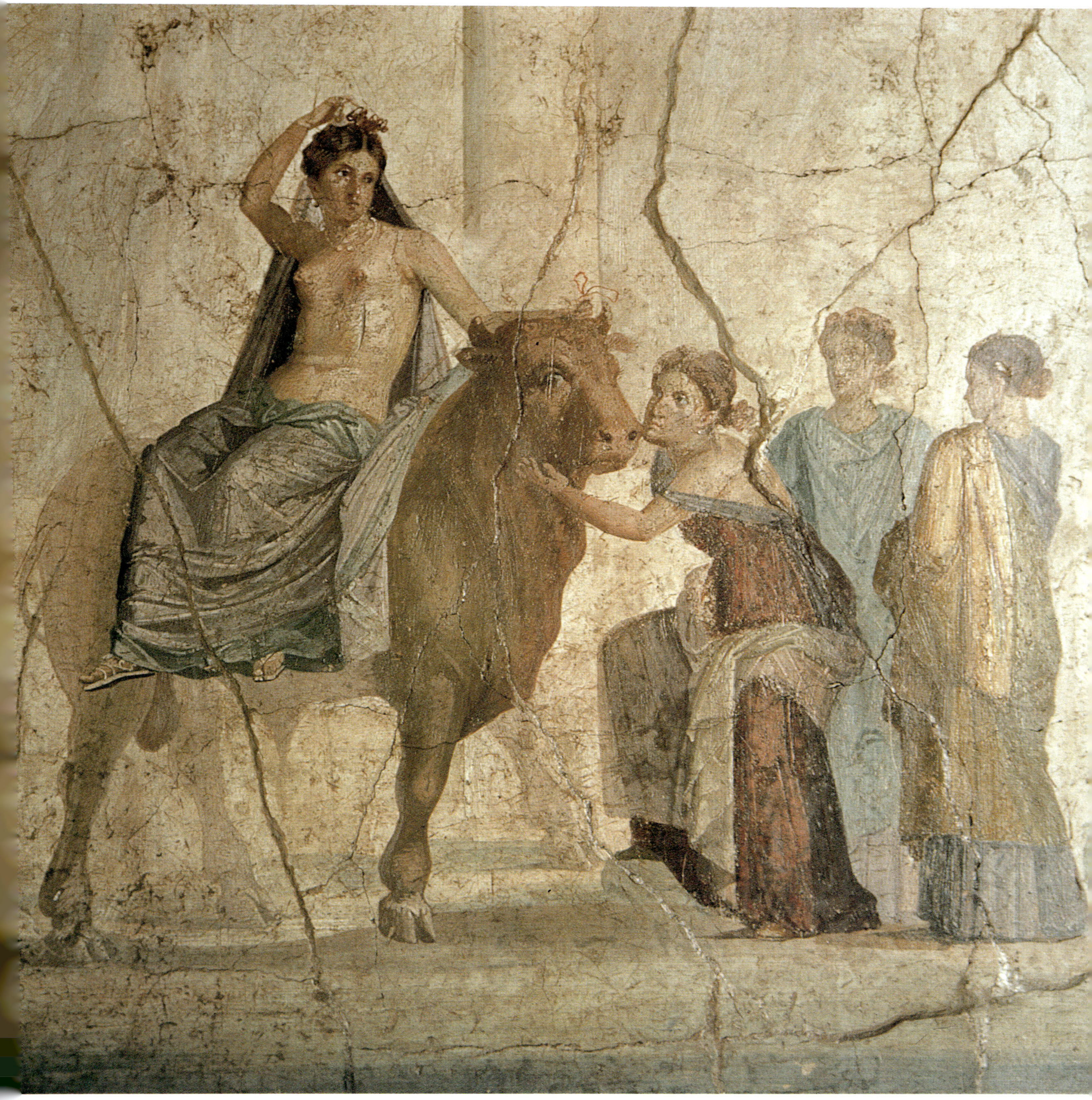

A-Z
CODEX GODS

solution and set the metal-working dwarves to fashioning him a chain made from intangible elements: a fish's breath, a mountain's roots, the stealth of a moving cat, etc. No amount of strength nor force could break this chain, although it appeared to be little more than a silken cord. The next problem was to get it on the monster. This was finally accomplished with the loss of only one hand, belonging to Tyr.

Fenrir went on to wreak havoc at Ragnarok, actually eating Odin before being killed by Vidarr.

FINN MACOOL
Also known as: Finn mac Cumaill, Fionn MacCumal

Hero of the ancient Irish *Fianna* epic, which tells of his own and his son Oisin's reigns and their heroic adventures in the 3rd century BC, Finn gathered around him other heroes and fighters all of whom had to undergo very extreme tests of physical endurance and mental hardship. They then gained admission into Finn's elite special forces and took part in countless magical and monstrous adventures.

FREYA
"Lady"
Also known as: Frigg

The most important fertility and mother goddess of Scandinavia and the equivalent of the great mother goddesses of the Mediterranean area such as Ishtar, Isis, Cybele, and Demeter. A further similarity with ancient West Asian cults was one of her ritual objects, her necklace Brisingamen.

In Norse legend the outstandingly beautiful Freya was the sister of Freyr and the daughter of the sea god Njord. She was married to Odin and her fertility aspect was emphasized by various accusations of incest and promiscuity that were leveled at her in a number of the Icelandic sagas, with Loki especially prominent. In her steamy sex goddess role she was closely involved in love, courtship and marriage rituals, while the procession of her cult statue by wagon from place to place was credited with the gift of prophecy, sexual potency and childbirth.

Another aspect shared with her husband Odin was sovereignty over death, with the fallen heroes being divided between them.

FREYR
"Lord"

The Scandinavian water god, and son of Njord, Freyr had intimate connections with the sea, ships and sea voyages. He was the twin brother of the fertility goddess Freya, both being members of a divine group called the Vanir, which had origins and parallels in West Asia. His worship was closely connected with the idea of divine marriage and sacrifice — in Freyr's case to the young maiden Gerd, who lived in the underworld with the giants and was reluctant to accept him until cursed with sterility. As a result of this myth

Above left: This tapestry features the Scandinavian mythical characters Odin, Thor and Freyr. Right: A Scandinavian carving depicting Odin, the husband of Freya.

· EUROPE ·

A-Z
CODEX GODS

Freyr had no sword when the gods fought their last great battle, Ragnarok, where he was attacked and killed by the fire-giant Surtr. Like Balder he manifested as the young god who must be sacrificed for the sake of humankind.

FURIES
"The Angry Ones"
Also known as: Erinyes, Eumenides
Three avenging goddesses of Greek legend who meted out justice to those who wrongly shed blood. They were also named Eumenides, which actually translates as "the Kindly Ones" — presumably an attempt at appeasement. Another trio of sisters, they were named Alecto, Tisiphone and Megaira. These terrifying winged snake hags, born from the bloody wound that Saturn inflicted on Kronos, pursued such people as Orestes after he had killed his mother, but were purposeful and never randomly malignant.

GAWAIN
Gawain was the Arthurian paragon of chivalry and the opponent of Lancelot in the intrigue of mythical Camelot. However, his adventure with the Green Knight overturned his reputation somewhat. When the giant challenged the Knights of the Round Table to a beheading contest, Gawain accepted and decapitated the giant at a single stroke. The giant then calmly retrieved his head and named a time and place for the rematch. Gawain eventually managed to keep this appointment despite countless digressions and temptations, but flinched when the Green Knight struck, thereby revealing his own imperfection. He only suffered a slight neck wound, and so lived to be remorseful of his imperfection and less likely to judge others.

Perhaps of solar origin, Gawain's strength was said to astrologically wax and wane, and like the Irish hero Cuchulainn he possessed a stealth belt that made him invulnerable.

GORGONS
Another Greek trio of terrifying sisters, Stheno, Eurale, and Medusa, were the daughters of the sea god Phorcys. The first two were immortal but the third, Medusa, wasn't — yet she is the one who is best known and is often referred to as the Gorgon, as if solo. The Gorgons dwelt in the far west, close by the Kingdom of the Dead, and were hideous in appearance — having snake hair, hands of brass, wings of gold, long tusk-like teeth, bodies armored with impenetrable scales and eyes that could kill. All who met their stare were turned instantly to stone. Only Poseidon, of all the gods and men, was not afraid of them, fathering the giant Chrysaor and the winged horse Pegasus on Medusa. This liaison was the cause of her demise, for Athena was so incensed by her impiety when she made love to Poseidon in a temple dedicated to her that she sought out an assassin. She selected the hero Perseus, who finally killed Medusa with Athena's aid.

Right: The gorgon Medusa with snakes for hair, stares from a temple pediment. (c. 580 BC).

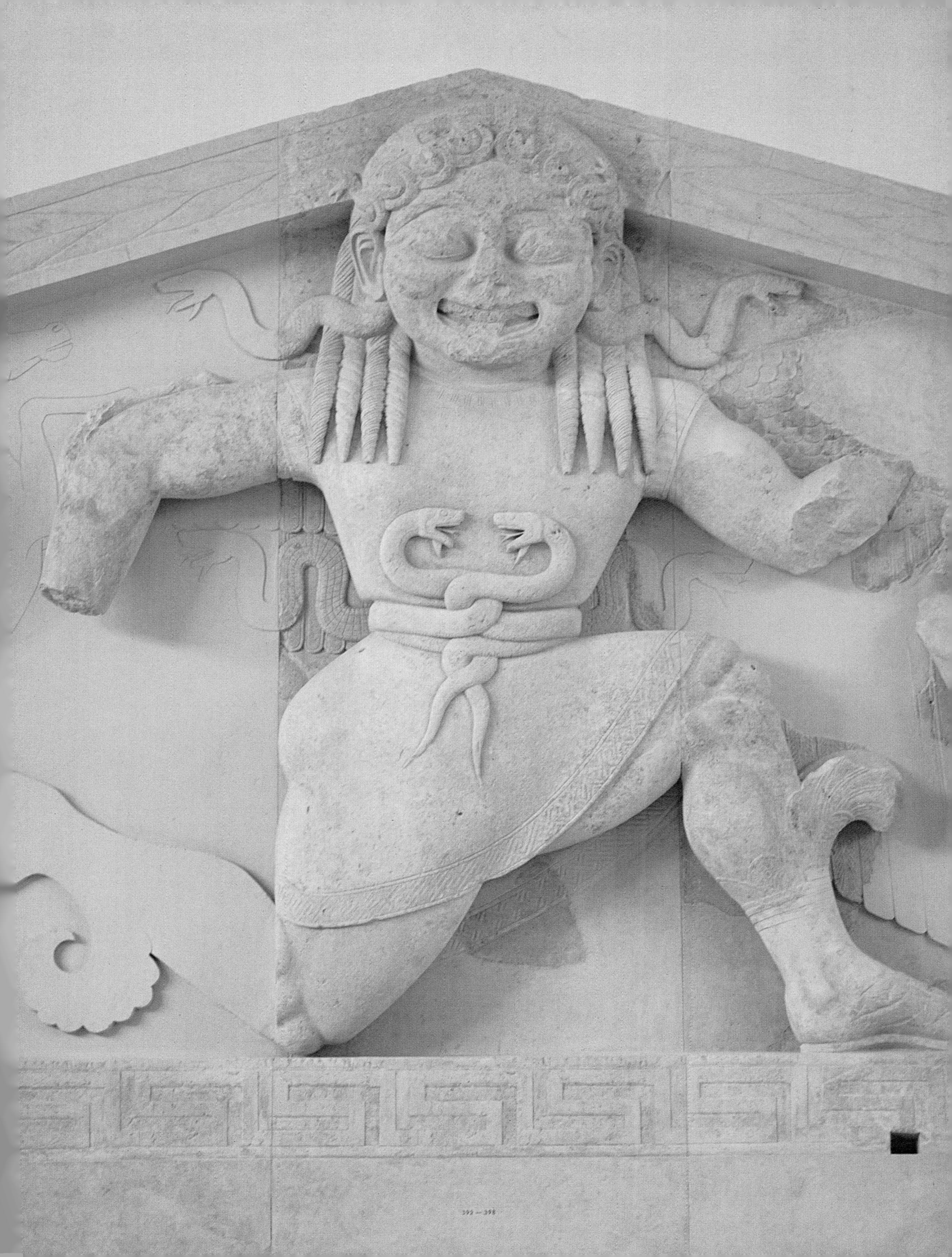

392 — 398

A-Z
CODEX GODS

HOLY GRAIL
Also known as: Sangreal

The mythical vessel of the Last Supper in Christian mythology, said to have received the blood of Christ as he bled on the cross. The Grail was supposed to have been brought to Britain by Joseph of Aramathea, the rich merchant who buried Jesus and went on to found a Christian settlement at Glastonbury. The grail was "mislaid" and vanished into the Limbo-realm of the wounded Fisher-King, its retrieval becoming an endless quest for the Knights of the Round Table, with Sir Galahad in particular being keen to find it.

The conventional Church hierarchy was disturbed by the Grail legend, linked as it was to fetish objects and the symbolism of older pagan religions, yet it could not curtail cup's potency.

HADES
Also known as: Pluto

Brother of Zeus and king of Hell, named Tartarus by the ancient Greeks, his name became synonymous with his kingdom. Unlike parallel gods of other religions Hades was seen as a pitiless and maleficent deity. Following the defeat of the Titans by the gods, Zeus took the earth and heavens as his dominion, giving his brothers Poseidon the sea and Hades the underworld.

Lacking a wife, Hades targeted his niece Persephone (the young daughter of Zeus and Demeter), and when her parents would not acknowledge him he took matters into his own hands and kidnapped her. Eternal winter and a barren earth were the result, as a forlorn Demeter sought her daughter and demanded her release. But shrewd Hades had foreseen this, and had given Persephone the seed of a pomegranate to eat — for anyone who had consumed anything whatsoever in the underworld could never return to the earth to live. Eventually a compromise was worked out, with Persephone dividing her time between sunlight and the realm of Hades, which neatly explained the turning seasons.

The name Pluto means "the rich" — a reference to the plentiful mineral resources beneath the ground and the fertility of the earth in which he dwelt.

HARPIES
Harpies were originally wind spirits but later they became winged monsters who snatched away food or carried people off to their deaths. In the story of the Argonauts they torment the blind seer Phineus. They were sometimes portrayed as birds with women's faces.

HECATE
"The Distant One"

Linked to the moon, the ancient Greek goddess Hecate might originally have been a fertility and agricultural deity, but her mainly beneficent role changed in time to that of a nocturnal witch, preoccupied with ghosts and magic, lingering in

Right: This detail of a larger work shows Hades, lord of the underworld, taking his neice Persephone by force to be his wife.

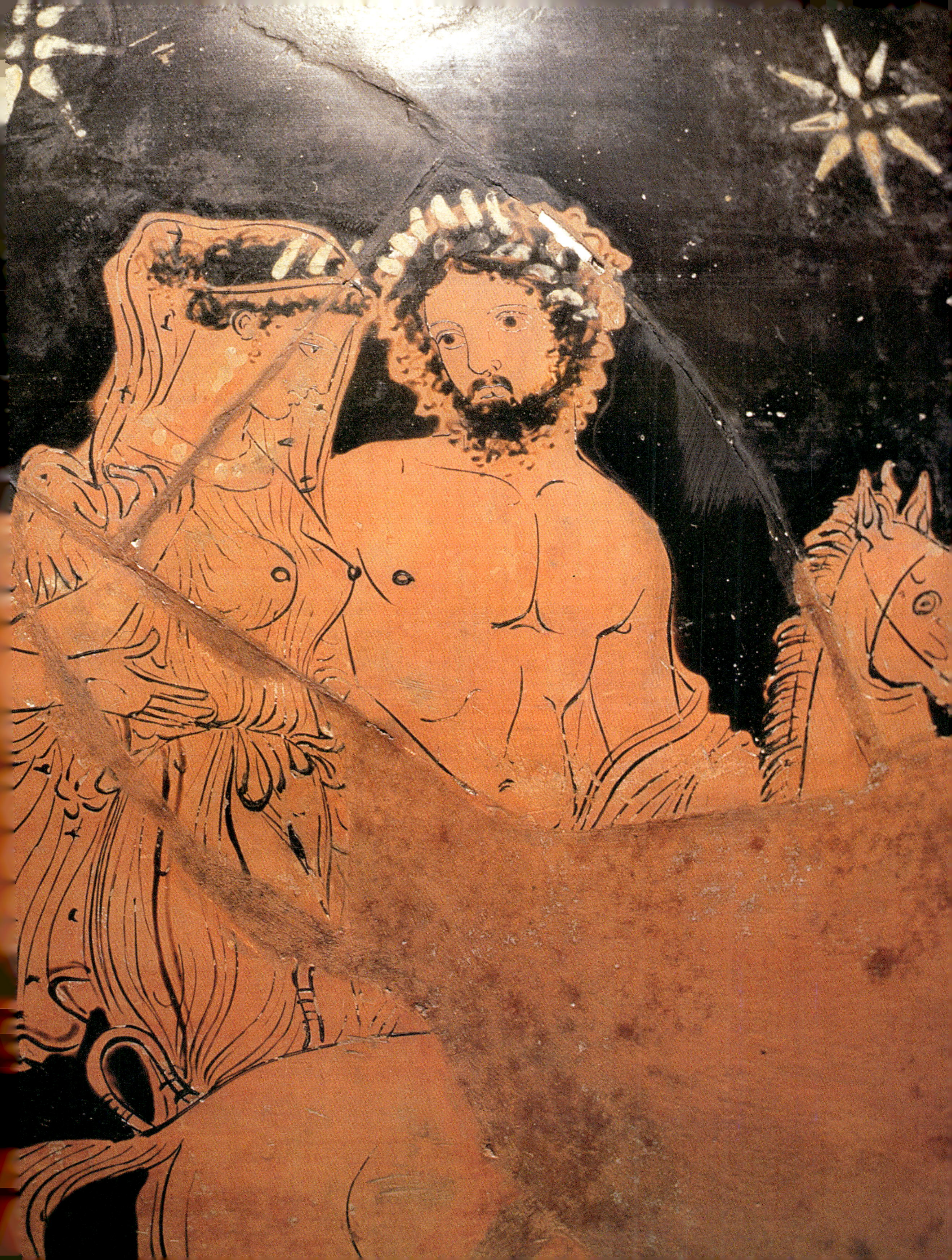

A-Z
CODEX GODS

cemeteries or places of murder and punishment. Attention from her could seriously damage your health and she was consequently appeased with offerings. Needless to say she was sister to the moon goddess Artemis.

HELIOS
Also known as: Sol
Helios was a Titan, a Greek sun god generally thought of as driving his chariot east to west across the sky. In later legend he is associated with Apollo or Hyperion.

Linked to the agricultural year, Sol, the Roman god of sun, was initially a relatively unimportant deity despite the importance of the sun in the growth of crops. The development of his cult occurred under the increasing influence of Oriental religions and under the Emperor Diocletian (who reigned from 284 AD until his abdication and retirement in 305) the cult of Sol was raised to one of the most important in the state.

HEIMDALL
Heimdall was the defender of Asgard, constantly scanning for the anticipated attack of the Giants, armed and ready to sound the alarm on his great horn at the launch of the Norse apocalypse: Ragnarok. He lived beside the Bifrost Bridge at Heaven's Edge where he often managed to thwart his cunning counterpart, Loki, who never stayed crushed for long and never stopped trying. At Ragnarok Heimdall, like almost all the other gods, went down fighting with flame, sword, tooth and claw against Loki's mad powers.

His manifestation as a beneficent fire god underlines these poised opposites, Loki symbolizing fire's destructive capability.

HEPHAESTUS
Also known as: Vulcan
The subterranean Greek smith and earth god, divine arms manufacturer and son of Zeus and Hera, Hephaestus is portrayed lame, clad in the leather apron of his metallurgical profession — his lameness the result of child abuse when his father Zeus angrily hurled him out of heaven. After falling for an eternity Hephaestus landed on the island of Lemnos, where he remained for a decade after he had recovered, learning the skills of metallurgy. He later produced some of the best equipment and munitions used by the gods — and kept a few ninja-type weapons up his sleeve too, including the almost invisible yet indestructible gossamer mesh net with which he caught his wife Aphrodite and his brother Ares red-handed in the act of their infidelity. His origins, as with many Greek gods, lie further to the east in West Asia and his myth later continued this westward trend — the Romans in turn transforming him into Vulcan.

Right: This close-up of a Corinthian vase, shows Heracles and the centaur Setos.

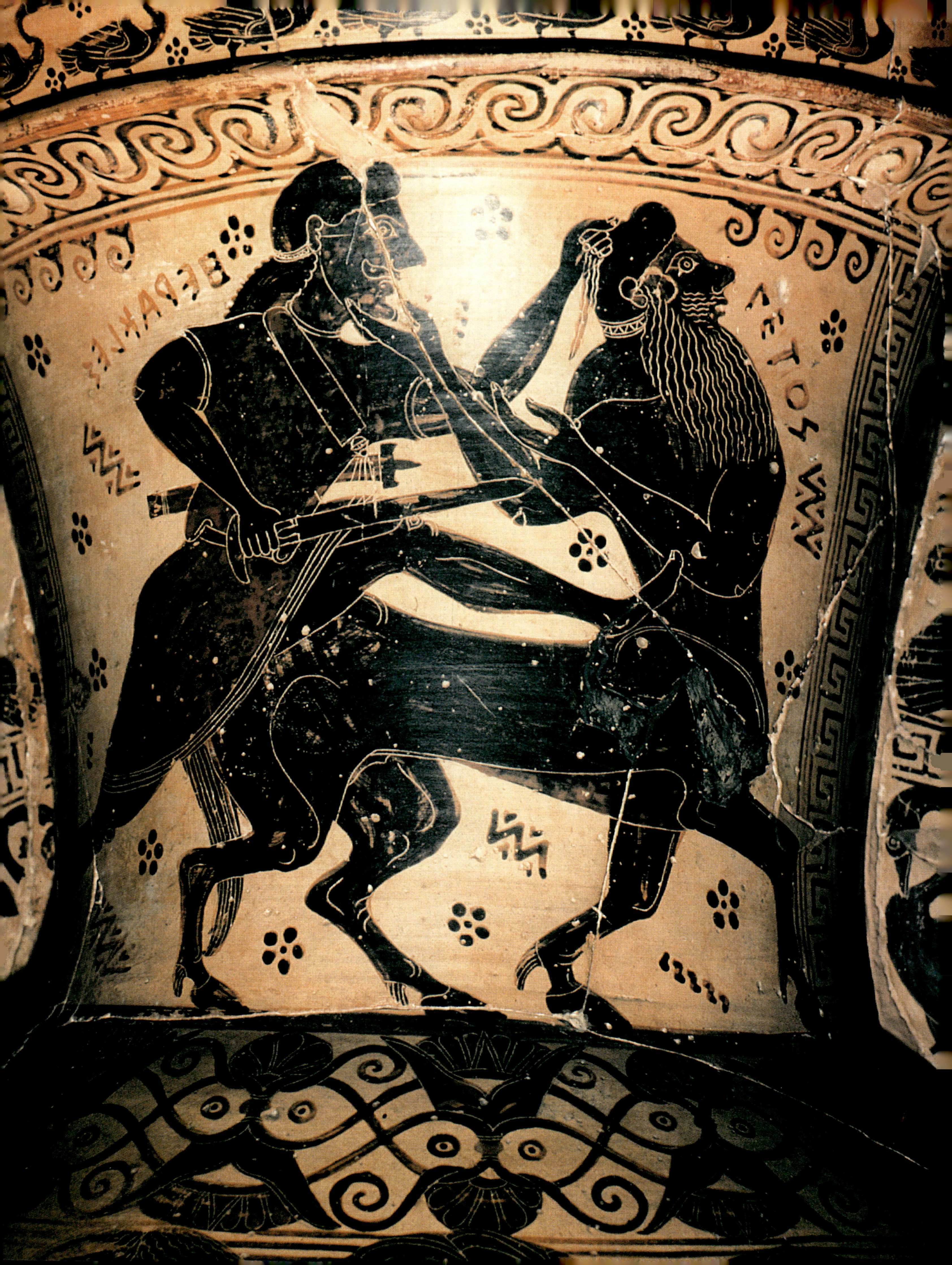

A-Z
CODEX GODS

HERA
"Lady"

Also known as: Juno

Manifesting the uneasy union of the older earth mother goddess with the dominant male sky deity, the marriage of Zeus and Hera was tempestuous to the say the least. His countless infidelities drove her beserk with jealous rage and motivated some horrendous acts of revenge. That Zeus could assert his superiority when she sometimes went too far reflects the inevitable passing of her power, though she remained a goddess of incredible destructive capability. The Roman counterpart was Juno, goddess of marriage and money.

HERACLES
Also known as: Hercules

The definitive superman hero of Greek mythology, the son of Zeus and a human girl Alcmena, who endured considerable trauma when giving birth. Hera singled out Heracles as the focus of her anger and resentment over the many extra-marital progeny of her errant husband. He survived assassination attempts that began simultaneously with his birth and went on to achieve various superhuman feats, until, finally driven mad by Hera, he killed his own family in a frenzy. In repentance he undertook his famous Twelve Labors. These were: the killing of the Nemean lion, the destruction of the seven-headed Hydra, the capture of the Arcadian stag, the capture of the Erymanthian boar, the cleaning of the Augean stables, the killing of the carnivorous Stymphalian birds, the capture of the bull Poseidon had sent to ravage Crete, the capture of the meat-eating Diomedian mares, the theft of the Hippolyta's girdle, the killing of the monster Geryon, bringing the apples from the garden of the Hesperides and finally, fetching the three-headed hellhound Cerberus from the underworld.

HERMES
Also known as: Mercury

Messenger of the Greek gods, son of Zeus and the nymph Maia, Hermes was originally a fertility deity who also led the souls of the dead down to the underworld and was thus later identified with Odin. He was the patron saint of merchants and seamen, good luck, thieves and pickpockets, but had a pronounced mischievous trickster aspect as well, often leading men astray. He wasn't above tricking gods as well — stealing the oxen of Admetus, which Apollo was looking after. He later quelled that

Left: The Greek god Heracles stands with his lion skin and club.
Right: This relief depicts Heracles battling the Lernaean Hydra (3rd century BC).

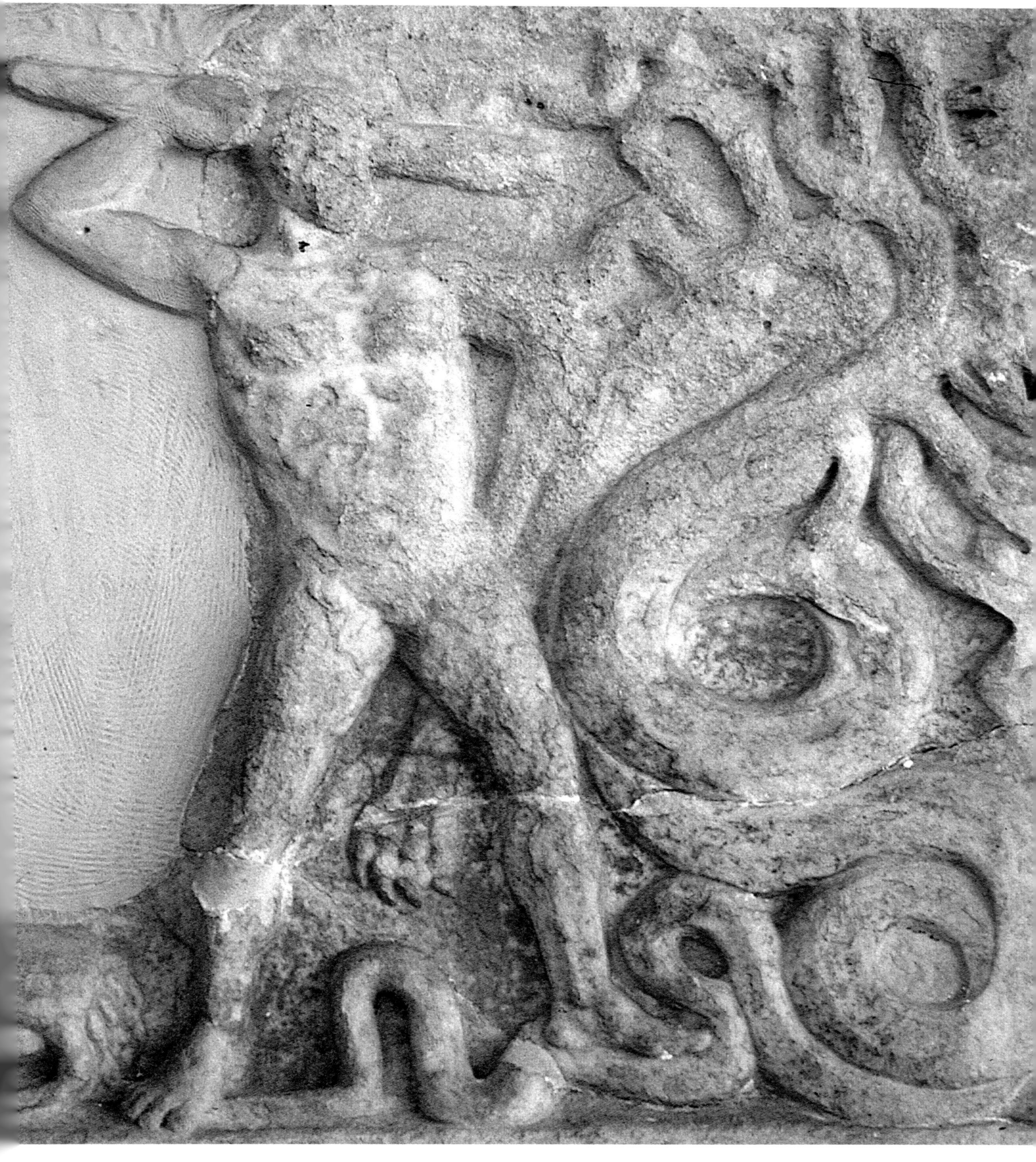

A-Z
CODEX GODS

god's rage by giving him the lyre — a musical instrument he had invented. For acting as Zeus's special go-between in his extra-marital affairs he was rewarded with the winged helmet and sandals in which he is usually portrayed, while holding his *caduceus* (wand). As the god of roads and travel he was represented by wayside shrines or *hermeia* — square pillars — with a bust of the god on top and a phallus carved below.

HESTIA

It is to Hestia's credit that she never took part in wars or disputes. This put her morally above the other great Olympians and she was widely worshiped for her humanity and for being the most benign of the gods. After the battle against the Titans and the ursurption of Cronus she was courted by both Apollo and Poseidon but she had taken an oath that she would remain a virgin. Zeus saw that this avoided any possible damaging conflict on Olympus and accordingly rewarded her by offering her the first victim of any mortal sacrifice. She was worshiped in the home as goddess of the hearth and most households would have had a small shrine to her.

HORATIUS

According to legend, Horatius, who was nicknamed the "one-eyed," prevented the army of an Etruscan leader, Lars Porsenna, from crossing the Sublician bridge. Once the bridge had been destroyed and Rome thus saved, Horatius was reputed to have swum across the River Tiber to safety. His exploits were made famous in English in Macaulay's *Lays of Ancient Rome*.

HYPNOS

The Greek god of sleep, son of Night and the brother of Death. He was generally thought of as a winged boy who touched the foreheads of the weary or poured a sleeping draught from a cup. In the *Iliad* he carries the dead warriors from the battlefield.

ICARUS

Son of the inventor Daedalus, who offended Minos the king of Crete. They escaped imprisonment together by means of artificial wings fastened by wax. Unheeding of his father's warnings Icarus flew too close to the sun, which melted the wax and he fell to a watery grave.

IO

Io was a priestess of Hera at Argos and a lover of Zeus who turned her into a heifer to protect her from the jealous Hera. Hera was not deceived and set the giant Argus to watch her. She then sent a gadfly which drove Io all over Europe and Egypt where she was eventually restored by Zeus.

JANUS

A legendary wise Italian king who founded a small town on the River Tiber called Janiculum, which became a core part of Rome and is still the

Right: This Roman lamp (1st century AD) shows Icarus falling to his death. Icarus had flown too close to the sun at which time his wings, fastened only by wax, melted.

289

A-Z
CODEX GODS

name of one of the Seven Hills of that city today. During his reign, Saturn, driven from Heaven by his son Jupiter, fled to Italy, and Janus promptly welcomed him as a co-ruler. He was portrayed with two faces — each looking in an opposite direction, because he was credited with knowledge of both the past and the future. His temple in the forum at Rome had another significance, for the gates were opened in time of war. Janus later developed into the god of all beginnings, and the month of January was sacred to him; while as four-headed Janus, or Janus Quadrifons, he presided over the four seasons.

JASON

Legendary leader of the Argonauts and son of Aeson, Jason should have inherited the throne of Iolcos after his father died, but was usurped by his half-brother, Pelias. For safety's sake Jason was then smuggled out of Iolcos and raised by the centaur Chiron. When he returned to claim his inheritance Pelias sent him on the quest for the Golden Fleece, convinced he would never return.

Jason gathered a crew of the noblest heroes in Greece, and with them and the indispensable witch Medea, succeeded in his mission, returned home, married Medea and gave the fleece to Pelias. At this point the traditions diverge dramatically, some saying that Jason ruled instead of Pelias, some that he lived quietly at Iolcos. One story is that Medea caused the death of Pelias by magic, tricking his daughters into boiling him in alive in cauldron in order to supposedly rejuvenate him.

This did not secure Jason the throne, as he was driven from Iolcos by Pelias's son. Jason and Medea then went to Corinth for a decade, after which he transferred his affections to Glauce, daughter of King Creon. In revenge Medea murdered the two children she had had by Jason and fled. Jason met his death when part of the stern of the *Argo* fell on him while he was asleep.

JESUS OF NAZARETH

Semi-legendary Son of God and the Virgin Mary in an "immaculate" conception, to whom many miracles and cures were attributed, as well as a strong moral and ethical stance. This militant young Hebrew, whose revolutionary message upset both Roman and Jewish authorities, eventually paid the price with his life, but was resurrected by his father, the Semite creator god Yaweh.

JUNO

Also known as: Hera

Along with Jupiter and Minerva, Juno was one of a trio of gods that were established by the Etruscans. She was the goddess of women and childbirth and was also the wife of Jupiter. Her ceremony, Matronalia, was held annually on March 1 — the month dedicated to Mars, who was Juno's miraculous offspring. She is remembered today in the name of the month June.

Right: This ivory panel, which shows the adoration of the Magi, probably originated in Syria (6th century AD).

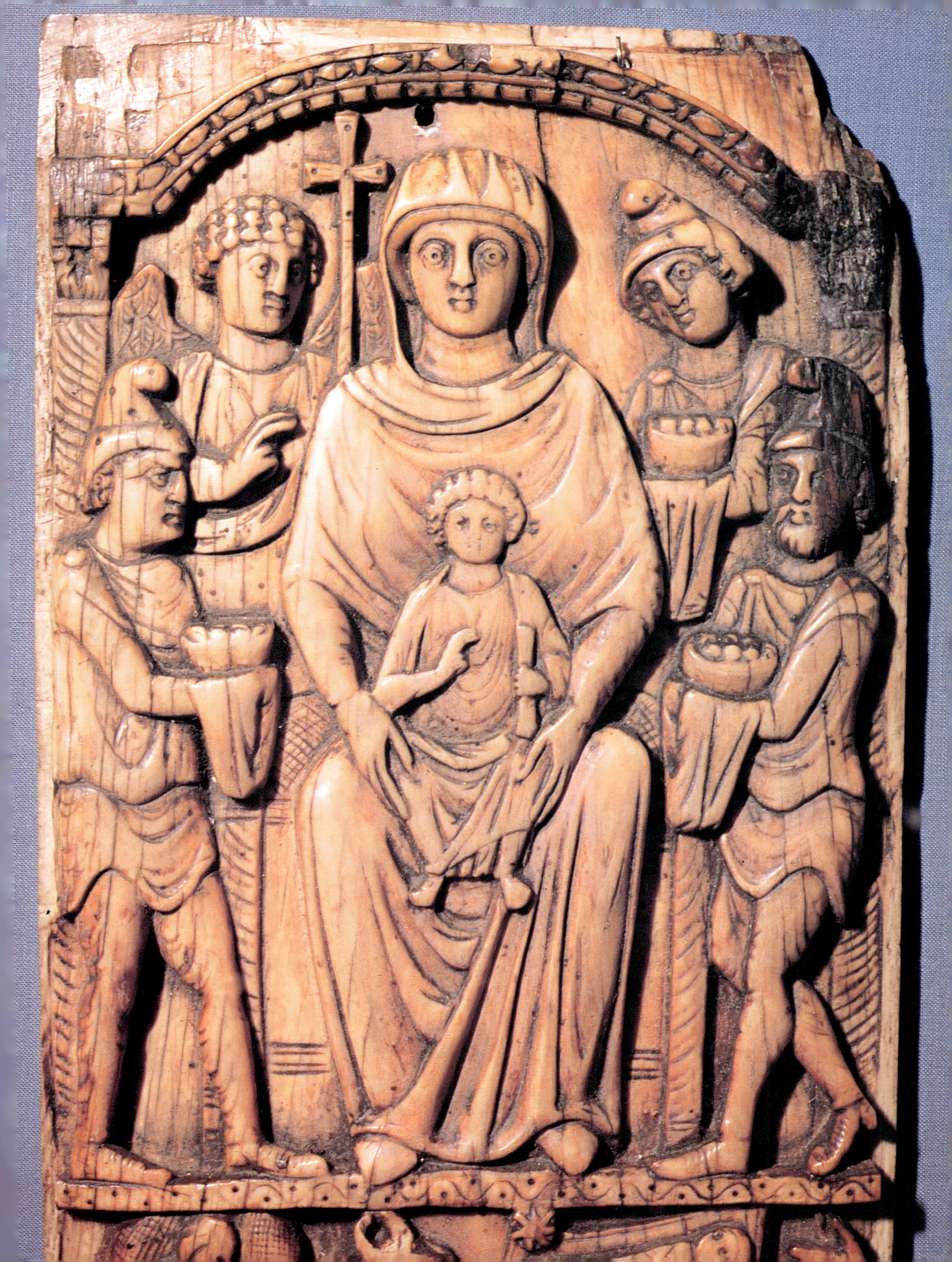

A-Z
CODEX GODS

Juno is often regarded as the Roman equivalent of the Greek goddess Hera and most of the myths surrounding her are derived from that attribution. One exception concerns the birth of Mars. In this version of the legend, Juno is upset following the birth of Minerva directly from Jupiter's head. She is placated when Flora massages her stomach with herbs leading Juno to become pregnant with Mars.

JUPITER
See Zeus.

KRONOS
Also known as: Chronos, Saturn

The Titan son of Ouranos and Gaia, Kronos committed patricide after his father, following a negative oracle, took to eating his children. Kronos then married his sister Rhea and proceeded to emulate his father, digesting his own progeny until Zeus, born in hiding, emerged to topple him. In the ensuing battle the gods led by Zeus defeated Kronos and the Titans, inaugurating a new age.

LANCELOT
Also known as: Lancelot du Lac

Stolen when only a year old and raised by the Lady of the Lake, Nimue, Lancelot was Arthur's elite swordsman who nevertheless ultimately betrayed him in his love and lust for the king's wife, Guinevere. After betraying his allegiance, he became impure and was thus excluded from the search for the Holy Grail. Lancelot represented the "all for love" ideal but in being so he disgraced the chivalric code and indirectly brought about the fall of Camelot. Guinevere ended her days in a convent as a nun and Lancelot as a monk, tending Arthur's grave.

LAOMEDON
The king of Troy and father of Priam, noted for his treachery. Laomedon refused payment to Apollo and Poseidon when they built his city walls so they sent a sea monster which would have devoured his daughter Hesione had not Heracles intervened. Laomedon had promised his famous horses to Heracles for rescuing his daughter but again did not keep his part of the deal. The horses in question were the ones Zeus had given to Troy in return for a Trojan prince called Ganymede who was carried off to be his cup bearer. When Laomedon refused to give up the horses Heracles sacked the city and killed all of Laomedon's sons except Priam.

LAPITHS
A primitive mountain tribe in Thessaly related to the Centaurs through common descent from Ixion. Ixion was a king of the Lapiths and, according to legend, the first man to kill a blood relative. For this he was purified by Zeus but, later, he tried to rape Hera. He was deceived by a cloud made in her image on which he begat the

Right: Athena and Hera of Samos were protectors of Athens and the Acropolis respectively. This Greek relief (403–402 BC) on an Athenian decree paid tribute to the Samian people.

ΗΓΗΣΩ ΦΑΝΙΑ ΑΛΑΙΕΥΣ

A-Z
CODEX GODS

father of the Centaurs. As a punishment for his sins Ixion was fixed to a revolving wheel in Hell to suffer for eternity. Lapiths were chiefly famous for their battle with the drunken Centaurs at the marriage of their king Pirithous.

LAVERNA

A very popular deity, Laverna was the Roman goddess of cheats and thieves. One of the city gates to Rome was called the Laverna due to its proximity to an altar dedicated to her worship.

LEDA

An Aetolian princess, the wife of Tyndareus, King of Sparta, and the mother of Clytemnestra, Helen, Castor and Polydeuces (Pollux), Leda was loved by Zeus who came to her in the form of a swan. She gave birth to an egg from which were hatched Helen and Polydeuces, while Castor and Clytemnestra were fathered by Tyndareus.

LEIB-OLMAI

"Alder Man"

Leib-Olmai was a Lapp bear god who was appeased by hunters in order to ensure success and gain protection from Ovda, a nasty counterpart to Leib-Olmai and a kind of naked transvestite wood ninja, who wandered the forests with its feet turned backward, looking for humans to torment prior to making supper out of them. A favored method was enticement to wrestle, cuddle or dance — people were then literally danced or tickled to death. Leib-Olmai was the only protection from this strange monster.

LETO

Mother of Artemis and Apollo.

LIBER

This god of fertility was linked with wine and, as with numerous other old Roman gods, was to inherit the mantle of his Greek counterpart, Dionysius. His festival, celebrated on March 17, was known as the Liberalia and was often the occasion when youths passed from adolescence to adulthood through the adoption of the *toga virilis*. Liber's cult was associated with those of Ceres and of Libertas.

Dionysius was also known as Bacchus, and it is from this name that the word Bacchanalian has derived. The festival of Bacchanalia was popular, particularly amongst the lower classes, and was often a time of great drunkenness. This led the senate to try and suppress the cult at the end of the 2nd century BC, but perhaps inevitably the cult survived until the end of the Roman empire.

LIBERTAS

The goddess of personal freedom. Following the expulsion of the tyrant Tarquinius Superbus, the last of the seven kings of pre-republic Rome, the state acquired "freedom" or "libertas." The basis of Roman freedom was the republican

Right: This Greek sculpture, now in the Vatican, depicts the tale of Laocoön, a priest of Apollo's who, along with his two sons, was killed by serpents sent by Apollo or Athena.

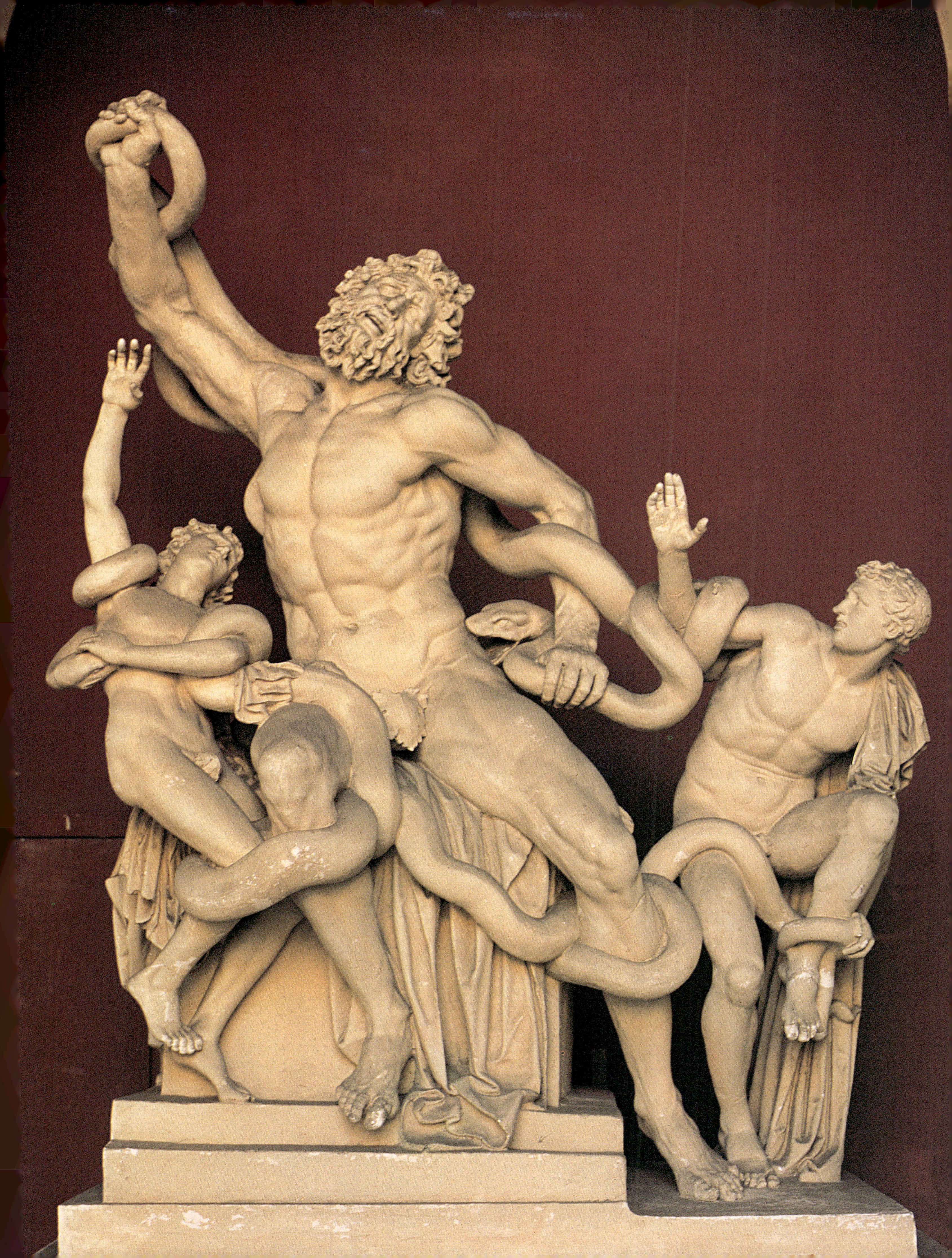

A-Z
CODEX GODS

constitution, although this was much modified over time and much of the opposition to Julius Caesar and the later emperors came from a belief that imperial power ran counter to the liberty enshrined in the constitution. To many Romans, appalled by the excesses of certain emperors, the republic represented a golden age to which the state should return.

LIBITINA

Just as the Romans had gods who looked after their entry into the world, so too did they have deities who looked after their death. Libitina was the goddess who watched over funerals.

LUNA

The goddess of birth and of the moon. She was worshiped at a number of temples, including one on the Aventine Hill that was burnt down during the reign of Nero (he who fiddled while Rome burned). Luna was the equivalent of the pre-Greek goddess Selene and of the Greek Artemis. In myth, Selene was the sister of Helios and Eos, and like her siblings was the possessor of a chariot on which she drove across the sky. There are various myths related to Selene. In one she falls in love with Endymion and, after bearing him fifty daughters, has him put into everlasting sleep so that she can continue to enjoy his beauty. Selene is also (with Zeus as the father) the mother of Herse (dew) and Pandia. Selene was also linked amorously with Pan.

LIMBO

An interim area of Hell inhabited by the virtuous pagan dead. Christian mythology came up with the idea of Limbo for those pagans who had lived a gentle, virtuous life prior to its own existence. These unfortunates reside in a part of Hell where people do not undergo pain and torment and yet are excluded from the bliss of Heaven.

LOKI

Malignant god of the destructive aspect of fire and mischief-maker/trickster supreme among the Norse gods, Loki is the conundrum of Norse mythology. He seems so vital to the whole show that if he had never existed there wouldn't really be much of a Norse mythology. He was invariably malicious but, having caused harm, he would then often somehow put matters right. He was the booby trap hidden by a callous Fate among the Asgard gods — permanently trying to go off. It seems that he was only tolerated because of an obscure blood-brother relationship with Odin but perhaps he reflected the awareness or attitude of the culture that gave birth to him — a certain fatalistic resignation that "it's all going to happen anyway, so go for it."

Ultimately it was through his incredibly destructive children Fenrir, Jormungand and Hel that Loki caused most trouble and Odin knew they would be triumphant at Ragnarok — the Doom of the Gods.

Right: A chess piece carved from walrus ivory into the shape of a Viking.

297

A-Z
CODEX GODS

LUCRETIA

Lucretia's rape and consequent suicide were the mythological root that led to the eclipse of Etruscan rule in Rome. It is told in her legend that the outcry generated brought about insurrection and ultimately the abolition of the monarchy, with the beginning of the republic not far behind. Nevertheless, while it seems plausible this was merely an exciting story concocted by later writers and poets to dramatize events lost in the mists of time.

LUG

Also known as: Lugus, Lugh

Lug was the solar deity in Irish Celtic mythology and leader of the legendary Tuatha. He was famous for his magical power and wisdom, but was also a musician of great renown. His qualities recommended him to the king of the Tuatha, who made him ruler for a set time in order to use his powers and organizational abilities to rid the kingdom of the evil Formoirian spirits that were assaulting it. Under Lug's control the various elements of Tuatha society — sorcerers, warriors, druids and weapon manufacturers — all worked together with such precision that victory soon came about. From that time Lug was seen as the patron of the Tuatha.

MARS

See Ares.

MEDEA

The daughter of Aeëtes, king of Colchis, a priestess of Hecate and a witch, Medea famously helped Jason win the Golden Fleece. Following this adventure Jason and Medea went to Corinth where he abandoned her for the king's daughter. In revenge Medea destroyed the girl and her father, killed her two children then escaped in a dragon-drawn chariot, first to Athens, then to Asia.

MEDUSA

See Gorgons.

MERCURY

See Hermes.

MERLIN

The wizard of Arthurian legend who brought about the king's birth. In fact Merlin's origins go even deeper into a Celtic past where various strands attribute magical feats of power to him, from overcoming dragons to the building of Stonehenge. It was only in the 12th century AD that the now familiar story was first recorded — the bringing together of Arthur's parents by the use of magic, transforming Uther into a double of Gorlois, Ygraine's husband. Merlin then raised Arthur, developing him for the kingship for which he was destined. The wizard was counterbalanced by a witch, Queen Mab, both of them representing a last flowering of pagan culture that was losing

Right: A scene from the Scandinavian doomsday myth Ragnarok. Here, Odin, armed with a raven and spear waits for death at the jaws of the wolf Fenrir.

299

A-Z
CODEX GODS

ground before a pugnacious Christianity, which was in the process of consigning them to folklore. Merlin's end came through another enchantress, Nineve, to whom through falling in love he imparted enough of his magic to enable her to trap him forever in an enchanted coppice.

MIDAS

Midas, the legendary king of Phrygia, has a variety of legends attributed to him, the most famous being that of his golden touch. This he won from Dionysius who granted his wish after he had aided Silenus, the satyr companion of that god. Having wished that everything he touched would turn to gold, Midas regretted his greed when he found this also applied to his sustenance. He subsequently asked to be relieved of his wish. Another version tells of Midas deviously making Silenius drunk in order to learn his wisdom. The knowing satyr then gives him a parable with the theme that riches do not bring happiness.

MINERVA

See Athena.

MINOS

Minos, the legendary Cretan king, was the son of Europa and Zeus but was brought up by Asterion, king of Crete, after whose death he became sole ruler, with an ensuing reign that was famous for its wisdom and justice. In total contrast to this are the Attic myths concerning Minos, which cast him as an evil tyrant exacting tribute and a womanizer who was also supposed to have originated homosexuality. Daedalus too, first worked for him and then had to escape with his life after an argument. This discrepancy is explained by the real-life contest for dominance between Attica and Crete, two fiercely competitive maritime states.

In later times Minos was portrayed as an underworld figure and an aggressive and severe judge of dead.

MINOTAUR

The mythical monster of the Labyrinth, with the head of a bull and the body of a man, the Minotaur was fruit of the union between Pasiphae, wife of King Minos of Crete, and the bull sent by Poseidon. Following his birth Minos had the Athenian architect Daedalus, construct a vast maze (the Labyrinth) and shut the bull/man hybrid away, feeding him seven young men and seven young women, which was the annual tribute exacted from Athens. The hero Theseus volunteered himself to be one of these victims and, with the help of Ariadne, the daughter of Minos who had fallen in love with him, was able to slay the monster and effect his own escape.

Right: Detail of a Greek vase featuring Theseus and the Minotaur, painted by Hermonax, during the 5th century BC.

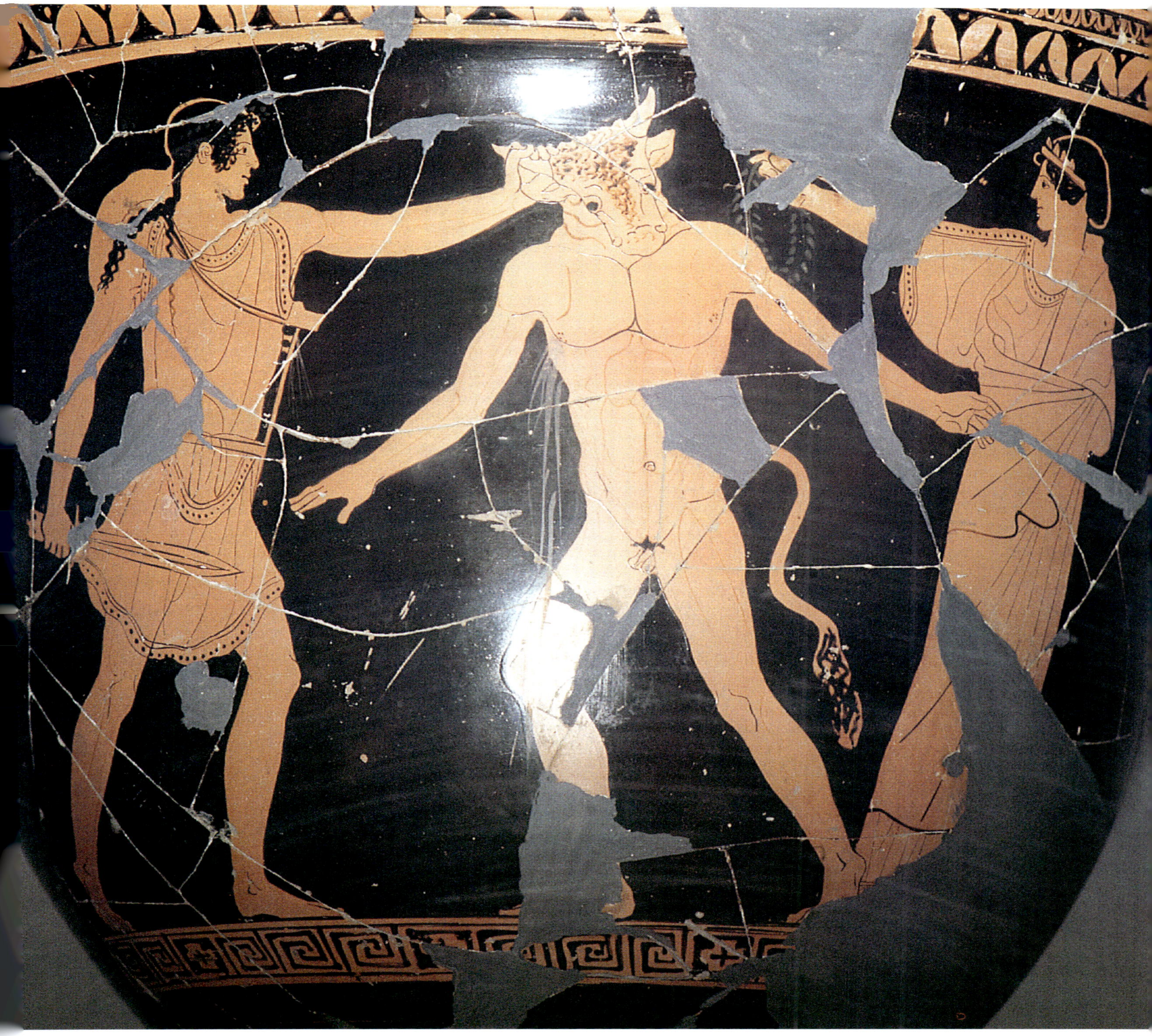

A-Z
CODEX GODS

MORRIGAN
"Phantom Queen"
Also known as: Nemhain, Badbh, Macha
Another Celtic mother goddess, who often combined her sexual role with that of a female war and horse deity, she regularly occurred in triple format. Although they did not fight themselves, they affected the armies in combat with their fearsome aspects and magic abilities. These goddesses also appeared in animal and bird avatars and Morrigan was especially famed for this facility, usually appearing as a raven or crow on the battlefield to signal immanent change and fulfillment of prophecy. As a fertility divinity she appeared as a beautiful young girl making advances, and as a mate to the Dgahda she advised him tactically.

THE MUSES
The Muses, of whom there were nine in number, were the daughters of Zeus and Mnemosyne (memory). Each of them had a particular area of art or science to control: Calliope was the muse of epic poetry; Clio that of history; Erato that of love poetry; Euterpe of lyric poetry; Melpomene of tragedy; Polyhymnia of sacred music; Terpsichore of song and choral dance; Thalia of comedy; and Urania of astronomy. Calliope was the mother of Orpheus (the father was Apollo) and she was normally portrayed holding a book and crowned with laurels. Clio was also portrayed with a book, in which she recorded the acts of the heroes. Erato was regarded as the inventor of the lute and the lyre and was normally portrayed as being crowned with roses and myrtle. Euterpe was regarded as the inventor of all wind instruments.

MYSTERIES
Many of the ancient cults of Classical society were secret societies, into which only the initiated — known as the mystai — could enter. Initiation rites were often graded and each initiate had to advance from one stage to the next. A number of the Eastern cults adopted by the Greeks and Romans, such as that of Cybele and Mithras, were also primarily secret in organization. Little is known about the actual ceremonies, as they were held in secret and only the initiated could attend. Those who revealed the secrets of the Mysteries were liable to punishment.

NARCISSUS
Narcissus was a beautiful youth in Greek mythology who was condemned to fall in love with his own reflection. Thinking that the reflection was a water-spirit he bent over to kiss it. The reflection disappeared but, as he backed away, it reappeared. Having fallen passionately in love with Narcissus only to be rejected by him, the nymph Echo died of grief. Echo had been punished by Hera with the loss of speech and she finally pined away to nothing but a voice. Like Echo, Narcissus died of pining for an impossible love. The nymphs prepared a funeral pyre for

Right: The mystery of the Mysteries ... here brides in an initiation ceremony are depicted recieving the rites of Dionysus.

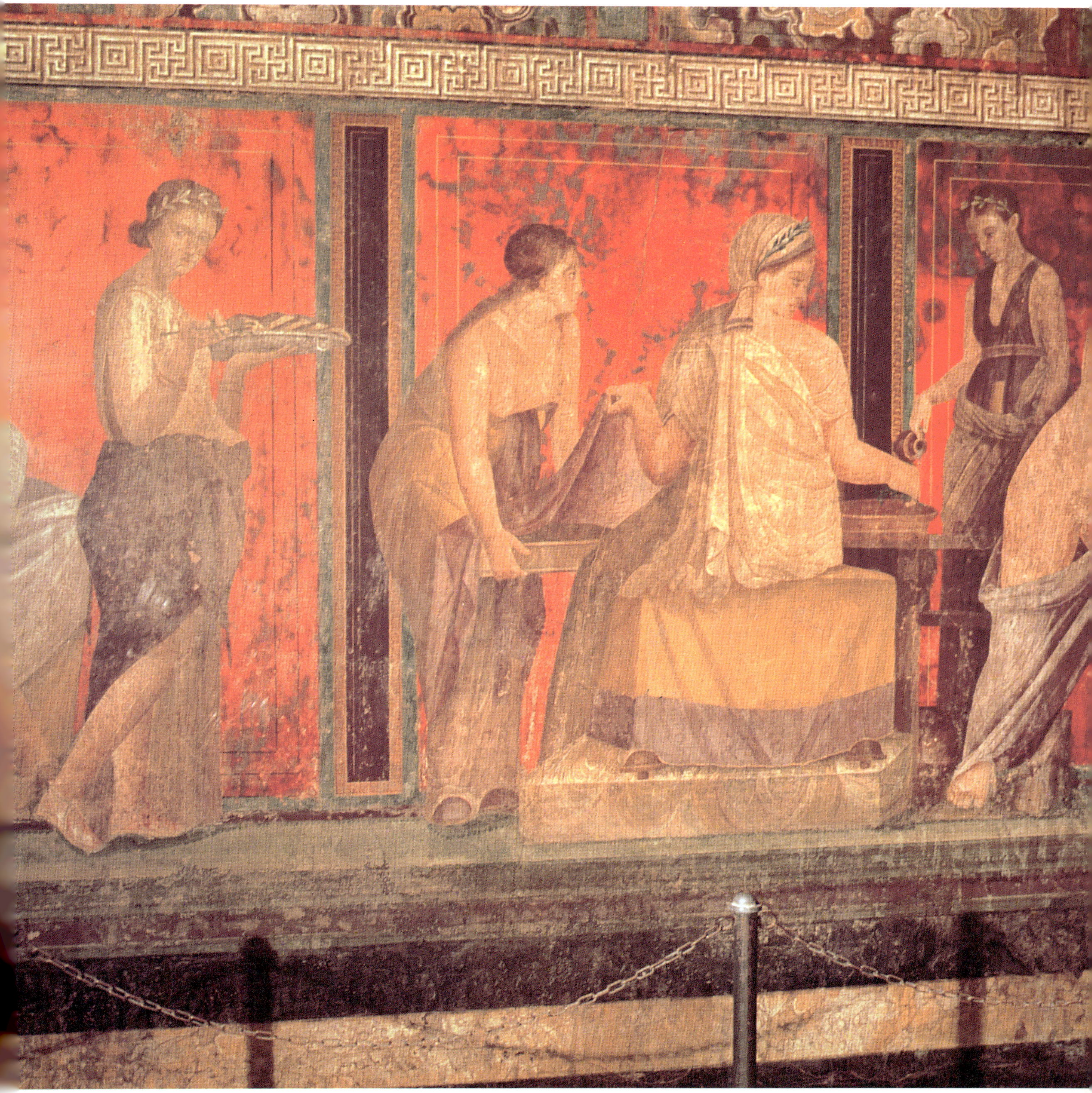

A-Z
CODEX GODS

him, but when searching for his body they are unable to find it; all that was left was a flower of white and purple — the narcissus.

NEMESIS

Nemesis was the daughter of Nyx (Night) and the agency of retribution and vengeance whose role was to curb all excessive good fortune, pride and arrogance. She reflected a fundamental concept of Greek thought — hubris — which taught that any man who rose above his condition exposed himself to divine reprisals. Thus Croesus, who grew too wealthy and powerful, was enticed by Nemesis into his expedition against Cyrus, which brought about his own downfall.

Nemesis was targeted and pursued by Zeus, this myth having two variants. In one she changed form innumerable times and successfully evaded him, in the other she was finally caught in goose format by Zeus in swan mode. From the resulting egg Helen of Troy and the Dioscouri were born.

NEPTUNE

See Poseidon.

NIKE

Also known as: Victoria

Greek winged goddess of victory, honored by Zeus since she fought on the side of the gods against the Titans but also inevitably amorously pursued by him. A statue at Delphi and a temple dedicated to her on the Athenian acropolis commemorate the Greek victory over the Persians. To the Romans she was Victoria.

NUADU

Also known as: Nudd

Supreme king of the Irish Celtic pantheon, Nuadu was the legendary ruler of the Tuatha, who lost an arm in the first battle of the Magh Tuired between the Tuatha and the Fir Bolg and consequently had to give up the kingship as he no longer possessed the required physical perfection. However, the divine smith Dian Cecht made Nuadu a magic arm of silver and he was able to reclaim the throne. In subsequent wars with the Fir Bolg he lost his courage and had to retire, ceding the throne to Lug.

NUM

Also known as: Numitorem

Num was the paramount creator sky deity of the Finnish Samoyeds. The Vogels believed their beneficent sky god Numitorem peopled the earth with humans and animals. Intriguingly no image of him was ever made, but the stories tell of his ceaseless efforts to provide for and help humans, firstly making land and then filling it with a living menu.

Right: Nike, the winged goddess of victory.

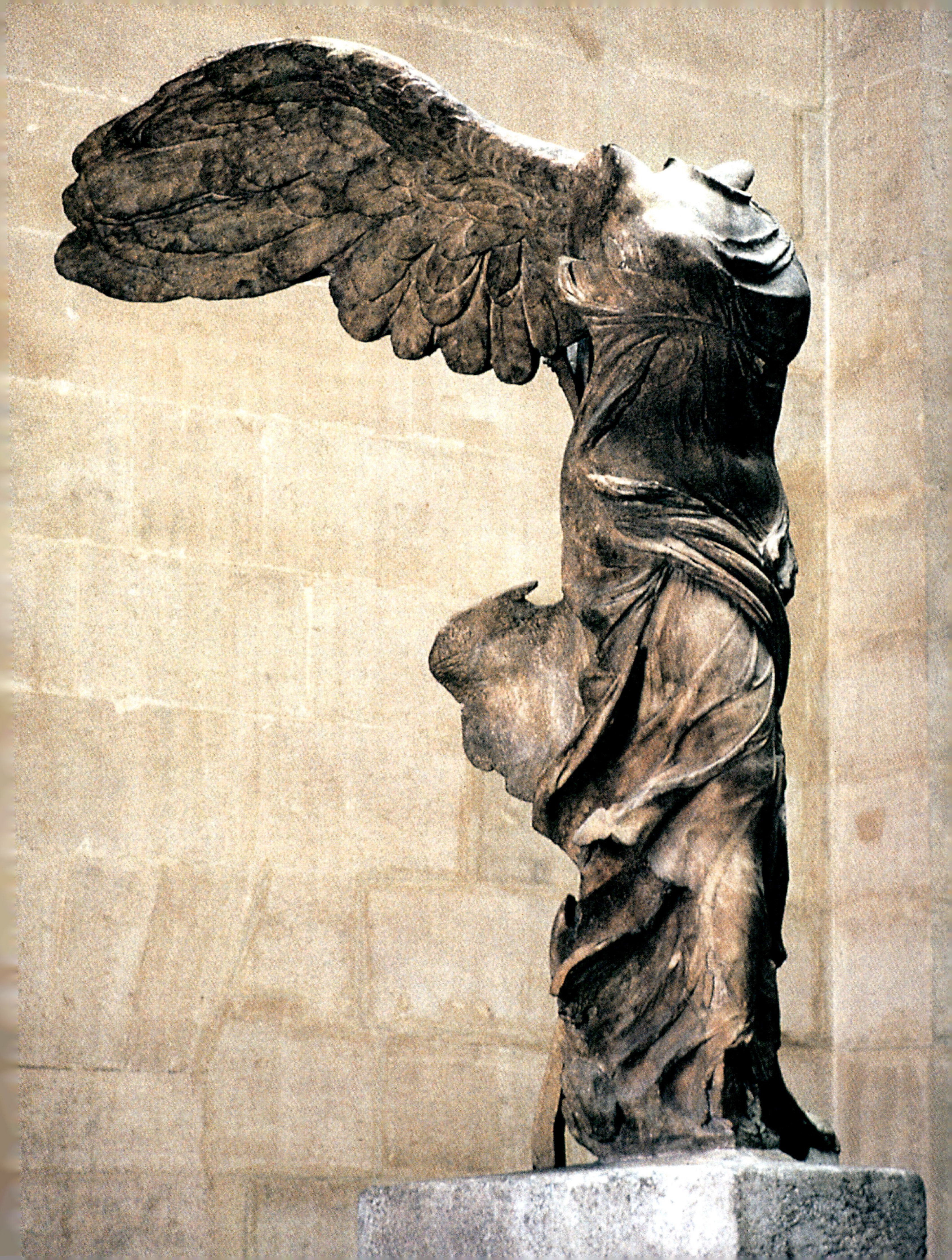

A-Z
CODEX GODS

ODIN

Also known as: Woden, Wotan

The supreme Viking sky and wind deity, omniscient Odin, father of the gods and men, hailed as "Allfather," appeared in a variety of camouflage, the prime one being as a hunched old man with one eye, wearing a deep slouch hat. Though the equivalent of Zeus and Jupiter in the Norse pantheon, he was in fact equated with Mercury in Classical times, as they were both leaders of souls of the dead. But Odin had many more functions than that — by his wife Freya he produced the Aesir race, the Norse Gods. His sons were Balder, Heimdall, Hermod, Hoder, Tyr and Vidarr (also known as Vali), some of whom in fact pre-date him and represent the classic syncretistic layering mode of religion and mythology. His omniscient facility was acquired through effort and sacrifice: to learn the Runes of Wisdom he had himself hung upon the World Tree Yggdrasil, though in another version he gained wisdom after drinking from the sage Mimir's well, paying the fee with one of his eyes. His information was also updated each dawn by two ravens — Huginn and Muninn — who circled the world keeping him up to date on all events. Of all his artifacts three pieces of equipment were pre-eminent: the powerful eight-legged stallion Sleipnir, the magic spear Gungir and his gold ring Draupnir. The latter two were made by the dwarf arms manufacturers. Gungir once thrust could not be stopped and Draupnir would clone itself nine times every ninth night.

Odin knew everything, but the knowing was sometimes tragic. He foresaw that the death of Balder would be the trigger for the apocalyptic Ragnarok yet none of his counter-measures produced more than a slight delay.

ODYSSEUS

Also known as: Ulysses

The most famous and charismatic hero of Greek mythology, and son of Laertes, king of Ithaca, Odysseus was critical to the success of the Trojan war, in which he was involved at every stage, particularly in subtle missions of diplomacy or espionage. From binding the suitors of Helen with a communal defense oath to the design of the Wooden Horse that got the Greeks into the city at the end of the campaign, Odysseus was the key figure, though the emphasis in the *Iliad* is on the mood and honor of others. The sequel was the *Odyssey*, another Homer epic, which thrust Odysseus even more firmly center-stage and dealt with his return journey from Troy. Ten years filled with adventure and ordeal were to elapse before he stepped ashore on Ithaca again; events which proved time after time the depth of character and skill of this extraordinary man. When finally home he had then to dispose of fifty greedy suitors, all seeking the hand of his own wife Penelope — a simple task for a man of this caliber.

Right: This gold bracteate was discovered with a Norwegian hoard (c. 500 AD).

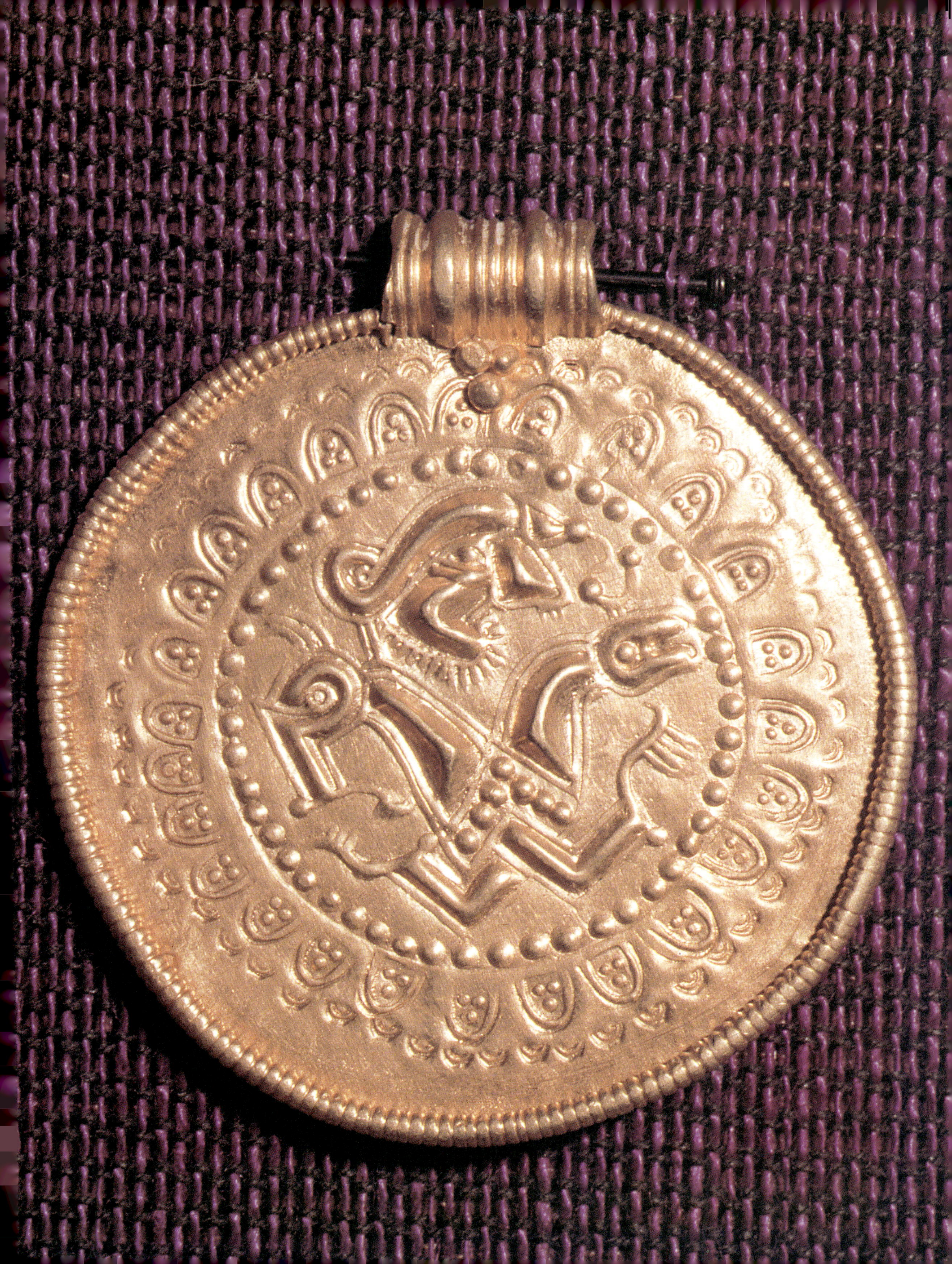

A-Z
CODEX GODS

OEDIPUS
"Swollen foot."

The doomed protagonist of one of the best known legends of Greek mythology, whose life was dramatized by Sophocles, Aeschylus and Euripides. It is difficult not to feel an overwhelming sympathy for Oedipus, who could not escape his excruciating fate. His tale unfolds with a chilling inevitability: his father exposed him on a hillside following the oracle that foretold his own doom by his son's hand and he was subsequently discovered by shepherds and adopted by King Polybus of Corinth. The Delphic oracle Oedipus then consulted foretold that he would kill his father and marry his mother and in a mistaken attempt to cancel this out he left Corinth and wandered — ignorant of the fact that he was actually heading to his real hometown and the unavoidable consequences. On the way he unknowingly killed his father in a road incident and then answered the riddle and thus disposed of the Sphinx who had been terrorizing Thebes. For this he was made king — and married his mother. When the truth finally emerged his mother killed herself and Oedipus, having gouged out his own eyes, wandered as a beggar until finally obtaining in death the peace that had eluded him in life.

OISIN
"Little Deer"

This legendary Irish hero ruled the mythical Land of Eternal Youth — Tir na n-Og — for three centuries. This came about when Oisin met a strange creature with the body of a gorgeous female and the head of gross pig. The creature promised an imminent change back to a particularly beautiful human form if he would only marry her. This he did and so it came to pass. Oisin then dwelt with his beautiful princess for 300 years in Tir na n-Og. After all this time in a mythical heaven, Oisin pined to see the land of his fathers again, so his wife provided a superb, magic-enhanced white stallion, but also warned him many centuries had passed, and guaranteed his safety only if his feet never touched the ground. Inevitably he eventually slipped and fell, with the result that the steed died instantaneously and Oisin suffered an accelerated aging process, becoming an old blind man in a matter of seconds.

ORPHEUS
In Greek mythology Thracian Orpheus was a master musician and singer-songwriter, to whom a variety of exploits are attributed. This son of Apollo could play so sweetly that he charmed the god Hades and won his wife back from the dead. Unfortunately he broke the only condition stipulated: that he would not look back at Eurydice until they had left the underworld. At the last moment he couldn't resist and so his wife was lost to him, becoming a vanishing shadow. Another myth has Orpheus as an Argonaut crewmember on the quest for the

Right inset: This piece of a vase shows Odysseus and a companion blinding Polyphemus (7th century BC).
Right: This Roman mosaic has Ulysses (Odysseus) passing the sirens (3rd century AD).

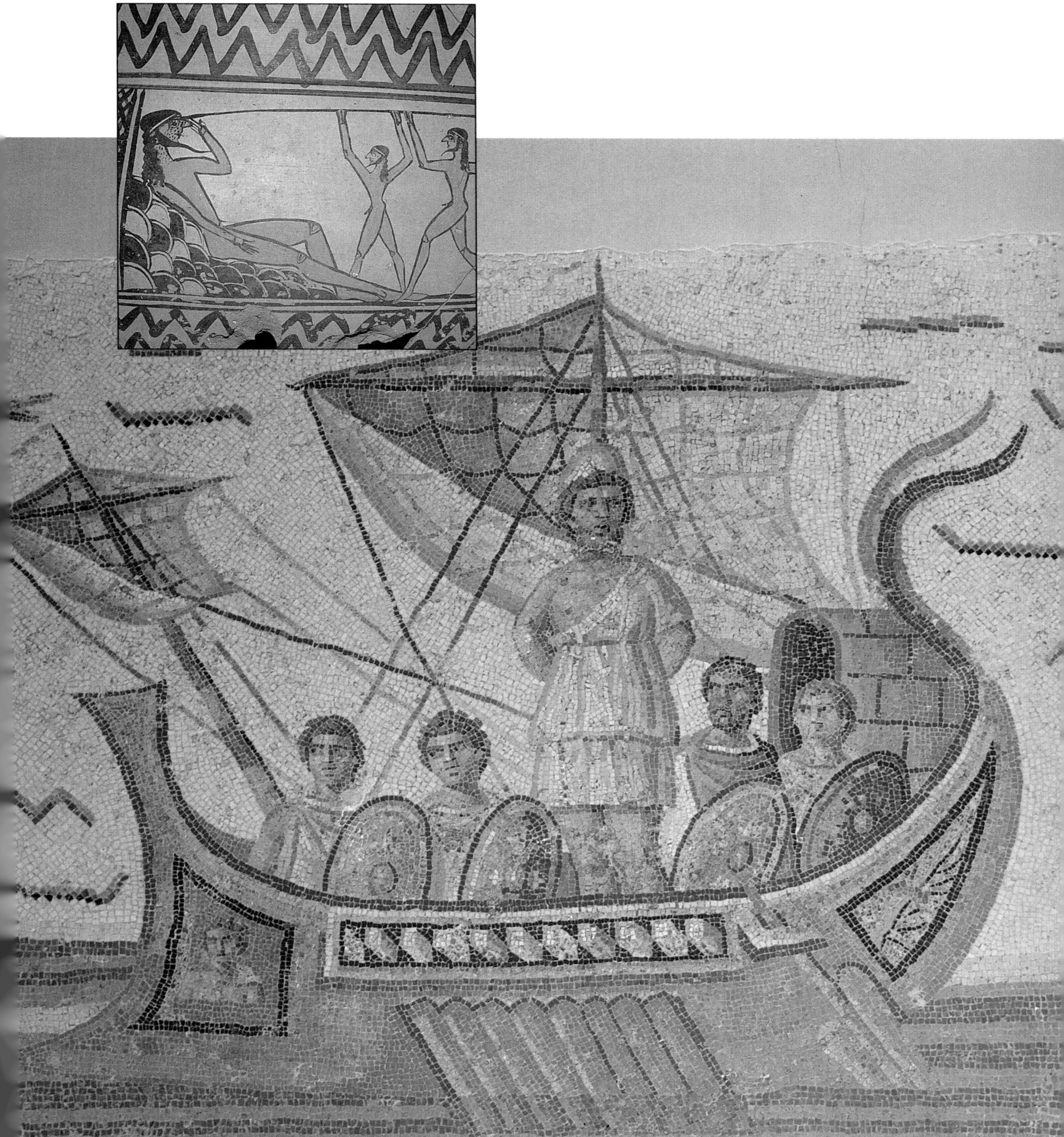

A-Z
CODEX GODS

Golden Fleece, where again his musical talent saved the mission more than once — calming stormy seas, synchronizing rowing and stifling the beautiful but deadly sirens.

His death occurred because he was a one-woman man who could not get over the passing of his beloved wife. Resentful and hysterical women apparently tore him to pieces during a Dionysian ritual.

OURANOS
Also known as: Uranus
The ultimate ancestor of the Greek divinities, Ouranos has West Asian connections in concept and consequence. Like the Egyptian Geb and Nut, Ouranos and Gaia were locked in a permanent sexual embrace, with their children remaining trapped within Gaia's womb unable to threaten his precedence. One of these, Kronos, equipped and advised by his mother, finally escaped and castrated his father. Emasculated thus, the sky was separated from the earth and life accelerated. Kronos married his sister Rhea, and from the spilt blood of Ouranos grew the Titans, Erinyes and Aphrodite. A brief golden age then ensued, which lasted until Kronos began to repeat his father's behavior, reabsorbing his own children. The Roman variant, Uranus, follows the Greek myth in every respect.

PAN
Also known as: Faunus
Pan is generally represented as having goat's ears, horns and legs. He was a fertility god and could be dangerous especially if disturbed in the heat of the day when he was asleep.

The origin of Pan is somewhat confused, but he probably derived from a more primitive culture than the Greek one which had him as the son of Hermes. According to this myth Hermes fathered him on a nymph who was so terrified at the sight of him at birth that she ran away. Hermes kept him on Olympus for the amusement of the other gods who exploited his easy-going nature. Apollo learned the art of prophesy from him whilst Hermes discovered how to make the Pan pipes which, incidentally, he claimed as his own invention and sold to Apollo as such.

In later mythology Pan was a lustful fun-loving god who lived in Arcadia with the wood nymphs and shepherds. They spent most of their time in this rustic idyll in revelry and tending to the herds of goats and sheep. Pan was generally a lazy character although he was a patron of hunters and would often help them in their pursuits. He liked nothing better than his afternoon sleeps after a night of lustful revelry and would frighten the life out of anyone who woke him with a terrible roar. Included amongst his many amorous conquests were the nymph Syrinx and the goddess Selene. His seduction of

Right: This Italian dish shows Orpheus charming the beasts with his music (c. 1525).

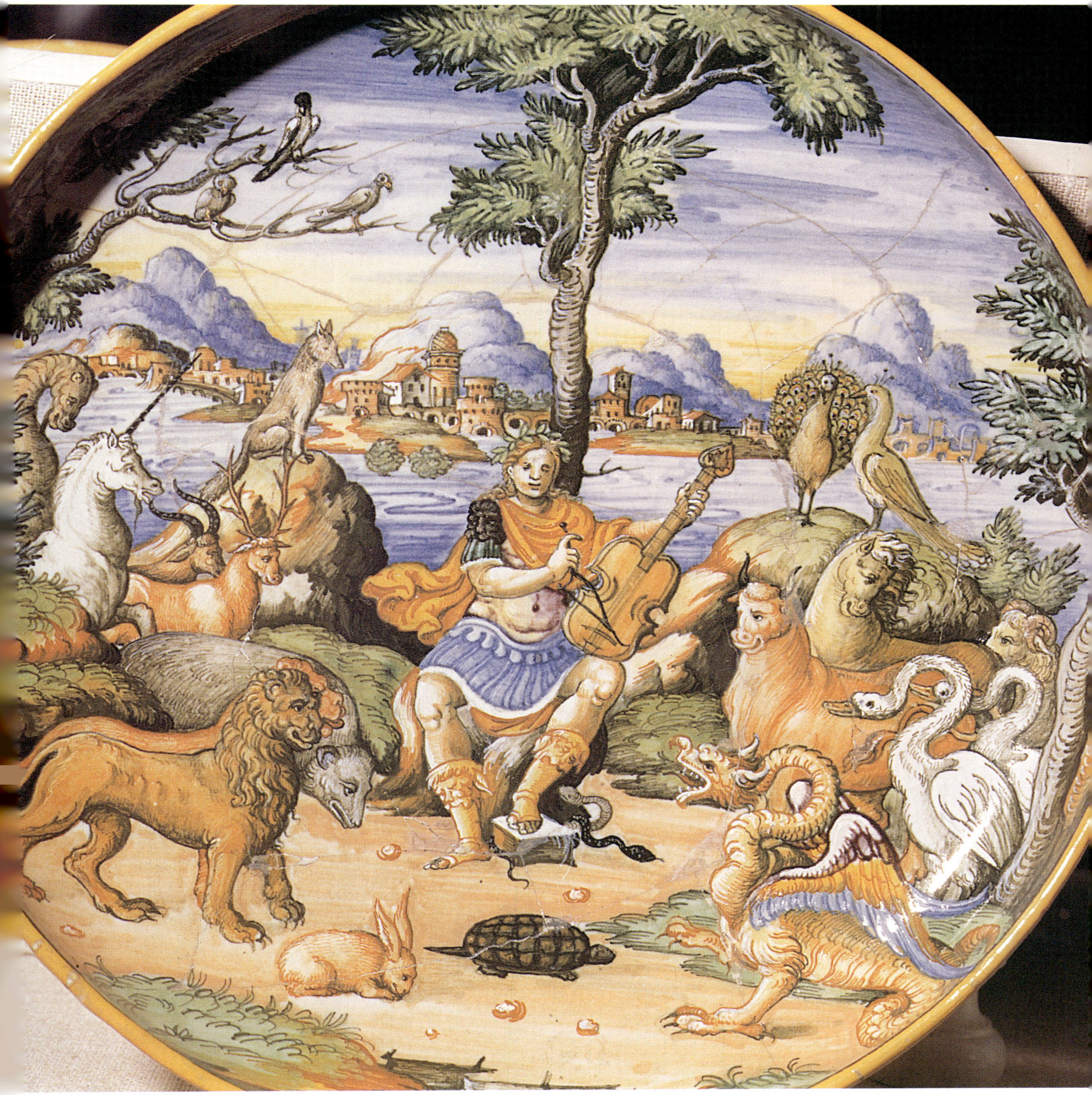

A-Z
CODEX GODS

the chaste Syrinx was the origin of his famous Pan pipes; he chased her to the banks of the River Ladon where she pleaded with Mother Earth to disguise her as a reed. Pan could not distinguish her from all the other reeds so he cut several stems which, together, formed his famous pipes. In his seduction of Semele he disguised his hairy black body with a beautiful white fleece, Selene was so enamored by this that she rode upon his back and was quite happy to let him do as he pleased with her not realizing who he really was.

PANDORA
"All Gifts"

Pandora was the first woman on earth. When Prometheus stole the secret of fire for humankind a furious Zeus ordered Hephaestus to make a woman out of earth who, with her charm and beauty, would bring misery to all men. The result was Pandora. This new creation was slyly introduced to Prometheus' brother, Epimetheus, who was completely smitten and instantly forgot his brother's warning to reject gifts from Zeus. It was only a matter of time until this beautiful woman began disrupting everything.

The story of Pandora's box gives a further explanation of human misery. Curious as to the contents of a large earthenware pot belonging to Epimetheus, Pandora lifted the lid. From the pot all the evils of the world Greed, Jealousy, Sloth etc. escaped, leaving only Hope at the bottom.

PANTHEON

It was normal in Greek and Roman religions to supplement an entreaty to an individual god with an appeal to all of the gods. The word *pantheon* is derived from the Greek words for all (*pan*) and god (*theos*). There still exists in Rome a temple, called the Pantheon, which has its origins in the 1st century BC when it was built for Agrippa. It was called the Pantheon because it had altars to many of the gods and, being circular, was believed to represent the sky. The building that survives today is largely the work of the Emperor Hadrian.

PEGASUS

A fabulous winged horse which was said to have sprung from the body of Medusa after Perseus had beheaded her.

PELEUS

Peleus was involved in many of the great heroic stories including the Calydonian Boar Hunt, the battle between the Lapiths and the Centaurs and the voyage of the Argonauts. He is probably best remembered for his marriage to Thetis by whom he fathered Achilles. Peleus first met Thetis and her sisters, the Nereids, when he was returning home on the *Argo*. It was at his wedding that the uninvited Eris threw down the fateful apple that led to the Judgment of Paris and the Trojan War.

Right: This vase, found in an Etruscan tomb, also depicts the blinding of Polyphemus by Odysseus.

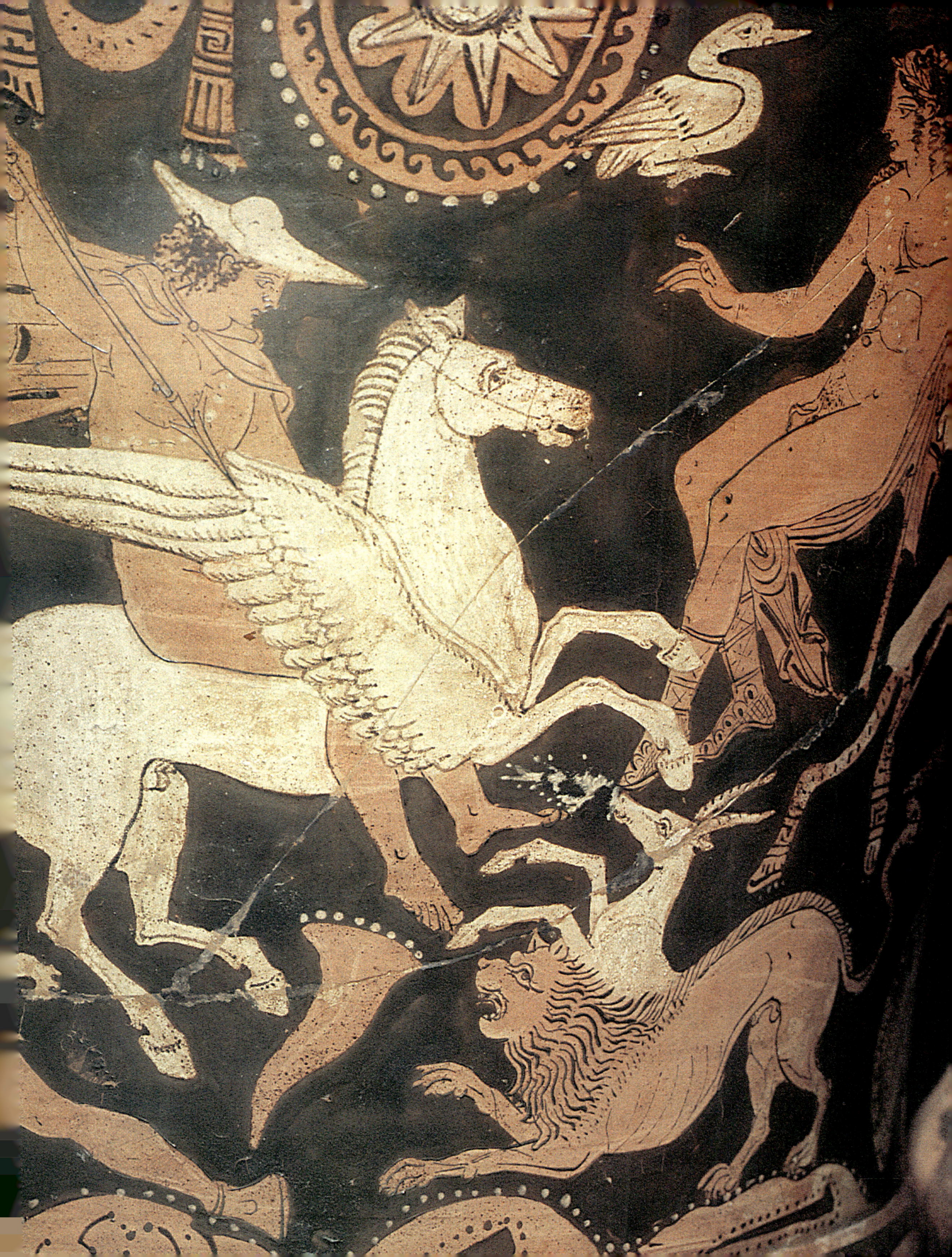

A-Z
CODEX GODS

PERSEUS

Perseus was the mythical Greek hero from Argos, the son of Zeus and Danae, famed for decapitating the Gorgon Medusa. His grandfather, Acristus, had received a prophecy that if his daughter bore a son, this son would kill him. When she in time gave birth to a Perseus, he then dumped mother and son at sea. They survived and came ashore on the island of Seriphos. There the ruler Polydectes fell in love with Danae, and finding that Perseus guarded his mother so well, sent him to destroy the Medusa. With the aid of Athena, Hermes and the Muses and their various gifts of special equipment (a shield to act as a mirror, winged sandals to fly and Hades' helmet of invisibility), Perseus easily escaped being turned to stone and won the head of the Gorgon.

On his way home with the head he used it to rescue Andromeda, who had been offered as sacrifice on seashore rocks. Returning to Seriphos he found that Polydectes had tried to rape Danae and turned him to stone with Medusa's head.

He then fulfilled the prophecy by accidentally killing his grandfather with a discus when the two were both present at funeral games. Unable because of this to claim his grandfather's kingdom he swapped with his cousin Megapenthes, who became king of Argos, while he himself became king of Tiryns.

PERUNNU

Supreme Slavic creator sky god, ruler of the Slavic pantheon. Perunnu, Lord of Thunder had his main cult center at Kiev. He had connections and parallels with Thor and Zeus, but his roots were Russian chthonic — of the earth. His name links him to the oak tree, and rituals enacted around it in his name consisting of semi-clad young girls whirling and much drinking — more of a party than a ritual. He was portrayed anthropomorphically, with a silver head and a gold moustache.

POSEIDON

Also known as: Neptune

Another son of Kronos and Rhea. His sphere of control covered the seas and also earthquakes. Within these fields he had similar powers to his brother Zeus. Poseidon played a key role in events leading up to the Trojan War. He built the walls of Troy with Apollo, but on being cheated of his pay became ill disposed toward the Trojans and actively helped the Greeks — though his participation was counterbalanced and curtailed by Zeus.

The Roman counterpart god was called Neptune. He was a water god and since the Romans were not in early times a sea-faring people, he was of little importance, having no specific legend until the assimilation of his Greek variant.

Right: This bronze statue of Poseidon or Zeus was found in the sea at Cape Artemision.

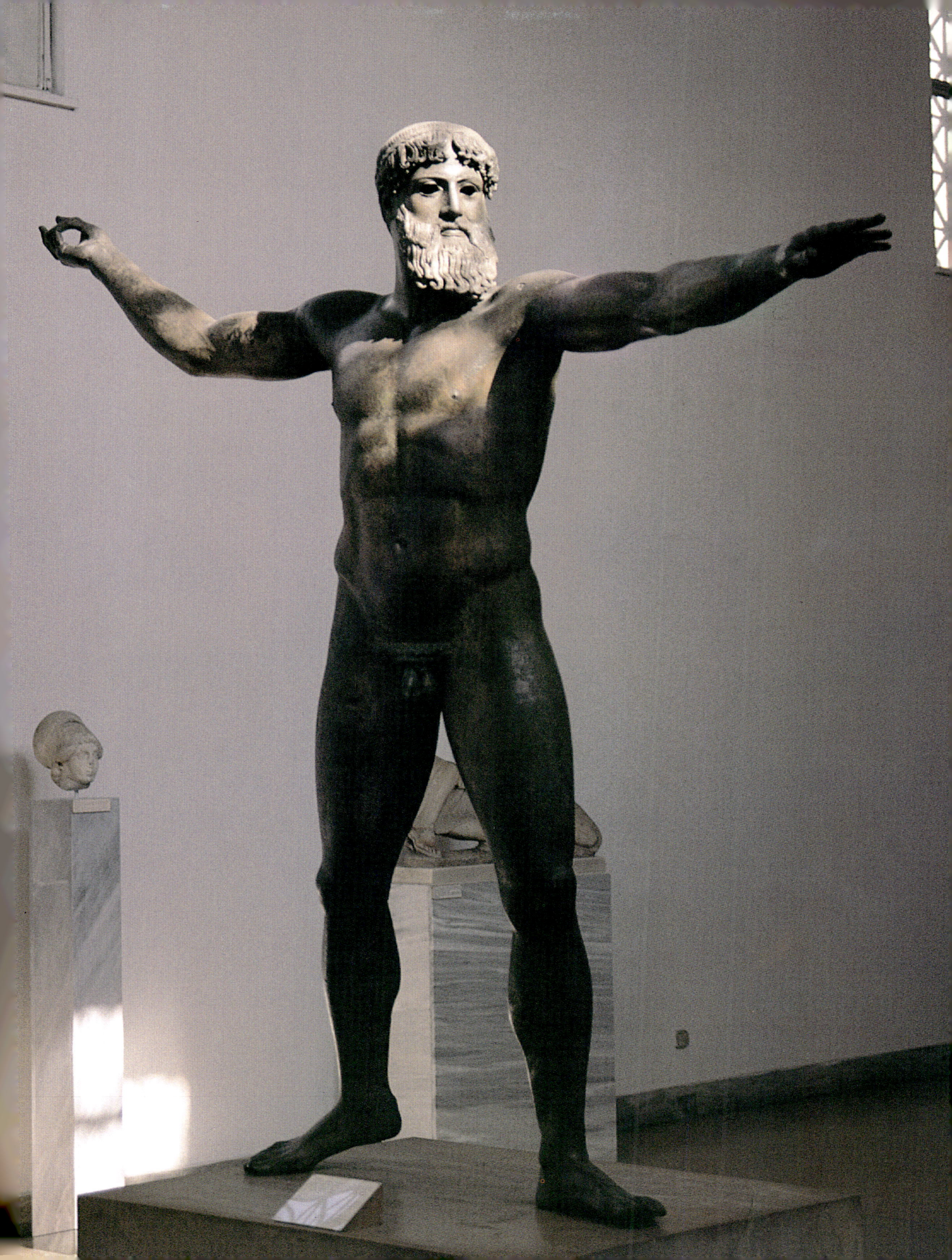

A-Z
CODEX GODS

PRIAM

King of Troy in the time of her Great War and destruction, Priam was perhaps guilty of hubris, for which he suffered long and hard, his sons and his city destroyed before his eyes. Maybe if we look behind the famous story of the *Iliad* we can discern reasons other than the one given — the fight over a woman. Troy's geographic situation was the real cause of war. The city was strategically placed to dominate her side of the Aegean as well as access to the Hellespont (Bosphorous) and Black Sea. She also had monopolies on various essential minerals and luxury goods coming from the older more sophisticated cultures of West Asia. Her tight control over these advantages ill-disposed her to the mainland Mycenaean Greek world, who uniquely forgot their differences for long enough to ultimately destroy her and expand itself.

PRIAPUS

A Greek fertility god of West Asian origin, Priapus was portrayed as a dwarf with an out of scale phallus which became his symbol. He was the son of Aphrodite but Hera, jealous of her rival's beauty, made him deformed at birth and he was consequently abandoned by his mother. His elephantine lingam became a popular charm with which to ward off evil. In some stories Priapus was connected to Dionysius as his son and their cults and functions have certain similarities.

PROMETHEUS
"Forethought"

This semi-divine, benevolent and prophetic fire spirit was the son of a Titan and a nymph — and therefore no friend of Zeus, Prometheus was thus an ally of humankind. After outmaneuvering Zeus and gaining for man the better portion of the sacrifices (humans gained the meat, while Zeus was left with fat, skin and bones) and smuggling the secret of fire from Heaven, he was punished in a particularly painful way. Chained to a rock, with an eagle sent each day to peck out and eat his liver which then promptly regrew each night, Prometheus was in perpetual agony. Heracles eventually freed him, and he gained immortality from Chiron the centaur, who wished to lose his and die.

Prometheus represented will-power and intelligence, resolute in the face of overwhelming odds, constructive and redemptive in their calm application.

PSYCHE
"Soul"

The soul was first seen as a separate "double" dwelling within the body. Later it progressed to be a winged spirit that departed the body at death. All such winged souls were believed to be female, and were visualized as butterflies. The story of Psyche elaborates this theory.

She was a beautiful princess, her wealth and looks intimidating any would-be suitors. Her

Right: Lovers Cupid and Psyche strike a romantic pose (c. 3rd century AD).

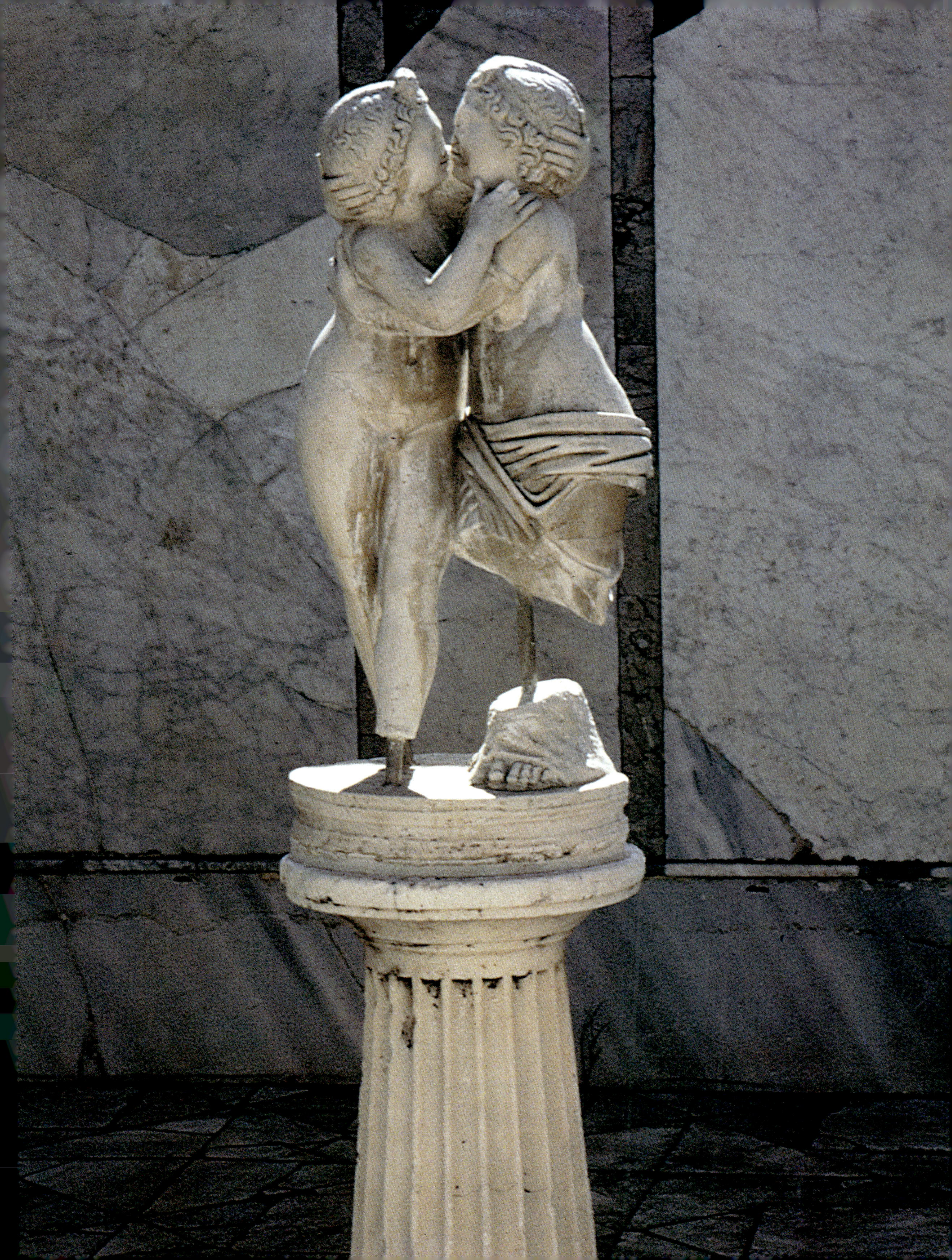

A-Z
CODEX GODS

desperate father, following oracular instructions, dressed her for marriage and left her on a rock, awaiting a "monster." Psyche fell asleep and was then carried away on the wind. On waking she found herself near a large palace, in which she was to live with her monster husband. She was never to see him, for if she did she was told she would lose him forever. However, at being teased on a visit home by her sisters, she resolved to look and discovered that he was Love incarnate — Eros, who awoke and fled. Desolate, Psyche wandered the earth, attracting the jealous attention of Aphrodite, who imprisoned and enslaved her. Her final task was to fetch a flask of the water of youth from the underworld, but on her way back she opened it and fell into a deep sleep. While asleep, Eros discovered her, and the couple were reunited. This myth climaxed with their marriage and Aphrodite was at last reconciled to her rival.

PURGATORY

A long-lived and still current medieval Christian myth concerning Hell's subdivisions. Purgatory is a kind of Limbo for sinful believers, whom prayer may help, for they are not entirely beyond redemption. Through repentance and penance they can even ascend to the perpetual bliss of Heaven. Purgatory then is more a last chance for the mildly sinful than the last resort for the evil.

PWYLL
"Wisdom"

A Welsh prince of Dyfed and one of the heroes of the *Mabinogion*, a Medieval cycle of legends, though his origins are far older. Pwyll met the magician and underworld king Arawn and they both agreed to swap bodies and lives for a year. After this Pwyll kept his underworld connection. He later married Rhiannon, but lost her for a while to the deceitful Gwawl, who had the support of her family. He recovered her eventually through his own ingenuity and they had a son, but the curse from Gwawl's family ensured a depressing time for the couple.

QUIRINUS

One of the oldest of all Roman gods, Quirinus was probably a war god of the Sabines. The Quirinal Hill was probably named after him. His festival was held on February 17. However, his importance declined with the rise of Mars as the war god. There are some indications that Quirinus was a deity derived from Romulus.

RHEA SILVIA

There are a number of legends about the origins of Romulus and Remus, the founders of Rome. Rhea Silvia was, according to tradition, the daughter of Numitor, the king of Alba Longa. In this version of the foundation story, Numitor is overthrown by his brother Amulius, who forces Rhea Silvia to become a Vestal Virgin in the

Right: This Viking cross stands at Gosforth in the north of England (10th century AD)

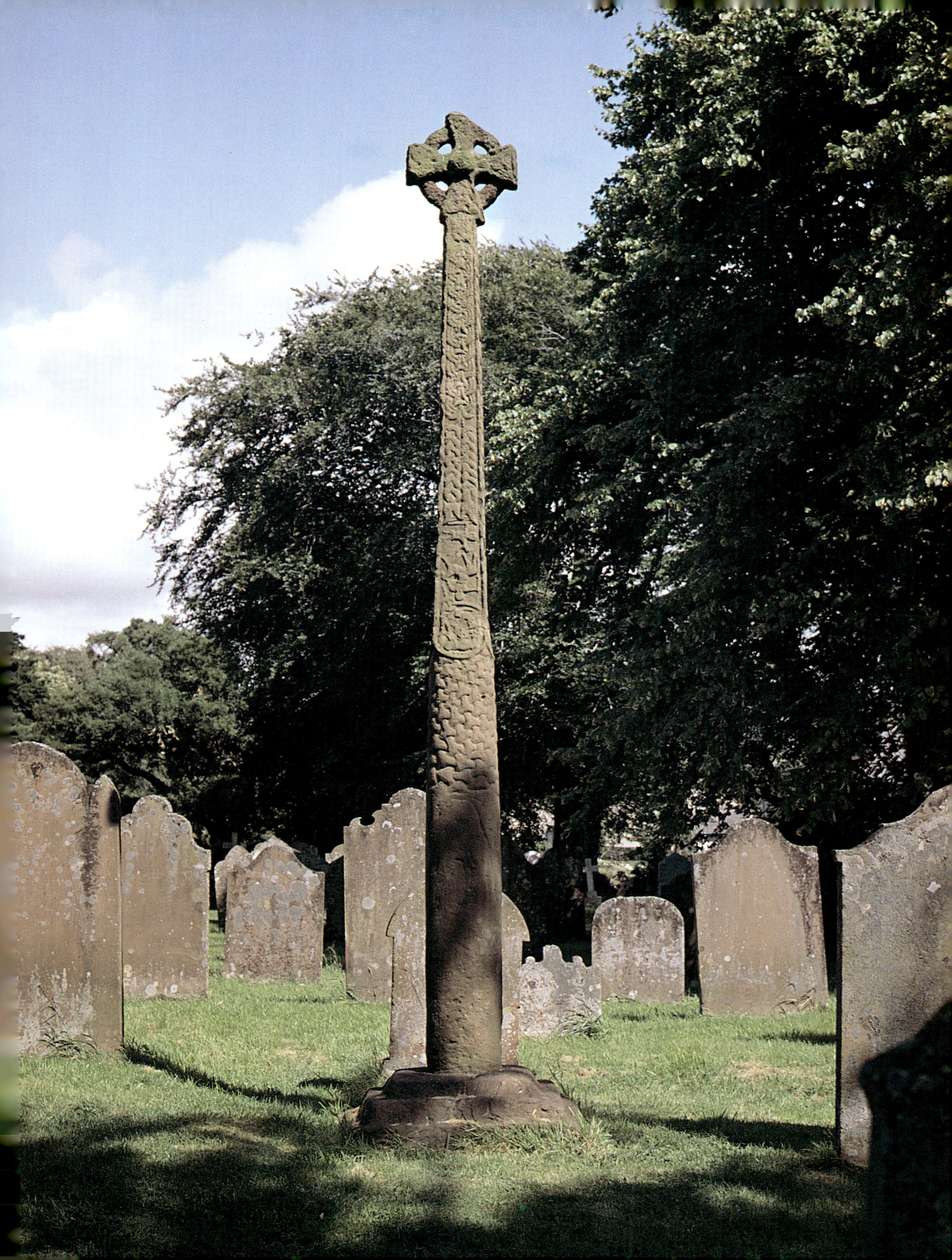

A-Z
CODEX GODS

hope of ensuring that there is no threat to his usurpation of the throne through Rhea Silvia's relationship with Mars. However, Rhea Silvia becomes pregnant and as a result she and her twin boys are thrown into the Tiber. Romulus and Remus are rescued.

RELICS

Preserved body parts of saints as well as artifacts of religious relevance, such as pieces of the original cross on which Jesus was crucified, were imbued with significance and healing power, containing the virtue or attributes of their original saintly owner. The collection of relics started early in Christian cults following the official pagan martyrdom of so many of their number, and continued throughout the Middle Ages. Belief in the holiness of these things spread far and wide — until a church without one was cut off in the wilderness, away from the kudos and the financial advantages of attracting the many pilgrims who would travel to see such artifacts. A black market in these ambiguous fetish objects soon began to exploit gullible pilgrims and priests alike and there was an explosion in the number of relics across Europe. Where they were genuine people proudly paraded them at festival times, harking back to rites practiced over millennia, and confidently expecting miracles. They were also carried as conventional talismans — by individuals as well as armies.

ROLAND

At the battle of Roncesvalles in 778 AD the Basques destroyed the rearguard of Charlemagne's army. The Frankish commander of that rearguard was Roland, who through a mixture of pride and bravery refused to summon reinforcements until it was too late. He died in the encounter. Legend then spun its gilded thread around this defeat, with the result that in the ensuing *Chanson de Roland* the fallen warrior was raised to the level of a religious hero killed by the Moslems, revealing an abiding Christian hatred of and competition with Islam.

ROMULUS AND REMUS
"Roman"
Also known as: Quirinus

According to legend, Rome was founded by twin brothers, Romulus (after whom Rome was supposed to have been named) and Remus. The legend was that the twins, the grandsons of Numitor, king of Alba Longa, were the sons of Rhea Silvia and the god Mars. Prior to their birth Numitor had been deposed by his brother Amulius, who, to protect himself, made Rhea Silvia a Vestal Virgin. Following the birth the twins were thrown into the River Tiber from where they were rescued and then suckled by a she-wolf, finally they were brought up by a shepherd and his wife. Growing to maturity, they killed Amulius and restored Numitor to his throne before departing to found their own city.

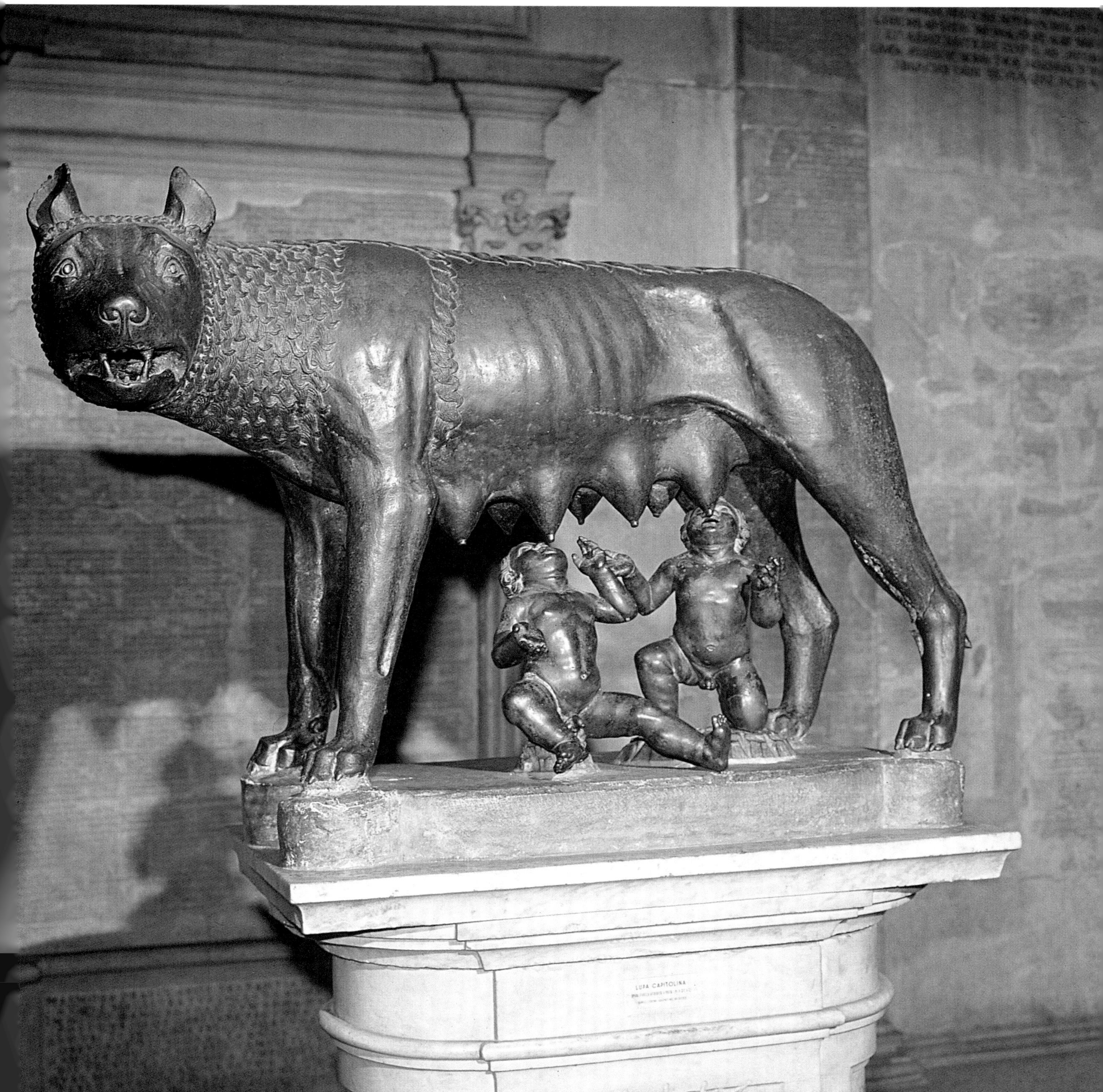
LUPA CAPITOLINA

A-Z
CODEX GODS

Remus was eventually killed by Romulus in a fit of anger during a town planning disagreement, after the former had crossed a sacred earthwork built by his brother. The Roman historian Livy ascribed the foundation of Rome to the year 753 BC and the motif of the she-wolf suckling the two baby twins has been found on coinage dating from the second half of the 3rd century BC.

Romulus also planned and executed his "Rape of the Sabine women" in order to provide wives for his Romans, kidnapping them after inviting the Sabines to a peace festival.

He later disappeared in a thunderstorm, becoming the god Quirinius.

SABINES

The Sabines were a race that lived to the east of Rome. According to tradition, a group of Sabines were the original inhabitants of the settlement built on the Quirinal Hill in Rome. Also according to legend, Romulus and a band of followers abducted a group of Sabine girls and raped them, a theme that has been much explored in Western art ever since. The Sabines were finally defeated by Rome in 299 BC and Romanized shortly thereafter.

SARAPIS

An example of a Egyptian god that came to have a cult in Rome, Sarapis was a god of healing. A temple dedicated to him existed in Rome from the 1st century BC, but his cult was gradually overtaken by another import from Egypt, the cult of Isis.

SATURN
"Sown"

The Saturnalia, held annually on December 17, was the greatest festival of the agricultural year and links Saturn, about whom little is really known for certain, into agrarian life. It is probable that he was linked with sowing. To Romans he was related to the Greek god Kronos, the father of Zeus, and, therefore, in Roman terms the father of Jupiter. The Saturnalia was one of the most important Roman festivals in the calendar and one in which, unusually, slaves were permitted to take part. This was a cheerful celebration involving role-reversal, where masters took orders from their slaves. From about the 4th century these celebrations were absorbed into those of New Year's Day and the Christian festival of Christmas.

Saturn was known as the god who civilized Italy. Following on from Janus he taught cultivation and with agriculture so central to wealth-creation it was natural for him to be regarded as a god of plenty. He ruled over a golden age of contentment and then suddenly disappeared, in the way of mythical kings. Saturn also shared all the attributes of Demeter.

Right: A bronze of the Alexandrian deity Sarapis (1st century AD).

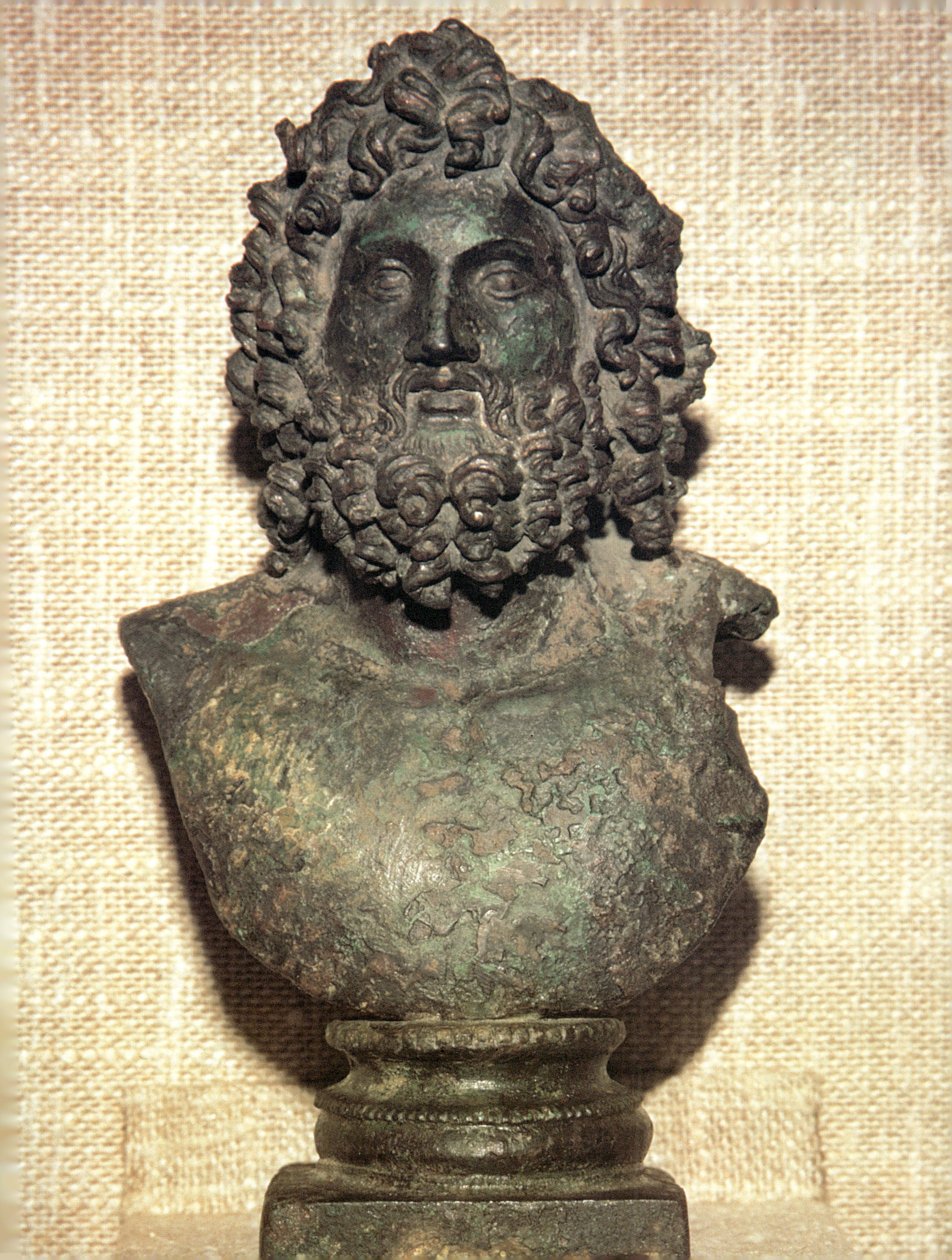

A-Z
CODEX GODS

SATYRS
In early mythology satyrs were half-bestial spirits of the woods and hills. They were mischievous and amorous and they often appeared chasing nymphs or reveling with Dionysus at his drinking parties. In later mythology, in Hellenistic Arcadia, their more sinister aspect is forgotten.

SEMELE
Daughter of Cadmus, king of Boetian Thebes, and mother (by Zeus) of the god Dionysius. Her affair with Zeus was interrupted by the jealousy of Hera, who persuaded her to test her lover's divinity by asking him to appear in his true shape. He appeared as a thunderbolt (his true shape), and Semele was struck dead, but her newly-conceived son was made immortal by the thunderbolt. Zeus lodged Dionysius in his thigh until he was born. When he was old enough Dionysius went down into Hades to fetch Semele and took her back up to Olympus to be a goddess. Semele was also loved by Actaeon, who was punished for rivaling Zeus.

SIBYL
Originally there was only one Sibyl, a prophetess who lived near Troy, but Classical literature gradually expands the number. Of the known Sibyls, one of the most famous is the Cumaean Sibyl, who guided Aeneas through the underworld in Virgil's *Aeneid*. According to legend, this Sibyl also possessed nine books of prophecies, which she offered to sell to Tarquinius Priscus, the last king of Rome. He refused to buy them, whereupon she destroyed three and offered him the remaining six at the original price. Again he declined the offer and she burned three more. She then offered the three remaining volumes at the same price; this time Tarquinius accepted the offer. These volumes were then preserved and used as a reference by the Senate until their destruction in 83BC.

SIGURD
Also known as: Siegfried
The quintessential Norse hero and dragon-slayer, son of Volsung and one of a line of doom-laden kings. The curse of the Niebelungs for the theft of their treasure by the Aesir eventually devolved onto Sigurd, with its grisly legacy of betrayal and murder. Sigurd killed the dragon Fafnir with his sword Gram, and then fell in love with the Valkyrie Brunhilda after he had woken her from an enchanted sleep. Tragically he then betrayed her by marrying Gudrun, as a result of being given a magic drink of forgetfulness. Brunhilda in turn married Gudrun's brother Gunnar and plotted Sigurd's death as vengeance. So the Niebelungs' curse was fulfilled.

Left: A Norwegian wood portal of the smith reforging Sigurd's father's sword.
Right: A Norwegian wood portal of Sigurd killing the dragon Fafnir (late-12–13 century AD)

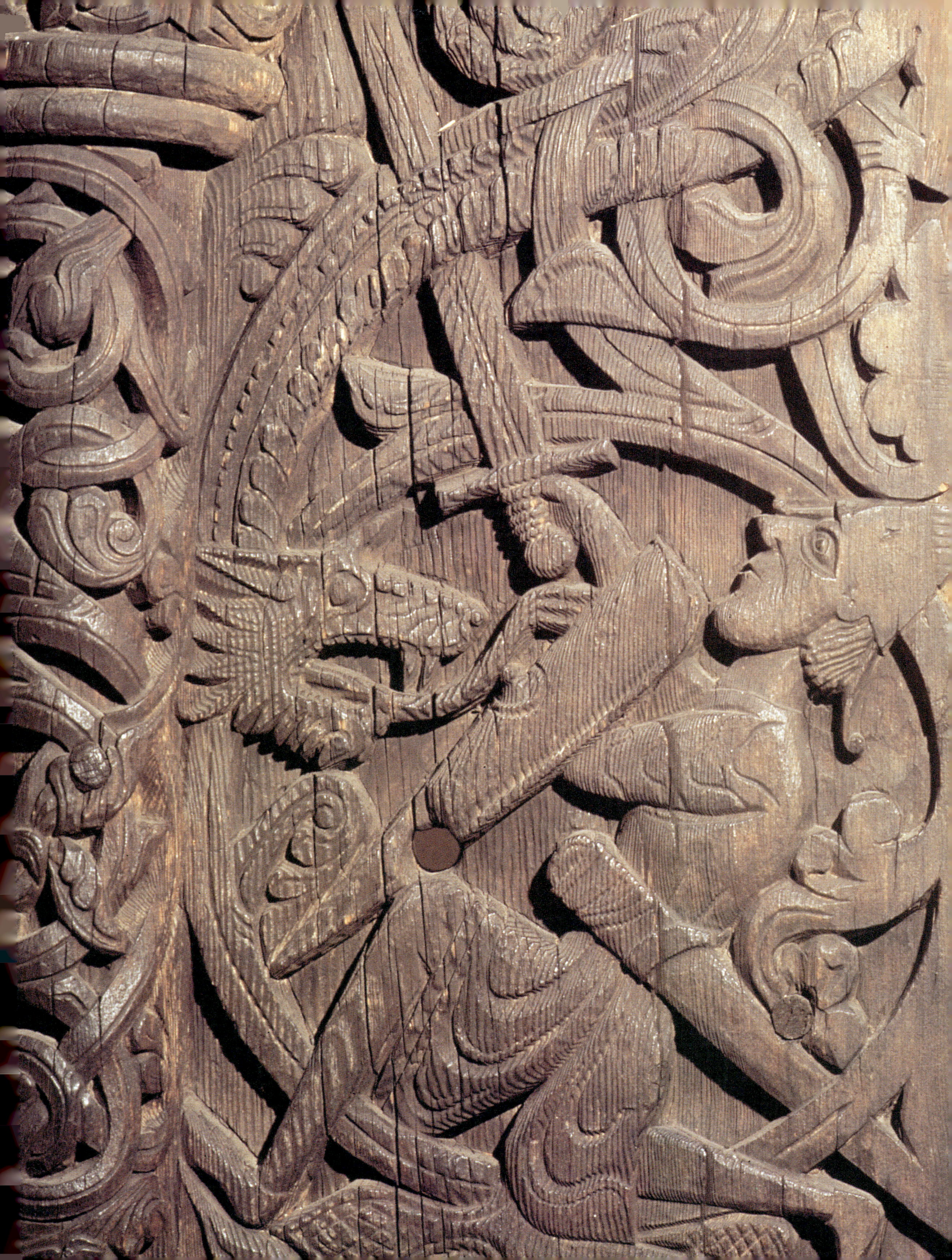

A-Z
CODEX GODS

SILVANUS
The son of a shepherd and a goat, Silvanus was a god of gardens and woodland. Portrayed with the body of a man and the legs of a goat, he can also (like Faunus) be seen as the equivalent of the Greek deity Pan.

SOMNUS
The Roman god of sleep can be seen as the equivalent of the Greek god Hypnos, who was the son of Nyx (the god of night). To the Greeks Hypnos lived, in one version of the legend, in a cave on the island of Lemnos.

STYX
The Styx is the river of the underworld over which the souls of the dead are traditionally ferried by Charon. Achilles was dipped into it to make him invulnerable. One legend purports that Alexander the Great was killed by water from the Styx sent to him in a mule's hoof.

TALIESIN
"Shining Brow"
A welsh wizard and bard famed for his knowledge, whose legends and poems are included in the *Mabinogion*. His origins are linked to the witch Caridwen, who prepared a magic brew in her cauldron, which was reduced to a potent elixir consisting of only three drops. Whoever drank them would possess all knowledge of the past, present and future combined. By complete accident the recipient was an unknown boy, one Gwion Bach, who was tending the fire underneath the simmering potion. When some boiling drops landed on his finger he instinctively sucked it, and then realizing his danger, fled. Caridwen pursued him remorselessly, constantly transforming both the boy and herself into various shapes and creatures in her efforts to consume him. Eventually she succeeded, by turning him into a grain of wheat and herself into a hen. Finally thrown into the sea he was caught in a fishing net and called Taliesin by those who saw him, because of his shining forehead.

TARPEIA
The Tarpeian Rock — a cliff on the south west face of the Roman Capitol — was the location from which traitors and conspirators were thrown off. The legend behind the Tarpeian Rock was that Tarpeia, the daughter of a Roman commander, was so greedy that she was prepared to allow the Sabines to capture the city in exchange for their gold bracelets. Rather than hand these over, however, the Sabines killed her with their shields.

TELLUS
An old Roman goddess of earth, Tellus had a festival — the Fordicidia — celebrated on April 15, when a cow in calf was sacrificed to her. Tellus was the Roman equivalent of Gaia who was one of the first to be born from Chaos in the creation myth, alongside Erebus (darkness), Nyx

Right: Silvanus, the offspring of a shepherd and goat.

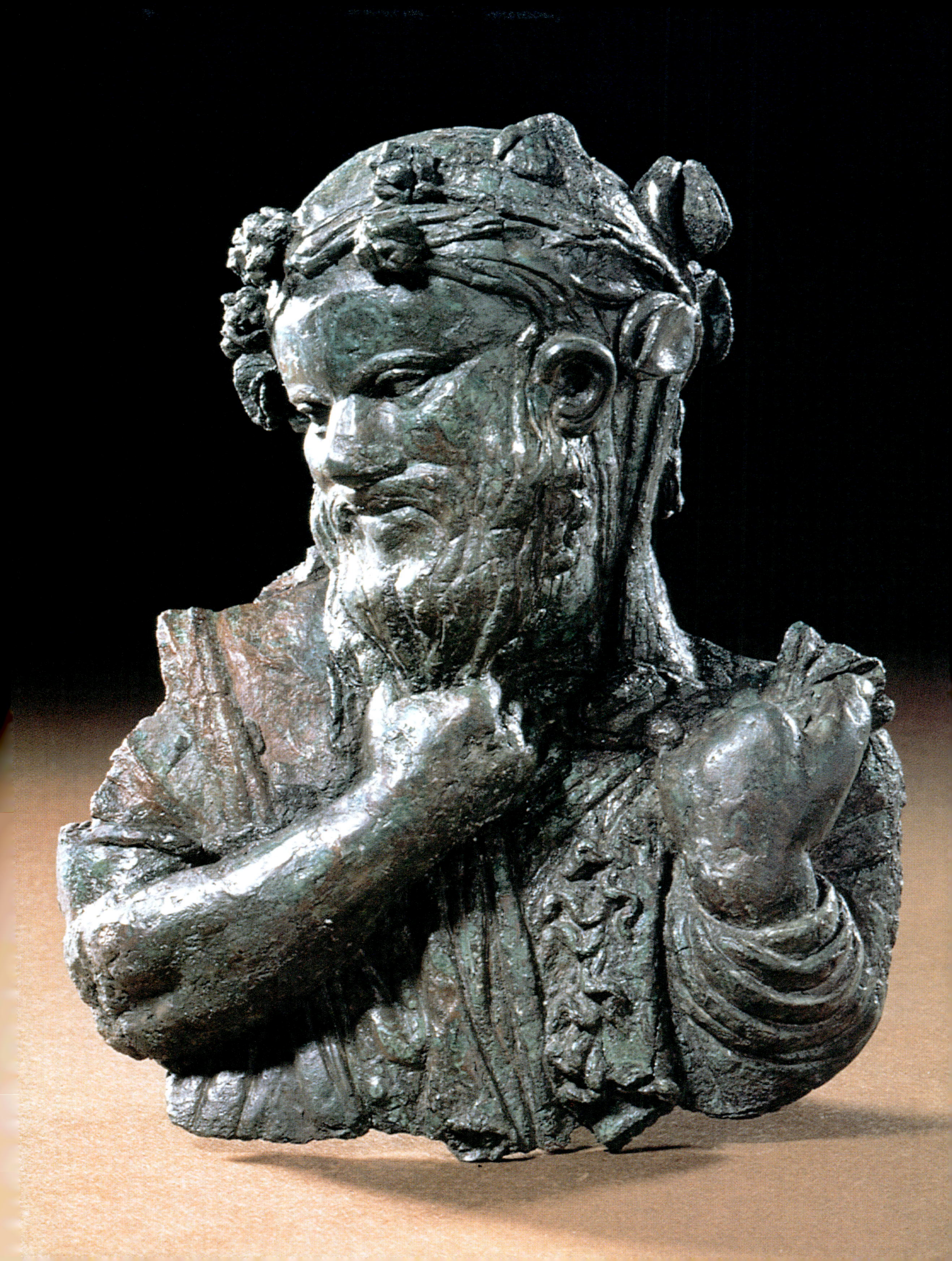

A-Z
CODEX GODS

(night) and Tartarus (the Underworld). Gaia was the mother of Ouranus (the sky) and Pontus (the sea). She was then the consort of Ouranus with whom she conceived the twelve Titans. Kronos was the youngest of these; he defied Ouranus, castrated him and took his place. However, the blood of Ouranus had fallen on Gaia and impregnated her with the Furies, the giants and the nymphs. When Kronos (Saturn) proved to be a tyrant, Gaia ensured that Zeus (Jupiter) survived to overcome his father. Following a further relationship with Tartarus, the monsters Titan and Echidna were born; they rebeled against Zeus but were defeated. According to myth, it was Gaia who provided the first oracle at Delphi, but her cult gradually declined in importance through antiquity to be replaced by those of others, for example, Demeter.

TEUTATES
"Thunderer"

Also known as: Esus, Taranis

A powerful Celtic war god from Gaul, equivalent to Mars and sometimes Mercury, he was singled out for special mention by the Roman writer Lucan, who noted that human sacrifices were carried out in his honor. Like Mars, Teutates was also a fertility god, and a protective deity against enemies and disease. Except for mention by Lucan and seven altars dedicated to him from Roman times almost nothing remains of this mysterious Celtic god.

THESEUS

A legendary Greek hero, particularly of Athens and Attica, where he was seen as an ancestral king and the founder of Athenian democracy. As a hero he was identified closely with Heracles, and is said to have joined him on some on his labors. It was Theseus who freed Athens from Cretan dominion, by volunteering to be one of the annual tribute group sent to Crete for inclusion on the Minotaur's menu. There, with the help of the priestess Ariadne, the daughter of King Minos, he managed to kill the beast and escape intact, though he later abandoned Ariadne on another island. Entering Athenian waters, he forgot to change his sails to a pre-agreed color (denoting mission success), and his father King Aegeus, presuming the worst, threw himself off the Acropolis. This story represents the passing of Cretan power to mainland Greece and the beginnings of Athenian ascendancy.

THETIS

Chief of the Nereids, it was prophesied that she would bear a son mightier than his father. Because of this Zeus and Poseidon decided to marry her to a mortal, Peleus in order that her offspring would not eclipse a deity. Their son was Achilles. In the *Iliad* Thetis is humanized as a mother whose only concern is her son, and she is always aware that he is doomed to die young.

Right: This Roman wall painting shows Theseus after killing the minotaur

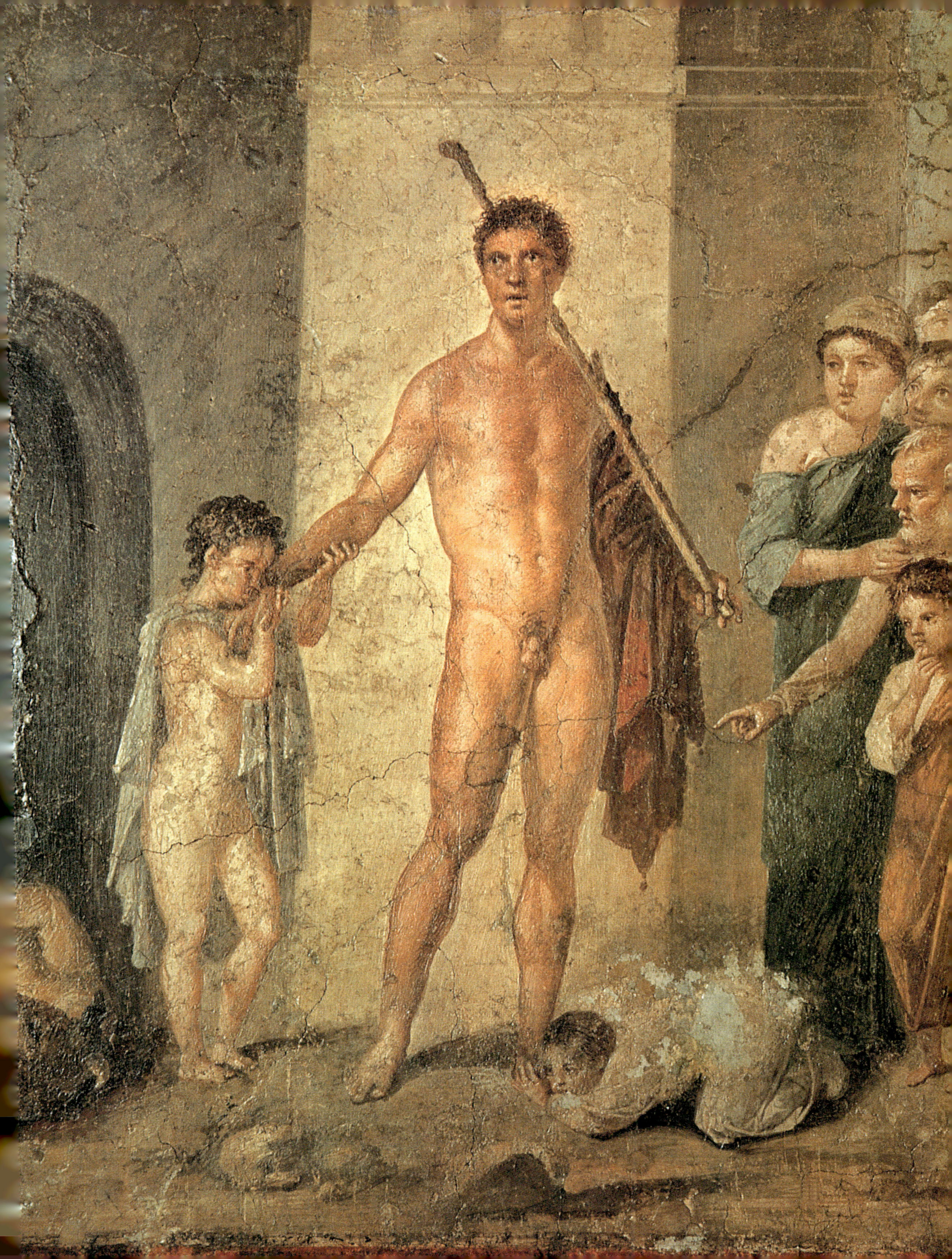

A-Z
CODEX GODS

THOR
"The Thunderer"

The most famous Norse weather god, with the closest parallels in the early Aryan religions of West and Central Asia (Anatolia and India). Handsome Thor was a great adventurer, often skirmishing with the giants. His specialist weapon and emblem was his hammer, Mjolnir, but he possessed two other interesting pieces of equipment — a strength-increasing belt and a pair of iron gauntlets with which to wield his deadly hammer.

On his travels he was often hoodwinked into performing astonishing feats by seemingly simple challenges. A rather long drinking horn could hardly be touched by his deepest draught — it ended in the sea and the difference he made to the sea level in attempting to swallow it is now known as the foreshore. Goaded into lifting a large gray cat off the ground and only managing one paw, he found it was really the World Serpent disguised and the world nearly fell apart. In a wrestling match with an old crone he stood firm and only eventually dropped to one knee — the contest was against old age itself. In another major myth Thor's hammer was stolen by the giants and he had to resort to a Lokian proposal of dressing up as Freya in order to get close enough to the giant king to be able to retrieve Mjolnir.

At Ragnarok Thor and Jormungand, the World Serpent, cancelled each other out.

TITANS
Name for the earliest Greek gods, the children of the sky god Ouranus and the earth goddess Gaia. They feature heavily in the mythology of Greece.

TYR
The archetypal warrior, Tyr was a Norse war deity identified with Mars and one of the Aesir god group. In the legends it was Tyr who sacrificed his hand in the jaws of the wolf Fenrir, providing time for the gods to disable the beast. At Ragnarok Tyr died like Odin — swallowed by the wolf, Garm, whom he simultaneously disemboweled. In fact the two gods have a lot in common and Tyr could even be an earlier version of the same deity, displaced into warrior status by the dominance of the Odin variant.

VALKYRIES
In Norse myth these were beautiful maidens who waited upon Odin in the underworld. They brought the dead to Valhalla.

VESTAL VIRGINS
Vesta was the Roman goddess of the hearth and was one of the many household gods. Initially her cult was primarily domestic, but with the growth of the cult of the king, the royal hearth came to have greater significance. Surviving in Rome, at the Forum Boarium, is a circular temple dedicated to Vesta (it is said that the temple was modeled on the hut of Romulus). Here an eternal

Above right: This Viking carving (10th century AD) has Thor and the giant in a boat, fishing for the serpent.
Below right: These silver Viking figures are of a horsemen (left) and Birka (right) holding a drinking horn

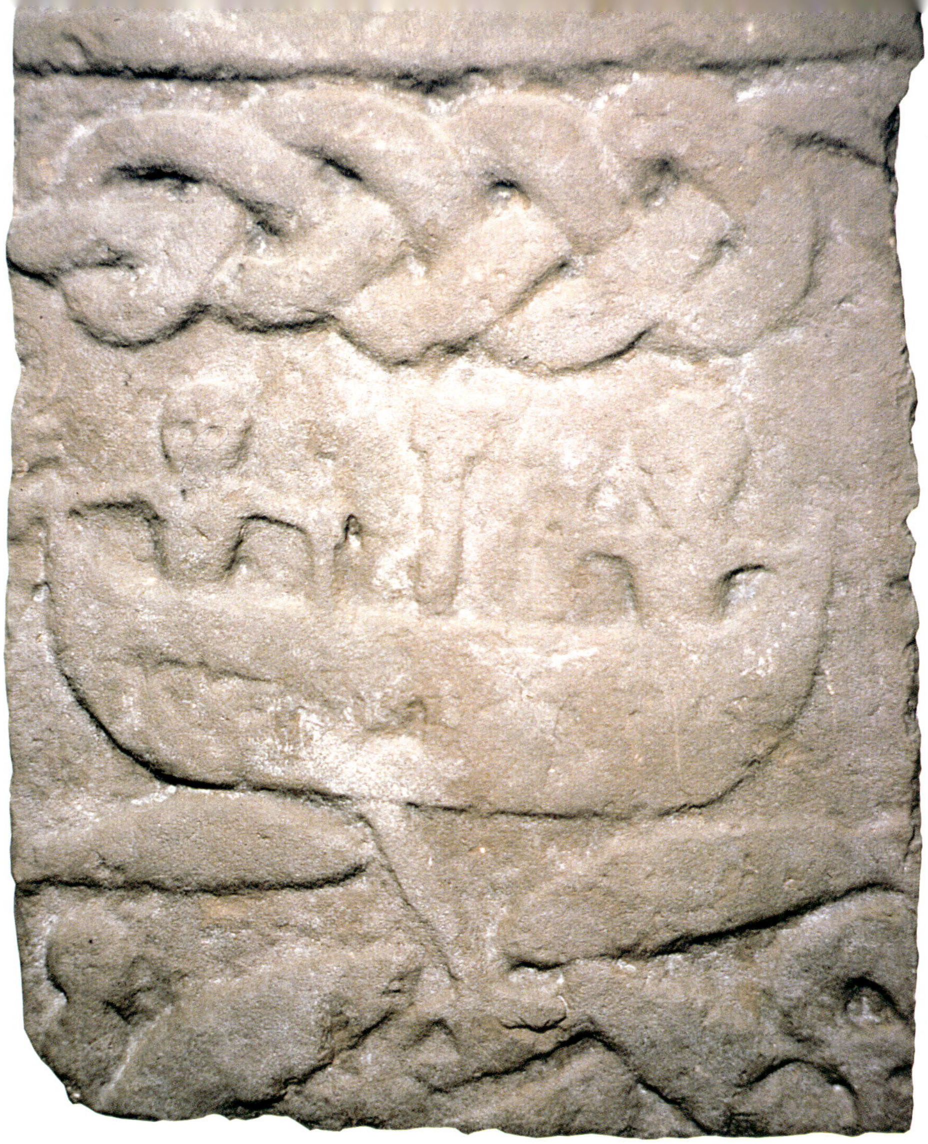

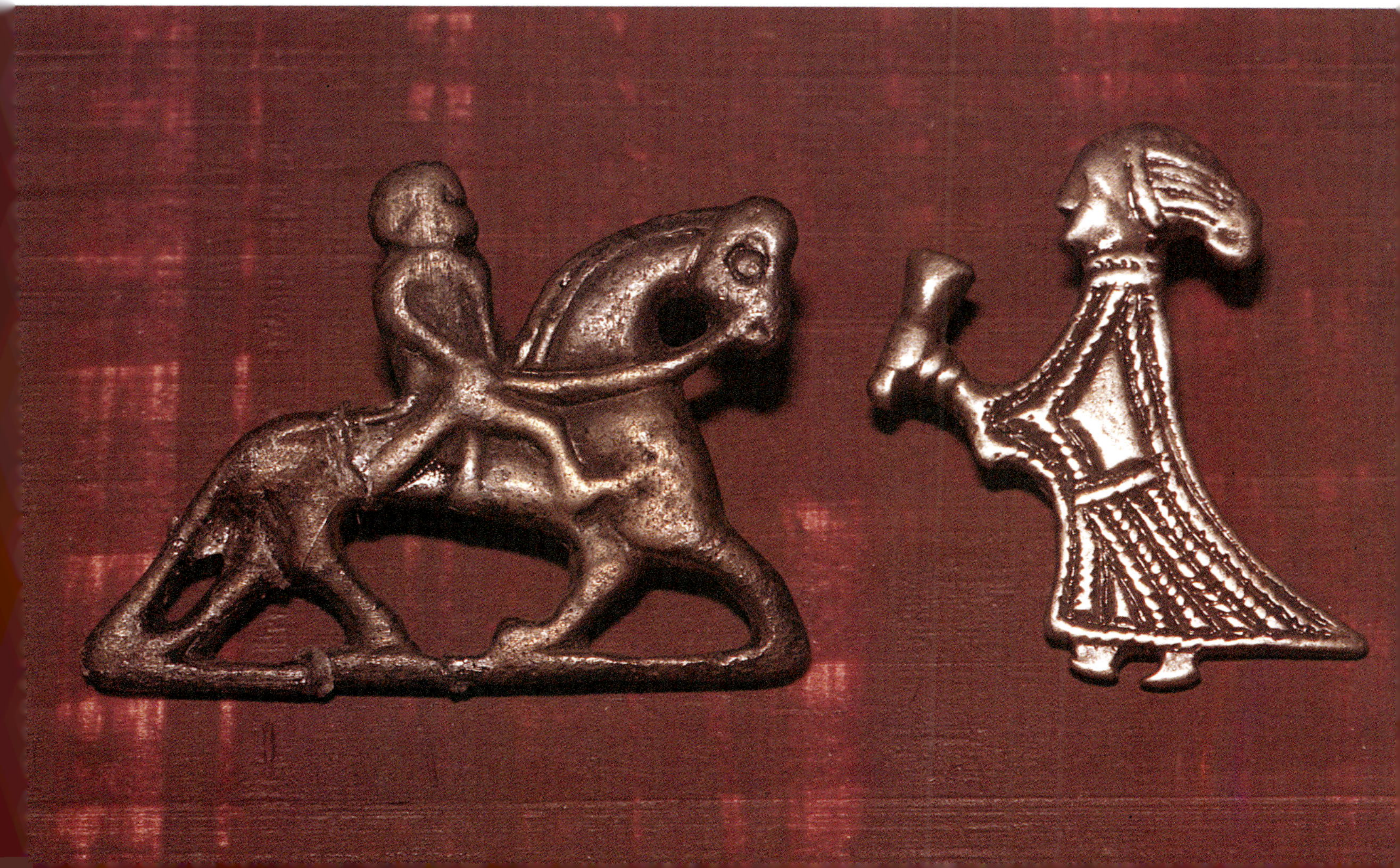

A-Z
CODEX GODS

flame was kept alight by the goddess's priestesses, the Vestal Virgins (the *Vestales*). The Vestal Virgins, who normally numbered six, were selected by the Pontifex Maximum. Although they were highly honored and served for 30 years (after which they could marry), they could also be severely punished if they allowed the eternal flame to die and could be buried alive if they forgot their vow of chastity. According to legend, the mother of Romulus and Remus, Rhea Silvia, was made into a Vestal Virgin by her uncle Amulius when he deposed her father from the throne of Alba Longa.

VICTORIA

The Roman equivalent of Nike, Victoria was the goddess of victory and was popular with and primarily worshiped (inevitably) by the army. In Greek myth Nike was supposed to be the daughter of the Titan Pallas, but supported the Olympian gods in their struggle against Kronos. It was Nike that accompanied Hercules to Olympus after he was deified. She was normally portrayed with huge wings flying at great speed to aid the victory of those favored by the gods. It was her altar in the senate in Rome that witnessed one of the last struggles in the city between the Christians and the pagans when in 382 AD the altar was removed on the orders of the Emperor Gratian. A campaign, led by Quintus Aurelius Symmachus was unsuccessful in its demands for the altar's restoration.

VIRGIN MARY

Within this Christian saint, the ancient earth mother goddesses continue to exist. A look at ancient Egyptian iconography of Isis and Horus amply illustrates the point. Initially Mary was not esteemed above others around Jesus, but from the 4th century onward her cachet increased dramatically. In 431 the Council of Ephesus confirmed on her the title of *Theotokos* — "God-bearer." She was of course a virgin mother — a contradiction in terms or a miracle, and other folklore and myths have grown consistently around her, despite the Church's attempts to play them down. She was particularly highly veneratedin the East, whose history includes so many variations of this sustaining maternal figure. It was later in the West that cult centers came into being, especially at Lourdes (France) and Fatima (Portugal), following visions of her.

WAYLAND

The hero smith god of northern legend, linked to both Hephaestus and Daedalus. Gifted in his craft of metalwork, this prince was captured in his workshop by the evil king, Nidud, who took his sword and one of his magic golden rings and had him hamstrung and marooned as a slave laborer in a tiny island workshop.

Wayland worked ceaselessly, plotting the return of his things and his revenge. Finally when the king's two young sons came to him demanding his treasure chest, he killed and

Right: This bronze statue has the Viking god, Thor holding his hammer, Mjolnir (c. 1000 AD) Following pages: This whalebone detail illustrates the Norse legend of Egil fighting off his attackers (c. 700 AD).

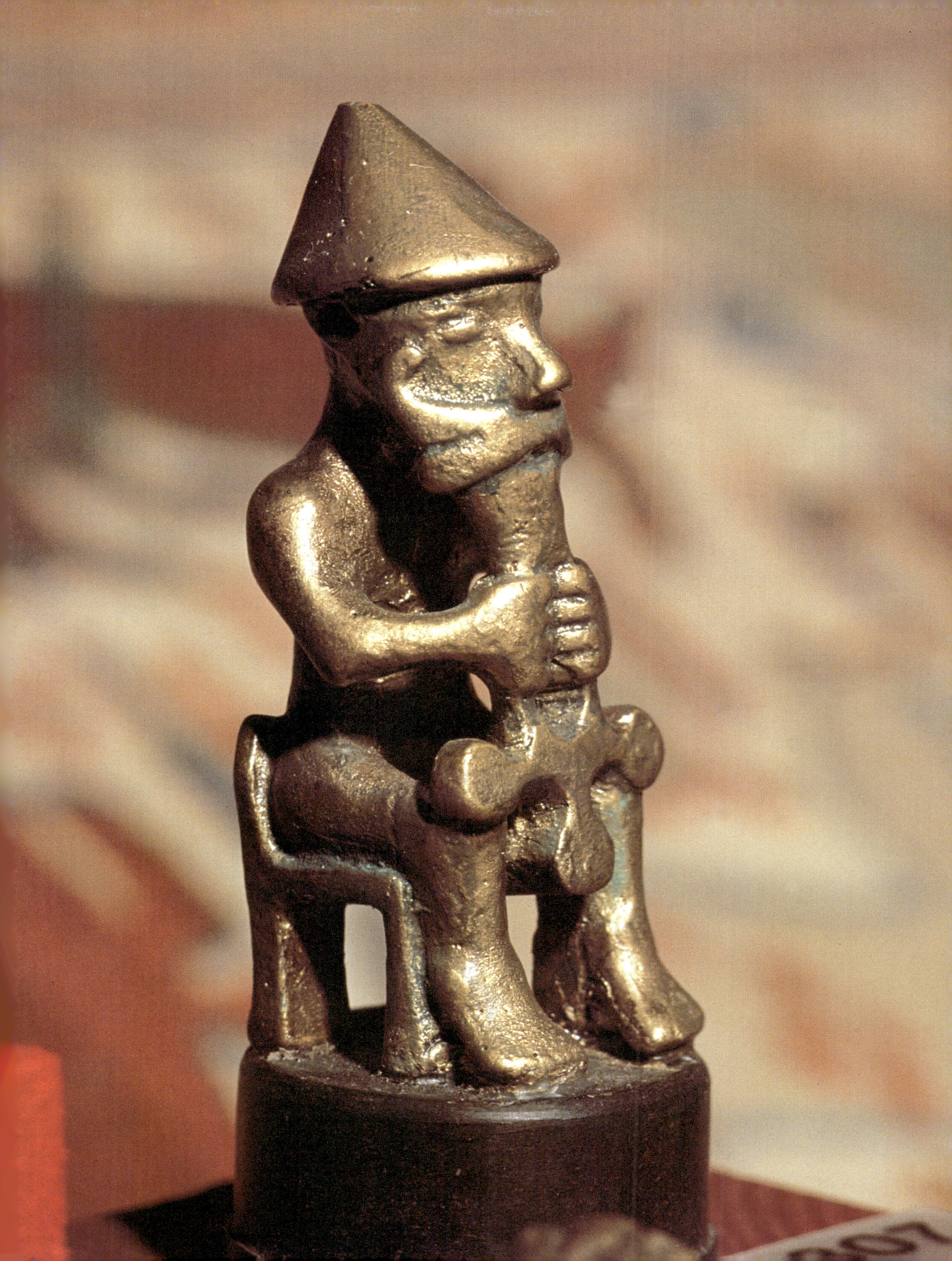

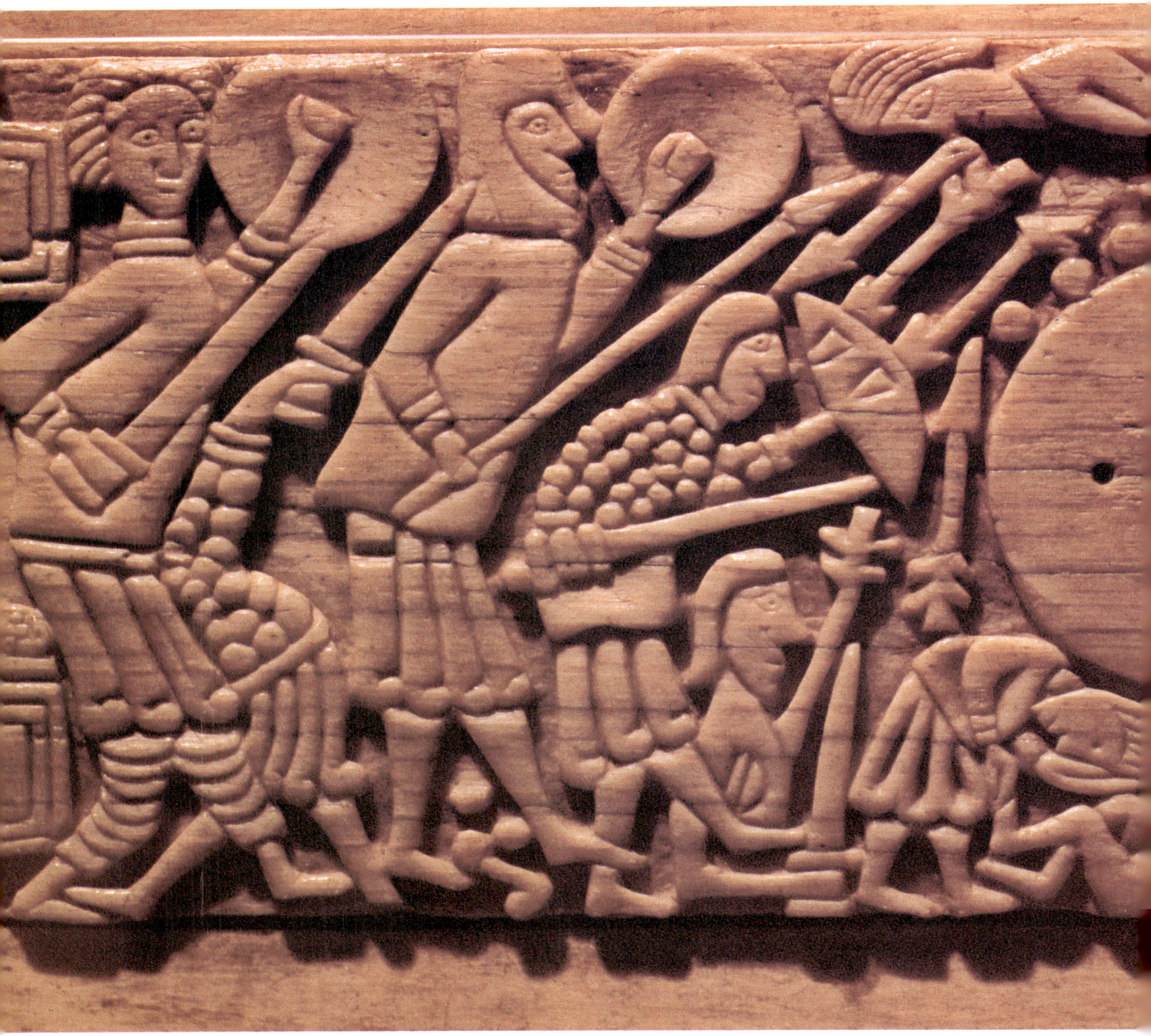

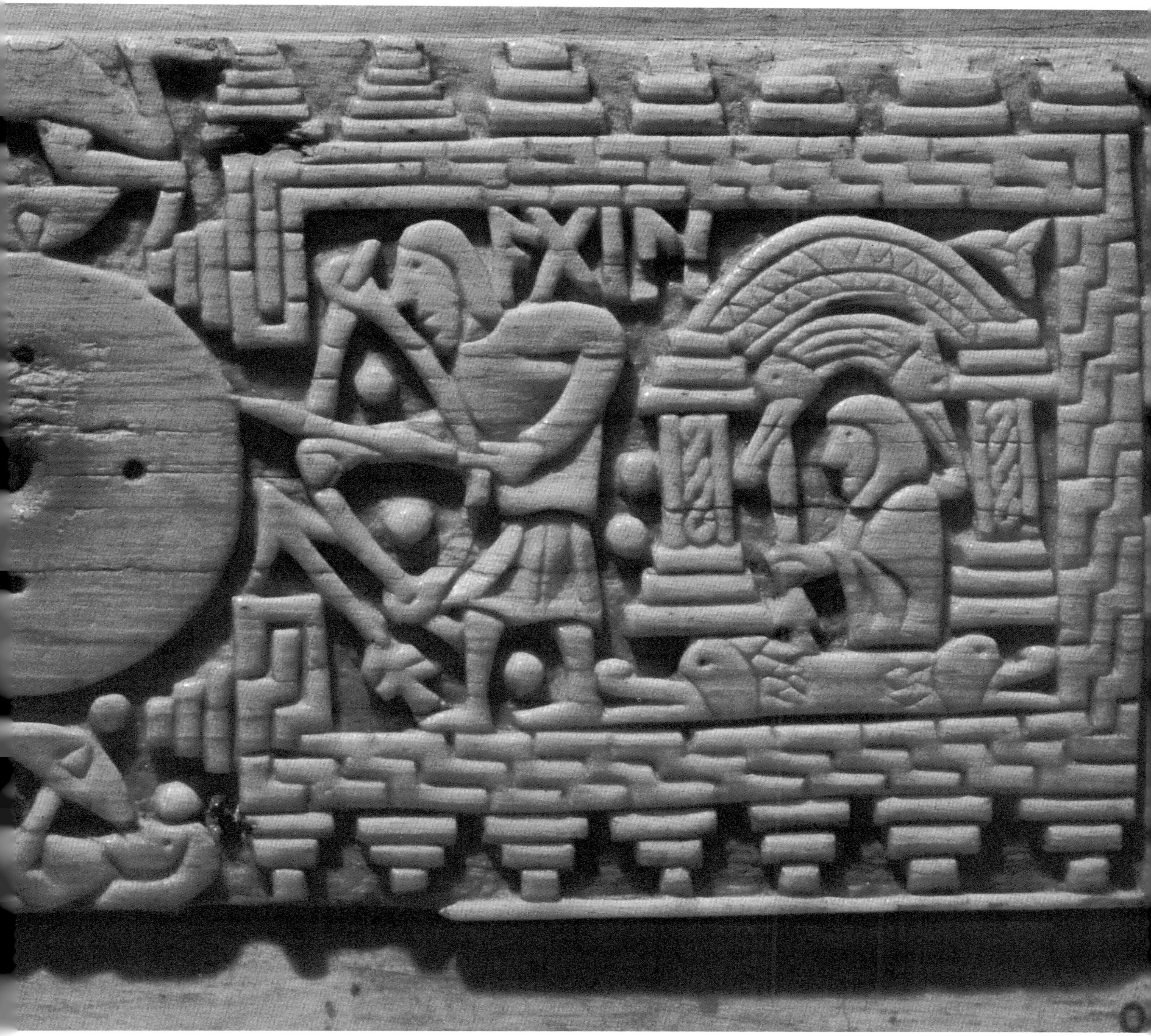

A-Z
CODEX GODS

skinned them, incorporating various parts into jewelry for the royal family. When Nidud's daughter visited his workshop, Wayland raped her and got his ring back. His revenge complete he escaped on specially made wings.

WITCHES

The old wise women of folklore with a knowledge of herbs and natural remedies, witches became the scapegoats of a Medieval Europe in full flight from paganism and increasingly obsessed with religious protocol. They were almost always female and practiced their arts by occult means — supposedly in league with the devil and possessing flight capability, they met in out of the way secret places to eat human flesh. It was with the Inquisition in the 13th century that they began to be targeted — the Church pronounced against a variety of heresies, with the use of torture to obtain the "truth" and prove witchcraft being frequent. By the time of the 15th and 16th centuries witch-burning was at the height of fashion, carried out by Catholics and Protestants alike, fuelled by guilt and fear and looking for explanations for the foul plagues that had more than decimated Europe.

YGGDRASIL

The great World Tree of Norse legend, a concept shared and envisioned by different mythologies. Yggdrasil's branches reached into and connected every layer of the world, while its canopy bloomed over the heavens. Its three massive roots reached down into giantland and the well of wisdom, another to Nifheim, the Norse Hades and the third linked to heaven, the gods and the well of Fate. Yggdrasil was an ash, the tree of knowledge from which Odin hung himself in sacrifice, to gain knowledge and understanding.

ZEUS

Also known as: Jupiter, Jove

Thunder god son of Kronos and supreme ruler of the Greek pantheon, manifesting power from his arsenal of weather weapons — thunderbolts, lightning and storms, Zeus toppled his child-swallowing father to seize power. Initially taking control of the sky and the earth's surface, he grew to become the all-powerful arbiter and judge, intervening in all aspects of human and divine life. He also possessed a shape-changing capability which he used extensively for covert female acquisition, for Zeus above all loved women and fathered many other gods and semi-divine heroes on a wide variety of partners. His wife Hera was driven berserk with rage by these infidelities, often stalking his mistresses, she would pursue and thwart the children of these unions too. Through this interplay the friction between the older chthonic mother-goddesses and the new Indo-European sky gods was enacted.

The Roman counterpart Jupiter was the Latin variant of this Aryan sky deity. From agricultural weather god beginnings he developed in conjunction with the city-state to become the paramount national god.

Right: A Greek bronze of Zeus holding a thunderbolt and a dove (6th century BC).

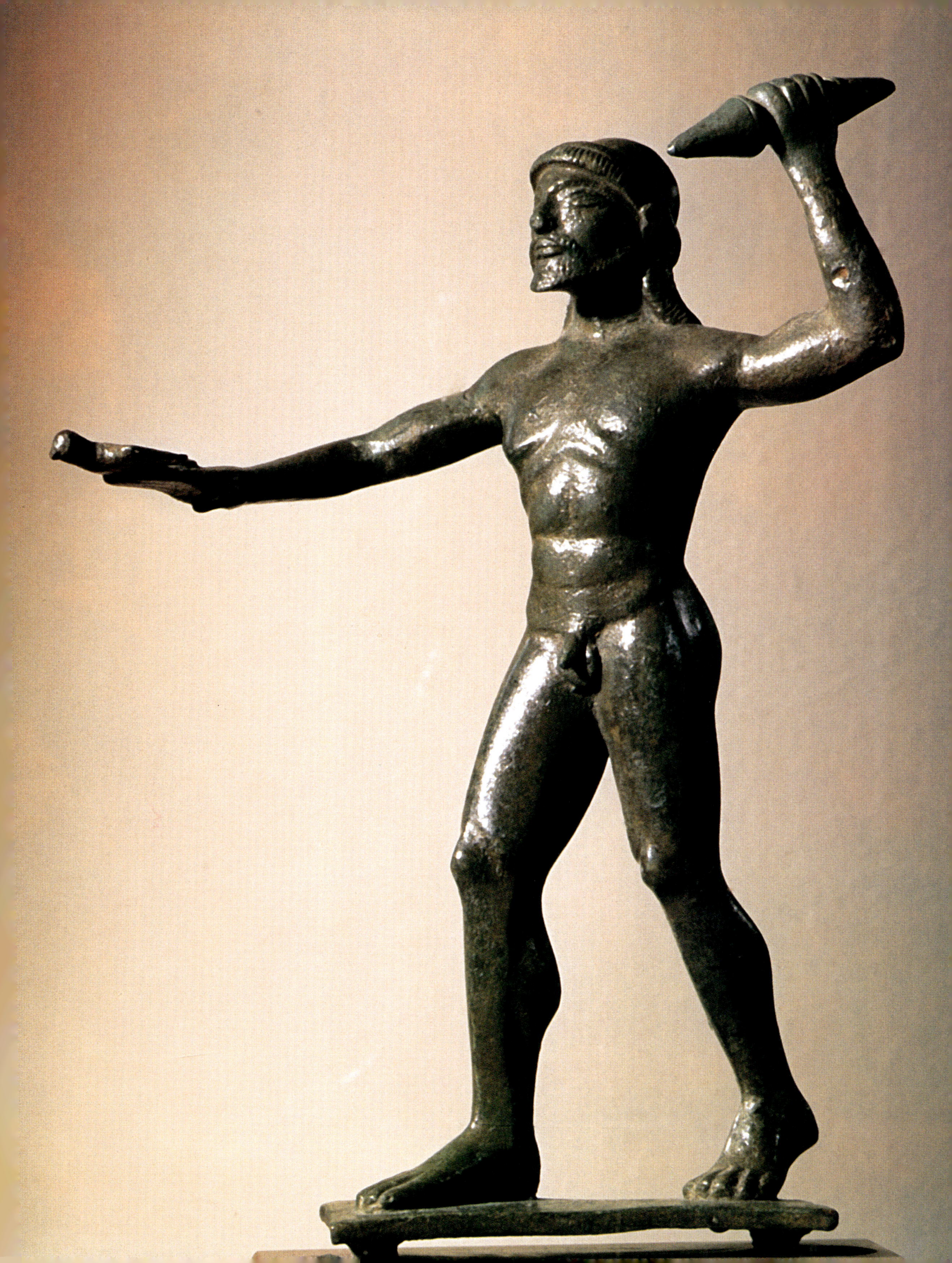

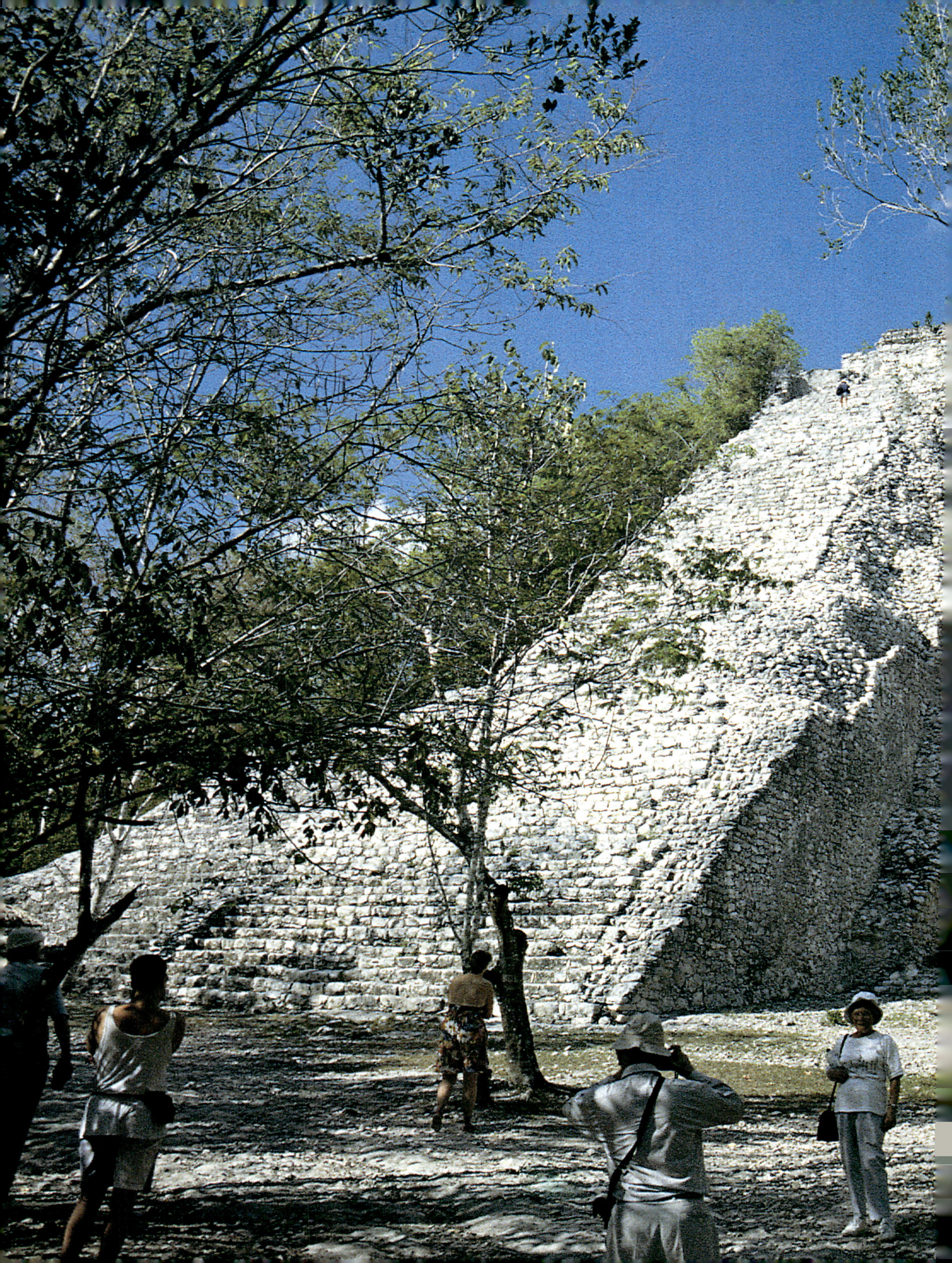

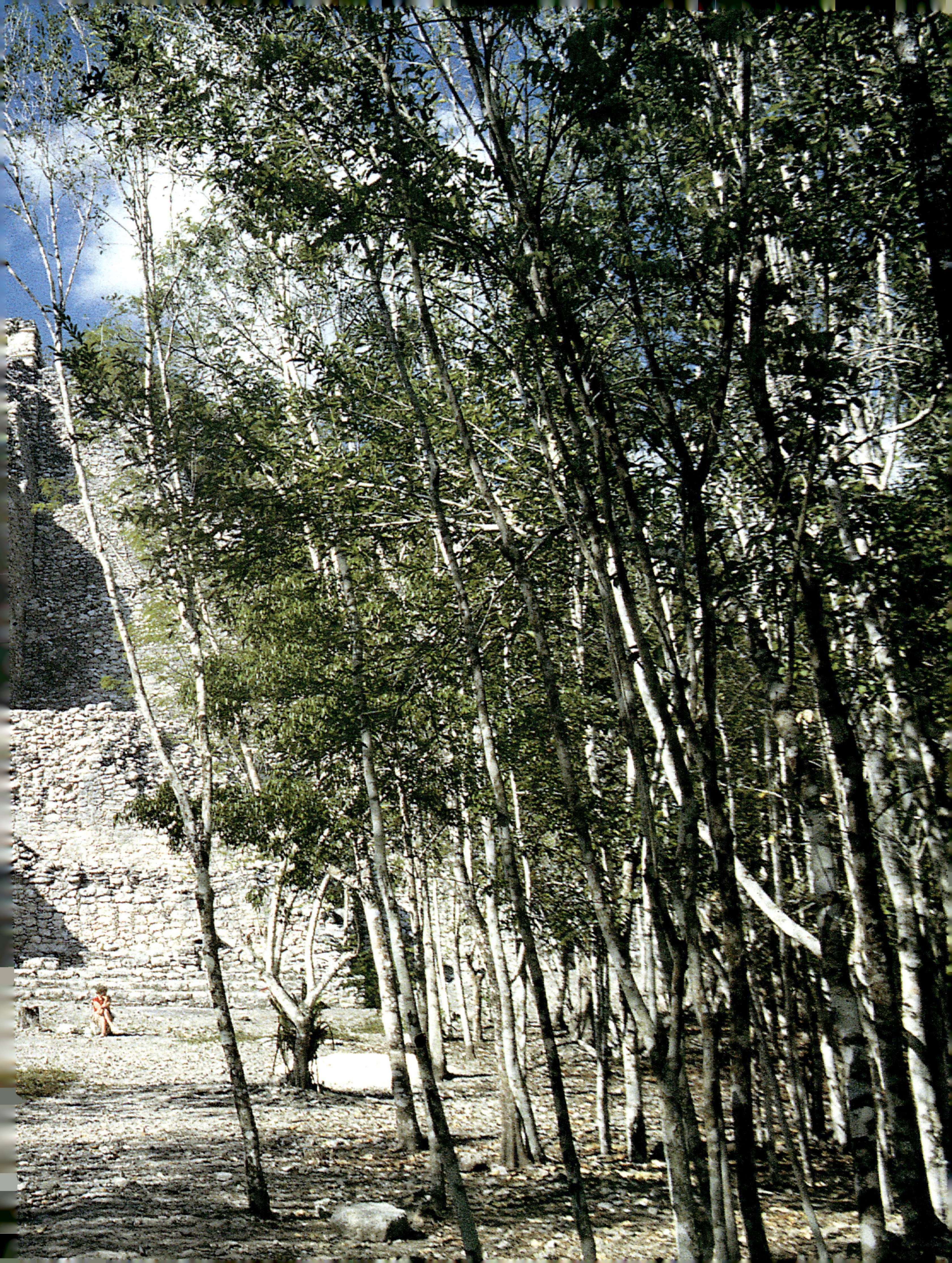

THE AMERICAS

NORTH AMERICA

It is thought that humans first entered continental America over the land bridge that connected it to Siberia during the last ice age some twenty thousand years ago, although this is an uncertain figure. Subsequently they migrated and settled ever southward, in a nomadic epic that would take people to the tip of Tierra del Fuego — journeying completely on foot. These immigrants were of a Mongoloid stock in keeping with their continent of derivation. Their belief systems were animist and shamanistic, relying upon a spirit world that was appeased and manipulated by gifted initiates. As these people dispersed across the vast lands of the Americas both environment and experience inevitably modified their culture. In the Great Plains and the Woodlands they became nomadic hunters, whereas further south and westward they became settled agriculturists. The oral cultures of these peoples were connected and suffused with nature, and almost every reaction and code of behavior was imbued with a simultaneous sacred agenda that gave every-day life meaning and function. Myths were used to explain and integrate the human, heaven and spirit worlds, to underline tribal, clan and family ties, to propitiate weather gods and other spirits and ensure fertility as well as bravery in battle. Accordingly, certain myths were only told to coincide with certain events or times of the year. It is interesting to note that the myths of these cultures differ from many others in that there were relatively few creation myths — the culture was still manifesting a variation on its original animist/shamanist beliefs when it encountered Europeans.

When the first trans-Atlantic voyagers arrived in the middle of the 16th century there were some 2,000 North American tribes who had evolved a range of societies from the

Previous pages: The largest pyramid in Yucatan.
Right: This chipped stone spearhead, a North American Indian flint tool, dates back to the Paleolithic Period.

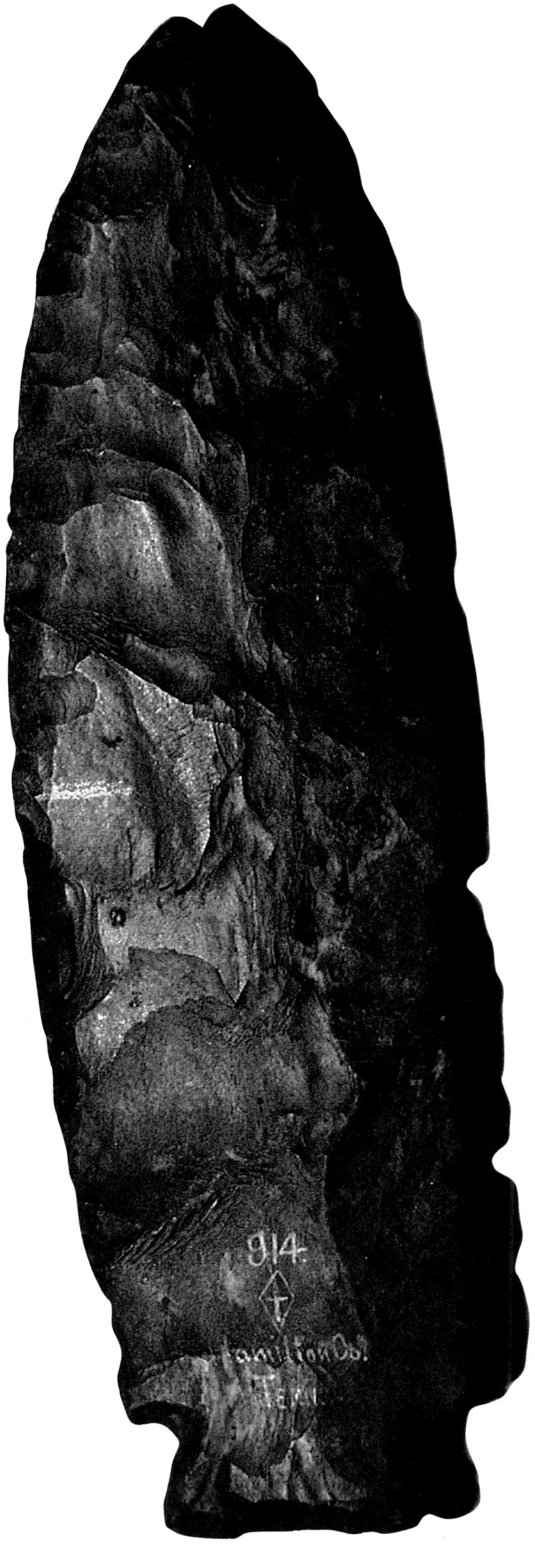
914

nomadic to the urban. The variety of tribal development was dictated by the diversity of habitats available on a continent spanning Arctic, Atlantic and Pacific spheres and including every terrain from deserts, forests, plains and mountains, to swamps and river valleys. Today, only some 300 tribes still exist on reservations. The majority of these indigenous peoples were hurried into the void by callous, land hungry, unsympathetic and competitive European settlers. Coming from lands of high population, technology and a culture that encouraged these advancements worldwide, they exploited the native peoples mercilessly. Perhaps it was fitting that many of these tribes lived in a constant state of raid and war, in a culture that emphasized bravery and feats of arms.

A few tribes had evolved a more complicated religious process including a supreme deity, but for the most part although variations were great, there are linking analogies that enable North American mythology to be seen in a single context. Almost all were totemic for instance, the totem being at once an object similar in capability to an African fetish in that it was imbued with spirit power and therefore was also a being of sorts, alive. It manifested as ancestral tribe and clan members as well as having an individual identity, and also represented animal and spiritual alliance, worship and propitiation. The totem was then a coat of arms, an altar, shrine flag and a family tree all rolled into one.

Common to all was the underlay of the original shamanism, imported across the ancient land bridge. Among the woodland tribes a Great Spirit was defined; sometimes identified as Sky Father, the creation of the whole universe was not always accredited to him but rather certain areas of influence. For instance he controlled the various agencies of earthly power — animal and elemental — as well as those

Above left and Right: Clay fertility figurines from the Brazilian Caraja tribe.

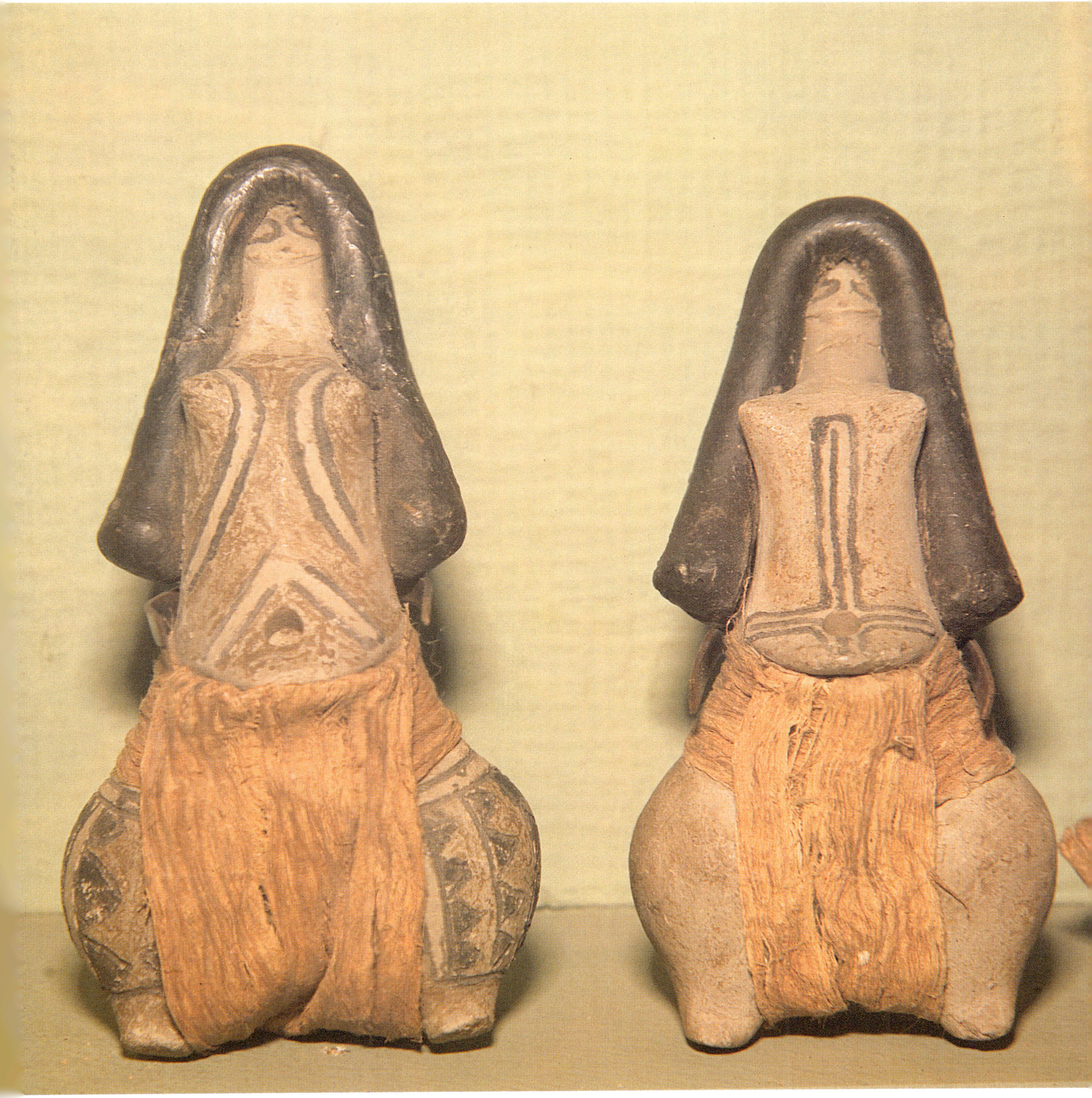

of his home turf, heaven. The making of the earth and its inhabitants was usually attributed to a trickster hero. The trickster was cunning, brave and resourceful, though also vindictive, spiteful and selfish. He created man, stole fire from heaven, formed the worlds, survived the flood, defeated monsters and sometimes just adventured. He could take human or animal form, and in fact was more often an animal — raven, crow, coyote, hare, rabbit etc. — a truly theriomorphic spirit. The Earth Mother was also worshiped and defined fertility with her grandchild twins — trickster heroes who played important roles in the myths and legends that recounted the reasons for life. Sometimes the twins were war gods, good and evil — the classic worldwide format for coping with duality and contradictory opposites and the attempt at reconciling them.

The native North Americans often viewed the universe as being made up of various stratified levels with the earth and its supported sky at the center. This was conceived as the second world to exist — as the first was drowned and submerged. At other times it was interpreted as the highest of worlds, and the last, anticipating an apocalypse scenario.

INUIT

Inhabiting the Arctic coasts stretching from Alaska to Greenland, the Inuit led their semi-nomadic hunting lifestyle, primarily because their environment allowed for little else. They lived during the winter on whale, seal, walrus and fish, and in the summer something that walked rather than swam — the caribou. Religious life was

Above left and Right: This North American Indian wrapping of a war bundle is made of white-tanned deerskin. It illustrates thunder birds and other supernatural beings sacred to the Eastern woodlands tribes.
Bottom left: Shamans of the Pacific northwest coast used this thunder bird rattle.

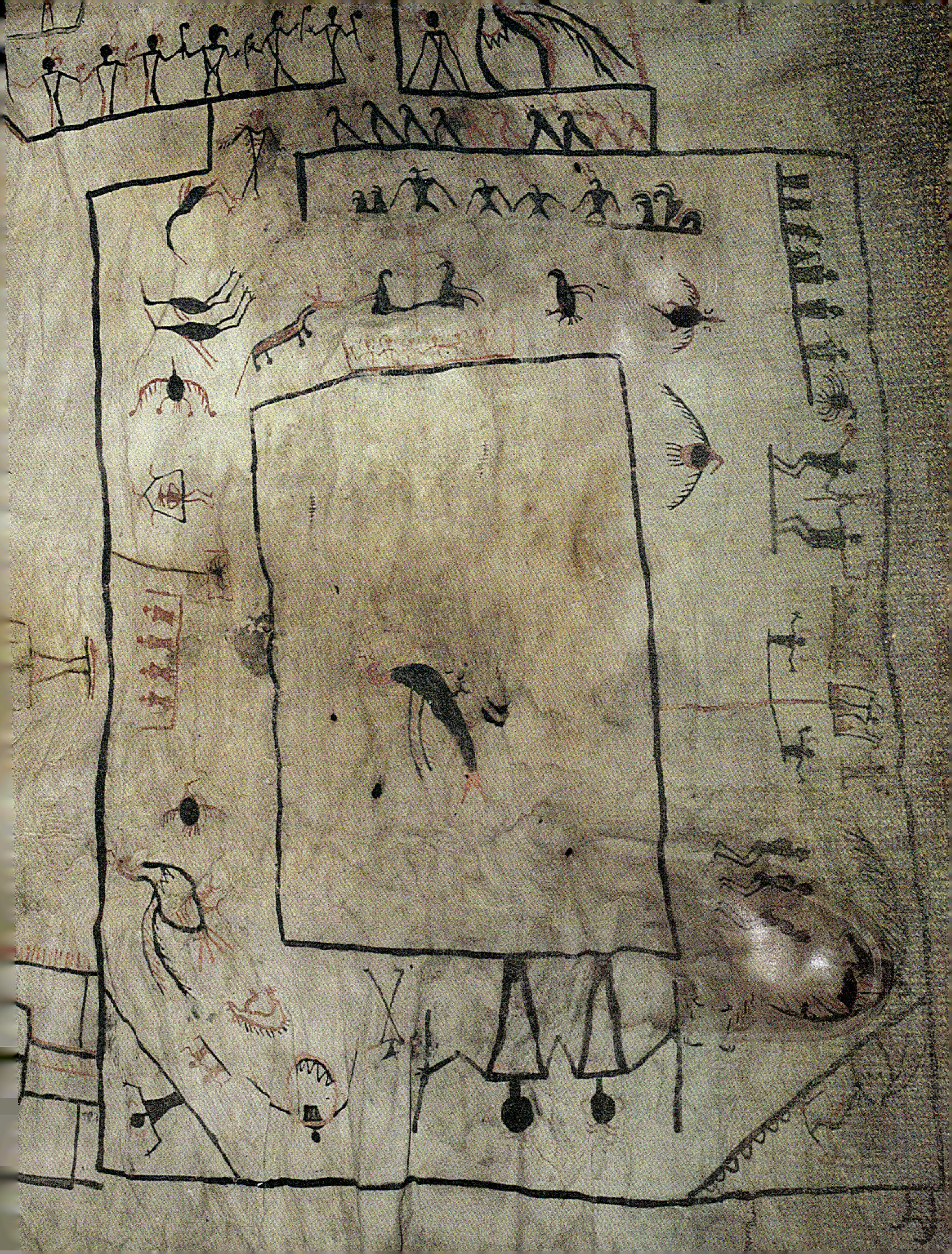

dominated by the concepts of animist shamanism, and these peoples had a busy and delicately balanced spirit world with which to contend. Hunters had their guardian spirits and shamans countered evil spells.

NORTHWEST

Tlingit, Tsimshian, Bella Coola, Kwakiutl, Nootka, Salish, Chinook.

The Northwestern tribes lived in large wooden villages in a mild climate with rich, fertile land and various food sources, particularly the sea. This easy subsistence saved time finding food which could instead be spent developing intricate ceremonies and a complex social life with detailed protocols and high quality symbolic artifacts and equipment. Clans each had a mythical animal founder, which acted as a symbolic badge of identity. The Thunderbird, Raven and Cannibal Spirit were the most powerful spirits. The settled existence of these people made them very aware of their lineage and history, which expressed itself in their rituals and artwork. Spectacular totem poles were a feature of their villages.

PLAINS

Blackfoot, Assinibone, Shoshoni, Cheyenne, Arapaho, Sioux, Pawnee, Kiowa, Comanche, Caddoan, Mandan, Omaha, Osage, Ariko.

Initially these tribes were nomadic buffalo hunters, but the influx of Woodland Indians being pushed westward by European settlement, forced the classic Plains culture into existence. Their emphasis was on individual and personal relationships with spirits and appeasement

Above left and Right: This blanket, with a totemic bear design, was made for a Tlingit tribe chief (Pacific northwest coast). Left: An Inuit (Eskimo) wooden mask representing a fish and its spirit.

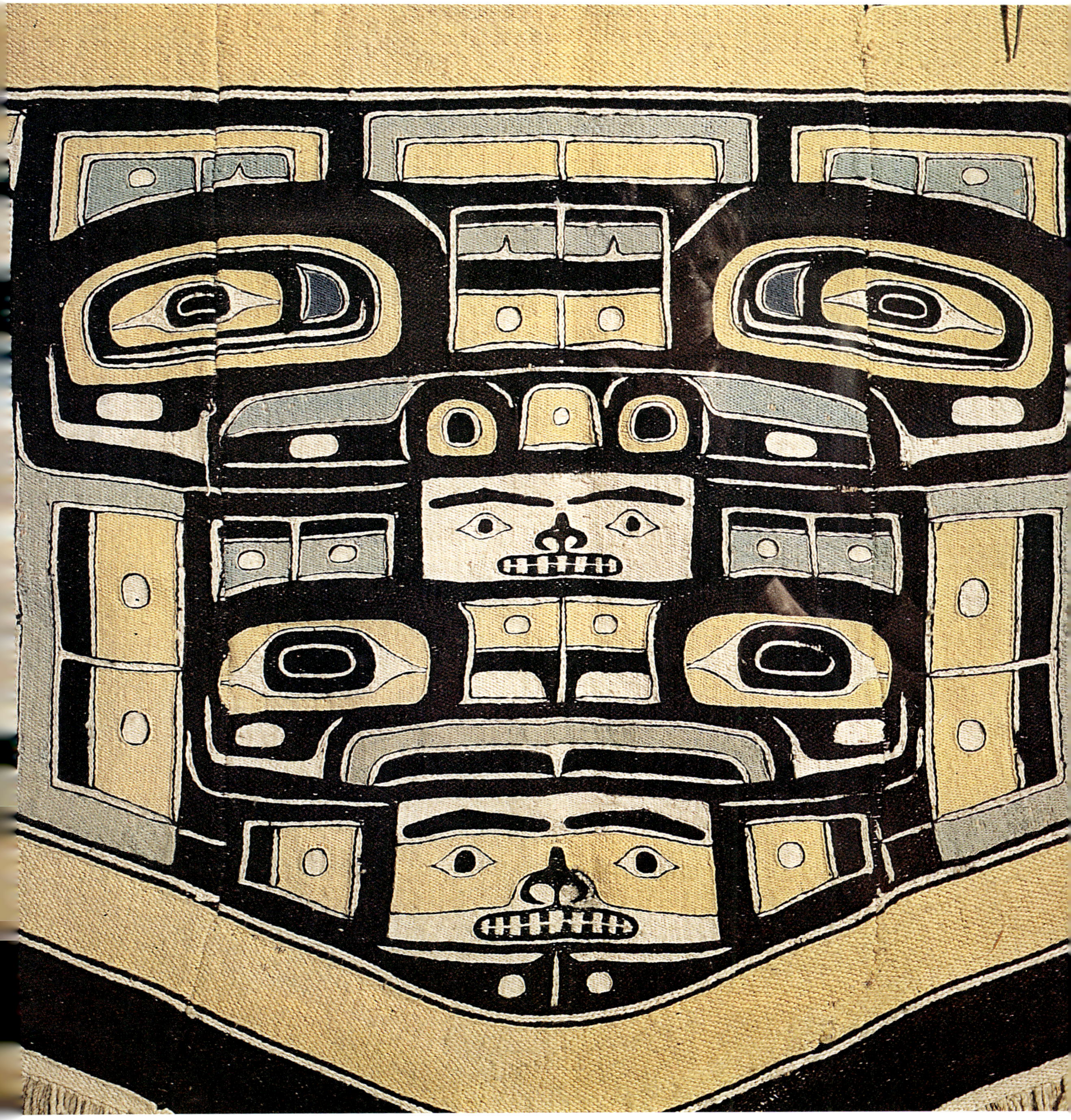

of weather gods, but there was also a developing idea of a Supreme Being. Prominent myths concerned animals and the origins of the ceremonies that underpinned correct procedure.

With the introduction of the horse and the gun from Europeans in the 16th century the Plains Indians were made still more martial and mobile. Being nomadic or semi-nomadic, they were organized and disciplined and the rituals and the rites enacted among hunters and warriors were focused on military success.

SOUTHWEST

Hopi, Navajo, Papago, Pueblo, Apache.

The Southwest contained a vital desert culture, including the most sophisticated "urban" builders, the Pueblo, whose mudbrick tower blocks were the most evolved of American Indian constructions. Their communities were closely-knit and therefore socially adept — a requirement for the careful husbanding of water resources and comparative isolation. This independence is why so much of their culture remains intact. Like all agricultural communities they had an intimate bond with their land and a conservative sense of history. Their myths detail precise and specific features coupled with an emergence mythology — from the fertile nourishing ground came the creator spirits and ancestors. During their rituals masked impersonators drew animal spirit providers down to bless crops and ensure a fruitful harvest.

SOUTHWEST WOODLANDS

Algonquian, Ottawa, Winnebago, Huron, Iroquois, Shawnee, Cherokee, Mikasuki, Cree, Delaware, Menominee, Potowatomi, Chippewa, Montagnais, Oneida, Senca, Mohawk, Muskhogean, Creek, Chicksaw.

Above left and Right: This colorful textile belonged to the Southwest Hopi tribe.

· THE AMERICAS ·

The dense forest of northern and eastern North America was reflected in the mythology of these forest dwellers — consisting as it did of spirits, demons and monsters. There were also elemental gods and a Supreme Being, along with differentiated upper and lower worlds. When pushed from their original tribal lands by European settlement, they drifted onto the plains but kept much of their mythology and culture intact. This became influential on the original Plains Indians, and went on to feature strongly in what became the classic period of that area. These peoples were divided into three main linguistic groups, some peaceable but others (the Iroquois for instance) warlike — inevitable in a culture where physical prowess was desperately required and highly prized.

CENTRAL AMERICA

In complete contrast to the North American Indians were the societies of Central or Meso America, which mainly consisted of ancient and decayed civilizations. The remains of these are often now accessible only through archeology, or from the secondary sources of European observation and record. (The Spanish did log some of what they were destroying.)

The first civilizations were those of the Olmecs and Teotihuacans, neither of whom left any written records, though they possessed a complicated symbol system, which betrays the complexity of their social and religious organization. However they did leave behind huge pyramid constructions, the precursors of later Mayan and Aztec edifices and the jaguar and mother goddess seem to have had especial significance. The Olmecs peaked around 800–400 BC, the Teotihuacans in 200 AD. Three of their biggest

Above left and Right: This Mayan pottery of a standing man is probably from the Yucatan.

351

structures were the Temple of the Sun, the Temple of the Moon and the Temple of the Feathered Serpent, which featured symbols characteristic of the later Aztec deities: rain god Tlaloc and the feathered serpent Quetzacoatl. This illustrates aptly the syncretistic process, for these mythical remains heavily influenced the Aztecs.

MAYA

Mayan culture occupied a wide and geographically varied area. In the south it spanned the highlands and the coast, in the north the Yucatan peninsula and in between a heavily forested semi-tropical jungle area. It was in this middle area that their civilization reached its peak. Though lacking a great river system to sustain them, their society seems to have West Asian parallels with Mesopotamia and Egypt. Their cities were primarily religious and cult centers, dominated by an educated priest elite. The earliest remains found so far indicate a commencement around 400–300 BC, their last temples falling into disuse between 750-900 AD.

The intellectual achievements of the Mayans were astonishing — including a complex calendar system using mathematical and astronomical data. Their script remains undeciphered today. Only three manuscripts remain but translation of these writings is one of archeology's holy grails. Interpretation of monuments, hieroglyphics and sculpture are thus constrained by this fundamental lack of information. The Spanish did record some things as they systematically destroyed the Mayan culture, but the three late works written after conquest seem to have more in common with Toltec culture. By then the Mayan had atrophied to such an extent that even its own people, shadows of their former selves, knew very little of their own past.

Above left and Right: This clay of a squatting man, was unearthed from a Mayan burial on the island of Jaina off Campeche.

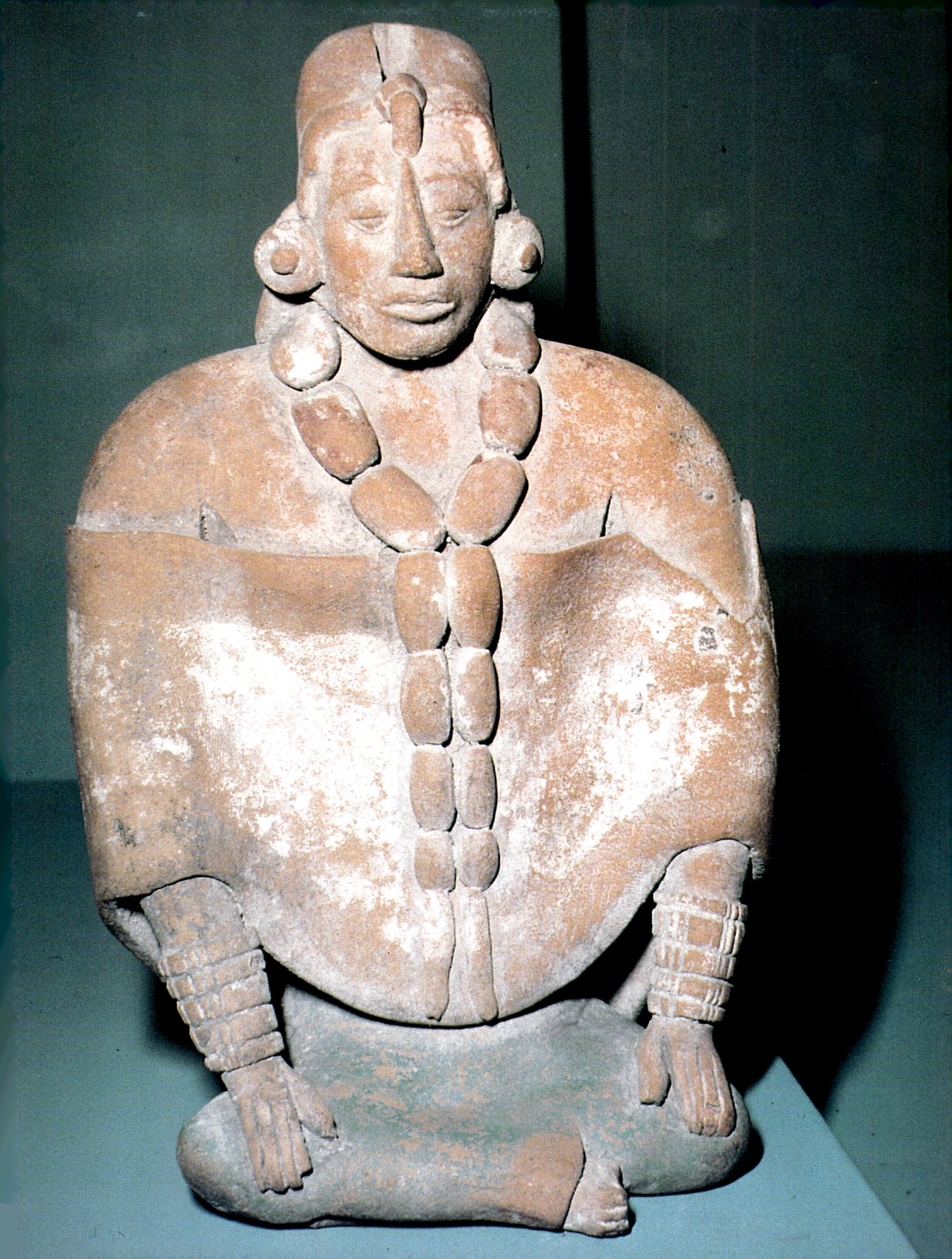

TOLTEC/CHICHIMEC

From the 8th to the 12th centuries AD successive bands of warrior Nahuatlan tribes entered the central Mexican plain. First to arrive were the Toltecs, followed by the Chichimecs and then the most famous or infamous of all, the Aztecs or Mexica, (they changed their name to suit their new place). The Toltecs founded their great city of Tollan, worshiped the earth mother and the sky god Mixcoatl, — the Cloud Serpent who was identified with the war leader under whom they were triumphant. Mixcoatl had an even more important son, named Quetzacoatl — the Green Feathered Serpent who again was a culture hero, war leader, priest-king and a god, all rolled into one. Tollan eventually fell to the Chichimecs, whose ascendance was soon eclipsed by the most extreme and warlike of these wandering groups — the Aztecs.

AZTEC

The extraordinary rise and fall of the Aztecs began when the tribe left their mythical ancestral lands and journeyed to the central Mexican plain. They do not seem to have dominated immediately, but rather as a poorer vassal state their manpower and military ferocity made them much in demand as mercenaries. From these beginnings they leapt to a grisly prominence that has seldom been equaled in its bloodthirsty brutality and bleakness. They finally settled according to their omens, on the marshy ground of Tenochtitlan, where they built a magical futuristic floating city, which contained over a million inhabitants at a time when the biggest European cities were a fraction of this size. Mythical study of the Aztecs reveals their syncretistic approach — they were much influenced by Olmec and Toltec culture, absorbing and modifying gods to suit their own purposes. Perhaps they were

Above left and Right: A Zapotec priest sits on a pyramid in full regalia holding his sacrificial knife (300–900 AD).

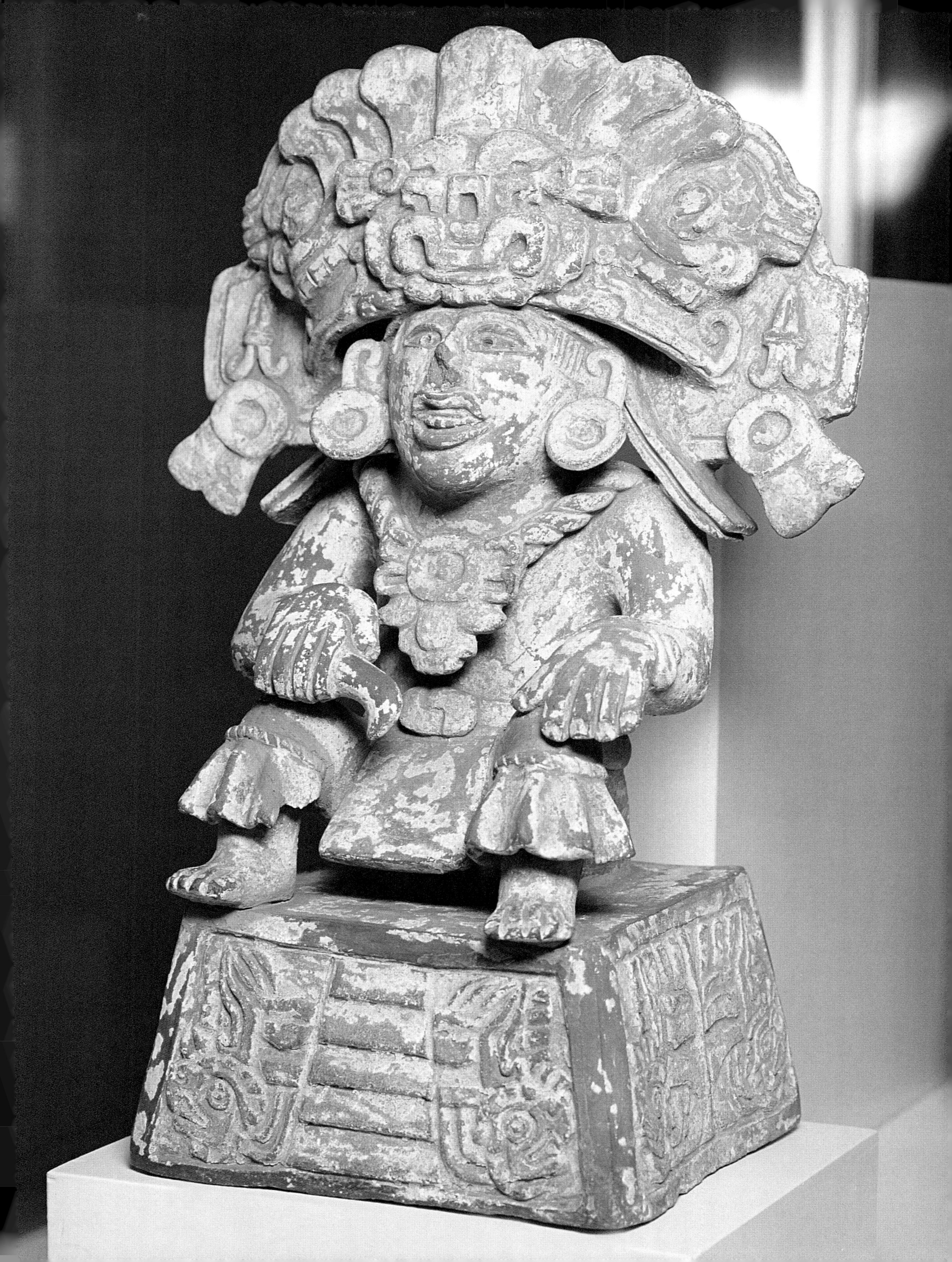

just a more extreme version of other societies of the time — the South American propensity for blood sacrifice was terrifying. It was thought to ensure fertility, and was also a responsibility, feeding the gods and thereby winning their continued allegiance. Given that the Toltec deity Quetzacoatl was revered by the Aztecs to an extreme degree, they must have seen themselves as the inheritors of that legendary older culture. Like the Romans the Aztecs absorbed and tolerated the gods of all those whom they conquered. (Believe what you want but pay your taxes...) One temple at Tenochtitlan contained statues of all the deities belonging to subject peoples. The ultimate example of the Aztec outlook was their one indigenous god Huitzilopochtli, who had led them from their mythical homeland, shown them the route, selected the city site and prophesised the brief greatness for which they had been selected. Born fully armed and furious, Huitzilopochtli — "the Humming Bird of the South" (humming birds were the souls of those warriors fallen in combat: the highest and most honorable death for an Aztec) — required a constant supply of fresh hearts cut out of live bodies. These were supplied from prisoners taken when on campaign. The Aztecs' meteoric rise was cut short by the Spanish conquest. In a live performance of an active myth, it was believed that Quetzacoatl had returned in the form of Cortez, the Spanish conqueror, to invert everything and seal the Aztec fate. A huge empire thus fell to a few scheming Europeans — because of the fatalistic nature of its people.

THE CARIBBEAN

The original native cultures of the Caribbean Islands have been so badly damaged by sustained contact with Europeans since the 16th century that almost nothing remains with

Above left and Right: This drinking vessel in the shape of a fox with cap and earflaps is an example of Peruvian pottery.

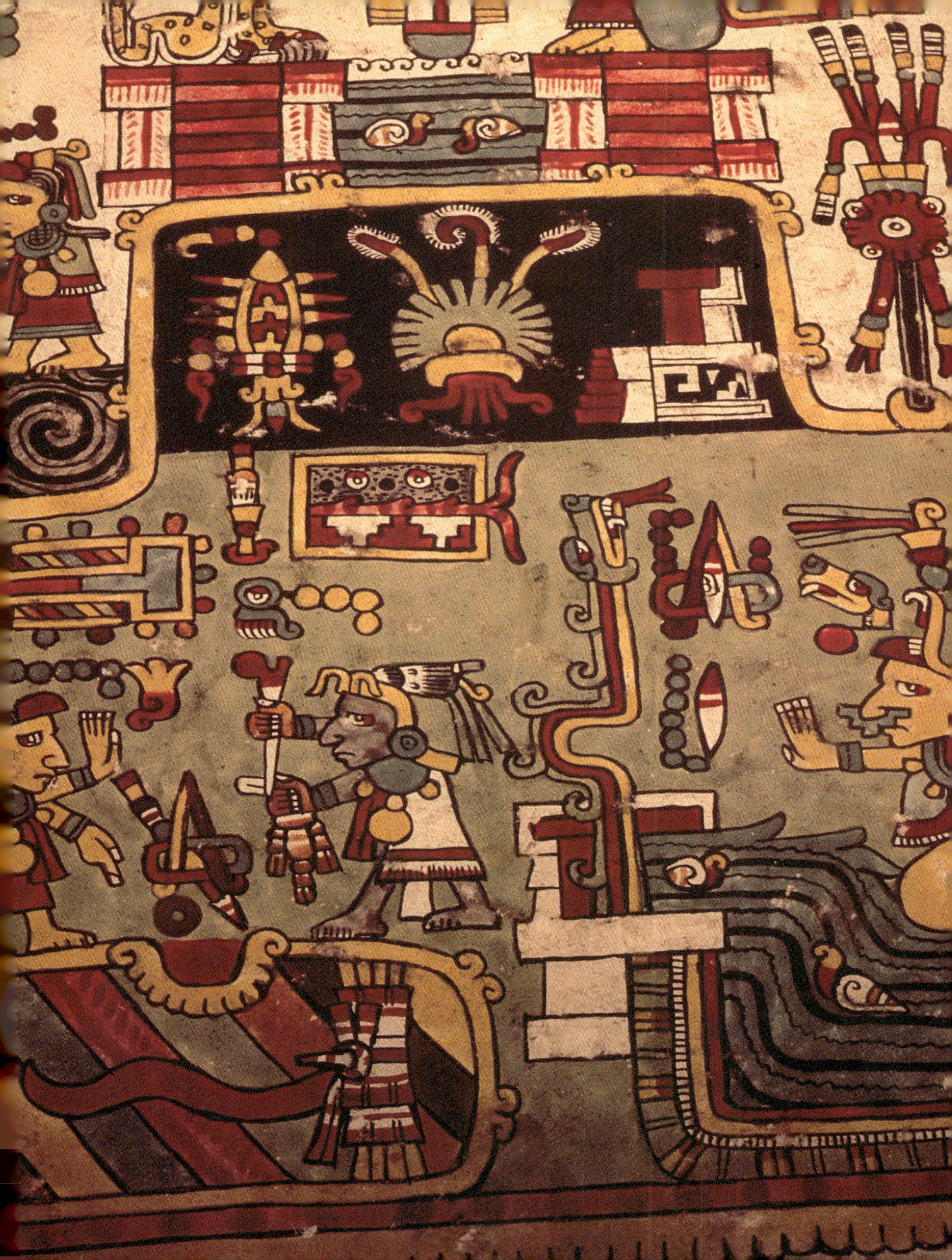

which to assess them. The tiny amount of data that is left of the Taino and Carib culture, speaks of a society that was similar to those South Western Indians of North America.

Since the days of the slave trade and the huge influx of Africans into the area a mix of shamanist, West African and Christian beliefs led to the rise of the Voodoo religion, which manifests as a series of cults based around a hybrid spirit or *loa*. In a Voodoo temple a priest or priestess leads the ritual invoking spirits of the Voodoo world to possess the members. From the utterings of those possessed knowledge is drawn.

SOUTH AMERICA
Chavin

Knowledge of this region is entirely dependent on archeological evidence and is therefore fairly limited — there is no record of any script or written data. However, it can be deduced from these remains that Chavin culture spread over much of the Andean region. Grouped in small agricultural and fishing communities their largest centers were religious, where a jaguar god was worshiped along with a mother fertility goddess. The sudden disappearance of this early civilization in about 33 BC is a complete mystery.

MOCHICA

The Mochican civilization took root and prospered in the coastal valleys of northern Peru, where it depended on a complex irrigation system for its agricultural survival. It also had large centers of civil and religious buildings, including great pyramid temples. The sun and moon were important celestial deities to the Mohicans, with perhaps the moon being dominant. There was also a mysterious jaguar god, whose worship included human sacrifice.

Above left and Right: This drinking vessel in the shape of a fox with cap and earflaps is an example of Peruvian pottery.

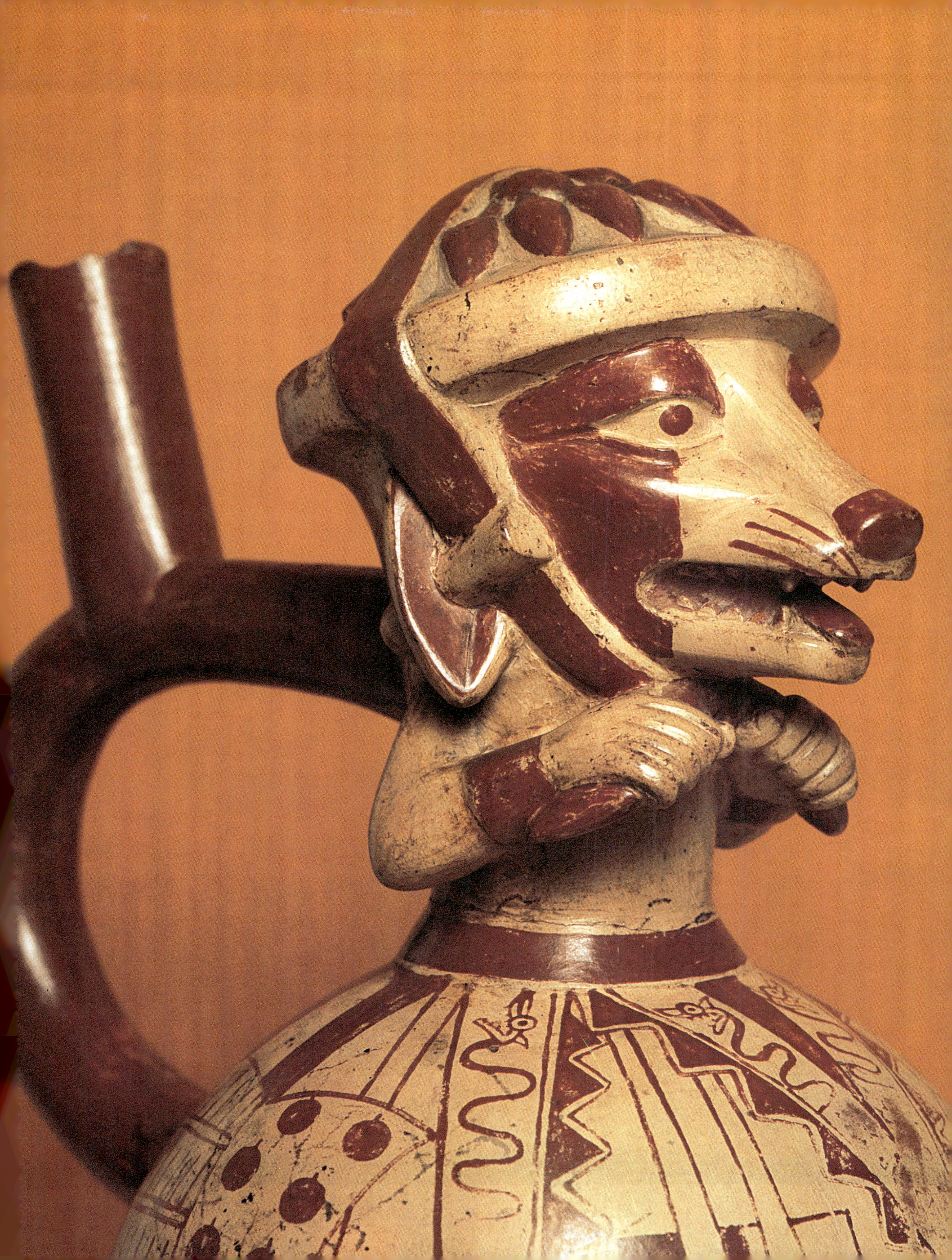

TIHUANACO

The first civilization of great size in the high Andes was centered on Tiahuanaco, near Lake Titicaca in Bolivia. There the buildings, dating from about the 1st century AD, include four pyramids and a huge complex platform which is entered from a monolithic portal known as the Gateway of the Sun. Pumas, condors, jaguars and other animal predators exist in massive stone sculptures. These creatures had a lasting influence on Andean culture, becoming the syncretistic prototypes for many of the religious cultures — but, again, details and documents of these people do not exist and it is impossible to be certain of their meaning. Though no sign of conquest or destruction is observable the Tihuanacoan civilization abruptly terminated sometime around 1000 AD.

CHIMOR AND CHUICUITO

Between the emergence of the Inca and the previous large-scale Tihuanaco society, a few much smaller societies briefly flourished, such as the Chimor and Chuicuito. The Chimor culture was highly centralized and had a deified ruler as well as moon and sea gods and totemic sculpture. Chuicuito by contrast was a smaller, loosely knit federation of related groups who seem to have occupied their time with in-fighting. Again, there is no data to inform us of their rationale.

INCA

The most famous and recent of the Andean civilizations, legend has the mythical origin of the Incas also at Lake Titicaca, but the consensus is that their roots were at Cuzco, their highland capital, circa 1200 AD. After a delicate moment in their history, when the original city almost entirely collapsed on them they went on to overcome any local

Above left and Right: An Inca man plays the pan pipe.

• THE AMERICAS •

opposition and competition. Their successful bid for supremacy was launched and decided within a timeframe of a few decades — an achievement of extraordinary proportions given that this was a people without knowledge of the wheel or writing, a bronze age empire run on foot.

Inca myth and culture were transmitted orally by a special class of bard-priests. As with most empire-builders, the Inca absorbed the gods and cultures of their victim peoples whilst maintaining their supremacy. This was not always an effortless condescension, but motivated perhaps by the meteoric rise of their supremacy and by a deep insecurity. They adapted and suppressed, modified, mutated and rewrote history to fit their own relative size.

After the Spanish conquest not a great deal survived; such that did was recorded by magnanimous conquerors or slave natives and reflects the same process that the Incas themselves had carried out — with the inevitable leaps and bounds of expediency. The fact that most of the important "primary" sources were written by Europeanized natives or Europeans gives the game away. These people could not hope to record the indigenous truths of that moribund culture in the evening of its existence, more a ghost of a reflection already fading in a dying sun overwhelmed by cloud. Biased perspectives, blood, beliefs and dogmas all intruded into any account. What can be said is that no minutely structured pantheon existed. The system that existed was linked to the requirements of the time, the place, the situation and the circumstances — further adulterated by expediency.

However, it can be said that generally Inti the sun god dominated, with a moon goddess and a rain god not far behind. The creator deity Viracocha absorbed all other influences and parallels to become supreme in the pantheon.

Above left and Right: This boiled head belonged to the South American tribes of the Amazon.

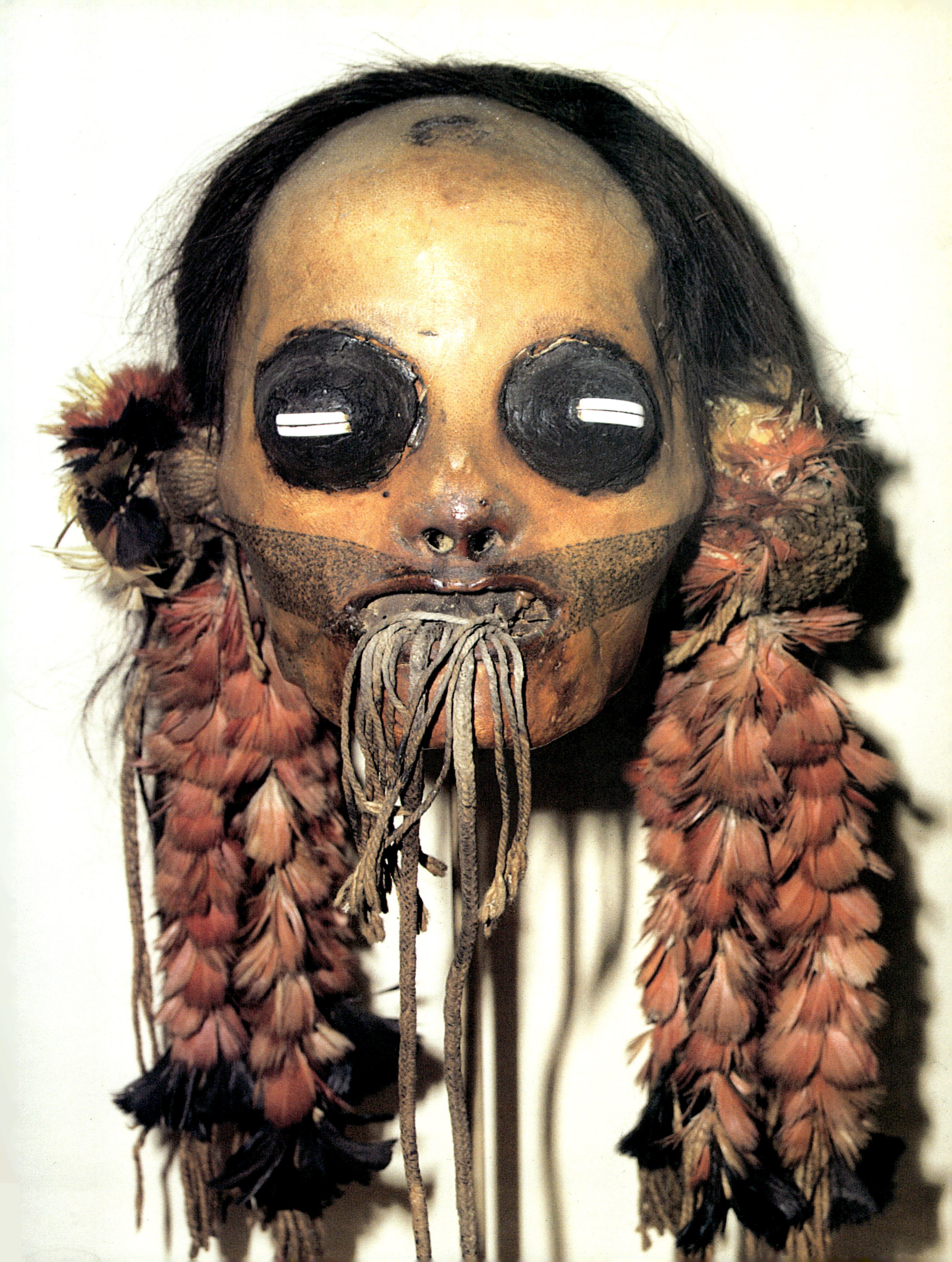

A-Z
CODEX GODS

ABA
The chief deity of the Chocataw tribe from the southeastern woodlands of North America. A mixture of creator-god and woodland spirit, Aba was supposed to have led the Chocataw people up onto the earth from the lower world in which they were conceived.

AGWE
Also known as: Ague, Agwe Woyo, Agoue Oyo
The most elaborate ceremonies took place to propitiate this *loa*; the regal Haitian god of the Sea. The Voodoo cult practices would include sinking ships laden with gifts and offerings down to his submarine palace.

AHAU KIN
The Mayan sun god, who in the creation story is referred to as the "Beginner of Time." Through this he also came to represent Judgement Day, when evil men would be returned to eternal suffering in a hell that existed prior to the creation of the sun, moon and earth.

AH PUCH
"The Lord of Death"
Also known as: Hunhau, Ah Kinchel, Yum Cimil
Identified as the god A in the Mayan Codex, Ah Puch was the Mayan god of death and took the form of a skeleton or a bloated corpse adorned with bells. In his avatar Hunhau he was the king of demons, ruling the ninth and lowest level of the underworld, known as Mitnal. Today he survives as Yum Cimil for the modern Yuacatec Mayans, and continues to loiter with intent in the houses of the sick. The ancient Mayans had a different attitude to death from their neighbors — they feared it greatly and grieved in an ornate manner. Poor people were buried equipped with food and money for the next world, whilst the rich were cremated and buried in shrines. There was a reverence for life and a fear of death quite heartening amongst the bloodthirsty South Americans.

AI APAEC
A late name for an active god of the Mochica, who seemed to share certain features with and have been the son of an indifferent creator/sky deity below whom he ranged at will. He was usually portrayed sporting a jaguar headdress and snake head earrings.

AIRSEKUI
Airsekui was the Great Spirit of the Huron tribe, to whom the first of all fruits and meat were offered. The Hurons are a North American woodlands tribe neighboring the Mohawks, the Cherokee and the Selish, with whom they are linguistically and culturally related. The Hurons were almost exterminated by the Iroquois, presently surviving in a very small group.

Right: A terracotta figure of the Mayan sun god.

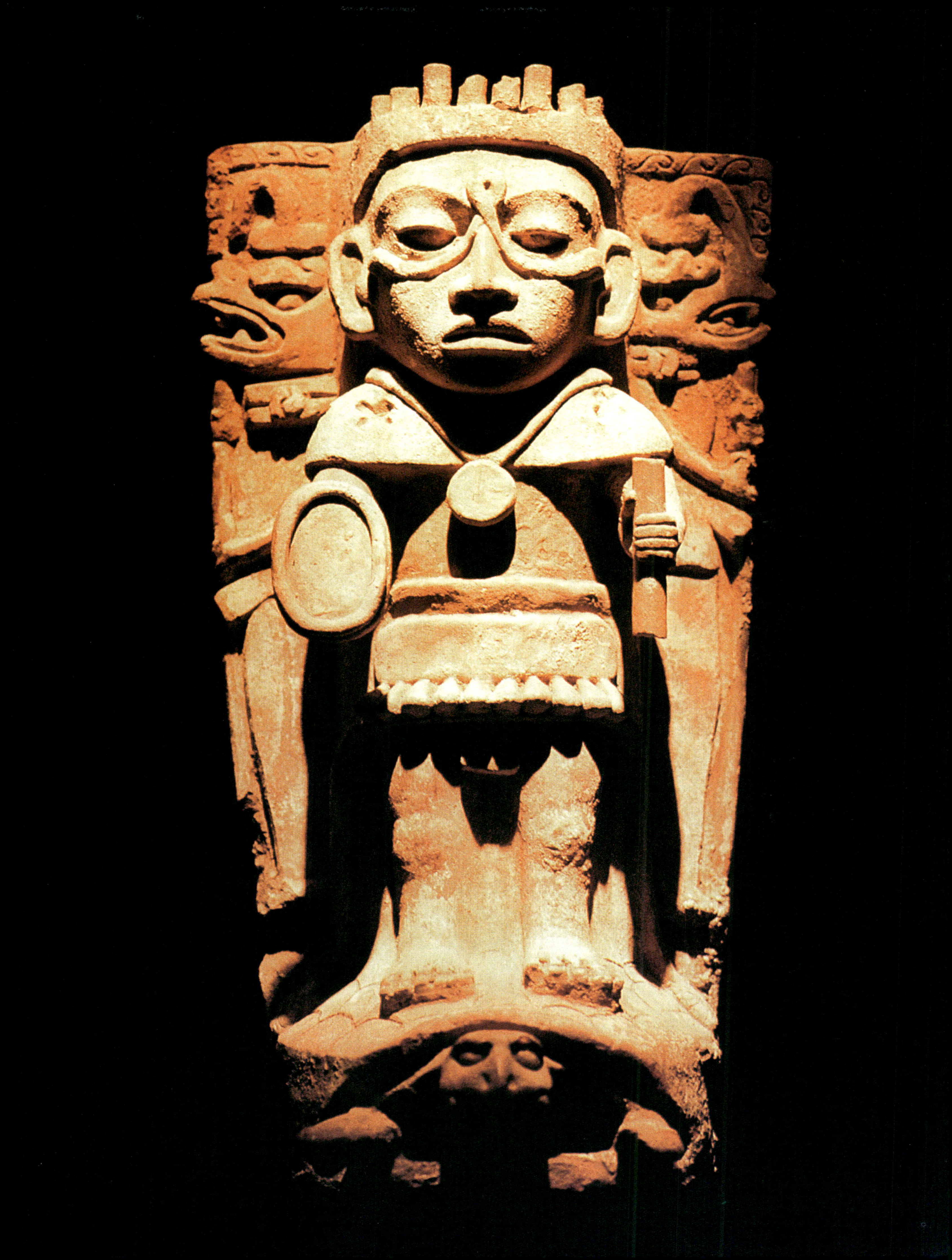

A-Z
CODEX GODS

AMOTKEN

The supreme spirit of the Selish tribes from the woodlands of North America, he dwelt high above mankind. He was the Selish version of the Great Spirit creator god common to many North American tribes. Often this type of god was of a very generalized nature and, having formed the elements of life, required help from animal/culture heroes who were more proactive and around whom myths and stories were woven. In this case Amotken's messenger/helper was Coyote who behaved unusually well, for the benefit of the Selish.

ANGAKOQ

A name for the Inuit tribe's medicine man or shaman. Given their scattered living conditions the Inuit mythology was never formalized and thus each local Angakoq was the repository of lore and magic, with personal communication links to the spirit world, the keeper and arbiter of tradition. A person (predominantly but not exclusively men) would become an Angakoq through the sponsorship of a tornac or guardian spirit, of which there were three particular kinds: those shaped like stones, those like human beings and the most powerful of all, those in the form of polar bears. Through the efficacy of their guardian they would then cure the sick, control the weather, interpret auguries and lead propitiatory sacrifices to appease the Great Spirits.

ARNARKUSAGA

Also known as: Nerrivik

Arnarkusaga was the Great Goddess of the Inuit. She was primarily a water and sea spirit, who as the source of all life ruled over alive and dead alike. The Inuit are the indigenous inhabitants of North America's Arctic coasts.

ASCENT OF THE NAVAHO

The prime creation myth of the Navaho tribes, from the southwest of North America. Like many other local tribes and peoples, the Navaho believed in a structured plurality of worlds and this myth details their gradual ascent to the earth, passing through various other colored worlds peopled by other races — Red, with bat-people, Blue, with swallow-people and Yellow, with grasshopper-people. Next they emerged into a multi-colored world already inhabited by farmers (the Kisani), who worshiped four color-coded gods. These gods made the first man and woman, who began to breed. Coyote and badger then arrived from the next world to cause various problems, culminating almost in the destruction of man. But the children of Aste Hastin and Aste Estsan ultimately survived, though doomed to suffer death. The myth is incredibly intricate, with many sections containing numerous gods and characters, including Rock Crystal Boy and Girl, Ground-heat Girl, Turquoise Boy and Corn Girl to name but a few.

Right: This Mayan painted jar was found in Guatemala (550–950 AD).

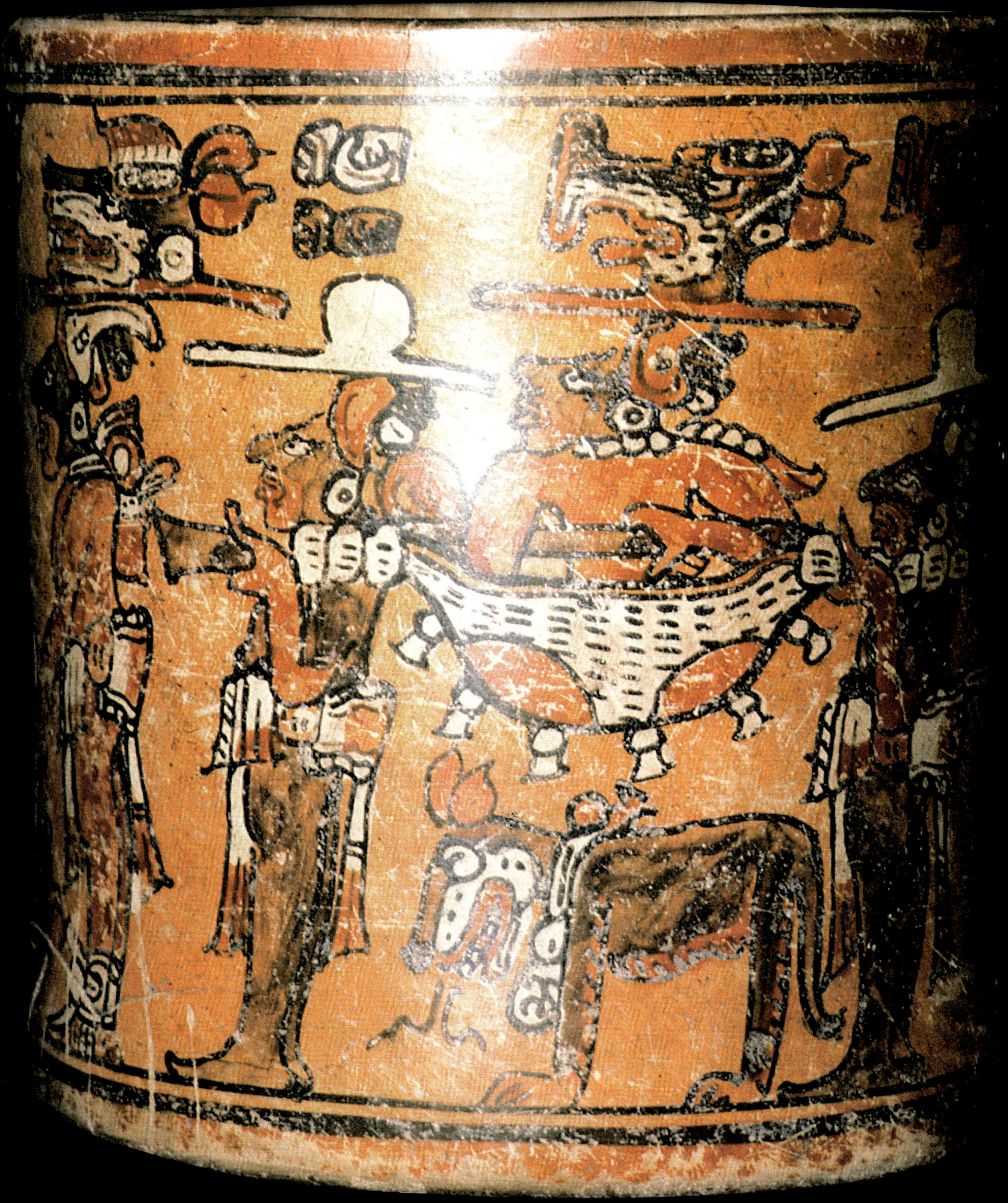

A-Z
CODEX GODS

ASGAYA GIGAGEI
Thunder god of the Cherokees from the North American woodlands. The Cherokee also suffered at the hands of the Iroquois. Asgaya Gigagei was their prime deity, with a group of lesser godlets known as the "Thunder Boys" serving under him.

ATIUS TIRAWEA
Also known as: Tirawa
Creator god of the Pawnee, who believed that it was Atius Tirawea who set the sun, earth, moon and stars in their courses. His conception or incarnation perhaps owed something to the Christian tales told by European settlers whom the Pawnee encountered on the Great Plains, but astral worship had always been at the center of their beliefs.

AWONAWILONA
As the supreme androgynous creator god of the Zuni Indians, from the Southwest of North America, Awonawilona possessed both male and female characteristics. From him/her came two children, each with separate sex and different powers; these were the Earth Mother, Awitelin Tsita and the Sky Father, Apoyan Tachu. From this divine couple the rest of creation was then born. Again the American Indians manifested a concept of a deity that prepared the world, but left that creation to his progeny to cultivate.

AZTLAN
The mythical island homeplace of the Aztecs. The legends surrounding it tell the story of migration southward, and foretold a return to their origin. The fifth ruler of the Aztecs, Montezuma, decided to send for advice to the ancestral homeland where Huitzilopochtli's mother still lived. Led by spirits, the delegation of ambassadors arrived at the island. That they spoke the same language yet were not recognizably the same surprised the islanders, who it turned out lived forever as long as they stayed on the island. When the delegation attempted to ascend to Coatlicue their feet sank into the ground. Through a change of diet and departure they had foregone their immortality and could not make such an ascension. Her steward instead acted as go-between. Coatlicue asked the the travelers to remind Huitzilopochtli of the oracle that foretold his eventual defeat and his promise to return home, to Aztlan. The entirity of Aztec adventure was in other words a foregone conclusion: a brilliant brief glory but ultimately defeat and retreat.

BOCHICA
The legendary ancestor patriarch and hero savior of the Chibca Indians, whose advanced early civilization in Colombia was second only to the Incas. The bearded Bochica came wandering from the east, teaching the Chibcas moral law and religious protocol as well as

Right: An Iroquois face mask.

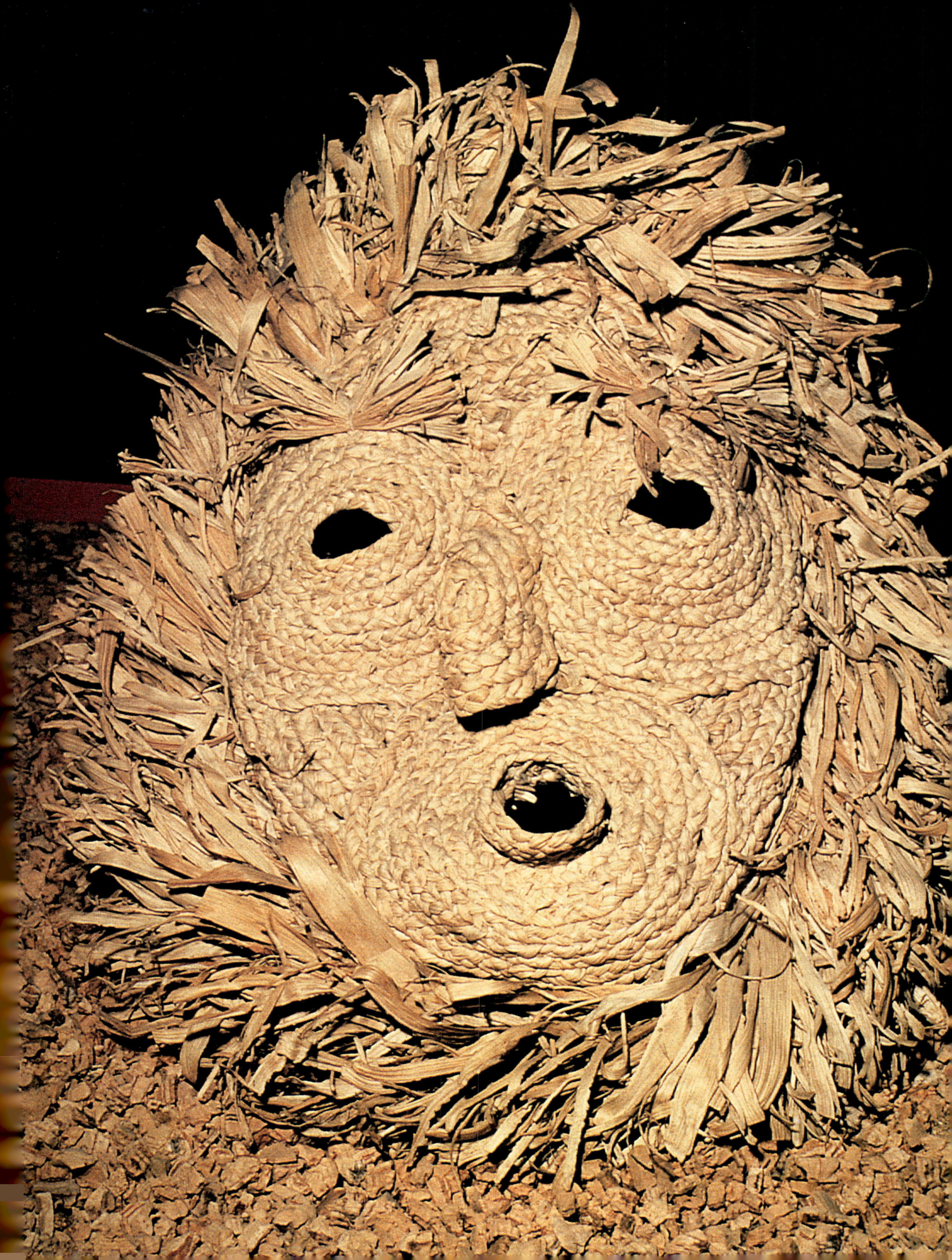

A-Z
CODEX GODS

more practical skills such as improved agricultural methods. He finally left, heading west, leaving only footprints on certain rocks. His severe manner had been criticized and opposed by a woman named Chie, who advocated a more laid back hedonistic approach to life. The serious Bochica didn't see the funny side of this and turned Chie into an owl. Understandably distressed by this Chie appealed to the work god Chibchacum, who flooded the whole country. The Chibcas then turned to Bochica, who forced Chibacum underground and drained and dried the land.

CHAC

Also known as: Chaac, Ah Toya, Ah Tzenul, Hopop Caan

The Mayan fertility and rain-god, equivalent of the Aztec Tlaloc, Chac was portrayed with wide staring eyes starting with tears, a prominent nose and two curled fangs. In fact there were four variant color-coded Chacs, each living at the four corners of the world, supervising the distribution of storms and global water management. They were honored at a springtime festival, along with the four wind gods — the Bacabs — who held up the world, and with whom they sometimes combined. The name Chacs was also given to the four old men chosen each year to assist the priests in their rituals. There were some truly grisly ceremonies attributed to this water deity, one involving the sacrifice of babies, who were then eaten by the priests officiating the rites. Despite this, Chac was essentially a beneficent deity generally well disposed to man, and in line with his irrigation attributes he was credited with the teaching of agriculture.

CHALCHIHUITLICUE

"Lady Precious Green"/"Lady of the Turquoise Skirt"/"Lady of the Jade petticoat"

The Aztec water goddess and patroness of chastity, marriage and babies, Chalchihuitlicue was portrayed either as a river from which a laden pear tree grew or as a beautiful young woman whose dress had an aquatic pattern and feel. She married her brother Tlaloc, and ruled over the Fourth Sun period which ended in flood and with all people transformed into fish. She then had a son with Quetzacoatl, Xiuhtecuhtli, who would emerge as the Fifth Sun. Although obviously an important member of the Aztec pantheon, Chalchihuitlcue does not occur often in Aztec narrative and folktales.

CHIMINIGAGUA

The supreme creator of the Columbian Chibca. From within the initial darkness of the void Chiminigagua created four huge birds whom he equipped with light and sent on a mission to spread it far and wide. He next created the sun so that the light itself could have a base from

Right: This stone cuahxicali (Eagle vase) is carved into the Mayan-Toltec rain god and was perhaps used as an offering bowl for hearts cut out in human sacrifice. (c. 10th century AD).

371

A-Z
CODEX GODS

which to operate and then the moon so that the birds could have a rest. Aside from this he withdrew, leaving the completion of creation to other more active gods. The creatrive deity Bachue became the mother of humankind.

CINTEOL

Cinteol was the Aztec god of maize, son of Tlazolteotl and husband of Xochiquetzal. In the spring festival held in his honor the people gave offerings of blood to him. Through his penitence he ensured continuity of the food supply for humankind. He was also associated with Tlaloc, and had various female avatars.

COATLICUE

"Serpent Lady"/"Goddess of the Serpent petticoat"
Coatlicue was a creator earth goddess, the mother, wife and sister of the sun and the fertile force from which everything is created, including both humans and the gods.

One day whilst doing penance in a valley, a ball of feathers fell onto Coatlicue, impregnating her. This filled her many sons with fury and they demanded to know who the father was. Their sister, Coyolxauhqui, urged them not to put their mother to death, but when the warriors arrived, Huitzilopochtli emerged in armor and slew almost everyone. An earth serpent goddess, Coatlicue was rather gruesome to behold, her skirt was made of writhing snakes, her necklace of human hearts with a skull pendant. She had clawed hands and feet, pendulous breasts and fed on corpses.

COYOLXAUHQUI
"Golden Bells"

A child of Coatlicue. When her mother fell mysteriously pregnant and her other siblings were furious in the condemnation of their mother, demanding the ultimate sanction of death, she ran ahead to try and warn her mother. As the awesomely devastating Huitzilopochtli appeared, he saw her only as the vanguard and ripped Coyolxauhqui's head off, going on to massacre all the other star children. When he returned to his mother she put him right about his sister, so to make amends he threw her head up into the sky to become the moon.

COYOTE

The trickster deity of southwestern Amerindian myth. Following the completion of the world Coyote and his dog Rattlesnake emerged from the ground. He then observed whilst the creator god Wonomi made the first man and woman, Kuksu and Laidamlun-kule. In an attempt to imitate Wonomi, Coyote then created some people himself, but during the process laughed, with the result that they were born with eyes of glass. Later observing the ease of

Right: A snake deity belonging to Mexico's Mayan people

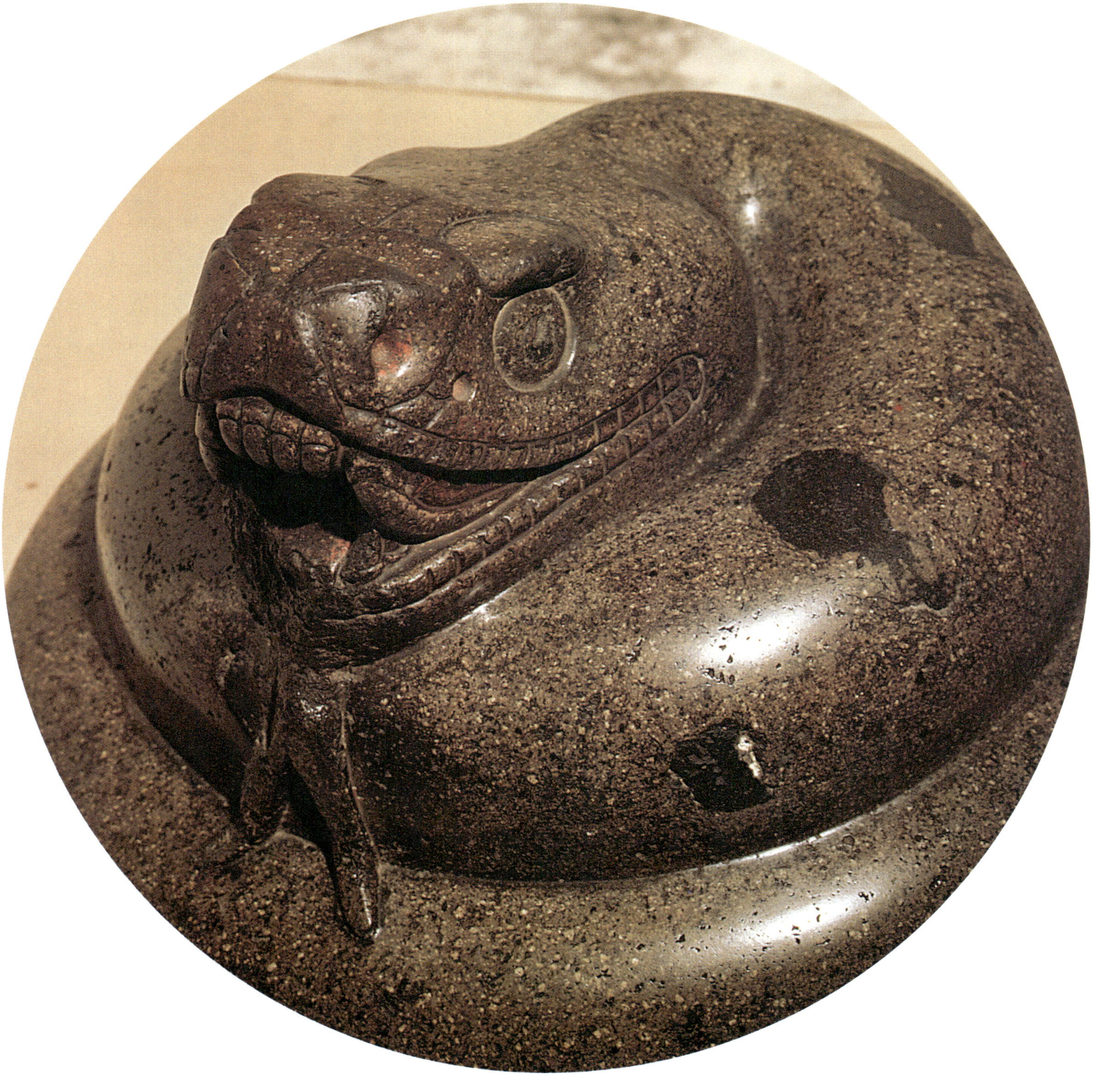

A-Z
CODEX GODS

life which Wonomi had made for man Coyote perversely decided to make things more difficult, creating sickness, suffering, sorrow and death. He was a cunning mischievous destructive force, the random element within creation. Everyone expected at some point to suffer from his trickery which was a manifestation of the contradictions in life.

DAMBALLAH
Also known as: Damballah Wedo, Simbi, Dan Petro

The immensely powerful snake god of Voodoo mythology, who dwells in the sky above Haiti with his wife Ayida. These two encom-pass the world as a pair of entwined serpents manifesting sexual unity. On earth he has an aquatic avatar in the form of a river snake named Simbi, the patron of rivers and springs and also Dan Petro. These three make a triumvirate of life affirming snake deities.

DOHKWIBUHCH
The creator deity of the northwestern Amerindian tribe the Snohomish. After Dohkwibuhch had finished making the world man was originally not particularly impressed with the work that Dohkwibuhch had done in his terraforming capacity, for he had built the sky so low that everyone continually banged their heads. Finally someone came up with a plan: if every living thing pushed simultaneously perhaps the sky could be lifted up. With the cry of "Ya-Hoh!" this project was initiated and proved successful, though a few creatures who did not realize what was going on ended-up skybound.

DZELARHONS
In Canadian Pacific Haida mythology, Dzelarhons was the Frog Princess and the Volcano Woman. She was married to Kaiti, the bear god, and arrived from the sea with six canoes full of people — virtually an entire tribe ready for settlement.

DZOAVITS
A demonic ogre from the mythology of the Shoshonean Amerindians from Utah and Nevada. Dzoavits stole Dove's two children, who were only rescued with the aid of Eagle and Crane after a scary covert mission that almost went wrong — at one point everyone had to hide as Dzoavits counter-attacked. But with the aid of Weasel and Badger things were then turned at the last moment, Badger tricking Dzoavits into a specially prepared hole, where she was then stoned with hot rocks and then sealed up.

Right: This Mayan relief shows a serpent god appearing before a priest.

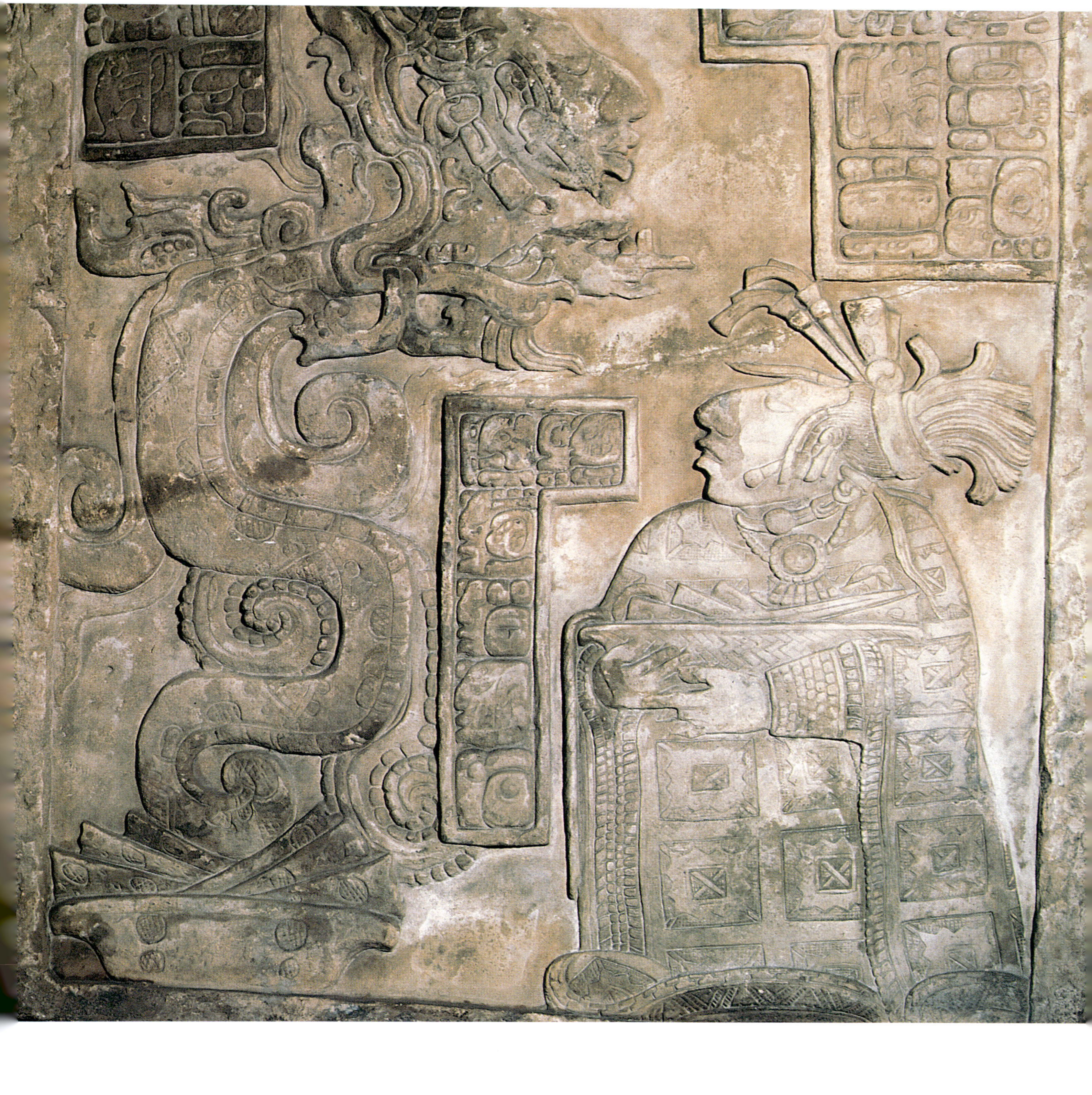

A-Z
CODEX GODS

EK CHUAH
"Black war Leader"
Ek Chuah was the fierce black-eyed war god of the Maya, concerned with war and those who fell in battle. He did possess a friendlier aspect though, as the patron of merchants, being portrayed as a door-to-door salesman with his produce in a sack. It was his war god status that was of most importance to the Maya though.

EL DORADO
"The Golden King"
El Dorado was a mythical magnet for the Spanish Conquistadores arriving in the 16th century. This legend told of a city paved and plated in gold, ruled over by a priest king named El Dorado because he was dressed head to foot in gold. This weird story emanating from the Incas fired the Spanish up so much that it sealed the fate of the Aztec and Inca Empires, since the greed these myths engendered elicited a brutality that would overwhelm them.

EL-LAL
El-Lal was the legendary hero of the Patagonian Indians. When his father, Nosjthj, had seized him from his mother in preparation for consuming him as a light lunch, El-Lal was rescued from his predicament by Rat, who hid him in his hole and taught him the sacred lore. Having completed his studies and become empowered El-Lal emerged once more into the world becoming its ruler through the invention of a new weapons system — the bow and arrow. He then made war on his cannibal father and his giant allies, defeating them all. Having gained supremacy he subsequently decided to leave the planet. After telling humankind to look after itself, he vanished.

ENUMCLAW
"Thunder"
One of two brothers (the other being Kapoonis) who sought guardian spirits to make them powerful medicine men. They were eventually successful and Kapoonis found a fire spirit who enabled him to make lightning. Meanwhile Enumclaw was instructed by another spirit and became an expert rock launcher. The sky father then elevated these two into the gods of thunder and lightning.

ERZULIE
Also known as: Erzulie Ge-Rouge, Erzilie
Erzulie is the love goddess in the Voodoo pantheon and a powerful *loa* of elemental force. She is portrayed as a beautiful yet tragic young woman — for she mourned the shortness of life and the limitations of love. Lavish with her gifts, she wears the rings of her three marriages to the snake deity Damballah, the sea god Agwe and the warrior hero Ogoun.

Right: A face-mask, found in Alaska, shows a little frog emerging from the mouth.

· THE AMERICAS ·

A-Z
CODEX GODS

ESTANATLEHI
"The woman who changes"
One of the most respected deities of the Navaho Indians of Arizona, Estanatlehi was constantly changing. Never remaining in one form or state for long, she changed from a young woman to an old crone and back again — a constantly shifting spectrum of age. She thus passes through an endless round of lives without dying; manifesting seasonal cyclic change growth and decay. She dwelt in a floating house in the west, where the sun visited her at the end of each day. It was said that she created man and woman from her own skin after she became aware of her loneliness.

THE FIVE SUNS
The myth surrounding the Aztec calendar. There were four eras known as "suns" before the present current one. The first was ruled by Tezcatlipoca, god of the north whose familiar was a tiger, and which was brought to an end when it was consumed by these beasts after its allotted span. The second was ruled over by Quetzalcoatl, god of the west and witchcraft and ended with hurricanes and men transformed into monkeys. The third was ruled by Tlaloc as god of the south and ended in a shower of fire, with men transformed into birds and the fourth was ruled over by Chalchihuitlicue, goddess of the east and water, ending in flood, with man changed to fish. It was believed that the fifth and present sun, ruled by Xiuhtecuhtli, the fire-god, would end in earth-quakes.

GA-GAAH
The wise crow god of the Iroquois tribe, G-Gaah brought them corn through a seed stashed in his ear. When this was planted in the earth goddess' body maize grew, and became the staple diet of the Iroquois.

GHEDE
The god of Death in Voodoo mythology, Ghede is portrayed as a skimpy figure dressed in black with a tall black hat and sunglasses. He waits at the crossroads where all the souls of the dead pass on their way to Guinee, the legendary place of origin and abode of the gods. Ghede is very wise, and knows all who have lived. He also possesses fertility god attributes and is sometimes portrayed with an erect phallus and at his place of worship a carved phallus lies next to his ceremonial gravedigger's equipment. He thus sustains the living and increases their number as well as resurrecting the dead. As a lord of love he is also noted for his obscenity and fondness for alcohol. His female counterpart is Maman Brigitte. Known for disruption that the shamans cannot counter he represents the irresistible and anarchic forces of life coupled with the inevitability of death.

Right: This Iroquois "False-Face," was used in ceremonies to cure illnesses.

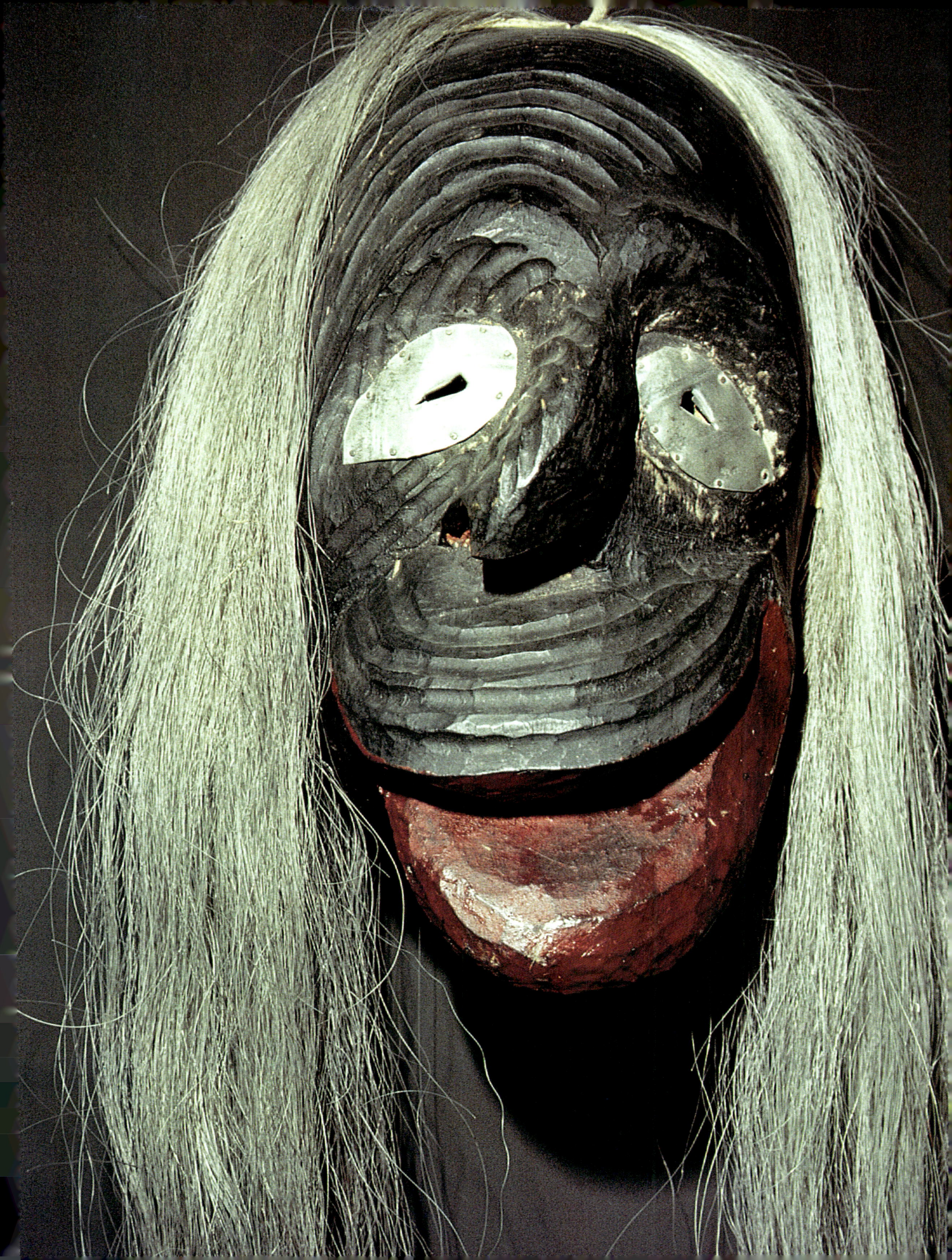

A-Z
CODEX GODS

GLUSKAP

Gluskap was the patriach and founding father hero of the Abnaki Indians, a tribe of Alonquin stock. After performing various heroic feats (including bareback whale riding), on behalf of the gods and men he retired from the world, awaiting his necessary return at a time of peril.

GREAT SPIRIT

An "allfather" creator god concept shared by many North American tribes, the Great Spirit was often merely the somewhat passive creator of all — the essence behind all things. The myths and legends that formed the culture of the tribes usually involved other god and characters. The Great Spirit could also occur in many forms: the Great Goddess, the Great Turtle, the Great Star, Great Hare, Great Hawk, etc.

GUINECHEN

"Master of Men"

Also known as: Guinemapun

The supreme creator deity of the Chilean Auca, who were the fiercely independent hardcore opponents of the Inca, and later the Spanish. To Guinechen is attributed the creation of all life, man, plants and animals, although weather systems were outside his fief, these being run by Pillan. The chief malefactor of the Auca pantheon was Guecufu.

HAHGWEHDIYU

Creator deity of Iroquois mythology, son of the sky goddess Ataensic and twin brother to the evil Hahgwehdaetgah. Hahgwehdiyu formed the sky and placed his dead mother's face in it which became the sun, making the moon and stars from her breasts. The earth was made fertile with her body. His brother naturally tried to counterbalance all this goodness with a little evil of his own, including the invention of earthquakes, hurricanes, floods and volcanic eruptions. Ultimately these two ended up in conflict, fighting using massive thorns from a giant tree. Fortunately for humankind, Hahgwehdiyu managed to defeat his evil sibling, banishing him to a murky underworld.

HIAWATHA

Also known as: Haiowatha

The legendary teacher/hero of the Onodaga tribe of the North American woodlands. Hiawatha united the six different nations of the Iroquois into a confederation, called the League of the Longhouse. These were the Onodaga, the Oneida, the Seneca, the Mohawk, the Cayuga and Tuscarora tribes. He was initially opposed by many of the leading figures in the individual tribes, but finally managed to curtail the bitter internecine war among the related tribes. Following his success many myths and legends were attributed to him.

Right: A gold mask unearthed from a pre-Colombian tomb.

• THE AMERICAS •

A-Z
CODEX GODS

HISAKITAIMISI
"The Master of Breath"
Also known as: Hisagitaimisi, Ibofanga
The supreme creator deity of the mound building Creek Indians from the Southeastern USA. Hisakitaimisi was also connected with the sun, and consequently was perhaps the closest thing to a powerful dominant creator deity that the North Americans tribe came up with.

HUACAS
These were sacred objects, usually rocks, that manifested and reflected religious/spiritual power. Beneath the remote Vira-cocha and the more active Inti, the Incas worshipped innumerable other deities and spirits, which were believed to be imbued in rocks, oracles and idols. This reflects the almost shamanist tendencies of the first native peoples which survived later incarnations.

HUITACA
Also known as: Chie
Huitaca was the Colombian goddess of indulgence, drunkenness and intoxication — a South American female Dionysius. She was also the moon goddess Chie who was turned into an owl when she opposed the severity of the Colombian hero Bochica. She was usually portrayed as a beautiful young woman.

HUITZILOPOCHTLI
"The Hummingbird Wizard on the Left"
A powerful necromancer and master of disguise, Huitzilopochtli was the original tribal god of the Aztecs, and with their success his role expanded to encompass both creator and war god status and he finally become the supreme deity of the pantheon. He sprang from his mother Coatlicue's womb spontaneously to defend her and killed his moon goddess sister, Coyolxauhqui. Huitzilopochtli had led the Aztecs to found their capital city Tenochtitlan, prophesying their future greatness: in return he demanded blood. Huitzilopochtli, above all gods of all races, required the biggest blood-price from man, and the militaristic Aztecs sated him with a never-ending supply of hearts, freshly cut from victims with an obsidian knife atop the Great Temple at the very center of Tenochtitlan. He was often identified with the Toltec Quetzacoatl whom he syncretistically absorbed.

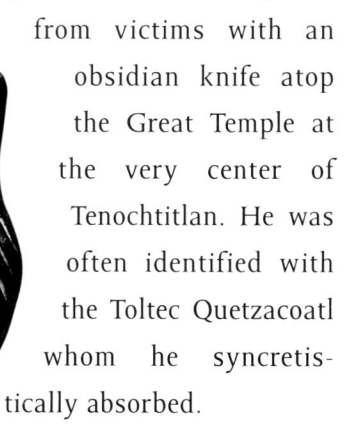

Right: A North American pottery figure of a man from the Spiro Mound, Oklahoma (Mississippi river valley culture 800–1400 AD). Left: A pot with bird figures, also of the Mississippi river valley.

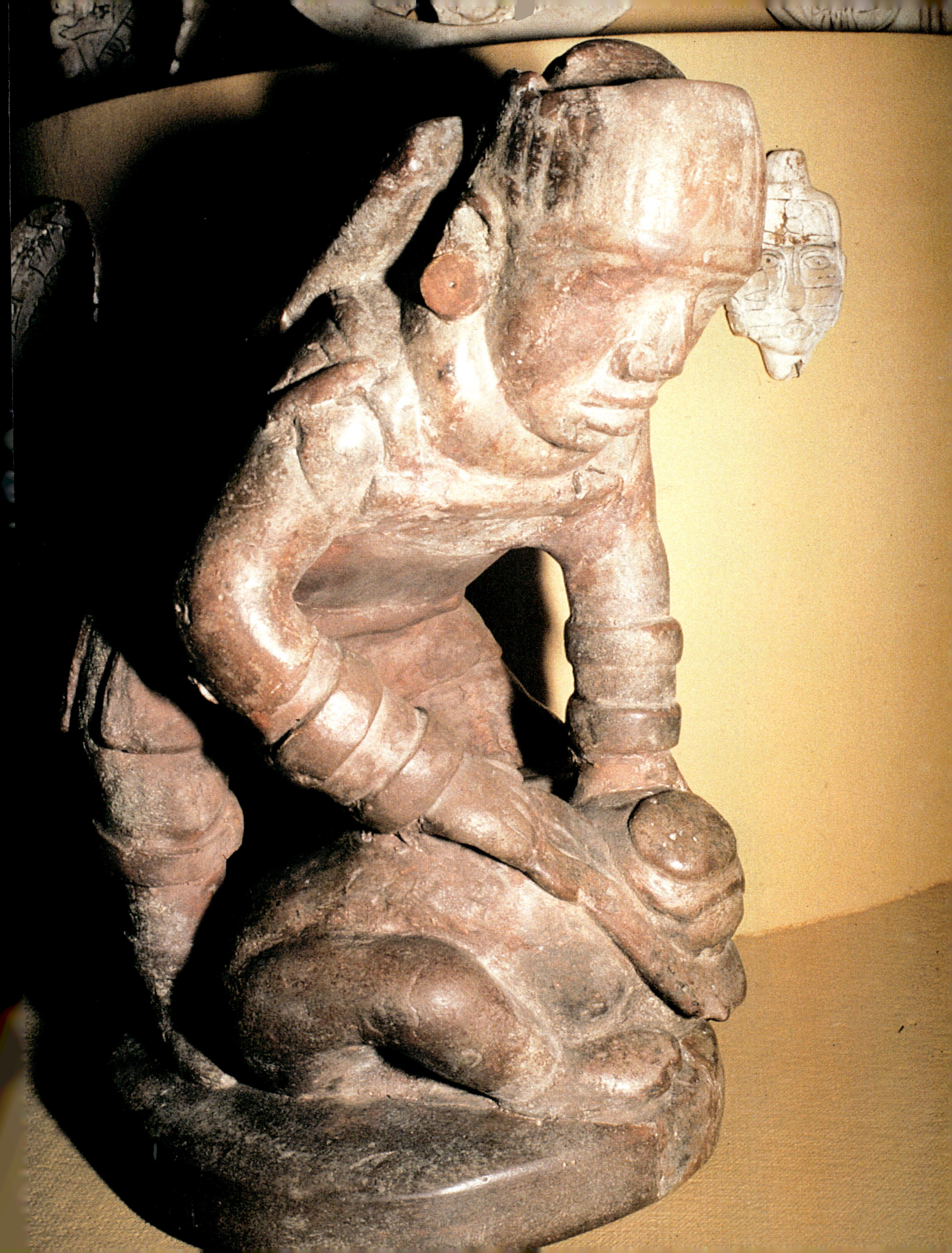

A-Z
CODEX GODS

HUNAB-KU
"Single God"
Also known as: Hunab
The distant creator god of the Maya, he renewed the world each time after three monster floods had engulfed it, pouring from the mouth of the great sky serpent. The first world had been populated by dwarves, builders of the great ruined cities; the second had been populated by an obscure race called the "offenders," so they obviously did something seriously wrong. The third race was the Maya themselves. This present world will also end in deluge. This alternating rhythm of construction and destruction expressed the duality and the contradiction inherent in life's fragility.

HURUING WUHTI
The dualistic creator god concept of the Hopi tribes of Pueblo, Southwest North America, Huruing Wuhti manifested as two old women between whom the sun traveled each day. They were responsible both for it and the creation of all else on the earth — plants, animals and humans — usually by modeling what they wanted out of clay and then blowing the breath of life into it.

ICTINIKE
Ictinike was the deceitful son of the Iowa Sioux solar deity, and a sometime war god. From him the North American tribes learned the arts and skills of warfare. In his mythological tales his deceit and treachery are paramount, with violence always just under the surface or around the corner.

IGALUK
The Inuit moon god, who was the supreme deity in Alaskan mythology, directing and controlling all other phenomena. The Inuits believed that the sun and the moon were brother and sister. Once, long ago in the depths of winter night, people began to "sport" in their igloos with the lights out. Only later when tapers were lit could anyone see who they had been with and to his horror Igaluk discovered that he had incestuously dallied with his sister the sun. In horror she tore off her breasts and rose into the sky. When he pursued her his taper extinguished to a glow. They eventually built a house in Heaven divided into two sections so that they could coexist.

INTI
Inti was the divine Inca ancestor of the royal family and the solar deity. He was portrayed as a solar disk that had a human face with rays emanating from it. His main center of worship was the great sun-temple at Cuzco, where his image was surrounded with a profusion of worked and beaten gold. He had three sons:

Right: A Maya stone relief showing a human sacrifice (c. 900 AD).

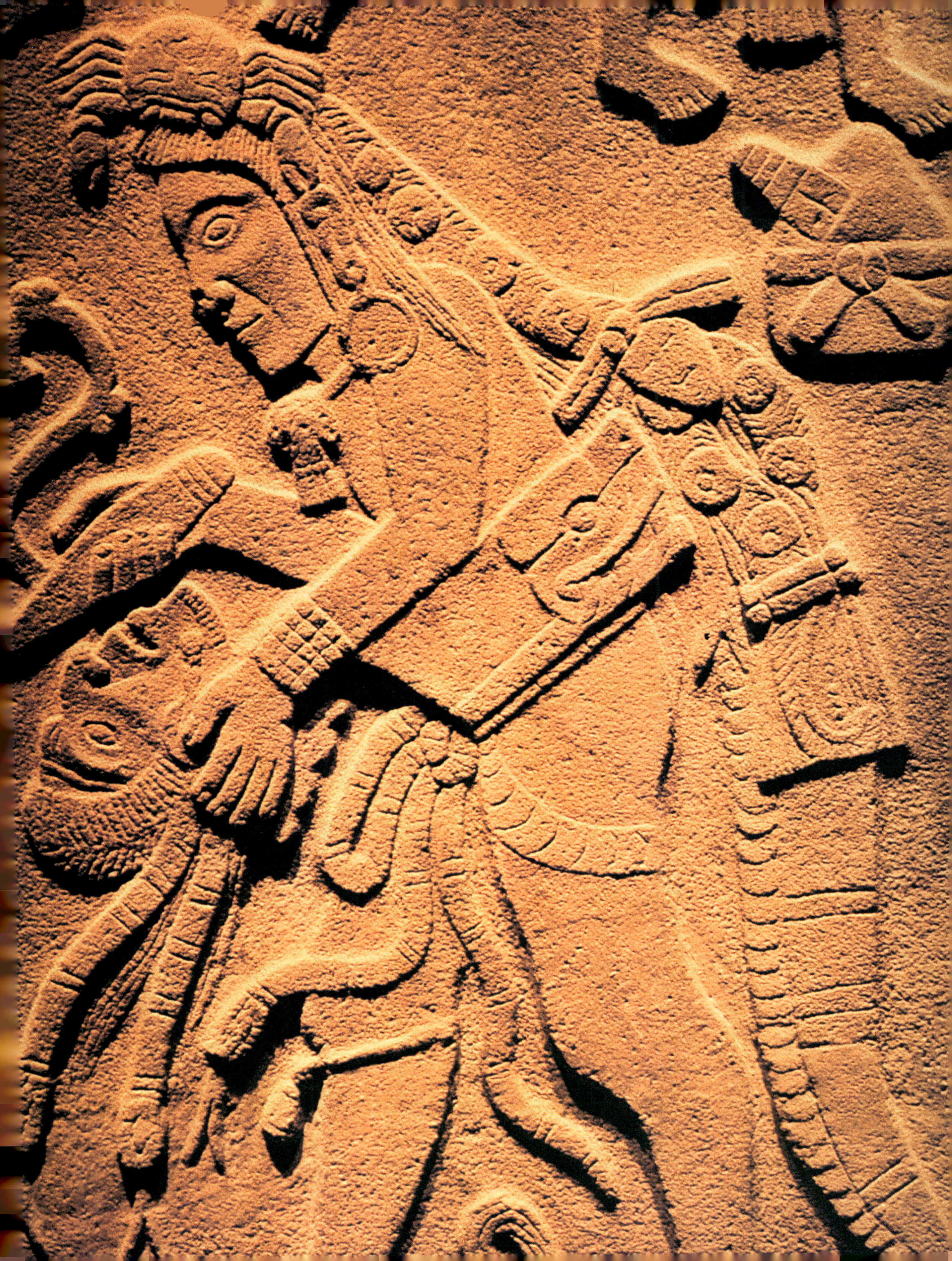

A-Z
CODEX GODS

Viracocha, Pachacamac and Manco Capac. Although his sons absorbed other gods in the syncretism of empire (becoming creator and fertility deities that could supercede him in certain myths), Inti's solar status and royal adoption gave his cult a vital central role in daily religious life. Again the same aspects of Andean and meso-American religion shared a similar preoccupation, with sun, rain, sky and earth deities all interlinked and associated — even sharing temple precincts and platforms.

ITZAMNA
"Lizard House"

The supreme creator deity of the Mayan pantheon, patron of writing and learning. An old man with a prominent nose, Itzamna was the son of Hunab Ku, the original creator god, and his consort was Ix Chel — "Lady Rainbow," goddess of medicine and childbirth. Itzamna was also a god of resurrection and a great healer, who introduced the skills of agriculture. He has also been identified by some with Kulkulkan and Quetzalcoatl.

IX CHEL
"Rainbow Lady"

Ix Chel was the mother goddess of the Mayan pantheon, a moon deity and patroness of weaving, medicine and childbirth. She was also depicted as a bitter old crone in Mayan mythology and aided the sky serpent in his deluge of the earth, emptying vials of anger and wrath upon the earth which manifested as cloudbursts and floods, along with the sudden furious destruction of tropical storms. As the consort of Itzamana, she was portrayed with claws and a writhing snake as a hat, a skull and crossbone patterned skirt, and was surrounded by symbols of death and destruction.

IX TAB

The Mayan goddess of suicide, Ix Tab was portrayed hanging from the sky, a noose around her neck, eyes closed in termination and already beginning to disintegrate. Mayan belief held that those who committed suicide, warriors killed in battle, women who died in childbirth and the priesthood all went directly to Heaven. Ix Tab came to convey the lucky souls who had made such a sacrifice to the paradise where all would be well, with no suffering en route.

IYATIKU

The corn/fertility/creatrive deity of the Keresan Puebloes. From Iyatiku's underground queendom, Shipap, the first men emerged, just as all babies continue to do so. At the time of each person's passing, it was believed that they returned from whence they came.

JAGUAR

The ancient fanged god of pre-Colombian religion in South America. Many statues have

Right: The Zapotec god of lightning and rain.

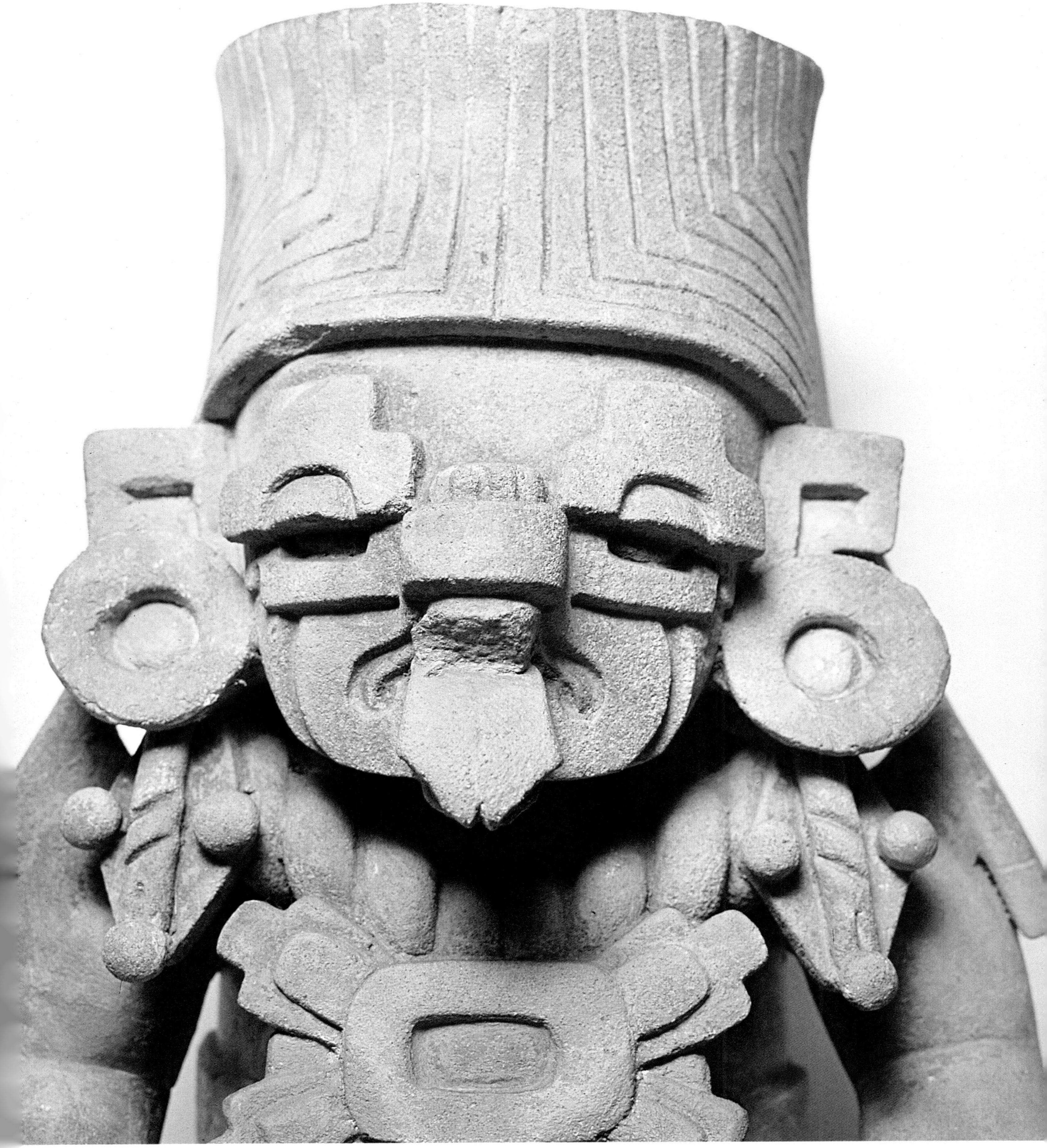

A-Z
CODEX GODS

been discovered of this ferocious and enigmatic god who had intense eyes and was sometimes even double fanged. In the Mochica Indian culture their distant creator god bore a feline aspect, and among the Bolivian tribes, where the jaguar is indigenous, men earned their warrior status through single combat with the jaguar, armed only with wooden spears. In fact, many South American societies used the Jaguar to denote a military grouping. There was also a close religious link between jaguars and the priesthood. Another role apart from the power manifestation was that of fertility deity — there are even statues of jaguar coupling with women.

KANASSSA

Creator deity of the Brazilian Kuikuru people, Kanassa was also credited with the gift of fire to humankind. As he was busy creating things out of the mud of a lagoon on the Xingu river, he drew a ray, which came to life and promptly stung him when he accidentally trod on it. Deciding it was too dark to work even with the light from a firefly, he decided to obtain an ember from the king of the vultures, who was the Master of Fire. This was accomplished by the expedient of grasping one of the vulture's legs until it agreed to fetch an ember from the sky. Successful in his aims Kanassa had fire, but the frogs and river animals tried to extinguish it, so with the aid of a snake he carried it away from the river to safety.

KASOGONAGA

The female rain deity of the Chaco tribes of the Pampas. These people seem to have had no ultimate creator deity, but instead a series of spirits in which all ceration was imbued. There was much individual tribal variation resulting in a conflicting hotchpotch of animism.

KITCKI MANITOU

Also known as: Kitshi Manitou

The supreme being of the Alonquin of the Eastern woodlands of North America, and their manifestation of the Great Spirit concept. The Alonquin came originally from Canada — around the Ottawa and St Lawrence rivers — and today live primarily on reservations in Western Quebec. They are an Atlantic coast Amerindian tribe, whose language and culture is related to the Blackfoot, Cheyenne, Cree and Arapaho tribes. Manitou is the Alonquin name for the divine energy intrinsic in all living things. Man tries to control the Manitous of small things — such as fire, wood and stones, in order that he might gain control over the bigger Manitous of storm, rain, sun and wind.

KONONATOO

"Our Maker"

The creator god of the Warau tribe from Guiana. The Warau believed that Kononatoo really wished his people to live alongside him in

Right: Many statues of the jaguar, such as this one from the Valley of Mexico (1400–1521 AD) have been found in South America.

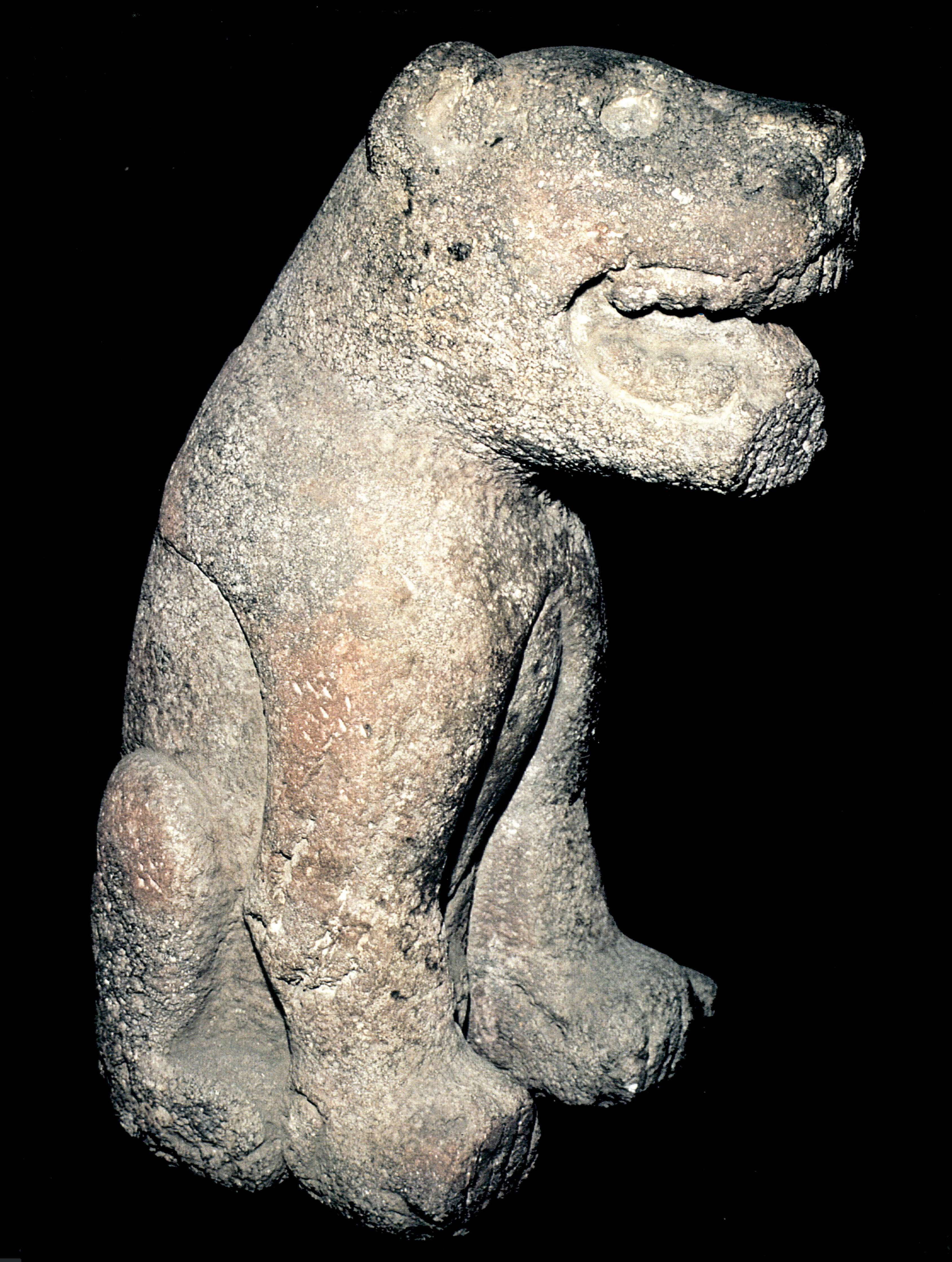

A-Z
CODEX GODS

Heaven as they originally did. They became separated from their creator when a young hunter discovered a hole in the sky through which the whole tribe descended to earth. This hole was then lost to use after an enormously obese woman got stuck in it. When Konomnatoo observed his progeny the Warau on earth with their disobedience, willfulness and belligerence, he went off the idea of restoring them to paradise. Two young Warau females even bathed in a taboo sacred lake and becoming pregnant from the water deity therein, gave birth to the race of snakes. This perhaps explains the extreme reluctance to bathe of the Warau.

KOSHARE

The Koshare were the creative clowns of the Pueblo people, they danced and entertained during ceremonies — a jester equivalent who were beyond punishment or censorship. Originally, the Koshare were the first men, made when a goddess wished to amuse her friends and so rubbed a ball of her own flesh together tightly and from it constructed these entertainers.

KUAT

Kuat was the solar deity of the Kamaiuran mythology. The Kamaiura hail from the Amazon Xingu river area. Their creation myth tells of a beginning with a dark void of endless night, in which people, though they existed, lived a nightmarish blind life of suffering. The brothers Kuat and Iae, who were the sun and moon, were in a quandary, for they did not know how to make light, but since the birds they observed already seemed to have daylight in their village, the two decided to steal it from the vulture king Urubutsin. They then sent a most peculiar but logical present of an effigy filled with maggots and transported by flies. Initially Urubutsin could not understand this message, but one of his vulture people interpreted it for him: the maggots were a tasty gift and the flies bore an invitation to visit the sun and eat many more. Thus the birds started out, after various depilatory maneuvers. Kuat and Iae were hidden in the next effigy, and as Urubutsin landed upon it his leg was seized and held fast. He was then held for ransom until the birds brought back daylight, which would alternate with night and solve their problem.

KUKULCAN

Kukulcan was the Mayan wind god and culture hero, the counterpart of the Aztec Quetzalcoatl. According to the Mayan codex, Kukulcan (God K) arrived in Yucatan from the sea and the west. His name obviously recalls that of the Toltec leader expelled by subject peoples who rebelled against his rule.

Right: This doll belonged to the Zuni people of western New Mexico.

· THE AMERICAS ·

391

A-Z
CODEX GODS

KUMUSH
"Old Man of the Ancients"

The creator deity of the northern Californian Modoc Indians, Kumush descended into a beautiful underground kingdom along with his daughter. This was where the spirits lived — partying all night and sleeping all day, at which time they reverted to dry bones. After a week in this spirit land Kumush decided to return to the upper world again, taking some of the spirits with him which he collected up in a bag. Several attempts were made by him to reach the surface along with his bag of bones/spirits, but each time he stumbled and the spirits took the opportunity to escape. Finally he spoke to them convincingly about the beauty of the surface world and after he had subdued or convinced them, he was able to transport them upward. When in sunlight once more he began to select bones to be the different tribes, his final choice being the Modoc, who were his chosen people. He then left with his daughter and built a home in the sky.

KURUMANY

As the creator god of the Arawak Indian of the Orinoco river basin Kurumany was believed to have created men, while his female counterpart Kuliminia made women. He also introduced death into the world when he learned of humankind's corruption. He then added other components to his project such as snakes, lizards, ants and fleas. There is a faint trace of another remote and indifferent god above Kurumany, named Aluberi, and some think that this mysterious god might have been controlling or directing Kurumany.

KWATEE
"Man who changes things"
Also known as: Kivati

The trickster god of the Puget Sound Indians in the Washington region, Kwatee changed the old world into that which we recognize today. The world was formerly filled with giant animal people such as Spider, Beaver, Eagle, Ant, Fox and Coyote; but Kwatee began getting things in place for real change. Of course he was discovered and the giant animal people attempted to prevent him, hatching an assassination plot. This was foiled by Kwatee's magic, which transformed the giants that came at him into smaller sized versions of themselves. He then rubbed balls of his own flesh together and made the first Indians from them. He next made more from some dogs he came across, and instructed his creations in the arts of building and making. He also killed a giant monster which dwelt in a nearby lake, by throwing hot rocks into its open jaws. Finally Kwatee grew old and tired. His work completed he sat on a rock to view his final sunset and then left the world to become one with the fading sun.

Right: The Zapotec bat god on this pottery urn appears to have a human head while on top he wears a helmet shaped like a bat.

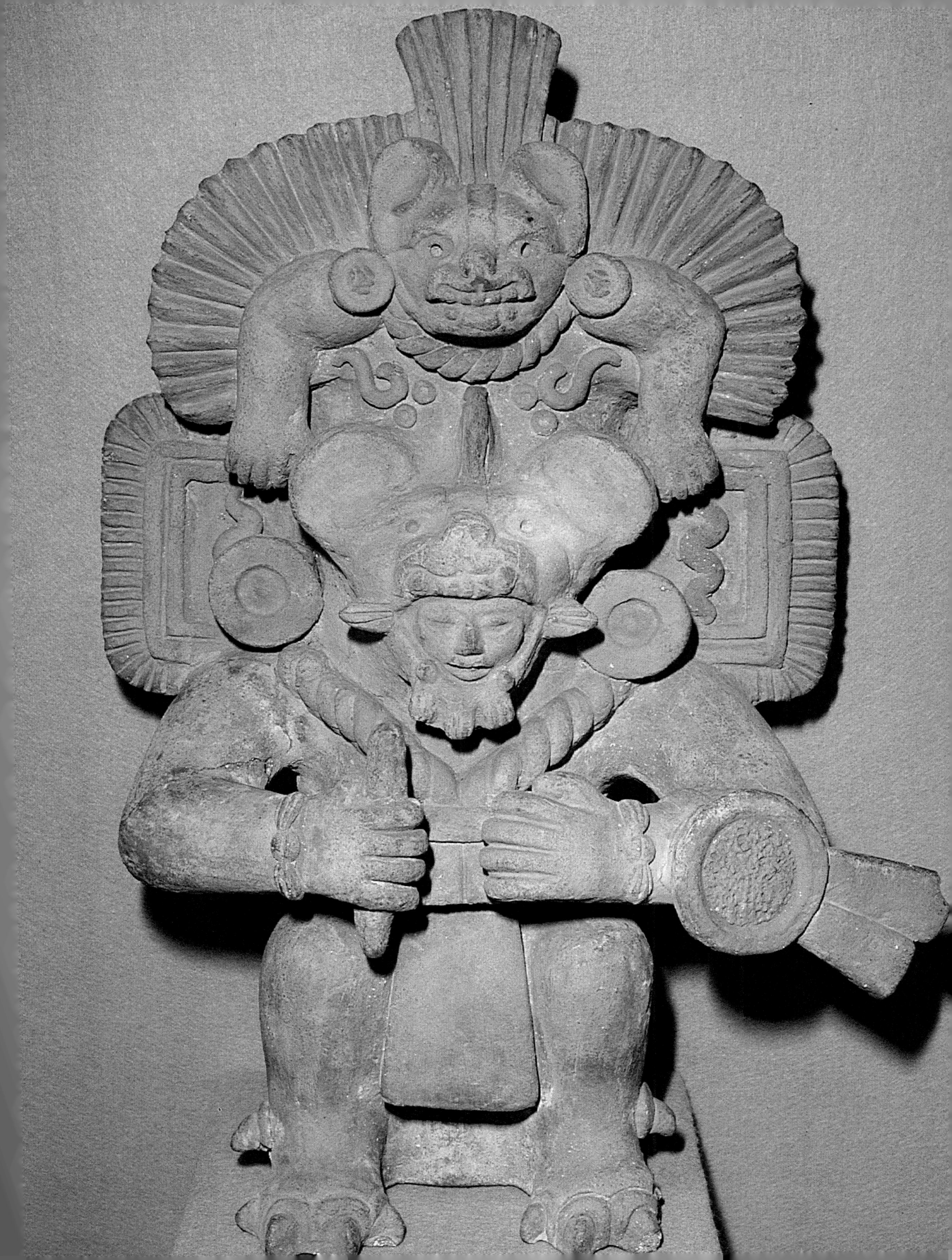

A-Z
CODEX GODS

LEGBA
Also known as: Papa Legba
Originally derived from the West African Fon ancestor god Lebe, Legba was the important and powerful Voodoo sun *loa*, who commanded the day, just as his counterpart Carrefour commanded the night.

MAMA QUILLYA
This Inca moon-goddess was the wife and sister to Inti, and therefore mother of the Inca race. She was also the patroness of married women. During eclipses it was said a monster demon or animal was attempting to swallow her and a service involving much noise was held to distract its attention.

MANCO CAPAC
Also known as: Ayar Manco
The legendary founder of the Inca royal house, Manco Capac's myth has three variants. The first tells the story of four brothers and four sisters who wandered toward Cuzco looking for somewhere to make their home. One of thee brothers, Ayar Cachi, the possessor of great magical strength, was so feared by his other brothers that they took the opportunity to wall him up in a cave as he slept. Two of the remaining brothers, Ayar Oco and Ayar Ayca became in turn a sacred stone and a protector of fields. This left only one brother to make the successful attempt to take Cuzco with his sisters, one of whom — Mama Ocllo — he married. A second variant had the sun god Inti feeling pity for the wretchedness and misery of humankind, and so deciding to send his children Manco Capac and Mama Ocllo to establish civilization. With them they had a large bar of gold complete with the instruction that wheresoever it fell to the ground they were to build a city. Cuzco was that place, and the dynasty they founded went on to conquer the Andes. The third variant, recorded by Spanish historians, concerns the divine status of the Inca crown and Manco Capac, where his rich clothes and splendid majestic demeanor impressed his gullible people.

MICHABO
The Great Hare — a version of the Great Spirit creator god belonging to the Alonquin of the North American woodlands. Michabo could also assume other animal shapes besides his natural hare form. He made the earth and filled it with plants and animals, and then produced humankind by mating with a muskrat! He later unusually developed into a hero/trickster who perpetrated various tricks to bring various things to the tribe, including the secret of fire.

MICTLANTECUHTLI
The Aztec god of death, who ruled over the dead in his silent soporific underworld kingdom called Mictlan. The emperor Montezuma,

Right: This pottery, belonging to the Chibca Indians of Colombia, depicts a goddess walking with a child while carrying another on her back (1200–1600 AD).

395

A-Z
CODEX GODS

gripped with fear and apprehension about the prophesized return of Quetzacoatl and its ensuing disaster, sent to Mictlantecuhtli, sumptuous gifts and the skins of the sacrificially slain, for he envied the god of death and was longing for the peace of Mictlan himself, fatalistically convinced that nothing could help or change the foretold path of events.

NA'API
"Old Man"
Also known as: Napi

The creator god of the Blackfoot Indians from the Great Plains of North America, Na'api was believed to have created the world, a woman and a son all from clay, and then breathed life into them. The woman was not satisfied for long before she began to demand whether life was transient or eternal. Na'api had not really thought about this aspect, and thought to let a test be the decider of human fate. The result of this test is our own mortality.

NAYENEZGANI
"Slayer of alien gods"

As the cultural hero and war god of the Navajo tribe, with his companion and counterpart Tobadzastsini, Nayenezgani would fight against any evil spirits that threatened the composure and continued existence of the world. He was the child of the sun god Tsohanoai and Estsanatlehi and therefore a Lord of Light. However, his counterpart and brother, Tobadzastsini, said to be linked with moistness and darkness, was a Lord of Shadow. The two brothers were on their way to visit their father when they saw smoke rising from a hole in the ground. Examining this hole more closely they perceived an underground chamber with an access ladder. Climbing down they encountered Naste Estsan the Spiderwoman, who revealed to them that on their way to see their father they would have various dangers to pass, and presented them with two magical feathers — one to subdue any enemy and the other to preserve any life. When they finally arrived at the sun god's house they certainly had need of their feathers, for their father tested them mercilessly, until finally acknowledging them.

OGOUN

The warrior hero of Voodoo mythology, whose ancestry traces back to the Nigerian iron god Ogun. There are many variants of Ogoun — fighter, politician, sacrificial victim, magician, gatekeeper and fire guardian to name but a few. His libations were never of water but of rum, which was then ignited, burning with his color — red. When his devotees are possessed by him he will insist that they drink rum as well.

Right: The Mayan god Mictantecuan, unearthed in Mexico.

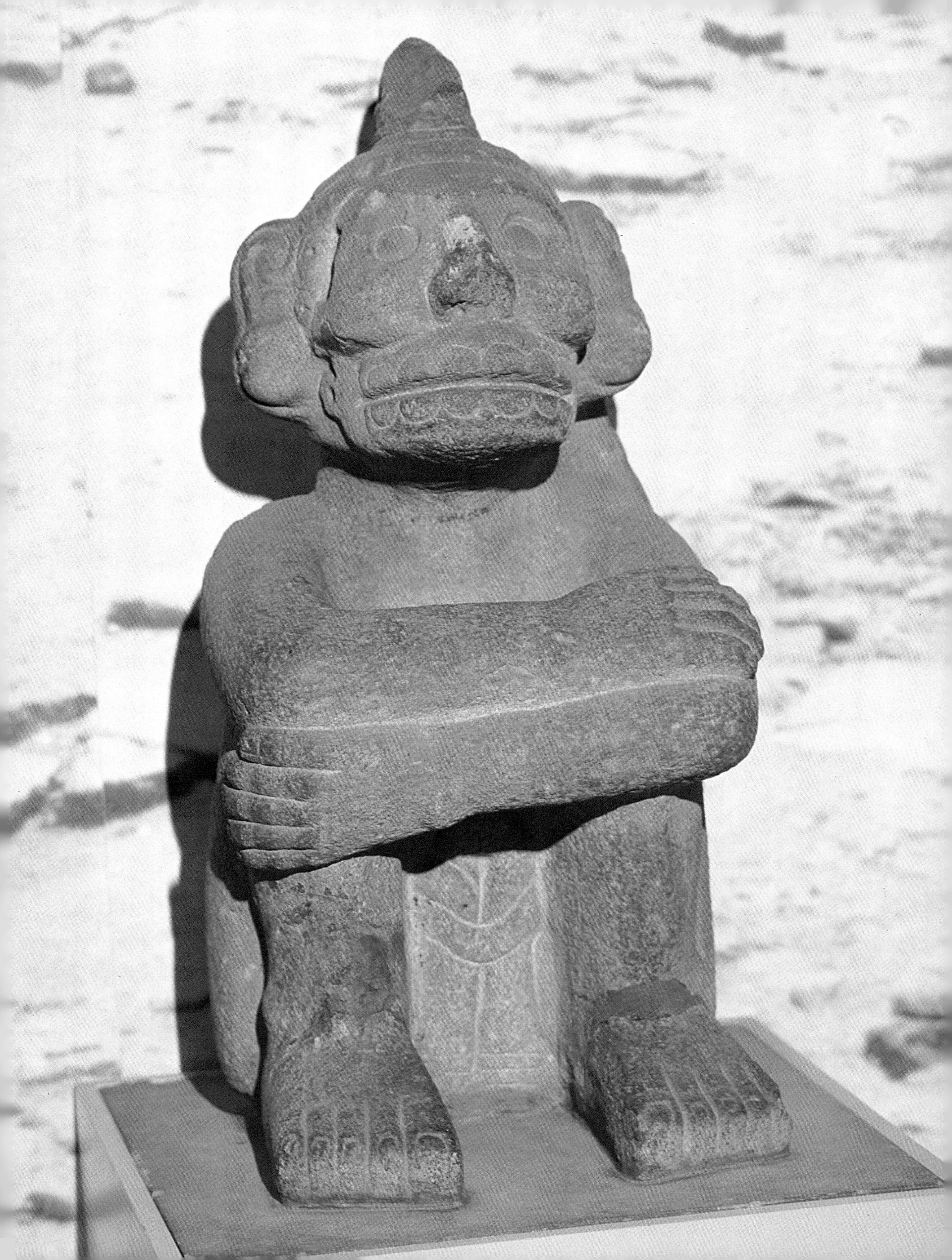

A-Z
CODEX GODS

OI
A legendary race who were the forebears of the Xingu river tribes of Brazil. The Oi were supposed to be very tall and to communicate through song. They disappeared only recently and so are remembered by the Native American tribes. Other mythical forbears also existed, including a tribe with holes in the tops of their heads.

OMETECUHTLI
"The Dual Lord"
High above all other Aztec gods and the world itself, remote in distance and outside the infinite spacetime matrix, exists the dual lord Ometecuhtli, androgynous master of duality and the source of all existence. A truly indifferent creator deity, the contraction of all opposites, beneath him the other more active gods lived their lives of struggle and competition, but he himself remains untouched and untouchable.

PACHAMAC
"Earth Maker"
An ancient creator god originating in Peru, he was adopted by the Inca and incorporated into their pantheon. His mythology tells that after creating the first man and woman he proceeded to neglect them, having forgotten to provide them with food. After some time the man died of starvation and his wife accused the sun of neglect, and in recompense he made her fertile. When she bore a son however Pachamac proceeded to rip him apart, and from the pieces grew fruit and vegetables. Her second son, who was named Wichama, Pachamac failed to catch, so he then destroyed his mother, the first woman. In revenge Wichama pursued him far, forcing him into the ocean.

PACHAMAMA
The Inca earth goddess Pachamama had many animals sacrificed to her, including llamas — a particularly symbolic animal. When the Incas were on the verge of entering Cuzco they sacrificed a llama to their goddess.

PAGE ABE
"Father Sun"
The creator god of the Tukano tribe from the upper Amazon. Their mythology tells of the time when there was Page Abe, the sun, and Nyami Abe the "night sun" — in other words the moon. Nyami Abe did not have a wife and so attempted to steal the wife of Page Abe. This infuriated the sun god and he banished his moon god brother from his home. Since then the two have never shared the same quarter of the sky. After this unpleasantness, Page Abe created the earth and filled it with flora and fauna and finally humankind. He was helped in his task by a semi-divine being named Pamuri-mahse. Later, Page Abe's daughter,

Right: A copper bear-mask belonging to the Pacific northwest tribes.

THE AMERICAS

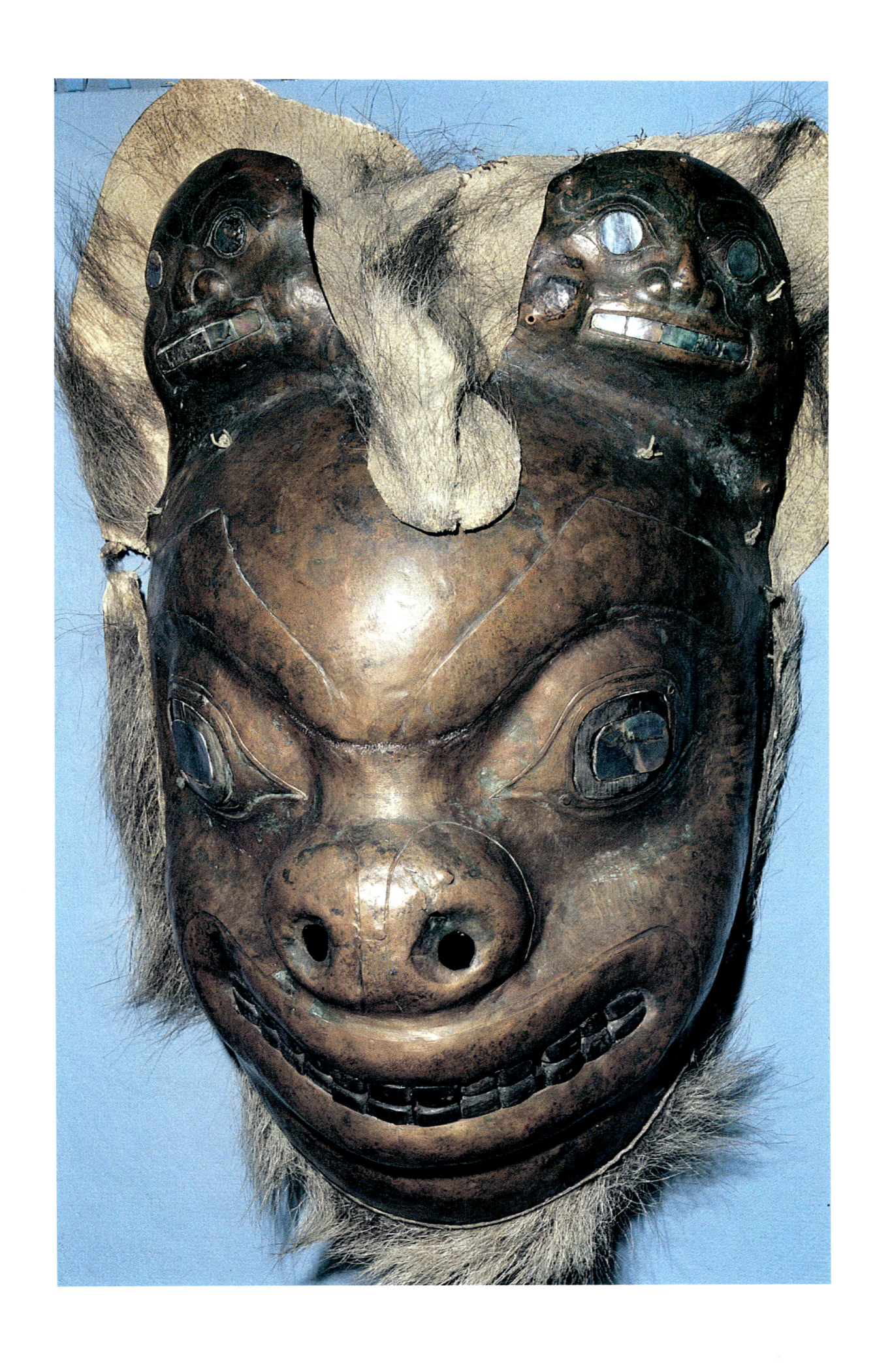

A-Z
CODEX GODS

Abe Mango, descended to become the teacher of the Tukano, bringing with her the gifts of construction, fire, ceramics, weaving and cookery.

QUETZALCOATL
"Plumed serpent" or "Precious Twin"

In many of the currently known myths, the ambiguous wind god Quetzalcoatl is the balancing adversary of Tezcatlipoca. His origins were as the principal fertility and creator god of the older Toltec civilization, but, as with many of the gods they came across, the Aztecs absorbed and modified him in a syncretistic mode that reflects meso-American cultural synthesis. It was said that he had pale skin, and that he would return for the End (as conceived by the Aztec Five Suns mythology) after he was ousted by Tezcatlipoca. This was a major reason for the sudden end of the Aztec Empire, as the Spaniard Cortez arrived with the correct skin tone at the correct time from the right direction.

Quetzalcoatl took part in the holy football game that was a part of Aztec religious practice, and lost the match to Tezcatlipoca, who expelled him from Tollan.

SEDNA
The sinister sea goddess of Inuit myhtology, only an angakoq can withstand the sight of her hideous one-eyed appearance. Legends recount her vile temper and savage control over the dead. Born from gargantuan parents, she was a terrible unmanageable child, who ate flesh whenever she could, including an attempt to digest her parents! Fortunately they awoke and in a rage took her out to sea where they then threw her overboard. When she clung to side of the boat her father cut off her fingers which as they touched the waters turned into whales, seals and fish. Her grisly domain was called Adlivun, and housed the spirits of those who had opposed her during life

SHAKARU
The sun god of the Pawnee tribe of the Great Plains. For the tribes of the Great Plains the annual Sun Dance festival was the most important time of the year, when inter-tribal discussions were held and young warriors proved themselves with tests of endurance and courage. Shakaru was the spirit of the sun who was created by the Tirawa. Tirawa also created the moon god Pah and required the two to mate. From this union a son was born, father to the ancestors of the Pawnee.

SI
The moon god of the Mochica Indians, Si replaced the fanged Ai Apaec. It is thought that he had also war god status, for he eventually assumed control of the Mochica pantheon through his control of weather, storms and water along with the calendrical system

Right: This form of a serpent god — perhaps Quetzalcoatl — belonged to the Zapotec people.

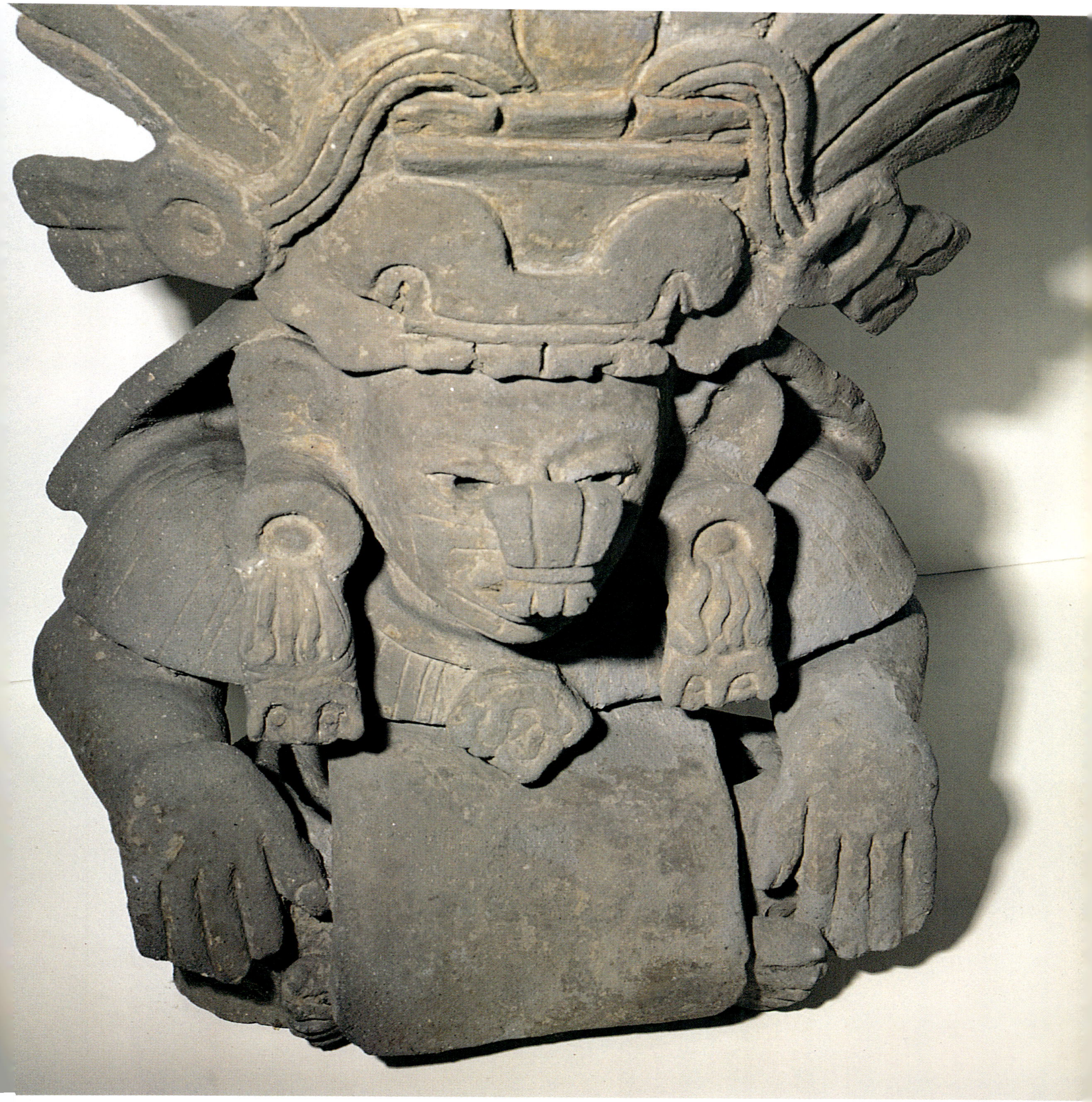

A-Z
CODEX GODS

SINAA
Sinaa was the feline ancestor of the Brazilian Juruna tribe. His father was a huge jaguar and his mother a woman. Both father and son possessed extra eyes in the back of their heads. It was foretold that the end of the world would occur when Sinaa finally pulled away the huge forked stick that holds up the sky. He was ancient but renewed himself through bathing, when he sloughed off his skin for a new one.

SPIDERWOMAN
Spiderwoman was a North American Navaho underworld spirit who aided the hero-twins and war gods Nayanezgani and Thobadzistshini in the search for their father Sakuru the sun-god. She first tried to dissuade them from their mission, but when they were adamant she aided them with protective charms and spells that enabled the twins to succeed. These spells also helped in the tests their father set the twins to prove themselves his sons.

TAWISCARA
The Huron devil god, he had an inimical twin brother Ioskeha, the two of them together representing the antagonistic forces of natural duality. In their savage combat they fought with any weapons they could lay their hands on. Unfortunately for Tawiscara his brother eventually used stag horns against him, driving him away bleeding profusely. Ioskeha then became the Huron guardian spirit.

TEZCATLIPOCA
"Smoking Mirror"
The foremost of the Mexican pantheon and a solar deity. Tezcatlipoca originated in the Olmec and Toltec past, and constantly changed into other gods. He was another wizard of great power — dark and nocturnal — who was greatly feared. At one stage he had four differently colored aspects, each possessing various attributes, but later this changed. The blue Tezcatlipoca became Tlacloc, the rain god, the red became Xipe Totec, the flayed god and the white became Quetzalcoatl, with the black Tezcatlipoca remaining. He was the ruler of the First Sun, before being overthrown by Quetzalcoatl. Myths about him from different tribes abound.

THUNDER BIRD
God of storms and thunder, revered by all North American tribes, took the forms of mythical birds. The Thunderbird has parallels with the Classical and Aryan thunder gods, manifesting the vital life energy of the male principle, represented in the storms that ravaged the land. The Thunderbird was an important totem figure, to which propitiating worship and respect was directed.

Right: A shaman's beautiful thunder bird rattle.

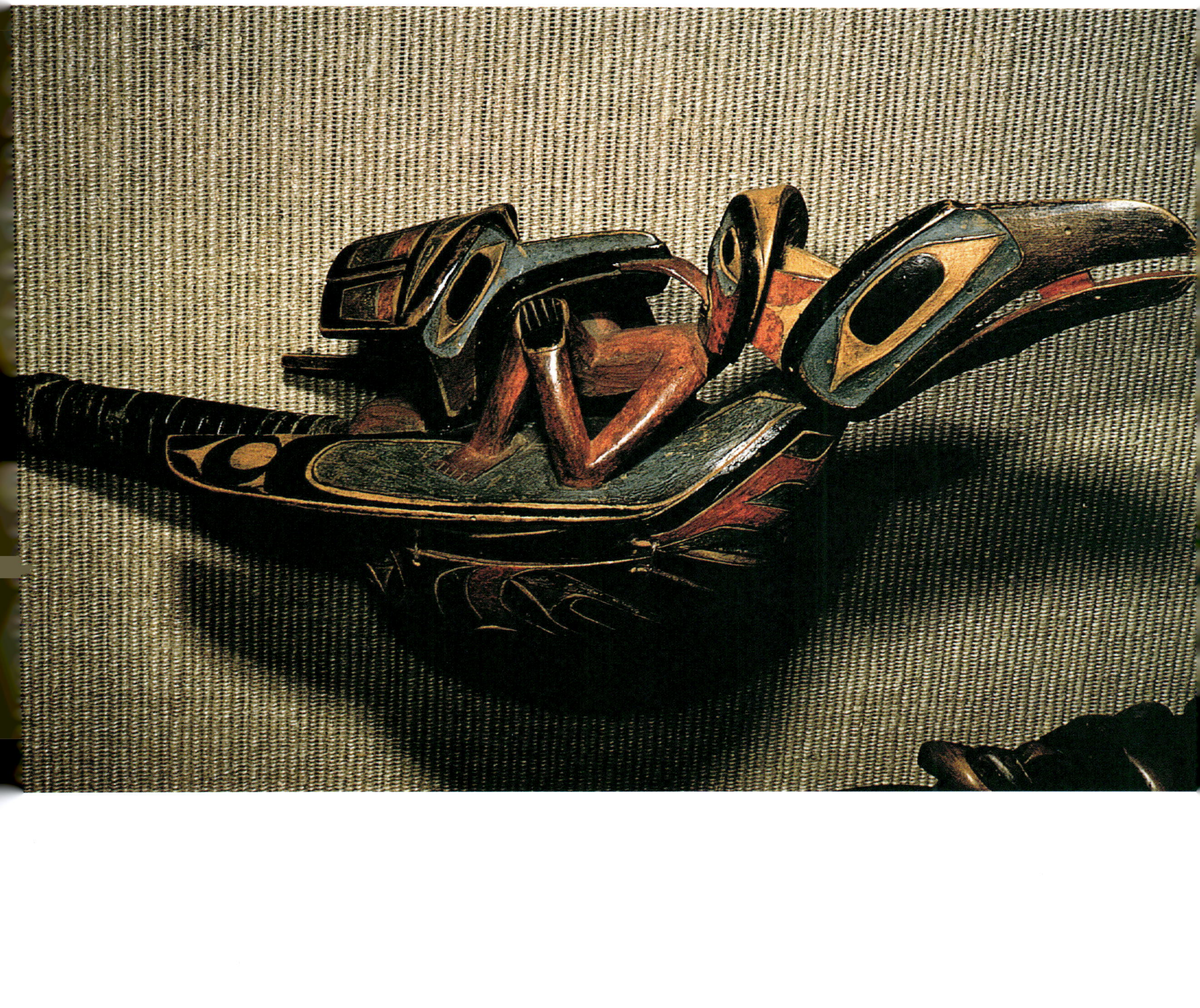

A-Z
CODEX GODS

TIRAWA

As the creator god and Great Spirit of the Pawnee and Delaware tribes of the North American Plains, Tirawa positioned the sun, moon and stars in the heavens and instructed the various spirits in their duties. These spirits — Sakuru, Pah and Bright, Evening, Great and Morning Stars — all carried out his plans, and from the resulting order the Earth came into being. Tirawa next ordered Sakuru and Pah to mate, and from this union and that of Great and Morning Stars, two children were born. They then had a son, called Closed Man, who was the mythical ancestor of the Pawnee.

TLALOC

Tlaloc was the Aztec rain and fertility-god to whom children were sacrificed — with the belief that if they cried copiously it foretold rain. His symbol was the double-headed serpent. His origins go back to the Toltecs and Zapotecs but within Aztec mythology he ruled the eastern sky with Mixcoatl, and was second only to Huitzilpochtli in importance, sharing the upper platform of the main temple at Tenochtitlan. He dispensed water onto the earth from four jars. The first nourished the earth and was good, the second brought cobwebs and blight, the third frost and the fourth a failed crop. Each mountain possessed its own Tlaloc, who was consequently also associated with volcanic eruptions. The Aztec heaven was called Tlalocan, Tlaloc's fertile and abundant domain.

TONATIUH

The Aztec god of the sun, heavenly warrior and ruler of Fate, closely associated with Huitzilopochtli and Tezcatlipoca. Tonatiuh had a bigger cult following than many of the other gods, for the souls of dead warriors and women who died in childbirth were looked after by him. His constant movement gave him a great thirst, for which he required daily sacrifice and much thirst-quenching blood.

TRICKSTER HEROES

The trickster hero of the North American Indians occured among all the tribes in all shapes and forms, but they were usually animals, including Rabbit, Coyote, Raven, Badger, Mink and Spider. Sometimes they had an individual name and combined roles, yet always they were slightly ambiguous — they aided or introduced events more as a humorous or ironic accident than by some design, or if by design then one completely of their own. Often they ended up dead or wounded as a result of their selfishness and treachery. They illustrated through unacceptable behavior the importance of rules and rationality within society. Ueuecoyotl for instance, was the ancient trickster god of Mexico whose spontaneity was

Right: This water vessel attributed to the Peruvian Mochica tribe clearly shows an example of human sacrifice.

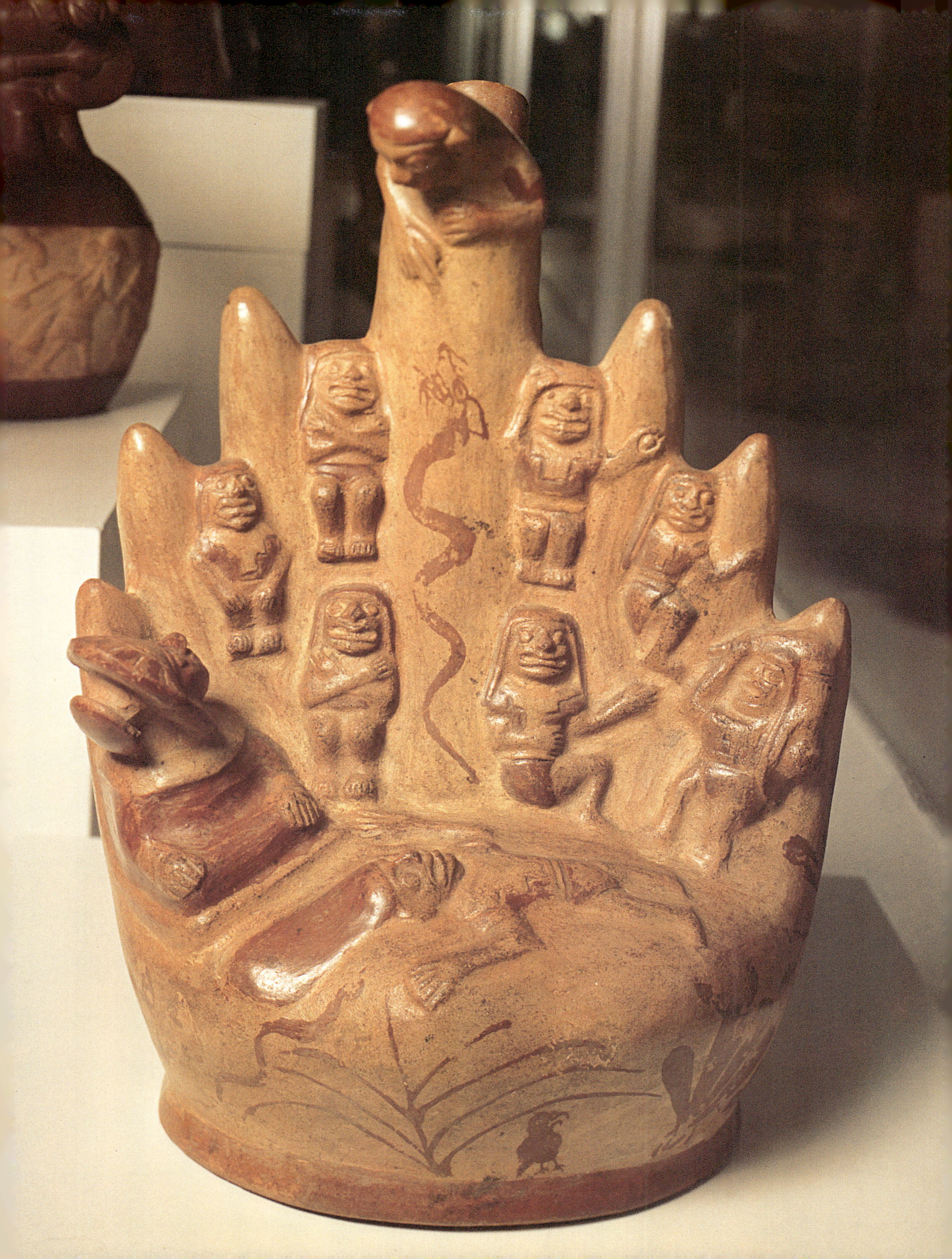

A-Z
CODEX GODS

feared by the puritanical Aztecs, especially when his irresponsible gaiety involved sex.

UAICA

Auica was a powerful medicine man of the Brazilian Jaruna. While out hunting one day he discovered many dead animals piled up under a particular tree. On approaching this strange heap he suddenly felt dizzy and collapsed into coma. He then experienced a visionary dream in which Sinaa the jaguar ancestor spoke to him. This was repeated at intervals, with Uaica following all Sinaa's instructions, which included making a potion made from the bark of the original Tree of Death. Through this he obtained much arcane knowledge and power, becoming a great medicine man and aiding his people in many ways. He was eventually persuaded to take a bride, but she proved to be unfaithful to him. When her lover made an attempt on his life Uaica had had enough and vanished.

VAI-MASHE

"Master of Animals"

Vai-Mashe was to the Amazonian Tukano tribe the most vital and important spirit of the forest. He was portrayed as a red dwarf, possessing a deadly red cane weapon. He controlled the movements of all the forest animals and even the medicinal plants and herbs. He also had a fertility aspect.

VIRACOCHA

Also known as: Con Ticci Viracocha
"The Foam of the Lake"

Viracocha's origins were pre-Inca, but with the Inca he grew in stature and attributes. He was the son of Inti and eventually the ultimate supreme creator god among the many tribes that made up the Inca Empire. He was supposed to live in Lake Titicaca, as the god of water, wearing a beard which symbolized his element, but he was also a sun and sky god, omnipresent and incomprehensible, giving life to all things, yet remaining aloof from creation. After making the world he journeyed through it, perfecting it and educating his creations. Sacrifice was required, but not on a daily basis.

WAKONDA

"Power Above"

Wakonda was the manifestation of the ultimate power behind all life and creation for the North American Great Plains Sioux. The source of all wisdom, knowledge and power which sustained the world and equipped the medicine men, Wakonda sometimes was envisioned as a huge thunder bird.

WISHPOOSH

The evil beaver spirit of the Washington Nez Perce Indians, who carried off fisherman who came to his lake. When the Nez Perce begged Coyote to help them, he fashioned a long

Right: This spectacular depiction of a Great Plains grass dance was drawn by a Sioux chief.

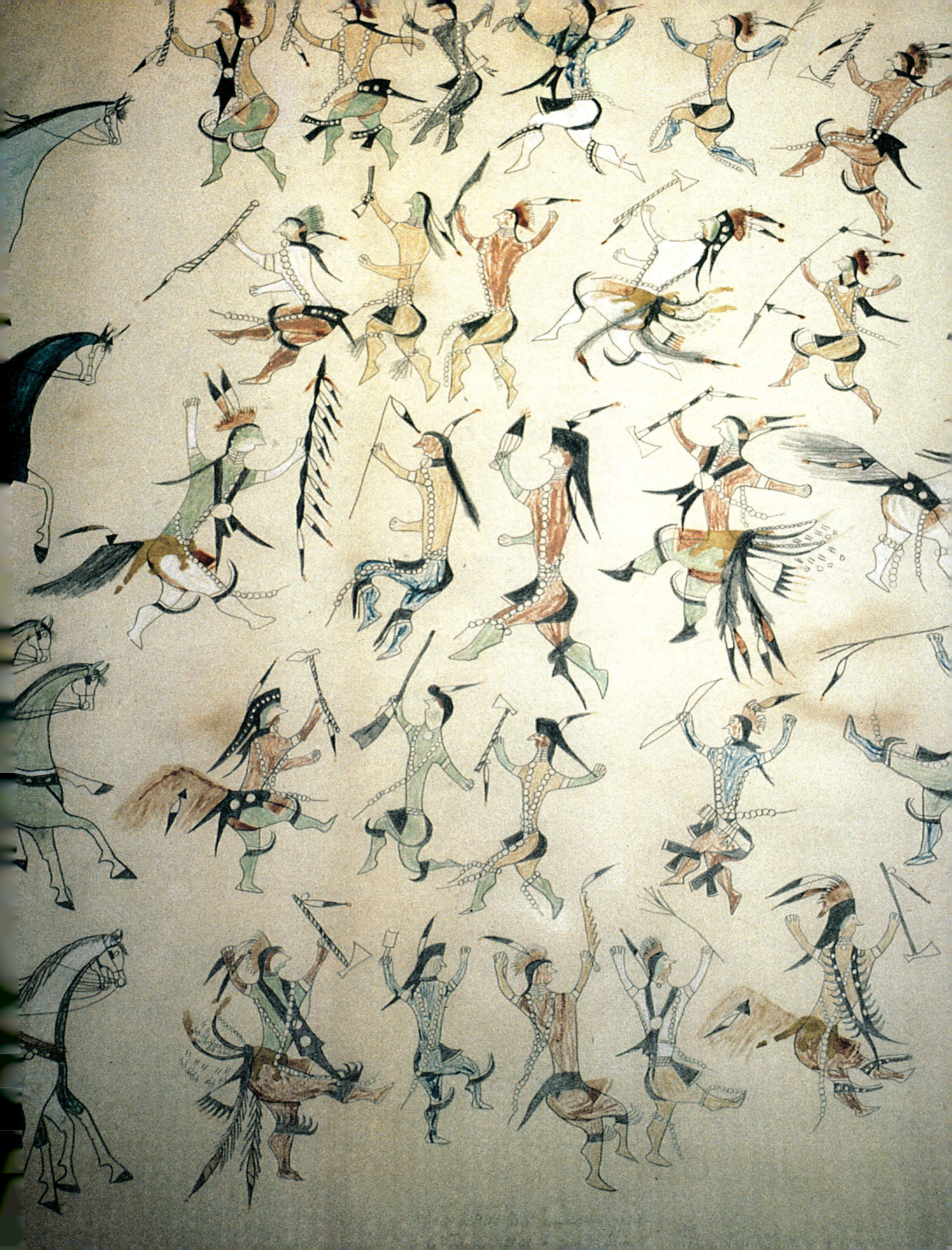

A-Z
CODEX GODS

spear and went fishing. When Wishpoosh grabbed Coyote and took him to bottom of the lake he received a shock, for his adversary fought back with alarming vigor. Indeed their battle — which spread over a large area as Wishpoosh attempted to lose his nemesis — was so intense that the waters were massively disturbed, rivers enlarged, hillsides torn asunder and gorges ripped out of the land. Eventually Wishpoosh managed to reach the ocean, where he ate whales to replenish his strength. The cunning Coyote then caught Wishpoosh out by changing himself into flotsam which the beaver monster inadvertently swallowed. Once inside his enemy's stomach Coyote was able to stab and slash Wishpoosh's insides to ribbons. Thus he died, and from the corpse Coyote created a new race of people: the Chinook, the Klickitat and the Yakima.

WONOMI
"No death"
Also known as: Kodo-yanpe, Kodo-yeponi
The supreme sky father and creator god of the Californian Maidu Indians, Wonomi was inviolate until the trickster Coyote appeared on the scene. Coyote managed to usurp the sky lord, because men were drawn to his energy and enthusiasm. Wonomi retreated to the sky, becoming the god of Heaven and leaving the earth to his wily adversary.

XIBALBA
The name of the nine-level Mayan underworld, ruled over by Hun Came and Vukub Came, along with other the other less superior lords. The Maya conceived the universe to exist on three major levels: Heaven, Earth and Hell, all joined in the center by a great tree, which enabled a certain amount of traffic and transportation between them. Like all South and meso-American cultures there was a special emphasis and correlation between color and numbers, which produced a complex calendrical system and advanced mathematics.

XIPE TOTEC
"Lord of the Seed Time"
The Flayed god — a penitential and agricultural deity of Zapotec origin. During his springtime festival - captives were sacrificed through flaying and then eaten at a ritual meal, their skins used to clothe images of the god and his priests. Xipe Totec fed humankind through being flayed, just as maize is skinned to reveal corn. He was one the four "sons" or cardinal points — a manifestation of the Red Tezcatlipoca. His other brothers were Camaxtli, Quetzalcoatl and Tezcatlipoca. Although he does not occur often in Aztec narratives, some events (flaying and eating of captives) are obvious references to him.

Right: This dance apron with a beaver totemic design belongs to a British Columbian tribe.

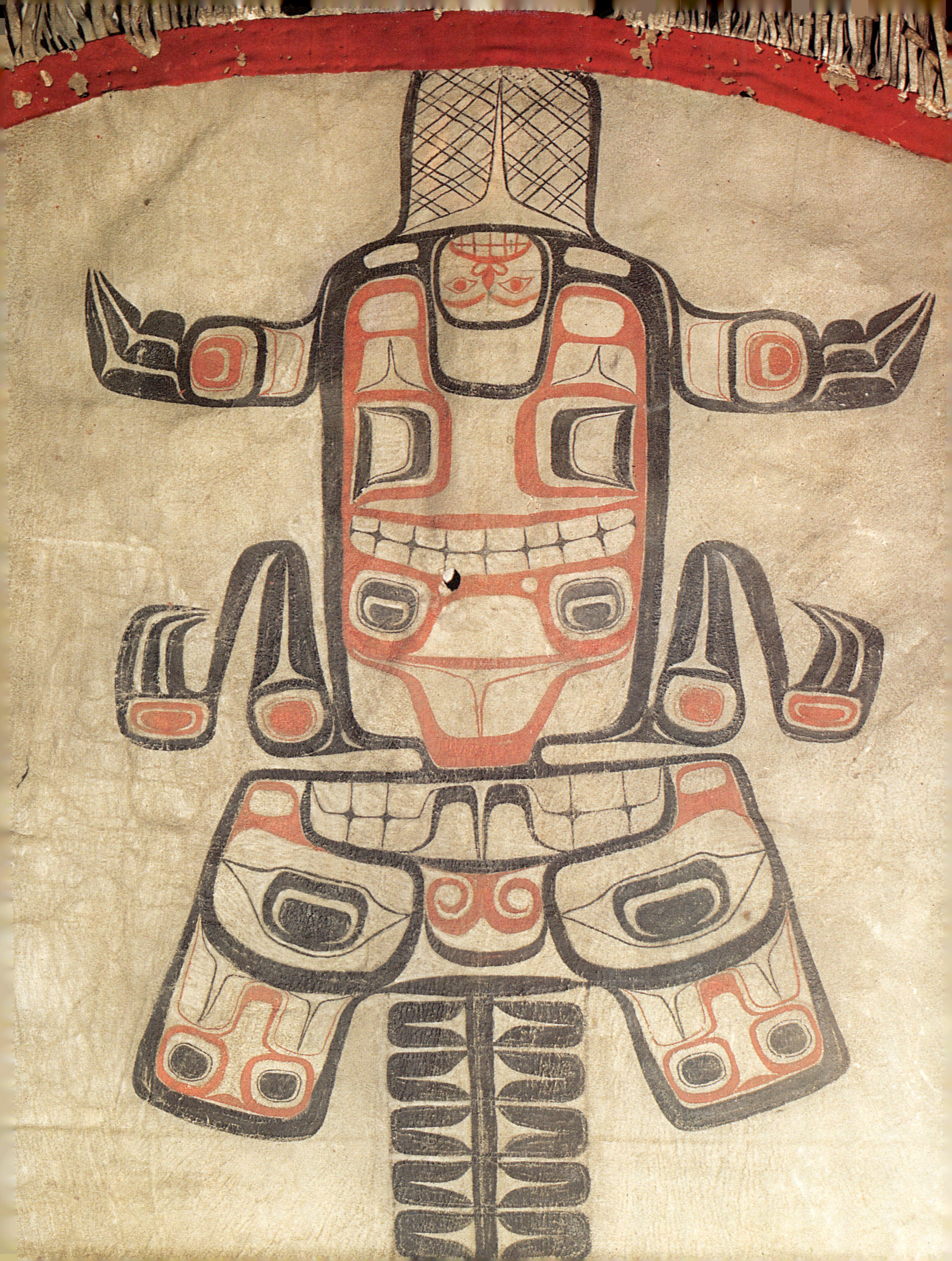

A-Z
CODEX GODS

XOLOTL
"The Animal"

A solar deity who governed the holy ball game, Xolotl was also the god of twins and deformed people who were sacrificed to the sun at the time of eclipse. He was portrayed deformed himself, with back to front feet. He was also the dispenser of bad luck who was responsible for bringing both man and fire from the underworld, into which he pushed the sun every night. He equates with the trickster type gods of other cultures and is of ancient derivation.

YANAULUHA
The legendary medicine man and teacher of the Zuni tribe of the Pueblo Indians. When men first emerged from the earth mother, they were strange in appearance and attitude having accustomed themselves to life underground. They put their faith therefore in the wisdom and skill of Yanauluha, who taught them the arts of agriculture and civilization. Yanauluha's staff — decorated with shells, feathers and stones, became the symbol of Zuni culture and religion, and was the symbolic emblem of power carried by the chief priest.

YUM CAAX
"Lord of the Forest"

The Mayan god of maize, who signified plenty — life, riches and the pleasure taken in participation of them. He was the god "E" in the Mayan codex, and also represented corn. Offerings of blood were made to him when the stalks were burnt.

ZOMBIE
In the Voodoo cult religion of Haiti a zombie is a body (often dead) which possesses no soul. This frightening state occurs if the soul is removed by magic from a living person, or a corpse whose soul had left after death and burial is re-animated. As the Lord of Death, Ghede had this power of reanimation.

Above left and Right: A box seat, where priests could view the games played in the Mayan ruins at Chichén Itzá. Left: The "goal" on the court at Chichén Itzá.

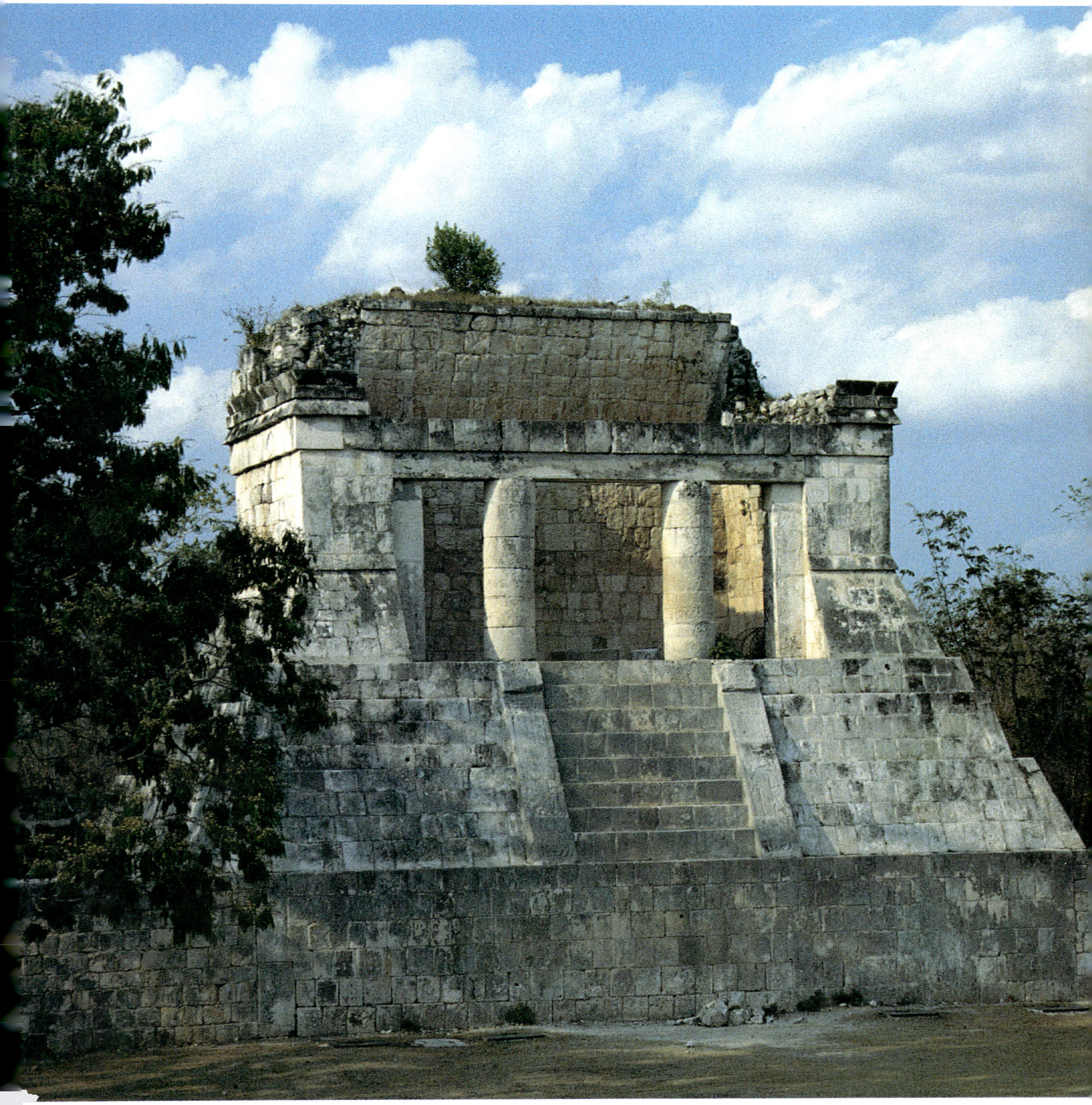

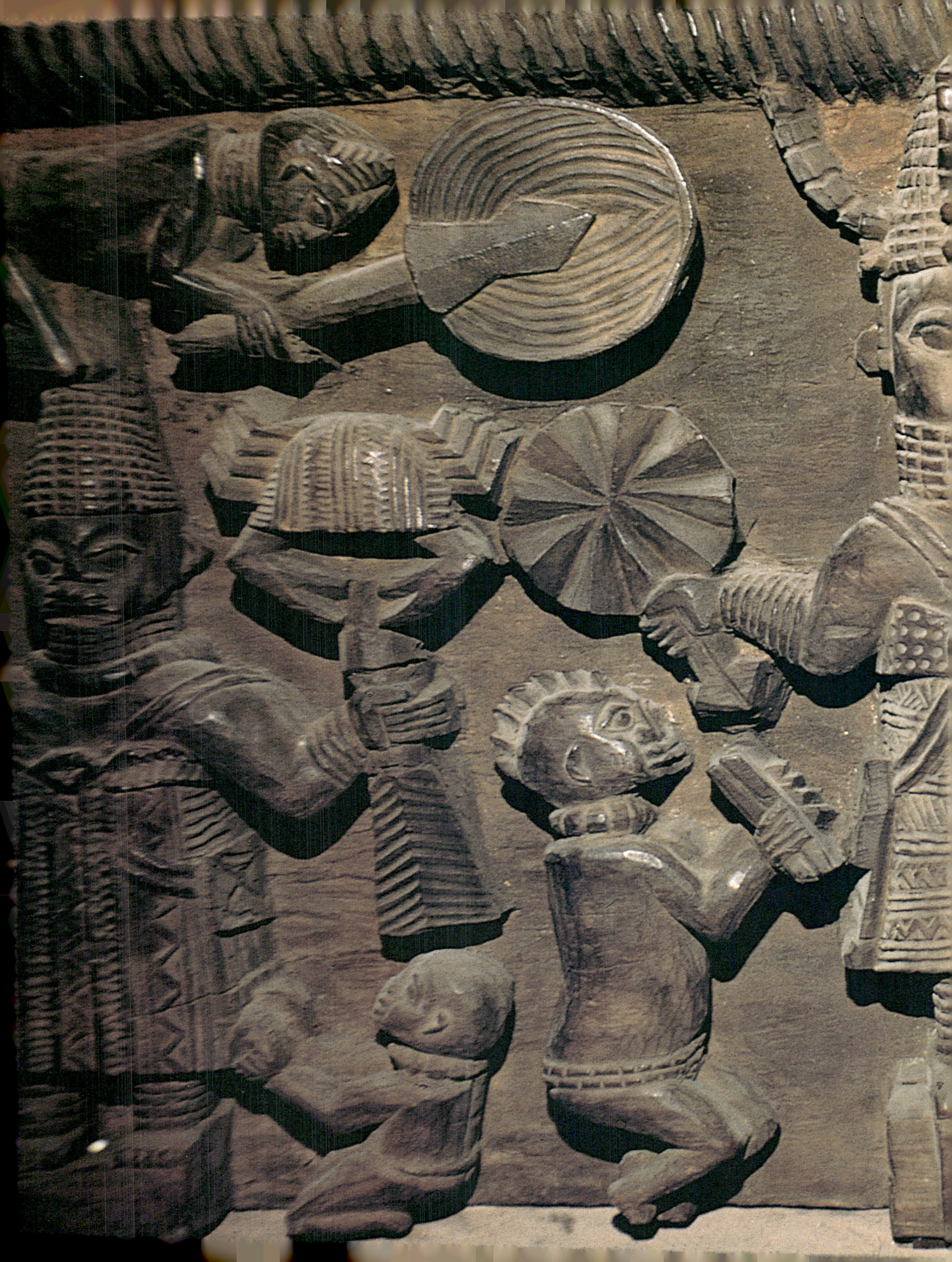

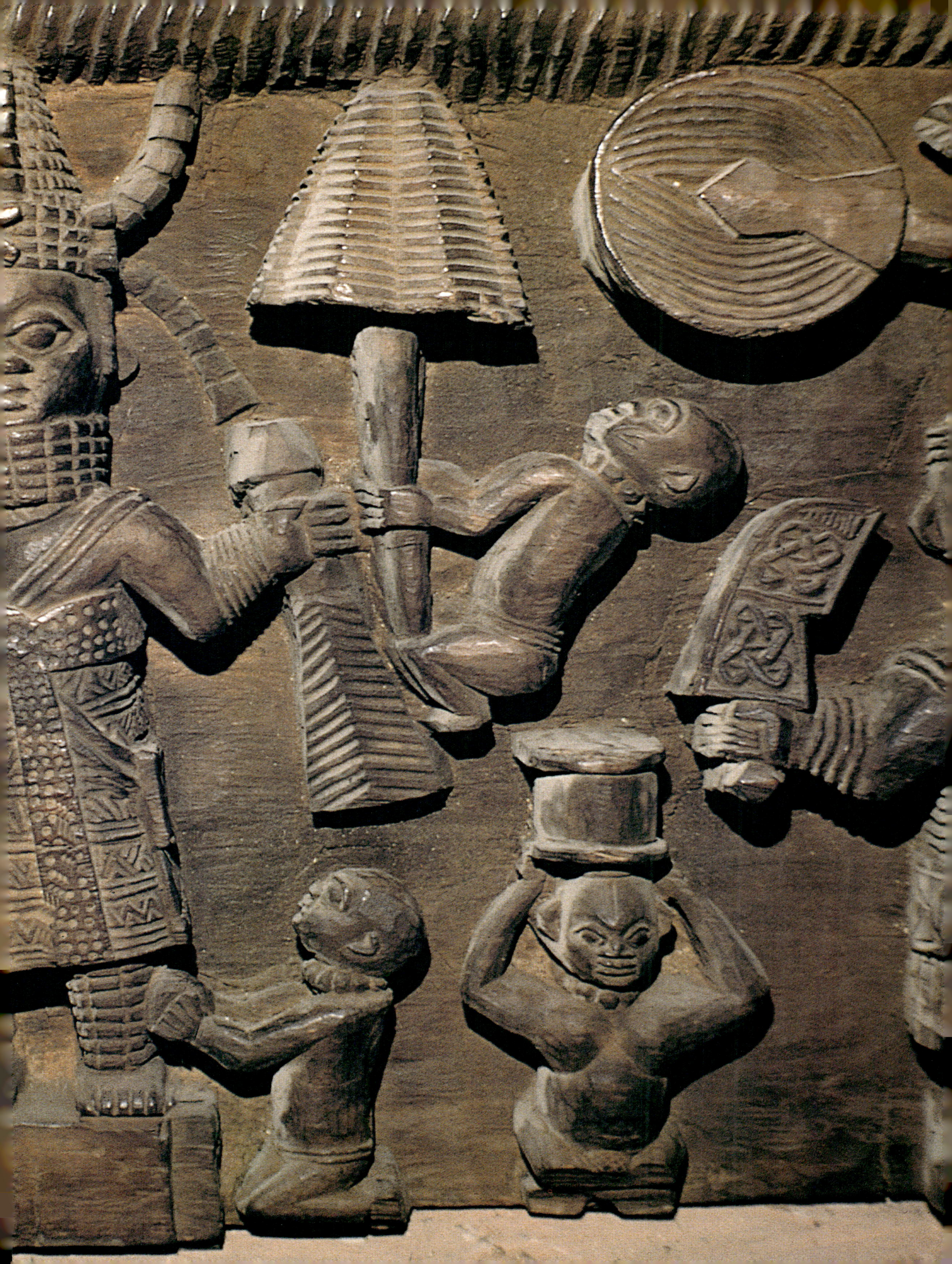

AFRICA

AFRICA is enormous and diverse, with over 2,000 languages spoken across its breadth. Despite the size, there is a startling element of basic mythical unity. There is the cosmic egg, the cosmic serpent, the great tower, the chameleon or trickster culture hero, the introduction of death through garbled or broken communications and the ancestor protocols. All of these bear more than a passing resemblance to each other, in spite of their sometimes massive racial discrepancies.

The size of the continent, the variety of its climate and its consequent effects on the different peoples perhaps account for the astonishing variety and differentiation amongst the tribes of Africa. Certainly another factor is the small scale of these societies. An oral tradition and varied lifestyle was generated by an environment in which people were often moving in migrations typical of any nomadic existence. This was similar to other nomadic groups of the world, the Aboriginals of Australia being just one example. In other ways these limitations have been a saving grace, enabling others to glimpse traditions that have given ancient peoples, still functioning in similar circumstances, so intimate a link with their history — this despite the vastness of time. However modern time has finally burst upon this once dark mysterious continent, bringing with it "slavery, imperialism, urbanization, money, communications, missionaries and most recently independence." And what a price she has paid to join the modern world. Christianity, Catholicism and Islam have followed the physical conquest of the continent and in so doing have modified certain areas to a lasting effect. There are, however, still a few parts outside these appropriations, where the culture has been strong enough to withstand the European attack. The Yoruba, the Fon, the Ashanti, and

Previous pages: A wooden bas relief of the king of Owo from his shrine in Eastern Yorobaland, Nigeria. Right: An ivory ceremonial mask from Benin, Nigeria.

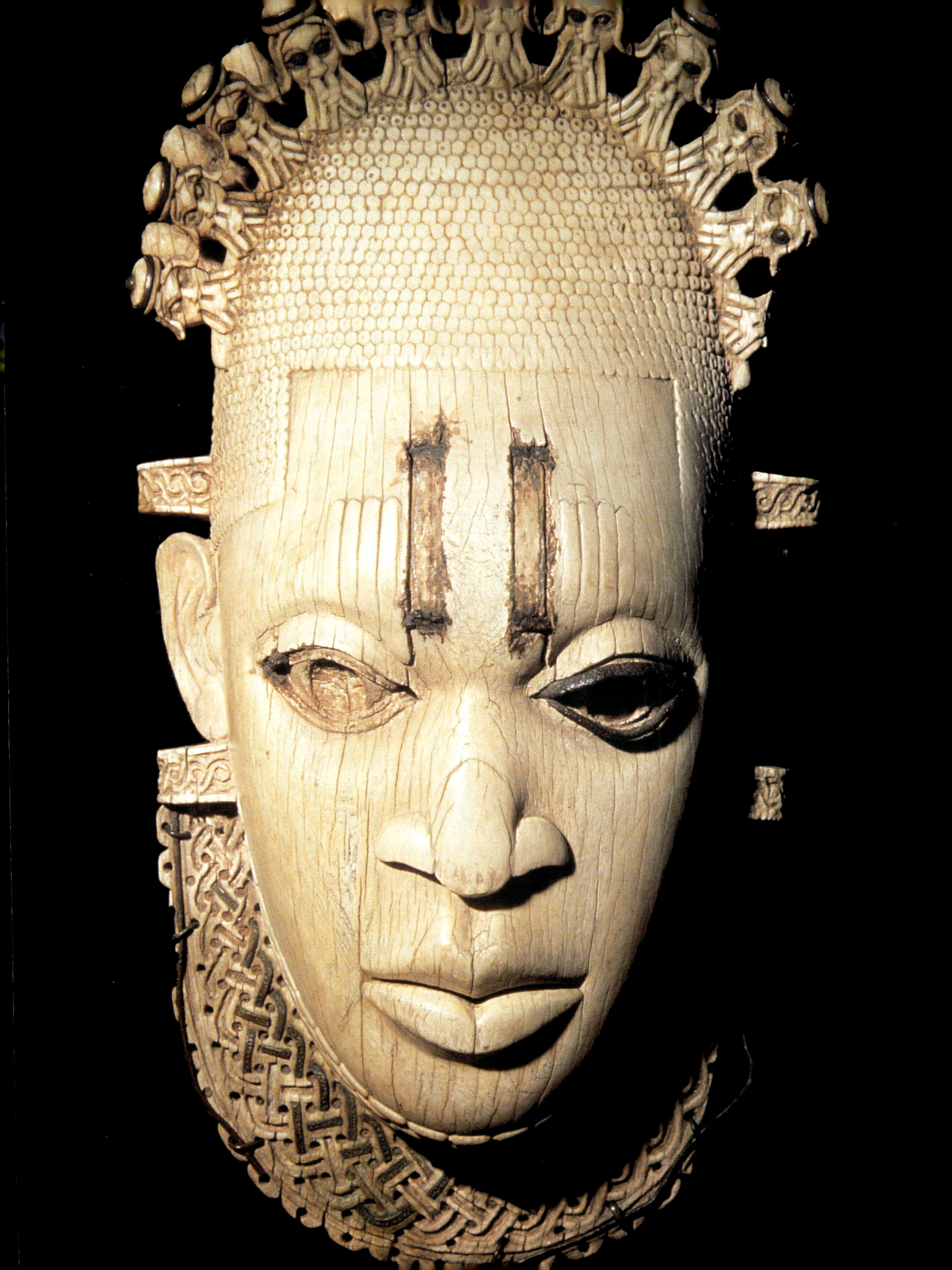

the Zulu all maintain their own cultural integrity, despite deep and lasting contact with the outside world.

Africa has always had to deal with condescending criticism inherent to colonialism and its "mission" of religious domination. In fact it was limited by the very design of that structure as envisaged by its builders, the western European nations. It was therefore a process rather than a situation, because in older societies who record their data, myths are often appropriated exclusively by the religious community until so old that they lose their meaning. Before the rise of international conquest and the spread of state religions, people were born into their belief, no matter how small. Hence the African plurality, diversity and tribalism. Linguistic linkage after all, does not presume there will be a shared religious culture, geography and other environments coupled with the inherently creative and participative aspect of true mythology ensured that there would be great diversity. Most of these magical mini-cultures are now in the void after 400 years of sustained attack. Only the strongest and usually largest or most hidden have survived The rest really is mythology in itself, murdered by the more contemporary myths of progress, conquest, and technology. The plurality of gods slowly gave way to more mundane monotheisms. A pantheon of gods, ones that had often evolved from animals through to anthropomorphic bodies that were combined with animal features, was reduced finally to mere humans.

In the tribal Africa the spirit world was never very far away, for the very air was humming with the agencies of witches, spirits, medicine men, Obia, Fa and magic. Concessions were offered and traded in this spirit world, where the balance between good mental health and disaster was thin, and where malign sorcerers and malevolent people

Above left and Right: This fantastic headdress belonged to a Dumazulu witch doctor from South Africa.

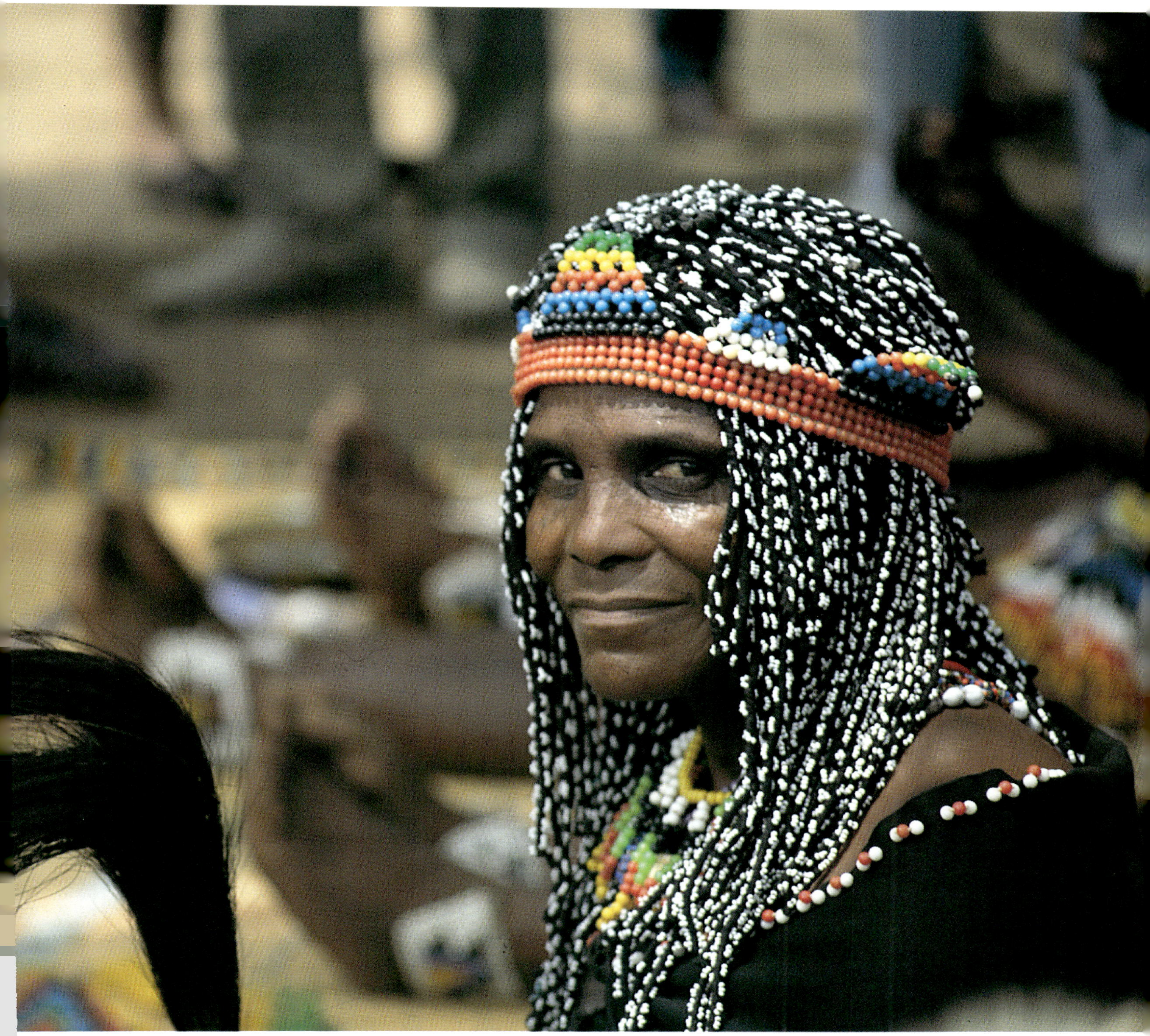

could constantly upset it. Divine favor was therefore sought through sacrifice and propitiation, especially during times of famine, drought, war, disease, misfortune and illness. Usually animals were sacrificed but obviously at one time humans were as well. Finally the Africa's isolation came to an end and the old religions were forced onto the retreat, with the newer world religions of Christianity and Islam coming into ascendance. Temples vanished but ancestor cults and magic still remained. The people, modified these strange new faiths with their own interpretation. While the few remaining living mythologies became a reminder of a once more diverse mythological environment.

African societies have a wide spectrum of different mythologies, each one reflecting the duration and current state of their own cultural evolution. These encapsulate the racial meetings, mixes and movements of history, as the original inhabitants and new arrivals melt into an historical reality of alliances, wars, feudal systems, monarchies and even empires (Zulu/Zimbabwe). The geographical variation of tribes gives mythical variation, but in the end these differences are not as great as the similarities of social texture and approach. Myths, as in India and other countries once deemed "Third World", have an active interface that stretches back into tribal history, constantly updated and retold they remain intrinsically the same — fulfiling the same vital role and function of maintaining physical and spiritual order within those societies. Perhaps it is this link to their own living past that personalizes their religion too, for there does not seem to be the gulf that exists between the sacred and profane in other cultures. Even if people were cut off from their pasts by the intervening millennia of recorded history, it still belonged to them. Maybe this sheer weight of data has

Above left and Right: A Yoruba carved ivory horseman from the Ogboni cult.

a wooden door from a shrine at Ijebu-Ode.
Yoruba. 98.5-18.1

something to do with it — maybe we have put too much "time" between us and our own ancient mythology, or the changes wrought have demanded starting again with new mythological constructs. Western rationalist thought has seen the development of the sciences and in essence, the death of god which has led in turn to new variants of the same old archetypes. It's as if the attempt to define civilization has led to displacement. Underneath, our ancient limbic systems still trace out their fears and desires. Lifestyles change much on the surface, but their underlying meaning and results are the same.

The classical concept of myth and rite as providing a framework on which one should conduct their life breaks down in the African prototype, where mythology is a way of life — a song eternally sung and a personal poem between the people and their gods, the manifestations of their spiritual selves. A series of collective participations and individual combinations that is absolutely all-inclusive. In fact all the layers of reality defined by their societies — celestial, mythical, spiritual, social and individual are overlapped or exist as simultaneous analogies of each other and therefore in the same place. Studies of any holistically functioning society (unmotivated by pure profit or material goods as the sole arbiters of value) reveal the astonishing level of minute detail which flows throughout its every part. Every item, every action is a symbol of a greater pattern that reflects the basic codas of existence. Everything and everyone is connected in a matrix of individual simplicity and cosmic complexity. The micro and macrocosms balance perfectly because size is just a matter of scale. The fact that it is there defines its own success, but set within the wider context, what happens when these different definitions meet? Why then like the continents

Above left and Right: This beautiful 13th century cast bronze head was made in Nigeria.

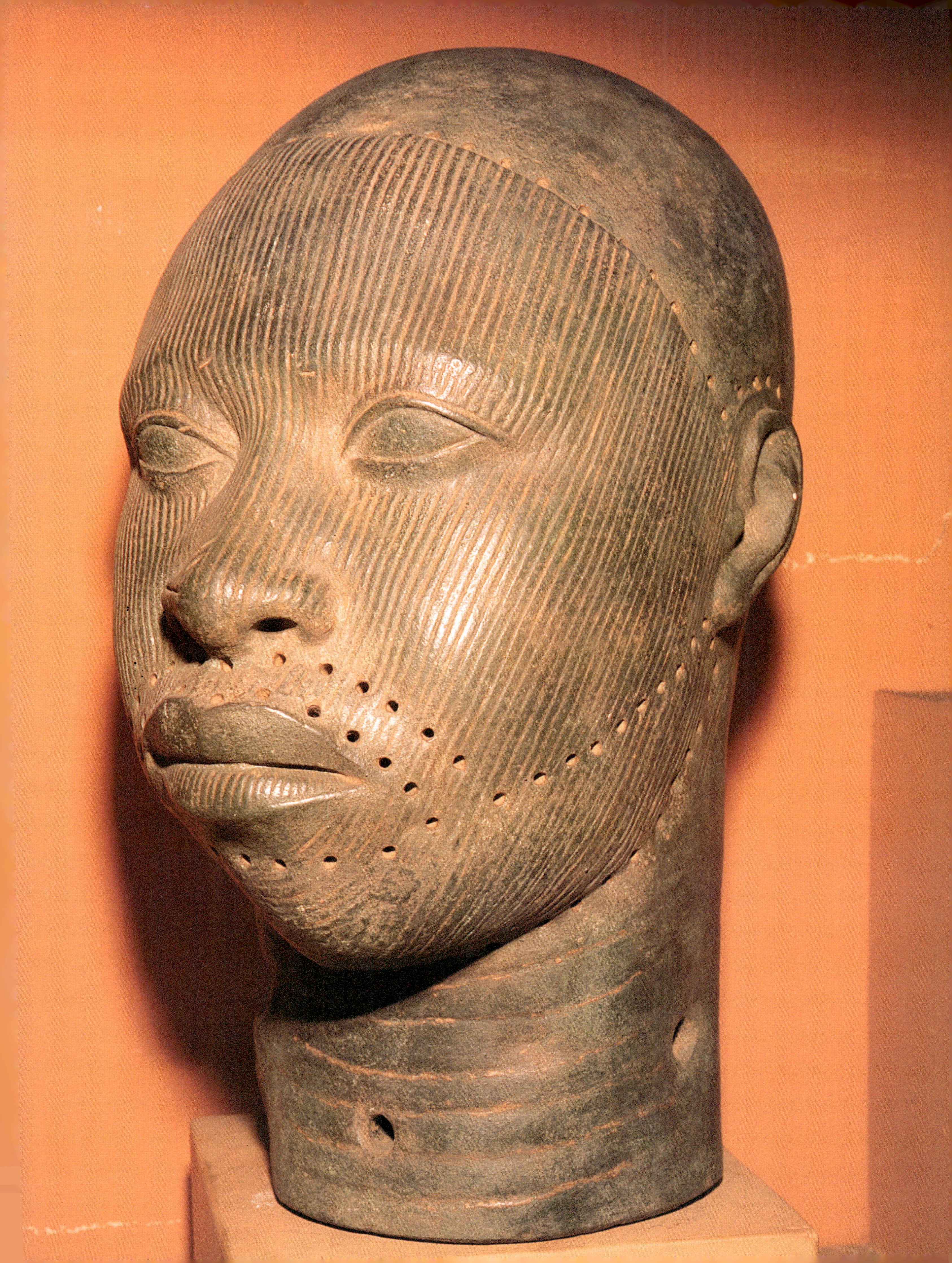

do they tectonically grind and clash. Ludicrous pieces get wrenched up out of context to form the features of a new landscape, which in turn gives way to fresh erosion.

African systems do have their science of numbers too — an almost alarming predilection for numerics that seem more western. However, most religions worldwide have this numerical preoccupation of existence. The sequences and codes of life's natural duality, contradiction and conciliation — the internal combustion engine of existence as codified in theory either numerical or visual. Like the simplistic cod-science of an advertisement these positive and negative attributes reflect the movement of the cosmos through the interaction of their tension.

WORLD ORIGIN

Many African mythologies start with the creation of the world already achieved, and their true beginning occurs with the appearance or introduction of humans. Some cultures trace the beginning of civilization to the manifestation of the dualistic energy of the cosmos, others to a cosmic egg or a more conventional ambiguous creator sky god. Ancestors fell or descended from the sky, or were born semi-divine from the often incestuous union of the creator with the first of his creations. Death and sex, share a common origin — they didn't initially exist (perhaps the awareness of them did not exist other than as an instinctive process involving no point of observation) but came about because of objectivity — or self-consciousness. The evolution of death is often outside the ambit of the creator too, caused rather as a result of human mistake, hero tricksters, creator god rage, garbled messages, communication breakdowns, competition between animals or just plain spite. The dead are the intermediaries, living in an

Above left and Right: Another similar Nigerian 13th century cast bronze head — this time from the Ipe tribe.

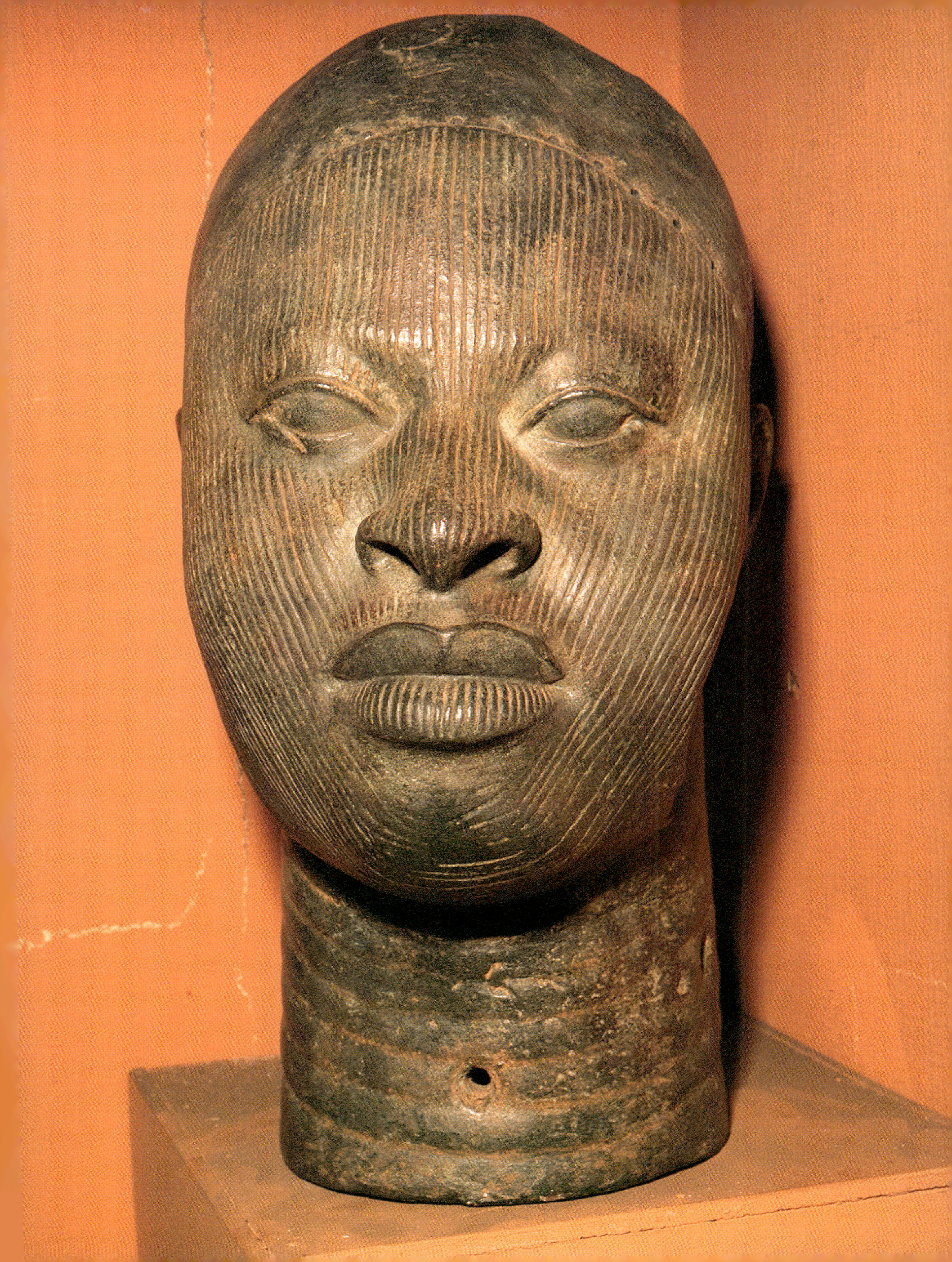

interim world that links the human and the divine. Sometimes these worlds are of the same thing — simultaneously manifested and mapped on each other, with their equivalent personalities, agencies and individuals. Sometimes the world is earthen in origin and other times of the sky. Important to some of the tribes are the origins and protocols of kingship, which in classic format becomes a position to justify and thereby maintain — keeping things just as they are through divine sanction in a linkage system perhaps inevitable in societies requiring the social cohesion of a hierarchical system. How else does one convince those less well off that it was meant to be so other than by divine or physical force? Other prevalent myths include the building of a giant tower — to reach heaven, recover immortality, challenge the gods, dispute arbitrary judgements, observe far situations and defend against invasion. Extraordinarily popular tricksters are the ones who create tension between everyone — humans, gods and spirits. Perhaps they are the manifestations of the intrinsically opposed dualisms of existence — the starting motor of the universal engine. These tricksters are morph-enabled they change shape and disguise themselves in order to deceive humans, gods and even natural phenomena. Essentially they are another human-divine interface whose borders blur — they represent both dualism and a link between its processes. An attempt to explain and therefore understand the contradictory/conciliative process required of all that exists — to get that existence-motor going. Animals are more prominent in African myths than just about anywhere else other than North America and Oceania, with great importance placed on the theriomorphic gods of spider, hare, dog, goat, chameleon, monkey and snake. Though human behavior patterns are often overmapped this

Above left and Right: This 13th century brass head is of a chief from the Yoruba of Ijgbu-Obi, a handle at the top allowed it to be carried through ceremonies.

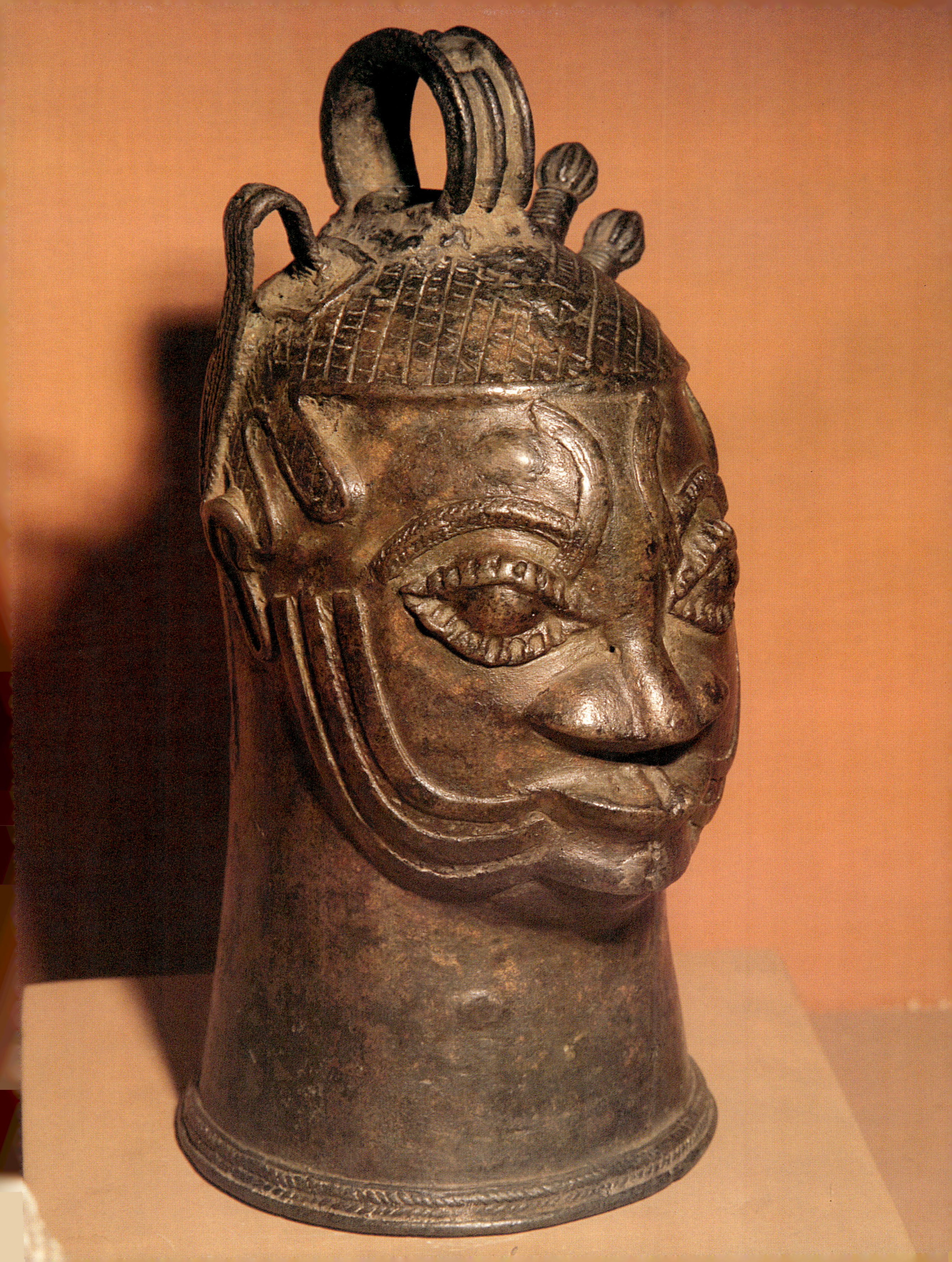

shows the link with the ancient ways that still existed/exists in Africa at least till very recently. Some animals assist in terraforming the earth, others are responsible for ancestor creation, the bringing of knowledge and skills through tricking someone else out of them, and some just for pure devillment.

Everything alive has spirit — an intangible double; spirits are worshiped, but also controlled by magic — necessary as there are both good and bad. A witch is a person with evil spirit. These are countered with recourse to a good magician, who can interpret the attack and prescribe the defense. The African concept of good and evil is far different from the Christian one of moral conscience. In Africa a person's importance is secondary to that of his social clan or tribe. Good nurtures it, evil threatens it. Illness is often perceived as the result of spiritual "Psy-Ops" (Psychological Operations against the enemy) — either ghosts or evil spirits released through the agencies of malevolent sorcerers, who absorb others' life energy as a way of nourishment and to increase their own power. In a continent of high infant mortality and poor health care this is certainly an alternative cultural explanation of the destructive or reducing process. One is born with the power or not, it cannot really be acquired. Sorcerers are the most powerful, doing it for their own evil kick, using fetishes — visual demonstrations and manifestations of their abilities. They thus conduct their Psy-Ops against already terrified victims. Belief seems to imbue power, as countless inexplicable circumstances and events bear witness.

Above left and Right: An elaborate African mask carved from wood and highlighted with metal studs.

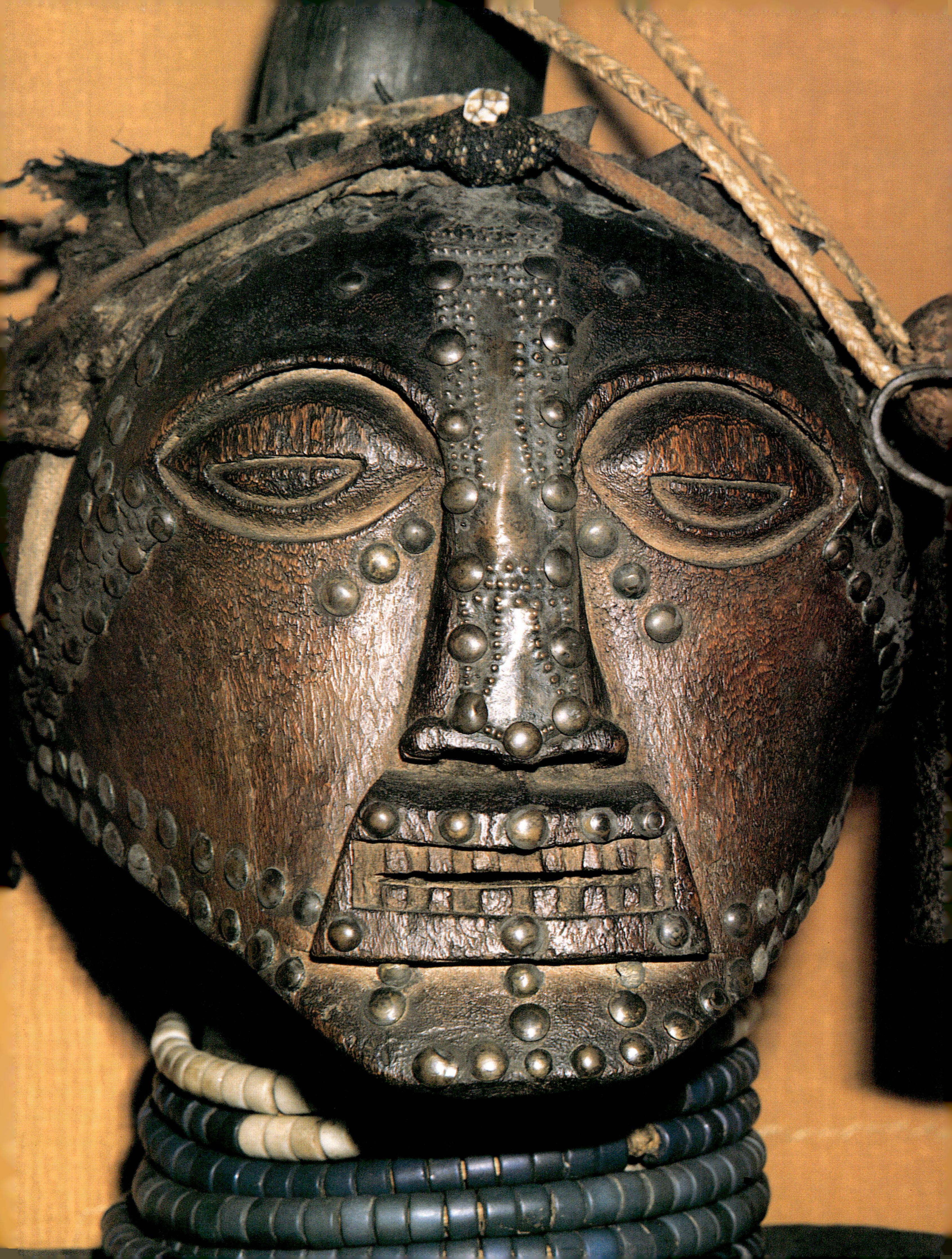

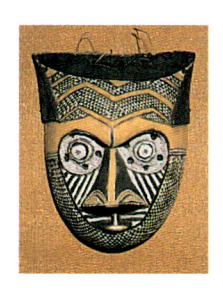

PYGMIES, BUSHMEN (SAN), HOTTENTOTS (KHOI), KHOISAN,

Anthropological and ethnological criteria define this grouping as the oldest of the continent, their small size and nomadic hunter-gatherer lifestyle set them apart from the other pastoralist, agriculturalist or militarist societies around them. Driven slowly from their original lands deep into the jungles and deserts in which they still survive after a fashion, these deceptively simple peoples, though now exposed to many outside influences, acknowledge a primitive monotheism coupled with their older, natural animistic tendencies. Thus sky creator deities, often complete with a borrowed foreign name, denote outside pollution of original sources. The dynamic animal, ancestor and spirit world represent the active interface of the indigenous culture. Here tales detail the endless struggle for balance between good and evil being played out with tricksters, heroes, monsters, magicians, animal avatars and archetypes, hunters, ghosts and ancestors all joining in an unendingly creative sequential dance. There are recognizable similarities with Oceanic religious and mythical development and the older animist religions of Siberia, North America and perhaps even pagan Celtic Europe. The fragmentary remains and the little people, are the leftovers of a richly imaginative life philosophy conveyed through animism.

BANTU

The Bantu had relatively little interest in creation mythology, which they attributed to a high god long since withdrawn. Instead emphasis was on the social order and divinely sanctioned kingship — the "business end" or control panel of society's

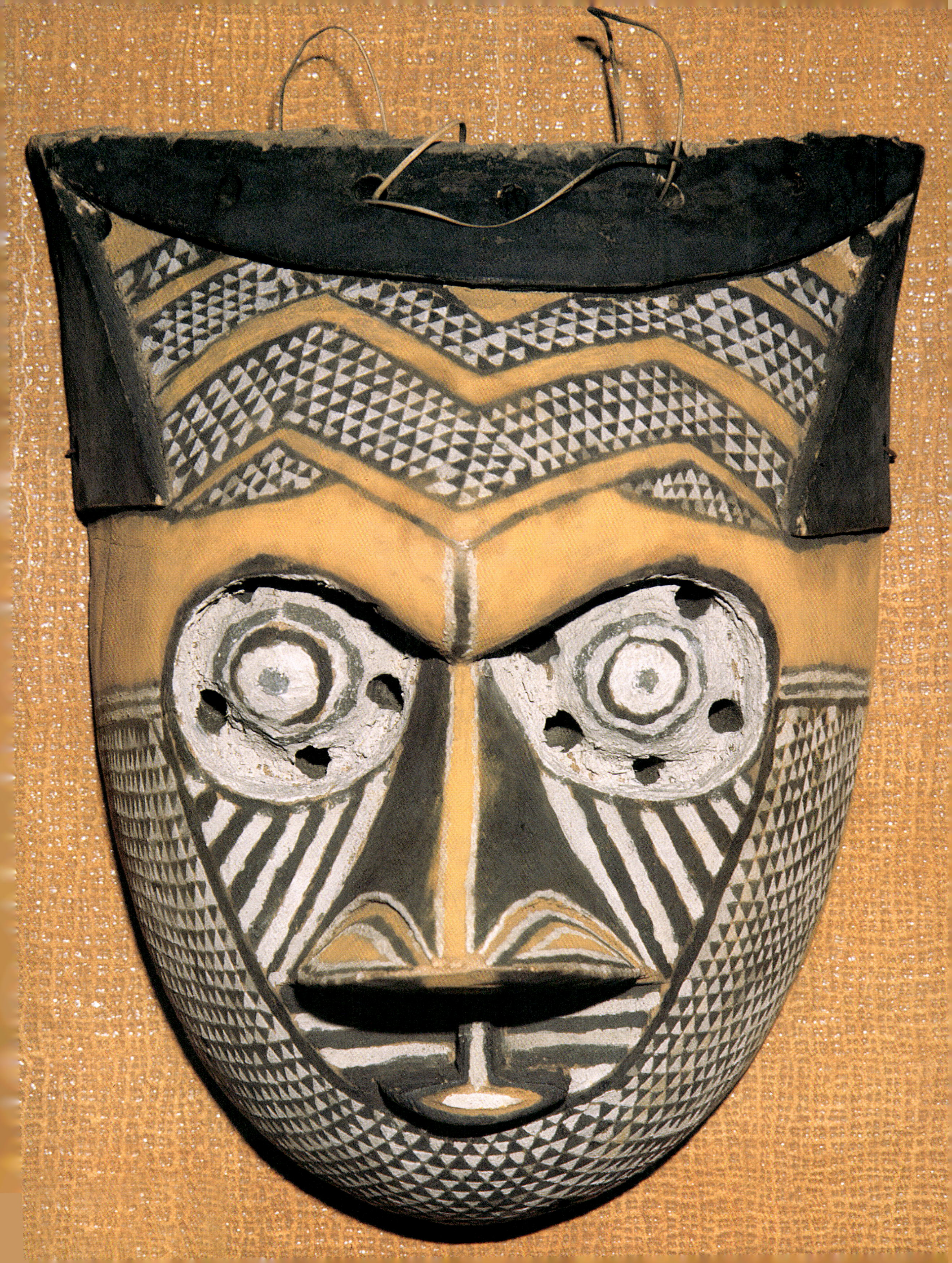

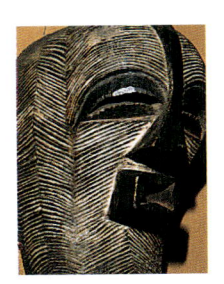

machine. Natural phenomena and animals were imbued with character too, and there were ornate ancestor cults.

Similar to ancient Egypt and other West and Central Asian civilizations, the Bantu emphasized the importance of the royal cult and ancestor worship within their own culture. As intermediaries between the human and divine worlds, the ancestors observe and insist on the correct forms and procedures so that the normal order of things may continue, undisturbed by chaos. These more evolved agriculturalist tribes acknowledged omnipotent sky deities, often but not always remote. Again the spirit world interface can improve connection between these worlds, but may also worsen it with tricks and games, playing out the hidden agenda of more random, willful, negative aspects.

The Bantu cover a wide range of different habitats and lifestyles, yet all acknowledge a supreme being, who drove out the other more ancient deities, giving them negative attributes in opposition to him or else converting them to the lower spirit world where they could avenge their drop in status on humankind. Even though there is undoubtedly a tinge of Christian influence here, it also represents the syncretistic mythological process combining legend, religion, myth and folklore. Creation cycles morph into a similar pattern, the supreme god's son often becoming the founding ancestor, with a flood variant. Women, as in the Greek mythology, seem to get the blame for the introduction of death, trickery and all the other evils into the world.

WEST AFRICA: ASHANTI, FON, YORUBA.

Polytheistic religions with ornate pantheons are the feature of these successful complex societies, with an underlay of African animism and ancestor worship. In fact these cultures

Above left and Right: An African dance mask.

contain some of the world's most complicated myths. All life animated by a duality often symbolized in twins of the opposite sex.

HAMIO-SEMITIC

This population spread covers the mainly Moslem area of Northern Africa. Common myths include that of a cosmic serpent whose body provides the material for the universe and the tertiary world format of earth, heaven and hell. Traces of the older ancient Berber culture lingers still in remoter places such as the Atlas region.

NILO-SAHARAN

This population spreads from the Nile's sources to the Lake Chad area in north-central Africa. With little interest in the origin of the world and life after death, their mythical origins delve mainly into the spirit world, ancestors and clan groups. Animals feature prominently in all these areas.

A-Z
CODEX GODS

ABASSI

Abassi is the creator sky deity of the Efik people. Despite his instincts to the contrary, Abassi let his wife's enthusiasm persuade him to allow a human couple to settle on the earth he had created. His fears were that they would eventually surpass him in ability and wisdom. In order to allay this insecurity the human couple were forbidden to grow food, work or breed, instead they would take their meals each day when they were summoned to heaven. Inevitably as time went on the human couple began to ignore these rules, developing their own agriculture and producing offspring. Abassi was quick to chastise his wife for persuading him to allow this state of affairs, whereupon she sent death and discord down to the humans. This myth details the basic life equation: the price of freedom is mortality.

ADROA/ADRO

"God in the Sky," "God on the Earth"

This was the dualistic creator sky god of the Lugbara from Zaire and Uganda. Adroa had two aspects, the first was as a remote but benevolent sky god who wished his people well but did not get involved in their lives. His second aspect, Adro, had more disturbing implications for humankind, for he was on the earth and at the same time ill-disposed towards them, requiring child sacrifices as appeasement though later substituting them with sheep. Although the father of their culture and social order the Lugbara returned this ambiguous feeling to their god and apart from the propitiating sacrifices did not acknowledge him beyond a token acceptance. Obviously the evil Adro version was the one to avoid. Usually invisible, he supposedly revealed himself to those at death's door. Tall and pale, he possessed only a half featured body (a single eye, ear, arm, leg etc) with his sky dwelling counterpart presumably using the other half of the body. He also had many children, known as Adroanzi, who were malignant spirits which followed people at night, killing them instantly if they ever looked back.

AJOK

Ajok was originally a benevolent creator god of the Sudanese Lotuko. His nature changed somewhat due to man's selfishness and hubris — yet again the theme of man's misbehavior causing all the world's problems returns. It became necessary therefore to appease Ajok with prayer and sacrifice. One myth tells of a mother begging him to restore her child to life, but when he did her husband chided her and killed the child. From then on death became permanent as the god would no longer co-operate.

AKONGO

This supreme deity belongs to the Ngombe of Congo. Akongo originally lived alongside people

Right: This carved horn head came from the shrine of a king of Owo in eastern Yorubaland, Nigeria.

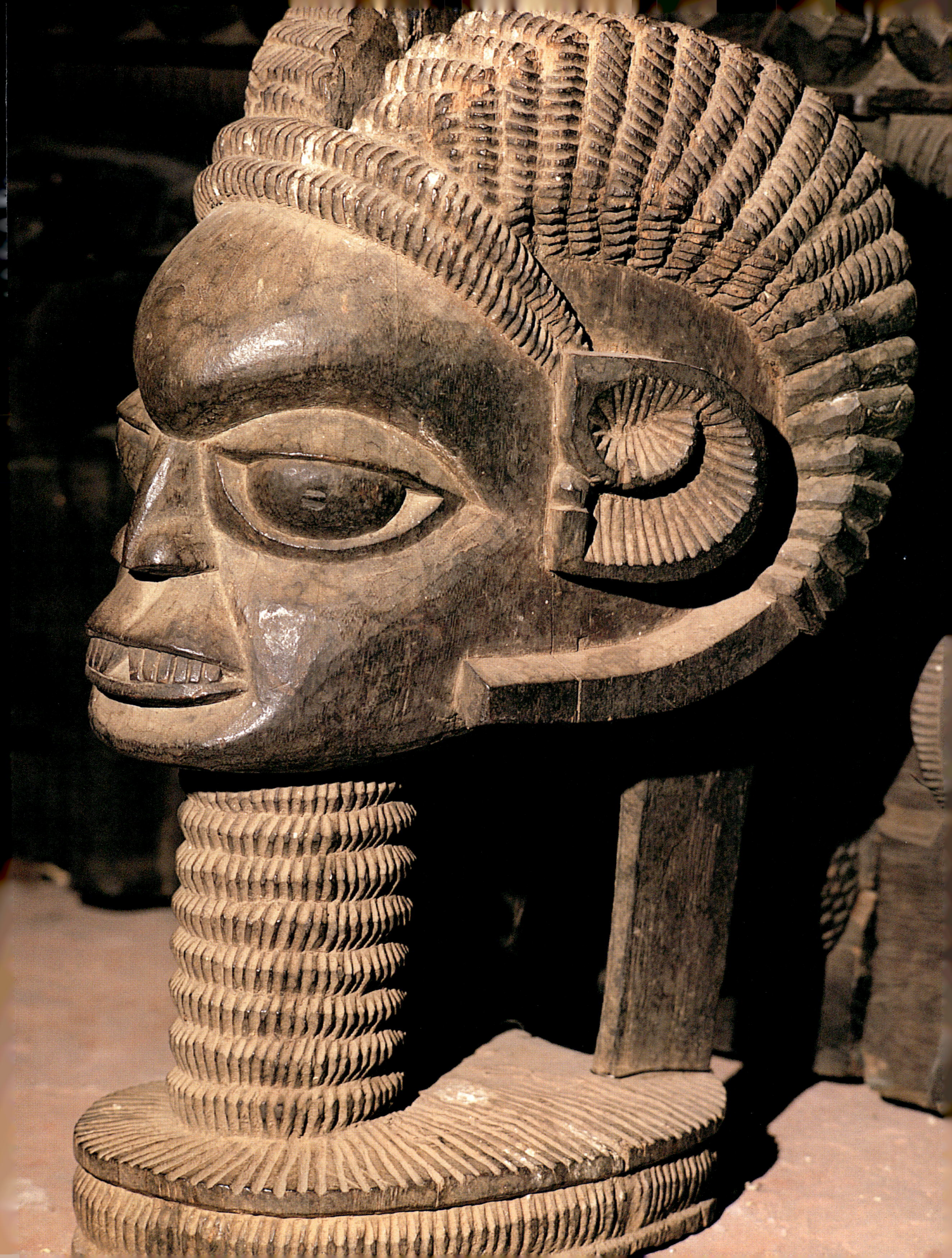

A-Z
CODEX GODS

until their bickering, divisiveness and violence disgusted him so much he vanished deep into the jungle, never to be seen again. It is through Akongo's auspices that the sky is held up above the earth, as he set two giants with large poles expressly for this purpose. Myth foretells of the end of the world when the giants tire of their task and let the sky drop.

AMMA

Amma was the chief creator god of the Dogon people of Mali, the potter who fashioned all creation from clay, beginning with the stars thrust into the firmament. He next formed a woman with which to mate, fathering first a jackal-monster (the trickster/devil figure counterpart to Amma), followed by the two serpent-like, asexual Nummo twins, who had to have their genitalia prepared in order to be capable of correct copulation. These twins invented speech and covered the bare Earth with plants and vegetation. Amma then coupled a third time with the Earth, producing yet another set of twins, who became the ancestors of the Dogon.

ANANSI

This trickster god was in the form of an Ashanti (now Ghana) spider. Anansi was originally a creator god but appears much more in his trickster role, with many roles in the Ashanti mythology attributed to him. In one, he was set a series of tasks to be accomplished before he could claim the Spider Stories as his own from the sky god Nyankopon. To win them he had to pay the price of a python, a hornet, a leopard and a nature spirit. He succeeded after tricking each creature into trapping itself. In this way he came to own the main collection of Ashanti tribal myths.

ANDRIAMBAHOMANANA

This primeval man in Madagascan mythology, he was married to Andriamahilala with whom he had many children. When asked by their god how they would like to die Andriambahomanana chose to die like the banana plant, which quickly grew to produce new shoots. His wife chose to go to the moon to be reborn each month.

ASASE YA

Asase Ya was the mother goddess figure of the Ashanti people. She was the wife of Nyankopon, and bore him four children.

ASA
"Father"

Asa is the creator god of the Kenyan Akamba tribes. He is believed to be an extremely strong but benevolent and merciful god who would often help humankind when things went wrong.

Right: African mask from Bamoun, Cameroon.

435

A-Z
CODEX GODS

AZRA'IL

Angel of death for the Tunisian Hausa peoples. Before Azra'il, people lived almost indefinitely — certainly for hundreds of years. One special virgin had been alive 500 years before she died. God was intrigued by this and asked a deity to show her to him. When the deity obliged the virgin was brought back to life from the grave, but was disturbed and unappreciative. It was then decided that people need not live so long that they suffered such depression and the 60–70 year life expectancy was agreed to. At this time Asra'il was called upon to separate the soul from the body.

BUMBA

Legend has it that Bumba, the chief creator god of the Bushongo people of the Congo, vomited the earth, sun, moon, heaven and stars, followed by various animals from which all life descended. Heaven and Earth were once a married couple who parted. Bumba appeared in a dream to a man called Kerikeri, showing him the secret of fire. Kerikeri then kept this secret to himself, charging others a high price for embers with which to cook their food. So the king's daughter, Mushanga, made him fall in love with her so that she might learn his secret. By pretending to be cold she forced him to reveal it when he built her a fire. After learning his secret she abandoned the marriage.

CAGN

Cagn is the prime creator god of the Kalahari Bushmen of south-central Africa. He was a wizard whose strength resided in one particular tooth and who could assume many forms, including a preying mantis and an antelope. He also possessed useful tools, which included a pair of sandals that became protective war-dogs. He was married to Coti, who bore him two sons — Cogaz and Gewi. Cagn faced many trials but his magic powers always came to his aid. Once he was killed by Thornbushmen, another time eaten by ants, each time his bones magically rejoined and he sprang back to life. Yet another time he was eaten by an ogre before being spat out.

CHIUTA

"Great Bow of Heaven"
Also known as: Mulengi ("creator"), Mwenco ("the owner of all"), Wamtatakuya ("eternal")
Chiuta was the paramount creator deity of Tunbuka of Malawi. Self-engendered and omniscient he was especially revered among the drought afflicted Tunbuka as a rain divinity.

CHUKU

"Great Spirit"
Also known as: Chineke
As the supreme creator of the eastern Nigerian Ibo, Chuku is renown for his benevolence and the Ibo refused to believe that he would harm

Right: An Ashanti gold mask made from a last wax casting.

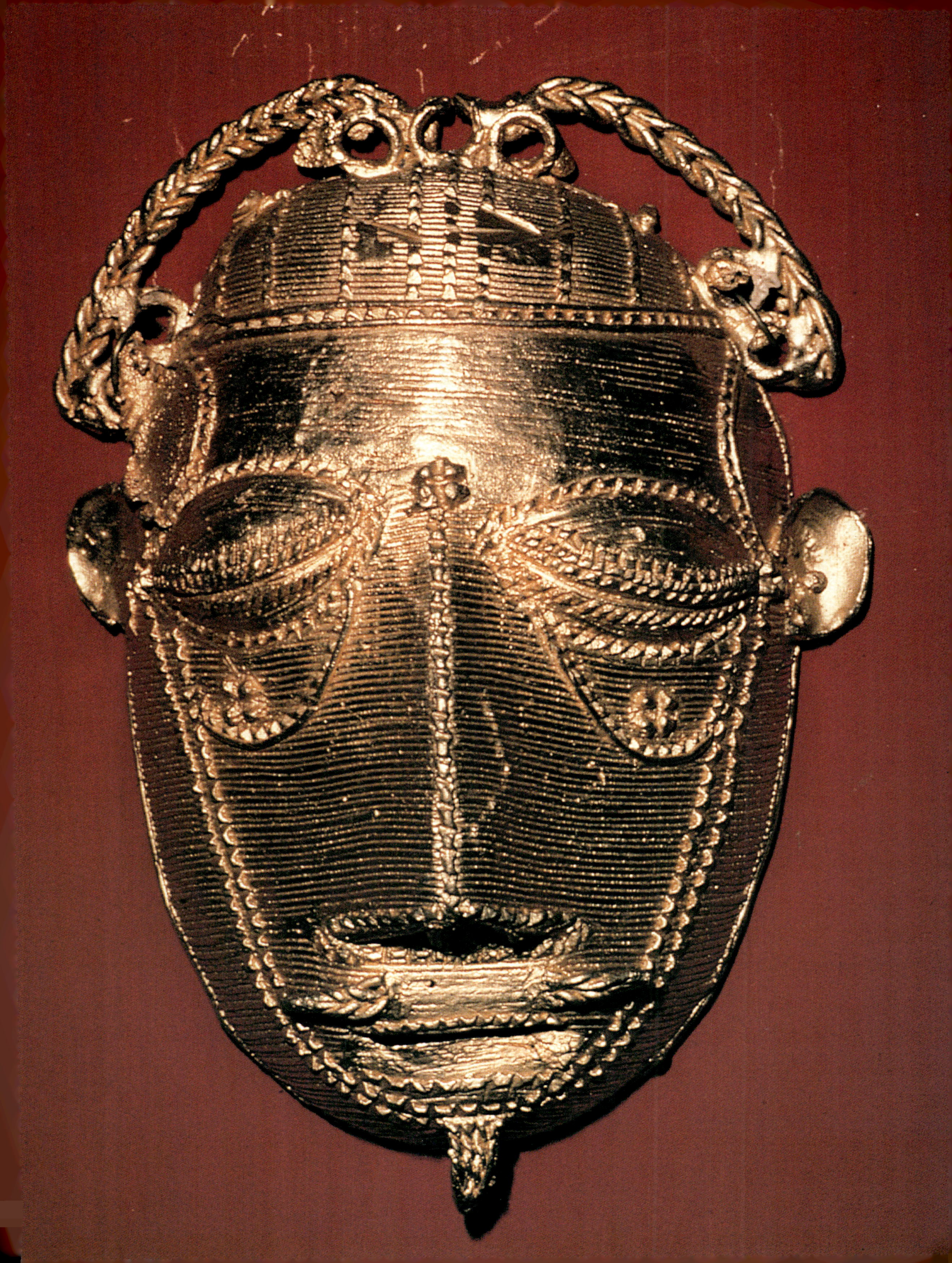

A-Z
CODEX GODS

anyone. They therefore attributed the existence of death to the familiar theme of garbled messages and communication breakdowns. Chuku sent a dog to his people with the following message: should anyone die acciden-tally, lay on the ground and have ashes scattered over top and soon they will come back to life. But this canine messenger grew hungry and weary and never completed his mission. Next Chuku sent a sheep, but this animal also stopped en route to eat and consequently got the message mixed up by suggesting that people bury their dead instead. The Ibo then followed those instructions and afterwards it was too late to change. Thus death came to humankind — and stayed.

EN-KAI
"Sky"
En-Kai was a vitally important rain and fertility god to the Masai of East Africa. The Masai were nomadic pastoralists and therefore rain was a constant concern since theirs and the lives of their livestock depended on it. As a result En-Kai was most carefully revered.

FA
Fa was the god of fate and destiny to the West African Dahomey people. Fa represented each man's individual fate and there was no room allowed for chance. To the Dahomey all that happened was a direct result of either human or divine action, and could never be attributed to random accident. Each person had to discover for themselves their own unique Fa. This was done primarily through divination or with the intervention of magic on his behalf to counter any misfortune or evil directed towards him. In fact the geomancy involved has parallels with the Chinese I-Ching or Book of Changes. Fa was also linked to the Ifa and Eschu of the Yoruba tribe, and the Legba of the Fon tribe. All were messengers and inter-mediaries between man and the gods.

GU
This mythical blacksmith and divine metalworker was sacred to the West African Fon. Following the creation of the world by the creator deity Mawu-Lisa, Gu was sent to earth to make it habitable for humankind. Since then he has never stopped working on his task. Gu has even appeared as a magical weapons platform of great capability and his association with metal runs through his iconography.

HEITSI-EIBIB
This mythical hero of Hottentot legend is a warrior, a great magician and the patron of hunters. He was conceived by a cow which had eaten some magic grass and was the antithesis of the evil monster Ga-gorib. Ga-gorib was a creature who loved to kill people by challenging them to throw stones at him — the stones would then automatically rebound and strike their

Right: This magic figure from the Congo has a body covered in nails

• AFRICA •

A-Z
CODEX GODS

throwers dead. When Heitsi-Eibib came across Ga-gorib he refrained from throwing his stone until the monster's gaze was diverted, with the result that Ga-gorib was struck and killed.

HOLAWAKA

In yet another message mix up, Holawaka — a mythical bird sent by the creator to the Ethiopian Galla people — was instructed to tell the Galla that when they were getting old they should slough off their skins and in this way rejuvenate themselves again. On the way to deliver this advice, however, Holawaka came across a snake eating a dead animal and unable to resist offered to tell the snake his message in return for a share of the meat. The snake was persuaded when Holawaka altered the message for its benefit, telling it that men would die but that it would rejuvenate through the shedding of its skin.

IMANA

"Almighty"

Also known as: Hategekimana, Hashakimana, Habyarimana

This omniscient creator deity was sacred to the Banyarwanda tribe of Rwanda. He was portrayed with exceedingly long arms and was generally kind to humankind, though he had a tendency to distance himself from them. Originally he coexisted with Death, but eventually decided to hunt him down and do away with Death. Imana instructed everyone to stay in their homes as he began to track Death down. However, an old woman, when begged by Death for protection, allowed him to hide under her skirt. Imana then decreed that Death should stay with humankind after all.

JOK

"Creator"

Also known as: Jok Odudu

This creator deity was paramount to the Ugandan Alur tribe, who believed sacrifices would produce rain. The Alur believed the earth to be filled with invisible spirits and that their ancestors manifested themselves in the form of serpents or large stones and rocks.

JUOK

Also known as: Nyikang

This multi-faceted creator deity was of the Shilluk people in the Upper Nile region. Their mythology viewed the universe as two divine loaves of bread represented by heaven and earth, with the river Nile in between. Juok supplied them with cattle, grain and fish and aided the sick and suffering. His very breath made the air in which they dwelt. The semi-legendary Shilluk king Nyikang is associated with Juok, and was believed to have become his avatar on earth. Through him Juok communicated with his people and upheld the laws that governed society successfully.

Right: Another nail fetish magic figure from the Congo.

• AFRICA •

A-Z
CODEX GODS

KALUMBA

Kalumba was the creator deity of the Luba tribe of Zaire in Central Africa. After Kalumba had created humankind he wished to protect them from death and disease. He therefore ordered the goat and the dog to guard the road down which life and death would come. Kalumba carefully instructed them to only allow life through and to turn back death. Unfortunately the two argued and split up, and while the dog was asleep at night death was able to sneak past. When the goat's turn to watch came the next day, he prevented life from passing with the result that man could not be saved from death.

KATONDA
"Creator"

Aka: Ssewannaku, Lugaba, Namuginga.

This supreme creator deity belonged to the Ganda tribe of East African. Katonda conceived the gods in ancestral and monarchical terms placing himself as the king of heaven and the final judge in all matters human and divine. The Ganda respected their active spirit world, with delicate protocols regarding the dead and their ghost spirits. They believed any mistakes could prove to have costly and even terminal results. As a result the Ganda controled this spirit world through the agencies of balubaale — fifty or so nature spirits who ranged from legendary heroes to personifications of natural phenomena.

KHONVUM

This holy spirit of Pygmy mythology, took no bodily form for he was omnipresent and eternal. Khonvum would sometimes visit earth but on those occasions he assumed the form of an animal, usually a chameleon. After having created the earth and sky he lowered mankind onto it and encouraging his creations by supplying forest, food, flora and fauna. He even revived the sun each night by collecting all the broken or damaged stars that it would take to restore the sun to its full glow.

KHUZWANE
"Creator"

Khuzwane was a remote creator deity of the Luvedu, a southern Bantu tribe in northeastern Transvaal. However, this tribe was as distant from their creator as he was from them. The Luvedu were relatively uninterested in the cosmological explanations behind their existence — the practical aspects of their surroundings and existence was much more important to them. It was their own monarch — always a queen in this matrilineal society — whom they viewed as the lynchpin of their physical and spiritual existence. Nature was equally important to the Luveda, but even the queen was believed to exert control over that.

Right: This magnificent 16th century of bronze metals belonged to the Benin or Dahomey tribe of Nigeria.

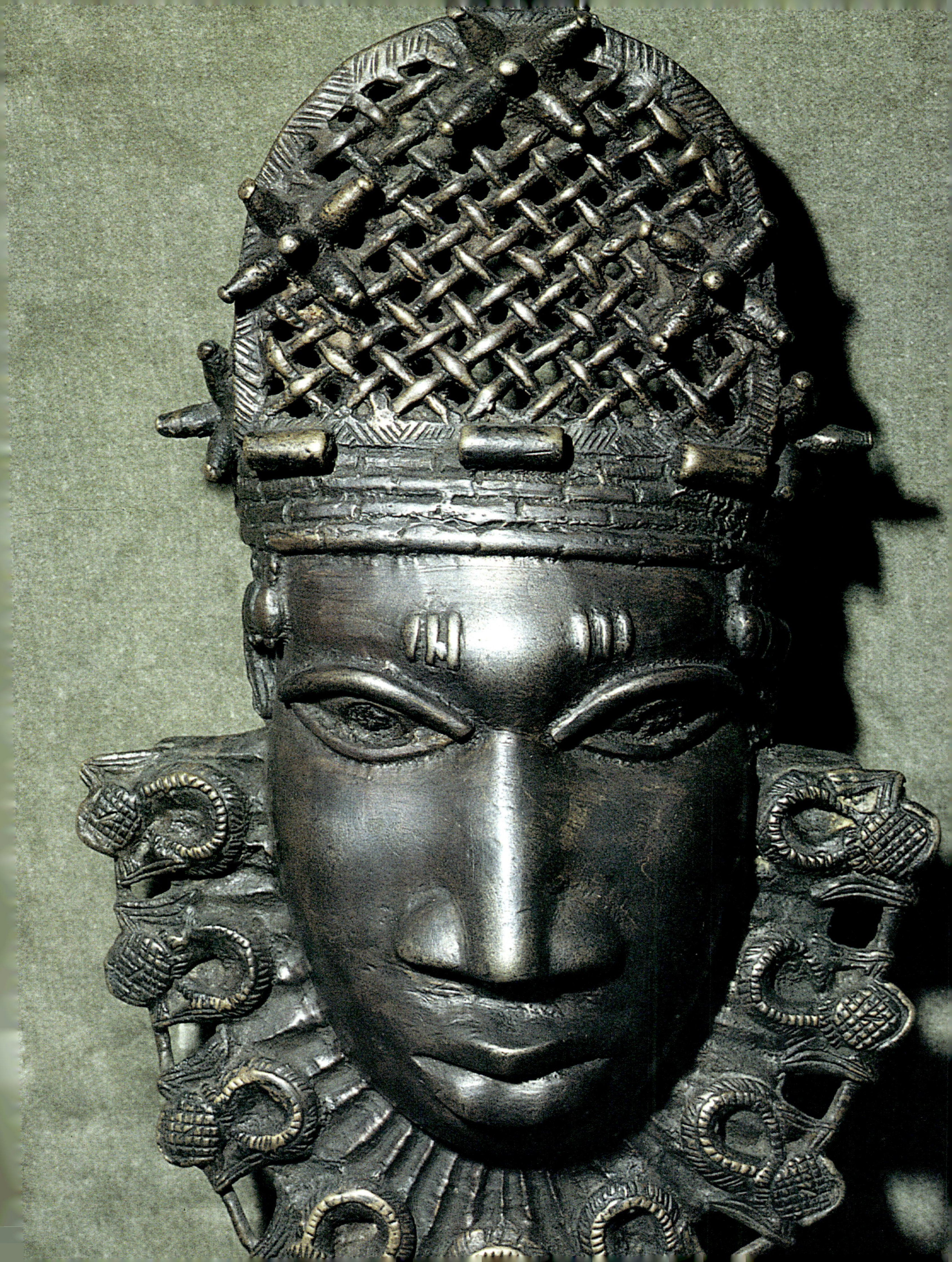

A-Z
CODEX GODS

KINTU

Kintu was a legendary semi-divine Ugandan monarch. He acted as steward to the creator deity Katonda, to whom he reported on the state of the earth below. One day, however, Katonda instructed him not to call again and as he departed he gave Kintu a strange sack with the instructions to guard it well and let no one else see it. For a while Kintu remembered to fulfil his duty, but eventually one night he got very drunk and left the sack behind somewhere. Katonda then revoked Kintu's divine status and this is how suffering and death came to Uganda.

KWOTH

Kwoth is regarded as the creator spirit of the Nuer tribe in the southern Sudan. He lacks any kind of physical form and therefore lives everywhere but nowhere, occurring in all natural phenomena. Kwoth's intrinsic life spirit is the root and fuel of all existence and he is viewed as essentially kind, especially to the needy and unfortunate.

LEGBA

This malevolent trickster hero of the Dahomey peoples is connected to the thunder god Heviosso, with whom he shares certain sacrifices and rituals. As Legba is considered evil and associated with death, it would seem to indicate he is a fallen older deity of some importance. Legba can appear outside a person's home in Indian lingam mode — a clay phallus looking something like a modern concrete road barrier, but with a thatched roof to protect it, which is propitiated daily.

LE-EYO

Le-Eyo is the supreme ancestor of the Masai, and responsible for the introduction of death into humankind. In a case of muddled spells Le-Eyo confused the correct formula — one which bid man to pass away and come back while the moon died — with its reverse. Once spoken this formula was activated and could not be removed, thus death arrived to claim man and the moon returned to glow again.

LEZA

Leza was the most important god of the Kaonde tribe of southern Africa, who manifested life's inherent ambiguity when he chose a honeybird as a courier to deliver three sealed packages to humankind. Two of these parcels contained seeds to grow food, but the third was to remain sealed and only opened in Leza's presence. The honeybird, like Pandora, was unable to restrain its curiosity and stopped en route to check the contents which unleashed all the evils of the world from the third parcel, which neither Leza nor the bird were able to recapture.

Right: A 16th century Benin bronze mask.

· AFRICA ·

A-Z
CODEX GODS

LIBANZA
This creator god was sacred to the Upoto tribe of the Congo. Libanza commanded all the people on both the earth and moon to attend to him at his court in Heaven. The moon people obeyed promptly, with the result that the moon died only briefly before being reborn each month. The earth people were much slower and sulkier in their response to the summons, and were consequently punished with death.

MASSIM-BIAMBE
This supreme creator god of the Congo Mundang people gave souls to all things. This meant they did not die with the body but escaped to join a new life as it was reborn. Massim-Biambe had no visible form and communicated with man through priests, holy objects or fetishes.

MAWU-LISA
Mawu-Lisa was the chief god of the Dahomey of West Africa. This god combined both male and female principles and could appear as either sex. Mawu-Lisa gave birth to a set of twins who came down to earth and began to populate it. Two of their offspring, Sagbata and Sogo, became rivals in their desire to rule. When Sagbata, as the eldest, was given precedence over Sogo, his younger brother stopped the rain from reaching the earth in retaliation. Soon people and animals alike were starving and thirsty because nothing would grow. When Mawu-Lisa sent Legba to check on things, the trickster god eventually reconciled the two brothers and Mawu-Lisa gained control of rainfall. The Dahomey, like the Yoruba, had a large pantheon of major and minor deities, culture heroes and tricksters.

MBOMBO
Mbombo was the creator deity of the Bakuba tribe in Zaire. He was known as the white god, who ruled over the earth when there was nothing but a primeval lake surrounded by black night. Apparently Mbombo had terrible stomach cramps and soon after vomited first the sun, the moon, the stars and then later animals and people. The Bakuba lived in a dense moist jungle, where white is the color of death and represented the spirit world. A rival related tribe, the Baluba, have their god Mbongo, who occurs in a similar series of creation myths.

MULUKU
Muluku was the paramount deity of the Macouas of Zambezi. Legend has it he terraformed the planet, then dug two holes in the earth and brought forth a man and a woman. He then furnished this couple with land and tools, giving them the knowledge and skills to maintain themselves. However, once the god had left, these humans threw down their tools, broke everything, ate their food raw and slept wild in the forest. When the god returned to view their

Right: This terracotta depicts an Ibo husband with his wives and children (c. 1880).

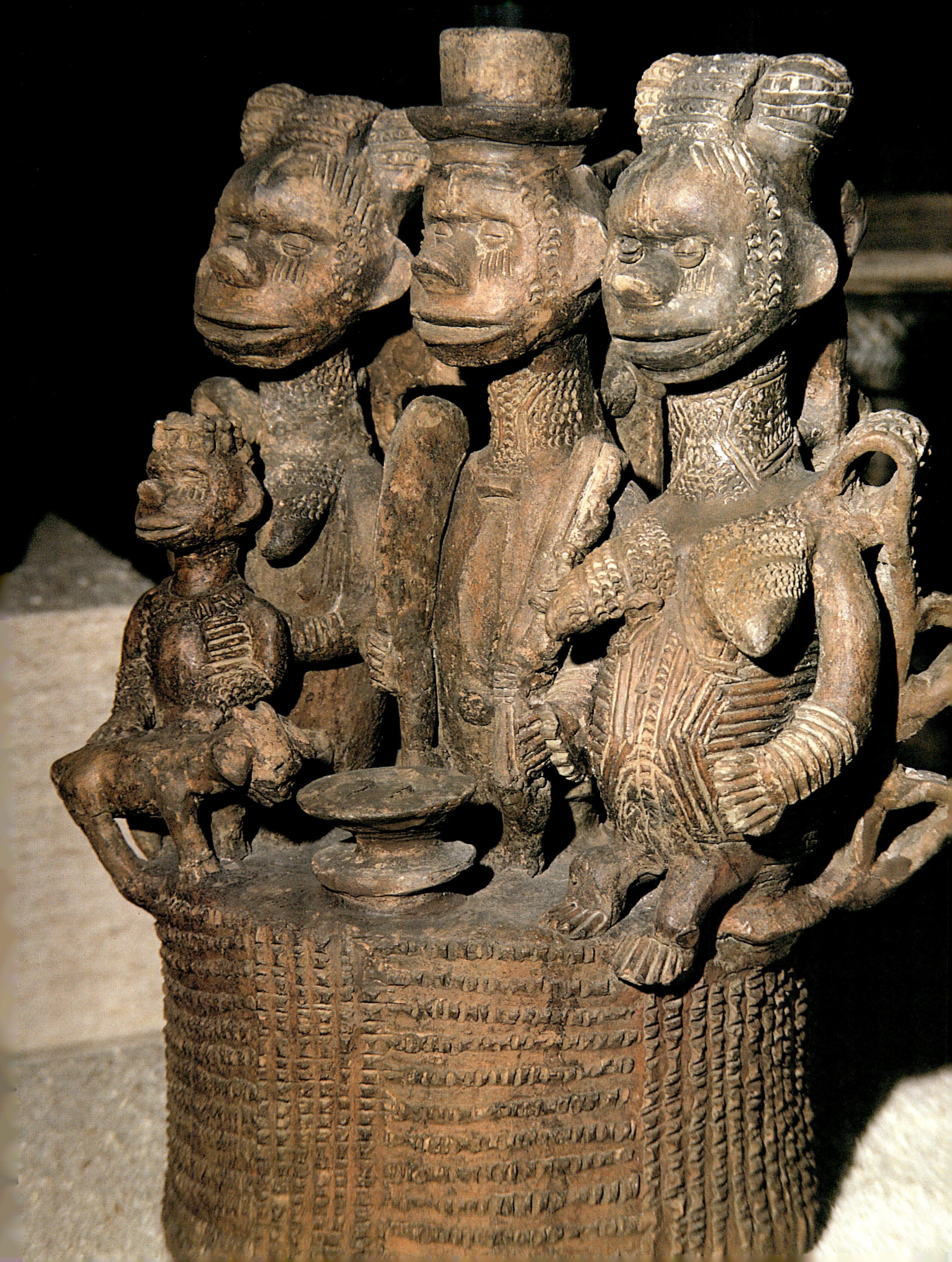

A-Z
CODEX GODS

progress he was initially dismayed and then enraged. Summoning two monkeys he equipped them as he had previously the humans. These clever animals began to do and use everything as Muluku had intended, so he cut off their tails and made them human, turning the original people into the monkeys.

MULUNGU

A remote creator deity of the Tanzanian Nyamwezi tribes, who having made the world remained very much in the background and not immediately accessible to man. In order to contact him they had to use the spirit world intermediaries, for there was no direct link between man and the gods — the spirits themselves, along with demons and monsters are the manifestation of this world beyond the grave. It is the evil spirits that bring forth disease and death.

Another Mulungu is the creator god of the Yao from Malawi, who dwelt contentedly with his animal creations on the earth, prior to the existence of humans. When humanity finally arrived it was in circumstances of great mystery, since Mulungu had not made them. He decided to observe this fresh species to see what should be done, and was aghast when he witnessed their destructive capacity as they set fire to things and killed animals. Mulungu knew it was time to leave and requested that a spider spin him a thread on which he escaped up to heaven.

MWUETSI

This moon god and prototype man was holy to the Makoni tribe of Zimbabwe. Mwuetsi was made by the creator deity Maori, who first of all placed him at the bottom of a lake, but he was discontented and made his bid for freedom in the air. Upon his arrival on dry land he discovered it barren and lonely, but Maori took pity on him and created a partner, Massassi, the morning star maiden. With her and his horn of magical ngona oil, Mwuetsi initiated a productive period which saw the land carpeted in vegetation. Eventually the time came for Massassi the morning star maiden to leave. This made Mwuetsi so distraught that Maori again felt he had to provide him with another wife — the evening star maiden, Morongo. These two then bred and produced animals and children, though when warned of his imminent death and advised to breed no longer, Mwuetsi ignored this advice and continued to sleep with Morongo, as a result of which the less pleasant and dangerous insects and animals came into being — including a snake which Morongo preferred to Mwuetsi. The snake eventually bit him and as he lay dying everything else began to grow ill, so having consulted Maori, his children returned Mwuetsi to the bottom of the sacred lake and took responsibility for the maintenance of all things.

Right: A Benin or Dahomey bronze plaque.

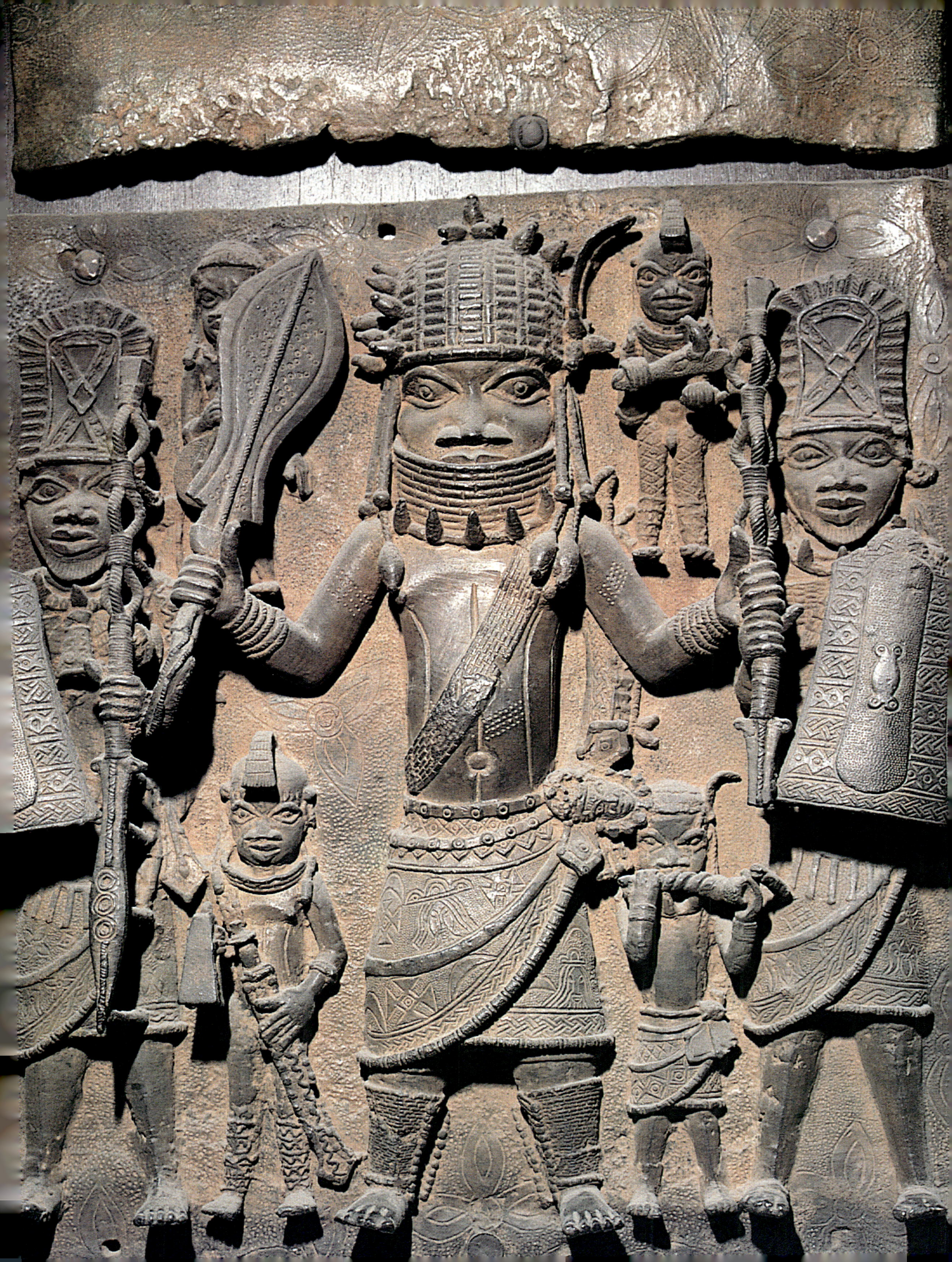

· THE WORLD OF MYTHOLOGY ·

This Benin bronze plaque shows the Oba of Benin in his divine state, his legs appear as mudpuppy fishes, a symbol of Olokun the sea god.

• AFRICA •

A-Z
CODEX GODS

NGAI
This is the supreme sky-god of the Masai of southeastern Africa. In the beginning of time there was only a single man on earth, whose name was Kintu. The daughter of Ngai saw him and fell in love. Kintu passed all the tests set out by Ngai to win his daughter's hand. Ngai only warned the couple never to return to the sky, and so the daughter came to live with him on earth, bringing with her plants and animals as her dowry. But Kintu had forgotten the grain for his chickens and so he returned to heaven, where he met a son of Ngai's — Death, who followed him home and lay in wait before he killed the couple's children. This illustrates a common African belief that the path between heaven and earth was destroyed by human error.

NGEWO-WA
Ngewo-wa was the supreme creator god of the Mende tribe of Sierra Leone. He created everything, including humankind, who at first called him Maanda (grandfather). These humans, however, were very demanding and constantly approached their god for things they needed before growing disatisfied after a short time. Finally Ngewo-Wa became disenchanted with his creations who needed to be more self-sufficient, and so he escaped to the sky. There his people could still see and worship him, but were unable to pester him directly. Humans were then forced to communicate through spirit world links. Alas, this spirit world was peopled with a variety of *dyinyinga*, some well disposed towards humans and others not. Through a mixture of boldness and reverence men could sometimes outwit these spirits to get what they required.

NJAMBI
This creator deity of the Lele tribe is believed to have made man, the arid Savannah and the vital forest/jungle — in other words all the resources that the Lele required. Njambi is wise and all seeing, the divine arbiter, protector and instructor of mankind. While the spirit world is the invisible matrix that binds the earthly and the heavenly planes, capable of influencing reality through propitiation and protocol.

NYAMBE
Nyambe was the chief deity of the Koko tribe of Nigeria, who, as with many African gods, was initially content to dwell among his creations, but grew tired of the endless bickerings in his midst. He gave humankind access to a magic tree which rejuvenated anyone who stayed for a set time beneath it, but when as time went on humans became too complacent about both it and him, he then uprooted the tree and left. Without their god and his magic tree, people could no longer cheat death and became mortal. Later Nyambe calmed down, he became more beneficent once he was more farther away.

A-Z
CODEX GODS

NYANKOPON
This was the supreme sky god of the Ashanti people of Ghana. Nyankopon initially got on well with humankind and lived in close proximity to them — a little too close. Apparently an old woman preparing yams kept hitting the mighty god with her pole. This eventually drove him away to seek somewhere more peaceful in the sky. As a result people tried to build a ladder up to him but this failed and led to many deaths. Nyankopon still cared for humankind however, and sent them a message that they would join him in the sky after death. The Ashanti pantheon is large and varied, containing many major and minor deities.

NYOKON
Nyokon is the supreme creator deity of the Nyokon of Cameroon in Central Africa. His firstborn was the spider and diviner Nyiko, who became his own mother's lover. Naturally he was expelled from heaven by his irate father but kept his divine powers and became a hero to the Nyokon tribes. This pattern of sons being expeled from heaven only to become a tribal hero is prevalent in African mythology.

NZAMBI
Also known as: Nzame
Nzambi was a creator god of the Bantu tribes of the Congo, who could also occur in female form, with various names. He created the first man, Fam, intending to place him above all else; but Fam became arrogant, misused the earth and damaged it severely, so Nzambi buried him in a hole and created a second man, Sekume — the ancestor of humankind. Sekume fashioned himself a wife called Mbongwe from a tree. But Fam had not died, and was still around to cause trouble for other human beings.

Nzambi then fell in love with a girl called Mboya with whom he had a son called Bingo. The parents competed for the child's affection and began to argue incessantly and in a rage Nzambi finally threw his son from heaven. He was found and raised by an old wizard called Otoyom. Nzambi and Mboya struggled to find Bingo but Otoyom used his magic to keep the boy concealed. When Bingo reached adulthood he became a teacher to all humankind.

OBASSI OSAW
This was the main deity of the Hausa tribes of the Niger. Obassi Osaw helped humankind by providing for all their wants — everything that is except the secret of fire, which remained exclusive to heaven. When he was asked to provide this too he became angry and refused the request, even from the king. A small boy was then sent and he too returned empty-handed. This boy was determined to succeed though, and so he returned to heaven. He ran small errands for Obasso Osaw, making himself indispensable to the god, until he was trusted completely. He

A-Z
CODEX GODS

then one night stole some embers and when all heaven was at rest, escaped back to earth triumphantly with the secret. When Obassi Osaw realized what had taken place he was furious and cursed the boy but the secret of fire remained with man on earth.

OGUN

Odun was the metal and war deity of the West African Yoruba and Ngao tribes. His origin was probably as a hunting deity for the smith god. Ogun was also the patron of hunters, barbers, and all those who used metal tools and weapons. He was also the god of justice with oaths sworn on his sacred metal of iron. Ogun was severe but fair and essentially dignified. As long as one observed protocol and acted honorably he was willing to help one achieve their goals.

OLORUN

The Nigerian Yoruba people, revered Olurun as their supreme god. Olurun joined with Olokun of the sea and from this union came two sons: Obtala the elder, and Odudua, the younger. Obtala was sent by his father to create the earth but failed on his mission because he got drunk and fell asleep. As a result Olorun sent Odudua, and he proved more successful. Another creation myth depicted Obtala and Odudua as male and female respectively. The Yoruban pantheon, consists of sixteen major deities, including Dada, Schango, Ogun, Ochossi and Shankpannan.

ONYANKOPON
"Great One"

Onyankopon was the supreme creator sky deity of the Ashanti people. Onyankopon was the source of all existence and those he created naturally ranked below. The order went along the lines of gods, spirits, lesser nature spirits, ancestors, man and animals. At first he actively aided and lived in close proximity to his creations, but in the familiar African theme of separation from the deity, man's continual noise and activity made him weary, and so he left for the more peaceful stratosphere. His departure had various repercussions, the main one being the introduction of death. His people then endeavored to build their way to heaven so they could reclaim their god but as they were tempting fate: the edifice collapsed and disaster followed. Although Onyankopon remained distant from humankind, he was accessible and not malevolent.

PEMBA

This creator deity was sacred to the Bambara tribes of the River Niger area. Though the Bambara believed the world to be in a continual state of evolution, they attributed various aspects of this continuous manifestation to Pemba. He was primarily a forest and vegetation god who also made and mated with the first woman. At first his offspring and wife worshiped him but later they became disenchanted and left.

Right: Another Benin bronze plaque showing the Oba of Benin and his warriors.

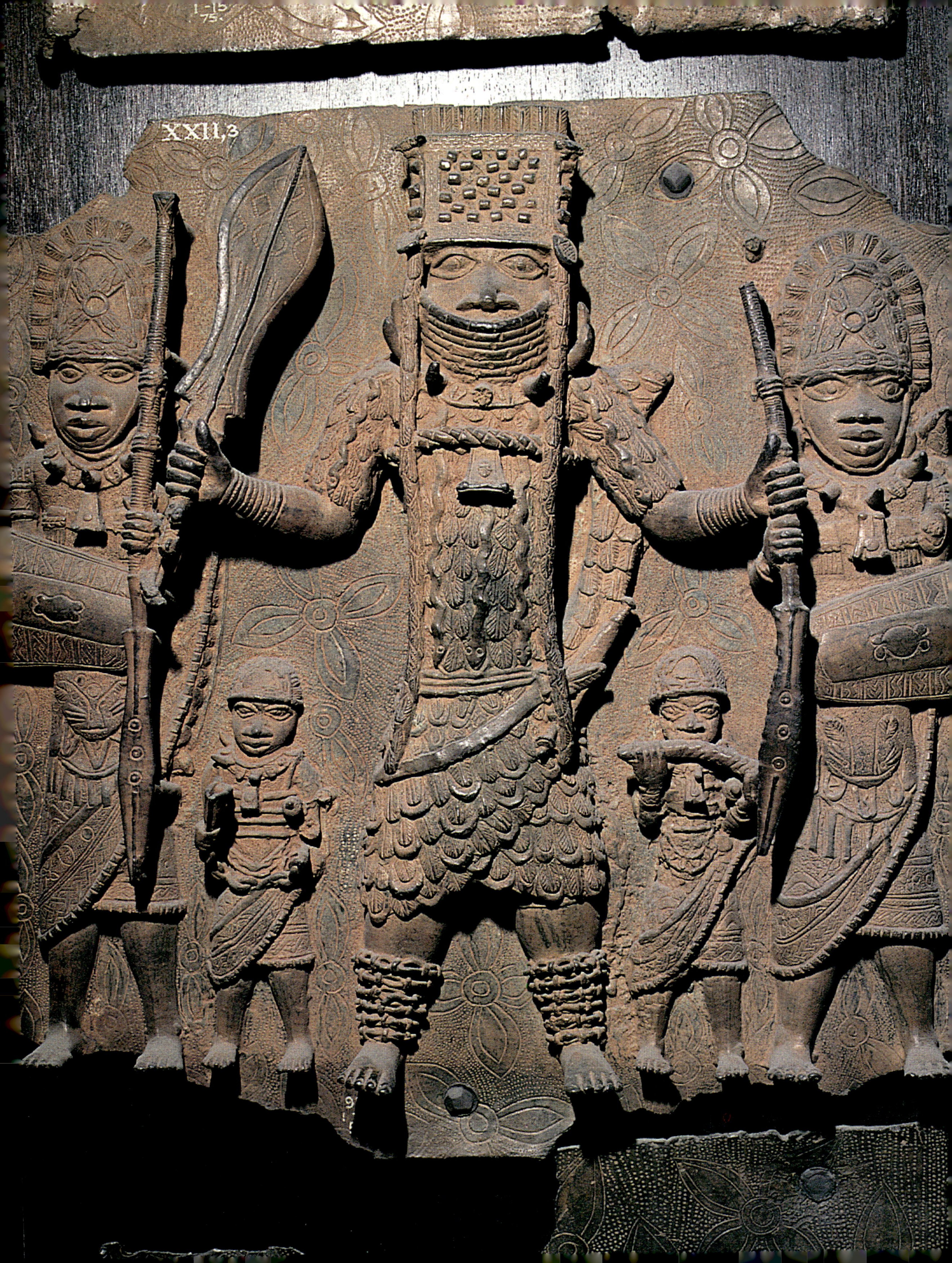
XXII,3

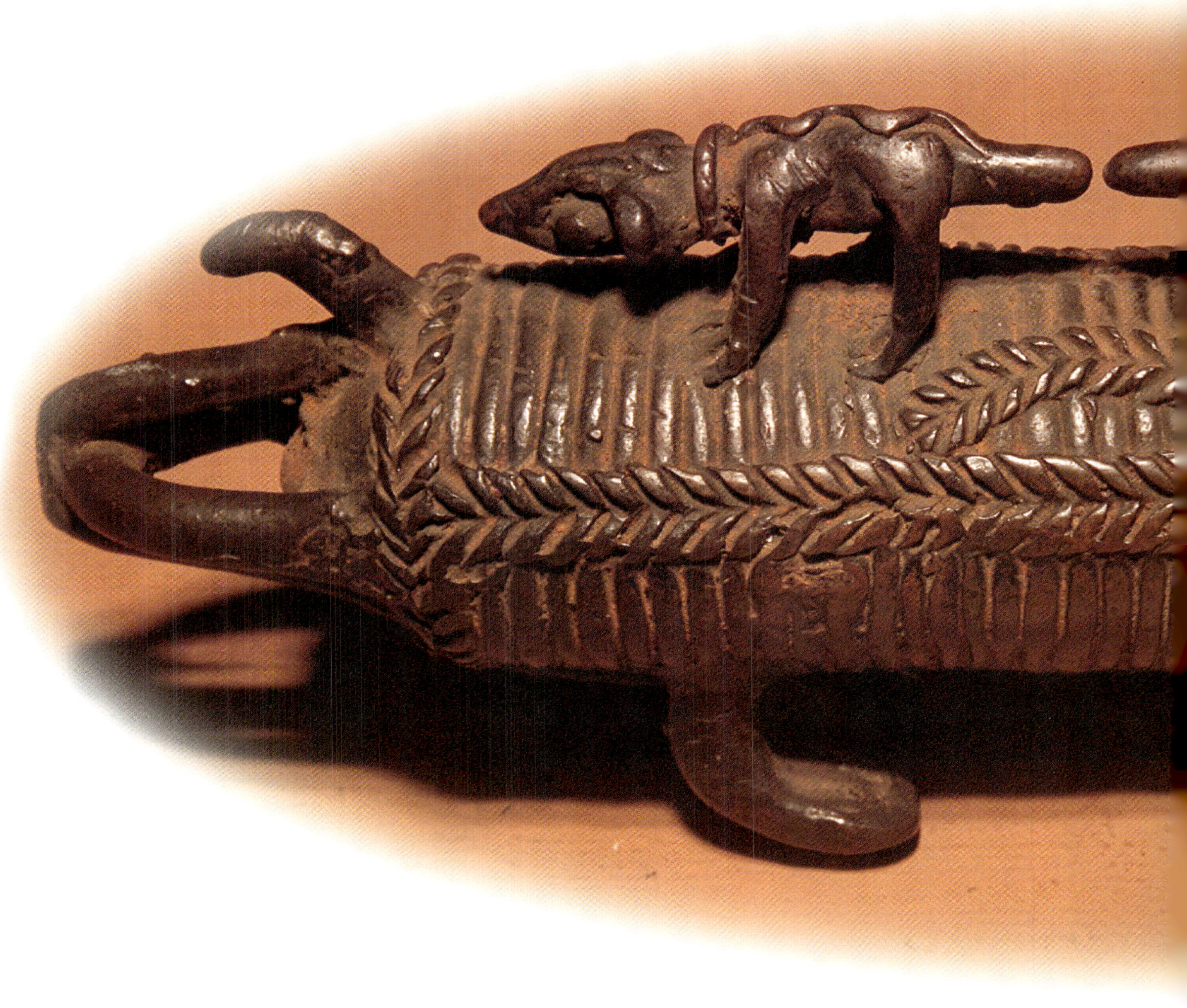

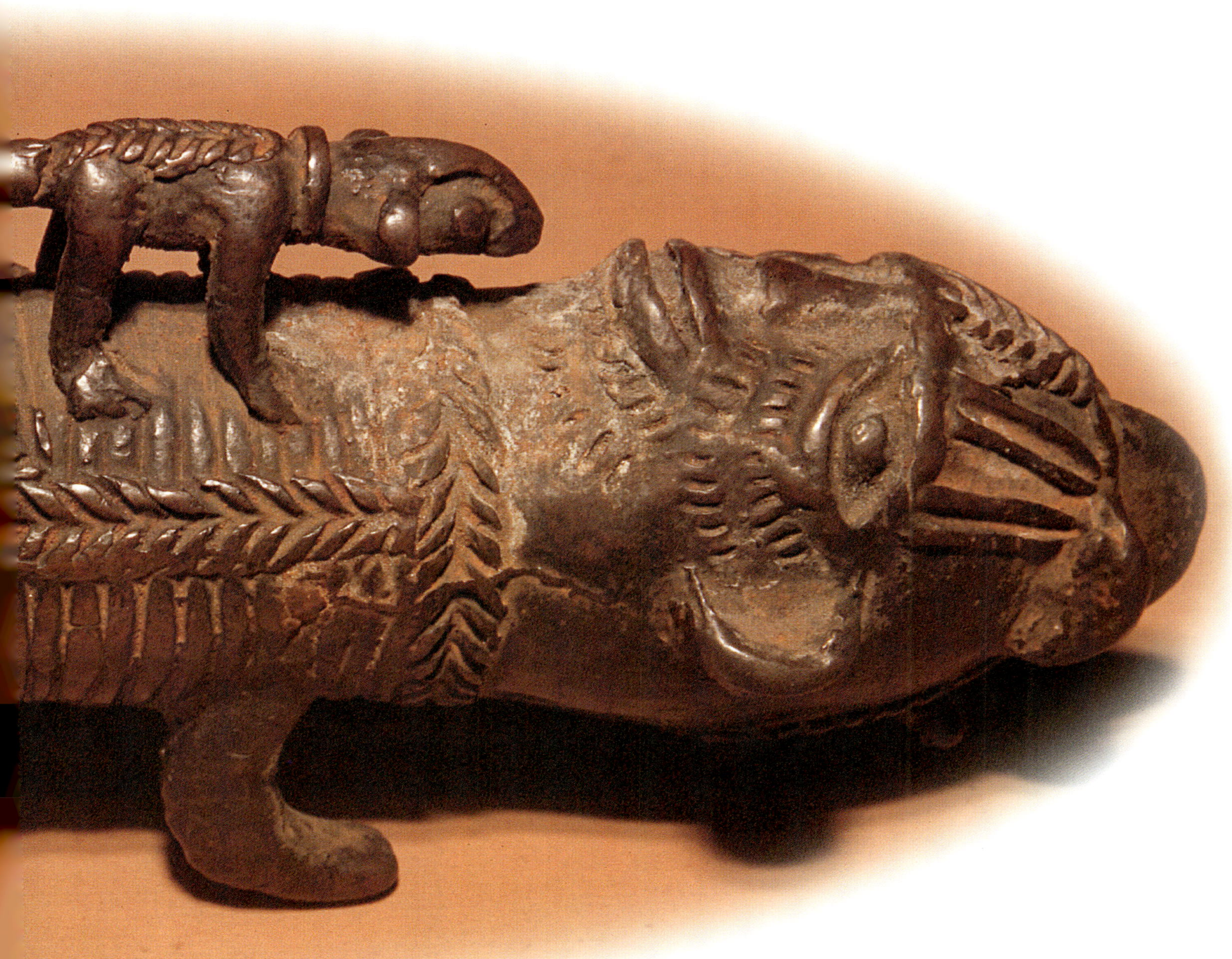

A-Z
CODEX GODS

Pemba had a brother too, the water deity Faro, who became jealous and supplanted his brother, eventually becoming the dominant partner.

RUGABA

Rugaba was the omnipotent creator god of the Ugandan Ankore tribe. As a sky god who also manifested as the sun, he controlled all the processes required of life. Though intrinsically benevolent his displeasure could kill. The Ankorean spirit world was divided into two opposing groups, the *emandwa*, protective guardians, and the *eminzu* — ancestral spirits who could be very aggressive and vindictive. Both Rugaba and man operated through these third parties, the protocols involved providing for a regulation of both divine and everyday human life.

RUHANGA

The Ugandan Banyoro people revered Ruhanga as a creator and fertility god. He had control over life and death and provided the Banyoro with food, health and children but also sickness and death. This negative aspect arose through another garbled message scenario — that popular theme in African mythology. At first all man had to do was enjoy his life and it would continue forever, but an old woman was responsible for a drastic change after she refused to be happy following the death of her dog. When Ruhanga came to know of her stubborn sadness he angrily decided that if life could not be appreciated, then for man it would have an end.

RUWA

Ruwa was the most holy deity of the Djaga tribe of Kilimanjaro. He brought the art of cultivation and civilization to humankind. In a Garden of Eden/loss of innocence scenario he had only one special yam tree from which man was forbidden. One day when he was absent a stranger came and convinced everyone that he had permission to eat the yams from the tree. When Ruwa discovered the betrayal he inflicted death and suffering upon man as punishment.

SOKO

This creator deity to the northern Nigerian Nupe had instructed people since the beginning of time. Soko taught people ritual and skills in a range of arts, by communicating through his special medium of magic. In this case it was the dead who acted as intermediaries between the living and the divine, though to make things more unpredictable these spirits could mischievously trick and dominate a man if he was not on his guard.

TILO

Tilo was the sky creator god to the Tongan tribes of Malawi and Zambia. In contrast to many African creator gods who tired of their creations and become much more distant, Tilo was actively

A-Z
CODEX GODS

involved in the world of his people. This god tried to help his creations as much as possible. Tilo managed to be both positive and negative — he was the maker of all life but balanced this with death, his approval guaranteed success but his anger yielded despair and disaster. This combination of the personal and the dispassionate made him a father figure of great depth who ultimately cherished his creations.

UMVELINQANGI AND UHLANGA

These male and female creator gods originated among the Zulu of Natal. They featured in a creation myth similar to that of ancient Greece. The sky (male) and earth (female) bonded and married to produce all things and people from their union. The first ancestor of the Zulu was Unkulunkulu, a child of the union between Umvelinqangi and Uhlanga and later a creator deity in his own right.

UNKULUNKULU
"Ancient One"

This Zulu and Xhosa god of created humankind in his image and was the bearer of civilization. Although mainly kind he did cause a few problems — death for instance. Unkulunkulu ordered the chameleon to go and inform mankind that they would be immortal but the creature dawdled. Angrily Unkulunkulu sent the lizard with the opposite message: that men would be mortal. By the time the chameleon arrived the lizard had already delivered his message, with death for man as the consequence. Unkulunkulu then balanced man's mortality with the introduction of civilization, with health treatment and fertility rites including marriage, so that man would prosper and his children succeed him, thus giving him a compensatory collective immortality.

WELE
"The One on High"
Also known as: Khakhaba, Isaywa

The Bantu Abaluyia tribe of Kenya looked upon Wele as the most paramount creator deity. Wele first made heaven, supported on columns above the primeval soup that would become the earth. He then created two brothers, the sun and the moon, who were to aid him in the next few stages of creation. These brothers, however, were jealous of each other and their competition spilled over into combat until forcibly separated by an irate Wele and assigned to their specific positions. The supreme deity then continued his task alone creating the earth and its climate he went on to make Mwambu and Sela — the first man and woman — the animals and anything else he had left out in a mere six days. Though mainly beneficent and compassionate Wele's temper meant did throw in the odd negative thing. However, most bad things were usually attributed to the meanness and duplicity of

A-Z
CODEX GODS

humans and various animals. The Abaluyia also have a version of the chameleon tale who brought death to humankind.

WERE
"Father"
Also known as: Wuonwa, Wuonji, Wuonkwere, Wuonoru

As supreme creator god of the Kenyan Luo tribe Were figured actively in the tribe's day-to-day life. The Luo revered him daily with songs and charms as well as sacrifices and prayers at shrines — everything was observed and declared to him in a culture firmly integrated within this divinity's scheme of things. Were controls the weather and he used a thunderbolt on wrongdoers but like an aged grandfather he had almost everyone's best interests at heart.

WULBARI

Wulbar was the main god of the West African Krachi tribe. Once again this African creator tired of living close to the people he created as they constantly pestered him with various demands. As with the deity Nyankopon where one old woman in particular was the final straw Wulbar was annoyed with the smoke that emanated from cooking fires — it made his eyes water. He eventually left and founded a court consisting only of animals, including the spider/trickster Anansi.

WUNI

Wuni was the supreme creator deity of the Dagamba tribe of Ghana. This story based on the theme of garbled messages was a bit different. This time it was the humans that sent a courier dog to Wuni. The humans begged to be relieved of their unending toil — unfortuneately they ended up with death instead of freedom because the dog got sidetracked by food and the goat who had overheard the original instructions even delivered the message incorrectly.

ZANAHARY

Zanahary was the prime creator god of the Madagascan pantheon, possessing a multiple bisexual avatar capability that had parallels with major Indian divinities. However, while Brahma, Vishnu and Shiva were all complementary aspects of the one Brahman, Zanahary manifested a more combative and contradictory exchange between the elements of existence. Thus the Zanahary earth manifestation (sometimes called Ratovoantany) goes his own way and conflicts with the sky variant Zanahary. After a bitter dispute a compromise was eventually reached: the sky Zanahary gave the earth Zanahary creations (mankind, animals etc) with life force, qualifying it with mortality and a conditional return of original components to each version of the god. Another version of this myth explains the reason for all these maneuvers as the Sky Zanahary's desire for a human wife.

Right: An unusual shaped plaque showing the Oba of Benin in a divine state.

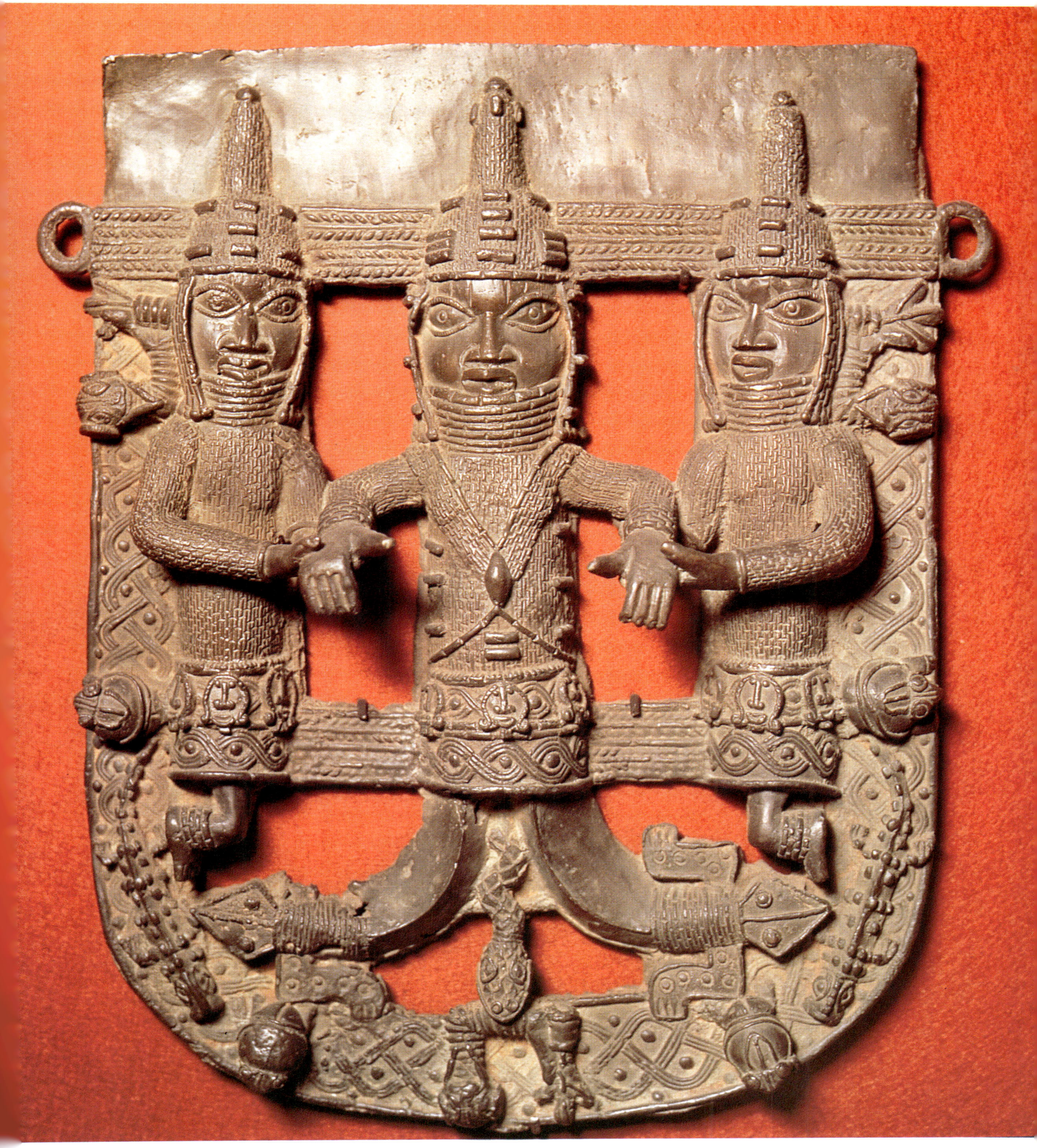

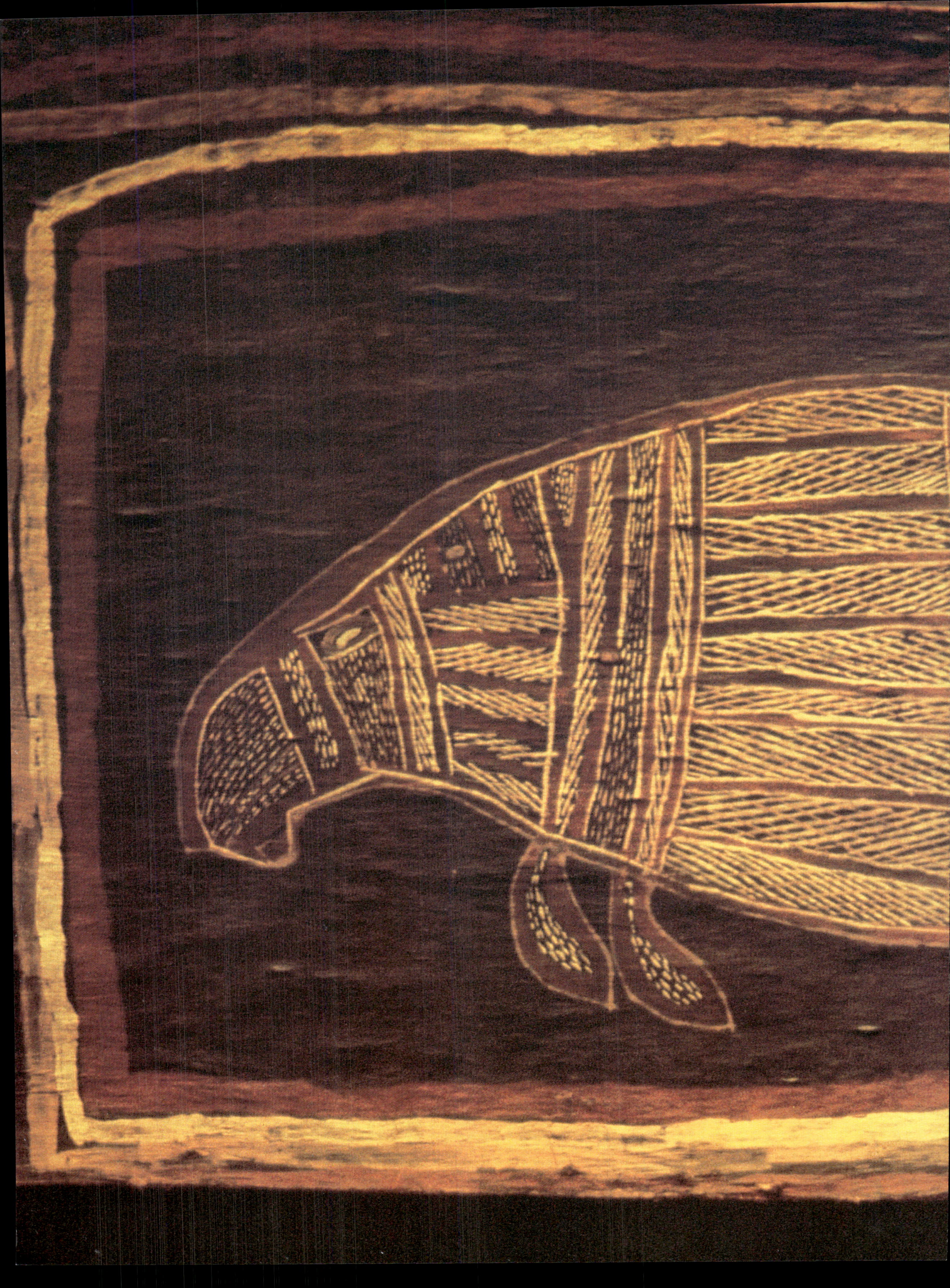

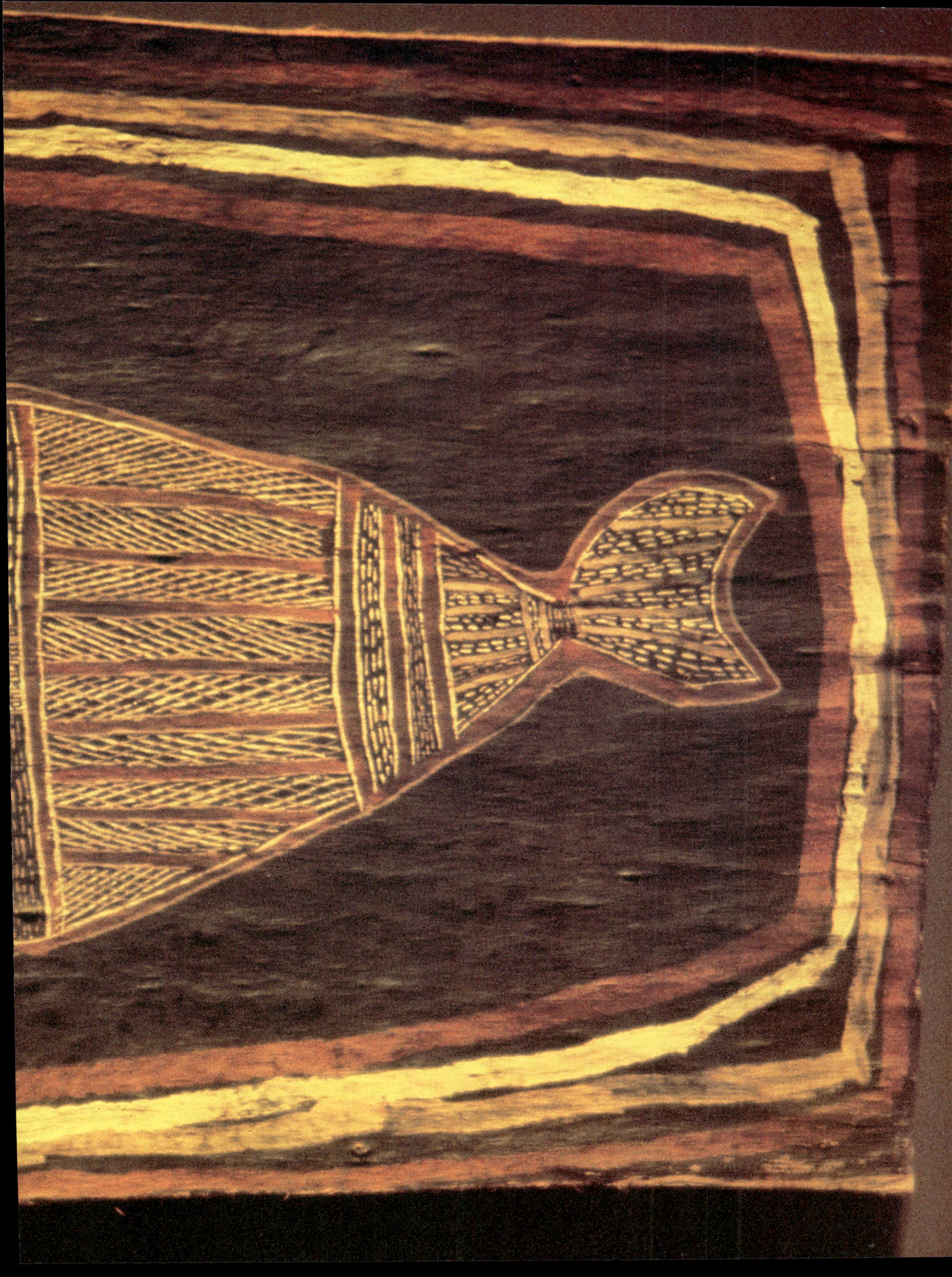

OCEANIA

OCEANIA, an area defined by the Pacific Ocean and one of the last areas of the world to be discovered and opened up, holds a strong fascination for Europeans, who see in its unspoiled ancient cultures a trace back to ancient, unrecorded societies, and the ways in which our ancestors might have lived. Thus many experts in the fields of anthropology and ethnography, as well as artists, painters and photographers, have swarmed over the islands and recorded the people in an attempt to get a fix on these cultures before they fade into oblivion under the relentless pressure of modern "civilization." Nevertheless, only a few parts of New Guinea and some remote Indonesian islands have managed to preserve any of their original culture. Otherwise the whole Oceanic area has been severely disrupted since the time of Magellan in the 16th century. European have since taken land, goods and labor, bringing in exchange European religions and diseases. Consequently, knowledge of many specific cultures has vanished forever after a policy of virtual extermination was carried out by the early colonists. Some native artifacts dug up or discovered have been preserved by benign administrators, who studied the native languages and preserved beliefs and customs in print.

The impact of missionaries cannot be underestimated. Trampling original religions under their proselytizing feet, only rare exceptions among their black dressed legions possessed the sensitivity and foresight to record what was dying before their very eyes.

When the Oceanics themselves learned to write they began to set down what they could before it vanished forever. At the beginning of this century various versions of myths and cultural lore were recorded, and museums have now been made in which to house cultural objects and artifacts.

Previous pages: Australian bark painting of a Dugong — sea cow — from Arnheimland.
Right: This Maori wood carving was taken from a plank lining a tribal meeting house in New Zealand (c. 1851).

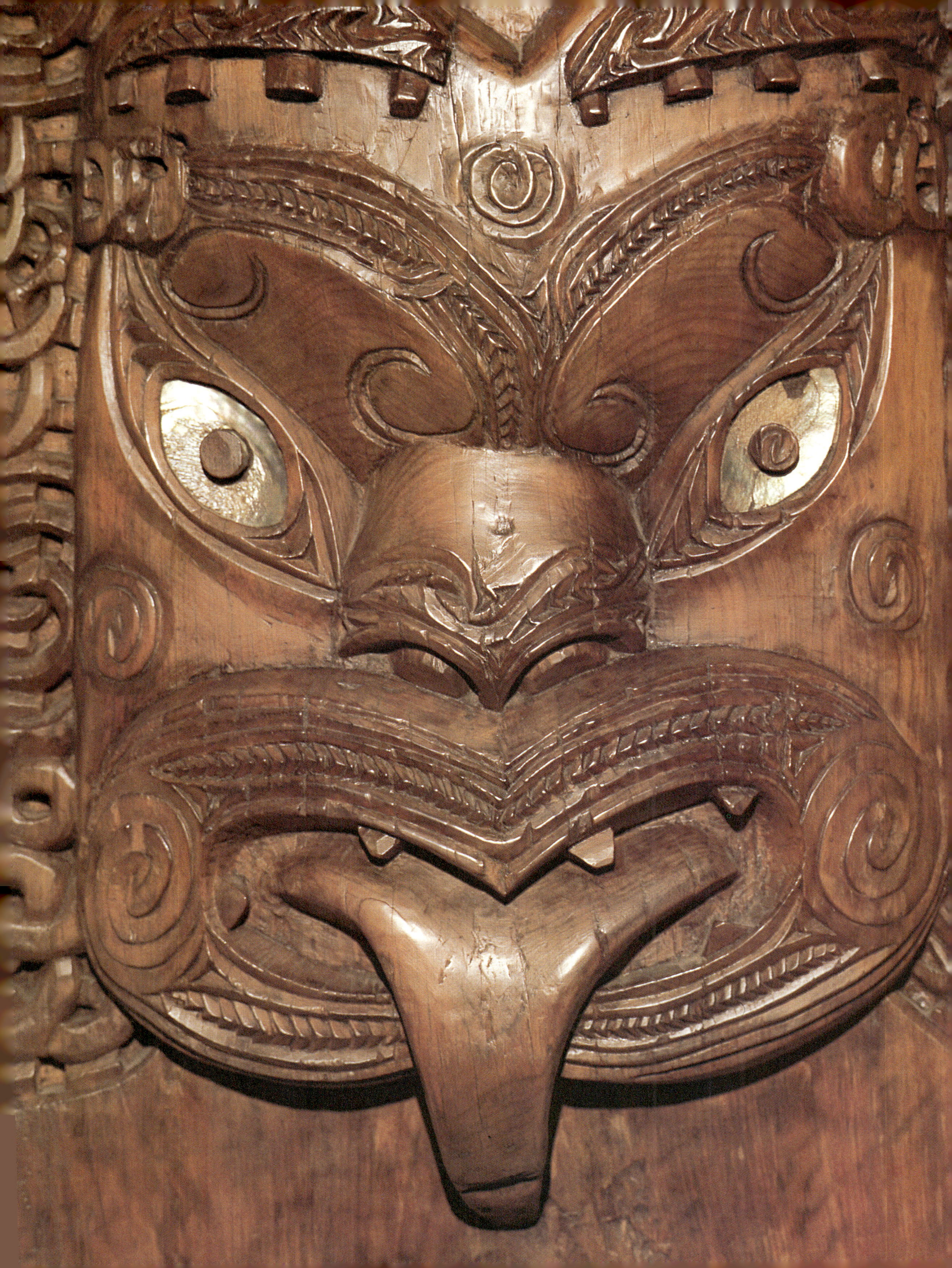

The origins and dispersals of the Oceanic population remain a controversial subject. South America and South East Asia are the current rival candidates for host countries from which the original ancestors set out. Now the population mix has undergone a thorough modernization, containing as it does almost every race of man in existence.

In the Oceanic region the absence of myths concerning the origin of life are not indicative of ignorance but rather of acceptance and a deliberate refusal to give an explanation — because the thing in question has always existed, and never had a beginning. Thus with the world already pre-existent, the more relevant laws of equilibrium and the development of spiritual power could be attended to, though in some cases an attempt was made to account for the existence of the planet. This could take one of two forms: creationist (the work of a creator god or goddess) or emergent (a spontaneous emergence out of the great void, in which the potential of everything else resides).

The sea also was so basic and essential it again was usually interpreted as having always existed — though it might have evolved from primordial beginnings into the more sophisticated, current version. A perusal of the major myths reveals that the question of origin is examined in a way analogous to various disciplines of contemporary science, for both use the one item that has remained the same: man's perception governed by his senses as they receive data from the enviroment. That they connect across millennia is really not so surprising at all.

Aboriginal myths center on the mythical travels of legendary nomadic characters, enjoying a creative role as they roamed, naming places, creating animals and humans as well as features of the landscape and establishing customs and

Above left and Right: This beautifully carved and painted head was used in ceremonies in Melanasia.

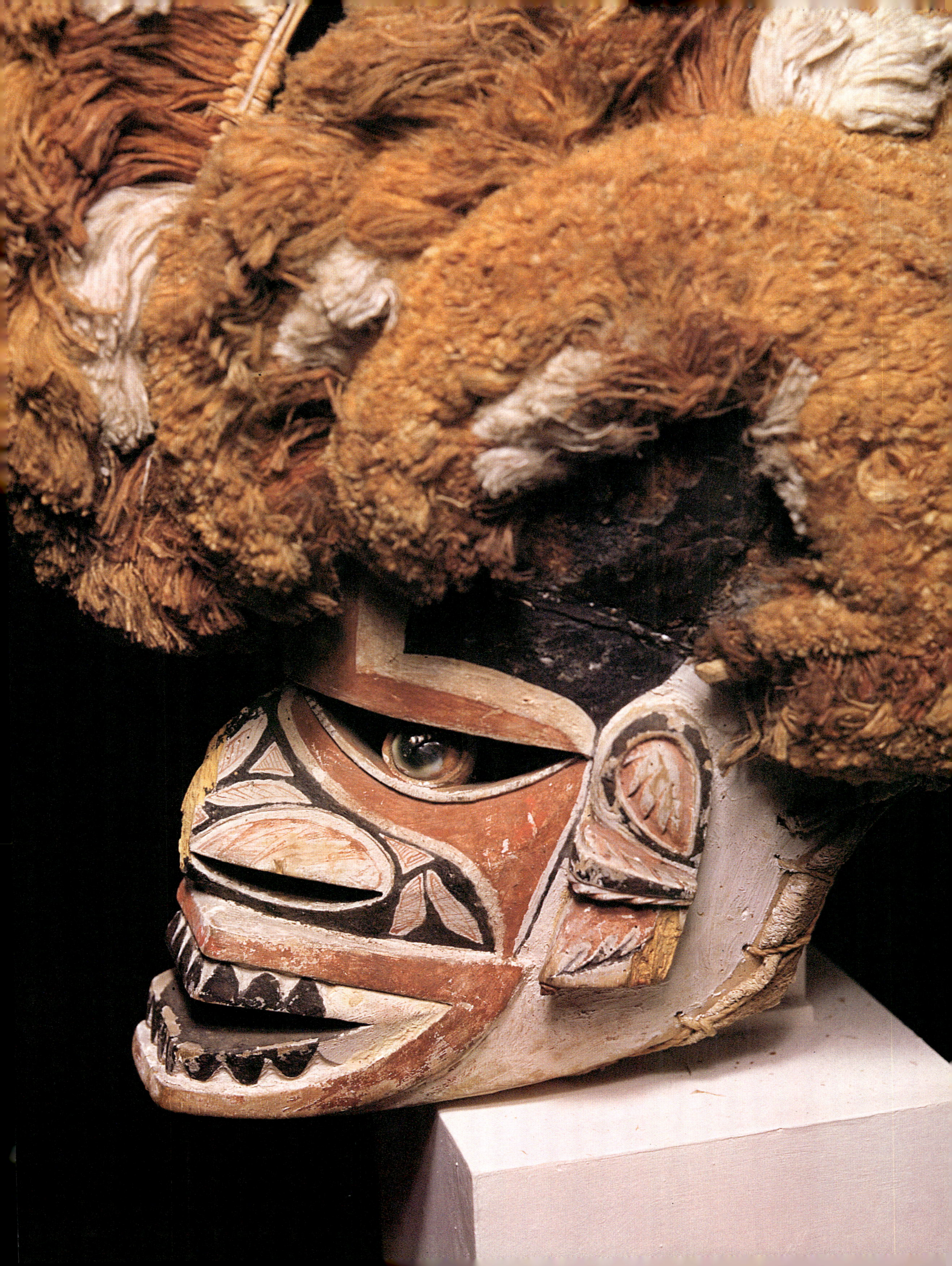

rituals. These myths focus outward, complementing the focus on outside features and sites of local identity. Regional variation merely reorders the sequencing, but the main myths by and large retain their form.

POLYNESIA

Polynesia is the easternmost cultural area of the Oceanic region, which forms a triangle from New Zealand to Hawaii and Easter island, and contains the island clusters of Tonga, Samoa, Tahiti and Tuamotu. This region also contains the largest population centers, with a rich fund of cosmological myths, including that of the strangers who come from the sea to conquer — thereby explaining the social divisions within societies. There have been several migration invasions launched into this massive area, but the main one was carried out by Polynesians from South East Asia by way of Micronesia over 2,000 years ago. They brought with them an already established culture, which gives the widely scattered islands an understandable mythological homogeneity, despite local variation. The best known Polynesian god/culture hero is the trickster Maui, who is common to all the island cultures of this widely spread group, all of whom have their legends and histories of migration. In a discernible format Maui leapfrogged the islands individually.

The New Zealand Maori, among the Earth's supreme mythical cosmologists, explain the progression from the one into many as the result of a conflict between the sky god Rangi and his offspring. In a similarity to the Greek god Ouranos, Rangi keeps his children squashed between himself and his wife, the two parents locked in an endless sexual embrace. Perhaps like Ouranos he was afraid that his children would eventually surpass him. Though not emasculated like his

Above left and Right: Stone figure of Hoa Haka Nana (Breaking Wave), the first ancestor of the Easter Islanders.

· OCEANIA ·

Greek counterpart, he is eventually forced to separate from Papa by his own progeny so that they can in turn free themselves from parental constrictions and begin the new cycle of existence that was intimated by their inception. Through rivalry and the subsequent warfare between the siblings various features of the world are then formed.

In Hawaii the composite sky deity Kane is credited with the creation of man, whom he later punished for the biblically similar transgression of sacred apple consumption, before withdrawing in high dudgeon, disgusted with his creations.

Polynesian heroes journeyed to the heavens, sun and the underworld to determine the question of mortality or to fulfil the quest for fire.

One thing almost all Oceanic island cultures shared was a reputation for cannibalism. Though now extinct, this practice was at one time a prevailing health hazard for European sailors and adventurers, who in turn engendered their own myths.

MELANESIA

This central cultural area consists of the world's second largest island — Papua/New Guinea, and a ring of volcanic archipelagos, including the Admiralty, Banks, Solomon, New Britain, New Hebrides and New Caledonia Islands, with the Fiji islands the most distant of the group. In stark contrast to Polynesia the mythology of this area has a great variety and individuality, perhaps as a result of there being no definitive supreme deity and that the inhabitants have a wider racial base. In fact, gods have no exalted status or purpose in Melanesian mythology, instead the emphasis is on an all-embracing supernatural energy known as Mana, which holds an vast spiritual importance. The myths tell of culture heroes who go on journeys to bring back customs which deal with

Above left and Right: Wooden figure of a man, from New Ireland.

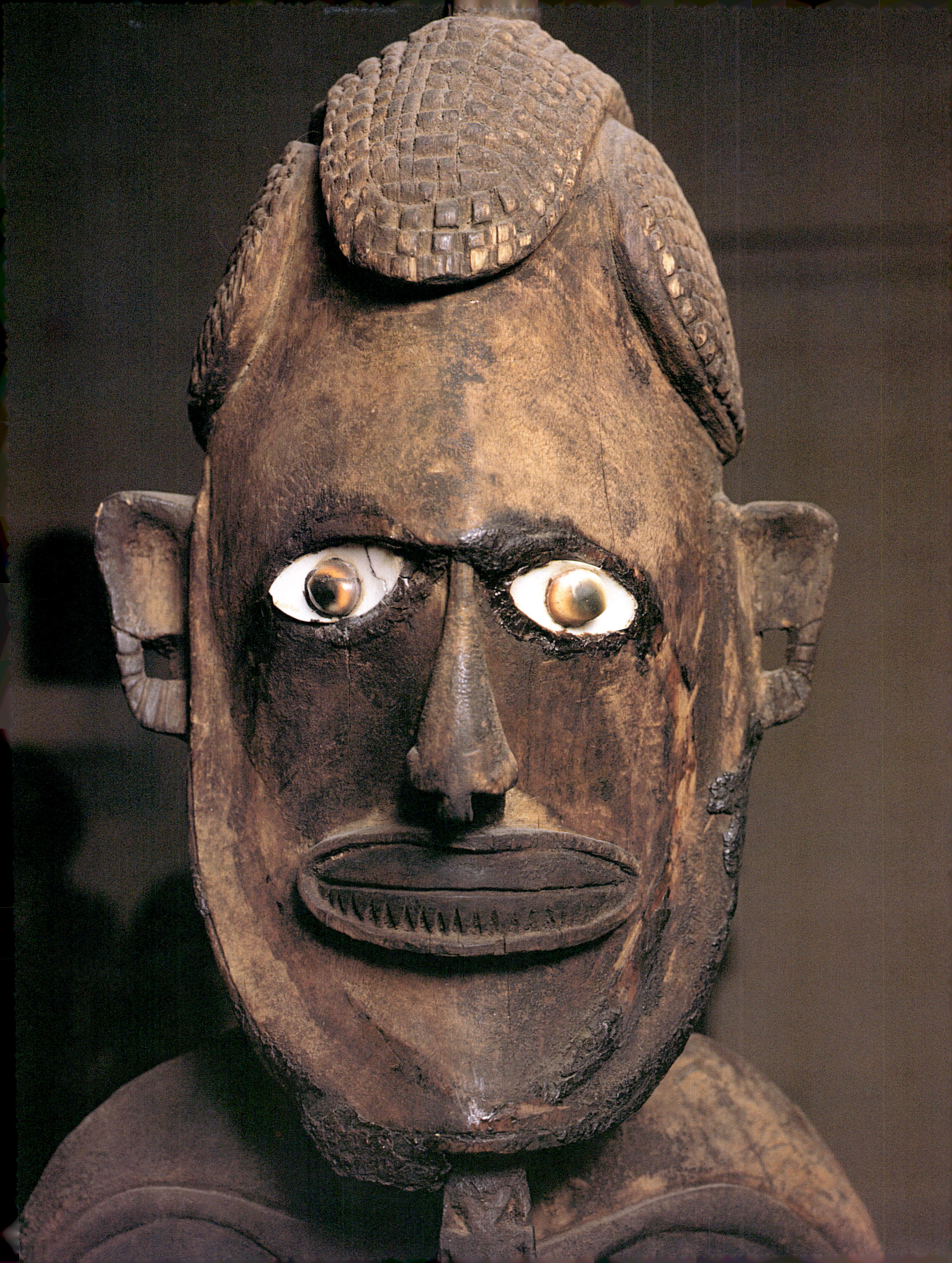

issues such as mortality, sex, mourning and warfare. Several important themes however do recur — one vital one being that the actions and kudos of culture heroes remain alive and effective among their living descendants so long as they maintain the correct protocols. Secret cosmologies do exist among some coastal peoples, but inland these are reinterpreted as examples of moral and cosmic dilemmas and expressed in allegory and metaphor.

The Melanesians accept the existence of a pre-formed world and concern themselves almost exclusively with the gain and the manipulation of Mana. This vital intrinsic energy has immense power and whoever can control it has the ability to achieve his desires. Almost like Chi or Ki, which is the East Asian variant, this unifying power source links and imbues all things.

Another Melanesian preoccupation is with good and evil and other contradictory concepts which are often explained and illustrated by using brothers and their sibling struggles of rivalry. This has more subtle undertones that go some way to explaining that evil or mishap arise as much from stupidity and human error as from a hostile environment. Men must strive for balance and maintain the natural equilibrium. On Papua however the emphasis is on fertility rather than balance. The Stone Age tribespeople of the island have maintained a way of life there that stretches back through inconceivable amounts of time as a result of their isolation — which is now no longer an option.

MICRONESIA

Micronesia is the northernmost area of the four, consisting of four main archipelagos — the Marshall, Mariana, Gilbert and Caroline Islands. Though for a long time isolated by distance

Above left and Right: This spirit mask made of wood and bark fiber was used in Malanggan ceremonies in New Ireland.

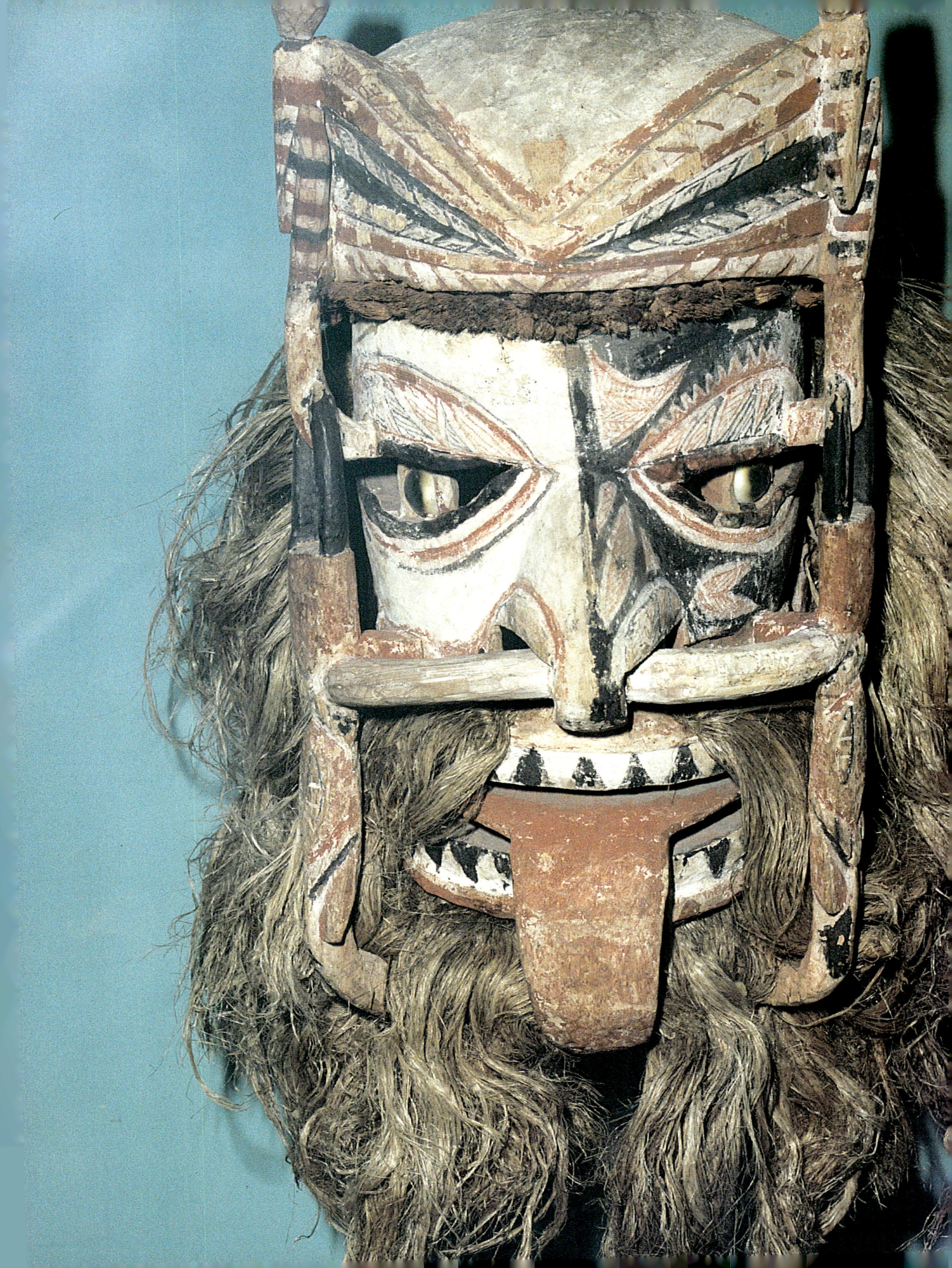

and size, it is now also possible to discern outside influence from such sources as Europe in the Micronesian cultures — Christian missionaries having muddied the waters in part of an inevitable process, as all cultures link slowly in the slow waltz called "civilization."

There is also great Micronesian emphasis on ancestor worship, with some even deified and propitiated, for they had animal avatars and through the use and manipulation of the cosmic Mana could become pretty nasty if offended. The "normal" dead went to one of two alternatives — a submarine paradise named Pachet, or a gloomy underworld called Pueliko, depending on their behavior in life.

The root of misfortune was again put down to a bloody-minded trickster/fire god, Olofat, who was responsible for most of the unpleasant things that existed or occurred. Other culture heroes, such as Lugeilan, were more benign and introduced the social arts of personal appearance — hairdressing and tattooing, which in fact had important cultural resonances.

AUSTRALIA

Australia is eons old in its isolation, possessing truly ancient and archaic animals and humans — the indigenous Aboriginals, flightless birds, the egg-laying mammals and marsupials.

When the English annexed Australia in 1788, it was still in its own time-warp, stretching back countless millennia. At the time there were approximately 350,000 Aborigines made up of some 400 tribes, who lived a nomadic hunter-gatherer existence that had barely changed since man had first arrived on the continent. They possessed intimate knowledge of landscape and bush, with animals and plants understood and exploited,

Above left and Right: An Australian Aborigine bark painting.

OCEANIA

but they had no agriculture, metallurgy, pottery nor writing. They probably originally island-hopped from the direction of the Indonesian archipelago, but an accurate date of their arrival is as yet impossible to give. Despite a low-level material culture these Aboriginal peoples developed a complex social and religious organization, with much variation — basically accepting the idea of a now remote original creator sky god, with the lesser but more active deities and culture founder heroes as the proactive mythological interface. Ritual and myth were linked as one was enacted in order to manifest the other. Thus initiation rites, ceremonies and totemism all confirmed identification and became regular practices.

According to Aboriginal creation mythology a primordial celestial being, the only pre-Dreamtime personality, created the world and then promptly left. This was followed by the Dreamtime phase itself, which consisted of ancestor animals and deities wandering the continent in creative mode, and is a manifestation of a still relevant and nostalgic cultural looking back and remembering, of great importance to those Aboriginals still left after three centuries of ill-treatment from the colonizing Europeans. These rites involved symbolic cannibalism (at one time real) as novices underwent a ritual that linked them to their primeval beginnings. Men were always the main executors of mythic protocol and tribal initiation, but women also had important roles and responsibilities.

Above left and Right: This Maori woodcarving was also removed from a tribal meeting house.

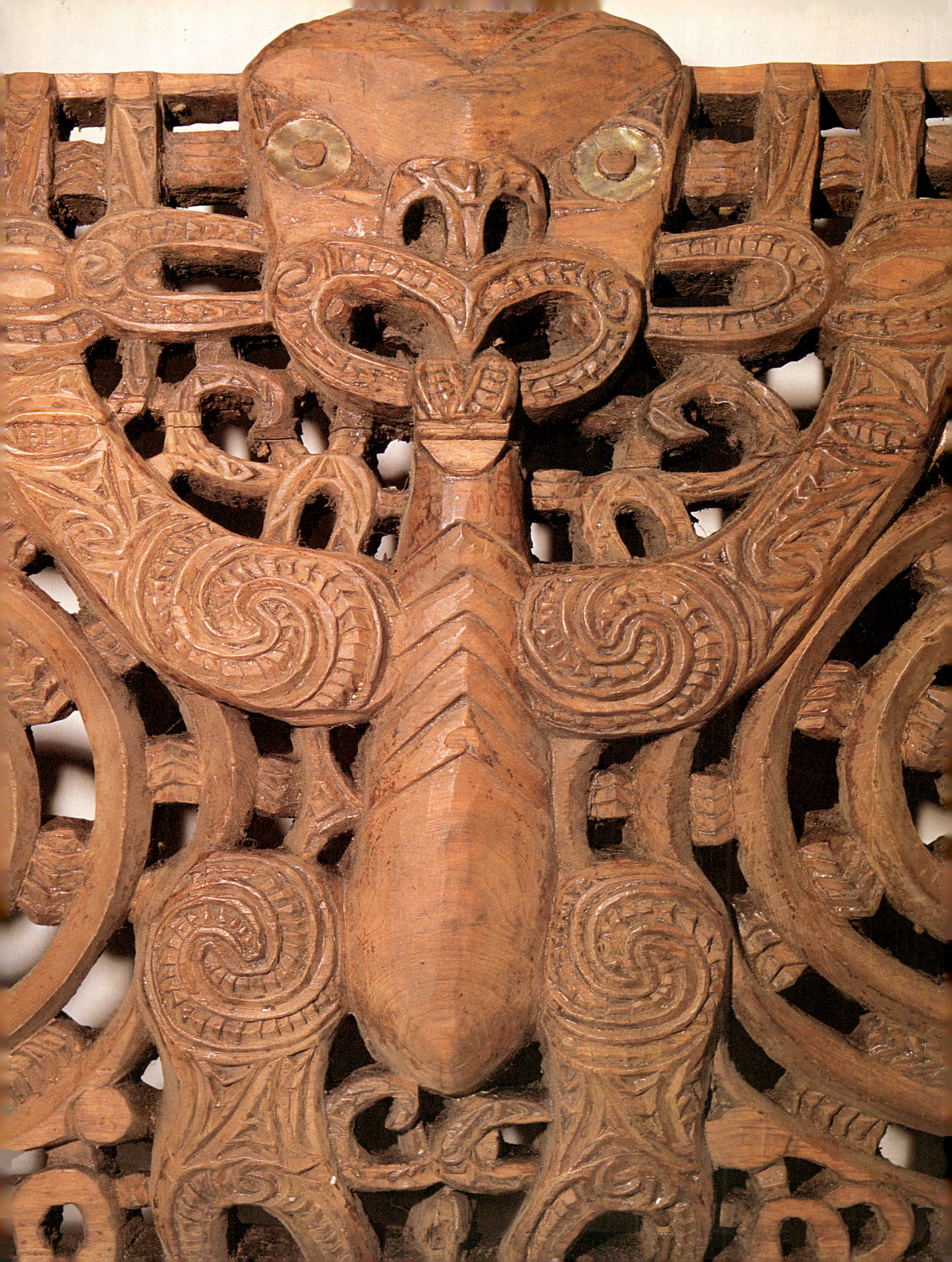

A-Z
CODEX GODS

AHOEITU
"Day has Dawned"

Ahoeitu was a mythical king of Tonga, the son of the supreme deity Eitumatupua and his human wife Ilaheva, descended from the original creator worm who first gave birth to humans. When Ahoeitu reached manhood he decided to visit his father in Heaven. His father was pleased to see him but his celestial half-brothers were resentful and jealous — so as soon as they could they ambushed, killed and ate him. Eitumatu-pua was not the paramount divinity for nothing — already knowing what had occurred he ordered his heavenly offspring to regurgitate their earthborn brother, reassembling the pieces as they haltingly arrived. When reassembled, Ahoeitu was given Tonga as his kingdom, with his brothers kept aloft until they had truly repented. All of Eitumutupua's sons were then to become mythical early kings of Tonga, but Ahoeitu the Earthborn was the first.

ALTJIRA
Remote creator sky god of the Aranda Aboriginal tribes of central Australia, Altjira was the original creator deity of the Dreamtime who went through the whole process of terraforming and populating the result, only to then remove himself to a detached height and ignore the rest of the proceedings. Altjira acknowledges no responsibility for the humankind that he made. His job done he allowed his creation free-reign to just get on with their existence, while cultivating a cool indifference.

ATANUA
Dawn goddess of the Polynesian Marquesas Islands, who arose from the conflict in which Mutuhei was finally destroyed by Ono, and Tanaoa was expelled by Atea. Atanua then became the wife of Atea. The sea was said to have been formed as a result of a later miscarriage she had.

ATEA
Atea is a creator sky deity of the Polynesian Tuamotu islanders, from whom they claim descent. Locked in embrace with the earth goddess Fa'ahtou he produced various children all of whom died until he took over the suckling of them — their mother not being nutritious enough.

The local variant of the sky/earth separation myth involves Atea and Tane-mahuta. Pursued off ground and starving, Tane-mahuta wanders the heavens, at one point initiating cannibalism when he opportunistically lunches on an ancestor. He successfully evades Atea and on reaching maturity defeats him using thunderbolt weaponry.

Right: Mask made of coconut fiber with eyes of coiled wire, from the Torres Straits Islands.

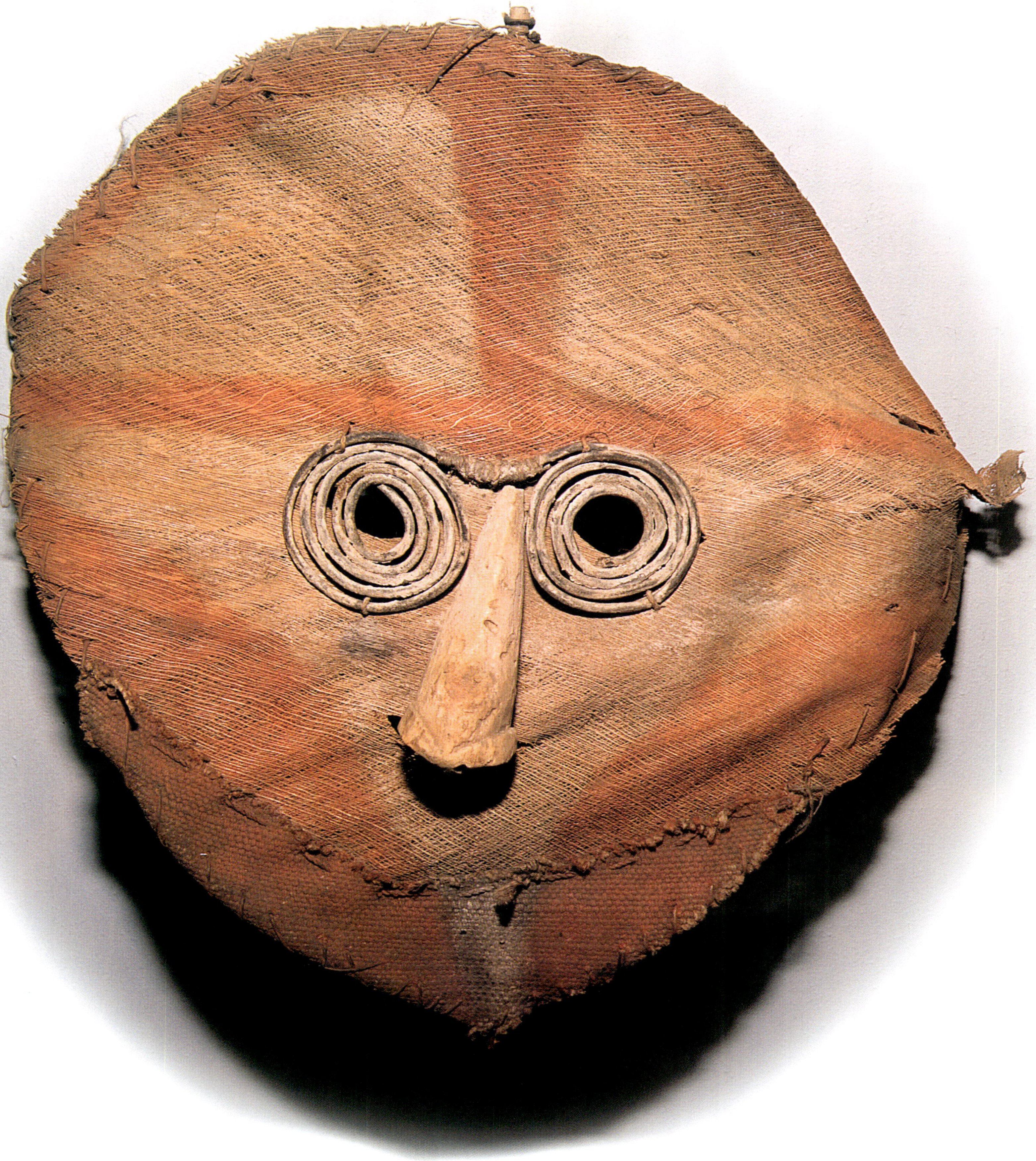

A-Z
CODEX GODS

AU
Au was the solar and sky creator deity of the Micronesian Gilbert Islands, who arose from the sea on the top of a tree. Only those fully initiated were allowed to know his true creation story, to others he was merely a culture hero called Auriaria.

BAGADJIMBRI
Identical twin creator god brothers of the Karadjeri tribes of northwestern Australia. Prior to them nothing existed, only a flat and featureless earth waiting for them to emerge and create. Initially as two dingoes they raced around making land features, water holes, trees and vegetation and finally people. By this time they had transformed again into two giants, who got into a fracas with the surly cat man Ngariman and his associates, who murdered them. They were revived by their earth mother's rejuvenating milk — which also drowned the murderers. They continued to live and change, eventually passing into the heavens as two clouds.

BAIAME
Baiame was the ancestral creator deity of the Kamilaroi tribe from Australia's New South Wales area. He was a beneficent sky god and medicine man, the great constructor of all things; who controlled the flow of life and its counterbalance, death. Having formed the world and its weather-systems he next populated it and then went on teach humans the skills of fishing and hunting.

BAMAPANA
Mischievous trickster hero of the Murngin tribes of northern Australia, Bamapana was the joker in the pack whose erratic behavior was guaranteed to stun. Often, if not always, obscene, he broke all rules and taboos — riding roughshod over tribal protocols. His radical and shocking tricks simultaneously charmed and revolted the other gods and the Murngin.

BOBBI-BOBBI
Divine ancestor and chthonic snake deity of the Binbinga tribe of northern Australia. Bobbi-bobbi helped mankind by providing various food sources, including the flying fox squirrel, even equipping men with a boomerang rib of his own with which to knock them down. This became a cause of friction between the god and his subjects when they overshot and made a hole in the sky, forcing him to repossess the weapon. Aboriginal ancestral creator deities often occurred in snake format, a common creature within the Australian geographical environment.

BUE
Semi-divine tribal ancestor hero of the Micronesian Gilbert Islanders, Bue was the son

Right: Stone figure of Moa Haka, from Easter Island.

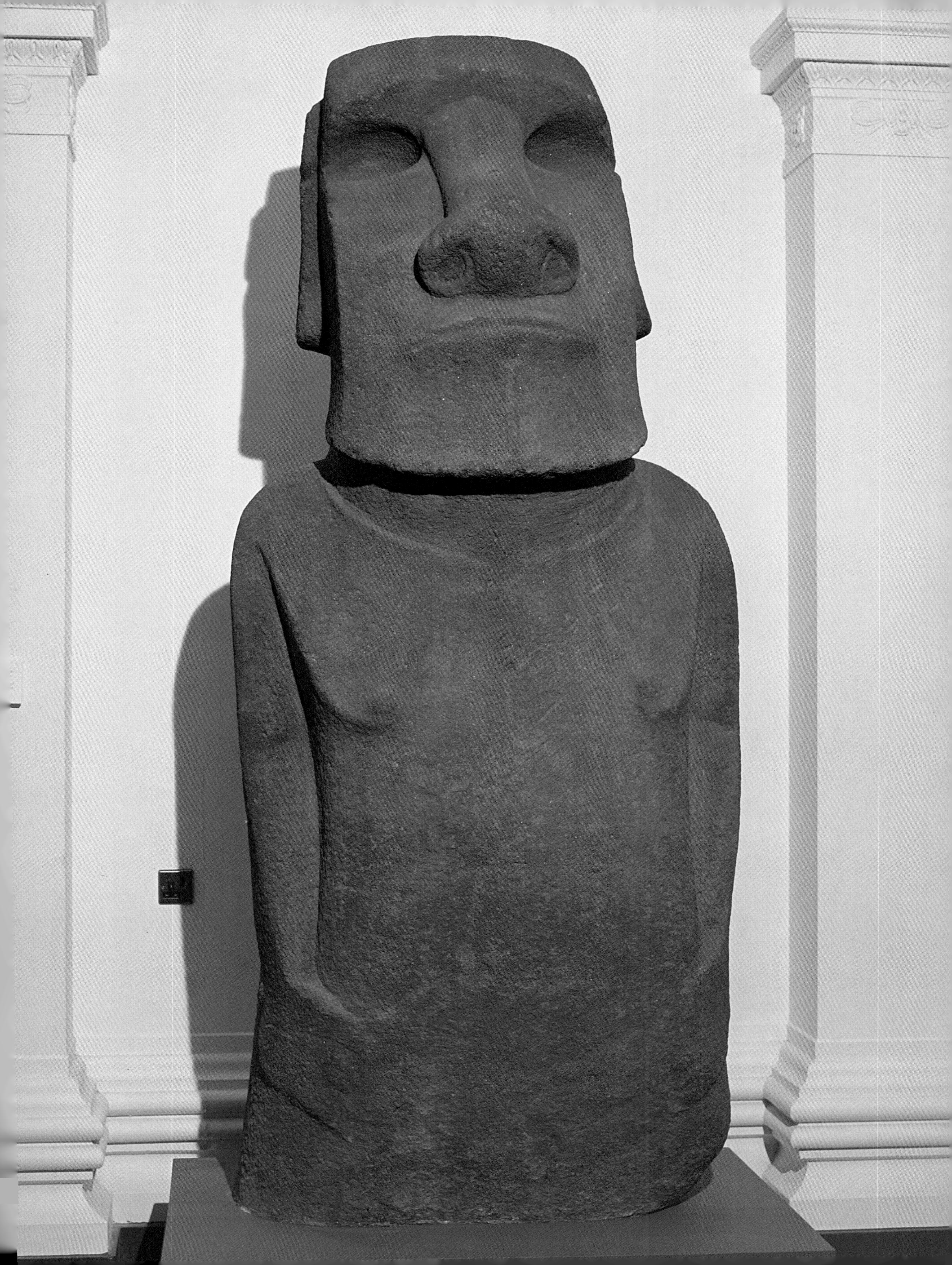

A-Z
CODEX GODS

of the sun god and a human woman. On reaching maturity he sought his father out to gain the knowledge and wisdom that were his birthright, though not without having to exert considerable physical and mental pressure. His father felt slightly eclipsed by his dynamic hero son, who went on to instruct his Gilbert Island tribes in the many skills and arts of construction, navigation, divination, divine communication and magic.

DJANGGAWULS

A trio of ancestral creator deities from northern Australia consisting of two sisters and a brother, born from the sun. The sisters represent the dual manifestation of fertility and mother goddess and the brother was perhaps a later addition to explain the change from a matriarchal to a patriarchal society.

The Djanggawuls came out of the northeast by canoe, accompanied by a prototype human, Bralbral. After they landed they began to create vegetation and animals with their sacred magic rangga sticks. Finally from their holy cone-shaped mat basket — *ngainmara* — they created and withdrew humans, instructing them in the arts of survival and fertility. The passing of power from women to men was explained in a myth which told of the sisters pausing one day to bathe. Hearing a commotion from the animals they ran back to their camp find that the men had stolen their sacred objects.

DREAMTIME

Also known as: Alchera, Ugud, Wongar, Laliya and Jukurpa

The Dreamtime is the name given to describe the mythical era when Australia was inhabited by the gods and totemic ancestors of the indigenous Aboriginal peoples. It is the timespan of the current universe and all the eventualities that are contained within it. Thus the Dreamtime is infinite, and so also a part of the present too, with those initial forms still sequencing the same patterns of existence that are manifested and modified in nature's endless matrix. Participation in these protocols still underlines Aboriginal lives. When submerged in these rituals, current individuals are connected to this "time outside time."

DUDUGRA

The aggressive solar deity of the Papuan tribes, born from the bizarre union of a giant fish with a human woman's leg. As this woman bathed in the sea her leg was brushed by a giant god-fish and later it began to swell alarmingly. Eventually her father lanced her leg — and out popped Dudugra, who because of unacceptable behavioral problems had to leave the human world. He was taken back down to the beach by his mother, picked up by his god-fish father and later climbed up into the sky to become the sun. In Papua the relentless sun is not appreciated solely as a life giver but as an exterminator too.

Right: Detail of a painting of spirits on the gable of a cult house in the Mafrik region of northern New Guinea.

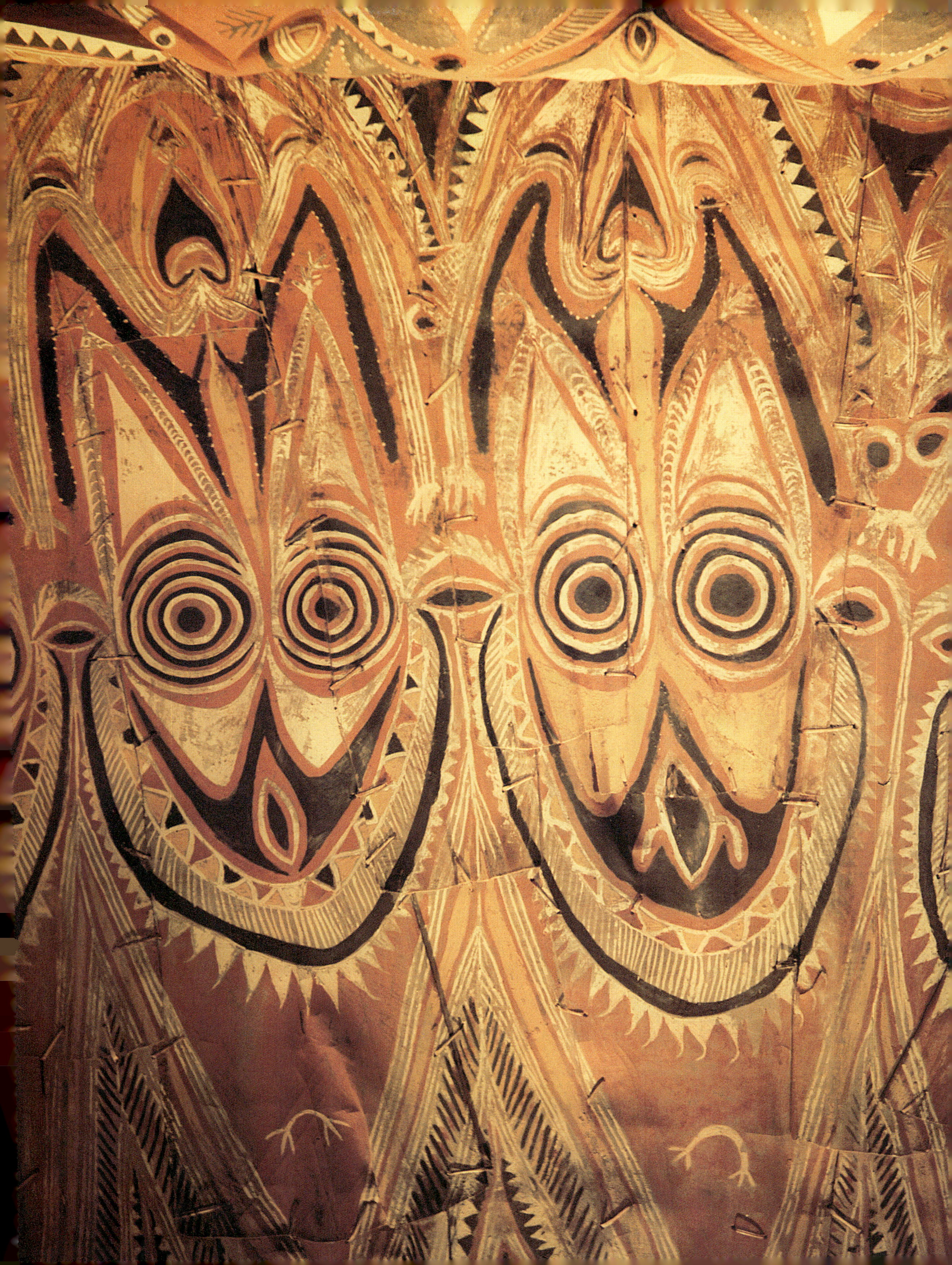

A-Z
CODEX GODS

Dudugra's intense rays were therefore partially screened when his mother threw lime into his face, causing him to blink and hide his glaring eyes.

GOGA

The ancient rain and fire goddess of the Massim tribe of Papua, Goga was a crone whose fire secret was eventually stolen by humankind. Enraged she sent a rainstorm to extinguish it, but a snake kept an ember and carried it to safety using its tail and so fire capability remained in the human world. In another version Goga lived on an island far out to sea which suffered a mixed animal commando assault in order to gain the secret.

GORA-DAILENG

God of the dead in the Micronesian Caroline Islands. Gora-daileng's job specification was to judge and punish the sinful and the wicked, choosing a punishment to fit the crime. Living by the subterranean river that bordered the underworld, he specialized in first roasting and torturing his victims with hellfire before slinging them in the river to be rushed away into oblivion.

HAKAWAU

Hakawau was a Maori medicine man and sorcerer supreme, reaching the height of his fame when he overthrew his rivals Puarata and Tautohito, whose magical fetish head had been terrorizing the population. By skilful use of his own powers and the aid of an army of familiars he stormed his rivals' fortress and after demonstrating his superiority clapped his hands to make his enemies die.

HAUMEA

Hawaiian ancestral goddess of fertility who introduced safer childbirth practices. Before she instructed women otherwise, children were delivered by being cut from their mothers, who died as a result. Haumea brought an end to this drastic custom. It was believed she possessed an age-changing power by which she could regenerate and continue her procreativity. In her agricultural fertility role she was connected to the sacred fruit trees that could produce food on demand. She also owned a magic stick that had the power to attract fish. Much of Haumea's constructive work was undone by the trickster Kaulu, who stole her plants and eventually was the cause of her death.

HINE

Also known as: Hina

A multi-faceted archetypal woman and goddess of life and death, a mother figure occurring in many island variants. She was the Maori wife of Tane and bore him a daughter of the same name, whom the god incestuously married. When the daughter learnt the truth she committed suicide and became the goddess of death, but

Right: Tangoroa, a Polynesian creator god.

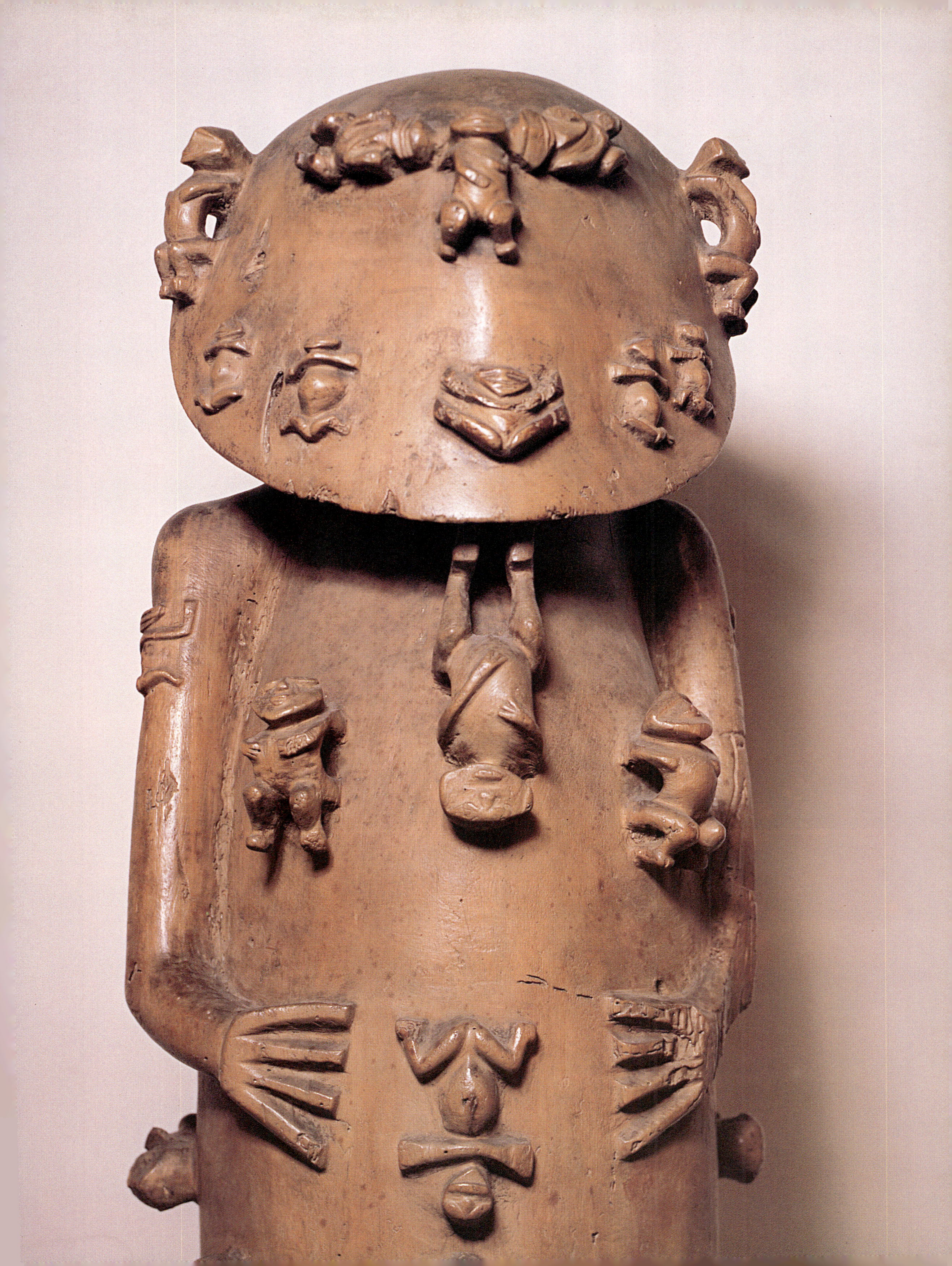

A-Z
CODEX GODS

this merely illustrates two sides of the same goddess.

The Tahitian variant accompanied her brother Ru on exploratory voyages, traveling as far as the moon, which she liked so much she elected to stay. An alternative version of this legend has Hine beating tapa cloth which gives the hungover Tana'aroa a thumping headache. Finally unable to tolerate the noise any further he hit her with the tapa mallet, killing her instantly, and her soul ascended to the moon.

Another Maori myth has her married to Tinirau an ambiguous sea god who shares her creative and destructive capabilities.

In Tumotuan legend it is the eel god Tuna she is married to but she becomes bored with him and seeks another lover among the other gods, finally selecting Maui.

IKI-HAVEVE

This is the native descriptive phrase for the Papuan cult that became the precursor of the more recent Cargo Cults of the Oceanic region. Beginning in the early 20th century, led by an old man named Evara, Iki-haveve involved ecstatic possession and the anticipated return of the ancestors. This was hearkening back to surer times in the face of extraordinary developments — the incursion of modern man and his technology into a previously Stone Age world. Cargo-cults developed over the next fifty years, reflecting the seemingly magical arrival of equipment and possessions from huge metal ships that seemed to have been made by the gods. These cults proclaimed the imminent dawn of a new age when the ancestors would return and expel the white invaders. Preparations included marching, drilling and moral regeneration.

KAHAUSIBWARE

The female creator deity of the Solomon Islands who, in a trait common within much of the Oceanic area, took the form of a serpent. It was Kahausibware who created the vegetation, wildlife and also the first men and women. She also introduced death into her creation, to balance the life that permanently filled it up. Having made the world she found herself rather irritated by its noisiness and hyperactivity. In fact, when the first woman left her child in Kahausibware's care, she found she could not tolerate its strident crying and strangled it in her coils. The frantic mother endeavored to save her baby by hacking up the snake goddess with an axe. Distinctly put out by the process of dismemberment the immortal Kahausibware departed forever to an island of her own.

KAI-N-TIKU-ABA

An Oceanic World Tree variant, Kai-n-tiku-aba was the sacred tree of the Samoa. It was said to have originated from the spine of Na Atibu, the father of all gods who sacrificed himself in

Right: A carved and painted Javanese mask.

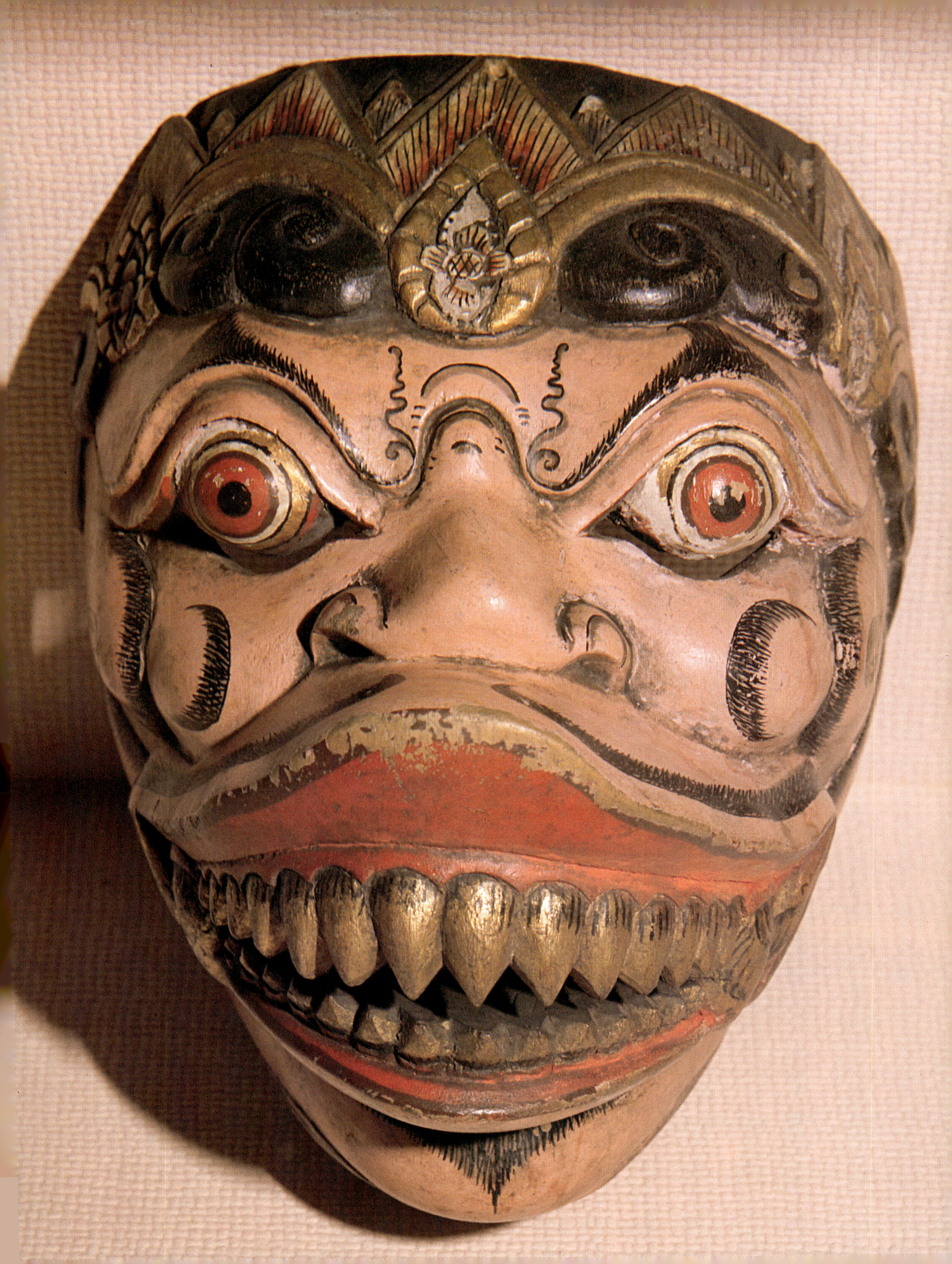

A-Z
CODEX GODS

order to form the world and heavens, with his spine as the World Tree linking them. The tree was productive in all its areas, even delivering fruit and having people live in its lower branches in the world of man. This came to an end when one man, named Koura-abi became enraged and broke the tree after being hit by excrement falling from someone above. As a result regret and sorrow entered the world.

KAMAPUA'A
"Hog Kid"

The popular pig deity of Hawaii, portrayed anthropomorphically, surmounted with a pig's head. Kamapua'a experienced various assassination attempts when young but survived them all to become a powerful and warlike god. He married into a king's family and distinguished himself on the battlefield, defeating many rival chiefs. He was also celebrated for his amorous adventures in which he wore women down with his perseverance, finally obtaining what he sought with a mixture of trickery, bluster, magic and intimidation. His enormous pig snout was so sensitive nothing could remain hidden from him for long.

KANE
"Husband"

The Ithyphallic fertility and creator god of Hawaiian mythology, similarly endowed to the Polynesian trickster Maui. Kane was one of a trio of top deities within the Hawaiian pantheon, along with Lono and Ku. It was in fact Lono who made the first man from red earth, but he fashioned him in the image of Kane. All three had a hand in the creation of the world and its species. It was Kane who brought the dual branches of knowledge from Heaven to Earth, containing data on the origin of everything from astronomy and genealogy to taboo. He was essentially a benevolent god, who never required human sacrifice, but was associated with all kinds of craftmanship, especially canoe building. His counterpart was the evil squid god Kanaloa, who vindictively opposed his creations, making life as unpleasant as he could.

KUMU-HONUA
"Earth Beginning"

Kumua-honua was the mythical first man and Adam-equivalent of Hawaiian legend. He and his wife, the first female Lalo-honua, lived in the Hawaiian variant of the Garden of Eden, the paradise created for them by Kane. As in Eden they were permitted to eat anything except the fruits of the sacred tree. In keeping with this international myth explaining the development of man's awareness from a state of innocence, the prototype couple eventually could not resist sampling the forbidden fruit. As an inevitable result they were expelled — driven out by a great seabird.

Right: Figure made of coral from the Torres Straits Islands. It would be placed near the fire when the occupants left their huts to prevent the fire from going out.

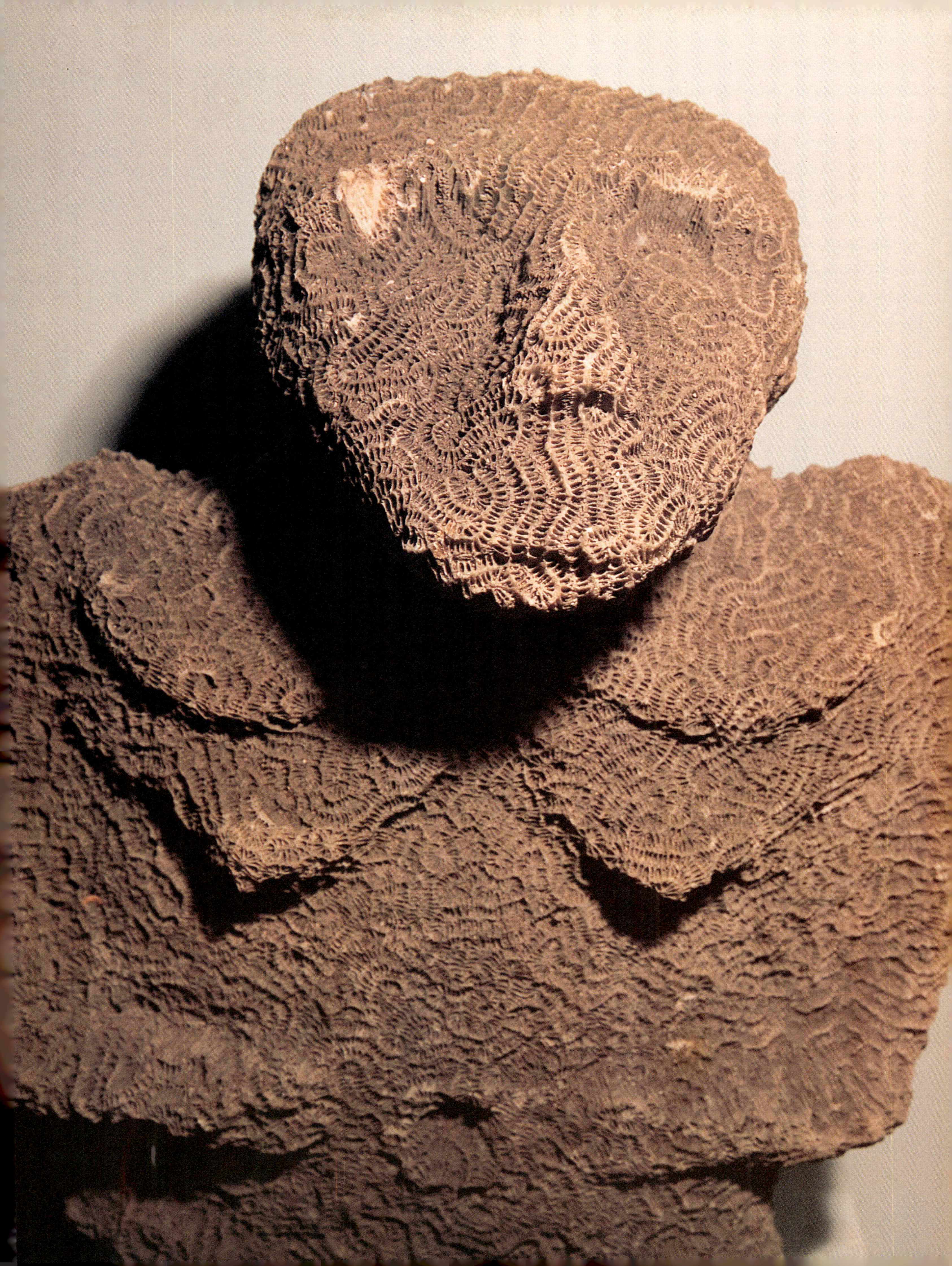

A-Z
CODEX GODS

KUNAPIPI
Also known as: Mamuna

An ogress mother goddess of northern Australia, who having created men and women as well as the animal kingdom, used her daughters to ensnare young men, who were then killed and eaten. Eventually the lack of eligible bachelors became critical and Yalungur the Eaglehawk was asked to resolve the situation, which he did by catching and killed the ogress. In another version of the myth men themselves stalk and kill her, cutting her open to rescue the victims and end her evil reign.

LAUFAKANAA
Wind god of the windswept Tongan island of Ata, responsible for the introduction of the banana tree and other technological innovations. In his role as a weather god Laufkanaa was propitiated whenever a fair wind was needed to sail, for this was his purpose as defined by the sky god with the mouthful of name: Tamapoulialamafoa.

LOA
Also known as: Lowa

Paramount creator deity of the Micronesian Marshall Islands. Before the world Loa lived alone in the primeval soup. Gradually through boredom as much as purpose he began to create features of land and sea, then creatures and finally mankind. Setting a god at each cardinal point he then withdrew, allowing the mechanism to function without further input from him. Another myth disputes how much of the actual creation process Loa was involved in, making him more remote from the start but still acknowledging his initial creator status.

LUGEILAN
Sky god of wisdom and instruction of the Micronesian Caroline Islands, Lugeilan was the trickster hero son of the Micronesian creator god Aluelop, who descended from the sky in order to teach mankind the arts of tattooing, dressing and the use of coconut and palm oil. Another brother brought the skills of carpentry and building. It was through Lugeilan's gift of tattooing that man was offered a way round his mortality — through the practice of this communal cultural art his continuity was assured. Lugeilan's beneficent reputation was irrevocably tarnished from the association with his manic trickster son, Olofat, whose antics eventually led to a more negative image for his father. After Olofat had challenged the sky gods themselves he was defeated and killed, but was revived by his father and used a communication link between himself and mankind.

Right: Australian Aborigine art in the form of a bark-painting.

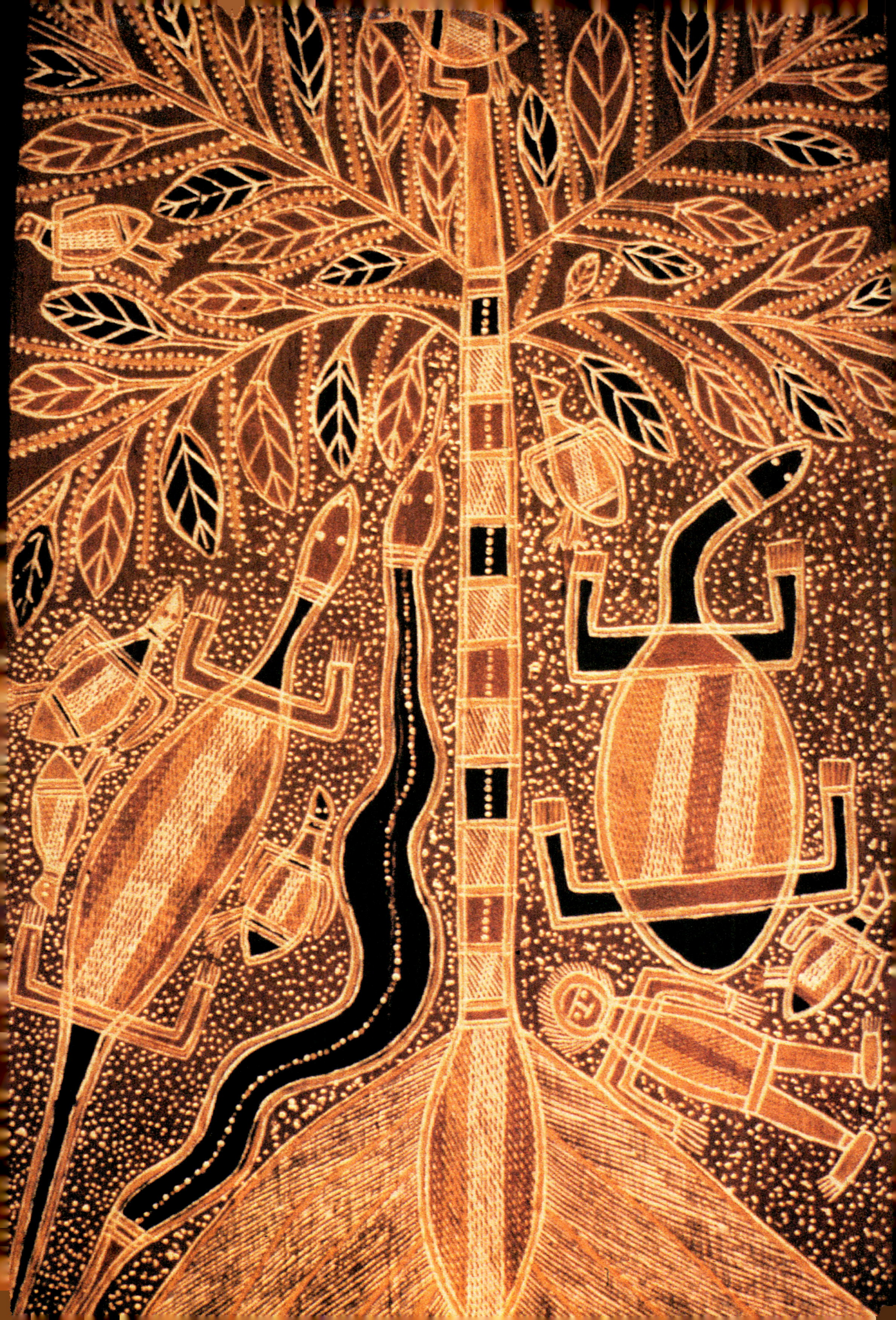

A-Z
CODEX GODS

MANGAR-KUNJER-KUNJA
"Fly Catcher"

Pivotal lizard-man ancestor of the Aranda tribes of central Australia. The Aranda creation myth begins with a world completely submerged other than a few tops of giant hills protruding from an endless sea. On the slopes, a single incomplete form consisting of two perceptible halves lay in a kind of comatose state. As the waters gradually receded Mangar-kunjer-kunja, the lizard avatar of the Arandan creator deity, emerged to cut the necessary orifices in the organism, separating the two halves into different beings — the first man and woman. Following this he provided them with tools and equipment and revealed the protocols of successful society for them to evolve.

MARAWA

Melanesian spider deity of the Banks Islands, Marawa was the companion and counterpart of Qat — whatever Qat did Marawa tried to imitate, usually getting things wrong in the process. When Qat made miniature figures out of wood and drummed the rhythm of life into them, creating humankind, Marawa tried himself but was so ashamed of the results he buried them — with the result that they decomposed, and death was introduced into the world. When Qat was making a canoe out of a tree trunk, Marawa drove him mad by putting each piece he cut out back in the trunk. Marawa was occasionally useful though, saving Qat from various uncomfortable predicaments, ultimately proving the reconciliation and mutual dependence of these two opposing figures.

MAUI

The legendary semi-divine Polynesian dwarf culture hero and trickster, Maui is a Lokian figure in Polynesian mythology, whose inventiveness, vitality and trickery have such a massive dynamic impact across the spectrum of the culture.

Originally abandoned to the sea by his mother, Taranga, soon after a premature birth, he was found by his ancestor spirit, the sky deity Tama, and taken up to dry out. Having grown and learnt fast he returned to earth to find his family, though his reception was mixed — his mother was overjoyed to see him but his brothers were just disgusted. His exploits then came thick and fast — fishing up many islands from the deep, raising the sky higher because it got in the way, beating up the sun to make him move more slowly and stealing the secret of fire for man. His legendary phallus won him Hina, the unfaithful wife of the eel deity Tuna. When that god tried to intervene he was killed and dismembered in a savage battle, his head becoming the first coconut tree.

Maui met his end when he voyaged to

Right: Rangda the "dreaded widow," Queen of the Witches, impersonated in the Barong dance from Bali, Indonesia (19th century).

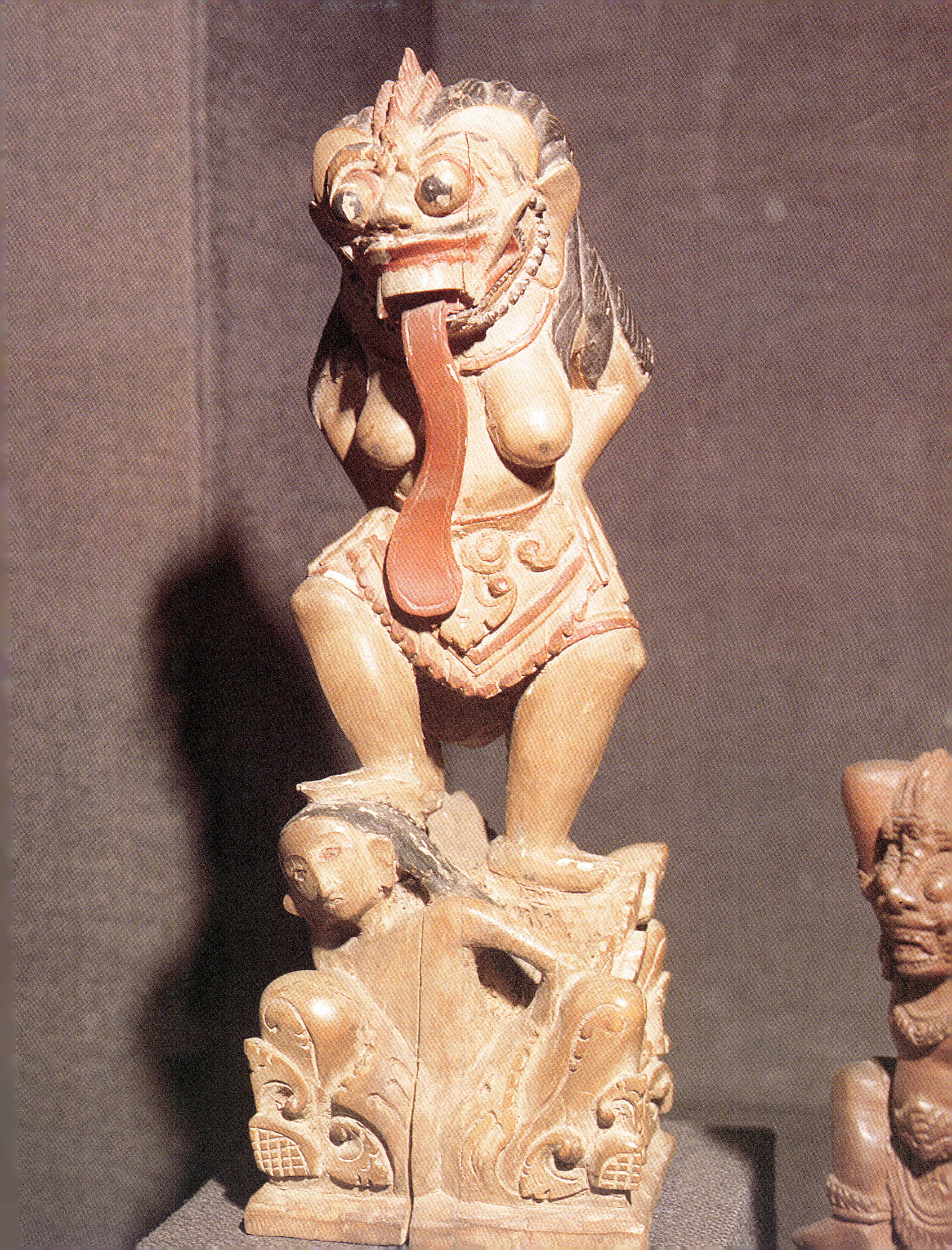

A-Z
CODEX GODS

Hawaii, killed by the islanders who grew sick of his endless tricks, though in another myth he was finally killed by the giantess Hine-Nui-Te-Po, when he went down into the underworld to discover immortality for humankind. As he sought to enter the goddess and defeat death she awoke and duly detroyed him.

MINAWARA/MUTULTU

Minawara and Mutultu were a pair of ancestral kangaroo men in the mythology of the Nambutji tribe of central Australia. Drifting on a raft of debris in the sea they arrived in Australia, where they traveled timidly at first, then headed into the center of the continent, evolving their own strange sexually oriented protocols which became part of the Nambutji male initiation ritual tradition.

MOKPOI

The Mokpoi were evil ghosts who prey on humankind in the mythology of the Murngin tribe of northern Australia. Within this culture death was never really seen as a naturally occurring phenom-enon, but rather as a result of an error in religious protocol, the evil intent of a sorcerer or undue attention from the Mokpoi. These malevolent spirits could be directed toward an intended target by a wizard of the black arts, the only practical defense being through counter measures by a good magician.

NAREAU
"Spider"

A pair of trickster arachnid creator deities from the Micronesian Gilbert Islands. The father and son were called Old Spider and New Spider respectively, both playing an important part in the creation of the world and its contents. Old Spider came from the primeval ocean, creating two beings from whom sprang all the other gods. This done he then sacrificed himself so that his son could build the rest of what was required, with the help of an octopus and an eel. One eye was thrown into the sky to become the sun and the other to be the moon, his flesh and bones scattered to turn into islands and trees and his brain crumbled in the sky to make the stars. When this was done New Spider then created the ancestors of mankind, whom he proceeded to torment with his trickery, as if they were made expressly for that purpose.

NDAUTHINA
"Torch Beare."

A Fijian fire deity and the guide of sailors and fishermen. The latter role came about when as a child his mother fastened a burning taper to his head so that he could find his way at night! From that time he patrolled the reefs with his headlight. Also as result of this nocturnal illumination, Ndauthina was known as the patron saint of adulterers, presumably because of their nighttime assignations.

Right: This carved wooden figurehead from the bow of a war canoe, represented a guardian spirit to ward off evil.

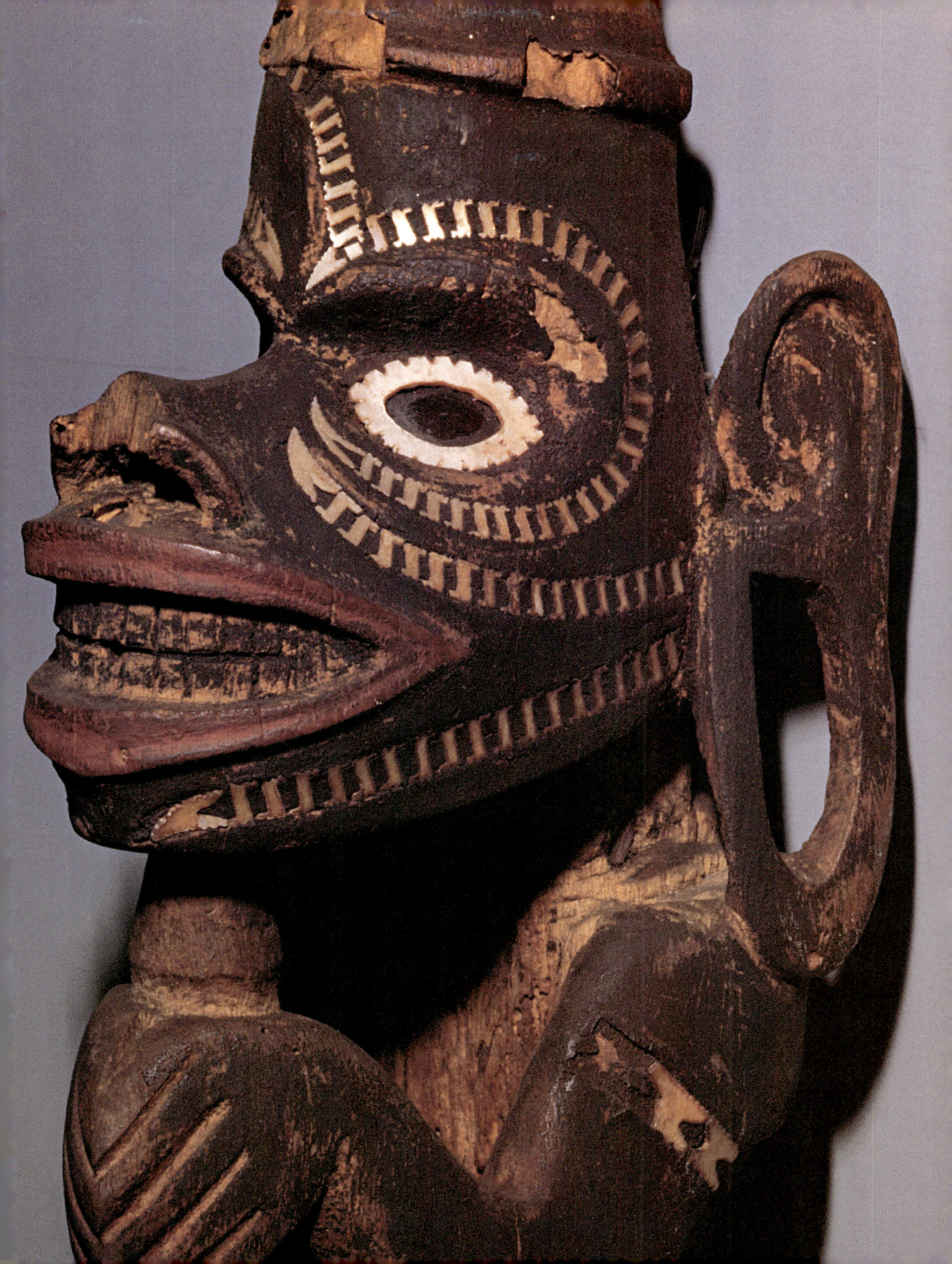

A-Z
CODEX GODS

NDENGI

The beneficent serpent creator deity from Fiji, whose flexing and turning within the earth were held to be the cause of earthquakes. Ndengi commanded his son Rokomotu to form land by scraping up mud from the sea bed. When this had been accomplished he then laid two eggs, from which the first human couple were hatched. Ndengi then coached them in life skills and provided food and fire. When the creator god slept it became night, and all existence was suspended until he awoke again. His boat builder nephews were disenchanted with these endless nights and killed the black dove that was Ndengi's alarm clock. In revenge the enraged god sent a huge flood to sweep them away, separating them onto different islands where they founded the different tribes and spread the arts of boat construction.

NEI TITUAABINE

Vegetation and fertility goddess of the Micronesian Gilbert Islands, Nei Tituaabine had a very brief life and a productive death. She was chosen by the king Auriaria, who fell passionately in love with her but their union bore no fruit, instead Nei Tituaabine took ill and soon died. When she was buried three trees grew from her grave — the coconut palm, the almond and the pandanus, her final gift to the islanders.

NJIRANA/JULANA

The Dreamtime wanderer and adventurer whose name is interchangeable with his personified phallus. This rather bizarre and exotic Dreamtime character was a famous mythical figure of the Western Desert Aboriginals. In keeping with his special equipment Njirana was dedicated to the pursuit of women, evolving some devious strategies in order to catch them — a favorite one was to travel swiftly underground and pop up suddenly to overwhelm them. He was connected to canines as well; filtering the bad ones out and favoring the good, he thus bred the prototype for the existing desert breeds.

NU'U

Nu'u was the Hawaiian Noah counterpart, whose righteousness and prayer saved him from an accidental flood. Like Noah, he escaped in an ark and eventually landed on the summit of one of Hawaii's mountains, where he continued to propitiate the gods. Kane then descended to explain that it had all been a mistake, caused by the movements of a massive undersea goddess, who caused tidal waves each time she shifted around too fast.

OLIFAT

Also known as: Olofat, Olofad, Iolofath, Wolphat, Yalafath

Right: This face-mask of carved and painted plum tree wood with fibre hair was worn in dances to celebrate the wild plum harvest, New Guinea, Torres Straits (19th century).

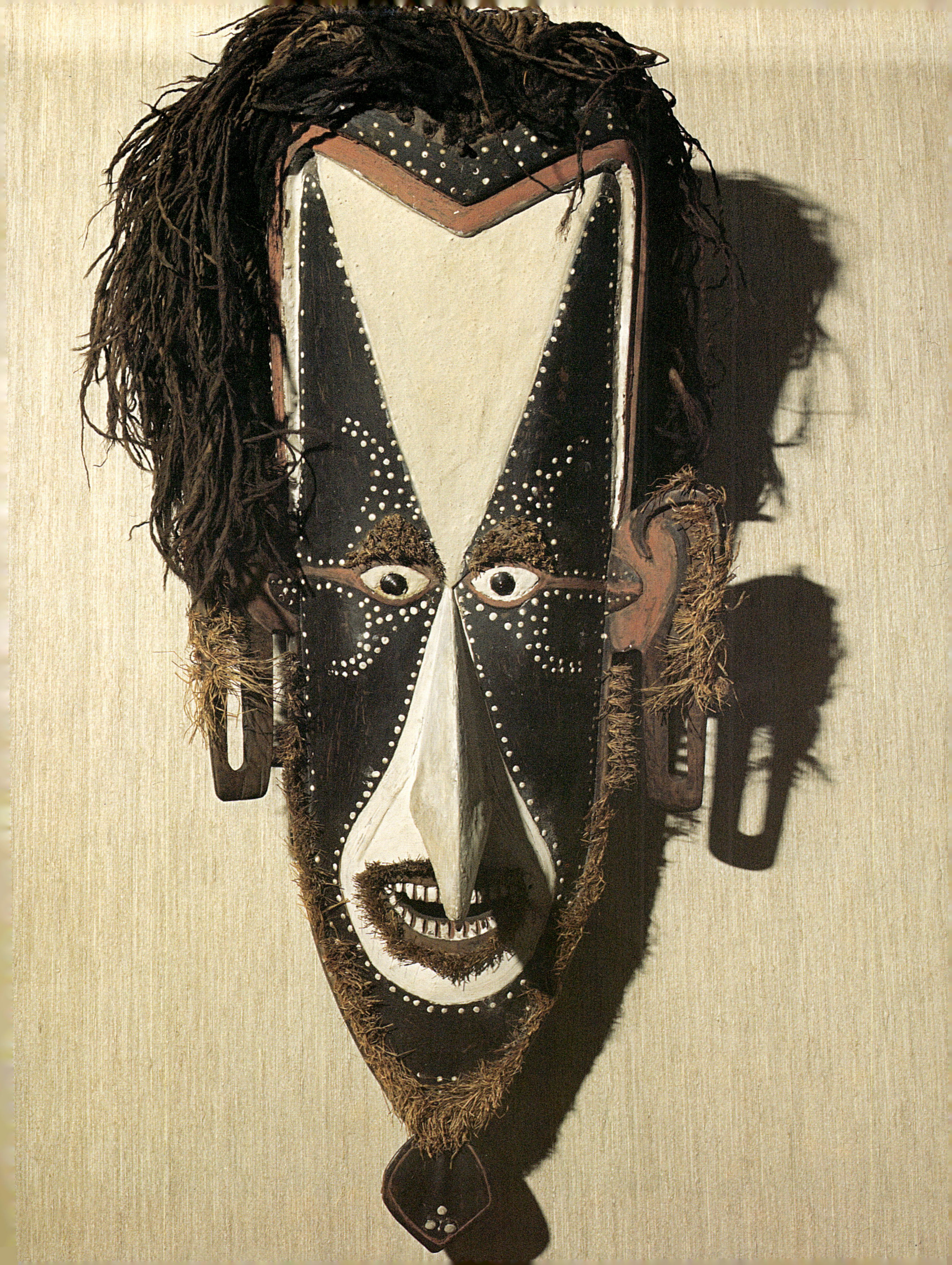

A-Z
CODEX GODS

The semi-divine hero son of the trickster god Lugeilan from Micronesia, Olofat inherited a lot of his father's mischievous temperament, and remorselessly teased and tantalized humankind.

Although of semi-divine parentage. Olifat had his mother's human half too, which rendered him mortal. When still young he sought his father out, ascending to Heaven on a column of smoke. The reception and his own reaction to it did not go well, he sabotaged the children's harmless fish games by equipping them with teeth, stings and spines, and finally caused an all out war with his divine relatives. The myth then splits into two variants, in one Olifat is killed, then resurrected by his father, before going on to act as an ambiguous communication link between gods and men. In another, he tricks his heavenly hosts, avoids being sacrificed and, defiant as ever, continues to make everyone the butt of his weird humor.

ORO

Oro is the Tahitian war deity, the son of Hinatuauta and Ta'aora, famously bloodthirsty in battle and sacrifice. He had three bellicose and bitchy daughters — Toimata, Aitupuai and Mahufaturau — who intimidated everyone and loved to join in their father's work. Ironically enough given his nature and progeny, he could also become a peace god when the necessity arose, his name being defined by whether he had picked up or put down his spear.

OMA RUMUFU
"Black Way"

Oma Rumufu was the intriguing pre-existent deity of the Siane tribes from New Guinea. In fact, he was their only deity, the pragmatic Siane possessed no cosmological or creation myths, but assigned control over obvious natural events — the movement of the sun, moon and tide etc — to the control of Oma Rumufu. He was also the Lord of the Dead.

PAKA'A

The Hawaiian wind and air god, who inherited his power from his grandmother, Loa. Paka'a was propitiated by seamen when a fair wind was needed, and in another maritime connection was also credited with the invention of the sail which he introduced to humankind so that they could make more of his wind power.

PAPA

Papa was the ancestral earth goddess of the Maori and other Polynesian peoples, and consort of the sky god Rangi. In a familiar archetypal myth, the other gods — their children — were initially compressed between

Right: Chalk ancestor figures from New Ireland, Melanesia.

• OCEANIA •

499

A-Z
CODEX GODS

them, barely able to breathe let alone move. Seeking more room they discussed many alternatives, including the murder of their parents, but settled for trying to prise them apart. All the gods tried and failed, until Tane resolutely forced them to separate. His brother, Tawhiri, upset at seeing their unwilling parents handled so roughly, sent storms and winds to oppose him — a cause of friction and then lasting enmity between the two. Nothing could stop the inevitable though — Papa and Rangi were forced apart so the world could exist.

In Hawaiian mythology Papa married the mortal king Wakea, who fell incestuously in love with their subsequent daughter. This led to the dissolution of the marriage and the introduction of death, as an embittered Papa retaliated.

PAPANG/ALLFATHER

Also known as: Sky-Hero, Daramulun, Nurundere and countless other names

The Allfather was the creator sky god of the Australian aborigines, another totemic deity, acknowledged by all tribes which each had their own particular tribal name for him, as well as accompanying myths and stories. Like most sky-gods thunder was his weapon, and he would hurl this from his stone axe when angry. The Allfather myth actually merges with that of the Rainbow Snake in its creative and destructive roles.

PELE

This tempestuous Hawaiian lava and fire goddess — a female manifestation of destructive power — was worshiped by those who claimed descent from her. Pele was very beautiful but fiery: her lava could envelop, burn and turn to stone any who roused her ire. Prior to her Hawaiian arrival she traveled extensively, supposedly looking for an old flame, but when she met the Hawaiian king Lohiau she knew that he was what she wanted. After a few days of blissful marriage Pele instructed him to wait and departed to prepare a new residence, unaware that time was rather more extensive for gods than it was for humans — by the time she summoned him he had died of old age. Undeterred he was revived and rejuvenated and brought by Pele's sisters to his new abode. However Pele's wild temper surged up due to impatience and jealousy, and unable to restrain herself she incinerated the whole party.

QAT

Qat was the prime Melanesian creator spirit, who fashioned humankind from a tree, and then infused them with life by drumming and dancing energy into them. Another spirit named Marawa sought to imitate him and also made people from a tree, but when they began to move he buried them and so brought mortality to man. Next, at the request of his brothers who were tired of the perpetual daylight, Qat inaugurated the rhythms

Right: Chalk ancestor figures from New Ireland, Melanesia.

• OCEANIA •

A-Z
CODEX GODS

and cycles of night and day and the seasons. For a long time everything was fine but eventually humans multiplied so much they became increasingly argumentative and competitive and Qat had to acknowledge the usefulness of his brother-spirit Marawa's invention of death, for without it chaos would ensue.

RAINBOW SERPENT

The Rainbow Serpent was the totemic water deity of the Dreamtime, responsible for the great Flood referred to in various Australian Aboriginal tribal myths. Although the Rainbow Serpent was acknowledged all over the continent, each tribe had a different name and accompanying myths for him. During the Dreamtime, the Rainbow Serpent built and shaped the water courses of Australia, which remain his holy places even now. He also sent rain and his special gift to mankind — blood, through which he controls all bodily functions. Sometimes all his different names could manifest as many individual snakes.

RONGO
"Sound"
Also known as: Ono, Lono

Rongo was a Polynesian agricultural deity and second of the sons of Papa and Rangi. In fact it was he who first tried to separate his fornicating parents whilst his other siblings were violently arguing about what to do. Rongo was also his mother's favorite and in arguments with his elder brother Tangora she invariably took his side. He came equipped with and was represented by his "godstick" — a totem of his divinity which was used by the priests in his ceremonies and agricultural rituals, and his other emblem was a large triton shell called "The Resounder." Rongo had three children who went on to become the ancestors of humankind.

In Hawaii he was known as Lono, who descended to earth down a rainbow to find a wife for himself. He succeeded in his quest and everything went well for while, but later believing his spouse was unfaithful he beat her to death. After this he was consumed with grief and organized a huge festival in her honor, touring the island challenging all who would to wrestling matches. His return was prophesied and Captain Cook was seen as his incarnation when he first arrived, for according to myth the Polynesian gods were fair-skinned.

SISIMATAILAA

The son of the sun god in Tongan mythology, whose human mother was impregnated when she fished continually with her back to the sun. When he reached maturity Sisimatailaa sailed off on his own to Samoa, where he fell in love with a local girl. Returning to Tonga to let his mother know of his impending marriage, at her behest he ascended a hill

Right: This human skull with clay modeled and painted features, New Guinea, Sepik River area.

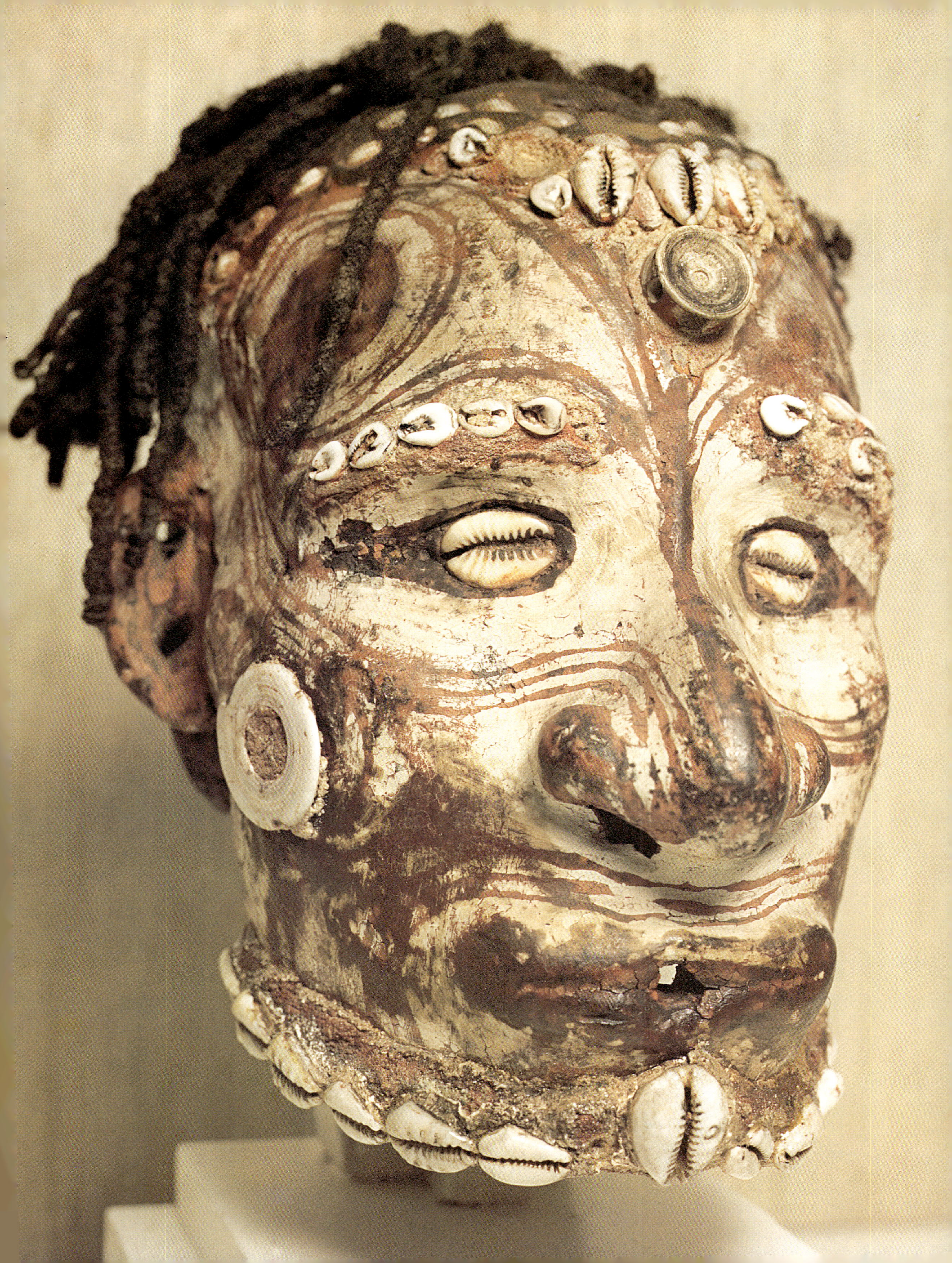

A-Z
CODEX GODS

and raised his arms in supplication to his father. The sun then gave him two parcels — one of which was never to be opened and the other that contained conventional riches. On the return journey to Tonga his new bride cajoled Sisimatailaa into opening the "forbidden" package. This magic packet then vomited such a quantity of things into their boat that it was overwhelmed and sank, drowning both of them in the process.

SOLAL AND ALUELOP

As Micronesian creator god, Solal planted the first giant primordial tree which he then climbed, stopping at different points to create the earth (in the middle) and the sky (at the top). The sky was allotted to Aluelop, whilst Solal descended and kept the lower underworld for himself. From the interaction between the upper and lower worlds all else took its form and function, with the decision made on high and the energy to carry it out coming from below. So the duality of life was balanced.

TA'AROA

Ta'aroa was the supreme creator god of Polynesian Tahiti. Myths tell of the initial dark void, with Ta'aroa contained within an egg-type shell, which he cracked open to emerge. When he called out in the darkness there was nothing to respond, so he retreated into a second egg, in which he let millennia pass. When he emerged for the second time he then used the shells to make the sky and the land, going on to summon the other gods from the void. In another myth he uses his own body parts to sculpt the land's features. Though mainly of beneficent aspect, occasionally in times of severe drought or some other potential disaster an angry Ta'aroa would be propitiated with human sacrifices.

TABURIMAI

Son of the semi-divine Micronesian Gilbert Island ancestor Baku. All his other brothers were all sea creatures, but Taburimai was human. This aroused their indignation and they plotted to murder him. His youngest brother, Teanoi the shark, wanted no part in this fratricide and helped Taburimai escape by carrying him on his broad back. Teanoi went on to become an astral deity, but Taburimai remained on earth, traveling extensively before getting married and having a child, the adventurous Tearikntarawa, who married the goddess of the sacred World Tree and another son who was so beautiful, he could spontaneously give birth without recourse to women.

TAGARO

Also known as: Takaro

A semi-divine culture spirit hero of the Melanesian New Hebrides Islands, concerning whom there are many myths, including his rather bizarre creation of man and woman.

Right: Tangaroa Upao Vahu was viewed as the creator and sea god of Polynesia, Rurutu Islands, Polynesia.

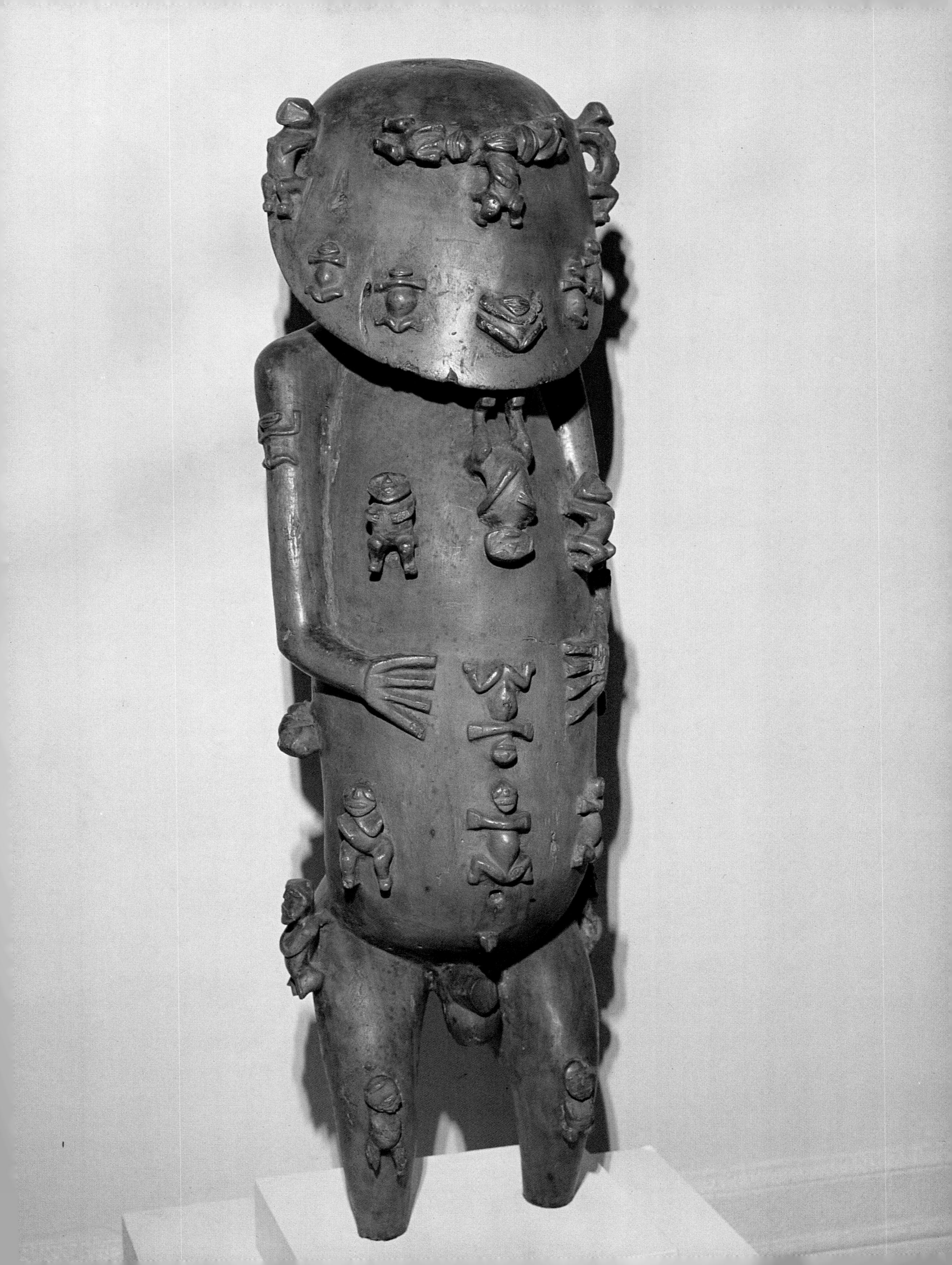

A-Z
CODEX GODS

From some mud he fashioned the first ten men, breathed life into them and having then formed them into a line he threw fruit at them. One man eventually was hit by a fruit on his phallus, which impaled it and as Tagaro pulled the fruit away it brought the phallus too, thus turning the man into a woman. Next he sent this woman away, later dispatching each man to visit her with a request individually. She greeted the first eight as relatives, but the ninth as husband and so Tagaro married them. His own wife was the swan maiden Vinmara, who flew from Heaven on wings which he later stole to force her to remain with him — though she later escaped along with their child.

In other myths Tagaro is opposed by the maleficent Suquematua, who ruled over the dead, but the sky hero always dominates his chthonic counterpart.

TANE
"Man" or "Husband"
Also known as: Tane-mahuta

Tane was the Maori variant of the Hawaiian Kane, a beneficent forest creator god who successfully levered his parents apart using his own bodyweight so that existence could manifest itself properly. Following this event, Tane and his wife Hine went on to become the creators of vegetation and ancestors of humankind, though an alternative legend has him displaced by his warlike brother Tu as man's creator. It was Tane also who brought the two sacred stones "Ocean Foam" and "Sea Mist" to the islands, whose replicas were the altars of Hawaiian religious ceremonies.

In other myths Tane creates man from clay and mud, woman from sand, and introduces cannibalism. His main opposition came from the maleficent squid god Tangaroa, who counterbalanced Tane's intrinsic goodness with a similar amount evil.

TANGAROA
Also known as: Tanaoa, Ta'aroa, Tangaloa, Kanaloa

Tangaroa was the malevolent Polynesian sea god who took the form of a squid and was balanced in eternal opposition to Tane. Both these gods occur with a variety of names and myths attributed to them that reflect the spread of population and belief in the Oceanic region. In the Society Islands of Western Polynesia Tangaloa was a creator deity, while in Hawaii his sweat made the sea as he labored to make the land. A Tahitian myth attributed the birth of Hine to his Ta'aroa variant, who then married his daughter in disguise, and on Easter Island he and Rongo were the only two Polynesian gods ever referred to as creator ancestors. In the Tumotuan legend Tagaroa sought and procreated with Faumea (also known as Haumea), had two children by her and then

Right: This wooden figure with boar's tusks warded off evil spirits. Nicobar Islands. Indian Ocean.

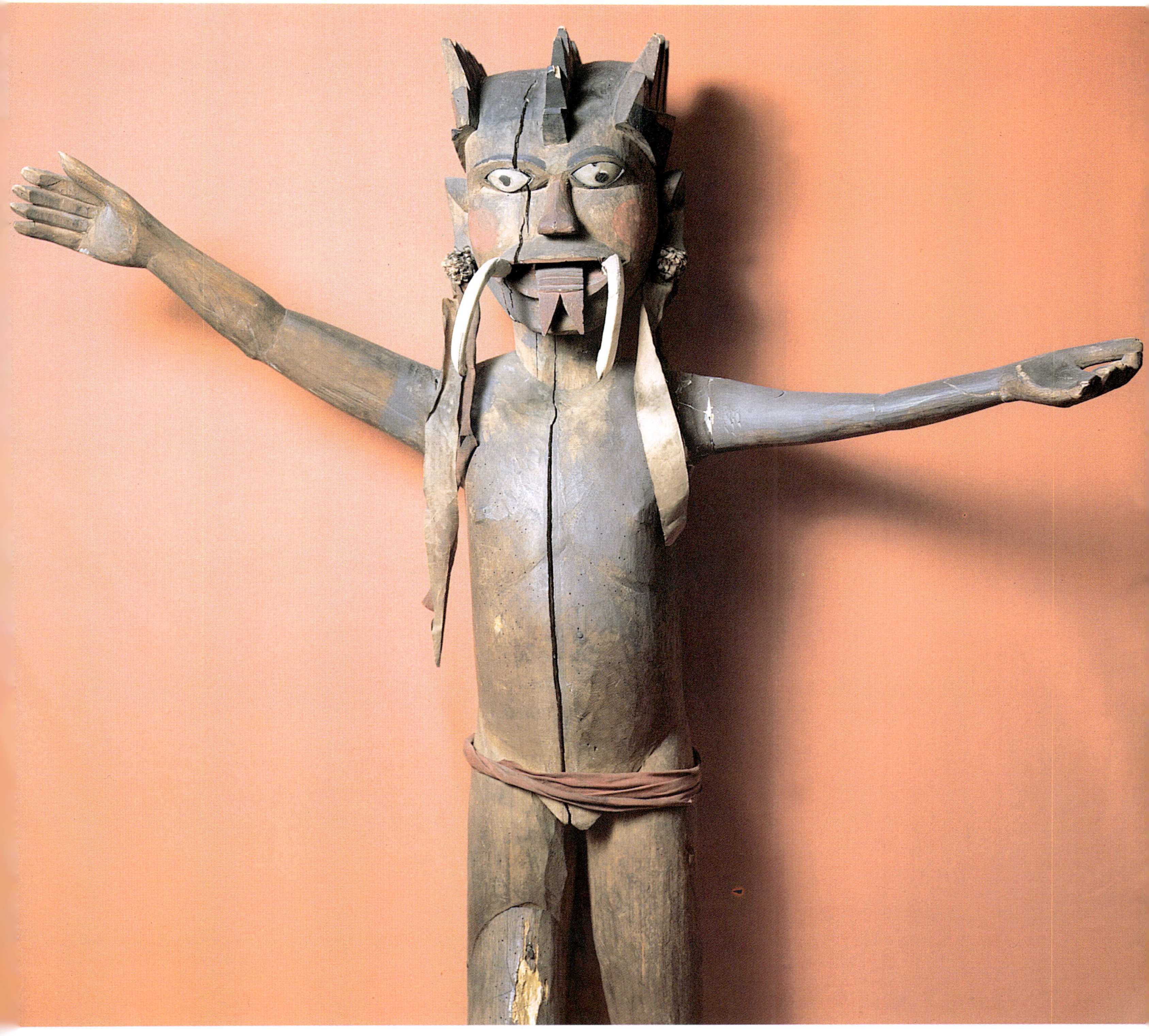

A-Z
CODEX GODS

fought an epic battle with the octopus demon Rogo, in order to rescue his daughter who had been swallowed by that creature.

TO-KABINANA/TO-KARVUVU

The Melanesian archetypal man and culture hero of the New Britain Islands. To-Kabinana and his brother To-Karvuvu were created by a nameless god who drew and animated pictures to bring them to life. These two manifested the duality of an inimical nature, one automatically doing things right and the other deliberately achieving the opposite, though he pretended to emulate his creative brother. When To-Kabinana dropped a light coconut and made a beautiful woman, his brother admiringly tried the same but with a dark coconut instead — which turned into a squat ugly female. To-Kabinana also carved and animated a wooden fish, which helped him to catch others effort-lessly, while To-Karvuvu's carved shark just ate them all. Another myth has To-Karvuvu responsible for the introduction of cannibalism, for after To-Kabinana requested him to look after their ancient mother he killed, roasted and ate her.

WANDJINA

The Wandjina were a collection of primal anthropomorphic animal deities from the formative Dreamtime of the Australian Aborigines. They occur in various famous rock paintings and were worshiped or referred to in relation to rain and fertility. Among them were: Warana the eagle-man, Wodoi the pigeon-man, Djunggun the owl-man, and Jarapiri the snake-man. They are portrayed anthropomorphically, yet lacking mouths and with other strange facial features. Haloes round their heads imbue them with power. These primordial beings helped to form the land and fill it with other living things during the Dreamtime.

WAWALUG

The Wawalug were a pair of fertility goddesses from the Arnhem Land in northern Australia. The sisters — Waimariwi and Boaliri — originally appeared from the north with rumors of incest hanging over them as one (Waimariwi) already had a small child and was pregnant when she arrived. As they traveled they gave names to the places they passed through, until they reached a sacred waterhole. This they managed to defile with blood when they washed the newly-born child of Waimariwi in the pool. The Great Serpent's guardian representative, Yurlunggur then emerged and swallowed both the women and children. He repeated this action a number of times, swallowing and regurgitating the women and children in a symbolic fertility rite.

Right: Head of a wooden figure from New Ireland, Melanesia.

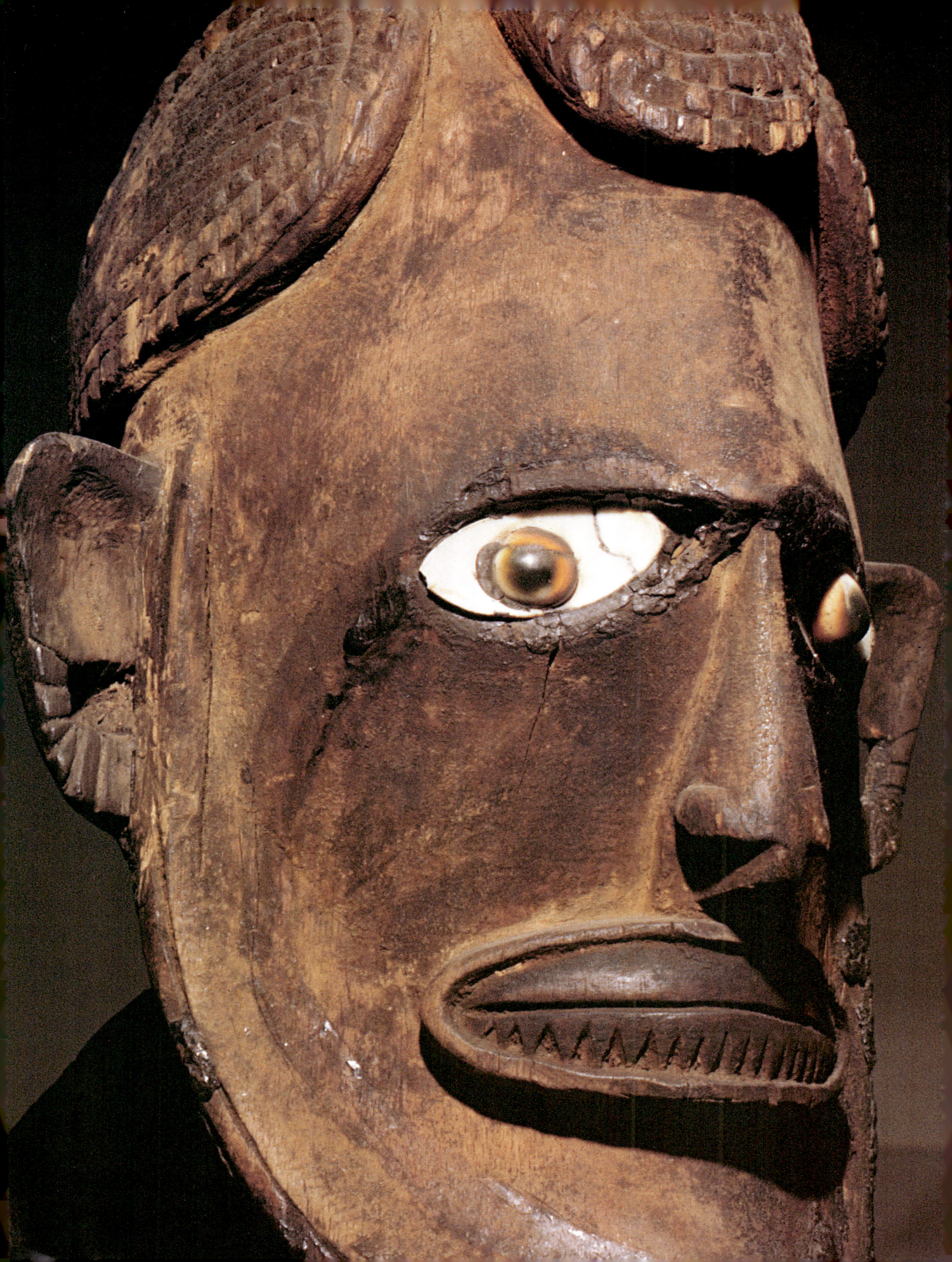

GLOSSARY

A

Acipitrine – Relating to or resembling a hawk.

Aceticism – The practice of withdrawal from the world and wordly pursuits in order to cultivate spiritual awareness.

Aerolite – A stony meteorite consisting of silicate minerals.

Ahuras – Beneficent divine beings.

Alchemy – Ancient predecessor of chemistry which sought to make gold from other substances.

Angakoq – The Inuit shaman, who was repository of lore and magic, with personal communication links to the spirit world, the keeper and arbiter of tradition.

Animism – The belief that natural objects, phenomena and the universe itself have desires and intentions.

Ankh — the Ancient Egyptian sign of eternal life.

Anthropomorphic – Resembling the human form.

Avatar – A visible and often corporeal manifestation of a deity.

B

Barque – boat.

Blackbox – A sealed data recorder placed within moving vehicles to track their procedures.

Bodhisattva – A divine being worthy of Nirvana who elects to remain on earth to aid others reach enlightenment.

C

Caduceus – A wand, signifying power and sometimes containing magic energy.

Chakra – Any of seven major energy centers in the human body.

Chi/ki – Intrinsic life energy present in all things.

City-state – A city and its environs run as a ministate, somewhat like present day Monaco.

Cornucopiae – Horn shaped containers filled with fruit, representing plenty.

Conquistadores – Spanish conquerors of South America.

Cyclops – A race of one-eyed giants in Greek mythology.

D

Daevas – Zorastrian devils and opponents of the Ahuras.

Daimyo – Feudal lords of old Japan.

Disinformation – False information intended to mislead or deceive.

Dux Bellorum – A war leader or general.

Dyinyinga – African spirits.

E

Edutainment – Education through entertainment.

The Great Ennead – A grouping of nine Egyptian gods.

F

Fa – Fate or destiny.

G

Geomancy – Phrophecy made by interpreting randomly generated patterns.

Gimokod – A manifestation of the soul within humans and in the spirit world

Golok – A machete or broad heavy knife.

GLOSSARY

H

Hamio-semitic – A combination of North African and Middle Eastern racial characterisics.

Heiroglyphics – Pictorial system of written communication.

Hellene and Hellenistic ages – The great age of Greek civilization, which lasted until Roman conquest of Greece.

Hermeia — Square pillars, with a bust of the god on top and a phallus carved below.

Hierachichal/Hierarchy – A system of things or people arranged in a specific order.

Homogeneity – Composed of similar parts of uniform nature.

Hubris – Pride or arrogance that brings retribution.

I

Indigenous – Native to the country of origin.

Infotainment – Information communicated through entertainment.

Involute – A complex, intricate psychological structure.

Ithyphallic – A prominently visible phallus.

J

Jihad – Moslem holy war unleashed on unbelievers or those outside the faith.

K

Kami – A divine being or spiritual force in the Japanese Shinto religion.

Karma – Hindu and Buddhist concept of retributive justice, similar to the Christian "Reap what you sow."

Khepresh – The War Crown of Ancient Egypt.

L

Liaison – Communication or contact, often clandestine.

Lingam – Hindu representation of the masculine member and a phallic representation of the god Shiva.

Loa – Voodoo spirit or god.

M

Matriachy – A female dominated family or society.

Matrix – A complex interconnected structure of many parts.

The Memphite Triad – A grouping of three gods from Memphis.

Mummiform – In the shape of a mummy (an Ancient Egyptian corpse wrapped in linen bandages).

N

Necropolis – City of the dead, a graveyard.

O

Obia – African system of magic.

Odyssey – Greek epic poem attributed to Homer, also any long eventful journey.

Ogdoad – An eight grouping.

P

Patriach – The male head of a tribe or family.

Pandanus – Oceanic tree/plant.

Pastoralist – Non-industrial rural agricultural society.

GLOSSARY

Paleolithic – The period of emergence of primitive man.
Paterae – Dishes of fruit representing plenty
Pantheon – All the gods collectively of a religion.
Persona non grata – Unwelcome, forbidden, banned.
Pharaoh – Title of Ancient Egyptian kingship.
Pogrom – Organized persecution or elimination on racial or ethnic lines.
Polychromic – Many colored.
Primary sources – Original sources of historical evidence.
Propitiation – To appease, conciliate or make sacrifice to a lord or god.
Pshkent – The Double Crown of Ancient Egypt, signifying the unity of the two original countries, Upper and Lower Egypt.
Psy-ops – Psychological operations conducted against an enemy.
Ptolemaic period – The period of the Ptolemies, a Greek derived family of Pharaohs in Ancient Egypt.

R
Rishi – A hermit

S
Saga – Epic poem or narrative.
Satori – A sudden illumination through a flash of insight.
Shaman – Priest or medicine man, who acts for the common man in the spirit world.
Sistrum – An ancient ceremonial rattle or shaking instrument.
Syncretism – The gradual process of accumulation and modification of ideas and culture into a single updating system.
Syrinx – A musical instrument akin to Pan pipes.

T
Tantric – A movement within Hinduism and Buddhism that combines magical and mystical elements.
Tapa – Oceanic tree/plant.
Telekinesis – Movement of a body or thing through thought power alone.
Terraforming – Planet forming.
Theriomorphic – Resembling animal form.
Tirthankara – "Makers of the crossing." The wise men, phrophets and leaders of Jainism.
Torc – A Celtic neck-ring.
Totem – An object, plant or animal that has ritual or clan associations, used to underline identity.
Trimurti – Indian concept of the ultimate divinity manifested in three forms representing birth, life and death.

W
Wyrd – Norse word for fate.

Y
Yogic – Of yoga — the Hindu meditation and exercise system aiming at mystical union with the supreme being.
Yoni – The female genitalia, regarded as the divine symbol of sexual pleasure and generation.